◀◀ **M**anagerial **E**conomics

◀◀ Managerial Economics

Second Edition

IVAN PNG

Blackwell
Publishing

BLACKWELL PUBLISHING
350 Main Street, Malden, MA 02148-5020, USA
108 Cowley Road, Oxford OX4 1JF, UK
550 Swanston Street, Carlton, Victoria 3053, Australia

First edition published 1998
Second edition published 2002
Reprinted 2002 (twice), 2003 (twice), 2004, 2005

Library of Congress Cataloging-in-Publication Data

Png, Ivan, 1957–
    Managerial economics / Ivan Png.—2nd ed.
      p.   cm.
    Includes bibliographical references and index.
    ISBN 0-631-22516-1 (alk. paper) — ISBN 0-631-22525-0 (pb. : alk. paper)
    1. Managerial economics.   I. Title.
  HD30.22. P62   2001
  338.5′024′658—dc21   2001035375

A catalogue record for this title is available from the British Library.

Set in 10 on 12 pt Galliard
by Graphicraft Ltd, Hong Kong
Printed and bound in the United Kingdom
by TJ International Ltd, Padstow, Cornwall

The publisher's policy is to use permanent paper from mills that operate a sustainable
forestry policy, and which has been manufactured from pulp processed using acid-free and
elementary chlorine-free practices. Furthermore, the publisher ensures that the text paper
and cover board used have met acceptable environmental accreditation standards.

For further information on
Blackwell Publishing, visit our website:
www.blackwellpublishing.com

◂◂ Brief Contents

◄◄ Contents

◀◀ 5 Competitive Markets 142

◀◀ 6 Economic Efficiency 184

Part II Market Power

◀◀ 7 Costs 223

◀◀ 8 Monopoly 260

◀◀ 9 *Pricing Policy* *299*

◀◀ **10 Strategic Thinking 344**

Part III Imperfect Markets

◀◀ **11 Externalities 385**

◄◄ 12 *Asymmetric Information* 419

◄◄ 13 *Incentives and Organization* 452

◀◀ 14 Regulation 487

◄◄ Preface

Managerial economics is the science of directing scarce resources to manage cost effectively. This book presents tools and concepts from managerial economics that practicing managers use. The book is aimed at business students as well as practitioners. Accordingly, it is deliberately written in a simple and accessible style. There is a minimum of technical jargon, complicated figures, and high-brow mathematics. The emphasis is on simple, practical ideas.

The book starts with the very basics. It presumes no prior knowledge of economics and only very elementary mathematics. As the orientation and content of this book differs substantially from traditional economics texts, it will also challenge readers with some background in economics.

Managerial economics is unique in integrating the various functions of management. In addition to presenting the essentials of managerial economics, this book includes many links to other management functions. Some examples are accounting (activity-based costing, statistical cost analysis, and transfer pricing), finance (opportunity cost of capital and takeover strategies), human resource management (incentives and organization), and marketing (brand extensions, promotion, and pricing). Fans of the World Wide Web may like to think of these links as jump points to other management functions.

In addition to the managerial focus, two features are worth emphasizing. First, the same principles of managerial economics apply in Africa, Asia, the Pacific, and Europe as in North and South America. Reflecting that unity, the book includes examples and cases from throughout the world. Second, the book uses examples from both consumer and industrial markets. The reasons are simple: a customer is as likely to be another business as a human being and likewise for suppliers.

For most readers, this may be their only formal book on economics. Accordingly, the book omits sophisticated theories and models, such as indifference curves and production functions, which are more useful in advanced economics courses. Further, the book recognizes that many topics traditionally covered by managerial economics textbooks are now the domain of other basic management courses.

Accordingly, the book omits linear programming, present-value analysis, and capital budgeting.

Regarding language, this book refers to *businesses* rather than *firms*. Realistically, many firms are involved in a wide range of businesses. In economics, the usual unit of analysis is a business, industry, or market rather than a firm. Also, the book refers to *buyers* and *sellers* rather than *consumers* and *firms*, since in most real markets, demand and supply do not neatly divide among households and businesses. To cite just one example, in the market for telecommunications, the demand side consists of businesses and households.

Finally, some comments on how to use this book are in order. Managerial economics is a practical science. Just as no one has learned swimming or tennis simply by watching a professional, no one can learn managerial economics merely by reading this book. Every chapter of this book includes a set of review and discussion questions. The review questions are to help the reader check and reinforce the chapter material. It is essential that new-found skills be practiced on the review questions. The discussion questions are intended to challenge, provoke, and stretch. They will be useful for class and group discussions.

Some chapters include suggestions for further reading. These are practical references for the typical reader, rather than academic journal articles intended for PhD economists.

Some chapters include mathematical supplements. These provide reinforcement to the text using algebra and calculus. The supplements will benefit students with a mathematics background.

Managerial economics is a science that is driven by data. Accordingly, the text and discussion questions frequently refer to actual data and the end of the book includes an appendix that lists many useful sources of data.

◀◀ Organization

This book is organized in three parts. Following the Introduction, Part I presents the framework of perfectly competitive markets. Chapters 2–6 are the basic starting point of managerial economics. These are presented at a very gradual pace, accessible to readers with no prior background in economics.

The book moves faster in Parts II and III. These are relatively self-contained, so the reader may skip Part II and go directly to Part III. Part II broadens the perspective to situations of market power, while Part III focuses on the issues of management in imperfect markets. Chapter 14 on regulation is the only chapter in Part III that depends on understanding Part II.

A complete course in managerial economics would cover the entire book. If time is limited, there are three possible shorter alternatives. One is a course focusing on the managerial economics of strategy, which would consist of chapters 1–10. Another alternative focuses on the managerial economics of organization and would consist of chapters 1–7 and 11–13. The third alternative focuses on modern managerial economics – strategy and organization – and would consist of chapters 1–3 and 7–13.

◄◄ Web-site

Please visit the web-site at http://www.comp.nus.edu.sg/~ipng/mecon.htm for on-line support to this book. The site contains updates and corrections to the book, links to data sources, a study guide, and an on-line form for your suggestions. The site also contains a link to resources for instructors, including transparencies, answers to discussion questions, and a testbank.

◄◄ Acknowledgments

First, I must acknowledge my deep gratitude to the reviewers: George Bittlingmayer (University of California, Davis), Margaret Capen (East Carolina University), Mike Granfield (University of California, Riverside), Bob Hansen (Dartmouth College), Douglas Lamdin (University of Maryland, Baltimore County), Lawrence Martin (Michigan State University), Mark Schupack (Brown University), and Mark Zupan (University of Southern California). With great patience, they encouraged and helped me nurture a rough sketch into a complete manuscript.

Next, I wish to thank various individuals, companies, and organizations that provided information and assistance. They include Pinelopi Koujianou Goldberg (Princeton University); Fred Kwan (Hong Kong University of Science and Technology); Lin Chu-chia (National Chengchi University); Frank Mathewson (University of Toronto); Robert Metcalfe, Gloria Pei, Jania Rosen, Fernando Salas, Tao Zhigang, and Wu Changqi (Hong Kong University of Science and Technology); the Australian Competition and Consumer Commission; Cisco Systems, Inc.; the Coalition for Vehicle Choice; the Commission of India, Hong Kong; Echo Bay Mines, Inc.; the office of the European Commission in Hong Kong; Honda Motor Company; the Hong Kong government; National Mutual Ltd., Hong Kong; the Prudential Insurance Company of America, Inc.; the Southern California Rapid Transit District; and Telstra Ltd.

For the second edition, I thank Luke Froeb (Vanderbilt University); Atreyi Kankanhalli, Victor Mustelier, Hong Nguyen (University of Scranton); Jorge Streb (CEMA); Tao Zhigang (University of Hong Kong); and Tom Pugel and Lawrence White (New York University). The Altavista and Google web search services deserve special mention as the starting points for many of the examples in this book.

Finally, I wish to thank the Hong Kong University of Science and Technology, National University of Singapore, and University of California, Los Angeles, the team at Blackwell Publishers (Al Bruckner, Colleen Capodilupo, Rolf Janke, Lisa McLaughlin, and Mary Riso), compositor Brian Smith, my economics teachers (Roger Witcomb, Oliver Hart, Mitch Polinsky, and John Roberts), and my family for their support and encouragement.

◄◄ About the Author

Ivan Png is a Professor and Dean of the School of Computing at the National University of Singapore. He graduated with a BA with First Class Honours in Economics from Cambridge University (1978) and a PhD from the Graduate School of Business, Stanford (1985).

Professor Png has previously taught at the Anderson School, University of California, Los Angeles (Assistant Professor, 1985–90, Associate Professor 1990–95, Professor 1995–96). He was also a visitor at the Hong Kong University of Science & Technology from 1993 to 1996.

Professor Png received the Outstanding Teaching Award from UCLA's MBA Program for Fully Employed Students, Class of '91, and Teaching Excellence Award, National University of Singapore (1998). His research has been published in leading scholarly journals including the *American Economic Review, Economic Journal, Journal of Political Economy, Management Science, Marketing Science,* and the *RAND Journal of Economics.* Professor Png is an Associate Editor of *Information Systems Research* and the *Journal of Industrial Economics.*

Chapter 1

Introduction to Managerial Economics

◀◀ 1 What is Managerial Economics?

Coca Cola and PepsiCo are the world's two pre-eminent soft-drink manufacturers. Coca Cola and Pepsi manufacture only concentrate, which they ship to networks of regional bottlers distributed throughout the United States and elsewhere in the world. The bottlers mix the concentrate with sweetener and water to produce the final product, which then is distributed to retailers, food service providers, restaurants, and other customers.[1]

Early in 1999, Pepsi spun off its American bottling operations as an independent company, the Pepsi Bottling Group. In this regard, Pepsi followed Coke, which had long been separate from its American bottlers. Coke's largest bottlers were Coca Cola Enterprises and the Coca Cola Bottling Company.

In early November 1999, following three years of vigorous competition for market share, Coca Cola announced that it would increase its price for concentrate to 7%. Later the same month, Pepsi made a similar announcement. Both Coke and Pepsi emphasized that they would step up expenditure on advertising and other marketing support in conjunction with the price increases.

Industry analysts predicted that the 7% increase in the price of concentrate would result in the $1.99 retail price of a 12-pack rising to $2.49 or higher. By contrast, the Pepsi Bottling Group estimated that the retail price would rise by 1 cent per can. The price increases were welcomed by *Beverage Digest* Editor, John Sicher, who remarked: "At this point, both systems need to improve margins and improve the overall profitability of the category." Other analysts, however, questioned the extent to which retail demand would fall as a result of the price increase. Sanford C. Bernstein analyst Bill Pecoriello concluded: "It's positive for the industry, but it's not without risk."

▼

---

[1] The following discussion is based, in part, on *Standard & Poor's Industry Surveys: Foods & Nonalcoholic Beverages*, 166, no. 22, section 1 (June 3, 1999), p. 3; "Pepsi to Increase Concentrate Prices by 6.9% Next Year," *Wall Street Journal*, November 22, 1999, p. B8; and "Following Coke, Pepsi will Raise Prices," *New York Times*, November 22, 1999, p. C2.

The November 1999 episode of price announcements presents several questions of business strategy. If Coke raises its price by 7%, should Pepsi follow? How would the price increase affect consumer demand? How should advertising expenditure be related to pricing? Pepsi's earlier decision to spin off its bottling group presents an organizational question: was it correct to follow Coca Cola to separate the bottling business from that of manufacturing concentrate?

Further, the profitability of Coke and Pepsi depends not only on their pricing and advertising, and the sensitivity of consumer demand to price increases. It also depends on the cost of sweeteners – sugar, corn syrup, aspartame – and other inputs. While Coke and Pepsi loom large in the market for soft drinks, they have a relatively smaller influence in the markets for some of their inputs. What price should Coke and Pepsi pay for these inputs? How are they affected by shifts in these markets?

> Managerial economics is the science of directing scarce resources to manage more effectively.

All of these are questions of managerial economics. **Managerial economics** is the science of directing scarce resources to manage cost effectively. Wherever resources are scarce, a manager can make more effective decisions by applying the discipline of managerial economics. These may be decisions with regard to customers, suppliers, competitors, or the internal workings of the organization. It does not matter whether the setting is a business, nonprofit organization, or home. In all of these settings, managers must make the best of scarce resources.

Pepsi has limited financial, human, and physical resources. Pepsi managers seek to maximize the financial return from these limited resources. They should apply managerial economics to develop pricing and advertising strategies, design their organizations, and manage purchasing. The same is true of Coca Cola.

In commercial jets, Airbus and Boeing are the world's two leading manufacturers. While Boeing is a publicly-traded company, Airbus is organized more like a cooperative with a tax-free status. Despite the differences in organization, the principles of managerial economics apply to Airbus and Boeing. Each needs to understand how they can influence the demand through price and advertising, how to compete effectively against the other, and what is the best organizational architecture.

Managerial economics also applies to the "new economy." Many of the challenges that confront management in the "new economy" are the same as those in the "old" economy. Consequently, the economic analysis and appropriate managerial solutions are similar. For instance, in pricing, airlines use differences in fare conditions to segment their market between business travelers and leisure passengers. Some analysts claim that the Internet is the ultimate segmentation tool: using online auctions, a seller can charge a different price to every buyer.

In competitive strategy, when Coke announces increases in price and advertising, Pepsi must consider whether to follow. Similarly, in the "new economy," when, in mid-1999, Microsoft threatened a price war in Internet access, America Online had to decide how to respond.

In organizational architecture, Airbus expects to generate several hundred million euros in profit by transforming itself from a marketing joint venture into a fully-integrated corporation. In the new economy, Amazon.com faced a similar issue: it decided to vertically integrate from being a "virtual retailer" and spent hundreds of millions of dollars on warehouses.

Given the many similarities, how then does the "new" economy differ from the old? The most obvious is the essential role of network effects in demand – the benefit provided by a service depends on the total number of other users. Network effects explain the growth of the Internet from an academic curiosity to a ubiquitous business platform in just five years. When only one person had email, she had no one to communicate with. With 100 million users online, the demand for email, ICQ, and other communications services mushroomed. Another reason for the feverish growth of the Internet was its open technology, which freely admitted developers of content and applications.

The other distinctive feature of the new economy is the importance of scale and scope economies. A recurring theme in the new economy is "scalability" – the degree to which the scale and scope of a business can be increased without a corresponding increase in costs. The information in Yahoo is eminently scalable: the same information can serve 100 as well as 100 million users. It is, in economic language, a "public good." To serve a larger number of users, Yahoo needs only increase the capacity of its computers and communications links. By contrast, a traditional library is less scaleable: a library must incur a relatively higher cost to serve a larger number of readers than the cost that Yahoo incurs to serve more users.

Managerial economics consists of three branches: competitive markets, market power, and imperfect markets. This book is organized in three parts, one part for each branch. Before discussing these three branches, let us first develop some background.

> **Progress Check 1A**   How is the managerial economics of the "new economy" different from that of the "old economy"?   *Progress check*

◂◂ 2 Preliminaries

To appreciate when and how to apply managerial economics, we should understand the scope and methodology of the discipline. We also need to understand several basic analytical concepts that are used throughout the three branches of managerial economics. This preliminary background is a necessary first step toward mastering the discipline.

> **Microeconomics** is the study of individual economic behavior where resources are costly.

Scope

First, we should distinguish managerial economics from **microeconomics** and **macroeconomics**. Microeconomics is the study of individual economic behavior where resources are costly. It addresses issues such as how consumers respond to

> **Macroeconomics** is the study of aggregate economic variables.

changes in prices and income and how businesses decide on employment and sales. Microeconomics also extends to such issues as how voters choose between political parties and how governments should set taxes. Managerial economics has a more limited scope – it is the application of microeconomics to managerial issues.

By contrast with microeconomics, the field of macroeconomics focuses on aggregate economic variables. Macroeconomics addresses such issues as how a cut in interest rates will affect the inflation rate and how a depreciation of the U.S. dollar will affect unemployment, exports, and imports. While it is certainly true that the whole economy is made up of individual consumers and businesses, the study of macroeconomics often considers economic aggregates directly rather than as the aggregation of individual consumers and businesses. This is the key distinction between the fields of macroeconomics and microeconomics.

Some issues span both macroeconomics and microeconomics. For instance, energy is such an important part of the economy that changes in the price of energy have both macroeconomic and microeconomic effects. If the price of oil were to rise by 10%, it would trigger increases in other prices and hence generate price inflation, which is a macroeconomic effect. The increase in the price of oil would also have microeconomic effects; for instance, power stations might switch to other fuels, drivers might cut back on using their cars, and oil producers might open up new fields.

Methodology

Having defined the scope of managerial economics, let us now consider its methodology. The fundamental premise of managerial economics is that individuals share common motivations that lead them to behave systematically in making economic choices. This means that a person who faces the same choices at two different times will behave in the same way at both times.

An **economic model** is a concise description of behavior and outcomes.

If economic behavior is systematic, then it can be studied. Managerial economics proceeds by constructing models of economic behavior. An **economic model** is a concise description of behavior and outcomes. By design, the model omits considerable information, so as to focus on a few key variables. In this regard, economic models are like maps: a map with too much detail is confusing rather than helpful. Imagine driving around Toronto with a map that included every pothole on the street. The map could not fit into the car! To be useful, a map must be less than completely realistic.

Economic models are like maps in another way. Different maps of Toronto serve different purposes: street maps for drivers, guides to main attractions for tourists, and charts of underground utility lines for builders. Likewise, there may be different economic models of the same situation, each of them focusing on a different issue.

Models are constructed by inductive reasoning. For instance, inductive reasoning suggests that the demand for new software increases with the amount that the publisher spends on advertising. We can build a model in which the demand for a product depends on advertising expenditure. The model should then be tested with actual empirical data. If the tests support the model, it can be accepted; otherwise, it should be revised.

Marginal vis-à-vis Average

In managerial economics, many analyses resolve to a balance between the marginal values of two variables. Accordingly, it is important to understand the concept of a **marginal value**. Generally, the marginal value of a variable is the change in the variable associated with a unit increase in a driver. By contrast, the **average value** of a variable is the total value of the variable divided by the total quantity of a driver.

> The **marginal value** of a variable is the change in the variable associated with a unit increase in a driver.

What is a *driver*? To explain, consider the following example. Alan and Hilda are clerks at the Luna Store. The store pays each clerk $10 per hour for a basic eight-hour day, $15 per hour for overtime of up to four hours, and $20 for overtime exceeding four hours a day. Suppose that Alan works 10 hours a day. Then he earns $10 per hour for eight hours and $15 per hour for two hours of overtime, which adds up to a total of ($10 × 8) + ($15 × 2) = $110.

> The **average value** of a variable is the total value of the variable divided by the total quantity of a driver.

With respect to Alan's pay, the driver is the number of hours worked. Hence, Alan's marginal pay is the amount that he could earn by working one additional hour. His marginal pay is $15 per hour. By contrast, Alan's average pay is his total pay divided by the total number of hours worked, which is $110/10 = $11 per hour. The marginal pay exceeds the average pay because the store pays higher rates for additional hours beyond the basic eight. Since the marginal pay is the pay for an additional hour of overtime, it is higher than the average pay.

Note that the marginal and average pay depend on the number of hours worked. Suppose that Hilda works 14 hours a day. She earns $10 per hour for eight hours, $15 per hour for the first four hours of overtime, and $20 per hour for the fifth and sixth hours of overtime, which sums to ($10 × 8) + ($15 × 4) + ($20 × 2) = $180. Her marginal pay is $20 per hour, while her average pay is $180/14 = $12.86 per hour. Hilda's marginal pay exceeds Alan's because she works four hours longer, which puts her into the $20 per hour overtime bracket.

Generally, the marginal value of a variable may be less than, equal to, or greater than the average value. The relation between the marginal and average values depends on whether the marginal value is decreasing, constant, or increasing with respect to the driver.

> A **stock** is the quantity of a given item at a specific point in time.

Stocks and Flows

Another important distinction in managerial economics is that between **stocks** and **flows**. A stock is the quantity at a specific point in time. By contrast, a flow is the change in a

> A **flow** is the change in a given item over a period of time.

stock over some period of time. While stocks are measured in units of the item, flows are measured in units per time period.

Every manager must understand the distinction between stocks and flows. A balance sheet represents the financial status of a business at a specific point in time, hence the items on a balance sheet – assets and liabilities – are stocks. By contrast, the income statement reports changes in the financial status of a business. The items in an income statement – receipts and expenses – are flows. An annual income statement reports flows over a year, while a quarterly income statement reports flows over three months.

Let us illustrate the distinction between stocks and flows with several other examples. The world's oil reserves at the beginning of the current year is a stock. This stock may be measured in billions of barrels. By contrast, the world's current production of oil is a flow. This flow may be measured in millions of barrels per day. Coca Cola Enterprises' inventory of concentrate on January 1, 2002 is a stock while its purchases and sales of concentrate during the period January 1–7, 2002 are flows.

Other Things Equal

Holding **other things equal** is the assumption that all other relevant factors do not change, made so that changes due to the factor being studied may be examined independently of those other factors.

The third basic concept in managerial economics is the device of holding **other things equal**. At any one time, the environment of business may be changing in several different ways. It would be difficult to analyze the implications of all the various changes together. The difficulty is compounded if the separate changes have conflicting effects. An alternative approach is to simplify the problem by analyzing each change separately, holding other things equal. Having analyzed the separate effects, we can then put them together for the complete picture.

For instance, a silver mine may be confronted with an increase in the price of electricity, a drop in the price of silver, and a change in labor laws, all on the same day. How should the mine adjust its production? The most practical way to address this question is to consider each change separately, holding "other things equal." Having understood each of the separate effects, the next step is to assemble them to get the complete picture.

Either explicitly or implicitly, almost every piece of managerial economics analysis holds other things equal. This usage is so close to being universal that we will not explicitly state the proviso. Nevertheless, it is always important to bear the proviso in mind when applying the results of some analysis to a practical managerial issue.

◂◂ 3 Organizational Boundaries

Throughout this book, we will take the viewpoint of an organization, which may be a business, nonprofit, or a household. All managers face the same issue of how to effectively manage costly resources. Since our analysis focuses on the organization, we first must identify the boundaries of the organization. We briefly discuss this issue here, while leaving the detailed analysis to chapters 7 and 13.

The activities of an organization are subject to two sets of boundaries. One is **vertical**, which delineates activities closer to or further from the end user. Members of the same industry may choose different vertical boundaries. For instance, the vertical chain in the automobile industry runs from produc-

> Vertical boundaries delineate activities closer to or further from the end user.

tion of steel and other materials, electrical and electronic components, tires and other parts to assembly of the vehicle to distribution. Both General Motors (GM) and Toyota are principally manufacturers of automobiles. Toyota did not produce electrical and electronic components, while GM did until 1999. Then, GM spun off Delphi Automotive Systems, which manufactures automotive components, systems and modules.

The vertical chain in the Internet runs from provision of content such as information, entertainment, and e-commerce, to Internet access, and to the telephone or cable service over which users access the Internet. America Online merged with Time Warner to become a provider of the entire vertical chain, including content, Internet access, and cable service. By contrast, Yahoo provides Internet content, but neither telephone nor cable service.

An organization's other set of boundaries is **horizontal**. The organization's horizontal boundaries are defined by its scale and scope of operations. Scale refers to the rate of production or delivery of a good or service, while scope refers to the range of different items produced or delivered. Just as members of the same industry may choose different vertical boundaries, they may also choose different horizontal boundaries.

> Horizontal boundaries define the scale and scope of an organization's operations.

For instance, in the sale of personal computers, Compaq and Dell operate on a much larger scale than the numerous small businesses that advertise generic machines in *PC Week*. Hence, in terms of scale, Compaq and Dell have wider horizontal boundaries than the generic suppliers. At the time of writing, however, Compaq and Dell differ in scope. Compaq manufactures a wide range of computers, including large highly fault-tolerant machines, servers, workstations, as well as personal computers, and it also provides consulting services. By contrast, Dell focuses on selling servers and personal computers. Accordingly, in terms of scope, Compaq has wider horizontal boundaries than Dell.

Progress Check 1B Explain the difference between the vertical and horizontal boundaries of an organization.

Progress check

The organizational boundaries of Coke and Pepsi

Historically, Coke was vertically separated: the Coca Cola Company, headquartered in Atlanta, owned the brand and sold concentrate to Coca Cola Enterprises, Coca Cola Bottling Company, and other franchised bottlers. By contrast, PepsiCo had been vertically integrated. Then, in March 1999, PepsiCo spun off the Pepsi Bottling Group (PBG) and shrunk its vertical boundaries. Following the spin-off, PepsiCo managed the brand and sold concentrate, while PBG used the concentrate to manufacture soft drink for sale in supermarkets and other distribution channels.

While the industry as a whole was vertically separating between concentrate production and bottling, the bottling part was consolidating horizontally. In 1978, Coke had 370 bottlers in the United States. By the end of 1998, that number had fallen to under 100. Likewise, one of Pepsi's leading bottlers, Pepsi Cola General Bottlers, acquired many smaller bottlers. Standard and Poor's Food and Beverage analyst remarked: "The recent spin-off of the . . . Pepsi Bottling Group is expected to further the trend towards consolidation."

Source: Standard & Poor's Industry Surveys: Foods & Nonalcoholic Beverages, 166, no. 22, section 1 (June 3, 1999), p. 3.

◂◂ 4 Markets

A **market** consists of the buyers and sellers that communicate with one another for voluntary exchange.

One basic concept of managerial economics – the market – is so fundamental that it appears in the names of each branch of the discipline. A **market** consists of the buyers and sellers that communicate with one another for voluntary exchange. In this sense, a market is not limited to any physical structure or particular location. The market extends as far as there are buyers or sellers who can communicate and trade at relatively low cost.

Consider, for instance, the market for cotton. This extends beyond the New York Board of Trade to growers in the Carolinas and textile manufacturers in East Asia. If the price on the Board of Trade increases, then that price increase will affect Carolina growers and Asian textile manufacturers. Likewise, if the demand for cotton in Asia increases, this will be reflected in the price on the Board of Trade.

In markets for consumer products, the buyers are households and sellers are businesses. In markets for industrial products, both buyers and sellers are businesses. Finally, in markets for human resources, buyers are businesses and sellers are households.

By contrast with a market, an **industry** is made up of the businesses engaged in the production or delivery of the same or similar items. For instance, the consumer electronics industry consists of all consumer electronics manufacturers, and the semiconductor industry consists of all semiconductor manufacturers. Members of an industry can be buyers in one market and sellers in another. The consumer electronics industry is a buyer in the semiconductor market and a seller in the consumer electronics market.

> An **industry** consists of the businesses engaged in the production or delivery of the same or similar items.

Competitive Markets

The global silver market includes many competing producers and thousands of buyers. How should a mine respond to an increase in the price of electricity, a drop in the price of silver, or a change in labor laws? How will these changes affect buyers? The basic starting point of managerial economics is the model of competitive markets. This applies to markets with many buyers and many sellers. The market for silver is an example of a competitive market. In a competitive market, buyers provide the demand and sellers provide the supply. Accordingly, the model is also called the *demand-supply model*.

The model describes the systematic effect of changes in prices and other economic variables on buyers and sellers. Further, the model describes the interaction of these choices. In the silver mine example, the model can describe how the mine should

The extent of e-commerce markets

A bricks-and-mortar bookstore serves a geographical area defined by a reasonable traveling time. By contrast, an Internet bookstore serves a much larger market – defined by the reach of telecommunications and the cost of shipping. In March 2000, Stephen King launched *Riding the Bullet*, which he described as "a ghost story in the grand manner," in digital format over the Internet. Readers paid $2.50 to download the 16,000-word story (about 33 printed pages). With digital distribution, Internet bookstores would be able to dispense with the logistics of shipping physical product. They would need only the telecommunications network.

In early 2000, the market value of Internet bookstore Amazon.com was ten times greater than that of America's leading bricks-and-mortar bookstore, Barnes and Noble. The vast disparity reflected the stock market's assessment of the difference in the long-term profitability of the two companies. An e-commerce business can reach a much larger market than a traditional bricks-and-mortar retailer. Further, by avoiding the costs of inventory and store rental, the e-commerce business may achieve lower costs.

Source: "E-Books King: Stephen the First," *Wired News*, March 14, 2000.

adjust prices when the price of electricity increases, the price of silver drops, and labor laws change, all on the same day. These changes affect all silver mines. Hence, the model also describes the interaction among the adjustments of the various mines and how these affect buyers.

Part I of this book presents the model of competitive markets. It begins with the demand side, considering how buyers respond to changes in prices and income (chapter 2). Next, we develop a set of quantitative methods that support precise estimates of changes in economic behavior (chapter 3). Then, we look at the supply side of the market, considering how sellers respond to changes in the prices of products and inputs (chapter 4). We bring demand and supply together and analyze their interaction in chapter 5, then show that the outcome of market competition is efficient (chapter 6).

Market Power

In a competitive market, an individual manager may have little freedom of action. Key variables such as prices, scale of operations, and input mix are determined by market forces. The role of a manager is simply to follow the market and survive. Not all markets, however, have so many buyers and sellers to qualify as competitive. **Market power** is the ability of a buyer or seller to influence market conditions. A seller with market power will have relatively more freedom to choose suppliers, set prices, and use advertising to influence demand. A buyer with market power will be able to influence the supply of products that it purchases.

> **Market power** is the ability of a buyer or seller to influence market conditions.

A business with market power must determine its horizontal boundaries. These depend on how its costs vary with the scale and scope of operations. Accordingly, businesses with market power – whether buyers or sellers – need to understand and manage their costs.

In addition to managing costs, sellers with market power need to manage their demand. Three key tools in managing demand are price, advertising, and policy toward competitors. What price maximizes profit? A lower price boosts sales, while a higher price brings in higher margins. A similar issue arises in determining advertising expenditure. With regard to other businesses, what are the benefits of cooperating rather than competing?

Part II of this book addresses all of these issues. We begin by analyzing costs (chapter 7), then consider management in the extreme case of market power, where there is only one seller or only one buyer (chapter 8). Next, we discuss pricing policy (chapter 9) and strategic thinking (chapter 10).

Imperfect Markets

Businesses with market power have relatively more freedom of action than those in competitive markets. Managers will also have relatively more freedom of action in markets that are subject to imperfections. A market may be imperfect in two ways:

when one party directly conveys a benefit or cost to others or where one party has better information than others. The challenge for managers operating in **imperfect markets** is to resolve the imperfection and, so, enable the cost-effective provision of their products.

> In an **imperfect market,** one party directly conveys a benefit or cost to others or one party has better information than others.

Consider the market for residential mortgages. Applicants for mortgages have better knowledge of their ability and willingness to repay than potential lenders. In this case, the market is imperfect owing to differences in information. The challenge for lenders is how to resolve the informational differences so that they can provide loans in a cost-effective way.

Managers of businesses in imperfect markets need to think strategically. For instance, a residential mortgage lender may require all loan applicants to pay for a credit check, with the lender refunding the cost if the credit check is favorable. The lender might reason that bad borrowers would not be willing to pay for a credit check because they would fail the check. Good borrowers, however, would pay for the check because they would get their money back from the lender. Hence, the credit check requirement will screen out the bad borrowers. This is an example of strategic thinking in an imperfect market.

Differences in information can cause a market to be imperfect. The same imperfection can arise within an organization, where some members have better information than others. Accordingly, another issue is how to structure incentives and organization.

Part III of this book addresses all of these issues. We begin by considering the sources of market imperfections – where one party directly conveys a benefit or cost to others (chapter 11) and where one party has better information than others (chapter 12), then the appropriate structure of incentives and organization (chapter 13). Finally, we consider how government regulation can resolve market imperfections (chapter 14).

◂◂ 5 Global Principles

We have mentioned that a market extends as far as there are buyers or sellers who can communicate and trade at relatively low cost. Owing to the relatively high costs of communication and trade, some markets are local. Examples include grocery retailing, housing, and live entertainment. The price in one local market will be independent of prices in other local markets. For instance, an increase in the price of apartments in New York City does not affect the housing market in Houston.

By contrast, some markets are global because the costs of communication and trade are relatively low. Examples include financial services, minerals, and shipping. In the case of an item with a global market, the price in one place will move together with the prices elsewhere. For instance, when the price of silver increases in London, the price will also rise in Tokyo.

We emphasize that, whether a market is local or global, the same managerial economics principles apply. For instance, when the price of fresh vegetables in Britain increases, consumers will switch to frozen vegetables. The same will be true in Japan, the United States, and any other place. An airline with market power in France will use that power to raise prices above the competitive level. The same will be true all over the world. A mortgage lender in Australia will act strategically to resolve the difference in information relative to borrowers. Again, the same will be true all over the world. Throughout this book, we shall give examples from different parts of the world to reiterate that managerial economics applies globally.

A related point is that the costs of and barriers to transport, communication, and trade have systematically fallen over time. This trend has caused many markets to become relatively more integrated across geographical boundaries. For instance, Canadian insurers sell life insurance and mutual funds in Asia, Israeli growers ship fresh flowers by air to Europe, and U.S.-based callback services offer cheap international telephone calls throughout the world.

As a result of the trend toward integration, managers need to pay increasing attention to markets in other places. Some markets may be similar, while others are different. In all cases, managers must not allow their planning to be limited by traditional geographical boundaries.

Global sourcing

Global integration means not only the opportunity to sell in new markets but also the opportunity to secure supplies from new sources. Foreign sources may provide cheaper skilled labor, specialized resources, or superior quality. These advantages allow a manufacturer to reduce production costs and improve quality.

Dell Computer manufactures personal computers at Austin, Texas, and Nashville, Tennessee. A typical Dell system might include a keyboard made in China, a monitor from Taiwan, and a mouse manufactured in Mexico.

◂◂ 6 Summary

Managerial economics is the science of directing scarce resources to manage cost effectively. It consists of three branches: competitive markets, market power, and imperfect markets. A market consists of buyers and sellers that communicate with each other for voluntary exchange. Whether a market is local or global, the same managerial economics principles apply.

A seller with market power will have freedom to choose suppliers, set prices, and use advertising to influence demand. A market is imperfect when one party directly conveys a benefit or cost to others or when one party has better information than others.

An organization must decide its vertical and horizontal boundaries. For effective management, it is important to distinguish marginal from average values and stocks from flows. Managerial economics applies models that are necessarily less than completely realistic. Typically, a model focuses on one issue, holding other things equal.

Key Concepts

managerial economics	average value	vertical boundaries
microeconomics	stock	horizontal boundaries
macroeconomics	flow	industry
economic model	other things equal	market power
marginal value	market	imperfect market

Review Questions

1. Amazon markets books and recorded music over the Internet, and delivers them by conventional means such as the United Parcel Service. Which of Amazon's activities are scaleable?

2. Explain the relation among the number of cars in service on January 1, 2002, the number in service on January 1, 2003, and the production, imports, exports, and scrappage of cars. Which of the variables are stocks and which are flows?

3. Using relevant examples, explain the distinction between macroeconomics and microeconomics.

4. "Managerial economics uses less than completely realistic models." Is this necessarily bad?

5. Kokusai Denshin Denwa (KDD) is Japan's leading provider of international telephone services. In November 1998, KDD's standard rate for calls from Japan to Singapore was ¥210 (yen) for the first minute and ¥120 for each subsequent minute. Yoko makes a five-minute call.
   (a) What is the average price per minute of Yoko's call?
   (b) What is the price of Yoko's marginal minute?

6. Which of the following are stocks and which are flows?
   (a) Monthly usage of laser printer toner cartridges.
   (b) Number of technicians on the payroll as of January 1.
   (c) Number of workstations in inventory as of July 31.

7. Explain the difference between
   (a) The market for electricity.
   (b) The electricity industry.

8. True or false?
   (a) In every market, all the buyers are consumers.
   (b) In every market, all the sellers are businesses.

9. Describe the vertical and horizontal boundaries of your university. In what ways could the vertical boundaries be expanded or reduced? What about the horizontal boundaries?

10. Why do economies of scale affect the horizontal boundaries of an organization?

11. Does a new economy business like Amazon need to consider its organizational boundaries?

12. Which of the following manufacturers has relatively more market power in its market?
    (a) Intel, which accounts for more than 50% of worldwide production of microprocessors for personal computers.
    (b) Compro, which has less than a 1% share of the global market for personal computers.

13. Managers operating in an imperfect market must (choose a or b)
    (a) Set high prices to make up for the imperfection.
    (b) Act strategically to resolve the imperfection.

14. Which of the following are consequences of the falling costs of international communication and trade?
    (a) Buyers can obtain products from a wider range of suppliers.
    (b) Sellers can market their products to a wider set of customers.

15. Explain the distinctions among the three branches of managerial economics.

Discussion Questions

1. Russell's savings consist of $10,000 in a savings account that yields 2% a year interest and another $10,000 in a money market fund that pays interest of 5% a year. Russell has just received a gift of $10,000 from his mother. His bank pays 4% interest on savings accounts with a minimum deposit of $20,000. The money market fund pays 5% interest on investments up to $100,000.
    (a) Calculate the average interest rate (= dollar amount of interest divided by amount of investment) from the savings account if Russell deposits the additional $10,000 in the savings account and qualifies for the higher interest rate.
    (b) Calculate the average interest rate if Russell deposits the additional $10,000 in the money market fund.
    (c) Calculate the marginal interest rate (= increase in dollar amount of interest divided by additional investment) from the savings account if Russell deposits the additional $10,000 in the savings account.
    (d) Calculate the marginal interest rate if Russell deposits the additional $10,000 in the money market fund.
    (e) From the viewpoint of maximizing his total interest income, where should Russell deposit the additional money?

2. Refer to the financial statements of any publicly listed company. Taking any page at random, identify which of the financial data are stocks and which are flows.

3. In each of the following instances, discuss whether horizontal or vertical boundaries have been changed, and whether they were extended or shrunk.
    (a) General Motors divested Delphi Automotive Systems, which manufactures automotive components, systems, and modules.
    (b) Internet content and service provider America Online (AOL) merged with Time Warner, a producer of films and music, and provider of cable television services.
    (c) The National Collegiate Athletic Association's (NCAA) Western Athletic Conference for basketball split into two smaller conferences.
    (d) DaimlerChrysler took over the import and wholesale distribution of Mercedes Benz cars in Hong Kong and Singapore from independent agencies.

4. Referring to the definition of a *market*, consider whether the following groups of buyers and sellers are part of the corresponding market.
    (a) After Iraq invaded Kuwait in August 1990, the United Nations banned Iraq from exporting oil to the rest of the world. During the ban, was Iraq part of the world market for oil?
    (b) Prisoners cannot freely work outside the jail. Do prisoners belong to the national labor market?

5. The recorded music industry is undergoing a transition from the compact disc (CD) to MP3 and other digital formats for online delivery. CDs are pressed from masters created from the original soundtrack and distributed through retailers and other channels. By contrast, MP3 titles can be delivered directly to consumers over the Internet. In 1999, the leading British publisher EMI decided to close all CD manufacturing facilities in North America in favor of contracting with specialist manufacturers to produce its CDs.
    (a) By considering the relative costs of transporting CD masters and pressed CDs, explain why music publishers arrange for CDs to be pressed in various regional centers throughout the world rather than in one central factory.
    (b) How would the shift from CDs to online digital delivery affect the extent of the market that EMI can economically serve from Britain?
    (c) Relate the changes in EMI's vertical boundaries to your discussion in (b).

Part *I*

Competitive Markets

Chapter *2*
Demand

◀◀ 1 Introduction

Steve Case founded America Online in 1985 to provide an online "walled garden" of content and services based on a proprietary technology. In the mid-1990s, America Online successfully managed the transition from proprietary system to the open-standard Internet. Growth mushroomed as new subscribers were attracted by America Online's chat rooms, instant messaging services (AOL Instant Messenger and ICQ), and specialized services such as Digital City, Moviefone, and MapQuest. At the time of writing, America Online had become the largest Internet service provider in the United States through its two brands, AOL with 24 million subscribers, and Compuserve with 2.8 million subscribers.[1]

AOL offered several alternative service plans, including an unmetered access plan at $21.95 a month (or $19.95 a month for customers who pre-paid for one year's service), and a limited usage plan for $9.95 a month providing 5 hours' free access and additional usage at $2.95 per hour. Compuserve catered to price-sensitive customers at $9.95 a month.

Ultimately, the size of the market for Internet access depends on the installed base of devices that can be connected to the Internet. To avoid being limited by the installed base of computers, America Online adopted its "AOL Anywhere" multi-platform strategy to offer AOL services "anywhere, anytime and at any speed – on emerging interactive platforms beyond the PC."

In October 1999, America Online signed an agreement with OpenTV, a developer of interactive software for digital set-top boxes allowing online access through television sets. The two companies agreed to develop OpenTV's software to provide

▼

[1] This analysis is based, in part, on "America Online and OpenTV Announce Plans to Develop Applications for OpenTV Platform," America Online, Inc., Press Release, October 25, 1999; and "America Online Delivers 'AOL Mobile' Services to AT&T Wireless Internet-Ready Phones," America Online, Inc., Press Release, September 5, 2000.

AOL email and instant messaging. OpenTV Chief Executive Officer Jan Steenkamp remarked: "With almost 99% of American households having one or more televisions, it makes the most sense to deliver the promise of convergence through the television."

Twelve months later, in September 2000, America Online concluded an agreement with AT&T Wireless to provide AOL service through Internet-enabled mobile phones. AT&T Wireless Vice President, Tom Trinneer, explained: "With our flat-rate pricing plans and extensive nationwide footprint, we're excited to be offering mobile access to AOL's popular features and service."

In the early years of the Internet, access providers charged subscribers by usage. Then, in March 1996, Netcom offered the first unmetered access plan for $19.95 a month. Microsoft Network quickly jumped on the bandwagon and America Online followed. Soon, unmetered plans dominated the Internet access market. How should a provider like AOL set the price for unmetered access? How should it price the limited access plan? Why did America Online embark on the "AOL Anywhere" strategy? For the "AOL Anywhere" strategy, why was it important that AT&T Wireless offered flat-rate pricing plans?

To address these issues, this chapter develops an analysis of consumer and business demand.

We begin with the demand curve of an individual buyer. This shows the quantity of the item that an individual will purchase as a function of its price. Next, we consider how demand depends on other factors, including income, the prices of other products, and advertising.

Then, we extend from the demand of an individual to the demand curve of the entire market. With the model of demand, businesses can identify factors that affect the demand for their products, and how to influence that demand. We can apply this analysis to explain the importance of the "AOL Anywhere" strategy. We then use the demand curve to show the maximum amount of money that the buyer is willing to pay for each unit of the item. Using this information, a seller can determine the maximum that a buyer is willing to pay for any specified quantity. We apply this method to explain how AOL should price its unmetered access plan. Finally, we highlight the important differences between consumer and business demand.

◂◂ 2 Individual Demand

The **individual demand curve** is a graph showing the quantity that one buyer will purchase at every possible price.

To understand how a price cut will affect sales, we need to know how the cut in price will affect the purchases of the individual buyers and, generally, how an individual's purchases depend on the price of an item. The **individual demand curve** provides this information: it is a graph that shows the quantity that one buyer will purchase at every possible price.

We shall present the concept of a demand curve with reference to an individual consumer. The principles underlying the demand curve for a business buyer are quite similar. Hence, this section focuses on consumer demand, and a later section highlights the important differences for business demand.

Construction

The basic issue is how to determine an individual's demand curve. Let us address the issue by considering Joy's demand for movies. We must ask Joy a series of questions that elicit her responses to changes in price, while holding other things equal.

We first ask, "Other things equal, how many movies would you attend a month at a price of $10 per movie?" Suppose that Joy's answer is, "None." We must add the proviso of "other things equal" because Joy's decision may depend on other factors, such as her income and the price of popcorn in the movie theater. When constructing Joy's demand curve for movies, we focus on the effect of changes in the price of movies and hold all other factors constant.

We then pose similar questions to Joy for other possible prices for a movie: $7.50, $5, $2.50, and 0. For each of these prices, Joy will tell us how many movies she would attend a month. We can tabulate this information as shown in table 2.1. This table represents Joy's demand for movies.

Next we graph the information from table 2.1 as shown in figure 2.1. We represent the price of movies on the vertical axis and the quantity in movies a month on the horizontal axis. At a price of $10, Joy says that she would go to no movies, so we mark the point where the price is $10 and quantity of movies is 0. Continuing with the information from table 2.1, we mark every pair of price and quantity that Joy reports. Joining these points, we then have Joy's demand curve for movies. This is the stepped curve drawn in bold.

The demand curve in figure 2.1 shows, for every possible price, the quantity of movies that Joy will attend. Knowing Joy's demand curve, a movie theater can predict how Joy will respond to changes in its price. For instance, if presently, the theater charges $5 per movie, Joy goes to two movies a month. If the theater reduces

Table 2.1 Individual demand

Price ($ per movie)	Quantity (movies a month)
10.00	0
7.50	1
5.00	2
2.50	4
0.00	7

Figure 2.1 Individual demand curve

The individual demand curve shows, for every possible price, the quantity of movies that Joy will attend. It also shows how much Joy would be willing to pay for various quantities.

its price to $2.50 per movie, it knows that Joy will increase her consumption to four movies a month. By contrast, if the theater raises its price to $7.50 per movie, Joy would cut back to one movie a month.

The demand curve in figure 2.1 is a series of steps. Later in this chapter, we will present demand curves that are smooth. The principles of demand curves are the same whether the curves are stepped or smooth.

Slope

The individual demand curve shows the quantity that the buyer will purchase at every possible price. Let us now consider the individual demand curve from another perspective.

Referring to Joy's demand curve in figure 2.1, we can use the curve to determine how much Joy would be willing to pay for various quantities of movies. Specifically, the curve shows that she is willing to pay $7.50 per movie for one movie a month. Further, it shows that Joy is willing to pay $5 per movie for two movies a month, and $2.50 per movie for four movies a month.

Generally, if the number of movies is larger, the price that Joy is willing to pay is lower. Equivalently, at a lower price, Joy is willing to buy a larger quantity (specifically, go to more movies). These two related properties of a demand curve reflect the principle of diminishing marginal benefit, which we shall explain next.

> The **marginal benefit** is the benefit provided by an additional unit of the item.

Any item that a consumer is willing to buy must provide some benefit, which may be psychic or monetary. We measure the benefit in monetary terms as we are interested in goods and services that are bought and sold. The **marginal benefit** is the benefit provided by an additional unit of the item. The marginal benefit of the first movie is the benefit from one movie a month. Similarly, the marginal benefit of the second movie is the additional benefit from seeing a second movie each month.

> **Principle of diminishing marginal benefit:** each additional unit provides less benefit than the preceding unit.

By the principle of **diminishing marginal benefit**, each additional unit of consumption or usage provides less benefit than the preceding unit. In Joy's case, this means that the marginal benefit of the second movie is less than the marginal benefit of the first movie, the marginal benefit of the third movie is less than the marginal benefit of the second movie, and so on.

Accordingly, the price that an individual is willing to pay will decrease with the quantity purchased. In terms of a graph, this means that the demand curve will slope downward. This is a general property of all demand curves: the lower the price, the larger will be the quantity demanded. Hence, demand curves slope downward. The fundamental reason for this downward slope is diminishing marginal benefit.

> **Progress Check 2A** Suppose that a movie theater is presently charging $7.50 per movie. By how much must the theater cut its price for Joy to increase her consumption by three movies a month?
>
> *Progress check*

Preferences

Our procedure for constructing a demand curve relies completely on the consumer's individual preferences. The individual decides how much he or she wants to buy at each possible price. The demand curve then displays information in a graphical way.

There are two implications of this approach. First, the demand curve will change with changes in the consumer's preferences. As a person grows older, her or his demand for rock videos and junk food will decline, while the demand for adult contemporary compact discs and meals in stylish restaurants will increase.

Second, different consumers may have different preferences and hence different demand curves. One consumer may like red meat while another is a vegetarian. We get the demand curve for each consumer from her or his individual responses to the questions regarding the quantity she or he would buy at each possible price.

Quantity demanded at a negative price: Hoover's free flight promotion

In Autumn 1992, the British home appliance manufacturer, Hoover, offered two free air travel tickets to every customer who purchased an appliance with a price of £100 or more. Each ticket was valid for round-trip travel to continental Europe or the United States. The market value of a pair of tickets exceeded £400.

For a £100 appliance, Hoover's effective price was £(100 − 400) = −£300; that is, the company was *paying* each customer £300 to take an appliance. As might be expected, huge numbers of consumers were willing to buy Hoover appliances on those terms. The promotion attracted over 100,000 customers.

Hoover's management, however, had not anticipated this response. It had to establish a special 250-person task force to deal with the flight bookings and set aside £48 million to cover the cost of over 200,000 free flights. William Foust, president of Hoover Europe, and two other senior executives were dismissed for their role in the promotion.

At the time of the promotion, Hoover was owned by the American appliance manufacturer Maytag. In May 1995, Maytag sold Hoover to an Italian home appliances group for £106 million.

Source: "Hoover 'Free Flights' Scheme Costs 48 Million Pounds," *Financial Times*, April 21, 1994, p. 7; "Hoover Sold after Free Flights Fiasco," *The Times*, May 31, 1995.

◂◂ 3 Demand and Income

We have mentioned that Joy's demand for movies may depend on other factors in addition to the price of such movies. For instance, if she gets a raise, she might spend more on movies. Her demand for movies will also depend on the price of alternative forms of entertainment such as video rentals.

The individual demand curve shows explicitly how the quantity that a person buys depends on the price of the item. The demand curve, however, does not explicitly display the effect of changes in income and other factors that affect demand. How do changes in these other factors affect an individual's demand curve? In this section, we focus on the effect of changes in the buyer's income and consider the impact of other factors in the next section.

Income Changes

Let us consider the effect of changes in income on demand in the context of Joy's demand for movies. Suppose that Joy's income is presently $30,000 a year.

Table 2.2 Individual demand with lower income

Price ($ per movie)	Quantity (movies a month)
10.00	0
7.50	0
5.00	1
2.50	2
0.00	7

Figure 2.2 Individual demand curve with lower income

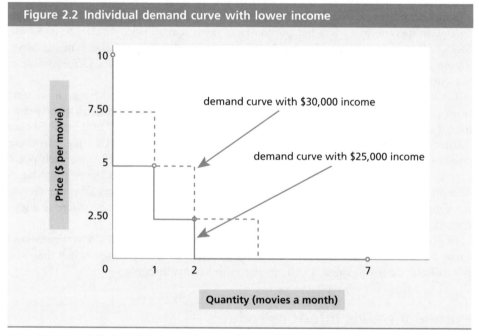

As Joy's income falls from $30,000 to $25,000, her entire demand curve shifts toward the left.

Table 2.1 and figure 2.1 represent Joy's demand curve for movies when her income is $30,000 a year.

We then ask Joy a series of questions. These questions probe the effect of changes in income as well as price: "Suppose that your income were $25,000 a year. Other things equal, how many movies would you buy a month at a price of $10 per movie?" We then pose the same question with other possible prices – $7.50, $5, $2.50, and 0 – and tabulate the information.

Suppose that table 2.2 represents Joy's answers. We also represent this information in figure 2.2, with the price of movies on the vertical axis and number of movies a month on the horizontal axis. Marking the pairs of prices and quantities, and joining the points, we have Joy's demand curve with an income of $25,000 a year. We can see that Joy's demand curve for movies with a $25,000 income lies to the left of her demand curve with a $30,000 income. At every price, Joy's quantity demanded with a $25,000 income is less than or equal to her quantity demanded with a $30,000 income.

The effect of a change in income on the demand curve is very different from that of a change in price. Recall that an individual demand curve shows the quantity that the person will buy for every possible price, other things equal. Referring to figure 2.1, if the price of movies drops from $7.50 to $5 per movie, while Joy's income remains unchanged at $30,000 a year, we can trace Joy's response by moving along her demand curve from the $7.50 level to the $5 level.

Suppose, however, that Joy's income drops from $30,000 to $25,000 a year. This change in income will affect her purchases of movies at all price levels – $10, $7.50, $5, $2.50, and 0. Accordingly, the drop in income will shift her entire demand curve. Figure 2.2 shows that, when Joy's income drops from $30,000 to $25,000 a year, her entire demand curve for movies shifts toward the left.

Let us understand the difference between a change in price and a change in income from another perspective. On figure 2.2, at the $5 level, we can mark two quantities: a quantity of two movies a month when Joy's income is $30,000, and another quantity of one movie a month when Joy's income is $25,000. Can we join these points to form a demand curve? The answer is definitely "no," because each point corresponds to a different income. A demand curve shows how a buyer's purchases depend on changes in the price of some item, holding income and all other factors unchanged. Accordingly, for each of the points that we have marked, there is a separate demand curve.

In general, a change in the price of an item will cause a movement along the demand curve for that item. By contrast, a change in income or any factor other than the price of the item will cause a shift in the entire demand curve.

Normal vis-à-vis Inferior Products

When Joy's income drops from $30,000 to $25,000 a year, her demand for movies shifts to the left. As Joy's income falls, her demand for movies also falls. By contrast, if her income were to rise, her demand would increase.

Let us compare Joy's demand for movies in general with her demand for afternoon matinees. Many movie theaters offer afternoon matinees at a cheaper price than their regular evening showings. If Joy's income falls, it is quite possible that she will substitute cheaper forms of entertainment for more expensive ones. In particular, the drop in her income may lead to an increase in her demand for afternoon matinees.

By contrast, when Joy's income increases, we can expect her to switch away from cheaper forms of entertainment and toward more expensive alternatives. So, as her income rises, Joy's demand for afternoon matinees will fall.

Goods and services can be categorized according to the effect of changes in income on demand. If the demand for an item increases as the buyer's income increases, while the demand falls as the buyer's income falls, then the item is considered a **normal product**. Equivalently, the demand for a normal product is positively related to changes in the buyer's income.

> For a **normal product**, demand is positively related to changes in buyer's income.

By contrast, the demand for an **inferior product** is negatively related to changes in buyer's income. This means that the demand falls as the buyer's income increases, while the demand increases as the buyer's income falls.

> For an **inferior product**, demand is negatively related to changes in buyer's income.

We can apply this classification to Joy. For her, movies in general are a normal product, while afternoon matinees are an inferior product. Generally, broad categories of products tend to be normal, while particular products within the categories may be inferior. Consider, for instance, transportation services. The entire category is probably a normal product: the higher a person's income, the more he or she tends to spend on transportation. Public transportation, however, may be an inferior product: with a higher income, the typical commuter switches from public transport to a private car.

Consumer electronics provide another example of the difference in the effect of changes in income on the demand for a category as compared with the effect on the demand for a specific product. While consumer electronics as a category is a normal product, particular products such as black-and-white TVs may be inferior.

The distinction between normal and inferior products is important for business strategy. When the economy is growing and incomes are rising, the demand for normal products will rise, while the demand for inferior products will fall. By contrast, when the economy is in recession and incomes are falling, the demand for normal products will fall, while the demand for inferior products will rise.

The normal–inferior product distinction is also important for international business. The demand for normal products is relatively higher in richer countries, while the demand for inferior products is relatively higher in poorer countries. For instance, in developed countries, relatively more people commute to work by car than bicycle. The reverse is true in very poor countries.

Progress Check 2B Draw a curve to represent an individual consumer's demand for black-and-white TVs. (1) Explain why it slopes downward. (2) How will a drop in the consumer's income affect the demand curve?

Progress check

How would you like your music?

In 1998, the value of worldwide sales of recorded music in the form of singles, music cassettes, and CDs was $38.7 billion. In Canada, with a 30.2 million population, sales of CDs were 77.2 million units, and sales of music cassettes were 11.2 million units. On average, each Canadian bought 2.6 CDs and 0.4 music cassettes. By contrast, in Argentina, with a slightly larger population of 36.1 million, CD sales were 18.5 million and music cassette sales were 6.7 million, which translated to 0.5 CDs and 0.2 music cassettes per capita.

Canadians enjoyed higher incomes than Argentine consumers. In 1998, Canadian GDP per capita was $19,831, while that for Argentina was $9,413. The difference in incomes explains why the average Canadian bought more of both CDs and music cassettes.

Canadians also bought relatively more CDs (and relatively fewer music cassettes) than Argentine consumers. The ratio of CD to music cassette purchases was 6.5:1 in Canada, and 2.5:1 in Argentina. One explanation of this disparity is that music cassettes were a relatively inferior product compared to CDs.

Another possible explanation of the disparity is a difference in the relative prices of music cassettes and CDs. In Canada, the average price of a music cassette was $6.06, while the average price of a CD was $11.55. In Argentina, the average prices were $7.80 and $13.80. Since CDs were relatively cheaper in Argentina, differences in prices probably do not explain why Canadians bought relatively more CDs than Argentine consumers.

Source: The Recording Industry in Numbers, 99, International Federation of the Phonographic Industry (London, 1999).

◂◂ 4 Other Factors in Demand

The individual demand for an item may depend on other factors in addition to the price of the item and the buyer's income. The other factors include the prices of related products, advertising, season, weather, and location. In this section, we focus on the prices of related products and advertising. The principles for the other factors are similar, hence we do not analyze each one of them explicitly.

Complements and Substitutes

Assume that Joy always eats popcorn when she goes to the movies. How will an increase in the price of popcorn affect Joy's demand for movies? Recall that Joy's demand curve for movies shows the quantity that she will purchase for every possible price of a movie, other things equal. A change in the price is represented by a movement along the demand curve. By contrast, a change in any other factor such

Figure 2.3 Individual demand curve with a more expensive complement

As the price of popcorn increases, Joy's entire demand curve shifts toward the left.

as the price of popcorn will affect Joy's purchases of movies at all prices of movies. Hence, it will cause a shift in the entire demand curve.

Suppose that, presently, the price of popcorn is $1. Figure 2.3 represents Joy's demand curve for movies when the price of popcorn is $1.

We next construct Joy's demand when the price of popcorn is $1.50. To do so, we ask Joy a series of questions to probe the effect of changes in the prices of both popcorn and movies: "Suppose that the price of popcorn is $1.50. Other things equal, how many movies would you attend a month at a price of $10 per movie?"

By repeating this question for all other prices of movies and marking the pairs of prices and quantities on a graph, we can obtain Joy's demand curve when the price of popcorn is $1.50. Figure 2.3 shows this demand curve: When the price of popcorn is higher, the demand curve for movies is further to the left.

In general, related products can be classified as either **complements** or **substitutes** according to the effect of a price increase in one product on the demand for the other. Two products are *complements* if an increase in the price of one causes the demand for the other to fall. By contrast, two products are *substitutes* if an increase in the price of one causes the demand for the other to increase.

In Joy's case, popcorn and movies are complements. The more movies that she sees, the more popcorn she will want. Hence, if the price of popcorn is higher, the price of the overall movie experience will be higher, and she will go to fewer movies.

> Two products are **complements** if an increase in the price of one causes a fall in the demand for the other.

> Two products are **substitutes** if an increase in the price of one causes an increase in the demand for the other.

How will an increase in the price of video rentals affect Joy's demand for movies? Instead of seeing a movie, Joy could watch a rented video. Accordingly, these two products are substitutes. If there is an increase in the price of video rentals, Joy's demand for movies will increase.

Generally, a demand curve will shift to the left if there is either an increase in the price of a complement or a fall in the price of a substitute. By contrast, a demand curve will shift to the right if there is either a fall in the price of a complement or an increase in the price of a substitute.

Home football games: to broadcast or not to broadcast?

In the 1999 National Football League (NFL) season, the Tennessee Titans won 13 games and lost 3 to qualify for the Super Bowl XXXIV in Atlanta. In what *NFL Insider Magazine* described as "perhaps the most exciting Super Bowl ever played," the Titans held down the St. Louis Rams for most of the game. However, in the final minutes, the Rams' Isaac Bruce caught a 73-yard touchdown pass and doomed the Titans to a 16–23 defeat.

Like other NFL teams, the Titans make money from sales of tickets and food, beverage, and other concession items at live games. Increasingly, however, gate and concession income has been overshadowed by earnings from television broadcasting. In 1998, CBS won the rights to broadcast the NFL's American Football Conference for a bid of $500 million a year, while the Fox Network won the NFL National Football Conference rights for $550 million a year. The broadcast fees are divided among the NFL teams.

What is the relationship between live broadcasting of away games and the demand to attend home games? Live broadcasting of away games entertains fans when their home team is playing away and stimulates popular support for the home team and interest in attendance at home games. Accordingly, live broadcasting of away games and attendance at home games are complements.

Live broadcasting of home games, however, may draw fans away from attending the game in person. To this extent, the two products are substitutes. On the other hand, live broadcasting of home games also stimulates popular support for the home team and hence attendance at home games. To this extent, the two products are complements.

Whether NFL team owners should allow live broadcasting of home games depends on the balance among these effects. The solution, enforced by federal law, is to allow broadcasting of home games only if they are sold out. Further, federal law requires that such broadcasts must show the entire game. This rule tends to squeeze out broadcasting of games from other cities and helps to focus the local television audience on their home team.

Source: Harris Molloy, Jr., *NFL Insider Magazine* (http://www.nfl.com/sb34/features/000130titansdefense.html)

To appreciate the business implications of complements and substitutes, let us consider the components of a personal computer. The basic components include the microprocessor, the memory, and the disk drive. Computer users need all three components; hence, these are complements. This means that when the price of memory or disk drives falls, the demand for microprocessors will rise, which increases the sales and profits of microprocessor manufacturers.

By contrast, a computer can generate sound through either a card or a chip; hence, sound cards and chips are substitutes. A drop in the price of sound cards will reduce the demand for sound chips, which cuts the sales and profits of manufacturers of sound chips. An increase in the price of sound cards will raise the sales and profits of chip manufacturers.

Progress Check 2C Referring to figure 2.1, how will a fall in the price of video rentals affect the original demand curve?

Progress check

Advertising

Advertising expenditure is another factor in demand. For instance, Joy's demand for movies may depend on advertising by the theater. Advertising may be informative as well as persuasive. Informative advertising communicates information to potential buyers and sellers. For instance, movie theaters list the movies that they are showing and their show times in the daily newspapers. These listings inform potential customers.

Persuasive advertising aims to influence consumer choice. Manufacturers of cigarettes and cosmetics, for instance, use commercials to retain the loyalty of existing consumers and attract others to switch brands. Marketers may also use persuasive advertising to promote new products.

Generally, an increase in advertising expenditure, whether informative or persuasive, will increase demand. Conversely, a reduction in advertising expenditure will cause demand to fall. The effect of advertising expenditure on demand may be subject to a diminishing marginal product, which means that each additional dollar spent on advertising has a relatively smaller effect on demand. (We will elaborate on the concept of a diminishing marginal product in chapter 4.)

The effect of advertising on a consumer's demand depends on the medium. TV commercials during football games will have more effect on male consumers, while those during cartoons will have relatively more effect on children. Print advertisements in women's magazines will have more effect on female consumers, while those in car magazines will have relatively more effect on auto enthusiasts.

Durable Goods

Durable goods, such as automobiles, home appliances, and machinery, provide a stream of services over an extended period of time. In addition to price, income, the prices of complements and substitutes, and advertising, three factors are particularly significant in the demand for durable goods. They are expectations about future prices and incomes, interest rates, and the price of used models.

By the very nature of durable goods, buyers have some discretion over the timing of purchase. Hence, the demand for durables depends significantly on buyer expectations about future prices and incomes. For instance, a consumer who is pessimistic about his future income may postpone replacing his car. A consumer who expects automobile manufacturers to cut prices at the end of the model year may delay a purchase until the price is cut.

In addition, many buyers need to finance their purchases of durable goods. Accordingly, the demand for durables depends significantly on interest rates. If interest rates are low, then the cost of buying a car or home will be lower; hence, the demand for these durables will be higher. By contrast, if interest rates are high, then the cost of buying a durable will be higher and the demand will be lower.

Finally, an important factor in the demand for "big-ticket" durable goods such as automobiles and machinery is the price of used models. Used cars are a substitute for new automobiles and, likewise, used machinery is a substitute for new equipment. A higher price for used cars affects the demand for new cars in two ways. First, the higher price makes the used car less attractive; hence, it increases the demand for a new car. Second, the higher price signals a higher resale value and so will encourage consumers to purchase new cars.

Demand for used cars

The American consumer's demand for used cars grew steadily over the 1990s. In 1990, the average passenger car in use was slightly over 7.5 years old. By 1997, the average age had risen to over 8.7 years. A major reason for the increasing demand for used cars was the fast rising price of new cars. Between 1990 and 1998, the median household income rose by 29.9%, and the consumer price index rose by just 24.7%. By contrast, over the same period the average price of a new car rose by 48.4%.

The demand for used cars also grew because of the increasing quality of used cars. A further reason was that automobile manufacturers reduced the frequency with which they changed designs. Car dealer David Ash remarked that consumers "often can buy a car 2 or 3 years old that looks pretty much like the newest model."

Historically, financial institutions charged higher interest rates on loans for used cars. Over time, however, with the improvement in automobile quality and the shift of middle-income consumers towards used cars, financial institutions began to offer more favorable rates. This gave a further lift to the demand for used cars.

Sources: "America's New Darling: the Used Car," *Asian Wall Street Journal*, November 2, 1994, p. 20; "Second Time Around," *Atlanta Journal and Constitution*, November 15, 1996, p. S01; and National Association of Automobile Dealers.

◂◂ 5 Market Demand

Businesses that deal with many different customers may determine their strategy on the basis of the entire market rather than individual customers. Such businesses need to understand the demand of the entire market. The **market demand curve** is a graph that shows the quantity that all buyers will purchase at every possible price. The analysis of a market demand curve is essentially similar to that for an individual demand curve, hence we need only highlight the key points in the following discussion.

> The **market demand** curve is a graph showing the quantity that all buyers will purchase at every possible price.

Construction

To construct the market demand for an item, we must interview all the potential consumers and ask each person the quantity that he or she would buy at every possible price. For each price, we then add the reported individual quantities to get the quantity that the market as a whole will demand.

Let us apply this procedure to construct the market demand for movies. Suppose that there are only three potential viewers: Joy, Max, and Lucas. We ask each of them, "Other things equal, how many movies would you attend a month at a price of $10 per movie?" Table 2.3 reports their answers. The market quantity demanded is 0.

We then repeat these questions for other possible prices: $7.50, $5, $2.50, and 0 per movie. At each price, we add the reported individual quantities to get the market quantity demanded. For instance, at a price of $5, Joy would go to two movies, Max would go to one movie, and Lucas would go to none; hence, the market quantity demanded is $2 + 1 + 0 = 3$ movies.

We represent the market demand on a graph, with the price of movies on the vertical axis and quantity on the horizontal axis, in figure 2.4. Joining the pairs of prices and quantities, we have the market demand for movies. This market demand curve is in bold.

Table 2.3 Market demand

Price ($ per movie)	Quantity (movies a month)			
	Joy	Max	Lucas	Market
10.00	0	0	0	0
7.50	1	0	0	1
5.00	2	1	0	3
2.50	4	2	3	9
0.00	7	6	4	17

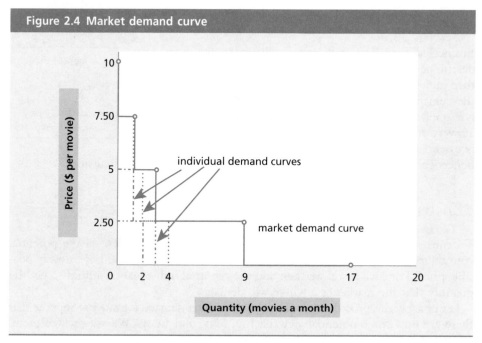

Figure 2.4 Market demand curve

The market demand curve is the horizontal summation of the individual demand curves. At every price, the market quantity demanded is the sum of the individual quantities demanded.

To do a **horizontal summation**, add the demand curves in the horizontal direction.

Another procedure for constructing a market demand curve is as the **horizontal summation** of the individual demand curves. On figure 2.4, we draw the individual demand curves of the three potential consumers: Joy, Max, and Lucas. *Horizontal summation* means that we add the curves in the horizontal direction. The individual demand curves show the number of movies that each of the three consumers will buy at every possible price. So, at every price, we add the quantities that the three consumers buy to arrive at the quantity that the market will buy.

Since the individual demand curves slope downward, the market demand curve also slopes downward. The fundamental reason is that all consumers get diminishing marginal benefit; hence, at a lower price, the market as a whole will buy a larger quantity.

The market demand curve in figure 2.4 has kinks where the quantity demanded rises in response to reductions in the price. As the number of consumers increases, the market demand curve will increase. Graphically, it will move further up and to the right. As the demand increases, we must reduce the scale of the figure and the kinks will gradually diminish in significance. Eventually, with a large number of consumers, the market demand curve will be an almost smooth curve. In the remaining chapters, we focus on smooth market demand curves.

Other Factors

Like individual demand, the market demand depends on other factors, including buyers' incomes, the prices of related products, and advertising. The market demand curve for an item shows explicitly only the effect of price on the quantity that the market wishes to buy. So, a change in the price of the item will cause a movement along the market demand curve from one point to another on the same curve.

By contrast, the market demand curve does not explicitly show other factors, such as incomes, the prices of related products, and advertising. Accordingly, changes in these factors will shift the entire market demand curve. In the math supplement to this chapter, we use algebra to explain how changes in the various factors affect a special type of smooth demand curve: a straight-line demand curve.

The directions of the effects of changes in the other factors on the market demand curve are similar to those for the individual demand curve. We will not repeat the discussion here. Instead, we focus on the key differences. An important application of demand analysis is to compare market demands in different countries. In each country, the market demand will depend on incomes as well as other factors. Let us discuss how to measure incomes in different countries.

Generally, there are two ways of measuring the income of an entire country: the gross national product (GNP) and the gross domestic product (GDP). Broadly, the GNP and GDP measure the total amount produced in a country for a given year. Since employers must pay workers, landlords, and lenders, the total value of production is also the total income of the country. The GNP is the GDP plus net income from foreign sources; hence, the two measures are closely related.

The average income of the residents of some country may be estimated by dividing either the GNP or the GDP by the population, which yields the GNP and GDP per capita, respectively. This can be converted into U.S. dollars by using the relevant exchange rate between the domestic currency and the U.S. dollar.

Income Distribution

Market researchers frequently take a shortcut when assessing market demand. Instead of considering the demand of all individual consumers and adding these individual demands, a common simplification is to estimate the demand for an individual with average income and multiply that by the number of buyers.

This simple approach ignores the distribution of income; that is, whether consumers have very similar or very disparate incomes. The distribution of income may have an important effect on the demand for particular items.

For instance, suppose that Northland and Southland have identical national incomes of $29.8 billion and populations of 1 million. In both countries, the average per capita income is $29,800. In Northland, 1% of the people earn $100,000 a year, while the other 99% earn $20,000 a year; in Southland, everyone has an equal income. Northland may have a substantial demand for cosmetic surgery, luxury cars, and designer clothing. By contrast, there will be no demand for these items in Southland.

Generally, the more uneven is the distribution of income, the more important it is to consider the actual distribution of income and not merely the average income when estimating market demand.

Progress check **Progress Check 2D** Referring to figure 2.4, show how an increase in the price of a complement would affect the market demand.

Who buys dishwashers in India?

With an average income of less than $500 a year, the people of India are among the poorest in the world. How could they afford to buy 28,000 units of $360 dishwashers? The answer to this question is that some people earn much more than the average income.

In India, income is less evenly distributed than in major developed countries such as the United States. India's National Council of Applied Economic Research classifies about 4% of urban households as "high income," with incomes exceeding $3,360 a year. It is these people who can afford to buy dishwashers.

Sources: "A Fresh Look at India," *McKinsey Quarterly*, no. 2 (1993), pp. 29–44; and *Euromonitor*.

Market Structure

We have analyzed how the individual demand curves of the various buyers can be horizontally summed to yield the market demand curve. The market quantity will be provided by one or more sellers. Hence, the market demand must be divided among the various sellers, each of whom faces its individual demand curve. Figure 2.5 depicts how the demands of individual buyers add up to the market demand and how the market demand divides into the demands facing individual sellers.

As figure 2.5 shows, the concept of an individual demand curve has two possible meanings: the individual demand curve of a buyer or the individual demand curve faced by a seller. It is important to maintain a clear distinction between the two meanings.

In chapter 4, we discuss in detail a seller's individual demand curve. Meanwhile, let us consider a question that managers frequently pose, "What is the demand for

Figure 2.5 Market structure

Demands from individual buyers add up to the market demand. The market demand divides into the demands facing individual sellers.

my product?" Our analysis of demand shows that this question has no answer. The answer can only be, "It depends." The quantity demanded depends on the selling price, buyers' incomes, the prices of related products, and other factors. Only when these variables are specified is it possible to gauge the quantity of demand.

◂◂ 6 Buyer Surplus

An individual buyer's demand curve shows the quantity that the buyer will purchase at every possible price. We now consider the buyer's demand curve from another perspective, which is to show the maximum amount that a buyer is willing to pay for each unit of the item. This perspective is important for business strategy as it shows how a seller can calculate the maximum price that the buyer can be charged for a given purchase.

Benefit

Recall that the marginal benefit is the benefit provided by an additional unit of an item. It can be measured as the maximum amount of money that the buyer is willing to pay for that unit. To illustrate, consider Joy's demand curve for movies, reproduced in figure 2.6. This shows that Joy is willing to pay $7.50 for the first movie; hence, her marginal benefit from one movie is $7.50. Similarly, Joy is willing to pay $5 for the second movie; hence, her marginal benefit from the second movie is $5, and so on.

In effect, Joy's demand curve is also her marginal benefit curve. This perspective also implies that the demand curve slopes downward. By the principle of diminishing marginal benefit, each additional movie gives less benefit than the one before. Hence, Joy's marginal benefit curve will slope downward. Since the marginal benefit curve is identical with Joy's demand curve, this means that Joy's demand curve will slope downward.

We have just seen how the demand curve shows the marginal benefit from each unit that a buyer purchases. Using this information, we can then calculate the buyer's

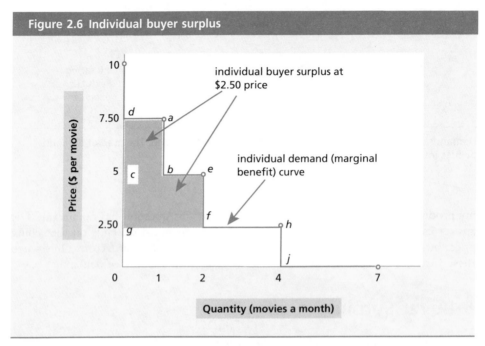

Figure 2.6 Individual buyer surplus

The individual buyer surplus is the buyer's total benefit from some quantity of purchases less the actual expenditure. At a price of $2.50, Joy's buyer surplus is the shaded area *gfebad* between the demand curve and the $2.50 line.

> The **total benefit** is the benefit yielded by all the units that the buyer purchases.

total benefit, which is the benefit yielded by all the units that the buyer purchases. The total benefit is the marginal benefit from the first unit plus the marginal benefit from the second unit, and so on, up to and including marginal benefit from the last unit that the buyer purchases.

A buyer's total benefit from some quantity of purchases is the maximum that the buyer is willing to pay for that quantity. Graphically, the total benefit is represented by the area under the buyer's demand curve up to and including the last unit purchased. Let us apply this concept to calculate Joy's total benefit from four movies a month. This is the area under her demand curve up to and including four movies a month. In figure 2.6, this is $7.50 + $5 + ($2.50 \times 2) = $17.50. Hence, the maximum that Joy would be willing to pay for four movies a month is $17.50.

Benefit vis-à-vis Price

Suppose that the price of a movie is $2.50. Then Joy goes to four movies a month. As already calculated, her total benefit would be $17.50. Joy, however, needs to pay only $2.50 \times 4 = \$10$, which is substantially less than her total benefit. The difference between a buyer's total benefit from some quantity of purchases and the actual expenditure is called the **buyer surplus**. At a price of $2.50 per movie, Joy's buyer surplus is $17.50 - \$10 = \$7.50$.

Referring to figure 2.6, Joy's total benefit from four movies a month is represented by the area 0*jhfebad* under her demand (marginal benefit) curve up to and including four movies a month. At a price of $2.50, her expenditure on four movies a month is represented by the area 0*jhg* under the $2.50 line up to and including four movies a month. Joy's buyer surplus is the difference between these two areas, that is, the area *gfebad* between her demand curve and the $2.50 line.[2]

> The **buyer surplus** is the difference between a buyer's total benefit from some quantity of purchases and her or his actual expenditure.

Generally, provided that purchases are voluntary, a buyer must get some surplus; otherwise, he or she will not buy. Hence, the maximum that a seller can charge is the buyer's total benefit. If a seller tries to charge more, then the buyer will walk away.

Progress Check 2E Suppose that the price of movies is $5. In figure 2.6, mark Joy's buyer surplus at that price.

Progress check

Price Changes

Referring to Joy's demand for movies, suppose that the price is $5 and Joy goes to two movies a month. Her buyer surplus is area *cbad*. Now suppose that the price drops to $2.50. Then Joy will raise her attendance from two to four movies a month. Her buyer surplus will increase by area *gfec*. The increase in buyer surplus can be attributed to two effects – she gets the two original movies at a lower price, and she goes to more movies.

Generally, a buyer gains from a price reduction in two ways. First, he or she gets a lower price on the quantity that the buyer would have purchased at the original higher price. Second, he or she can buy more, gaining buyer surplus on each of the additional purchases. The extent of the second effect depends on the buyer's response to the price reduction. The greater the increase in purchases, the larger will be the buyer's gain from the price reduction.

Similarly, a buyer loses from a price increase in two ways – the buyer must pay a higher price, and he or she will buy less.

---

[2] Changes in prices can affect a buyer's real income, hence shift the individual demand curve. Strictly, the buyer surplus must be measured from a demand curve that is adjusted for changes in real income. For simplicity, we ignore this detail.

Price promotions: the more you buy, the more you save?

Students at the University of California, Los Angeles, enjoy several privileges. One is a good education at a low price. Another is California's unbeatable weather, and a third is discounted movie tickets. Suppose that Alan buys 12 tickets a year at $4 rather than the full price of $7. By how much does he gain from the discount scheme?

One answer is that Alan "saves" $7 − $4 = $3 on each ticket, which adds to a total of $3 × 12 = $36. This answer, however, implicitly assumes that Alan would buy 12 tickets a year whether the price is $4 or $7.

For the correct answer, we apply the concept of buyer surplus. Figure 2.7 represents Alan's demand curve for movies. At the $7 full price, Alan would buy six tickets a year and get the buyer surplus of the shaded area *bac*. By contrast, at the discount price of $4, Alan buys 12 tickets a year and gets the buyer surplus of the shaded area *bac* plus the area *deab*.

Thus, the discount scheme increases Alan's buyer surplus by the area *deab*. This represents $(7 − 4) × 0.5(6 + 12) = $27, which is Alan's gain from the discount scheme.

We can analyze this $27 gain in two parts. First, Alan can buy six tickets (the number that he would have bought at the full $7 price) at a lower price. He gains $7 − $4 = $3 on each of these six tickets, or a total of $3 × 6 = $18. Second, the discount scheme induces Alan to increase his purchases to 12 tickets a year. Alan will get some buyer surplus on each of the additional tickets. In figure 2.7, the buyer surplus on the seventh through twelfth tickets is 0.5 × $(7 − 4) × 6 = $9.

Market Buyer Surplus

We have introduced the concept of buyer surplus for individual buyers. To see how the concept applies at the market level, let us consider the market demand for movies reproduced in figure 2.8. At a price of $2.50, the market quantity demanded is nine movies. The market's total benefit is the area under the market demand curve up to and including nine movies. By contrast, the market's expenditure for nine movies is the area under the $2.50 line up to and including nine movies a month.

The total benefit exceeds the expenditure; that is, the market as a whole is not paying the maximum that it would be willing to pay for that quantity of purchases. The difference is the market buyer surplus. Graphically, it is the area between the market demand curve and the $2.50 line.

Recall that the buyer surplus of an individual consumer at the price of $2.50 is the area between his or her demand curve and the $2.50 line. The sum of these

Figure 2.7 Value of discount movie tickets

The reduction in the price of movie tickets from $7 to $4 increases Alan's buyer surplus by the area *deab*.

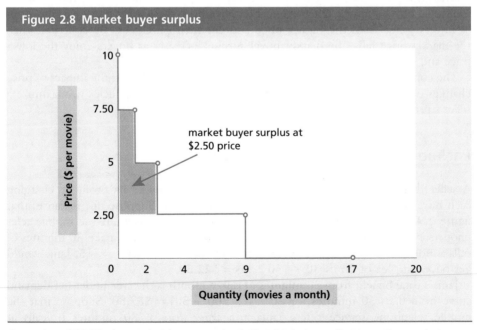

Figure 2.8 Market buyer surplus

At a price of $2.50, the market buyer surplus is the shaded area between the market demand curve and the $2.50 line.

Figure 2.9 Package deal

Jania will buy a package deal of 30 minutes of calls for any price not exceeding her total benefit of $37.50.

areas for all the individual consumers is the area between the market demand curve and the $2.50 line. Hence, the market buyer surplus is equal to the sum of the individual buyer surpluses.

The principles underlying the market buyer surplus are the same as those for the individual buyer surplus. When the market price rises, the market buyer surplus drops as buyers suffer from the higher price and cut their purchases. By contrast, when the market price falls, the market buyer surplus increases as buyers enjoy the lower price and expand their purchases.

The concept of market buyer surplus will be useful in analyzing the impact of price changes on the market as a whole and in developing pricing policies to maximize a seller's profit.

Package Deals and Two-Part Tariffs

A seller that has complete flexibility over pricing maximizes its profit by charging each buyer just a little less than his or her total benefit. Suppose, for instance, that figure 2.9 describes Jania's demand for mobile telephone calls. If the mobile telephone service charges a price of 50 cents per minute, Jania will make 30 minutes of calls a month. The service would earn a revenue of 30 × 50 cents = $15. Jania would get buyer surplus of 0.5 × 30 × 150 cents = $22.50.

Jania's total benefit from 30 minutes of calls a month is the area under her demand curve from 0 to 30 minutes, or 30 × 0.5(200 + 50) = $37.50. Suppose that the mobile telephone service offers Jania a *package deal* of 30 minutes of calls at $37 with no other alternative. The package deal will give Jania a buyer surplus of

$37.50 − $37 = 50 cents. Since there is no other alternative, Jania will buy this package. The service will earn $37 in
revenue, which is more than double the revenue from the
50-cent pricing policy. The package deal enables the service
to soak up almost all of Jania's buyer surplus.

> A **two-part tariff** is a pricing scheme consisting of a fixed payment and a charge based on usage.

The mobile telephone service could also extract Jania's
buyer surplus through a *two-part tariff*. A **two-part tariff** is
a pricing scheme consisting of a fixed payment and a charge based on usage.
Suppose that the mobile telephone provider offers a two-part tariff consisting of a
$22 monthly charge and an airtime charge of 50 cents a minute. Referring to fig-
ure 2.9, Jania would choose 30 minutes of calls a month. Her total benefit would
be the area under her demand curve from 0 to 30 minutes, which we earlier calculated to be $37.50. She would pay $22 in monthly charge and 30 × 50 cents = $15
in airtime charges. Hence, her buyer surplus would be $37.50 − $22 − $15 = 50
cents. Just like the package deal, the two-part tariff enables the service provider to
soak up most of the consumer's buyer surplus.

Providers of fixed-line and mobile telecommunications and Internet access make
widespread use of package deals and two-part tariffs in their pricing. They also
combine the two pricing techniques so that the monthly charge covers a specified
quantity of "free" usage while the user must pay a usage charge beyond the free
quantity. We study other ways of pricing to extract buyer surplus in chapter 9, "Pricing
Policy."

Pricing unmetered access at AOL

An unmetered plan for Internet access allows the subscriber to use the
service up to the quantity where her marginal benefit is zero. The service
provider, for instance AOL, should set the monthly charge slightly lower than
the area under the typical subscriber's demand curve up to the quantity
where her marginal benefit equals zero. This will extract most of her buyer
surplus, leaving just enough to persuade her to subscribe.

However, some users have lower demand curves than others. AOL caters to
users with lower demand through its $9.95 a month limited usage plan that
provides 5 hours' free access and charges for additional usage at $2.95 per hour.

In 1999, AOL raised the monthly charge for its unmetered access plan from
$19.95 to $21.95. AOL Chief Operating Officer Robert Pittman noted that
the raise did not affect the growth rate of AOL's subscriber population.
Presumably, the increase in AOL's content and services between 1996 and
1999 had raised subscribers' demand curves such that they were willing to
pay the higher monthly charge.

America Online embarked on the "AOL Anywhere" strategy to expand its
services beyond the population of computer users. Given AOL's emphasis on

unmetered access plans, it was important that other gateways to AOL also provide unmetered service. If a subscriber accessed AOL through a mobile provider that charged by usage, then the per-minute charge would negate AOL's unmetered pricing.

In this light, it was crucial for AOL to identify partners that provided unmetered access. Access through OpenTV and televisions would certainly meet this requirement. For access through Internet-enabled mobile phones, AT&T Wireless Vice President, Tom Trinneer, emphasized, "our flat-rate pricing plans and extensive nationwide footprint."

Sources: "America Online: Pricks and Kicks," *Economist*, August 14, 1999, pp. 52–5; and "America Online Delivers 'AOL Mobile' Services to AT&T Wireless Internet-Ready Phones," America Online, Inc., Press Release, September 5, 2000.

◄ 7 Business Demand

We have introduced the concepts of individual and market demand through the example of movies. Movies are a consumer good. By contrast, some items are purchased only by businesses. Examples include TV commercials, heavy trucks, machine tools, and human resources. Some items, such as gasoline and telephone calls, are purchased by both consumers and businesses.

Accordingly, it is important to understand the principles of business demand. In many ways, these principles are similar to those underlying consumer demand. Therefore, we will focus on the important differences between business and consumer demand.

Inputs

Consumers buy goods and services for final consumption or usage. By contrast, businesses do not purchase goods and services for their own sake but to use them as inputs in the production of other goods and services. We will make a detailed analysis of business operations in chapter 4. Here, we will review only the essentials necessary to understand the business demand for inputs.

For convenience, the inputs purchased by a business can be classified into raw materials, energy, labor, and capital. Businesses use these inputs to produce outputs for sale to consumers or other businesses. For example, a steel mill manufactures steel bars and sheets for sale to automakers and construction companies.

The inputs may be substitutes or complements. Consider, for instance, an express delivery service. Its trucks and drivers are complements: a truck without a driver is quite useless, as is a driver without a truck. Other inputs may be substitutes. For example, the service may use machines or workers to sort packages.

Similarly, operations such as loading and packing could be performed by machine or manually.

Demand

A business produces items for sale to consumers or other businesses. The business earns revenues from sales. By raising the quantity of inputs, the business can produce a larger output and hence a change in revenue. Accordingly, the business can measure its marginal benefit from an input as the increase in revenue arising from an additional unit of the input.

We suppose that, when the quantity of an input is larger, each additional unit of the input will generate a smaller increase in revenue. This means that the input provides a diminishing marginal benefit to the business.

Using the marginal benefit of an input, we can construct the individual demand curve of a business. This shows the quantity of the input that the business will purchase at every possible price. A business should buy an input up to the quantity that its marginal benefit from the input exactly balances the price.

To see why, consider the demand for labor of a delivery service. Figure 2.10 represents the marginal benefit of labor to the service. Let the wage be $10 per

Figure 2.10 Demand for labor

A business will buy 1,000 worker hours of labor a month, at which quantity its marginal benefit equals the $10 wage. If it buys only 900 worker hours, then, by raising the quantity of labor, it can increase profit by the shaded area *bac*.

worker hour. The quantity of labor that balances the marginal benefit with the wage is 1,000 worker hours a month. Suppose that the service buys only 900 worker hours. Then, the marginal benefit will exceed the wage. By increasing the quantity of the input, the business will increase revenue by more than the wage, hence it will raise profit by the shaded area *bac*. Similarly, we can show that, if the service purchases 1,100 worker hours, it can increase profit by reducing the input.

We have shown that a business should buy an input up to the quantity at which its marginal benefit from the input exactly balances the price. Generally, the input provides diminishing marginal benefit. Hence, when the price is lower, the business will buy a larger quantity, and conversely, when the price is higher, the business will buy a smaller quantity. Thus, as shown in figure 2.10, the demand curve for the input slopes downward.

General Motors' demand for aluminum

Aluminum is a strong, lightweight metal made from bauxite ore. By substituting aluminum for steel and other materials, automobile manufacturers can reduce vehicle weight, and so, improve fuel economy and thereby reduce emissions. Alcan, one of the world's leading aluminum manufacturers, estimates that a one-pound reduction in the weight of a car would reduce carbon dioxide emissions by 20 pounds over the life of the vehicle.

In 1998, General Motors used 1.7 billion pounds of aluminum, with an average of 210 pounds in each vehicle. However, the volatility of aluminum prices had discouraged GM's use of the metal. To address the price volatility, GM signed several long-term billion-dollar purchase agreements, including a 10-year contract with Alcan and a 13-year deal with IMCO Recycling. By 1999, GM's average consumption had increased to 271 pounds per vehicle. Automobile manufacturers as a group accounted for 18% of worldwide aluminum consumption of 25 million tons.

GM's increasing use of aluminum illustrates how business demand for an input depends on substitution among inputs and the demand for the final product. Through long-term contracts, GM effectively achieved a lower price for aluminum. Consequently, it increased its use of aluminum, at the expense of steel and other materials.

With the average price of unleaded gasoline rising from 98.6 cents a gallon in December 1998 to $1.617 in June 2000, auto buyers are becoming more conscious of fuel consumption. They would certainly appreciate and pay for improvements in fuel economy.

Sources: "GM Commits to Buy Aluminum in an Unusual Pact with Alcan," *Wall Street Journal*, November 8, 1998; and "General Motors Inks Long-Term Pact to Buy IMCO's Recycled Aluminum," *Wall Street Journal*, March 11, 1999.

Factors in Demand

A change in the price of an input is represented by a movement along the demand curve. By contrast, changes in other factors will lead to a shift of the entire demand curve. A major factor in consumer demand is income. Business demand does not depend on income but rather on the quantity of the output. If the output is larger, then the business will increase its demand for inputs. This is a shift of the entire demand curve because the increase occurs at all prices. If, however, the output is lower, then the demand for inputs will be lower.

The demand of a business for an input also depends on the prices of complements and substitutes in the production of the output. For instance, delivery trucks and drivers are complements, hence an increase in the drivers' wages will reduce the demand for trucks.

As we have outlined, business demand is derived from calculations of marginal benefit. On the whole, purchasing decisions of businesses are relatively less subject to impulse buying than those of consumers. Hence, advertising plays a smaller role in business demand, and is relatively more informative than persuasive advertising.

Progress Check 2F   Referring to figure 2.10, suppose that the service buys 1,100 worker hours of labor. How can the service increase its profit?

Progress check

◂◂ 8 Summary

A demand curve shows the quantity demanded as a function of price, other things equal. Generally, the demand curve slopes downward. Changes in price are represented by movements along the demand curve; changes in other factors, such as income, the prices of related products, and advertising, are represented by shifts of the entire demand curve. The market demand curve is the horizontal summation of the individual demand curves of the various buyers.

Buyer surplus is the difference between a buyer's total benefit from some quantity of purchases and his or her actual expenditure. Changes in price affect buyer surplus through the price changes themselves as well as through changes in the quantity demanded.

Key Concepts

individual demand curve	complement	total benefit
marginal benefit	substitute	buyer surplus
normal product	market demand curve	two-part tariff
inferior product	horizontal summation	

Further Reading

For the behavior of consumer and business buyers, see Philip Kotler's classic, *Marketing Management*, 10th ed. (Englewood Cliffs, NJ: Prentice Hall, 2000), Chapters 6 and 7.

Robert S. Pindyck and Daniel L. Rubinfeld present an economic analysis of demand using the model of indifference curves in *Microeconomics*, 5th ed. (Englewood Cliffs, NJ: Prentice Hall, 2001), Chapters 3 and 4.

? Review Questions

1. Define each of the following terms and give an example to illustrate your definition:
   (a) Substitute.
   (b) Complement.
   (c) Normal product.
   (d) Inferior product.

2. Name a good or service that you bought recently. Would you have bought less of the item if the price had been lower? Explain why or why not.

3. A new diaphragm protects women against pregnancy but not sexually trans- mitted diseases. How will the introduction of this product affect each of the following:
   (a) The demand for male condoms.
   (b) The demand for birth-control pills.

4. For many years, the government of Taiwan imposed tight controls on the news- paper and free-to-the-air broadcast television industries. Explain how these controls helped the growth of illegal cable television services.

5. The penetration of mobile telephony (number of subscribers per thousand people) is relatively high in wealthy countries like Finland and also in some very poor countries like Cambodia. Are mobile and fixed-line telephone service com- plements or substitutes?

6. How does Pepsi advertising affect the demand for the soft drink?

7. Suppose that there is a general increase in incomes. Compare the effect of this increase on the demand faced by the following two chains:
   (a) Marriott, a four-star hotel chain with properties throughout the world.
   (b) Motel 6, a chain of low-price motels.

8. Real per capita income in South Africa is much lower than in Britain. For which product is it more important to know South Africa's distribution of income when estimating demand (choose a or b)?
   (a) Bic disposable ballpoint pens.
   (b) Mont Blanc fountain pens.

9. Which of the following are important factors in the demand for new homes?
   (a) Interest rates.
   (b) Household incomes.
   (c) Expectations of future home prices.
   (d) The current price of building materials.

10. Explain how a long-distance telecommunications carrier can use the concept of buyer surplus to price a 1-hour package of long-distance calls.

11. The price of mobile telephone calls is 10 cents a minute. Antonella buys 200 minutes a month. Illustrate her demand curve and identify her buyer surplus.

12. "Summer sale: the more you buy, the more you save." Please comment.

13. How do the factors in demand for inputs such as advertising differ from the factors in the demand for end-user items such as Internet access?

14. Why are automated teller machines (ATMs) relatively more common in countries with higher labor costs?

15. Why do shipbuilders pay close attention to the prices of secondhand vessels and interest rates?

Discussion Questions

1. Using data from 93 countries, *The Economist* estimated a relationship between the literacy rate of women and the number of births per woman (fertility rate). When the literacy rate is 0%, the fertility rate is 8 per woman; and when the literacy rate is 100%, the birth rate is 2.5 per woman ("Population: Battle of the Bulge," *The Economist* [September 3, 1994], pp. 19–21).
   (a) Construct a diagram with literacy rate on the vertical axis and fertility rate on the horizontal axis. Mark the two points that *The Economist* estimated. Join the two points with a straight line.
   (b) Perhaps the largest cost of having a baby is the time that the mother must invest to bear and rear the child. For a more educated woman, is the value of this time higher or lower?
   (c) Returning to your diagram, mark "cost of child" on the vertical axis. Does your diagram have any relation to a demand curve? Please explain.

2. A disposable camera consists of a simple lens and a roll of film built into a cardboard box. It can be used only once: having finished the film, the consumer sends the entire camera to a photo finisher. Kodak and Fuji introduced disposable cameras to the U.S. market in 1987. Sales grew rapidly to 5 million units in 1989, to 9 million in 1990, and 15 million in 1991. By comparison, total film sales, including disposable cameras, were 706 million units in 1990 and 710 million in 1991 ("For Cardboard Cameras, Sales Picture Enlarges and Seems Brighter than Ever," *Wall Street Journal* (February 11, 1992), p. B1).

(a) How would the introduction of disposable cameras affect the sales of film for conventional (nondisposable) cameras?

(b) Based on the preceding data, Photo Marketing Association International's director of Marketing Research, Barry Harland, inferred that, if disposable cameras had not been available, total film sales would have dropped between 1990 and 1991. Do you agree?

3. In 1998, the value of worldwide sales of recorded music in the form of singles, music cassettes, and CDs was $38.7 billion. Americans bought 3.1 CDs and 0.6 music cassettes per capita, while Mexicans bought 0.5 CDs and 0.3 music cassettes per capita.

(a) Explain why per capita CD sales were relatively higher while per capita sales of music cassettes were relatively lower in the United States than in Mexico.

(b) On a suitable diagram, draw the U.S. demand for music CDs. Explain how the following changes would affect the demand curve: (i) increase in the price of CDs; (ii) rise in the ownership of CD players; and (iii) fall in the price of music cassettes.

(c) On another diagram, draw the demand for music CDs in Mexico. Explain how the following changes would affect the demand curve: (i) fall in advertising by music publishers such as Sony and Time Warner; (ii) reduction in the penalty for copyright infringement; and (iii) increase in the price of hamburgers.

4. In 1999, the Tennessee Titans moved to the new 67,000-seat Adelphia Stadium, on the west bank of the Cumberland River, overlooking Nashville. That season, the Titans charged $12–$52 for individual tickets and $250–$2,495 for season tickets. Considering that there were only 16 games in a regular season, the Titans were selling season tickets at a premium to individual tickets. By contrast, in the pricing of many other goods and services, consumers get a discount for buying in bulk.

(a) Explain how the individual demand for a home Titans game depends on the Titans' playing record, the identity of the opposing team, and the weather.

(b) By referring to the market demand curve for Titans' games, explain why some games sell out.

(c) A fan relying on individual tickets may not be able to see the more popular games. By contrast, a season ticket guarantees seating at all games. Explain why a fan is willing to pay more for a season ticket than the sum of the prices of individual tickets.

5. Color TVs are more expensive than black-and-white TVs. In 1989, American purchases of black-and-white TVs were 13 per thousand persons, while purchases of color TVs were 88 per thousand persons. By contrast, Canadian purchases of black-and-white TVs were 6 per thousand persons, while purchases of color TVs were 63 per thousand persons (*International Marketing Data and Statistics*, 17th ed. (London: Euromonitor, 1993), pp. 167 and 457).

(a) Compare the total purchases of TVs (color plus black-and-white) per thousand persons in Canada and the United States.

(b) How does the availability and quality of TV programming affect the demand for TVs? Use these factors to explain the difference in (a).

(c)   Compare the ratio of purchases of color to black-and-white TVs in Canada and the United States.

(d)   How does the distribution of income affect the demand for color relative to black-and-white TVs? Apply this factor to explain the difference in (c).

6.   The price of Chanel perfume is around $200 per fluid ounce, while the price of Arrowhead bottled water is $1 per gallon. Hilda buys 2 fluid ounces of Chanel and 10 gallons of bottled water a month.

(a)   Using relevant demand curves, illustrate Hilda's choices. Illustrate how the following changes will affect Hilda's demand for Chanel perfume: (i) a price increase to $220 per fluid ounce, and (ii) a cut in the price of another of Hilda's favorite perfumes.

(b)   Hilda spends more money each month on perfume than bottled water. Does this necessarily mean that perfume gives her more total benefit than water? Use appropriate demand curves to address this question.

7.   In June 1999, AOL had 17.6 million subscribers, and Compuserve had 2 million. By September 2000, AOL had grown to 24 million, and Compuserve to 2.8 million. Subscribers continued to be attracted by America Online's content and services, including chat rooms, instant messaging services (AOL Instant Messenger and ICQ), and specialized services like Digital City, Moviefone, and MapQuest.

(a)   With more people joining AOL Instant Messenger, each subscriber has more persons to communicate with. Using a suitable diagram, illustrate how growth of the AOL Instant Messenger subscriber base raises the individual demand curve of a typical AOL member.

(b)   In 1999, AOL raised the price for its unlimited access plan from $19.95 to $21.95 a month. Using the diagram in (a), illustrate how AOL might have determined the new price.

(c)   Compuserve kept its price at $9.95 a month. How might changes in AOL's content and services have affected the individual demand curve of a typical Compuserve member?

8.   The Coca Cola Company markets the Coke brand and manufactures concentrate for sale to regional bottlers. Coke bottlers mix concentrate with sweetener and water to produce the soft drink for supermarkets, restaurants, and other retail outlets. Possible sweeteners include corn syrup and sugar. Owing to federal restrictions against imports, sugar is relatively more expensive in the United States than the rest of the world.

(a)   Why do U.S. soft drink bottlers use relatively more corn syrup than bottlers elsewhere in the world?

(b)   Explain how the following changes would affect a Coke bottler's demand curve for corn syrup: (i) removal of the federal restrictions against sugar imports; (ii) fall in the price of corn syrup; and (iii) increase in the sales of Pepsi.

(c)   How would an increase in Pepsi advertising affect the demand for Coke?

9.   By substituting aluminum for steel and other materials, automobile manufacturers can reduce vehicle weight, and so, improve fuel economy. In 1998, General Motors used 1.7 billion pounds of aluminum, with an average of 210 pounds per vehicle. By the following year, its average usage had increased to 271 pounds. Automobile

manufacturers as a group accounted for 18% of 25 million ton worldwide aluminum consumption.

(a) Using a suitable figure, draw GM's demand curve for aluminum. (Strictly, this requires an assumption that GM is a small buyer and cannot affect the price of aluminum.) The price of aluminum fell from $1,476 per metric ton in 1997 to $1,303 in 1998 and $1,314 in 1999. Illustrate the effect of the price changes on your figure.

(b) Show how GM's demand curve for aluminum depends on the prices of gasoline and steel.

(c) Manufacturers of beverage cans also use large quantities of aluminum. Does GM's demand for aluminum depend on the sales of soft drinks and beer?

10. This question applies the techniques introduced in the math supplement. Suppose that the market demand for car rentals is represented by the equation

$$D = 50 - p + 0.2Y, \qquad (2.1)$$

where D is the quantity demanded in rentals a month, p is the price in dollars per rental, and Y is the average consumer's income in thousands of dollars a year. Assume that $Y = 50$.

(a) Draw the market demand curve. Show the effect of a cut in price, from $p = 30$ to $p = 20$.

(b) Show the effect on demand of an increase in income from $Y = 50$ to $Y = 60$.

11. This question applies the techniques introduced in the math supplement. Suppose that a typical household's demand for long-distance calls is represented by the equation

$$D = 200 - 4p + 0.4Y, \qquad (2.2)$$

where D is the quantity demanded in minutes a month, p is the price of calls in cents per minute, and Y is the household's income in thousands of dollars a year. Assume that $Y = 100$.

(a) Draw the household's demand curve.

(b) How many minutes will the household buy at a price of 25 cents a minute?

(c) What is the maximum lump sum that a long-distance carrier can charge the household for a package of 140 minutes of calls?

Chapter 2

Math Supplement

Individual Demand Curve

Using a little mathematics, we can reinforce our understanding of the individual demand curve, especially the effect of changes in price vis-à-vis other factors. Let the individual's demand for some item be represented by the equation

$$D = 30 - 2p + 0.04Y + 4s, \quad (2.3)$$

where D is the quantity demanded in units a year, p is the price of the item in dollars per unit, Y is the buyer's income in thousands of dollars a year, and s is the value of another factor.

This demand curve is a straight line. To explain, suppose that $Y = 100$ and $s = 0.5$. Then, substituting in (2.3),

$$D = 30 - 2p + 4 + 2 = 36 - 2p. \quad (2.4)$$

Differentiating (2.4) with respect to price

$$\frac{dD}{dp} = -2, \quad (2.5)$$

which means that the demand equation has a constant slope, or equivalently, that the demand curve is a straight line.

To sketch the demand curve, we consider two points on the curve. First, when the price $p = 0$, the quantity demanded $D = 36$. Next, if $D = 0$, $p = 36/2 = 18$.

Marking and joining these two points on figure 2.11, we have the buyer's demand curve.

As shown in figure 2.11, the demand curve is drawn with price on the vertical axis and quantity on the horizontal axis. Hence, the slope of the demand curve is the derivative of price with respect to quantity. From the demand equation, we can obtain the derivative of quantity with respect to price, which is −2. Inverting this, we find that the derivative of price with respect to quantity, or the slope, is −0.5.

The demand curve can be used to illustrate the effect of a change in price. By (2.4), when the price $p = 9$, the quantity demanded $D = 36 - (2 \times 9) = 18$. When the price is higher, $p = 10$, the quantity demanded $D = 36 - (2 \times 10) = 16$. We represent this change by a movement along the demand curve from the point where $p = 9$ and $D = 18$ to the point where $p = 10$ and $D = 16$.

This demand curve can be used to illustrate the effect of a change in income. Recall that, originally, the buyer's income was $Y = 100$. Suppose that the buyer's income rises to $Y = 150$. The other factor remains $s = 0.5$. Then, by (2.3), the demand curve becomes

$$D = 30 - 2p + 6 + 2 = 38 - 2p. \quad (2.6)$$

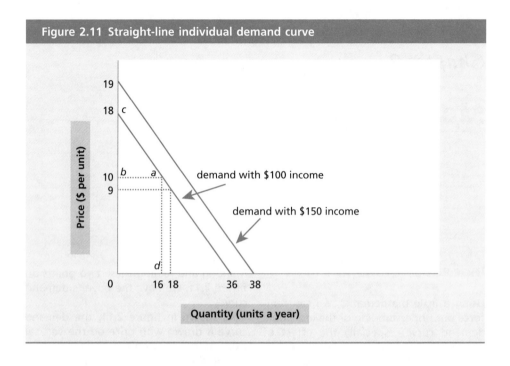

Figure 2.11 Straight-line individual demand curve

In this case, when the price $p = 0$, the quantity demanded $D = 38$, while if the quantity demanded $D = 0$, the price $p = 38/2 = 19$. Marking and joining these two points on figure 2.11, we have the demand curve with the income of $Y = 150$. This is a straight line that lies to the right of the demand curve with the income of $Y = 100$. By contrast to a change in price, the change in income is represented by a shift of the entire demand curve.

Recall that s is the value of another factor in demand. Originally, $s = 0.5$. Suppose that the other factor increases to $s = 0.6$, while income remains $Y = 100$. Then, by (2.3), the demand curve becomes

$$D = 30 - 2p + 4 + 2.4$$

$$= 36.4 - 2p. \qquad (2.7)$$

Accordingly, the change in the other factor is also represented by a shift of the entire demand curve. This other factor could be the price of a related product,

advertising expenditure, season, weather, or location. A change in any of these factors would shift the entire demand curve.

With the equation of the demand curve, we can calculate the total benefit and buyer's surplus. Recall the demand curve, with $Y = 100$ and $s = 0.5$ was

$$D = 36 - 2p. \qquad (2.8)$$

At the price $p = 10$, the buyer purchases quantity $D = 16$. The buyer's total benefit is represented by trapezium $0dac$, while the buyer's expenditure is represented by rectangle $0dab$. Hence, at the price $p = 10$, the buyer's surplus is represented by triangle bac. The area of this triangle is $1/2 \times \$(18 - 10) \times 16 = \$64$.

Market Demand Curve

Using a mathematical approach, it is very simple to see the relation between

Figure 2.12 Horizontal summation of straight-line individual demand curves

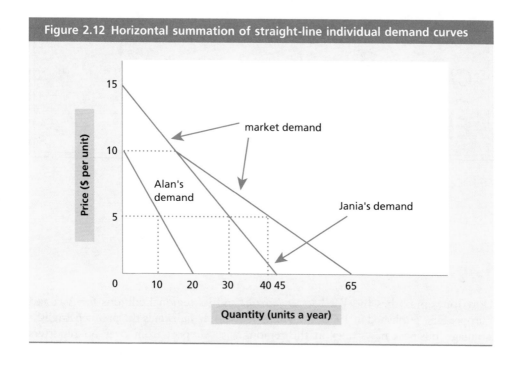

individual and market demand curves. Suppose that the market for some item has two buyers, Alan and Jania. Alan's demand for the item is

$$D_a = 18 - 2p + 0.02Y_a, \qquad (2.9)$$

while Jania's demand is

$$D_j = 42 - 3p + 0.01Y_j. \qquad (2.10)$$

To draw the curves, suppose that $Y_a = 100$ and $Y_j = 300$. Then

$$D_a = 20 - 2p, \text{ and} \qquad (2.11)$$

$$D_j = 45 - 3p. \qquad (2.12)$$

We draw these curves in figure 2.12.

Notice that Jania's quantity demanded is 0 for prices above 15, while Alan's quantity demanded is 0 for prices above 10. By horizontal summation, the market

demand curve has two segments. The upper segment covers prices between 10 and 15, where the market quantity demanded $D = D_j = 45 - 3p$. The lower segment covers prices of 10 or less, where the market quantity demanded $D = D_a + D_j = 65 - 5p$. We draw the market demand curve in figure 2.12.

We can check this market demand curve for the price $p = 5$. With $p = 5$, the individual quantities demanded are $D_a = 20 - 10 = 10$, and $D_j = 45 - 15 = 30$; hence, $D_a + D_j = 40$. This is exactly the quantity from the market demand curve in figure 2.12.

Just as for an individual demand curve, a price change is represented by a movement along the market demand curve, while a change in income or any factor is represented by a shift of the entire demand curve.

Chapter *3*
Elasticity

◄◄ 1 Introduction

Dow Jones publishes the *Wall Street Journal* and its regional editions for Asia and Europe. First published in 1976, the *Asian Wall Street Journal* is the premier English-language business newspaper in the region, with support from over 65 reporters and editors in 15 regional bureaus. The newspaper claims to deliver "the most comprehensive regional and global business news and financial information – with unparalleled clarity and accuracy."[1]

By June 1999, the *Asian Wall Street Journal* had achieved a circulation of 65,000, which was small by comparison with the main *Wall Street Journal*'s circulation of over 1.7 million. The *Asian Wall Street Journal*'s two single largest markets were Hong Kong (circulation of 12,800) and Singapore (circulation of 8,500). The content of the paper was transmitted by satellite from Hong Kong to eight other cities for printing and delivery throughout the region.

Like many other publications, the *Asian Wall Street Journal* derived the bulk of its revenue from advertising. The annual report of Dow Jones provides the combined revenues for all of the company's international publications, including the *Asian Wall Street Journal* and the *Wall Street Journal Europe*. In 1999, Dow Jones earned revenues of $116.9 million from international publications, of which $73.3 million was derived from advertising. Ignoring advertising in other international publications, the advertising revenue per copy of the *Asian Wall Street Journal* and the *Wall Street Journal Europe* was about $499 for the year.

In April 2000, Dow Jones relaunched the *Asian Wall Street Journal*. Management advanced the printing time so that the newspaper would be available to subscribers, airlines, and hotels at an earlier time, and on more newsstands. New subscribers were offered free access to the *Wall Street Journal Interactive Edition*, which previously

▼

[1] This analysis is based, in part, on "Publisher's Statement: *Asian Wall Street Journal*" (http://www.media.com.hk/kits/505.htm/); Dow Jones & Co. Inc., Form 10-K for 1999; and letter dated July 18, 2000, from Urban C. Lehner, publisher of the *Asian Wall Street Journal*.

was subject to an additional charge. The newspaper was also redesigned for easier reading.

A key element of the re-launch was substantial price cuts in four major markets. In Hong Kong, the cover price was reduced by 40% from HK$15 to HK$9, while the subscription price was reduced by 10% from HK$2,550 to HK$2,298. In Singapore, the cover price was reduced by 40% from S$3.50 to S$1.20, while the subscription price was reduced by 40% from S$510 to S$298. The newspaper cut its cover prices in the Philippines and Thailand by 40% and its subscription prices by 25–38%. The *Asian Wall Street Journal* kept advertising rates unchanged at $17 per agate line and $30,192 for a full-page black-and-white advertisement.

With each copy yielding up to 40% less revenue, Dow Jones management would have to carefully consider the impact of the substantial price cuts on the circulation. By how much would circulation increase? This would determine the impact of the relaunch on revenues from selling the newspaper. By increasing the demand to advertise in the *Asian Wall Street Journal*, it would also raise advertising revenue. Would the relaunched newspaper at least break even in terms of revenue?

To address these questions, we develop the concept of *elasticity*. The **elasticity of demand** measures the responsiveness of demand to changes in an underlying factor, such as the price of the product, income, the prices of related products, or advertising. There is an elasticity corresponding to every factor that affects demand.

> **Elasticity of demand** is the responsiveness of demand to changes in an underlying factor.

The *own-price elasticity of demand* measures the responsiveness of the quantity demanded to changes in the price of the item. With the own-price elasticity, a manager can tell the extent to which buyers will respond to a price increase or reduction. The *Asian Wall Street Journal* could apply this concept to gauge the impact of the price cuts accompanying the April 2000 relaunch.

We will show how elasticities can be used to forecast the effect of single as well as multiple changes in the factors underlying demand. Accordingly, a media industry analyst can use elasticities to consider how changes in both price and income will affect the demand for newspapers. We will also discuss how elasticities depend on the time available for adjustment. Finally, we consider the data and statistical methods to use in estimating elasticities.

In this chapter, we present elasticities in the context of demand. The same analysis applies to the supply side of a market as well. In chapter 4, we discuss the factors underlying supply and their corresponding elasticities.

◂◂ 2 Own-Price Elasticity

To address the issue of whether to raise price, we need a measure of buyers' sensitivity to price changes. The **own-price elasticity** of demand provides this information. By definition, the own-price elasticity of demand is the percentage by which the quantity demanded will change if the price

> The **own-price elasticity** of demand is the percentage by which the quantity demanded will change if the price of the item rises by 1%.

of the item rises by 1%, other things equal. Equivalently, the own-price elasticity is the ratio,

$$\frac{\text{percentage change in quantity demanded}}{\text{percentage change in price}}$$

or

$$\frac{\text{proportionate change in quantity demanded}}{\text{proportionate change in price}}.$$

Understanding the own-price elasticity of demand is fundamental to the management of a business. Indeed, this concept is so basic that it is often called simply the *price elasticity* or *demand elasticity*. In chapter 2, we distinguished the demand curve of an individual buyer, the market demand curve, and the demand curve faced by an individual seller. Every demand curve has a corresponding own-price elasticity. Before discussing how to apply this concept, let us first consider how it can be calculated.

Construction

> The **arc approach** calculates the own-price elasticity of demand from the average values of observed price and quantity demanded.

Generally, there are two ways of deriving the own-price elasticity of demand. One is the **arc approach**, in which we collect records of a price change and the corresponding change in quantity demanded. Then we calculate the own-price elasticity as the ratio of the proportionate (percentage) change in quantity demanded to the proportionate (percentage) change in price.

To illustrate, figure 3.1 represents the demand for cigarettes. Presently, the price of cigarettes is $1 a pack and quantity demanded is 1.5 billion packs a month. According to figure 3.1, if the price rises to $1.10 per pack, the quantity demanded would drop to 1.44 billion packs.

The proportionate change in quantity demanded is the change in quantity demanded divided by the average quantity demanded. Since the change in quantity demanded is $1.44 - 1.5 = -0.06$ billion packs and the average quantity demanded is $0.5 \times (1.44 + 1.5) = 1.47$ billion packs, the proportionate change in quantity demanded is $-0.06/1.47 = -0.041$.

Similarly, the proportionate change in price is the change in price divided by the average price. The change in price is $1.10 - $1 = 0.10 per pack, while the average price is $0.5 \times (1.10 + 1) = 1.05 per pack. Hence, the proportionate change in price is $0.1/1.05 = 0.095$.

By the arc approach, the own-price elasticity of the demand for cigarettes is the proportionate change in quantity demanded divided by the proportionate change in price, or $(-0.041)/0.095 = -0.432$. Equivalently, in this example, the percentage change in quantity demanded was -4.1%, while the percentage change in price was 9.5%; hence, the own-price elasticity is $-4.1/9.5 = -0.432$.

Figure 3.1 Arc approach

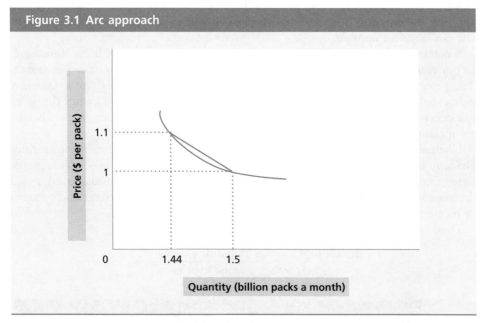

By the arc approach, the own-price elasticity of the demand for cigarettes is the proportionate change in quantity demanded divided by the proportionate change in price = (−0.041)/0.095 = −0.432.

An alternative way of calculating the own-price elasticity of demand is the **point approach**, which sets up a mathematical equation with quantity demanded as a function of the price and other variables. The own-price elasticity can then be derived from the coefficient of price in this equation. We illustrate this procedure later in the chapter.

The point approach calculates the elasticity at a specific point on the demand curve. By contrast, the arc approach calculates the elasticity between two points on the demand curve. In principle, as we consider shorter and shorter arcs, the estimate from the arc approach will tend to the point estimate. Thus, for an infinitesimally short arc, the arc and point approaches will provide identical numbers for the elasticity.

The arc and point approaches are the two ways of calculating the elasticity of demand with respect to all the factors that affect demand.

> The **point approach** calculates own-price elasticity from a mathematical equation, in which the quantity demanded is a function of the price and other variables.

Properties

The cigarette example illustrates several properties of the own-price elasticity of demand. First, as discussed in chapter 2, demand curves generally slope downward: if the price of an item rises, the quantity demanded will fall. Hence, the own-price elasticity will be a negative number. For ease of interpretation, some analysts report own-price elasticities as an absolute value, that is, without the negative sign. Accordingly, when applying the concept, it is very important to bear in mind that the own-price elasticity is a negative number.

Second, the own-price elasticity is a pure number, independent of units of measure. In our example, we measured the quantity demanded of cigarettes in packs per month. The percentage change in quantity demanded, however, is the change in quantity demanded divided by the average quantity demanded. It is a pure number that does not depend on any units of measure: the percentage change will be the same whether we measure quantity demanded in packs or individual cigarettes.

Likewise, the percentage change in price is a pure number. Since the own-price elasticity is the percentage change in quantity demanded divided by the percentage change in price, it is also a pure number. Thus, the own-price elasticity of demand provides a handy way of characterizing price sensitivity that does not depend on units of measure.

Third, recall that the own-price elasticity is the ratio

$$\frac{\text{percentage change in quantity demanded}}{\text{percentage change in price}}.$$

Table 3.1 Own-price elasticities of market demand

Product	Market	Own-price elasticity	Source (see References)
Automobiles			
Domestic compacts	U.S.	−3.4	Koujianou-Goldberg (1995)
Foreign compacts	U.S.	−4.0	Koujianou-Goldberg (1995)
Domestic intermediates	U.S.	−4.2	Koujianou-Goldberg (1995)
Foreign intermediates	U.S.	−5.2	Koujianou-Goldberg (1995)
Consumer products			
CDs	Australia	−1.83	Bain & McKenzie (1999)
Cigarettes	U.S.	−0.2, −0.4	Becker et al. (1994) Tegene (1991)
Liquor	U.S.	−0.2	Baltagi & Griffin (1995)
Utilities			
Electricity (residential)	Quebec	−0.7	Bernard et al. (1996)
Telephone service	Spain	−0.1	Garin Munoz (1996)
Water (residential)	U.S.	−0.2, −0.3	Williams & Suh (1986)
Water (industrial)	U.S.	−0.7, −1.0	Williams & Suh (1986)

If a very large percentage change in price causes no change in quantity demanded, then the elasticity will be 0. By contrast, if an infinitesimal percentage change in price causes a large change in quantity demanded, then the elasticity will be negative infinity. Accordingly, the own-price elasticity ranges from 0 to negative infinity.

Table 3.1 reports the own-price elasticities of the market demand for several product categories, while table 3.2 reports the own-price elasticities of the demand for individual sellers of several products. We say that the demand for an item is price **elastic** or *elastic with respect to price* if a 1% increase in price leads to more than a 1% drop in quantity demanded. Equivalently, demand is price elastic if a price increase causes a proportionately larger drop in quantity demanded.

> The demand is price **elastic** if a 1% increase in price leads to more than a 1% drop in the quantity demanded.

We say that demand is price **inelastic** or *inelastic with respect to price* if a 1% price increase causes less than a 1% drop in quantity demanded. An alternative definition is that demand is price inelastic if a price increase causes a proportionately smaller drop in quantity demanded.

> The demand is price **inelastic** if a 1% increase in price leads to less than a 1% drop in the quantity demanded.

From table 3.1, the own-price elasticity of the market demand for domestic compacts is −3.4. This means that a 1% price increase will reduce the quantity demanded by 3.4%. So, the demand for domestic compacts is elastic. The own-price elasticity of the market demand for foreign-made compacts is −4.0. This indicates that the demand for foreign compacts is more elastic than the demand for domestic makes.

Table 3.2 Own-price elasticities of individual seller demand

Product	Seller	Own-price elasticity	Source (See References)
Automobiles			
Chevette	Chevrolet	−3.2	Koujianou-Goldberg (1995)
Civic	Honda	−3.4	Koujianou-Goldberg (1995)
Escort	Ford	−3.4	Koujianou-Goldberg (1995)
Century	Buick	−4.8	Koujianou-Goldberg (1995)
Fleetwood	Cadillac	−0.9	Koujianou-Goldberg (1995)
Ferrari	Ferrari	−1	Koujianou-Goldberg (1995)
Consumer products			
Breakfast cereal	Columbus, OH supermarkets	−0.6, −0.7	Jones & Mustiful (1996)
Gasoline	Boston, MA stations	−3, −8.4	Png & Reitman (1994)

By contrast, the own-price elasticity of the market demand for liquor is −0.2. This means that a 1% increase in the price of liquor will reduce the quantity demanded by 0.2%. The demand for liquor is inelastic.

Progress check **Progress Check 3A** Referring to table 3.1, is the United States' residential demand for water relatively more or less elastic than the industrial demand?

Intuitive Factors

Managers can consider several intuitive factors to gauge whether demand will be relatively more elastic or inelastic. The first factor is the availability of direct or indirect substitutes. The fewer substitutes are available, the less elastic will be the demand. People who are dependent on alcoholic drinks or cigarettes feel that they cannot do without them; hence, the demand for these products is relatively inelastic. For the image-conscious teenager, sporting a pair of the "in" athletic shoes is the only way to gain peer acceptance, so teenage demand for the shoes is very inelastic.

In many countries, the Post Office has a legally established monopoly over carriage of letters. Hence, there are no direct substitutes for the Post Office letter service. Indirect substitutes, however, are popping up all over the world. With the spread of electronic mail and fax machines, the demand for a Post Office letter service is becoming relatively more elastic.

By considering the availability of substitutes, we can conclude that the demand for a product category will be relatively less elastic than the demand for specific products within the category. The reason is that there are fewer substitutes for the category than for specific products. Consider, for instance, the demand for cigarettes compared with the demand for a particular brand. The particular brand has many more substitutes than the category as a whole. Accordingly, the demand for the brand will tend to be more elastic than the demand for the category. This means that, if cigarette manufacturers can raise prices collectively by 10%, their sales will fall by a smaller percentage than if only one manufacturer increases its price by 10%.

Another factor that affects the own-price elasticity of demand is the buyer's prior commitments. A person who has bought an automobile becomes a captive customer for spare parts. Automobile manufacturers understand this very well. Accordingly, they set relatively higher prices on spare parts than on new cars. The same applies as well in the software business. Once users have invested time and effort to learn one program, they become captive customers for future upgrades. Whenever there is such a commitment, demand is less elastic.

A third factor that affects the own-price elasticity of demand is the cost relative to the benefit from searching for better prices. Buyers have limited time to spend on searching for better prices, so they focus attention on items that account for relatively larger expenditures. Families with toddlers, for instance, spend more time economizing on diapers than Q-tips. Similarly, office managers focus attention on copying paper rather than paper clips. Marketing practitioners have given the name *low involvement* to products that get relatively little attention from buyers.

The balance between the cost and benefit of economizing also depends on a possible split between the person who incurs the cost of economizing and the person who benefits. Almost everyone who has driven a damaged car to a body repair shop

Buyer price sensitivity: Escort vis-à-vis Civic

Ford and Honda cater to the subcompact segment of the automobile market with their Escort and Civic models, respectively. Are Ford Escort buyers more or less price sensitive than buyers of Honda Civics? One way to answer this question is to estimate the change in quantity demanded from a $100 increase in the price of each make. But this does not compare like with like.

A consistent way of comparing the price sensitivity of Escort and Civic buyers is to use the own-price elasticities of the demands. The own-price elasticities of the demands for Escorts and Civics have been estimated to be both −3.4. This indicates that Escort and Civic buyers are equally sensitive to price. For a 1% increase in price, both groups would reduce purchases by 3.4%.

Source: Pinelopi Koujianou-Goldberg, "Product Differentiation and Oligopoly in International Markets: the Case of the U.S. Automobile Industry," *Econometrica* 63, no. 4 (July 1995), pp. 891–951.

Shared costs: frequent flyer programs

Whenever there is a split between the person who pays and the person who chooses the product, the demand will be less elastic. In 1981, American Airlines established its AAdvantage program for frequent flyers. This program records each member's travel on American Airlines and awards free flights according to the number of miles that the member accumulates. The AAdvantage program does not give mileage credit for travel on competing airlines such as United or Delta, hence it provides members with a strong incentive to concentrate travel on American Airlines.

The AAdvantage program is especially attractive to travelers, such as business executives, who fly at the expense of others. Such travelers are relatively less price sensitive than those who pay for their own tickets. The AAdvantage program gives them an incentive to choose American Airlines even if the fare is higher. Among customers who fly at the expense of others, the program makes demand relatively less elastic. AAdvantage was a brilliant marketing strategy, and all of American's competitors soon established their own frequent flyer programs.

has been asked the question, "Are you covered by insurance?" Experienced repair managers know that car owners who are covered by insurance care less about price. In this example, the car owner gets the benefit of the repair work, while the insurer pays most or all the costs. A car owner who bargains over the repairs must spend his or her own time, while the insurer will get most of the saving.

Elasticity and Slope

When comparing the demands for different products or even quantities demanded of the same product at different prices, it is important to remember that these comparisons are relative. The reason is that the own-price elasticity describes the shape of only one portion of the demand curve. A change in price, by moving from one part of a demand curve to another part, may lead to a change in own-price elasticity.

Let us show this by considering the demand curve for cars in figure 3.2. This demand curve is a straight line. Suppose that, initially, the price is $7,000 per car and the quantity demanded is 22,000 cars a month. When the price increases to $8,000, the quantity demanded falls to 20,000 cars. The proportionate change in quantity demanded

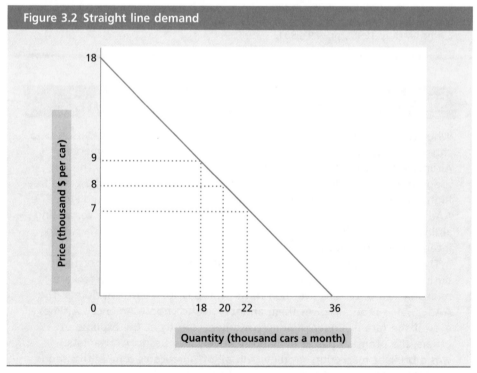

Figure 3.2 Straight line demand

Price (thousand $ per car) / Quantity (thousand cars a month)

By the arc approach, the own-price elasticity at a price of $7,000 is –0.1/0.13 = –0.8, and the own-price elasticity at a price of $8,000 is –0.11/0.12 = –0.9.

is $-2,000/21,000 = -0.1$, while the proportionate change in price is $1,000/7,500$ $= 0.13$. Hence, by the arc approach, the own-price elasticity is $-0.1/0.13 = -0.8$.

Now, suppose that the price increases from $8,000 to $9,000; then the quantity demanded falls from 20,000 to 18,000 cars. The proportionate change in quantity demanded is now $-2,000/19,000 = -0.11$, while the proportionate change in price is $1,000/8,500 = 0.12$. Hence, by the arc approach, the own-price elasticity is $-0.11/0.12 = -0.9$. Thus, the demand curve in figure 3.2 is inelastic at both prices of $8,000 and $7,000. It is relatively more elastic at the price of $8,000 per car than at a price of $7,000.

Generally, whether the demand curve is a straight line or curved, the own-price elasticity can vary with changes in the price of the item. In the case of a straight line demand curve, the demand becomes more elastic at higher prices. For demand curves with other shapes, the demand may become less elastic at higher prices.

Another point worth noting is that the own-price elasticity can also vary with changes in any of the other factors that affect demand. Recall that the own-price elasticity is the percentage by which the quantity demanded will change if the price of the item rises by 1%. If there are changes in any of the other factors that affect demand, then the demand curve will shift; hence, the own-price elasticity may also change.

A frequently asked question is the relation between own-price elasticity and the slope of the demand curve. In the math supplement, we show that the own-price elasticity is related to the slope, the price, and the quantity demanded. Thus, other things equal, where the demand curve is steeper, the demand is less elastic, and where the demand curve is less steep, the demand is more elastic. It is very important to stress that the price and quantity demanded are the "other things equal." To illustrate, let us consider again the straight line demand curve in figure 3.2. The slope of this curve is the rate of change of price for changes in the quantity demanded. The slope is $-18/36 = -0.5$. The demand curve is a straight-line; hence, it has the same slope throughout.

By contrast, as we have already shown, the own-price elasticity is -0.8 at a price of $7,000, and -0.9 at a price of $8,000. Generally, the own-price elasticity varies throughout the length of a straight-line demand curve.

If the own-price elasticity varies throughout the demand curve, while the slope is the same everywhere, what explains the difference? The answer is the price and quantity demanded. Even though the slope remains constant, the changes in price and quantity demanded along the demand curve mean that the own-price elasticity will vary. Thus, the own-price elasticity and slope are related but are not equivalent.

Progress Check 3B Referring to figure 3.2, suppose that the price increases from $11,000 to $12,000. Calculate the own-price elasticity of demand using the arc approach.

Progress check

Breaking even

In April 2000, Dow Jones re-launched the *Asian Wall Street Journal* with substantial price cuts in four major markets. In Hong Kong, where the paper had a daily circulation of 12,800, the cover price was reduced by 40% from HK$15 to HK$9, while the subscription price was reduced by 10% from HK$2,550 to HK$2,298. Management kept advertising rates unchanged at $17 per agate line and $30,192 for a full-page black-and-white advertisement. What must be the own-price elasticity of demand for the re-launch to break even just in terms of revenue?

Suppose that the proportion of regular subscriptions in daily circulation was 86%, which was the proportion for the main *Wall Street Journal*. Then, the *Asian Wall Street Journal*'s circulation in Hong Kong would have consisted of 11,000 regular subscribers and 1,800 single-copy sales. Advertising revenue would depend on the newspaper's circulation. We assume that annual advertising revenue was $499 (or HK$3,860) per copy.

Before the re-launch, the annual circulation revenue from subscriptions would have been HK$2,550 × 11,000 = HK$28 million. The advertising revenue from copies sold by subscriptions would have been HK$3,860 × 11,000 = HK$42.5 million a year. Total circulation and advertising revenue from subscribers was HK$70.5 million.

The re-launch reduced the subscription price by 10% to HK$2,298. Suppose that the price cut raised subscription volume to S thousands. Then the re-launch would break even in terms of circulation and advertising revenue from subscribers if $70.5 = 2.298 \times S + 3.86 \times S$, or $S = 11.45$. For the re-launch to break even in terms of all revenues from Hong Kong subscribers, the volume of subscriptions must rise to at least 11,450, which is a 4.1% increase. Since the price was reduced by just 10%, this means that the required own-price elasticity was −0.41 or lower.

Before the re-launch, the annual circulation revenue from single-copy (newsstand) sales would have been HK$15 × 250 × 1,800 = HK$6.8 million, assuming 250 publication days a year. The advertising revenue from single-copy sales would have been HK$3,860 x 1,800 = HK$6.9 million a year.

The re-launch cut the cover price of the newspaper by 40% to HK$9. In a similar way as for the subscription sales, we can show that, for the re-launch to break even in terms of all revenues from Hong Kong single-copy buyers, the volume of sales must rise to at least 2,242. This implies that the own-price elasticity must be −0.61 or lower.

In practice, Dow Jones should also consider the additional costs arising from the re-launch, and then assess the impact of the re-launch on profit. Further, it need not necessarily break even in each of the customer segments – subscribers and single-copy buyers – separately. All that it should consider is the overall profit.

Sources: "Publisher's Statement: Asian Wall Street Journal," (http://www.media.com.hk/kits/505.htm/); Dow Jones & Co. Inc., Form 10-K for 1999; and letter dated July 18, 2000, from Urban C. Lehner, publisher of the *Asian Wall Street Journal*.

◂◂ 3 Forecasting Quantity Demanded and Expenditure

The own-price elasticity of demand can be applied to forecast the effect of price changes on quantity demanded and buyer expenditure. Expenditure is related to the quantity demanded, since expenditure equals the quantity demanded multiplied by the price. The own-price elasticity can be applied at the level of an entire market as well as for individual sellers. From the standpoint of an individual seller, the quantity demanded is sales, while buyer expenditure is revenue. Hence, using the own-price elasticity of demand, the seller can forecast the effect of price changes on sales and revenue.

Quantity Demanded

Let us first consider how to use the own-price elasticity of demand to forecast the effect of price changes on the quantity demanded. Refer, for instance, to the demand for automobiles at a price of $7,000 in figure 3.2. How will a 10% increase in price affect the quantity of cars that buyers demand?

We have already calculated the own-price elasticity of demand at the $7,000 price to be −0.8. By definition, the own-price elasticity is the percentage by which the quantity demanded will change if the price rises by 1%. Hence, if the price of cars increases by 10%, then the quantity demanded will change by $-0.8 \times 10 = -8\%$; that is, the quantity demanded will fall by 8%.

To forecast the change in quantity demanded in terms of the number of cars, we should multiply the percentage change of −8% by the quantity demanded before the price change. By this method, the change in quantity demanded is $-0.08 \times 22,000$, that is, a drop of 1,760 cars. (In this calculation, we used the equality, 8% = 0.08.) The new quantity demanded would be 22,000 − 1,760 = 20,240 cars a month.

We can also use the elasticity method to estimate the effect of a reduction in the price on quantity demanded. Referring to figure 3.2, suppose, for instance, that the price of cars is initially $7,000 and then drops by 5%. The quantity demanded will change by $-0.8 \times (-5) = 4\%$; that is, it will increase by 4%. This example shows that it is important to keep track of the signs of the own-price elasticity and the price change.

Expenditure

Let us next see how to use the own-price elasticity of demand to estimate the effect of changes in price on buyer expenditure. Buyer expenditure equals the quantity demanded multiplied by the price. Hence, a change in price will affect expenditure through the price itself as well as through the related effect on quantity demanded.

Consider the effect of a small increase in price. By itself, the price increase will tend to raise the expenditure. The price increase, however, will reduce the quantity that buyers demand and so tend to reduce the expenditure. Hence, the net effect on expenditure depends on which effect is relatively larger.

This is where the concept of own-price elasticity is useful. Recall that demand is elastic with respect to price if an increase in price causes a proportionately larger fall in quantity demanded, while demand is inelastic if a price increase causes a proportionately smaller fall in quantity demanded. The own-price elasticity enables us to compare the relative magnitude of changes in price and quantity demanded.

If demand is price elastic, then the drop in the quantity demanded will be proportionately larger than the increase in price; hence, the small price increase will reduce expenditure. If, however, demand is price inelastic, the drop in quantity demanded will be proportionately smaller than the increase in price; hence, the small price increase will increase expenditure.

Generally, if demand is price elastic, a small price increase will reduce expenditure while a small price reduction will increase expenditure. By contrast, if demand is price inelastic, a small price increase will increase expenditure while a price reduction will reduce expenditure. (We prove these results in the math supplement.)

Whenever managers are asked to raise prices, their most frequent response is, "But my sales would drop!" Since demand curves slope downward, it certainly is true that a higher price will reduce sales. The real issue is the *extent* to which the price increase will reduce sales. A manager ought to be thinking about the own-price elasticity of demand.

To explain, consider the demand facing an individual seller and suppose that the demand is price inelastic at the current price. What if the seller raises price? Then, since demand is price inelastic, the price increase will lead to a proportionately smaller reduction in the quantity demanded. The buyer's expenditure will increase, which means that the seller's revenue will increase. Meanwhile, owing to the reduction in quantity demanded, the seller can reduce production, cutting its costs. Since revenues will be higher and costs will be lower, the seller's profits definitely will be higher. Accordingly, if demand is price inelastic, a seller can increase profit by raising price.

Pricing breakfast cereals

Eugene Jones and Barry W. Mustiful of Ohio State University studied the demand for breakfast cereals at six outlets of a national supermarket chain in the Columbus, Ohio, metropolitan area. They found that the demand was inelastic with respect to price: The own-price elasticity of demand for the top 10 brands was –0.7, while the elasticity for private label cereal was –0.6.

We have shown that, where demand is price inelastic, a seller can increase profits by raising price. The supermarket chain could have increased its profits by raising the prices of both branded and private label breakfast cereals at its Columbus area stores.

Source: Eugene Jones and Barry W. Mustiful, "Purchasing Behaviour of Higher- and Lower-Income Shoppers: a Look at Breakfast Cereals," *Applied Economics* 28, no. 1 (January 1996), pp. 131–7.

This discussion shows that, under the right conditions, a price increase can raise profits even though it may cause sales to drop. Therefore, when setting the price for an item, managers ought to focus on the own-price elasticity of demand. Generally, the price should be raised until the demand becomes price elastic. We will develop this idea further in chapter 9 on "Pricing Policy."

Accuracy

We have used the own-price elasticity of demand to forecast that, in figure 3.2, if the price of cars rises by 10% from $7,000, then the quantity demanded would drop to 20,240 cars a month. We can calculate the effect of the price increase in another way – directly from the demand curve. After a 10% increase, the new price would be $7,700. From the demand curve, the quantity demanded at that price would be 20,600 cars a month.

What explains the discrepancy between the quantities of 20,240 and 20,600? The reason for the discrepancy is that, as we have emphasized previously, the own-price elasticity may vary along a demand curve. Accordingly, the forecast using the own-price elasticity will not be as precise as a forecast directly from the demand curve. The same applies to forecasting changes in expenditure with the own-price elasticity.

Generally, the error in a forecast based on the own-price elasticity will be larger for larger changes in the price and the other factors that affect demand. Elasticities do not provide as much information as the entire demand curve. In many cases, however, managers do not know the entire demand curve. Their information is limited to the quantity demanded around the current values of the factors that affect the demand.

For many business decisions, however, managers do not need to know the full demand curve. The manufacturer of a luxury car, for instance, would never consider cutting the price to the level of a subcompact. So, it need not know the quantity demanded at such a low price. Likewise, the manufacturer of a subcompact would never consider raising the price to the level of a luxury car. Hence, the elasticities often provide sufficient information for business decisions.

◂◂ 4 Other Elasticities

In addition to price, the demand for an item also depends on buyers' incomes, the prices of related products, and advertising, among other factors. Changes in any of these factors will lead to a shift in the demand curve. There is an elasticity to measure the responsiveness of demand to changes in each factor. Managers can use these elasticities to forecast the effect of changes in these factors. In particular, the elasticities can be used to forecast the effect of changes in multiple factors that occur at the same time.

The analyses of elasticities of demand with respect to income, the prices of related products, and advertising are very similar. Accordingly, we will focus on the elasticity of demand with respect to income and discuss only the key differences for the other elasticities.

Income Elasticity

> The **income elasticity** of demand is the percentage by which the demand will change if the buyer's income rises by 1%.

The **income elasticity** of demand measures the sensitivity of demand to changes in buyers' incomes. By definition, the *income elasticity of demand* is the percentage by which the demand will change if the buyer's income rises by 1%, other things equal. In this case, the price of the item is one of the other things that must remain unchanged. Equivalently, the income elasticity is the ratio

$$\frac{\text{percentage change in demand}}{\text{percentage change in income}}$$

or

$$\frac{\text{proportionate change in demand}}{\text{proportionate change in income}}.$$

The income elasticity may be calculated using either the arc or point approach. (Since the demand curve diagram does not explicitly show income, we cannot draw a picture of the arc approach for calculating income elasticity.) For an infinitesimally small change in income, the arc estimate equals the point elasticity. Like the own-price elasticity, the income elasticity of demand varies with changes in the price and any other factor that affects demand.

By definition, the income elasticity is a ratio of two proportionate changes; hence, it is a pure number and independent of units of measure. In the case of a normal product, if income rises, the demand will rise, so the income elasticity will be positive. By contrast, for an inferior product, if income rises, demand will fall, so the income elasticity will be negative. So, depending on whether the product is normal or inferior, the income elasticity can be either positive or negative. Hence, it is important to note the sign of the income elasticity. Income elasticity can range from negative infinity to positive infinity.

We say that demand is *income elastic* or *elastic with respect to income* if a 1% income increase causes more than a 1% change in demand. Demand is said to be *income inelastic* or *inelastic with respect to income* if a 1% income increase causes less than a 1% change in demand.

The demand for necessities tends to be relatively less income elastic than the demand for discretionary items. Consider, for instance, the demand for food as compared with restaurant meals. Eating in a restaurant is more of a discretionary item. Accordingly, we expect the demand for food to be relatively less income elastic than the demand for restaurant meals.

Table 3.3 reports the income elasticities of the market demand for various items. In the United States, the demand for cigarettes and liquor hardly changes with income,

Table 3.3 Income elasticities of market demand

Product	Market	Income elasticity	Source (see References)
Consumer products			
Cigarettes	U.S.	0.1	Tegene (1991)
Liquor	U.S.	0.2	Baltagi & Griffin (1995)
Food	U.S.	0.8	Baye et al. (1992)
Clothing	U.S.	1	Baye et al. (1992)
Newspapers	U.S.	0.9	Bucklin et al. (1989)
Utilities			
Electricity (residential)	Quebec	0.1	Bernard et al. (1996)
Telephone service	Spain	0.5	Garin Munoz (1996)

while, in Quebec, the residential demand for electricity is also extremely inelastic with respect to income.

We can apply the income elasticity of demand to forecast the effect of changes in income on demand and expenditure. Suppose that, presently, the price of cigarettes is $1 per pack, the quantity demanded is 1.5 billion packs a month, and the income elasticity of demand is 0.1. How will a 3% increase in income affect the demand?

By definition, the income elasticity of demand is the percentage by which the demand will change if the buyer's income rises by 1%, other things equal. In the present case, the income rises by 3%; hence, the percentage change in demand will be $0.1 \times 3 = 0.3\%$; that is, demand will increase by 0.3%. Since the initial quantity was 1.5 billion packs, the increase in quantity is 0.003×1.5 billion = 4.5 million packs. Provided that the price remains at $1 per pack, this increase in demand will mean an increase in expenditure of $4.5 million.

A major difference between income and some of the other variables that affect demand such as price and advertising is that, generally, sellers have no control over buyers' incomes. While a seller can set price and advertising, it must take buyers' incomes as a given. Accordingly, we do not study how a seller should determine buyers' incomes.

Progress Check 3C Referring to table 3.3, is the demand for liquor relatively more or less income elastic than the demand for cigarettes?   *Progress check*

Products	Market	Cross price elasticity	Source (see References)
Table 3.4 Cross-price elasticities of market-demand			
Consumer products			
Clothing/food	U.S.	0.1	Baye & Beil (1994)
Gasoline at competing stations	Boston, MA	1.2	Png & Reitman (1994)
Utilities			
Electricity/gas (residential)	Quebec	0.1	Bernard et al. (1996)
Electricity/oil (residential)	Quebec	0.0	Bernard et al. (1996)
Bus/subway	London	0.0, 0.5	Gilbert & Jalilian (1991)

Cross-Price Elasticity

> The **cross-price elasticity** of demand is the percentage by which the demand will change if the price of another item rises by 1%.

Just as the income elasticity of demand measures the sensitivity of demand to changes in income, the **cross-price elasticity** measures the sensitivity of demand to changes in the prices of related products. By definition, *the cross-price elasticity of demand* with respect to another item is the percentage by which the demand will change if the price of the other item rises by 1%, other things equal. In this case, the (own) price of the item is one of the other things that must remain unchanged.

If two products are substitutes, an increase in the price of one will increase the demand for the other, so the cross-price elasticity will be positive. By contrast, if two products are complements, an increase in the price of one will reduce demand for the other; hence, the cross-price elasticity will be negative. The cross-price elasticity can range from negative infinity to positive infinity.

We say that demand is *elastic with respect to the price of another item* if a 1% increase in the price of the other item causes more than a 1% change in demand. Demand is said to be *inelastic with respect to the price of another item* if a 1% price increase in the other item causes less than a 1% change in demand. Generally, the more two items are substitutable, the higher their cross-price elasticity will be. Table 3.4 reports the cross-price elasticities of the demand for various items.

> The **advertising elasticity** of demand is the percentage by which the demand will change if the seller's advertising expenditure rises by 1%.

Advertising Elasticity

The **advertising elasticity** measures the sensitivity of demand to changes in the sellers' advertising expenditure. By definition,

Product	Market	Advertising elasticity	Source (see References)
Beer	U.S.	0.0	Franke & Wilcox (1987)
Wine	U.S.	0.08	Franke & Wilcox (1987)
Cigarettes	U.S.	0.04	Tegene (1991)
Anti-hypertensive drugs	U.S.	0.26–0.27	Rizzo (1999)
Clothing	U.S.	0.01	Baye et al. (1992)
Recreation	U.S.	0.08	Baye et al. (1992)

Table 3.5 Advertising elasticities of market demand

the *advertising elasticity of demand* is the percentage by which the demand will change if the sellers' advertising expenditure rises by 1%, other things equal. In this case, the (own) price of the item is one of the other things that must remain unchanged.

Table 3.5 reports the advertising elasticities of the demand for several consumer product categories. The advertising elasticity for beer is 0, which means that a 1% increase in advertising expenditure will not change the demand for beer. The advertising elasticity for cigarettes is 0.04, which means that a 1% increase in advertising expenditure will increase the demand for cigarettes by 0.04%.

Given these small elasticities, it may seem surprising that beer and cigarette manufacturers spend so much on advertising. Note that the advertising elasticities reported in table 3.5 pertain to market demand. Most advertising, however, is undertaken by individual sellers to promote their own business. By drawing buyers away from competitors, advertising has a much stronger effect on the sales of an individual seller than on the market demand. Accordingly, the advertising elasticity of the demand faced by an individual seller tends to be larger than the advertising elasticity of the market demand.

Forecasting the Effects of Multiple Factors

The business environment will often change in conflicting ways. For instance, the prices of substitutes may rise, but the prices of complements may rise as well. The only way to discern the net effect of factors pushing in different directions is to use the elasticities with respect to each of the variables.

To illustrate, suppose that the price of cigarettes is $1 per pack and sales are 1.5 billion packs a month. Then the price increases by 5% while income rises by 3%. What would be the impact on demand?

We have shown how to apply the own-price elasticity to forecast the effect of a change in price on quantity demanded and similarly to apply the income elasticity to forecast the effect of a change in income on demand. To calculate the net effect of the increases in both price and income, we simply add the changes due to each of the factors.

Suppose that the own-price elasticity of the demand for cigarettes is −0.4. Then, a 5% increase in price would change quantity demanded by $-0.4 \times 5 = -2\%$. We have already calculated that a 3% increase in income would increase demand by 0.3%. Therefore, the net effect of the increases in price and income is to change demand by $-2 + 0.3 = -1.7\%$. Originally, the quantity demanded of cigarette services was 1.5 billion packs. After the increases in price and income, the quantity demanded will be 1.475 billion packs.

We can use similar techniques to forecast the effects of changes in other factors, such as the prices of related products and advertising expenditures. Generally, the percentage change in demand due to changes in multiple factors is the sum of the percentage changes due to each separate factor.

Advertising and the demand for pharmaceuticals

The demand for prescription drugs differs from that for many other products in that it derives from the decision of possibly three persons – one who recommends the item (physician), another who consumes it (patient), and possibly another who pays for it (medical insurer or health maintenance organization). Pharmaceutical manufacturers spend up to 30% of sales on advertising. Most of this takes the form of "detailing", which is visits by sales representatives to physicians in their offices and hospitals. What is the effect of this advertising on the demand for prescription drugs?

Research into the demand for antihypertensive drugs has shown that the advertising elasticity of demand ranged between 0.26 and 0.27. The advertising elasticity for antihypertensive drugs covered by patents ranged between 0.23 and 0.25. This suggests that advertising has a smaller effect for drugs covered by patents.

Further, advertising caused the demand for antihypertensive drugs to become less price elastic. For all antihypertensive drugs, the own price elasticity ranged between −2.0 and −2.1 without advertising, while ranging between −1.5 and −1.7 in the long run with advertising.

Recall that, if demand is inelastic, a seller can increase profit by raising price. Hence, advertising helps a prescription drug manufacturer to raise profit in two ways – by directly increasing the demand, and by rendering the demand less price elastic.

Source: Rizzo (1999).

◂◂ 5 Adjustment Time

We have analyzed the elasticities of demand with respect to changes in price, income, the prices of related products, and advertising expenditures. We have discussed the intuitive factors that underly these elasticities. In addition, another factor affects all elasticities: the time available for buyers to adjust.

> The **short run** is a time horizon within which a buyer cannot adjust at least one item of consumption or usage.

With regard to adjustment time, it is important to distinguish the **short run** from the **long run**. The short run is a time horizon within which a buyer cannot adjust at least one item of consumption or usage. By contrast, the long run is a time horizon long enough for buyers to adjust all items of consumption or usage.

> The **long run** is a time horizon long enough for buyers to adjust all items of consumption or usage.

To illustrate the distinction, consider how Max commutes into Chicago. He does not have a car, so he takes the train. To switch from the train to a car, he needs time to buy or lease a car. Accordingly, with regard to Max's choice of transportation mode, a short run is any period of time shorter than that which he needs to get a car. A long run is any period of time longer than that which he needs to get a car.

We shall now discuss the effect of adjustment time on the elasticities of demand, and how the effect depends on whether the item is durable or nondurable.

Nondurables

Consider an everyday item like commuter train services. Suppose that one Monday morning, the local railway operator announces a permanent 10% increase in fares. Many commuters may have already made plans for that day, so the response to the higher fare may be quite weak on that day. Over time, however, the response will be stronger: as more commuters acquire cars, the demand for the railway service will drop.

Generally, for nondurable items, the longer the time that buyers have to adjust, the bigger will be the response to a price change. Accordingly, the demand for such items will be more elastic in the long run than in the short run. This applies to all nondurable items, including both goods and services.

Figure 3.3 illustrates the short- and long-run demand for a nondurable item. Suppose that the current price is $5 and quantity demanded is 1.5 million units. If the price drops to $4.50, the quantity demanded will rise to 1.6 million units in the short run and 1.75 million units in the long run.

Table 3.6 reports the short- and long-run own-price elasticities of market demand for several nondurables. Consistent with our analysis, the demand for these items is relatively more elastic in the long run than in the short run.

Two nondurable goods worth highlighting are alcohol and tobacco. To the extent that consumption of these items is addictive, the demand will be relatively inelastic. The effect of price changes on the quantity demanded will work through

Figure 3.3 Short- and long-run demand for a non-durable item

If the price drops from $5 to $4.50, the quantity demanded will rise to 1.6 million units in the short run and 1.75 million units in the long run.

Table 3.6 Short- vis-à-vis long-run elasticities

Product	Demand factor	Market	Short-run elasticity	Long-run elasticity	Source (see References)
Nondurables					
Cigarettes	Price	U.S.	−0.2, −0.4	−3.3	Becker et al. (1994) Tegene (1991)
Liquor	Price	U.S. Canada	−0.2	−1.8	Baltagi & Griffin (1995) Johnson & Oksanen (1977)
Gasoline	Price Income	World World	−0.23 0.39	−0.43 0.81	Espey (1998) Espey (1998)
Antihypertensive drugs	Price	U.S.	−0.5	−1.6	Rizzo (1999)
Bus	Price	London	−0.8	−1.3	Gilbert & Jalilian (1991)
Subway	Price	London	−0.4	−0.7	Gilbert & Jalilian (1991)
Railway	Price	Philadelphia	−0.5	−1.8	Voith (1987)
Durables					
Automobiles	Price Income	U.S. U.S.	−0.2 3	−0.5 1.4	Pindyck & Rubinfeld (1995) Pindyck & Rubinfeld (1995)

discouraging new people from taking up smoking and drinking. Accordingly, the demand for alcohol and tobacco will be relatively more elastic in the long run.

Durables

The effect of adjustment time on the demand for durable items such as automobiles is somewhat different. As for nondurables, buyers need time to adjust, which leads demand to be relatively more elastic in the long run. However, a countervailing effect leads demand to be relatively more elastic in the short run. This countervailing effect is especially strong for changes in income.

Consider, for instance, the demand for cars. Most drivers buy cars at intervals of several years. Suppose that there is a drop in incomes. Then, drivers will plan to keep their cars longer. Some drivers, who were just about to replace their cars, will keep their cars longer. So, the drop in incomes will cause purchases to dry up until sufficient time passes that these drivers want to replace their cars at the new lower income. By contrast, in the long run, the effect on sales will be more muted: eventually, all drivers will replace their cars but less frequently. Thus, the drop in income will cause demand to fall more sharply in the short run than in the long run.

Similarly, if income rises, drivers will replace their cars more frequently. Some drivers will find that they want to replace their cars immediately, causing a boom in purchases. This boom, however, will last only as long as it takes all such drivers to adjust to their new replacement frequency. Thus, the increase in income will tend to cause demand to increase more sharply in the short run than in the long run.

Accordingly, for durable items, the difference between short- and long-run elasticities of demand depends on a balance between the need for time to adjust and the replacement frequency effect. Adjustment time has a similar effect on the own-price and other elasticities of the demand for durable items.

Referring to table 3.6, we see that, for automobiles, the demand is more price elastic in the long run than the short run, indicating that the need for time to adjust outweighs the replacement frequency effect. By contrast, the demand for automobiles is more income elastic in the short run than the long run, suggesting that the replacement frequency effect is relatively stronger for changes in income.

Forecasting Demand

In the preceding section, we showed how short-run elasticities can be used to forecast the effect of multiple (short-run) changes in the factors that affect demand. We can apply the same method to forecast the effect of long-run changes, using long-run elasticities in place of short-run elasticities.

Progress Check 3D Draw a figure, analogous to figure 3.3, showing the short- and long-run demand for a durable.   *Progress check*

> # Gasoline prices and the demand for big cars
>
> The real price of gasoline fell continuously through the early 1980s. In principle, this should have increased the demand for cars and persuaded drivers to switch from smaller to larger cars as well as from diesel-powered to sportier gasoline-powered cars. The immediate effect on consumer choice, however, was quite limited. When oil prices first began to fall, drivers did not adjust their expectations of future oil prices and did not change their auto-buying patterns.
>
> In line with consumer purchases, General Motors continued to focus production on smaller and diesel-powered cars. When, however, lower oil prices persisted into the mid-1980s, consumers did adjust their long-term expectations. They switched en masse to large cars with powerful, sporty, gasoline engines.
>
> When the adjustment came, General Motors was caught with excess inventories of four-cylinder (relative to six-cylinder) cars as well as too many diesel-engine automobiles. The auto manufacturer had overlooked the difference between the short- and long-run cross-price elasticities between the demand for automobiles and the price of gasoline.
>
> By the late 1990s, Americans had become accustomed to cheap gasoline and fell in love with large cars and especially sport-utility vehicles like the Jeep Cherokee and Ford Explorer. Then OPEC cut oil production, causing oil prices to surge. It remains to be seen whether auto manufacturers would be better able to predict consumer expectations of rising gasoline prices and their effect on the demand for small as compared to big cars.
>
> *Source*: Speech given by Vince Barabba, executive director, General Motors, at UCLA, February 5, 1987.

◄◄ 6 Estimating Elasticities[2]

We have seen how elasticities can be applied to forecast changes in demand and expenditure for entire markets as well as individual products. Tables 3.1 to 3.6 present various elasticities of demand. As we have emphasized, an elasticity can change with a change in any one of the factors that affect demand. Further, to the extent that businesses sell different products or cater to different buyers, they will face different demand curves; hence, they will also face different elasticities. Accordingly, managers may not be able to rely on "off-the-shelf" estimates of elasticities.

Suppose, for instance, that the management of the Moonlight Lube chain would like to know the sensitivity of the demand for its auto lubrication service to changes in price and advertising. In this section, we outline the data and statistical techniques

---

[2] This section is more advanced. It may be omitted without loss of continuity.

that can be used to estimate the elasticities of demand. We focus on an intuitive explanation of the basic concepts. For a detailed presentation, the reader should consult the Further Reading section at the end of the chapter.

Data

Generally, there are two sources of data. One is records of past experience, including published statistics as well as private records. The other source of data is surveys and experiments specifically designed to discover buyers' preferences. An experiment conducted with genuine buyers making actual purchases is said to be done on a *test market*.

The data from past experience or surveys and experiments can be collected in two ways. One way is to focus on a particular group of buyers and observe how their demand changes as the factors affecting demand vary over time. For instance, using this method, Moonlight Lube could compile year-by-year records of sales, prices, and advertising expenditures. This type of data is called a **time series**, as it records changes over time.

> A **time series** is a record of changes over time in one market.

Conjoint analysis: determining buyer preferences

Bank Luna is considering whether to offer an express teller service that guarantees no waiting for a charge of up to 50 cents. The bank's marketing department has selected a random sample of customers to determine how much they would pay for such a service. Presently, the average waiting time is 5 minutes.

The marketing department can apply the technique of conjoint analysis. This is a market research technique to determine buyers' preferences among various product attributes by asking them to rank alternative combinations of the attributes.

In Bank Luna's case, there are two relevant attributes: price and waiting time. Suppose that the price for express service can be limited to 25 or 50 cents. Combined with the price of nothing for regular teller service, the price can take three possible values – none, 25, and 50 cents. The waiting time can take two possible values: none and 5 minutes. A full factorial design would ask each sample customer to rate the $3 \times 2 = 6$ combinations in table 3.7. The results can then be analyzed using multiple regression (explained later) or other statistical techniques.

Conjoint analysis is especially useful for evaluating new products or new markets. In these cases, past experience is of limited help, and so, experiments and surveys are the main way to collect relevant data.

Table 3.7 Conjoint analysis

Alternative								
Price (cents)	Waiting time (minutes)	Least desirable						Most desirable
0	0	1	2	3	4	5	6	7
25	5	1	2	3	4	5	6	7
50	0	1	2	3	4	5	6	7
0	5	1	2	3	4	5	6	7
25	0	1	2	3	4	5	6	7
50	5	1	2	3	4	5	6	7

> A **cross section** is a record of data at one time over several markets.

The other way of collecting data is to compare the quantities purchased in markets with different values of the factors affecting demand. Using this method, Moonlight Lube would collect records of sales, prices, and advertising expenditures in each of its markets. This type of data is called a **cross section**, because it records all the data at one time.

Just as time series or cross-section data can be compiled from records of past experience, the same applies to surveys and experiments. For instance, a program of test marketing can be designed to yield either time series or cross-section data.

Specification

Moonlight Lube would like to estimate the own-price and advertising elasticities of the demand for its auto lube service. Suppose that it selected 15 outlets as test markets and, in each market, set different levels of price and advertising expenditure for one week and recorded the corresponding sales.

As chapter 2 suggests, however, the demand for Moonlight's lube service may depend on other factors. To obtain accurate estimates of elasticities, it is important to specify all the factors that have a significant effect on demand and the mathematical relationship between demand and the various factors.

> The **dependent variable** is the variable whose changes are to be explained.

The mathematical relationship can be specified in a number of ways. In a relationship, the **dependent variable** is that whose changes are to be explained, while an **independent variable** is a factor affecting the dependent variable. A common specification is a linear equation in which the dependent variable is equal to a constant plus the weighted sum of the independent variables.

> An **independent variable** is a factor affecting the dependent variable.

In the case of a Moonlight outlet, the other factors affecting demand may include the number of cars in the area, and the price of competing lube services. Many factors, however, can safely be ignored. These include the weather, the prices of groceries, and the number of schoolchildren in the area. Table 3.8 records the test market data.

As for the mathematical form, the following is a linear equation relating the demand for lube service with four independent variables:

$$D = b_0 + b_1 \times p + b_2 \times N + b_3 \times A + b_4 \times c + u \qquad (3.1)$$

where D represents the quantity demanded; p, the price of lube service; N, the number of cars; A, the advertising expenditure; and c, the average price at competing lube services. In equation (3.1), b_0 is a constant, while $b_1, \ldots, b_4$ are the coefficients of quantity demanded, the price of lube service, the number of cars, and the average competing price, respectively. The variable u represents the collective effect of other factors.

Table 3.8 Test market data

Market	Quantity	Price ($)	Number of cars (thousands)	Advertising spending ($)	Average competing price ($)
1	86	30	22.00	500	20
2	87	35	23.00	550	29
3	93	28	23.40	430	31
4	92	25	23.00	400	35
5	86	30	23.60	500	29
6	93	20	24.00	400	30
7	88	29	24.10	300	35
8	89	31	24.50	450	28
9	88	35	25.00	430	25
10	93	29	25.60	500	30
11	87	35	26.00	400	29
12	89	40	26.00	570	31
13	88	47	26.70	520	35
14	82	34	27.30	300	29
15	93	35	28.00	450	35
Average	**88.93**	**32.20**	**24.81**	**446.67**	**30.07**

Multiple Regression

Referring to table 3.8, we see variations in all the independent variables among the 15 test markets. To estimate the own-price elasticity of the demand for lube service, we need some way to isolate the effect of price on quantity demanded from the effects of the other variables; we need a similar procedure for estimating the advertising elasticity of demand.

> **Multiple regression** is a statistical technique to estimate the separate effect of each independent variable on the dependent variable.

The statistical technique of **multiple regression** can estimate the separate effect of each independent variable on the dependent variable. Essentially, multiple regression operationalizes the "other things equal" condition needed to estimate an elasticity.

Multiple regression aims to determine values for the constant and the coefficients. To explain the technique, we denote the estimates for the constant and the coefficients by $\hat{b}_0$, $\hat{b}_1$, $\hat{b}_2$, $\hat{b}_3$, and $\hat{b}_4$. Using these values and the corresponding records of p, N, A, and c, we can calculate the *predicted value* of the dependent variable,

$$\hat{b}_0 + (\hat{b}_1 \times p) + (\hat{b}_2 \times N) + (\hat{b}_3 \times A) + (\hat{b}_4 \times c), \tag{3.2}$$

for each test market.

The predicted value may diverge from the actual quantity demanded, D, for the corresponding market. Let us call this difference the *residual*; that is, the residual is the actual value of the dependent variable, D, minus the predicted value:

$$D - [\hat{b}_0 + (\hat{b}_1 \times p) + (\hat{b}_2 \times N) + (\hat{b}_3 \times A) + (\hat{b}_4 \times c)]. \tag{3.3}$$

Figure 3.4 presents a simplified version of the demand for lube service with only one independent variable, the price. The straight line represents the predicted values of the demand, using the estimated constant and coefficient. We also mark the actual values for several markets. In market 3, the actual quantity exceeds the predicted value, hence the residual is positive. By contrast, in markets 1, 2, and 8, the actual quantity is less than the predicted value, so the residuals are negative.

Ideally, the estimates of the constant and the coefficients will be such that every predicted value equals the corresponding actual value. Then, all the residuals will be 0. Referring to figure 3.4, this would mean that every point would lie along the straight line.

Realistically, however, it is not likely that all the residuals will be 0. This leads to the question of what is the best way to determine the constant and estimates, and the line in figure 3.4. The most common approach is called the *method of least squares*. This is based on the view that positive residuals are equivalent to negative residuals and that large residuals are disproportionately bad.

The method of least squares seeks a set of estimates for the constant and the coefficients to minimize the sum of the squares of the residuals. Since equally large positive and negative residuals have identical squares, the method treats them

Figure 3.4 Multiple regression

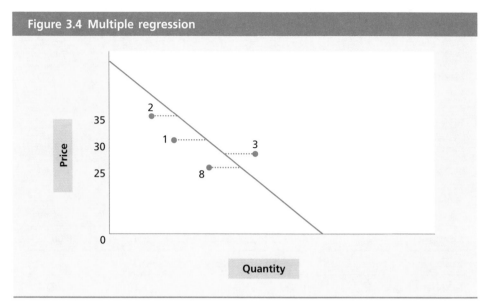

In market 3, the actual quantity exceeds the predicted value, hence the residuals are positive; in markets 1, 2, and 8, the actual quantity is less than the predicted value, so the residuals are negative.

identically. By squaring the residuals, the method gives relatively greater weight to large residuals. Least-squares multiple regression analysis is available in common spreadsheet programs as well as specialized statistical packages.

Interpretation

By applying least-squares multiple regression to estimate the equation for the lube service demand, we obtain the results in table 3.9. The estimates of the constant and coefficients are $b_0 = 63.48$, $b_1 = -0.48$, $b_2 = 0.65$, $b_3 = 0.03$, and $b_4 = 0.42$.

Using these estimates, we can calculate the elasticities of demand. In equation (3.1), the coefficient of price, b_1, is the rate of change of the quantity demanded with respect to changes in price. From table 3.9, the estimate of this rate of change, $\hat{b}_1 = -0.48$. The math supplement shows that the own-price elasticity is this rate of change multiplied by price and divided by quantity. From table 3.8, the average price is $32.20 and the average quantity is 88.93. Hence, the own-price elasticity at the average price and quantity is

$$-0.48 \times 32.20/88.93 = -0.17. \qquad (3.4)$$

We can use the same approach to calculate the elasticity of demand with respect to advertising and other independent variables.

Table 3.9 Multiple regression results

Regression statistics		
R-squared		0.65
Standard error		2.29
Number of observations		15
F-statistic		4.68
Significance		0.02

Independent variable	Coefficient	Standard error	t-statistic	significance
Constant	63.48	11.60	5.47	0.001
Price	−0.48	0.14	−3.31	0.008
Number of cars	0.65	0.51	1.28	0.242
Advertising spending	0.03	0.01	2.85	0.022
Competing price	0.42	0.17	2.53	0.036

Next, we use this example to discuss how to evaluate the significance of least-squares multiple regression results. The estimates of the constant and coefficients depend on the particular sample of observations in table 3.8. With another sample, we would obtain somewhat different estimates. By repeating the regression many times with different samples, we will obtain many sets of estimates. Using the probability distributions of these estimates, we can calculate measures to assess the significance of the regression estimates.

The F-statistic measures the overall significance of the independent variables. The statistic is computed on the assumption that there is no relationship between the dependent variable and the set of independent variables, meaning that the coefficients are all 0. The F-statistic ranges from 0 to infinity.

Using the probability distributions of these estimates, we can calculate the probability of obtaining any particular value for the F-statistic if the constant and coefficients are all 0. If this probability falls below a specific benchmark, then we say that the regression estimates are statistically significant. The conventional benchmarks are 1% and 5%.

From table 3.9, the F-statistic is 4.68 and the significance is 0.02 = 2%, which meets the 5% benchmark. We can be fairly confident that the regression estimates are statistically significant.

Related to the F-statistic is R-squared. This statistic uses the squared residuals to measure the extent to which the independent variables account for the variation of the dependent variable. R-squared ranges from 0 to 1. An R-squared value of 1 means that all the residuals are exactly 0, or equivalently, that every predicted value is exactly equal to the corresponding actual value. By contrast, an R-squared value of 0 means that the independent variables account for none of the variation in the dependent variable.

From table 3.9, R-squared is 0.65. This means that the regression equation accounts for 65% of the variation of the dependent variable. This is a reasonably large part of the variation.

The F-statistic and R-squared are ways to evaluate the independent variables as a group. By contrast, we use the t-statistic to evaluate the significance of a particular independent variable. Specifically, the t-statistic is the estimated value of the coefficient divided by the standard error. The standard error measures the dispersion of the estimate of the coefficient.

The t-statistic will be negative or positive according to the sign of the estimated coefficient. It ranges from negative to positive infinity. Using the probability distribution of the estimate, we can calculate the probability of obtaining any particular

Waiting time and "price elasticity"

A multiple regression study of the demand for gasoline at individual Boston-area service stations found that the elasticity of demand with respect to the price of gasoline was −3.3.

Customers of service stations, however, pay two prices: one in money to the seller and another in the form of waiting time. Estimates of demand must take into account the customers' sensitivity to waiting. If a station raises its price by 1%, its customers must pay 1% more in money. But this tends to reduce customer purchases. Given the station's fueling capacity, the reduction in purchases will reduce waiting times, which tends to increase the quantity demanded.

Accordingly, the estimated "price elasticity" of −3.3 combines the responsiveness to an increase in price alone together with the responsiveness to a reduction in waiting time. After adjusting for the effect on waiting time, Png and Reitman estimate that the own-price elasticity ranged between −6.3 and −8.4.

Other businesses that serve randomly arriving customers from a fixed capacity include Internet service providers, banks hospitals, and supermarkets. In estimating the own-price elasticity of demand at any such business, an analyst must take care to adjust for the effect of price changes on waiting times.

Source: I. P. L. Png and David Reitman, "Service Time Competition," *RAND Journal of Economics* 25, no. 4 (Winter 1994), pp. 619–34.

value for the t-statistic if the coefficient is 0. If this probability falls below a specific benchmark, then the estimated coefficient is statistically significant. The conventional benchmarks are 1% and 5%.

In table 3.9, the t-statistic for the price of lube service is -3.31 and the significance is $0.008 = 0.8\%$, which meets both the 1% and 5% benchmarks. The t-statistic for advertising spending is 2.85 and the significance is $0.022 = 2.2\%$, which meets the 5% benchmark. By contrast, the t-statistic for the number of cars is 1.28 and the significance is $0.242 = 24.2\%$, which does not meet even the 5% benchmark. Accordingly, we infer that the price of lube service and advertising spending have significant effects on the demand for lube service, but the effect of the number of cars is questionable.

Progress check **Progress Check 3E** Referring to tables 3.8 and 3.9, calculate the advertising elasticity of demand at the average quantity and advertising spending.

◂◂ 7 Summary

The elasticity of demand measures the responsiveness of demand to changes in a factor that affects demand. Elasticities can be estimated for price, income, prices of related products, and advertising expenditures. The own-price elasticity is the ratio of the percentage change in quantity demanded to the percentage change in price, and is a negative number. Demand is price elastic if a 1% increase in price leads to more than a 1% drop in quantity demanded, and inelastic if it leads to less than a 1% drop in quantity demanded.

The own-price elasticity can be used to forecast the effects of price changes on quantity demanded and buyer expenditure. Elasticities can be used to forecast the effects on demand of simultaneous changes in multiple factors. All elasticities vary with adjustment time. The long-run demand is generally more elastic than the short-run demand in the case of nondurables, but not necessarily for durables.

Elasticities can be estimated from records of past experience or test markets by the statistical technique of multiple regression.

Key Concepts

elasticity of demand	income elasticity	cross section
own-price elasticity	cross-price elasticity	dependent variable
arc approach	advertising elasticity	independent variable
point approach	short run	multiple regression
elastic	long run	
inelastic	time series	

Further Reading

Ramu Ramanathan covers the details of econometrics, which is the application of statistical techniques to economic issues, in *Introductory Econometrics with Applications* (Fort Worth: Dryden, 1998). Paul R. Messinger reviews the techniques of market research in Chapter 11 of the *Marketing Paradigm* (Cincinnati: South-Western College Publishing, 1995).

Review Questions

1. Why is the demand for business travel less elastic than that for leisure travel?

2. The demand for medical services is price inelastic. Explain in terms of the split between the person who decides on the service (doctor/patient) and the person who pays (patient/medical insurer/health maintenance organization).

3. Explain why the own-price elasticity is a pure number with no units and is negative.

4. Consider a service that you buy frequently.
   (a) Suppose that the price was 5% lower and all other factors do not change. How much more would you buy each year?
   (b) Using this information, calculate the own-price elasticity of your demand.

5. Suppose that the own-price elasticity of the demand for food is −0.7 and that, as a result of a nationwide drought, the price of food rises by 10%. Will this cause expenditure on food to rise or fall?

6. Consider a good that you buy frequently.
   (a) Suppose that your income was 10% higher and all other factors do not change. How much more would you buy each year?
   (b) Using this information, calculate the income elasticity of your demand.
   (c) Is the good an inferior product or normal product for you?

7. True or false?
   (a) The income elasticity of demand can be estimated by either the arc approach or the point approach.
   (b) Changes in the price of an item will affect the income elasticity of demand.

8. Manufacturers such as Dunlop and Goodyear use both natural and synthetic rubber to produce tires. If the elasticity of the demand for natural rubber with respect to changes in the price of synthetic rubber is negative, then the two types of rubber are (choose a or b):
   (a) Substitutes.
   (b) Complements.

9. Suppose that the elasticity of the demand for Nike sports shoes with respect to changes in the price of Adidas sports shoes is 1.3. Do you expect the elasticity with respect to changes in the price of Ferragamo shoes to be a smaller or larger number?

10. Suppose that the advertising elasticity of the demand for one brand of cigarettes is 1.3. If the manufacturer raises advertising expenditure by 5%, by how much will the demand change?

11. Explain why the advertising elasticity of the market demand for beer may be smaller than the advertising elasticity of the demand for one particular brand.

12. Consider the effect of changes in fares on the quantity demanded of taxi services. Do you expect demand to be more elastic with respect to fare changes in the short run or the long run?

13. Why is the long-run demand for a nondurable item more elastic than the short-run demand? Why might the same rule not apply to the demand for a durable item?

14. This question applies the analysis presented in the section on estimating elasticities. Explain why the method of least squares multiple regression aims to minimize the sum of the squares of the residuals and not the sum of just the residuals.

15. This question applies the analysis presented in the section on estimating elasticities. Explain the difference between cross-section and time series data.

Discussion Questions

1. In April 2000, Dow Jones re-launched the *Asian Wall Street Journal* with substantial price cuts. In Hong Kong, the cover price was reduced by 40% from HK$15 to HK$9, while the subscription price was reduced by 10% from HK$2,550 to HK$2,298. Management kept advertising rates unchanged. Suppose that, prior to the re-launch, the newspaper sold 1,800 single copies (through newsstands) per day and that annual advertising revenue was HK$3,860 per copy.
   (a) Assuming that the newspaper published on 250 days a year, calculate its annual circulation revenue from single-copy sales before the re-launch.
   (b) Calculate the annual advertising revenue from single-copy sales.
   (c) Suppose that, after the re-launch and price cut, the sales of single copies rises to *N* thousands per day. Calculate the new annual circulation and advertising revenues from single-copy sales.
   (d) What must be the own-price elasticity of demand for the re-launch to break even just in terms of revenue?

2. A study of the demand for water among commercial users such as apartment buildings, hotels, and offices reported that the own-price elasticity was −0.36, the elasticity with respect to the number of commercial establishments was 0.99, and the elasticity with respect to the average summer temperature was 0.02 (Williams & Suh, 1986).

(a) Intuitively, would an increase in the number of commercial establishments increase or reduce the demand for water? Is the estimated elasticity consistent with your explanation?

(b) Intuitively, would a rise in the average summer temperature increase or reduce the demand for water? Is the estimated elasticity consistent with your explanation?

(c) By considering the own-price elasticity of demand, explain how the water company could increase its profit.

3. A study of the demand for gasoline at Boston-area service stations reported that the elasticity with respect to price (combining the pure price effect with the effect on waiting times) was –3.3, the elasticity with respect to station fueling capacity was 0.7, and the elasticity with respect to the average price at nearby stations was 1.2 (Png & Reitman, 1984).

(a) Explain why the elasticity with respect to the average price at nearby stations is a positive number.

(b) Amy's station is the only competitor to Al's. Al's station has 3% more fueling capacity. Originally, both stations charged the same price. Then Amy reduced her price by 2%. What will be the difference in quantity demanded between the two stations?

(c) If Amy raises capacity from 6 to 7 fueling places, by how much could she increase price without affecting sales?

4. Electric power producers have a choice of several fuels, including oil, natural gas, coal, and uranium. Once an electric power plant has been built, however, the scope to switch fuels may be very limited. Since power plants last for 30 years or more, producers must consider the relative prices of the alternative fuels well into the future when choosing a generating plant.

(a) Do you expect the cross-price elasticity between the demand for oil-fired power plants and the price of oil to be positive or negative?

(b) Will the cross-price elasticity between the demand for oil-fired power plants and the price of coal be positive or negative?

(c) Compare the short with the long-run own-price elasticity of the demand for oil-fired power plants.

5. Suppose that, at the current gasoline price of $1.50 per gallon and average household income of $100,000 a year, the quantity demanded is 200 million gallons a week. If the price were increased to $1.68, the quantity demanded would fall to 158.7 million gallons a week. If the household income were increased to $110,500 a year, the quantity demanded would rise to 208 million gallons a week.

(a) Calculate the own-price elasticity of demand.

(b) Calculate the income elasticity of demand.

(c) According to these estimates, is gasoline a normal or inferior product?

6. Drugs that are not covered by patent can be freely manufactured by anyone. By contrast, the production and sale of patented drugs is tightly controlled. A study of the demand for antihypertensive drugs reported that the advertising elasticity of demand was around 0.26 for all drugs, and 0.24 for those covered by patents.

For all antihypertensive drugs, the own price elasticity was about −2.0 without advertising, and about −1.6 in the long run with advertising.

(a) Consider a 5% increase in advertising expenditure. By how much would the demand for a patented drug rise? What about the demand for a drug not covered by patent?

(b) Why is the demand for patented drugs less responsive to advertising than the demand for drugs not covered by patent?

(c) Suppose that a drug manufacturer were to increase advertising. Explain why it should also raise the price of its drugs.

7. Table 3.6 presents the short- and long-run elasticities of the demand for automobiles in the United States. Suppose that the price of cars rises by 5% while per capita income rises by 3%. What will be the effect on purchases of cars in the (a) short run and (b) long run?

8. According to a study of U.S. cigarette sales between 1955 and 1985, when the price of cigarettes was 1% higher, consumption would be 0.4% lower in the short run and 0.75% lower in the long run (Becker et al., 1994).

(a) Calculate the short- and long-run own-price elasticities of the demand for cigarettes.

(b) Is demand more or less elastic in the long run than in the short run? Explain your answer.

(c) If the government were to impose a tax that raised the price of cigarettes by 5%, would total consumer expenditure on cigarettes rise or fall in the short run? What about in the long run?

9. This question applies the analysis presented in the section on estimating elasticities. Suppose that the government has just announced a revision to the data in table 3.8. The new data increases the number of cars in markets 11–15 by 10%. All other data remain valid.

(a) Use multiple regression to estimate the demand with (i) the original data and (ii) the revised data.

(b) Calculate the new estimates for the elasticities with respect to price, number of cars, and advertising expenditure at the average values of quantity, price, number of cars, and advertising expenditure.

10. An Australian telecommunications carrier wants to estimate the own-price elasticity of the demand for international calls to the United States. It has collected annual records of international calls and prices. In each of the following groups, choose the one factor that you would also consider in the estimation. Explain your reasoning.

(a) Consumer characteristics: (i) average per capita income, (ii) average age.

(b) Complements: (i) number of telephone lines, (ii) number of mobile telephone subscribers.

(c) Prices of related items: (i) price of electricity, (ii) postage rate from Australia to the United States.

11. This question applies techniques introduced in the math supplement to chapter 2. Suppose that Moonshine Car Rentals faces a demand represented by the equation

$$D = 30 - p + 0.4Y, \tag{3.5}$$

where D is the quantity demanded in rentals a month, p is the price in dollars per rental, and Υ is the average consumer's income in thousands of dollars a year. Use the arc approach in the following calculations.

(a) Suppose that income $\Upsilon = 100$ and Moonshine raises the price from $p = 30$ to $p = 35$. Calculate the own-price elasticity of demand.

(b) Suppose that income $\Upsilon = 110$ and Moonshine raises the price from $p = 30$ to $p = 35$. Calculate the own-price elasticity of demand.

(c) Suppose that the price $p = 30$ and that income rises from $\Upsilon = 100$ to $\Upsilon = 110$. Calculate the income elasticity of demand.

(d) Suppose that the price $p = 35$ and that income rises from $\Upsilon = 100$ to $\Upsilon = 110$. Calculate the income elasticity of demand.

References

Kevin Bain and Margaret McKenzie. 1999. *Parallel Imports of Sound Recordings: What Happens Now?* Australian Competition and Consumer Commission.

Badi H. Baltagi and James M. Griffin. 1995. "A Dynamic Demand Model for Liquor: The Case for Pooling." *Review of Economics and Statistics* 77, no. 3 (August), pp. 545–54.

Michael R. Baye and Richard O. Beil. 1994. *Managerial Economics and Business Strategy.* Burr Ridge, IL: Irwin.

——, Dennis W. Jansen, and Jae-Woo Lee. 1992. "Advertising Effects in Complete Demand Systems." *Applied Economics* 24, no. 10, pp. 1087–96.

Gary Becker, Michael Grossman, and Kevin Murphy. 1994. "An Empirical Analysis of Cigarette Addiction." *American Economic Review* 84 (June), p. 396.

Jean-Thomas Bernard, Denis Bolduc, and Donald Belanger. 1996. "Quebec Residential Electricity Demand: A Microeconometric Approach." *Canadian Journal of Economics* 29, no. 1 (February), pp. 92–113.

Randolph E. Bucklin, Richard E. Caves, and Andrew W. Lo. 1989. "Games of Survival in the U.S. Newspaper Industry." *Applied Economics* 21, no. 5 (May), pp. 631–49.

Molly Espey. 1998. "Gasoline Demand Revisited: an International meta-analysis of elasticities." *Energy Economics* 20, no. 3 (June 1998), pp. 273–95.

George R. Franke and Gary B. Wilcox. 1987. "Alcoholic Beverage Advertising and Consumption in the United States." *Journal of Advertising* 16, no. 3, pp. 22–30.

Teresa Garin Munoz. 1996. "Demand for National Telephone Traffic in Spain from 1985–1989: An Econometric Study Using Provincial Panel Data." *Information Economics and Policy* 8, no. 1 (March), pp. 51–73.

Christopher Gilbert and Hossein Jalilian. 1991. "The Demand for Travel and for Travelcards on London Regional Transport." *Journal of Transport Economics and Policy* 25, no. 1 (January), pp. 3–29.

James A. Johnson and Ernest H. Oksanen. 1977. "Estimation of Demand for Alcoholic Beverages in Canada from Pooled Time Series and Cross Sections." *Review of Economics and Statistics* 59 (February), pp. 113–18.

Eugene Jones and Barry W. Mustiful. 1996. "Purchasing Behaviour of Higher- and Lower-Income Shoppers: A Look at Breakfast Cereals." *Applied Economics* 28, no. 1 (January), pp. 131–7.

Pinelopi Koujianou-Goldberg. 1995. "Product Differentiation and Oligopoly in International Markets: The Case of the U.S. Automobile Industry." *Econometrica* 63, no. 4 (July), pp. 891–951.

National Income and Product Accounts of the United States (1986).

Robert S. Pindyck and Daniel L. Rubinfeld. 1995. *Microeconomics*, 3d ed., p. 37. Englewood Cliffs, NJ: Prentice Hall.

I. P. L. Png and David Reitman. 1994. "Service Time Competition." *RAND Journal of Economics* 25, no. 4 (Winter), pp. 619–34.

John A. Rizzo. 1999. "Advertising and Competition in the Ethical Pharmaceutical Industry: the Case of Anti-hypertensive Drugs." *Journal of Law and Economics* 62, pp. 89–116.

Abebayehu Tegene. 1991. "Kalman Filter and the Demand for Cigarettes." *Applied Economics* 23, pp. 1175–82.

Richard Voith. 1987. "Commuter Rail Ridership: The Long and Short Haul," *Business Review*, Federal Reserve Bank of Philadelphia (November–December), pp. 13–23.

Martin Williams and Byung Suh. 1986. "The Demand for Urban Water by Customer Class." *Applied Economics* 18, pp. 1275–89.

Chapter 3

Math Supplement

Own-Price Elasticity

By definition, the own-price elasticity of demand is the proportionate change in quantity demanded divided by the proportionate change in price. Let Q represent the quantity demanded; dQ, the change in quantity demanded; p, the price; and dp, the change in price. Then dQ/Q is the proportionate change in quantity demanded, while dp/p is the proportionate change in price. Thus, in algebraic terms, the own-price elasticity is

$$e_p = \frac{dQ/Q}{dp/p} = \frac{p}{Q}\frac{dQ}{dp}. \qquad (3.6)$$

Using this definition, we can study the relationship between the own-price elasticity and the slope of the demand curve. Rearrange the definition of the own-price elasticity as follows:

$$e_p = \frac{p}{Q} \Big/ \frac{dp}{dQ}. \qquad (3.7)$$

The variable dp/dQ is the change in price divided by the change in quantity demanded, that is, the slope of the demand curve. So, by (3.7), the own-price elasticity is (p/Q) divided by the slope of the demand curve. Clearly, the own-price elasticity and slope are related but are not the same.

Changes in Price

Let us now show how to use the definition in (3.6) to forecast changes in quantity demanded and buyer expenditure as a function of the own-price elasticity, percentage change in price, and the quantity demanded. Rearranging the definition in (3.6),

$$\frac{dQ}{Q} = e_p \times \frac{dp}{p}. \qquad (3.8)$$

This says that the proportionate change in quantity demanded is the own-price elasticity multiplied by the proportionate change in price.

Let $\%Q$ represent the percentage change in quantity demanded and $\%p$ represent the percentage change in price. Then $\%Q = 100 \times dQ/Q$, and $\%p = 100 \times dp/p$. Multiplying both sides of (3.8) by 100 and substituting, we have

$$\%Q = e_p \times \%p, \qquad (3.9)$$

which says that the percentage change in the quantity demanded is the own-price elasticity multiplied by the percentage change in the price.

To forecast changes in buyer's expenditure, note that the buyer's expenditure is the price multiplied by the quantity demanded,

$$E = p \times Q. \qquad (3.10)$$

Differentiating with respect to p,

$$\frac{dE}{dp} = Q + p\frac{dQ}{dp}. \qquad (3.11)$$

Substituting from (3.6),

$$\frac{dE}{dp} = Q \times (1 + e_p). \qquad (3.12)$$

Dividing both sides of this equation by $E = p \times Q$, we have

$$\frac{1}{E}\frac{dE}{dp} = \frac{1 + e_p}{p},$$

or

$$\frac{dE}{E} = (1 + e_p) \times \frac{dp}{p}. \qquad (3.13)$$

Let $\%E$ represent the percentage change in expenditure, hence $\%E = 100 \times dE/E$.

Multiplying both sides of (3.13) by 100 and substituting, we have

$$\%E = (1 + e_p) \times \%p. \qquad (3.14)$$

If demand is elastic, so that $e_p < -1$, then $1 + e_p < 0$. So, an increase in price $\%p > 0$ will cause $\%E < 0$, meaning a drop in expenditure, while a fall in price $\%p < 0$ will cause $\%E > 0$, which is an increase in expenditure.

Similarly, if demand is inelastic, so that $e_p > -1$, then $1 + e_p > 0$. In this case, an increase in price $\%p > 0$ will cause $\%E > 0$, while a fall in price $\%p < 0$ will cause $\%E < 0$.

Changes in Multiple Variables

Generally, the analysis of income, cross-price, and advertising elasticities is similar to that for the own-price elasticity, so there is no need to repeat the analysis. Here, we will focus on showing how to use the elasticities to forecast the effect of multiple changes in the factors that affect demand.

Let Y, Z, and A represent income, the price of a related item, and advertising expenditures, respectively. Then, supposing that demand is a function of the price of the item itself, income, the price of a related item, and advertising expenditures, we have

$$Q = Q(p, Y, Z, A). \qquad (3.15)$$

By definition, the income elasticity is

$$e_y = \frac{dQ/Q}{dY/Y} = \frac{Y}{Q}\frac{dQ}{dY}; \qquad (3.16)$$

the cross-price elasticity with respect to a related item,

$$e_z = \frac{dQ/Q}{dZ/Z} = \frac{Z}{Q}\frac{dQ}{dZ}; \qquad (3.17)$$

and the elasticity with respect to advertising expenditure,

$$e_a = \frac{dQ/Q}{dA/A} = \frac{A}{Q}\frac{dQ}{dA}. \qquad (3.18)$$

Taking the total derivative of equation (3.15),

$$dQ = \frac{dQ}{dp}dp + \frac{dQ}{dY}dY$$
$$+ \frac{dQ}{dZ}dZ + \frac{dQ}{dA}dA. \qquad (3.19)$$

Dividing throughout by Q,

$$\frac{dQ}{Q} = \frac{1}{Q}\frac{dQ}{dp}dp + \frac{1}{Q}\frac{dQ}{dY}dY$$
$$+ \frac{1}{Q}\frac{dQ}{dZ}dZ + \frac{1}{Q}\frac{dQ}{dA}dA. \qquad (3.20)$$

Consider the term on the left-hand side of equation (3.20). Multiplying by 100, it becomes the percentage change in quantity. Next, consider the first term on the right-hand side. Multiplying the term by $100p$ and dividing by p, it becomes

$$100 \times \frac{p}{Q}\frac{dQ}{dp}\frac{dp}{p}$$
$$= 100 \times e_p\frac{dp}{p} = e_p\%p, \qquad (3.21)$$

that is, the own-price elasticity multiplied by the percentage change in price.

Similarly, each of the other terms on the right-hand side of equation (3.20) simplifies to the product of an elasticity and the percentage change in the corresponding factor. Accordingly, equation (3.20) simplifies to

$$\%Q = e_p\%p + e_y\%Y$$
$$+ e_z\%Z + e_a\%A. \qquad (3.22)$$

This says that the percentage change in demand due to changes in multiple factors is the sum of the percentage changes due to each factor separately.

Chapter *4*
Supply

◄◄ ## 1 Introduction

Dynamic random access memory (DRAM) chips are an essential component of personal computers, mobile telephones, and other electronic devices. Over the course of the 1990s, DRAM technology evolved through several generations – from 4 through 16 and 64 Megabits to the present state-of-the-art 256 Megabit chips. Semiconductor manufacturers are now researching the production of the next-generation 1 Gigabit (1024 Megabit) DRAM.[1]

Along with the evolution of technology, dominance in manufacturing has shifted from the United States to Japan, and now to Korea. In the early 1990s, Japanese DRAM manufacturers, Fujitsu, Hitachi, Mitsubishi, NEC, and Toshiba, dominated the industry. In the mid-1990s, three Korean manufacturers challenged the Japanese dominance. Supported by a government policy of low-interest financing, Hyundai, LG, and Samsung invested heavily in new DRAM production capacity. Hyundai Electronics corporate planning director Yoo Kook Sang asserted, "The Japanese hesitated, and now they are falling behind Korean companies . . . We will invest continuously without hesitation."

Asia accounts for about half of total DRAM sales. The massive increase in Korean supply and the Asian economic crisis caused DRAM prices to plummet. In just 30 months between December 1995 and June 1998, the price of 16-Megabit chips fell over 90% from $45 to less than $2. Similarly, the price of 64-Megabit chips fell 70% from $30 in the first half of 1997 to below $10 12 months later.

The drastic price decline forced all semiconductor manufacturers to review their DRAM businesses. In early 1998, Fujitsu decided to shut its plant in Durham, England,

---

[1] The following analysis is based, in part, on "Korean Firms Outrace Japan in the Memory-Chip Market," *Asian Wall Street Journal*, March 15, 1995, p. 1; "Fujitsu to Curb Output of DRAMs in Europe," *Asian Wall Street Journal*, April 1, 1998, p. 6; "TI Plans to Trim 3,500 jobs" and "Texas Instruments will Also Sell its Money-losing Memory-Chip Business," *Orange County Register*, June 19, 1998, p. c1; "Fujitsu Microelectronics' Durham Plant to Cease Operations," *M2 Presswire*, September 7, 1998; and "Japanese Semiconductors: and Then There were Two," *Economist*, January 23, 1999, p. 58.

which had been producing 2.5 million units of 4- and 16-Megabit DRAMs a month. By contrast, Fujitsu decided to continue production of 64-Megabit chips in Gresham, Oregon. Mitsubishi idled its Fukuoka and Kumamoto plants for seven days in early May, reducing production by 800,000 units of 64-Megabit chips.

Texas Instruments (TI) decided to quit the DRAM industry altogether. It sold plants in Avezzano (Italy), Richardson (Texas), and Singapore, as well as interests in two Asian joint ventures to Micron Technology. TI sold its share of a joint venture Taiwanese factory to partner Acer. It shut the remainder of its DRAM production facilities including one in Midland, Texas. The company's exit left Micron as the United States' only significant DRAM manufacturer.

The drastic fall in DRAM prices posed important managerial issues and led to drastic adjustments by Fujitsu, TI, and other manufacturers. Why did Mitsubishi decide to stop production temporarily? Why did Fujitsu shut its Durham factory while continuing production at Gresham? How did TI's sale to Micron affect the worldwide supply of DRAMs?

To address these questions, we need to understand how a seller determines the quantity that it will supply and the price at which it breaks even. In this chapter, we first consider the relation between costs and the production rate and how a business will adjust its production rate to changes in the price of its output. We also analyze whether an enterprise should continue in business. This provides the foundation for the concepts of the individual supply curve and seller surplus, which are the seller-side counterparts to the demand curve and buyer surplus.

Then, we compare supply in the short run, when businesses are restricted in the extent to which they can adjust inputs, with supply in the long run, when businesses can freely adjust all inputs. Using this analysis, we can explain why Fujitsu shut its Durham factory while continuing production at Gresham.

Next, extending from the individual seller to the market, we examine the market supply curve and market seller surplus. This enables us to explain the effects of TI's sale to Micron on the worldwide DRAM supply. Following this, we introduce elasticities of supply, which measure the responsiveness of quantity supplied to changes in various factors. Finally, we highlight the special aspects of supply in human resource markets.

◂◂ 2 Short-Run Costs

Two key decisions of a business, whether to continue in operation and the rate at which to operate, both depend on the length of the time horizon. In chapter 3, we introduced the concepts of short run and long run in relation to buyers. The same concepts apply to sellers as well. A **short run** is a time horizon in which a seller cannot adjust at least one input. In the short run, the business must work within the constraints of past commitments such as employment contracts and investment in facilities and equipment. Over time, however, these commitments expire. A **long run** is a time horizon long enough for the seller to adjust all inputs.

> The **short run** is a time horizon within which a seller cannot adjust at least one input.

> The **long run** is a time horizon long enough for the seller to adjust all inputs.

The difference between the short run and long run depends on the circumstances. For instance, if a building contractor has just engaged 100 workers on a 12-month contract, then the employment of these workers cannot be adjusted until the expiration of the contract. Hence, the contractor's short run is at least 12 months long. By contrast, a contractor that has hired workers on a daily basis could adjust its workforce every day. Similarly, a contractor who has purchased construction equipment has committed to a relatively longer horizon than one who has rented the equipment on a weekly contract.

In this and the next section, we focus on short-run business decisions; we consider long-run behavior in the fourth section.

Fixed vis-à-vis Variable Costs

> The **fixed cost** is the cost of inputs that do not change with the production rate.

> The **variable cost** is the cost of inputs that change with the production rate.

To determine its production rate, a business needs to know the cost of delivering an additional unit of product. To decide whether to continue in operation, a business needs to know how shutting down will affect its costs. An important factor in both decisions is the distinction between fixed and variable costs. The **fixed cost** is the cost of inputs that do not change with the production rate. By contrast, the **variable cost** is the cost of inputs that change with the production rate.

Let us consider the distinction between fixed and variable costs in the context of Luna Farm, which produces eggs. Like those of most businesses, Luna's financial and accounting records do not classify expenses into fixed and variable. Rather, the records organize expenses according to the type of input: rent, wages, and payments for supplies. By interviewing Luna's management, we can learn the costs required for alternative short-run production rates. Table 4.1 presents this information.

To distinguish between fixed and variable costs, a business must analyze how each category of expense varies with changes in the scale of operations. Referring to table 4.1, we can perform this analysis for Luna. Luna cannot adjust the size of its facility, so the rent does not vary with the production rate. The rent is $2,000 whether Luna produces nothing or 9,000 dozen eggs a week; hence, it is a fixed cost. Wages vary with the production rate, but even when Luna produces no eggs, it incurs wages of $200. Hence, the wages include a fixed component of $200, while the remainder is variable. Finally, the cost of supplies is completely variable.

In table 4.2, we assign Luna's expenses – rent, wages, and cost of supplies – into the two categories of fixed costs and variable costs. As the production rate increases from nothing to 9,000 dozen eggs a week, the fixed cost is always $2,200. By contrast, the variable cost increases from nothing for no production to $6,696 for 9,000 dozen eggs a week.

> **Total cost** is the sum of the fixed and variable costs.

Total cost is the sum of fixed cost and variable cost. Algebraically, if we represent total cost by C, fixed cost by F, and variable cost by V, then

$$C = F + V. \tag{4.1}$$

Table 4.1 Short-run weekly expenses

Weekly production rate	Rent	Wages	Cost of supplies	Total
0	$2,000	$200	$0	$2,200
1,000	$2,000	$529	$100	$2,629
2,000	$2,000	$836	$200	$3,036
3,000	$2,000	$1,216	$300	$3,516
4,000	$2,000	$1,697	$400	$4,097
5,000	$2,000	$2,293	$500	$4,793
6,000	$2,000	$3,015	$600	$5,615
7,000	$2,000	$3,870	$700	$6,570
8,000	$2,000	$4,862	$800	$7,662
9,000	$2,000	$5,996	$900	$8,896

Table 4.2 Analysis of short-run costs

Weekly production rate	Fixed cost	Variable cost	Total cost	Marginal cost	Average fixed cost	Average variable cost	Average cost
0	$2,200	$0	$2,200				
1,000	$2,200	$429	$2,629	$0.43	$2.20	$0.43	$2.63
2,000	$2,200	$836	$3,036	$0.41	$1.10	$0.42	$1.52
3,000	$2,200	$1,316	$3,516	$0.48	$0.73	$0.44	$1.17
4,000	$2,200	$1,897	$4,097	$0.58	$0.55	$0.47	$1.02
5,000	$2,200	$2,593	$4,793	$0.70	$0.44	$0.52	$0.96
6,000	$2,200	$3,415	$5,615	$0.82	$0.37	$0.57	$0.94
7,000	$2,200	$4,370	$6,570	$0.95	$0.31	$0.62	$0.94
8,000	$2,200	$5,462	$7,662	$1.09	$0.28	$0.68	$0.96
9,000	$2,200	$6,696	$8,896	$1.23	$0.24	$0.74	$0.99

Figure 4.1 Short-run total cost

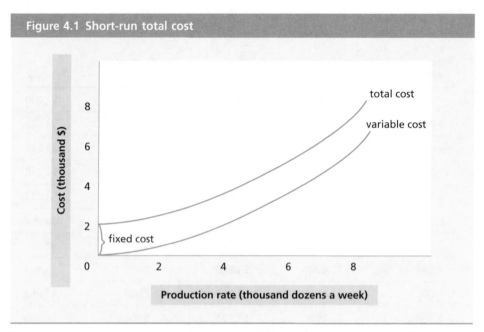

The total cost curve is the variable cost curve shifted up by the amount of the fixed cost.

Provided that there are some variable costs, then total cost will increase with operations. In Luna's case, referring to table 4.2, the total cost is $2,200 for no production, and rises to $8,896 for production of 9,000 dozen eggs a week.

It is helpful to illustrate the concepts of total, fixed, and variable costs. In figure 4.1, the vertical axis represents cost, while the horizontal axis represents the scale of operations. We draw a curve representing variable cost. The total cost curve is the variable cost curve, shifted up everywhere by the amount of the fixed cost. In particular, the fixed cost is represented by the height of the total cost curve at the zero production rate.

By analyzing its costs as fixed and variable, the management of a business can understand which cost elements will be affected by changes in the scale of operations. The distinction between fixed and variable costs is important whether the business is growing or shrinking. For instance, suppose that management is planning to reduce costs by downsizing. Downsizing will have no effect on fixed costs and will only reduce the variable costs. Hence, in a business whose costs are mostly fixed, downsizing may have relatively little effect on costs.

Progress check   **Progress Check 4A**   In figure 4.1, if the fixed cost were higher, how would that affect the total and variable cost curves?

Marginal Cost

To determine the scale at which it should operate, a business needs to know the cost of making an additional unit of product. Then, the business can see whether selling the additional unit will add to or subtract from its total profit. The change in total cost due to the production of an additional unit is the **marginal cost**. The marginal cost can be derived from the analysis of fixed and variable costs.

> The **marginal cost** is the change in total cost due to the production of an additional unit.

Let us derive the marginal cost in the case of Luna Farm. Referring to table 4.2, as the production rate increases from none to 1,000 dozen eggs a week, the total cost increases from $2,200 to $2,629. The increment $2,629 − $2,200 = $429 is the additional cost of producing the 1,000 dozen eggs. Hence, the marginal cost is $429/1,000 = 43 cents per dozen.

Notice that, as the production rate increases from none to 1,000 dozen a week, the fixed cost remains unchanged; only the variable cost increases. Hence, we also can calculate the marginal cost from the increase in variable cost. Using this approach, as the production rate increases from none to 1,000 dozen eggs a week, the variable cost increases from $0 to $429. Therefore, the marginal cost is $429/1,000 = 43 cents per dozen.

Similarly, as the production rate increases from 1,000 to 2,000 dozen eggs a week, the variable cost increases from $429 to $836. The marginal cost is now $407 for 1,000 dozen eggs, or 41 cents per dozen. With each increase in the production rate, the marginal cost increases, reaching $1.23 at the rate of 9,000 dozen eggs a week. In Luna's case, each additional dozen requires more variable cost than the one before. We display this information in table 4.2.

Average Cost

The marginal cost is the cost of producing an additional unit. A related concept is **average cost**, which is the total cost divided by the production rate. The average cost is also called the *unit cost*. Given the scale of operations, the average cost reflects the cost of producing a typical unit.

> The **average cost** (unit cost) is the total cost divided by the production rate.

Let us derive the average cost in the case of Luna Farm. Referring to table 4.2, we can obtain the average cost as total cost divided by the production rate. At 1,000 dozen eggs a week, the average cost is $2,629/1,000 = $2.63, while at 2,000 dozen a week, the average cost is $3,036/2,000 = $1.52. The average cost continues to fall with increases in the production rate until it reaches a minimum of 94 cents at 6,000–7,000 dozen a week. Thereafter, it increases with the production rate. At 9,000 dozen a week, the average cost is 99 cents.

To understand why the average cost first drops with increases in the production rate and then rises, recall that the total cost is the sum of the fixed cost and the variable cost:

$$C = F + V. \tag{4.2}$$

If q represents the production rate, then dividing throughout by q, we have

$$\frac{C}{q} = \frac{F}{q} + \frac{V}{q}. \tag{4.3}$$

In words, the average cost is the average fixed cost plus the average variable cost. The average fixed cost is fixed cost divided by the production rate. So, if the production rate is higher, the fixed cost will be spread over more units; hence, the average fixed cost will be lower. This factor causes the average cost to fall with increases in the production rate.

The other element in average cost is the average variable cost, which is the variable cost divided by the production rate. In the short run, at least one input is fixed; hence, to raise the production rate, the business must combine increasing quantities of the variable inputs with an unchanged quantity of the fixed input.

The increase in output arising from an additional unit of an input is called the **marginal product** from that input. At low production rates, there is a mismatch between the variable inputs and the fixed input. Owing to the mismatch, the marginal product is low and the average variable cost is high. With a higher production rate, the variable inputs match the fixed input relatively better, and the average variable cost is lower.

> The **marginal product** is the increase in output arising from an additional unit of the input.

As more of the variable inputs are added in combination with the fixed input, there will be a mismatch again. Eventually, there will be a *diminishing marginal product* from the variable inputs. This means that the marginal product becomes smaller with each increase in the quantity of the variable input. With a diminishing marginal product from the variable inputs, the average variable cost will increase with the production rate.

In Luna's case, table 4.2 shows that the average variable cost first drops from 43 cents to 42 cents as the production increases from 1,000 to 2,000 dozen eggs a week. Then, the average variable cost rises from 42 cents to 74 cents as the production increases from 2,000 to 9,000 dozen a week.

Recall that the average cost is the average fixed cost plus the average variable cost. While the average fixed cost falls with the production rate, the average variable cost falls and then increases. Accordingly, where the average variable cost is increasing, the relationship between the average cost and the production rate depends on the balance between the declining average fixed cost and the increasing average variable cost.

If the fixed cost is not too large and the average variable cost increases sufficiently, the average cost will first decline with the production rate and then increase. As table 4.2 shows, this is the case for Luna.

In figure 4.2, we graph the marginal, average, and average variable costs against the production rate. The marginal cost curve falls from 43 cents at 1,000 dozen a week, to reach a minimum of 41 cents at 2,000 dozen a week, and rises thereafter. The average variable cost curve falls from 43 cents at 1,000 dozen a week, to a minimum of 42 cents at 2,000 dozen a week, and then rises. Similarly, the average cost curve falls from $2.63 at 1,000 dozen a week, to a minimum of 94 cents at

Figure 4.2 Short-run marginal, average variable, and average costs

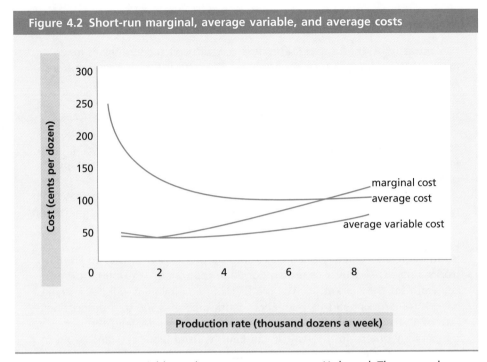

The marginal, average variable, and average cost curves are U-shaped: The curves decrease at low production rates, reach a minimum, and then increase for higher production rates.

6,000–7,000 dozen a week, and then rises. The graphs of the marginal, average variable, and average cost curves are each shaped like the letter *U*.

Progress Check 4B   In figure 4.2, if the fixed cost were lower, how would that affect the marginal, average variable, and average cost curves?

Progress check

Technology

In the preceding analysis, we derived the information about costs by asking the seller for the cost of producing at various rates. Accordingly, at every production level, the total, average, and marginal cost depend on the seller's individual operating technology.

There are two implications of this approach. First, the curves will change with adjustments in the seller's technology. For instance, a seller that discovers a technology

DAF trucks: Avoiding fixed labor costs

By contrast with the United States, it is very difficult for businesses in many Western European countries to lay off workers for economic reasons. Accordingly, labor can become a fixed cost for a very long horizon. As the example of DAF Trucks shows, some European businesses try to reduce fixed costs by substituting temporary workers for permanent employees.

DAF Trucks NV is one of Europe's largest truck manufacturers. It was established in 1993 to take over production in Belgium and the Netherlands from DAF NV, which had collapsed under pressure from a falling European demand for trucks.

DAF Trucks retained only 2,500 of its predecessor's 13,300 workforce. Within two years, by late 1995, growth in demand had enabled the new organization to increase daily production to 70 trucks. It expanded employment to a permanent workforce of 3,500 plus 2,200 temporary workers.

Although the company planned to step up production further to 80–85 trucks a day, DAF Trucks chairman Cor Baan cautioned, "Flexibility is the key word for the market. . . . The old levels of employment will never come back." DAF Trucks gears its permanent workforce of 3,500 to a production rate of 60 trucks, while the company meets additional demand through temporary workers. In this way, it can limit its fixed labor cost and avoid excess labor during economic downturns.

Source: "DAF Is Back on the Road," *International Herald Tribune*, September 20, 1995, p. 15.

involving a lower fixed cost will lower its average cost curve. A seller that uses a technology with a lower variable cost will lower its average, average variable, and marginal cost curves.

Second, different sellers may have different technologies and, hence, different cost curves. They may differ in the structure of fixed vis-à-vis variable costs. Some may have better technologies and hence lower costs than others.

◂◂ 3 Short-Run Individual Supply

Costs are one dimension of the short-run decisions whether to continue in operation and how much to produce. The other side to these decisions is revenue. We now consider the revenues of a business.

In analyzing revenues, we shall assume that the business aims to maximize profit. Realistically, of course, managers may pursue a number of objectives in addition to maximizing profit. We maintain the assumption of profit maximization because it is enough to account for a wide variety of common business practices and provides a foundation for a useful model of market competition.

Further, we assume that the business is so small relative to the market that it can sell as much as it would like at the going market price. We need this assumption to construct individual and market supply, which are the counterparts to individual and market demand. In chapter 5, we explain the need to assume that the business can sell as much as it would like at the going market price.

Production Rate

Supposing that the price of eggs is 70 cents a dozen, how much should Luna produce? Generally, the profit of a business is its total revenue less its total cost, and in turn, **total revenue** is the price multiplied by sales.

> The **total revenue** of a business is the price of its product multiplied by the number of units sold.

In table 4.3, we show Luna's cost and revenue at different production rates, with the assumption that the price is 70 cents. For instance, if sales are 1,000 dozen a week, then Luna's total revenue will be $0.70 × 1,000 = $700. If sales are 2,000 dozen a week, then Luna's total revenue will be $0.70 × 2,000 = $1,400. Similarly, we can calculate the total revenue at other production rates. From table 4.3, the highest profit is a *loss* of $1,293, which comes from producing at a rate of 5,000 dozen a week. (Later, we will explain why it makes sense for Luna to produce "at a loss.")

We can derive a general rule for the profit-maximizing production rate by illustrating cost and revenue with a diagram. In figure 4.3, we draw the cost curves

Table 4.3 Short-run profit

Weekly production rate	Variable cost	Total cost	Total revenue	Profit	Marginal cost	Marginal revenue
0	$0	$2,200	0	−$2,200		
1,000	$429	$2,629	$700	−$1,929	$0.43	$0.70
2,000	$836	$3,036	$1,400	−$1,636	$0.41	$0.70
3,000	$1,316	$3,516	$2,100	−$1,416	$0.48	$0.70
4,000	$1,897	$4,097	$2,800	−$1,297	$0.58	$0.70
5,000	$2,593	$4,793	$3,500	−$1,293	$0.70	$0.70
6,000	$3,415	$5,615	$4,200	−$1,415	$0.82	$0.70
7,000	$4,370	$6,570	$4,900	−$1,670	$0.95	$0.70
8,000	$5,462	$7,662	$5,600	−$2,062	$1.09	$0.70
9,000	$6,696	$8,896	$6,300	−$2,596	$1.23	$0.70

Figure 4.3 Short-run profit

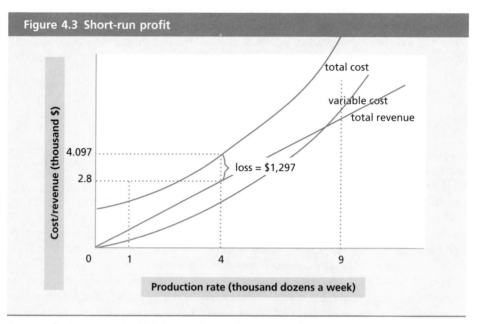

At a production rate of 4,000 dozen, the total revenue is $2,800 and the total cost is $4,097; hence, the vertical difference between revenue and cost is a loss of $1,297. Marginal revenue is represented by the slope of the total revenue line, while marginal cost is represented by the slope of the total cost curve.

from figure 4.1, adding a line to represent Luna's total revenue at a price of 70 cents. The line rises at a rate of $700 for every increase of 1,000 dozen in the production rate. Equivalently, the slope of the line is 0.70. For instance, one point on the total revenue line is at a production rate of 4,000 dozen and revenue of $0.70 × 4,000 = $2,800.

Using figure 4.3, we can measure the difference between the total revenue and the total cost at any production rate. In the figure, the vertical difference between the total revenue line and the total cost curve represents the profit. For instance, at a production rate of 4,000 dozen a week, the height of the total revenue line is $2,800, while the height of the total cost curve is $4,097. Hence, the vertical difference is a loss of $1,297.

Generally, to maximize profit, a business should produce at that rate where its marginal revenue equals its marginal cost. The **marginal revenue** is the change in total revenue arising from selling an additional unit.

> The **marginal revenue** is the change in total revenue arising from selling an additional unit.

To explain the rule for maximizing profit, consider figure 4.3. Graphically, the marginal revenue is represented by the slope of the total revenue line. Similarly, since marginal cost is the change in total cost due to the production of an additional unit, the marginal cost is represented by the slope of the total cost curve.

At a production rate such as 1,000 dozen a week, the total revenue line climbs faster than the total cost curve, or equivalently, the marginal revenue exceeds the marginal cost. Then, an increase in production will raise the profit. Wherever the marginal revenue exceeds the marginal cost, Luna can raise profit by increasing production.

By contrast, at a production rate of 9,000 dozen a week, the total revenue climbs more slowly than the total cost curve, or equivalently, the marginal revenue is less than the marginal cost. Then, a reduction in production will increase profit. Wherever the marginal revenue is less than the marginal cost, Luna can raise profit by reducing production.

Thus, Luna will **maximize profit** at the production rate where its marginal revenue equals marginal cost. At that point, the total revenue line and the total cost curve climb at exactly the same rate. Hence, a small change in production (either increase or reduction) will affect both total revenue and total cost to the same extent. Accordingly, it is not possible to increase profit any further.

> The **profit-maximizing** scale of production is where marginal revenue equals marginal cost.

We can use another approach to explain why a business maximizes profit by balancing marginal revenue and marginal cost. By definition, the marginal revenue is the change in total revenue arising from selling an additional unit. For a business that can sell as much as it would like at the market price, the change in total revenue arising from selling an additional unit is exactly equal to the price. Hence, the marginal revenue equals the price of the output.

In figure 4.4, we draw the marginal and average cost curves from figure 4.2 and also include the marginal revenue line. The marginal revenue line also represents the price.

Figure 4.4 Short-run production rate

Given the price of 70 cents, the seller maximizes profits by producing at the rate of 5,000 dozen a week, where marginal cost equals the price.

Where the price exceeds the marginal cost, Luna can increase profit by raising production. By contrast, where the price is less than the marginal cost, Luna can increase profit by cutting production. Therefore, Luna will maximize profit by producing at 5,000 dozen a week, a rate at which its marginal cost just balances the price.

Break even

Our discussion of the profit-maximizing production rate assumed that the business is continuing in operation. To decide whether to continue production, the business needs to compare the profit from continuing in production with the profit from shutting down. We shall see that the key factor in this comparison is the composition of fixed vis-à-vis variable costs.

Suppose that a business continues production. Let the revenue from the profit-maximizing production rate be R, while the fixed cost is F and the variable cost is V. Then, the maximum profit is $R - F - V$.

> A **sunk cost** is a cost that has been committed and cannot be avoided.

Now suppose that the business shuts down. Clearly, this will reduce its total revenue to 0. How will the shutdown affect its costs? We assume that the entire fixed cost, F, of the business is also **sunk** in the short run. A cost is *sunk* if it has been committed and cannot be avoided. The opposite of sunk is avoidable.

By assumption, the entire fixed cost, F, is also sunk. This means that, even if the business shuts down, it must still pay the fixed cost, F. In contrast to the fixed cost, the variable cost is avoidable. Hence, if the business shuts down, it need not pay anything in variable cost. Thus, if it shuts down, the profit will be the zero revenue minus the fixed cost, that is, $-F$.

The business should continue in production if the maximum profit from continuing in production is at least as large as the profit from shutting down. Algebraically, this break even condition is

$$R - V - F \geq -F, \tag{4.4}$$

which simplifies to

$$R \geq V. \tag{4.5}$$

Because the fixed cost is sunk, it drops out of the condition for continuing in production. The business should continue in production so long as its revenue covers the variable cost.

> The short-run break even condition is that price covers average variable cost.

Recall that revenue is the price multiplied by sales, $R = p \times q$. We can divide the break even condition (4.5) throughout by sales (or the production rate) to obtain

$$p \geq \frac{V}{q}. \tag{4.6}$$

Hence an equivalent way of stating the short-run break even condition is that the price must cover the average variable cost.

To summarize, in the short run, a business maximizes profit by producing at the rate where the marginal cost equals the price, provided that the price covers the average variable cost. Otherwise, it should shut down.

Let us apply the short-run break even analysis to Luna Farm. Suppose that Luna continues production. Then, from table 4.3, by producing at a rate of 5,000 dozen eggs a week, Luna will operate at a loss of $1,293. By assumption, Luna's entire $2,200 fixed cost is also sunk, while if Luna shuts down, it need not pay anything in variable cost. Thus, if Luna shuts down, its profit will be the zero revenue minus the $2,200 fixed cost, that is, a loss of $2,200. Clearly, Luna is better off continuing in production.

Another way to make this decision simply ignores the fixed cost. Table 4.3 shows the variable cost and total revenue. If Luna produces 5,000 dozen a week, it will earn a total revenue of $3,500, while its variable cost would be $2,593. Since the revenue exceeds the variable cost, Luna should continue in production. Thus, we have explained why it makes sense for Luna to produce "at a loss" – the reason is that the "loss" includes a sunk cost that should be ignored.

Individual Supply Curve

> The **individual supply curve** is a graph showing the quantity that one seller will supply at every possible price.

Using the rule for profit-maximizing production, we can determine how much a business should produce at other prices for its output. This is the information needed to construct a seller's individual supply curve. The **individual supply curve** is a graph showing the quantity that one seller will supply at every possible price.

For every possible price of its output, a business should produce at the rate that balances its marginal cost with the price, provided that the price covers the average variable cost. Referring to figure 4.4, if the price is 80 cents rather than 70 cents a dozen, Luna should expand production to the rate where the new price equals the marginal cost.

Indeed, by varying the price, we can trace out the quantity that Luna should supply at every possible price and, hence, construct Luna's individual supply curve. In fact, the individual supply curve is identical with the portion of the seller's marginal cost curve that lies above the average variable cost curve.

Following the marginal cost curve, the individual supply curve slopes upward. If the seller is to expand production, then it will incur a higher marginal cost. Hence, the seller should expand production only if it receives a higher price. Accordingly, the individual supply curve slopes upward. Further, the slope of the supply curve is identical to the slope of the marginal cost curve.

The individual supply curve shows how a seller should adjust its production in response to changes in the price of its output. Hence, a change in the output price will be represented by a movement along the supply curve.

Progress Check 4C Using figure 4.4, show the quantity that Luna should produce at a price of 75 cents per dozen eggs. *Progress check*

Demand for Inputs

We can now explain in detail how to obtain an individual seller's demand for inputs. We have derived the seller's marginal cost from its total cost, which in turn was derived from the estimates of the expenses on rent, wages, and other supplies needed at various production rates. These estimates depend on the prices of the various inputs.

Suppose, for instance, that table 4.1 assumes a wage of $10 per hour. The calculations in tables 4.2 and 4.3 and figures 4.3 and 4.4 are based on a wage of $10 per hour. What if the wage is $9 per hour? Then, we must go back to adjust tables 4.1–4.3 and figures 4.3–4.4 using the new wage rate.

Intuitively, as we show in figure 4.5, the marginal cost curve will shift downward. The profit-maximizing production rate increases from 5,000 to 5,600 dozen. From the new production rate of 5,600 dozen, we can go back to determine the corresponding quantity of the labor input. With a higher production, the quantity of labor demanded will also be higher.

By varying the wage rate, we can determine the quantity demanded of labor at every possible wage rate. This will allow us to construct the individual seller's demand for labor. As we have just shown, the quantity demanded will be higher at a lower wage; hence, the demand curve for labor will slope downward. The same method can be used to derive the individual seller's demand for every other input.

Figure 4.5 Lower input price

With a lower input price, the marginal cost curve will shift downward; hence, the seller will increase the production rate from 5,000 to 5,600 dozen.

Whether to produce DRAMs in Golden Week

Owing to the conjunction of several national holidays, the week beginning April 29 is called "Golden Week" in Japan. In 1998, faced with depressed DRAM prices, Mitsubishi Electric decided to idle its Fukuoka and Kumamoto plants for seven days, and so reduced production by 800,000 units of 64-Megabit chips. Among Japan's other four major DRAM manufacturers, Fujitsu and Toshiba also decided to stop operations during Golden Week, while Hitachi and NEC announced that they would continue in production.

The differences among the five big DRAM manufacturers regarding whether to produce during 1998 Golden Week might be explained by differences in their short-run break even conditions. For Fujitsu, Mitsubishi, and Toshiba, the short-run price had fallen below their average variable costs, so they chose to shut down temporarily. By contrast, for Hitachi and NEC, the short-run price still covered their average variable costs, so they continued to produce.

Source: "Toshiba, Mitsubishi, Fujitsu Halt DRAM Output in Golden Wk," *Dow Jones Newswires*, April 29, 1998.

Organizing production at multiple facilities

Echo Bay Mines has gold mines at Lupin in Canada as well as Cove in Nevada. How should it organize production at the two mines? Assuming that it can sell as much as it would like at the market price, Echo Bay Mines could simply direct each mine to produce at a rate balancing the price of gold with its marginal cost.

Another, more general approach applies even to sellers that are large enough to affect the market price. These should organize production so as to equalize the marginal cost at every facility. By doing so, the seller will minimize its companywide production cost.

To explain this rule, suppose that Echo's marginal cost at Lupin is $370 per ounce, while its marginal cost at Cove is $350 per ounce. If Echo reduced production at Lupin by one ounce and increased production at Cove by one ounce, it could reduce total cost by $370 − $350 = $20. These adjustments would not affect the total production of the entire company. Generally, if the two mines have different marginal costs of production, the company can always reduce costs by switching production between the mines.

Therefore, to minimize the companywide cost of production, a seller should organize production so as to equalize the marginal cost at every facility.

◂◂ 4 Long-Run Individual Supply

In the short run, a business must work within the constraints of past commitments such as employment contracts and investment in facilities and equipment. Over time, however, contracts expire and investments wear out. With sufficient time, all inputs become avoidable. A long-run planning horizon is a time frame far enough into the future that all inputs can be freely adjusted. Then the business will have complete flexibility in deciding on inputs and production.

How should a business make two key decisions – whether to continue in operation and how much to produce – in the long run? To address these issues, we first analyze the long-run costs and then look at the revenue.

Long-Run Costs

Let us analyze long-run costs in the context of Luna Farm. We ask the management to estimate the costs of producing at various rates when all inputs are avoidable. Suppose that table 4.4 presents the expenses classified into rent, wages, and cost of supplies.

In the long run, Luna can vary the size of its facility. The rent is $250 at zero production and increases to $2,500 for production of 9,000 dozen eggs a week. Similarly, the wages are $200 at zero production and rise to $5,289 at a production rate of 9,000. The cost of supplies rises from nothing for zero production to $900 at a production rate of 9,000.

Table 4.4 Long-run weekly expenses

Weekly production rate	Rent	Wages	Cost of supplies	Total
0	$250	$200	$0	$450
1,000	$500	$279	$100	$879
2,000	$750	$461	$200	$1,411
3,000	$1,000	$757	$300	$2,057
4,000	$1,250	$1,176	$400	$2,826
5,000	$1,500	$1,722	$500	$3,722
6,000	$1,750	$2,403	$600	$4,753
7,000	$2,000	$3,221	$700	$5,921
8,000	$2,250	$4,182	$800	$7,232
9,000	$2,500	$5,289	$900	$8,689

Table 4.5 Analysis of long-run costs			
Weekly production rate	Total cost	Marginal cost	Average cost
0	$450		
1,000	$879	$0.43	$0.88
2,000	$1,411	$0.53	$0.71
3,000	$2,057	$0.65	$0.69
4,000	$2,826	$0.77	$0.71
5,000	$3,722	$0.90	$0.74
6,000	$4,753	$1.03	$0.79
7,000	$5,921	$1.17	$0.85
8,000	$7,232	$1.31	$0.90
9,000	$8,689	$1.46	$0.97

As this example shows, in the long run, the business may incur some cost even at production levels close to zero. For instance, it may not be possible to build an egg-producing facility smaller than some minimum size. The $250 is the rent associated with a facility of the minimum size. Similarly, Luna's owner must work at least 20 hours a week. At a wage of $10 per hour, the minimum labor cost is $10 × 20 = $200 a week. Extracting the relevant information from table 4.4, we can compile the long-run marginal and average costs in table 4.5. We draw the long-run marginal and average costs in figure 4.6.

Comparing the short-run and long-run average cost curves, the long-run average cost curve is lower and has a gentler slope. The reason is that, in the long run, the seller has more flexibility in adjusting inputs to changes in the production rate. Accordingly, it can produce at a relatively lower cost than in the short run, when one or more inputs cannot be changed.

Production Rate

Let us now consider how much the business should produce in the long run. We can apply the general rule derived for short-run production: to maximize profit, a business should produce at that rate where its marginal cost equals the price of its output. In the long run, however, we use the long-run marginal cost.

The reasoning for this rule is the same as before. Where the price exceeds the long-run marginal cost, the seller can increase profit by raising production. By contrast, where the price is less than the long-run marginal cost, the seller can increase

Figure 4.6 Long-run production rate

Given a price of 70 cents, the seller maximizes profits by producing 3,400 dozen, where the long-run marginal cost equals the price.

profit by cutting production. Thus, the seller will maximize profit by producing at the rate such that its long-run marginal cost just equals the price.

For Luna Farm, table 4.6 shows the long-run cost, revenue, and profit. The profit column shows that profit reaches a maximum at a production rate of 3,400. The marginal cost at a production rate of 3,400 is 70 cents. Since the price is 70 cents, this confirms that the production rate of 3,400 maximizes profit.

Break even

We next analyze the break even condition under which a business should continue in long-run production. Combining this with the profit-maximizing production rate, we can derive the long-run individual supply curve.

In the long run, a business should continue in production if the maximum profit from continuing in production is at least as large as the profit from shutting down. In the long run, all costs are avoidable; hence, if the business shuts down, it will incur no costs and so its profit from shutting down is nothing.

Let $(R - C)$ represent the maximum profit from continuing in production. Then the business should continue in production if

$$R - C \geq 0, \tag{4.7}$$

which simplifies to

$$R \geq C. \tag{4.8}$$

Table 4.6 Long-run profit

Weekly production rate	Total cost	Total revenue	Profit	Marginal cost	Marginal revenue
0	$450	0	–$450		
1,000	$879	$700	–$179	$0.43	$0.70
2,000	$1,411	$1,400	–$11	$0.53	$0.70
3,000	$2,057	$2,100	$43	$0.65	$0.70
4,000	$2,826	$2,800	–$26	$0.77	$0.70
5,000	$3,722	$3,500	–$222	$0.90	$0.70
6,000	$4,753	$4,200	–$553	$1.03	$0.70
7,000	$5,921	$4,900	–$1,021	$1.17	$0.70
8,000	$7,232	$5,600	–$1,632	$1.31	$0.70
9,000	$8,689	$6,300	–$2,389	$1.46	$0.70

This break even condition says that the business should continue in production so long as total revenue covers total cost.

Since total revenue is price multiplied by sales, $R = p \times q$, we can divide the break even condition throughout by sales (or the production rate) to obtain

$$p \geq \frac{c}{q}. \tag{4.9}$$

An equivalent way of stating the **long-run break even condition** is that the price must cover the average cost.

Referring to table 4.5, Luna's lowest average cost is 69 cents. It attains this cost at a production rate of 3,000. Hence, if the price of eggs falls below 69 cents, then Luna should go out of business.

> The **long-run break even condition** is that price covers average cost.

Individual Supply Curve

A seller maximizes profits by producing at the rate where its long-run marginal cost equals the price of the output. By varying the price, we can determine the quantity that the seller will supply at every possible price. We have also shown that the seller should remain in business only if the price covers its average cost. Thus, the seller's long-run individual supply curve is that part of its long-run marginal cost curve, which lies above its long-run average cost curve.

Progress check

Progress Check 4D Referring to table 4.5, if the market price of eggs is $1.31, how much should Luna produce and what will be its profit?

Fujitsu: Durham vs Gresham

By 1998, Fujitsu had invested $590 million for production of 4- and 16-Megabit DRAMs at its Durham factory. A further $1 billion investment was needed to enable the plant to produce the state-of-the-art 64-Megabit DRAMs. Meanwhile, the industry was already working on 256-Megabit designs.

Given the development of technology, the Durham plant was close to being obsolete. The $1 billion investment for production of 64-Megabit chips was a long-run decision. Fujitsu had to ensure that the long-run price would cover its average cost (including the $1 billion investment).

At that time, however, Fujitsu had already equipped Gresham to manufacture 64-Megabit chips, hence the decision to continue production at Gresham was a short-run issue. Fujitsu only had to consider whether the short-run price covered its average variable cost.

The *average cost* of producing 64-Megabit chips at Durham would definitely have been higher than the *average variable cost* at Gresham. Further, given the tendency for the prices of semiconductors to fall over time, the long-run price of DRAMs would have been lower than the short-run price. Accordingly, we can understand why Fujitsu shut the Durham factory while continuing production at Gresham.

Sources: "Fujitsu to Curb Output of DRAMs in Europe," *Asian Wall Street Journal*, April 1, 1998, p. 6; "Fujitsu Microelectronics' Durham Plant to Cease Operations", M2 Presswire, September 7, 1998; and "Japanese Semiconductors: And Then There were Two," *Economist*, January 23, 1999, p. 58.

Oil: To produce or not to produce?

In the oil industry, production is the activity of extracting crude oil from the ground. The cost of producing oil from small wildcat sites in Texas is relatively high. High-cost producers must carefully consider the relation between the long-run price and their average cost.

Figure 4.7 shows year-by-year percentage changes in the price of the benchmark West Texas Intermediate crude oil, and the numbers of active drilling rigs in Canada and Texas over the period between 1988 and 1999. The changes in the number of Texas drilling rigs tracked the changes in the oil price very closely. More dramatic was how the change in the number of Canadian drilling rigs tracked and amplified changes in the oil price, except for the period between 1993 and 1994.

Figure 4.7 Oil price and drilling rigs

1988

1999

◆ Texas rig count ■ Canadian rig count ▲ Oil price

Sources: Baker-Hughes, US Energy Information Administration.
The change in the number of Texas oil rigs tracked the change in the oil price very closely.
The change in the number of Canadian oil rigs tracked and amplified changes in the oil price,
except for the period between 1993 and 1994.

◂◂ 6 Market Supply

If the price of eggs is 70 cents a dozen, how much will be produced by the market as a whole? To address this question, we need to know the market supply curve of eggs. The **market supply curve** of an item is a graph showing the quantity that the market will supply at every possible price. At any particular price, the quantity that the market will supply is the sum of the quantities supplied by each individual seller.

> The **market supply curve** is a graph showing the quantity that the market will supply at every possible price.

The market supply is the counterpart to the market demand, which we introduced in chapter 2. Together, supply and demand constitute a market. We first analyze the short-run market supply, and then consider the long-run supply.

Short Run

To construct the market supply, we can draw an analogy from our analysis of market demand. Recall that the market demand curve is the horizontal sum of the individual demand curves. Similarly, the market supply curve is the horizontal sum of the individual supply curves. At any particular price, each seller's individual supply curve shows the quantity that seller will supply. The sum of these quantities is the

Figure 4.8 Market supply

The market supply curve is the horizontal summation of the individual supply curves. At a price of 70 cents per dozen, the market quantity supplied is 5,000 + 8,000 = 13,000 dozen. At a price of 80 cents per dozen, the market quantity supplied is 5,800 + 9,200 = 15,000 dozen.

quantity supplied by the market as a whole. By varying the price, we can get the information needed to construct the market supply curve.

A seller's short-run individual supply curve is the portion of its marginal cost curve that lies above its average variable cost curve. Hence, the market supply curve begins with the seller that has the lowest average variable cost. The market supply curve then gradually blends in sellers with higher average variable cost.

In figure 4.8, we assume that there are just two producers of eggs: Luna Farm and Venus Farm. We draw the individual supply curves of the two producers and sum these horizontally to obtain the market supply curve. This shows that, at a price of 70 cents, the market as a whole will supply 5,000 + 8,000 = 13,000 dozen a week.

Our analysis of individual supply showed that the higher the price of the output, the more the seller will wish to produce. Since each seller will produce more, the market as a whole will also produce a larger quantity. Accordingly, the market supply curve slopes upward.

The market supply curve shows how market production responds to changes in the price of the output. Hence, the effect of a change in the output price is represented by a movement along the supply curve. Suppose, for instance, that the price of eggs rises from 70 to 80 cents per dozen. Then, referring to the market supply curve in figure 4.8, the market quantity supplied increases from 13,000 to 15,000.

The supply of an individual seller depends on the prices of all inputs, including labor, equipment, and supplies. A change in an input price will affect the seller's marginal cost at all production levels. The change will shift the entire marginal cost curve and hence the entire individual supply curve.

Since the market supply curve is the horizontal summation of the various individual supply curves, the change in the input price will also shift the entire market supply curve. Specifically, an increase in the price of an input will shift the market supply up, while a reduction in an input price will shift the market supply down.

We can apply this analysis to predict how an increase in the price of animal feed would affect the market supply of eggs. The higher price of feed will raise each seller's marginal cost of production and shift up its individual supply curve. Hence, the market supply curve will shift up.

In general, a change in the price of the output is represented by a movement along the market supply curve, while a change in the price of any input will cause a shift of the entire market supply curve.

Progress Check 4E In figure 4.8, show how a fall in the price of animal feed would affect the market supply of eggs.

Progress check

Long Run

The principles of long-run market supply are somewhat different from those underlying short-run supply. In the long run, every business will have complete flexibility in deciding on inputs and production. This flexibility implies that existing sellers can leave the industry, and new sellers can enter. The freedom of entry and exit is the key difference between the short run and long run.

We have shown that, for a seller to break even in the long run, its total revenue must cover its total cost. If a seller's total revenue does not cover the total cost, then the seller should leave the industry. Hence, the seller's individual supply will reduce to zero. This departure will reduce the market supply, hence raise the market price and the profits of the other sellers. Sellers that cannot cover their total costs will continue to leave the industry until all the remaining sellers break even.

By contrast, an industry where businesses can make profits, in the sense that total revenue exceeds total cost, will attract new entrants. Each of the new entrants will contribute its individual supply and so add to the market supply. The increase in the market supply will push down the market price and hence reduce the profits of all the existing sellers. If the existing sellers continue making profits, new entrants will continue to enter the industry until all the sellers just break even.

Accordingly, in the long run, when there is a change in the market price, the quantity supplied will adjust in two ways: first, all existing sellers will adjust their quantities supplied along their individual supply curves, and second, some sellers may enter or leave the market.

Let us apply this analysis to understand how producers of eggs will respond to an increase in the market price from 70 to 80 cents. Referring to figure 4.9, when the price rises from 70 to 80 cents, the short-run quantity supplied will increase from 13,000 to 15,000. Further, the price increase will raise the profits of the existing producers.

Figure 4.9 Short- vis-à-vis long-run market supply

If the price rises from 70 to 80 cents per dozen, the quantity supplied will increase from 13,000 to 15,000 in the short run and to 20,000 in the long run. If the price falls from 70 to 65 cents per dozen, the quantity supplied will fall from 13,000 to 12,000 in the short run and to 10,000 in the long run.

Over time, however, the higher profits will attract new producers to enter the industry. The new entrants will add to the market supply; hence, in the long run, the quantity supplied will increase from 13,000 to 20,000. As this example shows, for a given increase in price, the long-run market supply slopes more gently than the short-run market supply.

How will producers respond to a fall in the market price from 70 to 65 cents? Referring to figure 4.9, when the price drops from 70 to 65 cents, the short-run quantity supplied will drop from 13,000 to 12,000. In the short run, a business will continue to produce so long as the price covers its average variable cost.

Over time, however, producers for whom the price is below average cost will leave the industry. The departures will reduce the market supply. So, in the long run, the quantity supplied will drop relatively more, from 13,000 to, say, 10,000. This example shows that, for a price reduction, the long-run market supply slopes more gently than the short-run market supply.

Accordingly, for any change in price, the long-run market supply slopes more gently than the short-run market supply. Using terminology that we will introduce later in the chapter, we say that the long-run market supply is *more elastic* than the short-run supply.

Properties

While the short-run market supply generally slopes upward, the long-run market supply may be flat. In the long run, new businesses can enter and existing businesses can leave. Specifically, in the long run, the quantity supplied can expand through replication of existing businesses, and, hence, the long-run supply should be completely flat.

There is, however, a reason why the long-run market supply may slope upward. The resources available to the various suppliers may vary in quality. New entrants may not be able to replicate the resources of existing suppliers; hence, the new entrants must incur higher costs. This is especially true of resource-based industries such as minerals and agriculture. Resource differences also are signficant in markets where location plays an important role. For instance, in air transportation, suppliers with access to more convenient airports will have relatively lower costs.

The long-run market supply curve shows the quantity that the market will supply at every possible price. Hence, the effect of a change in the output price is represented by a movement along the market supply curve. By contrast, a change in wage

Texas Instruments and worldwide DRAM supply

The year 1998 was a watershed for the U.S. semiconductor memory industry. Micron Technology celebrated its 20th anniversary and also suffered its first net loss in a decade. Micron bought factories in Avezzano (Italy), Richardson (Texas), and Singapore from Texas Instruments (TI). Micron also bought TI's 25% ownership and 100% production interests in two Asian joint ventures, one in Singapore and the other in Japan. TI shut the remainder of its DRAM production facilities including one in Midland, Texas.

TI's deal with Micron simply transferred its ownership of the factories and interests in the joint ventures. Since no plants were dismantled, the sale did not affect worldwide capacity for production of DRAMs. By contrast, the closure of the Midland plant did reduce production capacity and hence the long-run worldwide supply of DRAMs.

Sources: "TI Plans to Trim 3,500 jobs" and "Texas Instruments Will Also Sell its Money-Losing Memory-Chip Business," *Orange County Register*, June 19, 1998, p. c1.

or any factor other than the price of the output will cause a shift of the entire market supply curve.

◂◂ 6 Seller Surplus

We derived the individual supply curve by asking a seller how much it would supply at every possible price. Another way to interpret the supply curve is to view it as showing the minimum price that the seller will accept for each unit of production. Using this approach, we can explain how a seller benefits or suffers from changes in the price of its output, and how a seller's profit varies with the price of its output.

Price vis-à-vis Marginal Cost

> The **seller surplus** is the difference between a seller's revenue from some production rate and the minimum amount necessary to induce the seller to produce that quantity.

In the case of Luna, referring to figure 4.10, the marginal cost of producing 1,000 dozen eggs a month is 43 cents. This is the minimum price that Luna will accept for the first 1,000 dozen. At a market price of 70 cents, however, Luna receives 70 cents for each unit of production. The difference of $(0.70 - 0.43) \times 1,000 = \$270$ is a surplus for the seller. Generally, the **seller surplus** is the difference between a seller's revenue from some quantity of production and the minimum amount necessary to induce the seller to produce that quantity. Luna receives a seller surplus on all production up to the marginal unit.

We will show that the short-run seller surplus can also be defined as the difference between the seller's revenue from some production rate and the variable cost. The minimum amount sufficient to induce a seller to deliver some production rate is the minimum that it requires for each unit up to the specified quantity. The minimum that a seller requires for each unit is the marginal cost. Hence, the minimum amount sufficient to induce a seller to deliver some production rate is the sum of the marginal costs for each unit up to the specified quantity.

The sum of the marginal costs for each unit up to some specified quantity is the variable cost. Accordingly, in the short run, the minimum amount necessary to induce a seller to deliver some production is the variable cost. Graphically, this is the area under the marginal cost curve up to the specified production rate. Thus, the seller surplus is the difference between the seller's revenue from some production rate and the variable cost, or $R - V$.

To illustrate, let us consider Luna's seller surplus at the price of 70 cents. Referring to figure 4.10, the revenue is represented by the area of the rectangle $0abc$ under the price line up to the quantity of 5,000. The variable cost can be represented by the area $0abd$ under Luna's marginal cost curve up to 5,000 dozen a month. The shaded area dbc between the price line and the marginal cost curve represents the seller surplus.

In the short run, a seller breaks even where total revenue covers the variable cost; hence, the *short-run* seller surplus is equal to total revenue less variable cost. In the

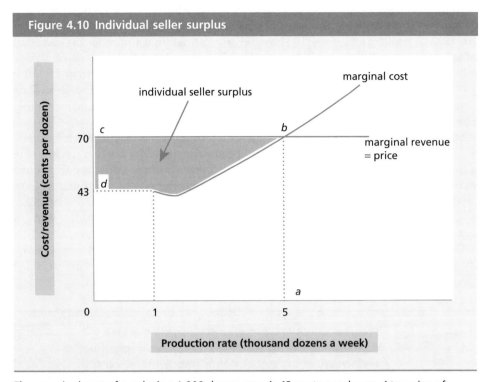

Figure 4.10 Individual seller surplus

The marginal cost of producing 1,000 dozen eggs is 43 cents per dozen. At a price of 70 cents per dozen, the seller receives a surplus of $(0.70 – 0.43) × 1000 = $270 for that production. At the 70 cent price, the seller will produce 5,000 dozen a week. The individual seller surplus is the shaded area *dbc* between the price line and the marginal cost curve.

long run, however, total revenue must cover total cost for the seller to break even. Hence, the *long-run* seller surplus is equal to total revenue less total cost.

Profit/Price Variation

Let us now analyze how a seller benefits or suffers from changes in the price of its output. Generally, a change in the price of the output will affect a seller's profit in two ways. The price change will affect the seller's revenue at the original production rate. Further, the price change will induce the seller to adjust production. We can illustrate these effects with the Luna example. Our example will also explain why a seller's profit varies relatively more than the price of its output.

Recall from table 4.2 that, when the price of eggs is 70 cents per dozen, Luna maximizes short-run profit by producing 5,000 dozen. If the price is 80 cents, however, Luna should increase production up to 5,800 dozen a week, where its marginal cost is 80 cents. The price increase raises Luna's profit in two ways: first, Luna gets 10 cents more for the original 5,000 production, and second, Luna expands production to 5,800 dozen, thus earning some additional profit.

In this example, the price of eggs increases by $10/70 = 14\%$. For each of the 5,000 dozen that it produced at the original price of 70 cents, Luna was making different amounts of profit. In figure 4.10, however, we can see that the profit on each unit of production would definitely be less than 70 cents. Accordingly, a 10-cent price increase would raise the profit on each unit of production by more than $10/70 = 14\%$. In addition, at the higher price of 80 cents, Luna chooses to expand production to 5,800 dozen, further increasing its profit. Hence, the 14% price increase raises Luna's profit by more than 14%.

Suppose instead that the price of eggs drops by 10 cents or 14% to 60 cents a dozen. Then, in table 4.2, Luna should cut production to 4,200 dozen a week, where its marginal cost is 60 cents. This would reduce Luna's profit in two ways: first, Luna would get 10 cents less for every unit that it produces, and second, Luna will cut production by 800 dozen. By the same reasoning that we used to consider the effect of a price increase on Luna's profit, we can show that the 14% cut in the price of eggs would reduce Luna's profit by more than 14%.

Generally, a change in the price of the output will affect the seller surplus by changing the revenue at the original production rate and inducing the seller to adjust production.

Progress check

Progress Check 4F In figure 4.10, shade the area representing the increase in seller surplus arising from an increase in the price of eggs from 70 to 90 cents.

Profit/price variation: Lihir Gold

One of the world's 15 largest gold mines is located on Lihir Island, off the northeast coast of Papua New Guinea. In October 1995, the owners of the Lihir gold mine launched an initial public offering of shares. The prospectus for Lihir Gold's offering projected the mine's profit in 1999 to be $52 million if the price of gold turned out to be $400 per ounce, while the projected profit was $24 million or 46% higher if the price of gold turned out to be just $50, or 12.5%, higher.

These projections are consistent with the general principle that a seller's profit varies relatively more than the price of its output. Lihir Gold's prospectus also included a production forecast of 584,000 ounces a year. At this production rate, a $50 increase in the price of gold would change revenues by $50 × 584,000 = $29.2 million. Taking into account increases in production, royalties, and taxes, the company projected that a $50 price increase would actually raise profit by $24 million.

Source: "Lihir Sparks a Gold Rush with Hot Stock Offering," *Asian Wall Street Journal*, September 12, 1995, p. 13.

Purchasing

An important application of the concept of seller surplus is in the management of purchasing. Suppose, for instance, that Speedy Foods is a large dairy manufacturer. It buys eggs as an input into manufacturing confectionery and ice cream. Presently, Speedy pays 70 cents per dozen to suppliers such as Luna Farm. We have shown that the 70-cent price gives Luna the area *dbc* in seller surplus.

Speedy can use the analysis of seller surplus to reduce the cost of its purchases and hence raise its own profit. Referring to figure 4.10, the minimum amount of money necessary to induce Luna to sell 5,000 dozen eggs a month is the area *0abd* under Luna's marginal cost curve. Speedy should offer Luna a lump sum equal to area *0abd* plus $1 to supply a bulk order of 5,000 dozen eggs. This amount of money leaves Luna with $1 of seller surplus and is just enough to induce Luna to supply the order. Through the bulk order, Speedy saves an amount represented by area *dbc* less $1.

The foregoing example illustrates how a buyer can apply the concept of seller surplus to reduce the cost of its purchases. The buyer should design a bulk order that extracts the seller surplus and pay the seller the minimum amount of money necessary to induce production of the desired quantity of output. Essentially, the buyer is purchasing up the seller's marginal cost curve.

Market Seller Surplus

The seller surplus for an individual is the difference between its revenue from some production rate and the minimum amount necessary for it to produce that quantity. The seller surplus for the whole market is the sum of the individual seller surpluses. It is the difference between the market revenue from some production rate and the minimum amount necessary for the market to produce that quantity. Graphically, the market seller surplus is represented by the area between the price line and the market supply curve. This concept applies in both the short run and the long run.

Figure 4.11 shows a short-run market supply curve. For example, at a price of 70 cents, the short-run market seller surplus is represented by the shaded area between the price line and the short-run market supply curve.

We have mentioned previously that, in the long run, the market supply curve may be flat. In this case, there will be no market seller surplus. If, however, the long-run market supply curve slopes upward, then there will be some market seller surplus.

The seller surplus accrues to those who own the superior resources.

◀◀ 7 Labor Supply

So far, we have discussed supply in the context of businesses that sell goods and services. In human resource markets, however, the sellers are individual persons.

Figure 4.11 Market seller surplus

At a price of 70 cents, the market seller surplus is the shaded area between the price line and the market supply curve.

The principles of human supply are similar to those underlying business supply. Accordingly, for brevity, we will focus on the special aspects of supply by individual persons.

Marginal Cost of Labor

The basis of individual supply by a business is maximization of profit. The business supplies the production rate where its marginal cost equals the market price. As we now explain, the individual supply of services by a person has a different basis.

A person's time is limited to $24 \times 7 = 168$ hours a week. The person must divide this time between labor and leisure, where *leisure* means any use of time that does not produce income. Hence, leisure includes time devoted to sleep as well as shopping and sport. Leisure is a consumer good. We suppose that, like other consumer goods, leisure provides diminishing marginal benefit. (At this point, the reader may wish to review the second section of chapter 2 on diminishing marginal benefit.)

In figure 4.12, we draw a curve representing a person's marginal benefit from leisure. The horizontal axis represents time, while the vertical axis represents the marginal benefit. By the principle of diminishing marginal benefit, the marginal benefit of leisure starts high and declines with increasing leisure time.

Figure 4.12 Marginal cost of labor

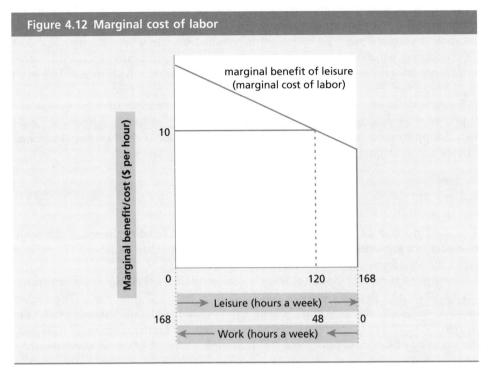

The marginal benefit of leisure declines with increasing leisure time; hence, the marginal cost of labor increases with the hours of labor. Given a wage of $10 per hour, the individual chooses 48 hours of work, or 120 hours of leisure.

Owing to the constraint of 168 hours a week, if a person spends more time on labor, there will be less time for leisure. Conversely, if a person spends less time on labor, there will be more time for leisure. Referring to figure 4.12, the quantity 0 hours of leisure is equivalent to 168 hours of labor, while the quantity 168 hours of leisure is equivalent to 0 hours of labor.

Accordingly, in figure 4.12, we can interpret the curve for the marginal benefit from leisure as the marginal cost of labor by viewing the horizontal axis from right to left. Viewed this way, the marginal cost of labor begins from a low level for 0 hours of labor and rises with increases in the hours of labor. Essentially, the diminishing marginal benefit from leisure time translates into an increasing marginal cost of labor.

Supply

The procedure for constructing a person's individual supply curve of labor is similar to that for constructing a business' individual supply curve of output. Suppose that the person can choose to supply any quantity of labor at the market wage of $10 per hour. In figure 4.12, we draw a horizontal line representing the market wage of $10 per hour.

Then, the person maximizes net benefit by choosing the quantity of labor where the marginal cost of labor equals the wage. The reasoning is the same as for why a business maximizes profit by choosing the production rate where the marginal cost of production equals the price of the output. Referring to figure 4.12, if the wage is $10 per hour, the individual chooses 48 hours of work, which means 168 − 48 = 120 hours of leisure.

By varying the wage, we can determine the quantity of labor that the person will supply at every possible wage. With this information, we construct the person's individual supply curve of labor. The market supply of labor is the horizontal summation of the individual curves of all the people supplying labor.

Slope

The marginal cost of labor increases with the quantity of labor; hence, if the wage is higher, an individual will tend to supply a larger quantity of labor. This would cause the individual supply curve to slope upward.

However, figure 4.12 does not show a countervailing effect: for any given quantity of labor, the person's income will be higher with a higher wage. The higher income will raise the marginal benefit from leisure and, equivalently, raise the marginal cost of work. Owing to this "income effect," a higher wage tends to reduce the quantity of labor supplied, making the supply curve of labor slope downward.

Paying for overtime

Typically, employers must pay workers 50–100% more than the regular wage rate for overtime work. Let us understand why employers must pay such a large premium for overtime work.

A worker's marginal cost of labor increases with the quantity supplied. The typical employer, however, does not allow its workers to choose any quantity of labor for some specified wage rate. Instead, the employer purchases a bulk order of 40 hours a week. Through the bulk order, the employer can extract some of the worker's seller surplus.

The regular wage rate reflects the worker's average cost of labor for 40 hours a week. The average cost of 40 hours of labor will be less than the marginal cost of the 40th hour, to an extent that depends on the steepness of the worker's marginal cost of labor.

If the employer wants to purchase overtime of an additional 5 hours of labor, it must pay the worker's marginal cost for the 41st–45th hours. As we have already explained, depending on the steepness of the worker's marginal cost of labor, the marginal cost of these hours may be substantially more than the regular wage. This explains why overtime rates are 50–100% higher than the regular wage.

Accordingly, the net effect of a higher wage on the quantity of labor that a person will supply depends on the balance of the two effects: the increasing marginal cost of labor and the income effect. This balance determines whether the supply of labor will slope upward at all wage levels.

◂◂ 8 Elasticity of Supply

Consider a typical issue for an industry analyst: If the price of gasoline and wages increases by 5 and 10%, respectively, what would be the effect on the short-run supply of gasoline by oil refineries? The analyst could answer this question with the market supply curve. In practice, however, analysts seldom have sufficient information to construct the entire market supply curve.

Another way of responding to the question applies the **elasticities of supply**, which measure the responsiveness of supply to changes in underlying factors such as the prices of the item and inputs. The elasticities of supply are the supply-side counterparts to the elasticities of demand, which we introduced in chapter 3.

> The **elasticity of supply** is the responsiveness of supply to changes in an underlying factor.

There is an elasticity corresponding to every factor that affects supply. Further, the elasticity can be estimated for individual supply curves as well as the market supply.

Price Elasticity

The **price elasticity of supply** measures the responsiveness of the quantity supplied to changes in the price of the item. The price elasticity of individual supply reveals how a seller will respond to a price change. Moreover, the price elasticity provides a simple way to compare the price sensitivity of sellers providing different items.

> The **price elasticity of supply** is the percentage by which the quantity supplied will change if the price of the item rises by 1%.

By definition, the price elasticity of supply is the percentage by which the quantity supplied will change if the price of the item rises by 1%, other things equal. Equivalently, the price elasticity is the ratio

$$\frac{\text{percentage change in quantity supplied}}{\text{percentage change in price}}$$

or

$$\frac{\text{proportionate change in quantity supplied}}{\text{proportionate change in price}}.$$

We can estimate the price elasticity of supply by either the arc or point approach. Let us apply the arc approach to calculate the price elasticity of Luna's short-run supply of eggs. Referring to figure 4.13, at a price of 70 cents, Luna produces 5,000 dozen. If the price increases to 80 cents, Luna would increase production to 5,800 dozen.

Figure 4.13 Price elasticity of supply

The proportionate change in quantity supplied is 15%, while the proportionate change in price is 13%. Hence, the price elasticity of supply is 0.15/0.13 = 1.15.

The proportionate change in quantity supplied is the change in quantity supplied divided by the average quantity supplied. The change in quantity supplied is 5,800 − 5,000 = 800 dozen a year, and the average quantity supplied is (5,800 + 5,000)/2 = 5,400 dozen a year; hence the proportionate change in quantity supplied is 800/5,400 = 0.15 = 15%.

Similarly, the proportionate change in price is the change in price divided by the average price. The change in price is 80 − 70 = 10 cents, while the average price is (70 + 80)/2 = 75 cents. Hence, the proportionate change in price is 10/75 = 0.13 = 13%. Accordingly, the price elasticity of Luna's short-run supply is 0.15/0.13 = 1.15.

Properties

The price elasticity of supply is a pure number that does not depend on any units of measure. Generally, the individual supply curves of businesses selling goods and services slope upward. Hence, the price elasticity of supply is a positive number that ranges from 0 to infinity.

If the price elasticity is less than 1, then a 1% increase in price will lead to less than a 1% increase in quantity supplied. In this case, the supply is inelastic. By contrast, if the price elasticity is more than 1, then a 1% increase in price will lead to more than a 1% increase in quantity supplied. Then, the supply is elastic.

In the case of human beings selling labor, the price of the service is the wage; hence, we measure sensitivity by the wage elasticity of supply. As mentioned in the preceding section, the supply curve of labor may slope downward at some wage levels. Then, the wage elasticity is negative.

From a managerial standpoint, the price elasticity is a handy way of characterizing the sensitivity of sellers to changes in price without worrying about choosing appropriate units of measure. For instance, a human resource manager may want to know whether unionized workers are more or less sensitive to changes in wages than nonunion workers. The manager can address this question by comparing the wage elasticities of the two groups.

When comparing the supplies of different items or even quantities supplied of the same item at different prices, it is important to remember that these comparisons are relative, because the price elasticity may vary along the same supply curve. A change in price, by moving from one point on a supply curve to another, may lead to a change in the price elasticity. Similarly, a change in any of the factors that affect supply may affect the price elasticity.

Intuitive Factors

The price elasticity of supply depends on the extent of capacity relative to current production. For instance, a seller that has considerable excess capacity will step up production in response to even a small increase in price. In this case, the individual supply will be relatively elastic. On the other hand, if capacity is tight, the seller may not increase production very much even if the price rises substantially. Hence, when capacity is tight, the individual supply will be relatively inelastic. Capacity utilization affects the elasticity of both individual and market supply.

The price elasticity of supply also depends on time. In the short run, some inputs may be costly or impossible to change. Consequently, the marginal cost of production is very steep. For instance, a factory wishing to step up production immediately may have to engage the workforce on overtime. Since overtime rates are 50–100% higher than regular wage rates, the marginal cost of overtime work is relatively high. With sufficient time, however, the factory could hire more workers at the regular wage. Accordingly, in the long run, the marginal cost of production will slope more gently.

Generally, the long-run supply is relatively more elastic than the short-run supply. This applies to both individual and market supply. Table 4.7 presents the price elasticities of the market supply for several products in the United States.

Forecasting Quantity Supplied

We can use the price elasticity of supply to calculate the effect of changes in price on quantity supplied for an individual seller as well as the entire market. To illustrate, let us calculate how a 5% increase in the price of eggs will affect Luna's production. Earlier, we estimated that the price elasticity of Luna's short-run supply was

Table 4.7 Price elasticities of supply

Product	Time horizon	Price elasticity	Source
Distillate (heating oil)	Short run	1.57	Considine (1992)
Gasoline	Short run	1.61	Considine (1992)
Pork	Long run	0.23	Holt & Skold (1989)
Tobacco	Long run	7.0	Fulginiti & Perrin (1993)
Housing	Long run	1.6–3.7	Blackley (1999)

Sources: Dixie M. Blackley, "The Long-Run Elasticity of New Housing Supply in the United States: Empirical Evidence for 1950 to 1994," *Journal of Real Estate Finance and Economics* 18, no. 1 (January 1999), pp. 25–42. Timothy J. Considine, "A Short-Run Model of Petroleum Product Supply," *Energy Journal* 13, no. 2 (1992), pp. 61–91. Lilyan Fulginiti and Richard Perrin, "The Theory and Measurement of Producer Response Under Quotas," *Review of Economics and Statistics* 75, no. 1 (February 1993), pp. 97–105. Matthew T. Holt and Karl D. Skold, "Dynamic Elasticities and Flexibilities in a Quarterly Model of the U.S. Pork Sector," *Applied Economics* 21, no. 12 (December 1989), pp. 1683–700.

1.15. The price elasticity of supply is the percentage by which the quantity supplied will change if the price rises by 1%. Hence, if the price of eggs increases by 5%, the quantity supplied will change by $1.15 \times 5 = 5.8\%$; that is, the quantity supplied will increase by 5.8%.

Progress check

Progress Check 4G Referring to figure 4.13, suppose that, if the price were 90 cents per dozen, Luna would supply 6,500 dozen. Calculate the price elasticity of supply for an increase in price from 80 to 90 cents.

Gasoline Supply

Using the relevant elasticities of supply, we can calculate the impact of changes in multiple factors that affect supply. For instance, we can calculate how a 5% increase in the price of gasoline and a 10% increase in wages would affect the short-run supply of gasoline by oil refineries.

The price elasticity of gasoline supply has been estimated to be 1.61, while the elasticity of gasoline supply with respect to wages has been estimated to be –0.05. Hence, a 5% increase in the price of gasoline would change quantity supplied by $1.61 \times 5 = 8\%$, while a 10% increase in the wage would change supply by $-0.05 \times 10 = -0.5\%$. Thus, the net effect of both changes is to change the quantity of gasoline supplied by $8 - 0.5 = 7.5\%$.

◂◂ 9 Summary

A small seller, which cannot affect the market price, maximizes profit by producing at a rate where its marginal cost equals the price. In the short run, at least one input cannot be adjusted. The business breaks even when total revenue covers variable cost. In the long run, the business can adjust all inputs and leave or enter the industry. It breaks even when total revenue covers total cost.

The supply curve shows the quantity supplied as a function of price, other things equal. The effect of a change in price is represented by a movement along the supply curve to a new quantity. Changes in other factors such as wages and the prices of other inputs are represented by shifts of the entire supply curve.

Seller surplus is the difference between revenue from some production rate and the minimum amount necessary to induce the seller to produce that quantity. Elasticities of supply measure the responsiveness of supply to changes in underlying factors that affect supply.

Key Concepts

short run	average (unit) cost	individual supply curve
long run	marginal product	market supply curve
fixed cost	marginal revenue	seller surplus
variable cost	profit maximizing	elasticity of supply
total cost	total revenue	price elasticity of supply
marginal cost	sunk cost	

Further Reading

For the role of individual persons in supplying labor and savings, refer to chapter 5, "The Household as Supplier," of the book by

Michael Katz and Harvey Rosen, *Microeconomics*, 3rd ed. (Homewood, IL: Irwin, 1998).

Review Questions

1. Explain the distinction between the short run and long run. How is this related to the distinction between fixed and variable costs?

2. Comment on the following statement: "It costs our factory an average of $2 to produce a piece of clothing. If you ask me how much it would cost to step up the production rate, I would say $2 per piece."

3. Farmer John's fixed cost of growing corn is higher than that of Farmer Jill. What does this imply for the difference in their marginal costs of growing corn?

4. Consider a business that can sell as much as it wants at the market price. Explain why its marginal revenue equals the market price.

5. Presently, Mercury Oil is producing 2,000 barrels of crude oil a day. The price is $15 per barrel. Its marginal cost is $20 per barrel. How can Mercury increase its profit?

6. Does the following analysis under- or over-estimate the change in profit? Presently, the price of eggs is 60 cents per dozen. Sharon's farm is producing 10,000 dozen eggs a month with a profit of $2,000. If the price of eggs rises to 70 cents a dozen, Sharon's profit will rise by $1,000.

7. Luna Metals uses diesel powered excavators and dump trucks in its silver mine. How will the following changes affect Luna's average and marginal cost curves?
   (a) An increase in the price of diesel fuel.
   (b) A drop in the price of silver.
   (c) A cut in the wages of workers.

8. Advertising is an important input into marketing most consumer products. Explain why the profit generated by an additional dollar of advertising will diminish with the total amount of advertising.

9. Some companies continue in business even though they are losing money. Are they making a mistake?

10. Following an increase in the price of diesel fuel, which was expected to be temporary, one bus operator suspended operations, while another continued in business. Explain this disparity in terms of the short-run break even condition.

11. Consider the market supply curve of new apartments. For each of the following changes, identify whether the change will cause a movement along the curve or a shift of the entire curve.
    (a) An increase in the price of new apartments.
    (b) An increase in the price of building materials.
    (c) A cut in the wages of construction workers.

12. How can a buyer use the concept of seller surplus to reduce the cost of its purchases?

13. True or false?
    (a) When capacity is tight, a seller's supply will be relatively more elastic.
    (b) Except for labor, the price elasticity of supply is always positive.

14. Consult a friend who works part-time, say, in the college bookstore or cafeteria.
    (a) Suppose that wages are 5% higher. How many more hours would your friend work each year?
    (b) Using this information, calculate the wage elasticity of your friend's supply.

15. Consider the price elasticity of the market supply of taxi service. Do you expect supply to be relatively more elastic with respect to fare changes
    (a) in the long run?
    (b) in the short run?

Discussion Questions

1. Lego invented its eponymous brick in 1949. Within 50 years, the company had produced over 200 billion bricks at factories in Denmark, Korea, Switzerland, and the United States. Lego bricks are made from acrylonitrile butadinese styrene (ABS). The raw material is melted at around 235 degrees Celsius, molded under high pressure, and then cooled. Lego manufactured the molds at its own factories in Germany and Switzerland.
   (a) Which of the following costs are fixed and which are variable: (i) production of the mold, and (ii) raw material?
   (b) In a short-run planning horizon, which of the costs in (a) must the manufacturer cover to remain in business?

2. A typical bank's sources of funds include savings deposits, certificates of deposit (CDs), and checking (demand) deposits.
   (a) Obtain the current interest rates on savings and checking accounts and CDs from a local bank. Suppose that the bank incurs an additional 1% cost to administer checking accounts. There are no additional administrative costs for savings accounts and CDs. List the three sources of funds in ascending order of annual cost per dollar of funds.
   (b) Suppose that the bank has equal amounts of savings and checking deposits and CDs. Compare its average cost of funds with its marginal cost of funds.

3. Table 4.1 shows the weekly expenses of the Luna Farm. Suppose that wages are 5% higher, increasing the cost of labor by 5%.
   (a) By recalculating tables 4.1 and 4.2, explain how the increase in wages will affect the (i) average variable cost and (ii) average cost.
   (b) Luna's management claims that it needs a 5% higher price to make up for the wage increase. Assess whether this claim is valid in the (i) short run and (ii) long run.

4. Jupiter Oil produces crude oil from two fields, one in the north and another in the south. Table 4.8 reports the total costs at the two fields for various rates of production.

Table 4.8 Jupiter Oil

Production rate (barrels/day)	Total cost from:	
	Northern field	Southern field
1,000	$5,000	$8,000
2,000	$11,000	$16,000
3,000	$18,000	$24,000
4,000	$26,000	$32,000
5,000	$35,000	$40,000

(a) To produce a total of 5,000 barrels per day in the cheapest way, how much should the company produce from the northern field and how much from the southern field?

(b) At the production rates that you give for (a), what is the cost of the last thousand barrels from the northern and the southern fields?

5. Barrick Gold, a Canadian corporation listed on the New York Stock Exchange, owns the Bousquet mine in Northwest Quebec and the Tambo mine in Chile. Table 4.9 reports information on selling prices and costs for the two mines. Barrick's selling price of gold differs from the spot price as some production is sold through long-term contract and also owing to the company's use of hedging. The "average cash cost" includes operating cost, royalties, and taxes, while the "average cost" includes the cash cost as well as depreciation and amortization.

Table 4.9 Barrick Gold

	Tambo 1996	Tambo 1997	Tambo 1998	Bousquet 1998
Production (thousand ounces)	160	133	167	176
Selling price ($ per ounce)	415	420	400	400
Average cash cost ($ per ounce)	307	309	273	194
Average cost ($ per ounce)	417	456	392	400

Source: Barrick Gold Corporation, 1997 and 1998 Annual Reports.

(a) Suppose that the Tambo mine always produces at the scale where its marginal cost equals the selling price of gold. Its marginal cost curve, however, shifts with changes in wages, equipment, and other factors. Using the data from table 4.9, illustrate the shifts in Tambo's marginal cost curve, the selling price, and profit-maximizing scale of production between 1996 and 1998.

(b) In 1997, management continued to produce from the Tambo mine even though the selling price of gold, $420 per ounce, was less than its average production cost of $456 per ounce. Was this a mistake?

(c) Use Barrick's 1998 data to compare the (i) short-run break even conditions for Bousquet and Tambo; and (ii) the long-run break even conditions for the two mines.

6. In 1984, Pennzoil entered into an agreement to acquire 1.008 billion barrels of Getty Oil's reserves for $3.4 billion. Shortly after, however, Getty accepted a higher offer from Texaco. Pennzoil then sued Texaco for interference with contract. Pennzoil claimed that its damages were 1.008 billion barrels times $10.87, which had been its average exploration cost, less the proposed acquisition cost of $3.4 billion. The price of West Texas Intermediate Crude was $30 per barrel in 1984. (*Texaco, Inc. v. Pennzoil, Co.*, Court of Appeals, First District, Houston, 729 S.W. 2d, p. 768.)

(a) Suppose that the future price of oil is $30 per barrel, while the production cost from the Getty fields is a constant $5, $10, or $15 per barrel. In each case, what is the profit from producing 1.008 billion barrels of oil? (Ignore the fact that the profit will be received in the future.)

(b) For each case, deduct $3.4 billion from your profit in (a).

(c) Which is a more accurate way to estimate Pennzoil's damages, the approach in (b) or that used by Pennzoil?

7. Until 1998, there were two major American manufacturers of DRAMs. Then, Texas Instruments (TI) sold its factories in Avezzano (Italy), Richardson (Texas), and Singapore and interests in two Asian joint ventures to Micron Technology. TI shut the remainder of its DRAM production facilities including one in Midland, Texas.

(a) Compare the effects on the worldwide long-run supply of DRAMs of TI's sale of the Richardson plant with its closure of the Midland factory.

(b) Which probably had the higher average cost – the Richardson or Midland plant?

(c) Following TI's exit, Micron Technology was left as the United States' only significant DRAM manufacturer. Did that necessarily imply that there was only one company manufacturing DRAMs in the United States?

8. Compile two series of data, one for the price of physical gold and another for an index of gold mining shares, on a monthly basis for the most recent 10-year period. Convert the two series into comparable indexes by rebasing both series to 100 at the beginning of the period.

(a) Graph the two series against time.

(b) Compare the volatility of the two series.

(c) Explain the difference in the volatility.

9. Several studies have estimated the wage elasticity of the market supply of labor among women to be 0.2.

(a) By what percentage must wage rates increase for women to supply 10% more labor?

(b) How would an increase in the price of childcare affect the market supply of women's labor?

(c) Suppose that the elasticity of the market supply of women's labor with respect to the price of childcare is –0.5. If the wage rises by 5% and the price of childcare also rises by 5%, what would be the effect on the hours worked by women?

10. Suppose that a study of the ocean tanker industry shows that, when tanker rates are 5% higher, the market quantity supplied is 1% higher in the short run and 25% higher in the long run.

(a) Calculate the short- and long-run price elasticities of supply.

(b) Is supply more or less elastic in the long run than in the short run? Explain your answer.

(c) If tanker rates were to fall by 2%, what would be the effect on industry quantity supplied in the (i) short run and (ii) long run?

11. This question applies the techniques presented in the math supplement. Let the market supply for aluminum be represented by the equation

$$S = p - 0.5z - 2,$$

where S is the quantity supplied in tons a year, p is the price of the aluminum in dollars per ton, and z is the price of electricity.

(a) Suppose that that $z = 5$. Sketch the supply curve.

(b) Illustrate the effect of a change in the price of aluminum from $p = 20$ to $p = 16$.

(c) Illustrate the effect of a change in the price of electricity from $z = 5$ to $z = 2$.

Chapter 4

Math Supplement

Production Decision

Let us prove that, for a business that can sell as much as it would like at the market price, the profit-maximizing production rate is the one where marginal revenue equals marginal cost. Let q be the rate or scale of production. We express total cost, $C(q)$, as a function of the production rate, q. Let F and $V(q)$ represent fixed and variable costs, respectively. Since the fixed cost does not vary with production, F is not a function of q. Then, total costs

$$C(q) = F + V(q). \qquad (4.10)$$

Let p be the price of the product, and $P(q)$ and $R(q)$ represent profit and total revenue, respectively. Profit equals total revenue less total cost:

$$P(q) = R(q) - C(q). \qquad (4.11)$$

Now, total revenue is price multiplied by sales (that is, the production rate), $R(q) = pq$; hence,

$$P(q) = pq - C(q). \qquad (4.12)$$

To find the profit-maximizing production rate, we differentiate profits with respect to the production rate and set the derivative equal to 0:

$$p - \frac{dC(q)}{dq} = 0. \qquad (4.13)$$

Hence, to maximize profits, the business must produce at a rate such that

$$p = \frac{dC(q)}{dq}. \qquad (4.14)$$

The right-hand side of condition (4.14) is the derivative of total cost, which is the marginal cost. Hence, the condition states that the business maximizes profit where the price of the product just balances the marginal cost.

Finally, by differentiating equation (4.10) for fixed and variable costs, we find that marginal cost is just the rate of change of the variable cost:

$$\frac{dC(q)}{dq} = \frac{dV(q)}{dq}. \qquad (4.15)$$

Market Supply Curve

Using algebra, we can reinforce our understanding of the market supply curve and especially the effect of changes in price vis-à-vis other factors. Let the market supply for some item be represented by the equation

$$S = p - 0.5z - 3, \qquad (4.16)$$

where S is the quantity supplied in units a year, p is the price of the item in dollars per unit, and z is the price of an input.

This supply curve is a straight line. To explain, suppose that $z = 2$. Then, substituting in equation (4.16),

$$S = p - 1 - 3 = p - 4. \qquad (4.17)$$

Differentiating (4.17) with respect to price,

$$\frac{dS}{dp} = 1 \qquad (4.18)$$

which means that the supply equation has a constant slope, or equivalently, that the supply curve is a straight line.

To sketch the supply curve, we consider two points on the curve. First, when the price $p = 10$, the quantity supplied $S = 10 - 4 = 6$. Next, if the quantity supplied is $S = 0$, the price, $p = 4$. Marking and joining the two points $p = 10$, $S = 6$, and $p = 4$, $S = 0$ on figure 4.14, we have the market supply curve.

We can use the supply curve to illustrate the effect of a change in price. For instance, when the price $p = 9$, the quantity supplied $S = 9 - 4 = 5$. When the price is higher, $p = 10$, the quantity supplied $S = 10 - 4 = 6$. We represent this change by a movement along the supply curve from the point at which $p = 9$ and $S = 5$ to the point at which $p = 10$ and $S = 6$.

The market supply curve in (4.16) can also illustrate the effect of a change in the price of an input. Recall that, originally, the price of the input was $z = 2$. Suppose that the price rises to $z = 3$. Then, referring to (4.16), the supply curve would become

$$S = p - 1.5 - 3 = p - 4.5. \qquad (4.19)$$

In this case, when the price $p = 10$, the quantity supplied $S = 5.5$; if the quantity supplied $S = 0$, the price $p = 4.5$. Marking and joining these two points on figure 4.14, we have the supply curve with the input price of $z = 3$. This is a straight line that lies to the left of the supply curve

Figure 4.14 Straight-line market supply curve

with the input price of $z = 2$. By contrast to a change in price, the change in the input price is represented by a shift of the entire supply curve.

Generally, a change in any factor other than the price of the item is represented by a shift of the entire market supply curve.

Forecasting Quantity Supplied

Using mathematics, we can derive a general formula with which to calculate changes in quantity supplied as a function of the price elasticity and percentage changes in price. Let S represent the average quantity supplied; $\%S$, the percentage change in the quantity supplied; p, the average price; and $\%p$, the per-

centage change in price. Then, by definition, the price elasticity of supply is

$$s_p = \frac{\%S}{\%p}. \qquad (4.20)$$

We can rearrange the price elasticity as follows:

$$\%S = s_p\, \%p, \qquad (4.21)$$

which says that the percentage change in quantity supplied is the price elasticity multiplied by the percentage change in price.

If there are multiple changes in the factors affecting the quantity supplied, then the net percentage effect on quantity supplied is the sum of the separate effects. Each separate effect is the corresponding elasticity multiplied by the percentage change in the factor.

Competitive Markets

◄◄ 1 Introduction

On March 24, 1989, the Exxon Valdez ran aground in the Prince William Sound, Alaska, spilling 11 million gallons of oil. The accident sparked wide and costly repercussions for the oil tanker industry. The U.S. Congress passed the Oil Pollution Act, requiring tankers using U.S. ports to have double hulls by 2010. Then, the International Maritime Organization (IMO) ordered single-hull tankers to be scrapped by their 30th year of service, and tankers over 25 years' old to be retrofitted against oil spills. Tankers with double hulls cost more to build and operate than comparable single-hulled vessels.[1]

Historically, major oil producers including BP Amoco, Exxon, and the Saudi Arabian Oil Company operated their own tankers to transport their oil. Some disbanded their fleets, in part to avoid legal liability for oil spills and other accidents. They now charter vessels from independent tanker companies. The independents are relatively small. For instance, in 1999, the fleet of Frontline, one of the largest independents, amounted to 5.5 million deadweight tons or less than 2% of the 285.4 million total industry tonnage.

Owing to a construction boom in the 1970s, by 1999, over a third of the world's tanker fleet was over 20 years old. These vessels must soon be retrofitted to comply with IMO rules, and also undergo the Fifth Special Survey, a drydock process costing $3–9 million. Tanker analyst Fred Doll predicted that some owners would rather scrap their vessels: "scrapping . . . will be sensitive to current and expected freight rates".

▼

[1] This discussion is based, in part, on Fred Doll, "Tanker Market Overview," *Lloyd's Nautical Yearbook 1999* (London: Lloyd's); *Platou Report 1999* (http://www.platou.com/platoureport.htm); and *Double-Hull Tanker Legislation* (Washington, DC: National Academy Press, 1998) (http://www.nap.edu/readingroom/books/tanker/).

The demand for tanker services depends on the quantity and distance of oil exports. Between 1997 and 1998, average daily production by the Organization of Petroleum Exporting Countries (OPEC) rose from 26.8 million barrels per day (bpd) to 27.9 million bpd. The price of oil fell from $16.16 per barrel in December 1997 to $9.39 per barrel in December 1998. By reducing the price of oil, OPEC's action also lowered tanker operating costs.

Changes in the market for tanker services pose important questions for the management of oil producers and independent tanker operators like Frontline. OPEC's production increase raised the demand for oil tanker services and lowered the cost of supply. What would be the impact of OPEC's action on tanker rates? Regulatory changes pose additional issues: would the owners of older tankers scrap their vessels? Were the IMO rules good or bad news for tanker owners? To answer each of these questions, we must understand demand, supply, and the interaction between the two sides of the market.

At first glance, the need to understand both demand and supply may seem surprising. The drop in the cost of fuel affects the supply of tanker service but not the demand. The increase in OPEC production affects the demand for tanker service but not the supply. Yet, as we shall see, in both of these cases, we cannot get a complete answer unless we consider both sides of the market. The same applies to many other managerial issues: although the initial change affects only one side of a market, it is necessary to consider the interaction with the other side to obtain a sensible and complete picture.

In this chapter, we combine our earlier analyses of demand and supply to understand how they interact in competitive markets. The central concept is that of market equilibrium. Applying this concept, we can understand the short- and long-run effects of changes in demand and supply. Further, we show how the relevant elasticities of demand and supply can be used to calculate the precise changes. Within this framework, we can explain the effects of a drop in the cost of fuel and an increase in OPEC production on the price and quantity of tanker service.

Finally, we consider the distinction between paying a price and bearing that amount. The demand–supply framework is the core of managerial economics. It can be applied to address business issues in a wide range of markets, including both goods and services, consumer as well as industrial products, and items sold in domestic and international markets.

◂◂ 2 Perfect Competition

In the preceding chapters, we developed the concepts of demand and supply. Recall that a market demand curve shows, for every possible price, the quantity that all buyers will purchase. When deriving a demand curve, we assume that every buyer can purchase as much as he or she would like at the going price and that all buyers pay the same price. Similarly, when deriving a market supply curve, we assume that every seller can deliver as much as he or she would like at the going price and that all sellers receive the same price.

A market is said to be in **perfect competition** if
1. its products are homogeneous;
2. it includes many buyers, each purchasing a small quantity;
3. it includes many sellers, each supplying a small quantity;
4. buyers and sellers can enter and exit freely;
5. all buyers and all sellers have equal information.

Let us now make explicit the assumptions underlying the concepts of demand and supply. Generally, demand–supply analysis applies to markets in which competition is very keen in the sense of the following five conditions: the product is homogeneous; there are many buyers, each of whom purchases a quantity that is small relative to the market; there are many sellers, each of whom supplies a quantity that is small relative to the market; new buyers and sellers can enter freely, and existing buyers and sellers can exit freely; and all buyers and all sellers have equal information about market conditions.

Collectively, these five conditions define **perfect competition**.

In principle, the concepts of demand and supply curves are valid only in a perfectly competitive market. In practice, however, the demand–supply framework can be applied even to markets that do not perfectly meet the five conditions. When applying the framework in such markets, we must check how the implications of the analysis might be sensitive to the particular conditions.

We shall treat the terms *perfect competition* and *demand–supply framework* as synonymous. Let us now review the five conditions for perfect competition.

Homogeneous Product

Competition in a market where products are differentiated is not as keen as that in a market where products are homogeneous. Gold is a homogeneous commodity. Gold mined in North America is a perfect substitute for gold from Australia, Brazil, South Africa, or any other part of the world. If Echo Bay Mines, a North American gold producer, tries to sell its gold at even 1% above the prevailing world market price, absolutely no one would buy. By the same token, if Echo Bay Mines offered its gold at 1% less than the market price, it would be swamped with more orders than it could meet. The price of gold from any source is exactly the same.

Let us contrast gold with mineral water. Mineral water is not homogeneous. Water from different sources has a different chemical composition and hence different taste and therapeutic effect. Even mineral waters that are chemically identical need not be homogeneous. For instance, two waters from nearby sources may be chemically identical but differentiated through brand marketing.

Owing to the chemical and marketing differentiation, Evian can raise its price by 1% without worrying that all its consumers would switch to other brands. Likewise, if Evian reduced its price by 1%, its sales would increase but not so much as to exhaust production capacity. The same is true for other manufacturers of mineral water. Consequently, there is no uniform price for mineral water: different manufacturers may charge different prices. In general, competition among manufacturers of mineral water is relatively weaker than competition among gold mines.

Many Buyers Purchasing Small Quantities

The second condition for perfect competition is that there are many buyers, each of whom purchases a quantity that is small relative to the market. In such a market, no buyer can get a lower price than others; hence, all buyers face the same price. This means that all buyers compete on the same level playing field.

To illustrate this condition, let us compare the market for gold with that for uranium. There are countless buyers of gold, ranging from Indian villagers to Paris jewelers. The purchases of each buyer are very small relative to the world stock. No one buys enough to get an especially low price. Rather, every buyer pays the same world price.

By contrast, buyers in the market for uranium are relatively few. Some buyers, such as the defense organizations of the nuclear powers, are so big that they have market power. In a market where some buyers have market power, different buyers pay different prices: the buyers with market power get lower prices. The buyers do not compete on a level playing field.

Let us now see why we must have the second condition to construct a market demand curve. A market demand curve shows, for every possible price, the total quantity that buyers will purchase. Suppose that all buyers are small buyers. Then, for every possible price, the quantity that buyers collectively will buy is the sum of the quantities that each individual buyer will purchase at that price. By considering all possible prices, we can construct a market demand curve.

Suppose, however, some buyers have market power and get lower prices. Then, different buyers pay different prices. Moreover, a buyer with market power can affect the price that it pays. A buyer with market power cannot answer the question, "How much would you buy, assuming that you could buy as much as you would like at the going price?" Such a buyer cannot answer this question because it can affect the going price. Thus, when some buyers have market power, it is not possible to construct a market demand curve.

Many Sellers Supplying Small Quantities

The third condition for perfect competition is that there are many sellers, each of whom supplies a quantity that is small relative to the market. The logic for this condition is similar to that for requiring many small buyers. In a market where there are many sellers, all of whom are small, no seller has market power. This means that no seller can get a higher price than others; hence, they all face the same price. All sellers compete on the same level playing field. The condition that there are many sellers supplying small quantities also is necessary to construct a market supply curve.

We can illustrate this condition by comparing the markets for silver and platinum. There are many producers of silver throughout the world, in North and South America, Africa, Asia, and Australia. None of these has market power. By contrast, a single Russian producer accounts for almost 70% of world production of palladium. The

Russian producer has substantial market power. Accordingly, the market for silver is much more competitive than that for palladium.

Free Entry and Exit

The fourth condition for perfect competition is that new buyers and sellers can enter freely, and existing buyers and sellers can exit freely. In particular, this means that no technological, legal, or regulatory barriers constrain entry or exit. To explain this condition, let us focus on free entry by new sellers and free exit by existing sellers. The logic for free entry and exit among buyers is quite similar.

Consider a market with free entry and exit. As we saw in chapter 4 on market supply, if the market price rises above a seller's average cost, then new sellers will be attracted to enter. This will add to the market supply and bring down the price. Hence, with free entry and exit, the market price cannot stay above a seller's average cost for very long. The market will be very competitive.

To illustrate, let us compare the markets for Internet service and content provision. Many jurisdictions require that Internet service providers be licensed. By contrast, there is relatively less regulation of Internet content provision. As a result, there are relatively more content providers and a higher degree of competition among them.

The degree of competition also depends on barriers to exit. Suppose that an Internet service provider must pay the government a compensation fee to cease service. It must consider this exit cost when deciding whether to enter the market. Therefore, the higher are the exit costs, the less likely new providers are to enter the market; hence, the less competitive the market will be.

Equal Information

The fifth condition for perfect competition is that all buyers and all sellers have equal information about market conditions such as prices, available substitutes, and technology. With equally distributed information, every seller or buyer will be subject to intense competition. If, for instance, a new supplier offers a key input at a lower price, then, immediately, every producer will get the same lower price. No seller can enjoy the privilege of secret information.

Photocopying service is a mature industry. Information about market conditions is widely and evenly available among buyers as well as sellers. As a result, the market is extremely competitive.

By contrast, information is not equally distributed in the market for medical services. Patients rely on their doctors for advice about their health problems and recommended treatment. In this market, sellers (doctors) have better information than buyers (patients). There may be differences in information on the supply side as well as between the two sides of the market. Doctors who attend continuing education and read the latest journals may have better information than others. Better-informed doctors may offer more effective advice and treatment than less well-informed doctors.

Markets where there are differences in information among buyers, or among sellers, or between buyers and sellers are not as competitive as those where all buyers and all sellers have equal information.

Progress Check 5A Explain why it is possible to construct a market supply curve only if there are many sellers, each of whom supplies a quantity that is small relative to the market.

Progress check

Regulatory barriers to competition: the Japanese beer market

With annual consumption of 5.2 billion liters (1.1 billion gallons), the Japanese beer market is one of the world's largest. Until the mid-1990s, however, the market was far from competitive. Four domestic manufacturers – Asahi, Kirin, Sapporo, and Suntory – controlled over a 95% share. The reason was government regulation. Until 1994, the Ministry of Finance would only license breweries that produced a minimum of 2 million liters a year. The Ministry limited retail licenses to small family-owned stores that tended to stick with the big four brewers.

The Ministry's regulations on breweries prevented the entry of new domestic brewers. Further the restrictions on retail sales hampered foreign brewers that could offer beer at half the Japanese price.

In April 1994, the Ministry lowered the threshold for brewery licenses to production of 60,000 liters a year. This led to the rapid entry of numerous specialty breweries. In addition, the Ministry also liberalized the regulations on retail sales of alcohol. In 1997, the Ministry allowed stores larger than 10,000 square meters (107,600 square feet) to sell beer. This further opened the market to competition from domestic as well as foreign brewers.

Source: "Only Here for the Biru," *Economist*, May 14, 1994, pp. 69–71.

◂◂ 3 Market Equilibrium

We have reviewed the five conditions for perfect competition. If a market meets these conditions, we can validly apply the concepts of demand and supply. We now introduce the concept of market equilibrium, which unifies demand and supply. **Market equilibrium** is the price at which the quantity demanded equals the quantity supplied. The concept of

Market equilibrium is the price at which the quantity demanded equals the quantity supplied.

equilibrium is the basis for all analyses of how changes in demand or supply affect market prices and quantities.

Demand and Supply

To illustrate the concept of equilibrium, consider the market for tanker service. Shippers generate the demand, and tanker lines provide the supply. Using a graph, we mark the price of tanker service in dollars per ton-mile on the vertical axis and the quantity of tanker service in millions of ton-miles a year on the horizontal axis. (One ton-mile represents the carriage of one ton over a distance of one mile.) Then, we draw the demand for and the supply of tanker service.

As emphasized in chapter 2, the demand curve slopes downward. From chapter 4, we know that, depending on the circumstances, the supply curve is flat or slopes upward. In this case, we suppose that the supply curve slopes upward. In figure 5.1, consider the point at which the demand and the supply curves cross. That point represents the market equilibrium: the price at which the quantity demanded just balances the quantity supplied.

Suppose that the equilibrium in the market for tanker service is at a price of $20 per ton-mile and quantity of 10 million ton-miles a year. Referring to figure 5.1, the demand curve shows that, at the price of $20, buyers want to purchase a total of

Figure 5.1 Market equilibrium

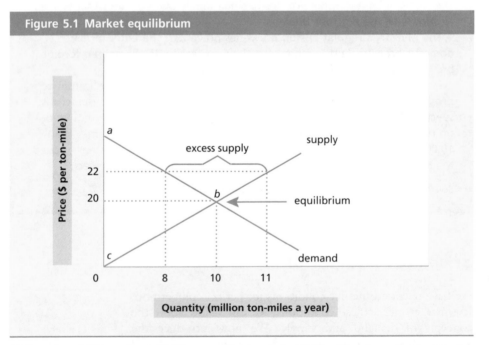

At the price of $20 per ton-mile, the quantity demanded is 10 million ton-miles a year and the quantity supplied is the same. When the price is $22 per ton-mile, the quantity supplied exceeds the quantity demanded by 3 million ton-miles a year.

10 million ton-miles a year. The supply curve in figure 5.1 shows that, at the price of $20, sellers want to supply a total of 10 million ton-miles a year. The quantity that buyers want to purchase exactly balances the quantity that sellers want to supply.

At the market equilibrium, there is no tendency for price, purchases, or sales to change. The price will not tend to change because the quantity demanded of 10 million ton-miles just balances the quantity supplied of 10 million ton-miles. Purchases will not tend to change because, at the price of $20, buyers (shippers) maximize benefits less expenditure by purchasing 10 million ton-miles. Further, sales will not tend to change because, at the price of $20, sellers (tanker lines) maximize profits by supplying 10 million ton-miles.

Excess Supply

What happens when the market is not in equilibrium? Then, generally, the market price will tend to change in such a way as to restore equilibrium. For instance, suppose that the market price is $2 above equilibrium, at $22 per ton-mile. Then, referring to the demand curve in figure 5.1, buyers would cut back purchases to 8 million ton-miles a year. The supply curve in figure 5.1 shows that, at a price of $22, sellers would supply more, specifically 11 million ton-miles a year.

Hence, at a price of $22 per ton-mile, the quantity supplied would exceed the quantity demanded by $11 - 8 = 3$ million ton-miles a year. In more colorful terms, there would be too many ships chasing too few customers. We give the name **excess supply** to the amount by which the quantity supplied exceeds the quantity demanded. So, at a price of $22, there would be an excess supply of 3 million ton-miles a year. In a situation of excess supply, the market price will tend to fall. Tanker lines would compete to clear their extra capacity and the market price would drop back toward the equilibrium level of $20.

> The **excess supply** is the amount by which the quantity supplied exceeds the quantity demanded.

From figure 5.1, it is clear that, if the price were even higher, at $25 per ton-mile, the excess supply would be even larger than the excess supply at a price of $22. Generally, the higher is the price above the equilibrium level, the larger will be the excess supply.

Excess Demand

Another way in which the market can be out of equilibrium is when the price is below the equilibrium level. In this case, the market price will tend to rise. To illustrate, suppose that in the market for tanker service, the price is $18 per ton-mile. Further, suppose that, at the price of $18, buyers would purchase 12 million ton-miles a year, and sellers would supply 9 million ton-miles a year. Then, the quantity demanded would exceed the quantity supplied by $12 - 9 = 3$ million ton-miles a year.

> The **excess demand** is the amount by which the quantity demanded exceeds the quantity supplied.

We give the name **excess demand** to the amount by which the quantity demanded exceeds the quantity supplied. Hence, at a price of $18 per ton-mile, there would be excess demand of 3 million ton-miles a year. Faced with this excess demand, buyers would compete for the limited capacity and the market price would rise toward the equilibrium level of $20. Generally, the lower is the price below the equilibrium level, the larger will be the excess demand.

Progress check

Progress Check 5B In figure 5.1, illustrate the excess demand if the price is $16 per ton-mile. Mark the quantities demanded and supplied.

Significance of Equilibrium

We focus on equilibrium for two reasons. First, as we have seen, if a market is not in equilibrium, either buyers or sellers will push the market toward equilibrium. Second, by comparing equilibria, we can address a wide range of questions like, "If the price of a related product, the cost of inputs, or government policy were different, how would that affect the market for my product?" To address such questions, we compare the market equilibrium under the original circumstances to the equilibrium under the new set of parameters. When prices are quite flexible, the market will adjust to the new equilibrium fairly quickly, so comparing equilibria is a fairly accurate method of analysis.

As earlier chapters have emphasized, the demand side of a market may consist of either people or businesses, and similarly, the supply side may consist of either people or businesses. The concept of market equilibrium is the same whether buyers are people or businesses and whether sellers are people or businesses. The market equilibrium is the price at which the quantity demanded just balances the quantity supplied.

For a market to be in equilibrium, both the quantity demanded and the quantity supplied must be the result of voluntary choices by buyers and sellers, respectively. Neither buyers nor sellers may face rationing.

In practice, very few markets exactly satisfy the five conditions for perfect competition. This means that demand–supply analysis does not precisely apply. Nevertheless, we can still apply this method of analysis: many of the managerial implications are the same even if a market is not perfectly competitive. However, we must be careful to check the implications against the conditions that the market does not satisfy.

⊲⊲ 4 Supply Shift

In general, changes in economic variables such as the prices of inputs or changes in government policies will cause shifts in demand, supply, or both. Even if the change superficially appears to affect only one side of the market, it is essential to analyze the effects on the other side as well. As we shall soon see, an analysis that ignores the other side of the market could be seriously misleading.

In this section, we consider the effect of a change that shifts the supply curve. Specifically, the introduction to this chapter asked how a drop in the cost of fuel would affect the price of tanker service. Let us apply the demand–supply framework to address this question.

We need to start from the equilibrium before the change in fuel cost. Suppose that, before the change in fuel cost, the price of tanker service was $20 per ton-mile and the quantity purchased was 10 million ton-miles a year.

Equilibrium Change

Fuel is a major input into the supply of tanker service. The supply curve of tanker service does not explicitly show the cost of fuel. Accordingly, any change in the cost of fuel will shift the entire supply curve. Suppose that the average fuel cost of tanker service was $4 per ton-mile, and that the cost of fuel drops by 15% or 60 cents per ton-mile. This would cause the entire supply curve of tanker service to shift downward by 60 cents per ton-mile. We represent this shift in figure 5.2.

The entire supply curve shifts down because the reduction in fuel cost affects sellers' marginal costs whatever the quantity that they supply. Another way of looking at the impact of the change in fuel cost is that it shifts the supply curve to the right: at every possible price, sellers want to supply more.

Figure 5.2 Supply shift

When the cost of fuel drops 60 cents per ton-mile, the entire supply curve shifts downward by 60 cents. At the new equilibrium, the price is $19.60 per ton-mile and the quantity is 10.4 million ton-miles a year.

The change in fuel cost, however, does not affect the demand for tanker service. Referring to figure 5.2, the new supply curve crosses the unchanged demand curve at a new equilibrium point d, where the price is $19.60 per ton-mile. The fall in price from $20 to $19.60 increases the quantity demanded from 10 to 10.4 million ton-miles a year. On the new supply curve, at the price of $19.60, the quantity supplied is 10.4 million ton-miles a year. The price of $19.60 is the new market equilibrium.

Price Elasticities

In the example of the tanker market, when the supply curve shifted down by 60 cents, the equilibrium price fell by only 40 cents. Generally, a downward or upward shift in the supply curve will change the equilibrium price by no more than the amount of the supply shift. What determines the extent of the change in price? We shall show that the change in the equilibrium price depends on the price elasticities of demand and supply.

Consider figure 5.3(a), which depicts an extremely inelastic demand. This means that buyers are completely insensitive to the price: they purchase the same quantity regardless of the price. Accordingly, when the supply curve shifts, the buyers do not change their behavior – they continue to purchase exactly the same quantity. In figure 5.3(a), when the supply curve shifts down by 60 cents, the equilibrium price drops by exactly 60 cents to $19.40 per ton-mile.

Regarding the market demand curve, the other extreme is an extremely elastic demand, as depicted in figure 5.3(b). This means that buyers are extremely sensitive to price. When the supply curve shifts, the buyers soak up all the additional quantity supplied. Consequently, the equilibrium price does not change at all. In figure 5.3(b), when the supply shifts down by 60 cents, the equilibrium price remains unchanged at $20 per ton-mile. The new equilibrium quantity is 10.6 million.

Realistically, however, the market demand probably is somewhat but not extremely sensitive to price. If there is an increase in supply, some buyers will switch from other forms of transport to tanker service, while existing buyers may purchase more. Hence, when the supply curve shifts down, the price will fall but by less than the downward shift. Likewise, if the supply curve should shift up, the market price will rise but by less than the upward shift.

By comparing figures 5.3(a) and (b), we can see the relationship between the price elasticity of demand and the price response to a shift in supply. Generally, if the demand is more elastic, then the change in the equilibrium price resulting from a shift in supply will be smaller.

Let us next see how the change in the equilibrium price depends on the price elasticity of supply. Figure 5.3(c) depicts an extremely inelastic supply. This means that sellers are completely insensitive to the price: they provide the same quantity regardless of the price. In particular, if their costs change, they will not change the quantity supplied. Referring to figure 5.3(c), tanker lines supply 10 million ton-miles a year whatever the market price. Consequently, the change in fuel cost does not change the equilibrium price.

Figure 5.3 Price elasticities of demand and supply

Extremely inelastic demand

(a) When demand is extremely inelastic, the supply curve shift reduces the price by exactly 60 cents but does not affect the quantity.

Extremely elastic demand

(b) When demand is extremely elastic, the supply curve shift does not affect the price but raises the quantity to 10.6 million.

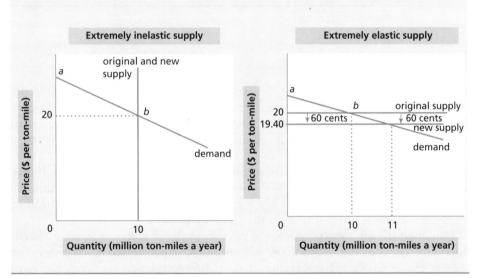

Extremely inelastic supply

(c) When supply is extremely inelastic, the supply curve does not shift.

Extremely elastic supply

(d) When supply is extremely elastic, the supply curve shift reduces the price by exactly 60 cents and raises the quantity to 11 million.

Regarding the market supply curve, the other extreme is an extremely elastic supply, as depicted in figure 5.3(d). This means that, essentially, the marginal cost of production is constant. Accordingly, if the cost of an input changes, the marginal cost changes by the same amount at all production levels. Then, the equilibrium price changes by exactly the same amount. Referring to figure 5.3(d) for the tanker services market, when the supply curve shifts down by 60 cents, the equilibrium price drops by exactly 60 cents per ton-mile. The quantity rises to 11 million ton-miles a year.

Realistically, however, the supply of tanker service is sensitive to price: to supply more service requires more capacity and, so, higher costs. An elastic supply means that sellers can increase service with some increase in costs. So, when the supply curve shifts down, the price will fall. Likewise, if the supply curve should shift up, the market price will rise.

By comparing figures 5.3(c) and (d), we can see that, generally, if the supply is more elastic, then the change in the equilibrium price resulting from a shift in supply will be larger.

Progress check

Progress Check 5C Which of (1) and (2) is true? For a given downward shift of the market supply curve, the drop in the equilibrium price will be larger if (1) the demand is more price elastic or (2) the supply is more price elastic.

Common Misconception

A common misconception is that, if sellers' costs fall by some amount, then the market price will fall by the same amount. For instance, a change in the cost of fuel affects only the supply side of the tanker service market. Does this mean that, if the cost of tanker service drops by 60 cents, then the price would fall by the same amount?

Such simple thinking overlooks the impact of the shift in supply on buyers. If they are insensitive to price, then they will not buy more; hence, the price will drop by the entire 60 cents. If, however, they are very sensitive to price, then the shift in supply would result in no change to the equilibrium price.

The simple thinking also overlooks the price sensitivity of sellers. If sellers are insensitive to price, then the drop in cost will not induce them to sell more; hence, the price of tanker service will not change at all. If, however, sellers are very sensitive to price, then the shift in supply would cause the price to fall by the entire 60 cents.

Generally, the effect of a change in costs on the market price depends on the price elasticities of both demand and supply.

Progress check

Progress Check 5D In figure 5.2, show how an 80 cent drop in the cost of fuel would affect the supply curve and the equilibrium price.

The demand for French products: foie gras vis-à-vis butter

France's agricultural exports include foie gras and butter. The supplies of French products to world markets depend on the exchange rate between the French franc and other world currencies, such as the U.S. dollar. If the franc becomes more expensive, the cost of providing French products to world markets and the supply curves will be higher. If, however, the franc becomes cheaper, then the supply curves will be lower.

Suppose that the franc becomes 10% more expensive, causing the supply curves of French foie gras and butter to shift up by 10%. How will these shifts affect the prices of foie gras and butter on world markets?

There are few substitutes for French foie gras; hence, the demand is relatively inelastic. The upward shift of the supply curve will result in a relatively large increase in the world price. By contrast with foie gras, butter is a relatively homogeneous product. There are many close substitutes for French butter, so that the demand is relatively elastic. Accordingly, the upward supply shift curve will result in a relatively small increase in the world price.

Retail competition and wholesale price cuts

A frequent complaint among consumer goods manufacturers is that, when they reduce wholesale prices, their retailers do not reduce retail prices by the same amount. The retailers take bigger margins instead of passing on the full reduction to consumers. Some marketing consultants believe that the cause of the problem is a lack of competition among retailers and claim that, if retailing were competitive, retailers would pass on the full amount of reductions in the wholesale price.

Let us apply the demand–supply framework to study this argument. Consider, for instance, the retail market for tissues. In this market, consumers generate the demand, while retailers provide the supply. We make the extreme assumption that the market is perfectly competitive. Figure 5.4 represents the demand and supply. The equilibrium is a price of $15 per carton and quantity of 200 million cartons a year.

Now suppose that tissue manufacturers reduce the wholesale price by $1 a carton. In the retail market, this will reduce the cost of supplying tissues by $1 at all quantities. Hence, the supply curve will shift down by $1.

Does the market price fall by $1? Only if either the market demand is extremely inelastic or the market supply is extremely elastic. In all other cases, the market price will fall by less than $1.

Figure 5.4 Wholesale price cut

A $1 cut in the wholesale price shifts down the retail supply curve by $1 and results in a lower retail price and larger quantity.

> Recall that we assumed that the retail market was perfectly competitive. And yet we found that, in most cases, the retail price will fall by less than $1 when manufacturers reduce the wholesale price by $1. Accordingly, the reason why retailers absorb part of a cut in wholesale prices is not a lack of competition. The explanation lies in the price elasticities of retail demand and supply.

◂◂ 5 Demand Shift

In the case of the market for tanker service, we saw that, to understand the impact of a shift in supply, we had to consider the interaction between supply and demand. Our next application begins with a change that shifts demand. To get a complete understanding of the final outcome, however, it is necessary to consider the supply side as well.

Equilibrium Change

The introduction asked how an increase in oil shipments would affect the price and quantity of tanker service. Figure 5.5 shows the original equilibrium at point *b*, with

Figure 5.5 Demand shift

A 1-million ton-mile increase in demand shifts the demand curve to the right and results in a higher price and larger quantity.

a price of $20 and quantity of 10 million ton-miles a year. Suppose that the demand rises by 1 million ton-miles at all price levels. Accordingly, in figure 5.5, the entire demand curve shifts to the right by 1 million ton-miles. The increase in oil shipments, however, does not directly affect the supply of tanker service. So, the supply curve does not change.

From figure 5.5, we see that the new demand curve crosses the unchanged supply curve at a new market equilibrium (point *f*). The new equilibrium has a higher price and a larger quantity of tanker service. By how much will the price rise and by how much will the quantity of tanker service increase? The answer depends on the price elasticities of both demand and supply.

Since the analysis is very similar to that for a shift in supply, we leave the details to the following progress check.

Progress Check 5E   Using figure 5.5 as a basis, construct a series *Progress check* of four figures to show the effect of the increase in the demand for tanker service on the market price when (a) demand is extremely inelastic, (b) demand is extremely elastic, (c) supply is extremely inelastic, and (d) supply is extremely elastic.

Common Misconception

If demand increases by some amount, then would the market quantity increase by the same amount? For instance, a change in oil shipments affects only the demand side of the tanker service market. Hence, it is easy to think that, if the demand increases by 1 million ton-miles, then the market equilibrium quantity would increase by the same amount.

This simple thinking overlooks the impact of the shift in demand on sellers: specifically, what is the marginal cost of providing additional tanker service? The simple thinking also overlooks the price-sensitivity of buyers: how much are they willing to pay for additional service?

Generally, as shown in the answer to Progress Check 5E, the change in market equilibrium resulting from a shift in demand depends on the price elasticities of both demand and supply. When the demand increases by 1 million ton-miles, the market equilibrium quantity would increase by between 0 and 1 million ton-miles. The precise change depends on the price elasticities.

Demand and supply on Valentine's Day

People buy greeting cards and roses throughout the year. As Valentine's Day approaches, however, cards and roses become necessities. The demand for both products jumps. Applying demand–supply analysis, we expect the prices of both products to rise. The price of roses, however, always increases much more sharply than the price of greeting cards. Why?

We can explain this disparity by considering the price elasticities of supply in the two markets. The supply of greeting cards on Valentine's Day is much more elastic than the supply of roses. Greeting cards can be stored, so manufacturers can easily step up production and prepare larger stocks ahead of Valentine's Day. This means that the supply of cards is relatively elastic; hence, an increase in demand has little effect on price.

By contrast, roses are perishable. Only roses maturing around Valentine's Day will be suitable for that day. It is relatively costly to increase the quantity supplied on Valentine's Day. This means that the supply is relatively inelastic, and consequently, the increase in demand causes the price to increase sharply.

Source: B. Peter Pashigian, "Demand and Supply on Valentine's Day," in *Price Theory and Applications* (New York: McGraw-Hill, 1995), p. 19.

OPEC and the tanker services market

Between 1997 and 1998, OPEC's average daily production rose from 26.8 million barrels per day (bpd) to 27.9 million bpd. The price of oil fell from $16.16 per barrel in December 1997 to $9.39 per barrel in December 1998. By reducing the price of oil, OPEC's action also lowered the operating costs for tanker services. Taken independently, the increase in demand pushed up tanker rates, while the cost reduction lowered tanker rates. The net effect was that tanker rates held steady.

In March 1999, OPEC members resolved to cut back production. Daily average output fell from 27.9 million bpd in 1998 to 26.7 million bpd in 1999. By October 1999, the price of oil had recovered to $21.62 per barrel. Between 1998 and 1999, the average daily charter rate for modern VLCCs (very large crude carriers, with capacity of over 175,000 deadweight tons) fell by 41% from $33,300 to $19,600, while the rate for older VLCCs fell by 54% from $23,700 to $11,000.

Why did the rates for older tankers fall more sharply? Older vessels are less fuel-efficient and hence were affected relatively more severely by the increase in the price of oil. While both new and old tankers faced the same fall in demand, the older tankers were hit harder by the increase in operating costs. Hence the charter rates for older tankers fell relatively more.

Source: Platou Report 1999 (http://www.platou.com/platoureport.htm).

◂ 6 Calculating Equilibrium Changes[2]

In the preceding sections, we have seen how to apply demand–supply analysis to analyze the effect of changes in demand or supply on the market equilibrium. We emphasized that the effect depends on the elasticities of demand and supply.

To obtain a precise estimate of the effect of the supply shift on the market price and quantity, we need to know either the entire demand and supply curves or the relevant elasticities. As we explained in chapters 3 and 4, information on elasticities is often more readily available than the entire demand and supply curves. Accordingly, it is important to understand how we can use the elasticities to calculate the effects of shifts in demand and supply on the market price and quantity.

Essentially, we combine the techniques presented in chapters 3 and 4. Chapter 3 showed how to use elasticities of demand to calculate changes in demand. Chapter 4 showed how to use elasticities of supply to calculate changes in supply. Now we must combine these methods to calculate changes in the market equilibrium.

▾

[2] This section is more advanced. It may be omitted without loss of continuity.

Figure 5.6 Supply reduction

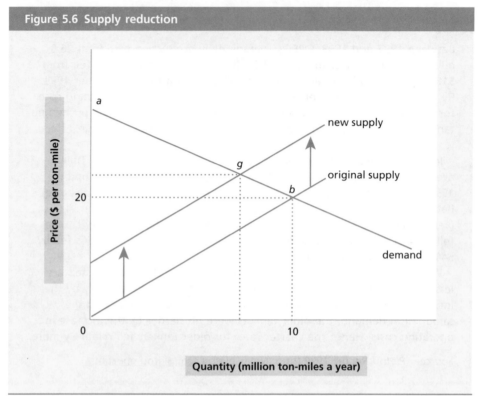

An increase in costs shifts up the supply curve and results in a higher price and smaller quantity.

Using Elasticities

Suppose, for instance, that we would like to know how a 5% increase in the cost of fuel would affect the price of bulk cargo service. Referring to figure 5.6, in the original equilibrium at point *b*, the price is $20 per ton-mile and the quantity is 10 million ton-miles. Suppose that the price elasticity of demand is −2, the price elasticity of supply is 1, and the elasticity of supply with respect to the cost of fuel is −0.4.

After the reduction in supply, the market will move to a new equilibrium at point *g*. Between the original and new equilibria, there will be changes in the market price and quantity demanded. Let %*p* represent the percentage change in the price. Since the price elasticity of demand is −2, the percentage change in the quantity demanded due to the change in price will be −2 × %*p*.

On the supply side of the market, two variables change. First, the quantity supplied will change with the change in the price. Since the price elasticity of supply is 1, the percentage change in the quantity supplied due to the change in price will be 1 × %*p*. Second, the quantity supplied will change with the 5% increase in the cost of fuel. Since the elasticity of supply with respect to the cost of fuel is −0.4, the percentage change in the quantity supplied due to the change in the cost of fuel will be $-0.4 \times 5 = -2$. Hence, the percentage change in the quantity supplied due to the changes in the price and fuel cost will be $1 \times \%p - 2$.

Referring to figure 5.6, when the market moves from the original equilibrium at point b to the new equilibrium at point g, the quantities demanded and supplied will change. In the original equilibrium, the quantity demanded equals the quantity supplied. Likewise, in the new equilibrium, the quantity demanded equals the quantity supplied. Accordingly, between the two equilibria, the change in the quantity demanded must equal the change in the quantity supplied.

This implies that the percentage change in the quantity demanded equals the percentage change in the quantity supplied. Since the percentage change in the quantity demanded is $-2 \times \%p$ and the percentage change in the quantity supplied is $1 \times \%p - 2$, the equality means that

$$-2 \times \%p = \%p - 2, \tag{5.1}$$

or $\%p = 0.67$. This means that the new price will be 0.67% higher. Now, in the original equilibrium, the price $p = 20$. Hence, in the new equilibrium, the price will be $\$20 \times 1.0067 = \$20.13$.

Since the percentage change in the quantity demanded is $-2 \times \%p$, it will be $-2 \times 0.67 = -1.34$; that is, a reduction of 1.34%. In the original equilibrium, the quantity was 10 million ton-miles; hence, in the new equilibrium, the quantity will be $10 \times 0.9866 = 9.866$ million ton-miles. Using the elasticities of demand and supply, we have calculated the new equilibrium (point g on figure 5.6).

Formula

Generally, the procedure for calculating the changes in the market equilibrium price and quantity is as follows. First, calculate the percentage change in quantity demanded due to changes in the price and other variables. Next, calculate the percentage change in quantity supplied due to changes in the price and other variables. Then, equate the percentage changes in quantity demanded and quantity supplied and solve for the percentage change in price. Finally, use the percentage change in price to calculate the percentage change in quantity. This procedure can be used to make precise estimates of the effects of changes in a variable that affects demand or supply or simultaneous changes in multiple variables.

To calculate changes in the market equilibrium,

1. calculate the percentage in the quantity demanded;
2. calculate the percentage change in the quantity supplied;
3. equate these percentage changes to solve for the percentage change in price;
4. calculate the percentage change in quantity.

Progress Check 5F Starting from the equilibrium with a price of $20 per ton-mile and quantity of 10 million, calculate the effect of a 10% reduction in the cost of fuel on the price and quantity of tanker service.

Progress check

Increasing demand and the market for gasoline

Suppose that the price of gasoline is presently 95 cents per gallon and sales are 500 million gallons a week. How will a 3% increase in household income affect the price and sales of gasoline? Referring to figure 5.7, the increase in household income will cause the demand for gasoline to shift to the right. The increase in household income, however, will not affect the supply of gasoline. Accordingly, there will be a new market equilibrium with higher price and quantity.

To calculate the new equilibrium using the procedure just given, we need the relevant elasticities. Previous research provides the following estimates. The price elasticity of the demand for gasoline is –0.23, while the income elasticity is 0.39.[1] Further, the price elasticity of the supply of gasoline is 0.62.[2]

The first step is to calculate the percentage change in the quantity demanded. Let %p represent the percentage change in price. Then, the percentage change in the quantity demanded due to the change in price will be –0.23 × %p. The percentage change in the quantity demanded due to the increase in income will be 0.39 × 3 = 1.17. Hence, the percentage change in the quantity demanded due to the changes in price and income will be –0.23 × %p + 1.17.

The next step is to calculate the percentage change in the quantity supplied. The percentage change in the quantity supplied due to the change in price will be 0.62 × %p.

The third step is to equate the percentage changes in quantity demanded and quantity supplied. This implies that

$$-0.23 \times \%p + 1.17 = 0.62 \times \%p.$$

Solving this equation, we have

$$1.17 = (0.62 + 0.23) \times \%p,$$

which implies that the percentage change in price, %p = 1.17/0.85 = 1.38, which is approximately 1.4%. Hence, the 3% increase in household income results in the market price rising by 1.4%. Since the original price is 95 cents per gallon, the new price will be 95 × (1.014) = 96.3 cents.

The fourth step is to use the percentage change in price to calculate the percentage change in quantity. In this case, the equilibrium quantity will increase by a proportion of 0.62 × 1.4 = 0.87, or approximately 0.9%. Since the original quantity is 500 million gallons a week, the new quantity will be 500 × 1.009 = 504.5 million gallons.

▼

[1] Molly Espey, "Gasoline Demand Revisited: an International Meta-analysis of Elasticities," *Energy Economics* 20, no. 3 (1998), pp. 273–95.
[2] Timothy J. Considine, "A Short Run Model of Petroleum Product Supply," *Energy Journal* 13, no. 2 (1992), pp. 61–91.

Figure 5.7 Gasoline market

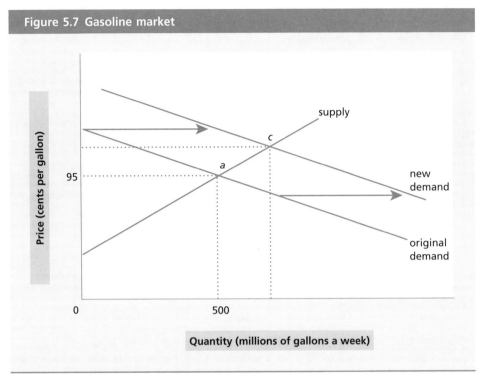

An increase in household income shifts the demand curve to the right and results in a higher price of gasoline and larger quantity.

◂◂ 7 Adjustment Time

Earlier, we studied the effects of shifts in demand and supply on the market equilibrium. An important factor in the size of these effects is the time horizon. Specifically, the elasticities of demand and supply vary with the time horizon. Accordingly, shifts in demand and supply may have different short-run and long-run effects.

To consider these differences, we start from a market that is in short- and long-run equilibrium. Generally, in equilibrium, each individual buyer purchases the quantity where her or his marginal benefit equals the price, and each individual seller provides the quantity where its marginal cost equals the price. Figure 5.8 represents the interactions among individual buyers and sellers in a market equilibrium.

The market demand curve is the horizontal summation of the individual demand curves, and the market supply curve is the horizontal summation of the individual supply curves. At the equilibrium price, the market demand curve crosses the market supply curve. The price then signals to each buyer how much to purchase and to each seller how much to provide. Figure 5.8 applies to both short- and long-run equilibria.

Figure 5.8 Market and individual equilibrium

Source: Adapted from Michael Katz and Harvey Rosen, *Microeconomics,* 1994 edition, p. 353. Reprinted by permission of Richard D. Irwin, Homewood, Illinois.

The individual demands add up to market demand, and individual supplies add up to market supply. The equilibrium price signals to each buyer how much to purchase and to each seller how much to provide.

Suppose that, originally, the market for tanker service was in short- and long-run equilibrium, with a price of $20 per ton-mile and quantity of 10 million ton-miles. Let us now analyze the short-run vis-à-vis long-run effects of an increase in demand by 1 million ton-miles.

Short-Run Equilibrium

Short-run market equilibrium is the price at which the short-run quantity demanded equals the short-run quantity supplied.

Figure 5.9 depicts the **short-run market equilibrium** at a price of $20 per ton-mile. Figure 5.9(a) shows the cost and demand curves of an individual seller. The short-run supply curve of any individual seller is that portion of its short-run marginal cost curve that lies above its short-run average variable cost curve.

By the assumption of perfect competition, each seller supplies a quantity that is small relative to the market. Equivalently, it has a small market share. Hence, the demand facing the seller is extremely elastic at the $20 market price. In the short run, the seller maximizes profit by operating at the point where its short-run marginal cost equals the market price. In Figure 5.9(a), the profit-maximizing scale of short-run operations is 100,000 ton-miles a year.

Figure 5.9(b) shows the short-run market equilibrium at point *a*. At the $20 equilibrium price, the short-run market demand curve crosses the short-run market supply curve. The short-run market demand curve is the horizontal summation of the short-run individual demand curves. Similarly, the short-run market supply curve is the horizontal summation of the short-run individual supply curves.

Figure 5.9 Short-run market equilibrium

(a) Individual seller

(b) Market

(a) An individual seller operates at 100,000 ton-miles a year, where the short-run marginal cost equals the market price.

(b) The market is in equilibrium at a price of $20, where the short-run demand crosses the short-run supply.

Long-Run Equilibrium

Figure 5.10 depicts the **long-run market equilibrium** at a price of $20 per ton-mile. Figure 5.10(a) shows the cost and demand curves of an individual seller. The long-run supply curve of any individual seller is that portion of its long-run marginal cost curve that lies above its long-run average cost curve. As each seller has a small market share, it faces a demand that is extremely elastic at the $20 market price. In the long run, it

> **Long-run market equilibrium** is the price at which the long-run quantity demanded equals the long-run quantity supplied.

maximizes profit by operating at the point where its long-run marginal cost equals the market price. By figure 5.10(a), the profit-maximizing scale of long-run operations is 100,000 ton-miles a year.

Figure 5.10(b) shows the long-run market equilibrium at point *a*. At the $20 equilibrium price, the long-run market demand curve crosses the long-run market supply curve. The long-run market demand curve is the horizontal summation of the long-run individual demand curves. Similarly, the long-run market supply curve is the horizontal summation of the long-run individual supply curves.

Figure 5.10 Long-run market equilibrium

(a) Individual seller

(b) Market

(a) An individual seller operates at 100,000 ton-miles a year, where the long-run marginal cost equals the market price.

(b) The market is in equilibrium at price of $20, where the long-run demand crosses the long-run supply.

Demand Increase

Starting from the short- and long-run equilibria, we suppose that the demand curve shifts to the right by 1 million ton-miles. For simplicity, we assume that the short- and long-run demand curves are the same.

Let us first consider the new short-run equilibrium. Referring to figure 5.9(b), the shift in demand will move the short-run market equilibrium to point *c*, with a higher price of $22. At the same time, referring to figure 5.9(a), every seller expands its operations to the scale of 105,000 ton-miles, where its short-run marginal cost equals the new market price of $22. This means operating service capacity more intensively; for instance, by delaying routine maintenance on ships and postponing annual vacations for crews.

Generally, the extent to which a seller expands its operations depends on the slope of its short-run marginal cost curve. If the short-run marginal cost curve is steep, then the price increase will not lead the seller to expand operations by very much. By contrast, if the short-run marginal cost curve is gentle, then the price increase will induce a large expansion of operations. The steepness of the short-run marginal cost curve depends on such factors as the availability of excess production capacity and the cost of overtime relative to standard wage rates.

Let us next consider the new long-run equilibrium. In a long-run horizon, there is enough time for all costs to become avoidable, for new sellers to enter the market, and for existing sellers to leave. Accordingly, as we have shown in chapter 4, the market supply tends to be more elastic in the long run than in the short run.

With regard to the tanker service market, the increase in demand raises the market price and hence each seller's profits. Over the long run, this will induce existing sellers to expand capacity and enlist additional crew members and also will attract new sellers to enter the market. The industry will expand along the long-run market supply curve. To the extent that the expansion will attract sellers with relatively less favorable resources, the long-run market supply will slope upward.

Referring to figure 5.10(b), the shift in demand will move the long-run market equilibrium to point *d* with a price of $21. Figure 5.10(a) shows the new long-run equilibrium for an individual seller. Although the price is higher than in the original equilibrium, higher input prices result in higher marginal and average cost curves. Accordingly, in the new long-run equilibrium, each individual seller just breaks even. No other sellers will wish to enter the industry, and no seller will wish to leave.

Figure 5.11 depicts both the short- and long-run market equilibria. The original equilibrium is point *a*, the new short-run equilibrium is point *c*, and the new long-run equilibrium is point *d*. The price in the new long-run equilibrium is lower than in the new short-run equilibrium but higher than in the original equilibrium. The

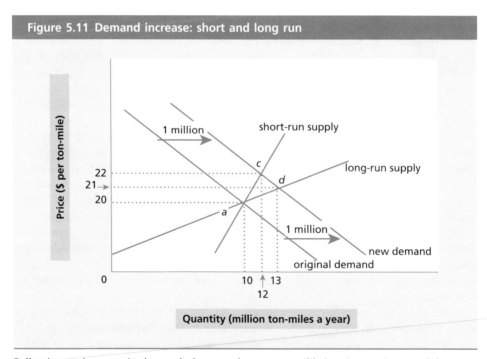

Figure 5.11 Demand increase: short and long run

Following an increase in demand, the new short-run equilibrium is at point *c* and the new long-run equilibrium is at point *d*. The price rises more in the short run than the long run. The quantity increases less in the short run than the long run.

quantity in the new long-run equilibrium is higher than in the new short-run equilibrium, which in turn is higher than in the original equilibrium. The basic reason for these differences is that the supply is more elastic in the long run than the short run.

In the new long-run equilibrium, there will be more sellers than in the new short-run equilibrium or the original equilibrium. The higher price attracts new sellers to enter and supports a larger number of sellers; hence, a larger industry.

Progress check

Progress Check 5G Suppose that the demand for tanker service increases by 2 million ton-miles. Use figure 5.11 to illustrate the short- and long-run effects on the market equilibrium.

Demand Reduction

We have considered the short- and long-run impacts of an increase in demand. We can apply the same approach to study the effects of a fall in demand. Figure 5.12 illustrates a 1 million ton-mile reduction in the demand for tanker service. The original equilibrium is at point *b*.

The reduction in demand will move the short-run market equilibrium to point *e*, with a lower price of $17. Those sellers whose average variable cost exceeds the price will shut down. In the tanker market, this means laying up their ships. Those sellers for whom the price covers their average variable cost will continue in business. Each will cut back operations to the scale where its short-run marginal cost equals the new market price of $17.

The extent of the cutback depends on two factors. One factor is the extent of sunk costs. If a seller has many prior commitments, most costs are sunk. It will continue to produce so long as the price covers its average variable cost. In this case, the price reduction will lead to a relatively minor cutback in operations. Generally, in an industry involving substantial sunk costs, the reduction in demand will translate into a relatively large drop in price and a small reduction in quantity.

The second factor is the slope of the seller's short-run marginal cost curve. If the short-run marginal cost curve is steep, then the price reduction will not induce the seller to cut back operations by very much. By contrast, if the short-run marginal cost curve is gentle, then the price reduction will have a relatively larger impact on quantity.

In the long run, there is enough time for all costs to become avoidable, for new sellers to enter the market, and for existing sellers to leave. Referring to figure 5.12, the shift in demand will move the long-run market equilibrium to point *f* with a price of $19. For some sellers, the long-run price is below their average total cost. These will exit the industry, which means scrapping their ships and dismissing all workers. The entire industry will contract along the long-run market supply curve.

Figure 5.12 Demand reduction: short and long run

Following a reduction in demand, the new short-run equilibrium is at point e and the new long-run equilibrium is at point f. The price falls further in the short run than the long run. The quantity drops less in the short run than the long run.

In the new long-run equilibrium, there will be a smaller number of sellers and each will exactly break even with average total cost equal to the market price.

Referring to figure 5.12, the price in the new long-run equilibrium is higher than in the new short-run equilibrium but lower than in the original equilibrium. Further, the quantity in the new long-run equilibrium is less than in the new short-run equilibrium, which in turn is less than in the original equilibrium. The basic reason for these differences is that the market supply is more elastic in the long run than the short run.

Price and Quantity over Time

Our analysis of the short- and long-run effects of shifts in the demand illustrates two general points. First, in response to shifts in demand, the market price will be more volatile in the short run than the long run. Specifically, if there is an increase in demand, the market price will increase more in the short run than in the long run. By contrast, if there is a reduction in demand, then the market price will fall more in the short run than in the long run.

Second, in response to shifts in demand, there is a greater change in the market quantity over the long run than in the short run. If there is an increase in demand, the quantity will increase more in the long run than in the short run. Likewise, if there is a reduction in demand, the quantity will drop more in the long run than the short run.

The distinction between the short run and long run is that, in the short run, some costs are sunk. Accordingly, the disparity between the short run and long run is relatively sharper in industries where operations involve substantial sunk costs. In such industries, the price will be relatively volatile, as the market adjusts to shifts in demand. When demand increases, the short-run price will exceed the long-run price. When, however, there is a fall in demand, the short-run price will be less than the long-run price.

Further, in industries with substantial sunk costs, the adjustment of production will be concentrated in the long run. Owing to the substantial sunk costs, relatively little adjustment can be made in the short run.

By contrast, in industries where sunk costs are minor, the adjustment to shifts in demand will be relatively smoother. The market price will be relatively less volatile. The adjustment of production will be spread through the short run and long run.

Frontline

With a fleet of 5.5 million tons deadweight, Frontline is one of the world's largest independent tanker owners. In 1996, it adopted a new strategy to build one of the most modern fleet of tankers. Frontline aimed to be a "consolidator within a highly fragmented industry . . . through acquisitions, mergers and market cooperation, the latter preferably in the form of pool arrangements."

In March 1999, OPEC successfully cut back production. In the short run, given the available tanker tonnage, the reduction in the demand for tanker services caused charter rates to fall. Between 1998 and 1999, the average daily charter rate for modern VLCCs fell by 41% to $19,600. Frontline's bottom line dropped from after-tax income of $31.9 million to an after-tax loss of $86.9 million.

However, the recession in the tanker services market bore a silver lining for Frontline. Charter rates for older VLCCs fell relatively more than those for modern VLCCs. The drop in rates prompted a significant long-run adjustment. Under the pressure of low charter rates, high operating costs, and the looming costs of the Fifth Special Survey and retrofitting, the owners of many older tankers decided to scrap their vessels. Tonnage scrapped rose from 7.0 million in 1998 to 16.4 million in 1999.

Frontline's management concluded, "The weak market over the last two years has reduced new ordering, increased scrapping and will most likely lead to a stronger and longer upturn in the market".

Sources: Platou Report 1999 (http://www.platou.com/platoureport.htm) Frontline Ltd., *Annual Report 1999.*

Texas Instruments, Micron, and the DRAM market

In 1998, following three years of continuously falling prices for dynamic random access memories (DRAMs), Texas Instruments (TI) decided to quit the industry. It sold plants in Avezzano (Italy), Richardson (Texas), and Singapore, as well as interests in two Asian joint ventures to Micron Technology. TI sold its share of a Taiwanese factory to joint-venture partner Acer. It shut all other DRAM production facilities including one in Midland, Texas. TI's exit left Micron as the United States' only significant DRAM manufacturer.

Why did Micron buy TI's production capacity at a time of tremendous excess supply in the market? One possible reason was that, with its increased size, Micron would command significantly more power over the DRAM market. We discuss market power in chapter 8.

Another possible explanation is that TI and Micron differed in their long-run expectations of DRAM prices. Micron may have been more optimistic, and hence viewed the purchase of TI's plants at a depressed time as a good deal.

Indeed, the demand for DRAMs recovered with Asia's emergence from its economic crisis and a general shift from 32 to 64 Megabytes as the standard memory for personal computers. (One Megabyte is made up of 8 Megabits.) In addition, Korean manufacturers reduced their investment as their Government cut back low-interest financing. The price of 64-Megabit DRAMs bottomed out at $7.50 in the autumn of 1998 and then recovered to $10 by January 1999. Subsequently, the price fluctuated between $5 and $15, and then ended 1999 at $8.50.

Source: Standard & Poor's Industry Surveys: Semiconductors 167, no. 41, section 2 (October 14, 1999).

Like the elasticity of the market supply, the elasticity of the market demand depends on the time horizon. Recall from chapter 3 that, depending on the nature of the item, the long-run demand may be more or less elastic than the short-run demand. Just as we analyzed the short- and long-run effects of shifts in demand, we can apply the same approach to consider the short- and long-run effects of shifts in supply.

◂◂ 8 Receipts vis-à-vis Incidence

We have applied the demand–supply framework to consider the effects of changes and in demand and supply in the short and long run. Another useful application of this framework is to understand the impact of the costs of transportation, brokerage, and other forms of intermediation on the market for the final good or service.

For instance, a typical issue for manufacturers of industrial products is whether to include the cost of shipment in the price to the customer. One approach is to set an "ex-works" or "free on board" price and leave the customer to pay the freight, while the alternative is to charge a price including freight. Using the demand–supply framework, we will show that both pricing methods have exactly the same impact on the manufacturer and customer.

Freight Inclusive Pricing

> The **cost and freight (CF) price** includes the cost of delivery to the buyer.

We begin by considering the cement market with freight inclusive pricing. A price that includes freight is called **cost and freight**, abbreviated CF. In the market for cement, the buyers are building contractors and the sellers are cement manufacturers. Suppose that all manufacturers set CF prices that include a freight cost of 25 cents. The market price is $1.50 per pound, at which price, the buyers purchase 1 million pounds a year. Figure 5.13 illustrates the market equilibrium at point *a*.

Figure 5.13 Pricing and freight cost

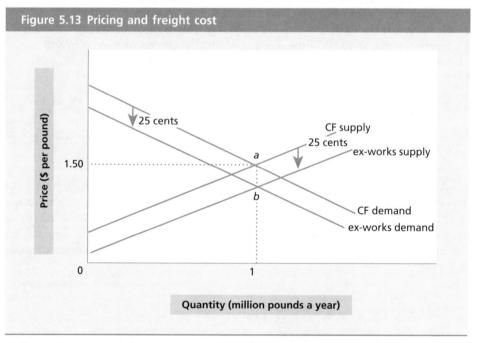

If all manufacturers switch to ex-works pricing, the supply curve shifts down by 25 cents and the demand curve also shifts down by 25 cents. The equilibrium quantity remains unchanged at 1 million pounds.

Ex-Works Pricing

Next, suppose that all cement manufacturers switch to ex-works pricing. An **ex-works price** does not include the freight cost: it literally means "the price at the gate to the works." Since the manufacturers no longer incur the 25-cent freight cost, the switch will shift the entire supply curve of cement down by 25 cents. In figure 5.13, the entire supply curve shifts down because each manufacturer's marginal cost of supplying cement is reduced whatever the quantity that it actually supplies.

> The **ex-works price** does not include the cost of delivery to the buyer.

The switch to ex-works pricing also affects the market demand. With ex-works pricing, each buyer must pay 25 cents a pound to obtain the cement. In figure 5.13, this can be represented by shifting the entire retail demand curve down by 25 cents. To explain this shift, recall that the market demand curve is the horizontal sum of the individual demand curves. In turn, each buyer's demand curve shows the amount that the consumer is willing to pay for each pound of cement. Since each buyer must pay 25 cents in freight for every pound, the buyer's willingness to pay will be 25 cents lower at all quantities. This means that the entire demand curve will shift down by 25 cents.

There is another way to confirm that the switch to ex-works pricing will shift down the demand curve. Consider the buyer of the 1 millionth pound. By the original demand curve, that buyer would be willing to pay exactly $1.50 for that pound. If, however, the buyer must incur a 25-cent freight cost, it will now be willing to pay $1.50 – $0.25 = $1.25 for the 1 millionth pound. The same 25 cent reduction in willingness to pay applies to all the inframarginal units as well. Hence, the entire demand curve shifts down by 25 cents.

In figure 5.13, the new demand and supply curves cross at point *b*. Relative to the original equilibrium at point *a*, the price is lower. The new demand curve is the original demand curve shifted down by 25 cents. Likewise, the new supply curve is the original supply curve shifted down by 25 cents. Hence, the new equilibrium point *b* must be vertically below the original equilibrium point *a*, and the vertical distance *ab* must be 25 cents.

Thus, in the new equilibrium, each buyer pays $1.25 to the seller and $0.25 in freight, making a "total price" of $1.25 + $0.25 = $1.50, which is exactly the price under freight-inclusive pricing. Further, the quantity of sales is exactly the same in the old and new equilibria. Generally, the price and sales are the same whether the sellers do or do not include the freight cost in their prices.

Incidence

When demand or supply shift, the consequent change in the price for a buyer or seller is called the **incidence** on that party. In the cement example, when manufacturers switch from freight-inclusive to ex-works pricing, the market price drops

> **Incidence** is the change in the price for a buyer or seller resulting from a shift in demand or supply.

by 25 cents to $1.25; hence, the net effect on buyers is zero. This shows that, although the switch in pricing method requires buyers to "pay" the freight cost, there is no net effect after we consider adjustments in both demand and supply.

Equivalently, whether manufacturers set prices that do or do not include the freight cost, the incidence is the same. The incidence does not depend on which side – buyer or seller – initially pays the freight cost.

In fact, the incidence of the freight cost depends only on the price elasticities of demand and supply. This analysis reflects common sense. If sellers pay the freight cost, the buyers would be willing to pay a higher price. By contrast, buyers that must pay the freight cost would insist on paying less to sellers.

The distinction between receiving or paying an amount of money and the incidence of the receipt or payment is a very fundamental economic concept. We have applied this distinction in the context of industrial pricing. The distinction is also important for understanding the effect of brokerage fees and government taxes.

Using demand–supply analysis, it can be shown that, regardless of whether buyers or sellers pay brokerage fees, the market price and quantity will be the same. Similarly, demand–supply analysis can show that, regardless of whether a tax initially is imposed on buyers or sellers, the market price and quantity will be the same. The incidence of brokerage fees and taxes depends only on the price elasticities of demand and supply.

Progress check

Progress Check 5H Using figure 5.13 as a basis, construct a series of four figures to compare the market equilibria with freight-inclusive pricing and ex-works pricing when (a) demand is extremely inelastic, (b) demand is extremely elastic, (c) supply is extremely inelastic, and (d) supply is extremely elastic.

Promoting retail sales: cents-off coupons

Some consumer marketing consultants suggest that cents-off coupons are more effective in lowering retail prices than cuts in wholesale prices. According to this suggestion, manufacturers should distribute coupons widely. Then, when consumers make purchases, they can redeem the coupons and get the full price reduction. This argument, however, overlooks the possibility that retailers will raise their prices when consumers use coupons. So, are coupons more effective than direct cuts in wholesale prices?

To address this question, we consider the retail market for a brand of shampoo, where consumers provide the demand and competitive grocery stores provide the supply. Figure 5.14 illustrates the market equilibrium at point s, with a price of $4 per bottle and quantity of 500,000 bottles a year.

First, we suppose that the manufacturer cuts the wholesale price of its shampoo by 25 cents. In the retail market, this wholesale price cut will shift the supply curve down by 25 cents. The entire supply curve shifts down because the wholesale price cut affects retailers' marginal costs of supplying the shampoo at all quantities. The cut in the wholesale price does not affect the retail demand. At the new equilibrium (point t), the price is lower and the quantity of sales is higher. Suppose that the price is $3.80 and the quantity is 550,000 bottles a year.

Next, suppose that, instead of cutting the wholesale price, the manufacturer maintains the wholesale price, while distributing 25-cent coupons to all consumers. Supposing that every consumer will cash in a 25-cent coupon for every bottle purchased, the consumer's willingness to pay will be 25 cents higher at all purchase levels. This means that each consumer's and hence the market demand curve will shift up by 25 cents.

The coupons, however, do not affect the supply curve. Referring to figure 5.14, the new demand curve crosses the original supply curve at point u. Relative to the original equilibrium, the price is higher, and the quantity of sales is higher.

In figure 5.14, compare the triangle vsu with the triangle swt. Line sv represents a 25-cent upward shift of the demand curve, and line sw represents a 25-cent downward shift of the supply curve. Accordingly, lines sv and sw are of equal length.

Curve st is a segment of the original demand curve, and curve vu is the same segment shifted up by 25 cents. Further, curve su is a segment of the original supply curve, and curve wt is the same segment shifted down by 25 cents. Accordingly, the triangles vsu and swt must be identical. This means that the point u must be vertically above the point t and the vertical distance tu must be 25 cents. Since the quantity at point t is 550,000 bottles, the quantity at point u also is 550,000 bottles.

Since the price at point t is $3.80, the price at point u must be $3.80 + 0.25 = $4.05. This is the retail price with coupons. Hence, the effective price to consumers is $4.05 − 0.25 = $3.80. The effective price with a coupon is identical to the price when the manufacturer directly cuts the wholesale price by 25 cents. This means that, in the new equilibrium, the price and sales are the same whether the manufacturer cuts the wholesale price or all consumers use coupons.

Assuming that all consumers use coupons, there is no difference between coupons and a direct cut in the wholesale price. Hence, there must be a different reason for using coupons. In chapter 9, we explain how coupons can be used to discriminate between consumers with different willingness to pay for a product.

Figure 5.14 Wholesale price cut vis-à-vis coupons

If the wholesale price is cut by 25 cents, the retail supply curve shifts down by 25 cents and the quantity increases to 550,000 bottles. If every consumer uses a 25-cent coupon, the retail demand curve shifts up by 25 cents and the quantity increases to 550,000 bottles. In both cases, the effective retail price and sales are the same.

◀ 9 Summary

How will an increase in demand and a reduction in marginal costs affect the market for an item? Questions such as these are commonplace. The answers, however, are not so simple. To understand the complete effect of a shift in demand or supply, it is necessary to consider both sides of the market. Generally, the effect of any change in demand or supply depends on the elasticities of both demand and supply.

The time horizon is a key factor affecting elasticities of demand and supply. Prices are more volatile and quantity adjustment takes relatively longer in industries where production involves substantial sunk costs.

Finally, it is important to distinguish a receipt or payment from incidence. A payment or receipt can be shifted from one to the other side of the market. Incidence is fundamental and depends only on the elasticities of demand and supply.

Key Concepts

perfect competition
market equilibrium
excess supply
excess demand
calculating equilibrium change

short-run market equilibrium
long-run market equilibrium
cost and freight price
ex-works price
incidence

Further Reading

Useful references on the economics of competitive markets include Michael L. Katz and Harvey Rosen, *Microeconomics*, 3rd ed. (Homewood, IL: Irwin, 1998, chapter 10, and Steven E. Landsburg, *Price Theory and Applications*, 4th ed. (South-Western College Publishing, 1998), chapter 7.

Review Questions

1. Several pairs of markets follow. For each comparison, which market better fits the model of perfect competition at the retail level (choose a or b)? Explain your answers.

   For entertainment,
   (a) cable television;
   (b) video rentals.

   For energy,
   (a) electric power;
   (b) gasoline.

   For investments,
   (a) publicly listed shares;
   (b) antiques.

2. True or false? If some sellers have market power, then it is not possible to construct a supply curve. Explain your answer.

3. The California Public Utilities Commission regulates airport shuttle services. License applicants must have liability insurance and satisfy standards of financial responsibility. How does such regulation affect the degree of competition in the market for airport shuttle services?

4. True or false? The assumptions of perfect competition are unrealistic, so the model is useless.

5. How would each of the following changes affect the market for sugar?
   (a) Development of a new zero-calorie sweetener.
   (b) An increase in the demand for milk.
   (c) A cut in the wages of farm workers.

6. If the market price exceeds the equilibrium price, what will be the consequences?

7. How would each of the following changes affect the market for new apartments?
   (a) An increase in the price of building materials.
   (b) A cut in the wages of construction workers.
   (c) A cut in mortgage rates.
   (d) An increase in household incomes.
   (e) An increase in the price of food.

8. Under what circumstances would an increase in household incomes have the least effect on the market price of air travel? Please state conditions in terms of the price elasticities of demand and supply.

9. Suppose that wages in the hotel industry are rising at the rate of 3% a year. Which determines the effect of an increase in wages on hotel room rates?
   (a) Price elasticity of demand.
   (b) Price elasticity of supply.
   (c) Both (a) and (b).

10. In the section on calculating equilibrium changes, we showed that a 3% increase in household income would cause the market price of gasoline to rise by 1.4%. Suppose that the price elasticity of supply were 0.8 rather than 0.62. How would the 3% increase in income affect the market price?

11. Consider the effect of a cut in mortgage rates on the price of new housing. Compare the short-run changes in price and quantity with the long-run changes.

12. True or false? Prices will be relatively less volatile in industries with substantial sunk costs. Explain your answer.

13. Older tankers are less fuel-efficient and so have higher operating costs than newer vessels. Older tankers must undergo expensive refitting. Explain why a drop in the demand for tanker service leads to the scrapping of older tankers and not newer ones.

14. Venus Paper is cutting the wholesale price of its tissues. Which of the following situations is better for consumers?
   (a) There are many other attractive brands, and hence the retail demand for Venus tissue is very elastic.
   (b) Venus tissue is quite special and has an inelastic demand.

15. Suppose that disposable diaper manufacturers cut their wholesale price by 50 cents a package. Consider the retail market. Explain the difference between receipt and incidence of the wholesale price cut for retailers.

Discussion Questions

1. Until 1979, almost all the oil exported from the Middle East was shipped by tanker through the Persian Gulf. When war broke out between Iraq and Iran, both countries attacked gulf shipping and oil production facilities. Between 1979 and 1988, Iraq's oil exports fell from 3 to 2.7 million barrels/day (bpd), while Iran's oil exports fell from 5.3 to 2.5 million bpd. To sustain its European exports, Iraq built oil pipelines to the Red Sea and the eastern Mediterranean.
   (a) Using an appropriate supply–demand diagram, illustrate the effect of (i) the production cut and (ii) the new pipelines on the market for tanker services.

    (b)   How would air and naval attacks on gulf shipping affect the market for tanker services?

    (c)   The net effect of the production cuts, pipeline construction, and military action was to increase the lease rates for tanker services. Using the supply–demand diagram, illustrate the net effect.

2.   At times, a major problem for Japanese consumer electronics manufacturers has been the appreciation of the yen against the U.S. dollar. This means that the yen is more expensive in terms of the U.S. dollar.

    (a)   Explain how the appreciation of the yen from ¥150 to ¥100 per U.S. dollar affects the wholesale cost of supplying Japanese consumer electronics to the United States.

    (b)   Suppose that the Japanese yen rises by one-third against the U.S. dollar. Which of the following are plausible explanations of why the U.S. retail price of Japanese-made CD players will rise by less than one-third: (i) the wholesale cost accounts for only part of retailers' costs, (ii) American retail demand for Japanese-made CD players is inelastic, (iii) American retail supply of Japanese-made CD players is inelastic?

    (c)   How will the appreciation of the yen affect the price and sales of Korean CD players in the United States?

3.   Consider any fresh fruit or vegetable grown in the United States.

    (a)   Using suitable demand and supply curves, explain how you expect the price of the item to vary over the four seasons of the year.

    (b)   Next, consider heating oil. Using suitable demand and supply curves, explain how you expect the price of heating oil to vary through the seasons.

    (c)   Compile two time series of monthly prices: one for the fruit or vegetable that you are considering and another for heating oil over the same 36-month period. Compare the seasonal variation in the two series.

4.   Manufacturers of paper products are major buyers of wastepaper. They use a combination of wood pulp and wastepaper to produce paper products. The supply of wastepaper comes from households and businesses. An issue in environmental policy is the effectiveness of price incentives in encouraging recycling of wastepaper. The price elasticity of the demand for wastepaper has been estimated to be −0.07, while the price elasticity of the supply has been estimated to be 0 (John A. Edgren and Kemper W. Moreland, "An Econometric Analysis of Paper and Wastepaper Markets," *Resources and Energy* 11 (1989): pp. 299–319).

    (a)   Consider a government policy that reduces the price of wastepaper to manufacturers by 5%. How will this affect the quantity demanded?

    (b)   Consider a government policy that increases the price of wastepaper to sellers by 5%. How will this affect the quantity supplied?

    (c)   Are price incentives an effective way of increasing the recycling of wastepaper?

5.   This question applies the techniques presented in the section on calculating equilibrium change. The elasticities of the demand for gasoline with respect to price and income are −0.23 and 0.39, respectively. The elasticities of the supply with respect to price and labor wages are 0.62 and −0.05, respectively. Suppose that the price of gasoline is $1 per gallon and sales are 400 million gallons a year. What will be the effect on the market price and quantity

   (a) If income rises by 4%.

   (b) If wages rise by 10%.

   (c) If both changes (a) and (b) occur.

6. The price of housing is a major issue in Hong Kong. Many blame speculators for wide swings in housing prices. To cool speculation, the Hong Kong government at one time prohibited banks from lending more than 70% of the value of new homes.

   (a) How do the following factors affect the demand for housing: (i) rising incomes, (ii) population growth, and (iii) trend away from multigenerational to single-generation households?

   (b) Is the supply of housing more elastic in the short run or in the long run?

   (c) How would the government's mortgage restrictions affect the rate of new construction, housing prices, and the housing stock in (i) the short run and (ii) the long run?

7. In March 1999, OPEC successfully cut back production. The OPEC action reduced the demand for tanker services.

   (a) Using suitable demand and supply curves, illustrate the short-run effects of the OPEC action.

   (b) Using your diagram for (a), illustrate the long-run effects of the OPEC action.

   (c) When charter rates are low, the owner of a tanker must decide whether to continue operating, temporarily lay up, or scrap the vessel. Explain how the owner should choose among these alternatives.

8. With January 1, 2000 heralding a new millennium, many predicted worldwide shortages of champagne, lobster, and other traditional New Year delicacies. New England and Canadian wholesalers began stockpiling lobsters in the first half of 1999. Boston dealer James Hook ordered 675,000 kilograms, 50% more than the previous year. The anticipated shortages, however, did not materialize. In early December, with just weeks to the New Year, the wholesale price of lobster fell 12% to $11.70 per kilogram ("Lobster Dealers Net Meager Sales on New Year Celebration Stockpile," *Asian Wall Street Journal*, December 29, 1999, pp. 1 and 7.)

   (a) On a suitable diagram, draw the long-run supply of lobster for New Year's Eve. In gauging the price elasticity of supply, note that lobster can be stockpiled for over 6 months.

   (b) Illustrate the effect of an increase in demand from 1998 to 1999. How would the increase in demand affect the price? How would the price effect depend on the price elasticity of supply?

   (c) Processors have developed a method to freeze whole lobsters in a plastic sleeve of brine that provides a quality almost equal to the fresh animal. How would this new technology affect the elasticity of long-run supply?

9. E-commerce is predicted to reduce the cost of intermediary services such as those of travel agencies, real-estate brokers, and investment advisors. Consider the market for air travel. Suppose that, with conventional travel agencies, the market equilibrium price is $300 per ticket, including a $15 intermediation cost. The quantity bought is 2 million tickets a year. With e-commerce, however, the intermediation cost falls to $2 per ticket.

(a) Using suitable demand and supply curves, illustrate the original equilibrium with conventional travel agencies. Represent the intermediation cost by shifting the supply curve.
(b) Illustrate the new equilibrium with e-commerce.
(c) What factors determine the extent to which consumers will benefit from e-commerce? Explain your answer with demand and supply curves.

10. Typical real-estate broker: "In California, the seller always pays the broker's commission, so, buyers get brokerage services free."

MBA: "If the custom were for the buyer to pay the commission, then would sellers get brokerage services free?"

Real-estate broker, clearly losing patience: "That is a purely hypothetical scenario, but if that situation were to arise, yes, I guess you're right."

(a) Assume that each seller pays a brokers' commission of $18,000. Then, the supply of houses includes the cost of brokerage. Illustrate the market equilibrium with a price of $310,000 per house and sale of 200,000 houses a year.
(b) Now suppose that buyers rather than sellers pay the $18,000 commission. Using your figure, illustrate the following: (i) shift the supply curve down by $18,000 since sellers do not pay the commission, and (ii) shift the demand curve down by $18,000 since buyers now pay the commission.
(c) Compare the market equilibria of (a) and (b) in terms of (i) the net price received by sellers and (ii) the net price paid by buyers. (Net prices are net of brokerage commission, if any.)

11. This question applies the techniques for solving equilibrium explained in the math supplement. Let p and w represent the price of new construction (in dollars per square foot) and a laborer's wage (in dollars per hour), respectively. Further, let the demand for new construction be represented by the equation

$$D = 40 - p, \tag{5.2}$$

and the supply be represented by the equation

$$S = 5 + 1.5\, p - w. \tag{5.3}$$

All quantities are in millions of square feet a year.
(a) Suppose that, initially, $w = 5$. Calculate the market equilibrium price and quantity.
(b) Next, suppose that a laborer's wage increases to 7. Calculate the new market equilibrium price and quantity. Does the price of new construction increase by the same proportion as the increase in the wage?

Chapter 5

Math Supplement

Market Equilibrium

Earlier, we used graphs to analyze the equilibrium in the market for tanker service. To reinforce our understanding, we now derive the market equilibrium using algebraic methods. Let p and f represent the price of tanker service and the cost of fuel, respectively. Further, let the demand for tanker service be represented by the equation

$$D = 30 - p, \qquad (5.4)$$

and the supply be represented by the equation

$$S = 4 + 0.5p - f. \qquad (5.5)$$

Suppose that, initially, $f = 4$. Then, the supply equation simplifies to

$$S = 0.5p. \qquad (5.6)$$

Before calculating the equilibrium, it is useful to graph the equilibrium. From the demand equation, when $D = 0$, $p = 30$, and when $p = 0$, $D = 30$. This gives us two points on the demand curve. Moreover, differentiating the demand equation with respect to price,

$$\frac{dD}{dp} = -1 \qquad (5.7)$$

which means that the demand equation has a constant slope, or equivalently, that the demand curve is a straight line. This is enough information to draw the demand curve.

Similarly, we can draw the supply curve. From the supply equation, when $S = 0$, $p = 0$, and when $p = 20$, $S = 10$. Further, by differentiating the supply equation with respect to price, we can show that the supply curve is also a straight line. This completes figure 5.1.

In market equilibrium, the quantity demanded equals the quantity supplied, that is,

$$D = S. \qquad (5.8)$$

Substituting from (5.4) and (5.6), this means

$$30 - p = 0.5p, \qquad (5.9)$$

which implies that

$$p = 20 \qquad (5.10)$$

and, hence, that

$$D = S = 10. \qquad (5.11)$$

Therefore, as depicted in figure 5.1, the market equilibrium occurs at a price of $20 per ton-mile and quantity of 10 million ton-miles.

Demand and Supply Shifts

We can also use an algebraic method to analyze the impact of shifts in demand or supply. Consider, for instance, the effect of a 15% drop in the cost of fuel. As the original cost is 4, the 15% drop will reduce the cost to $4 \times 0.85 = 3.40$. Substituting $f = 3.40$ in the supply equation, (5.5)

$$S = 4 + 0.5p - 3.40$$
$$= 0.60 + 0.5p. \qquad (5.12)$$

In market equilibrium, the quantity demanded equals the quantity supplied: that is,

$$D = S. \qquad (5.13)$$

Substituting from (5.4) and (5.12), this means

$$30 - p = 0.60 + 0.5p, \qquad (5.14)$$

which implies that

$$p = 19.60 \qquad (5.15)$$

and, hence, that

$$D = S = 10.4. \qquad (5.16)$$

Therefore, as depicted in figure 5.2, the new market equilibrium occurs at a price of $19.60 per ton-mile and quantity of 10.4 million ton-miles.

Chapter 6
Economic Efficiency

◀ ## 1 Introduction

In 1970, Stanford University professor Paul Ehrlich warned that the world's oil, natural gas, and uranium supplies would run out by 2000. Soon afterward, one of the most influential books of the decade was published. *The Limits to Growth* predicted that silver would be exhausted by 1988 and oil by 2003.[1] These dire predictions coincided with sharp increases in the prices of oil and other minerals. For instance, in just four months between September 1973 and January 1974, the price of crude oil jumped 350% from $2.59 to $11.65 per barrel.

The Limits to Growth sparked an intense debate among policymakers around the world. Many "experts" proclaimed that the sharp price increases signaled impending catastrophe and called for urgent government regulation. They argued for controls on oil consumption, and for the government to encourage the use of biomass, the sun, wind, and other renewable energy sources. By contrast, most economists were relatively sanguine and argued that the price increases were a good sign.

In 1978, the U.S. Congress passed the Public Utility Regulatory Policies Act (PURPA), which required electric power utilities to purchase (wholesale) electricity at a fixed price from producers of renewable energy. PURPA gave birth to the California wind power industry. In the early 1980s, the state Public Utilities Commission prepared standardized contracts for each utility, basing the fixed wholesale purchase price of electricity on the price of oil. At that time, the price of oil exceeded $30 per barrel. By 1985, a total of 1,000 megawatts of wind-powered electric generating capacity had been installed, mainly in the Tehachapi and Altamont Passes.

Meanwhile, the price of oil fell to a low of $10.91 in July 1986, and then oscillated between $10 and $20 over the next ten years. However, electric power utilities were

▼
---
[1] The following analysis is based in part on Donella H. Meadows, Dennis L. Meadows, Jorgen Randers, and William W. Behrens, III, *The Limits to Growth* (New York: Universe Books, 1972), pp. 56–60; Paul R. Ehrlich and Anne H. Ehrlich, *Population Resources Environment* (San Franscisco: W. H. Freeman, 1970), p. 60; and Richard T. Stuebi, "The Rise, Fall and Rebirth of Wind Energy in California: Lessons for the Renewable Energy Industry," *NextWave Energy*, March 1999.

contractually required to buy wind-generated electricity at prices fixed in the early 1980s. No further fixed-price contracts for wind-generated electricity were issued after 1984.

The consumption of fuel generates emissions that harm the environment. At the 1997 International Convention on Climate Change held in Kyoto, Japan, many of the world's leading economies agreed to a 5.2% reduction of greenhouse gases from 1990 levels by 2012. To achieve this target, they raised taxes on gasoline. In Germany, the government of Chancellor Gerhard Schroeder imposed a phased "ecology tax" on gasoline, with the tax rising by 6 pfennig per liter in each phase.

The extent of taxes on gasoline consumption varies internationally. At the time of writing, taxes accounted for 65–77% of the retail gasoline price in France, Italy, and the United Kingdom, but an average of only 24% in the United States. The percentage varied across the United States owing to differences in state sales taxes and state duties on gasoline.

Why did economists hail increases in the prices of minerals as good news, while technology experts believed that they signaled impending disaster? What was the effect of PURPA on the market for wind-generated electric power? How effective are "ecology taxes" in reducing the consumption of gasoline? In this chapter, we develop the concept of economic efficiency to address such questions.

A firm understanding of economic efficiency is important to every manager because it provides the intellectual foundation for the market system. We show that market prices allocate scarce resources in an economically efficient way. This efficiency is the reason why economists welcomed the increases in the prices of oil and other minerals in the 1970s. The price increases would motivate energy users to conserve and energy producers to expand supply.

The same concept of economic efficiency is also fundamental in management for two reasons. First, it provides a guide to managing resources within an organization. Second, it provides a guide to opportunities for profit. Whenever the allocation of resources is not economically efficient, there is a way to make money by resolving the inefficiency. This is a simple yet very powerful rule. In this chapter, we focus on the concept of economic efficiency. Later, in chapters 9, 11, and 12 on pricing, externalities, and asymmetric information, we apply the rule extensively to identify opportunities for profit in different contexts.

Finally, in this chapter, we apply the concept of economic efficiency to assess the various ways by which governments intervene in competitive markets. In particular, we consider the effects of ceilings and floors on market prices, and the impact of taxes. Applying these analyses, we can explain the impact of PURPA on the market for wind-generated electricity and analyze the effectiveness of ecology taxes on the consumption of gasoline.

‹‹ 2 Conditions for Economic Efficiency

Before discussing economic efficiency, we must define this concept. An allocation of resources is **economically efficient** if no reallocation of resources can make one person better off without making another person worse off. In this definition, persons may be human beings or businesses.

> An allocation of resources is **economically efficient** if no reallocation of resources can make one person better off without making another person worse off.

To appreciate the concept of economic efficiency, let us consider an allocation of resources that is not economically efficient. Then, by some reallocation of resources, it is possible to make one person better off without making another person worse off. Clearly, the original allocation of resources is undesirable. Accordingly, it seems very reasonable to aim for economic efficiency in the allocation of resources.

Sufficient Conditions

The concept of economic efficiency seems very reasonable. The definition, however, is difficult to apply in practice. It is easier to consider economic efficiency in terms of three sufficient conditions that are based on users' benefits and suppliers' costs.

An allocation of resources is economically efficient if, for every item,

1. All users achieve the same marginal benefit.
2. All suppliers operate at the same marginal cost.
3. Every user's marginal benefit is equal to every supplier's marginal cost.

For economic efficiency, every product and resource – consumer as well as industrial, goods as well as services, and domestic as well as imported – must satisfy these conditions.

Let us review these three conditions in the context of Russian passenger airlines operating under central planning.

*   *Equal marginal benefit.* The first condition for economic efficency is that all users receive the same marginal benefit. Consider two people in the city of Novosibirsk, Siberia. Mikhail, a senior Communist party official, can take any number of flights anywhere in Russia free of charge. Raisa works in a factory and, every year, pays one month's wages for a flight to visit her family in Moscow. In this example, Mikhail will fly so much that the marginal flight provides almost no benefit. By contrast, Raisa's annual flight is worth at least one month's wages. If the Russian government reallocated a flight from Mikhail to Raisa, Mikhail's loss would be less than Raisa's gain, so society as a whole would be better off. This shows that an allocation of resources is economically efficient only if all users of a product achieve the same marginal benefit.

*   *Equal marginal cost.* The second condition for efficiency is that all suppliers of an item must be operating at the same marginal cost. Suppose that the Central Planning Bureau has designated two airlines, Narodny Airways and Siberia Airlines, to serve the Novosibirsk–Moscow route. Owing to higher fuel efficiency and better allocation of personnel, however, Siberia Airlines' marginal cost on the route is 10% lower than that of Narodny Airways. In this case, society as a whole could reduce the cost of airline travel while maintaining the number of flights if Siberia Airlines were to expand its services and Narodny Airways were to shrink. This shows that an allocation of resources is economically efficient only if all suppliers operate at the same marginal cost.

*   *Marginal benefit equals marginal cost.* The final condition for efficiency ties together users and suppliers: for a resource allocation to be economically efficient,

the users' marginal benefit must balance the suppliers' marginal cost. Suppose that, in accordance with a Russian government policy of encouraging migration to Siberia, the Central Planning Bureau allocated more aircraft, fuel, and human resources to the two airlines and ordered them to increase service. To fill the extra seats, the Central Planning Bureau had to distribute free airline tickets to all factories in the Novosibirsk area. Not all the free tickets were used, which indicates that, for some passengers, the marginal benefit of flying was 0.

Under these circumstances, the marginal benefit of flying to passengers will be lower than the airlines' marginal cost. Since marginal benefit is less than marginal cost, society overall could benefit by reducing the number of flights. The cut in service will reduce the (marginal) benefit by less than it reduces the (marginal) cost. The difference between the marginal cost and the marginal benefit is a gain to society. Likewise, if the marginal benefit from some product exceeds the marginal cost of providing it, society should increase provision of that item. Accordingly, an allocation of resouces is economically efficient only if users' marginal benefit balances suppliers' marginal cost.

Philosophical Basis

We have presented the concept of economic efficiency. Let us review two aspects of this concept. The first is the distinction between economic efficiency and technical efficiency. **Technical efficiency** means providing an item at the minimum possible cost. Technical efficiency alone, however, does not imply

> Technical efficiency is the provision of an item at the minimum possible cost.

that scarce resources are being well used. For instance, an airline may be providing service at the minimum possible cost. These, however, may be flights that no one wants. The concept of economic efficiency extends beyond technical efficiency. For economic efficiency, the quantity of the item must be such that the marginal benefit equals the marginal cost.

The other important aspect of the concept of economic efficiency is that it assesses resource allocations in terms of each individual user's evaluation of the benefit. So, for instance, if Siberian residents like to fly and do not like to take the train, the concept takes these preferences as a given. By contrast, under communism, the central planners may disregard individual preferences and instead, impose their own view of what people should or should not consume. For instance, the Central Planning Bureau may dictate that Siberian workers should travel by train rather than plane or that only senior Communist party officials should be allowed to fly.

Progress Check 6A Referring to the market for oil, explain the difference between economic efficiency and technical efficiency.

Progress check

Internal Organization

Let us now see how to apply the same concept of economic efficiency within an organization. Suppose that Moonlight Paper has paper mills and forests in various locations. Paper is produced from wood pulp. Since Moonlight has multiple paper mills and forests, it must decide how to organize production at the various forests and delivery of wood to the various mills.

The concept of economic efficiency provides a guide to how Moonlight should use its scarce resources. Production will be efficient if all users achieve the same marginal benefit, all suppliers operate at the same marginal cost, and every user's marginal benefit balances every supplier's marginal cost.

Let us explain these three conditions in the context of Moonlight's production and delivery of wood. In this case, the users are the paper mills and the suppliers are the forests. The first condition for efficiency is that all users receive the same marginal benefit. This means that each of the company's paper mills must get the same profit from an additional ton of wood. If one mill could get more profit than another, the company should switch some supplies of wood to the mill that gets the higher profit. Then, the company's overall profit will be higher.

The second condition for efficiency is that all suppliers of an item must be operating at the same marginal cost. If one forest can produce wood at a lower marginal cost than another, then the company should direct the lower-cost forest to produce more and the higher-cost forest to produce less. This would increase the company's overall profit.

The final condition for efficiency is that the marginal benefit must balance the marginal cost. If the marginal benefit of wood to the paper mills is less than the marginal cost of producing wood, then the company should cut back production. The reduction in cost would be greater than the reduction in benefit, so overall profit would rise. By contrast, if the marginal benefit of wood is greater than the marginal cost, then the company should increase production. The company will maximize profit when the marginal benefit equals the marginal cost.

The concept of economic efficiency is very useful. It provides a guide to making the best use of scarce resources within individual organizations as well as across entire economies.

◂◂ 3 Adam Smith's Invisible Hand

"He intends only his own gain, and he is . . . led by an invisible hand to promote an end which was no part of his intention" (Adam Smith, *The Wealth of Nations*, vol. II, Book IV, p. 35, first published in 1776).

> The **invisible hand** that guides multiple buyers and sellers, acting independently and selfishly, to channel scarce resources into economically efficient uses, is the market price.

Although published over 200 years ago, Adam Smith's insight is no less valid today. In a competitive market, buyers and sellers, all acting independently and selfishly, will channel scarce resources into economically efficient uses. The **invisible hand** that guides the multitude of buyers and sellers is the market price. This invisible hand is a simple and practical way of achieving economic efficiency.

Figure 6.1 Air travel market

In equilibrium, the demand crosses the supply at a price of 100,000 rubles. Each consumer purchases up to the quantity where marginal benefit is 100,000 rubles. Each provider supplies the quantity where marginal cost is 100,000 rubles.

Competitive Market

Suppose that Russia privatizes airline travel and, as a result, the Novosibirsk–Moscow route becomes a perfectly competitive market. Let us see how the invisible hand will work in this market. Demand comes from individual persons and supply from airlines. Figure 6.1 shows the market equilibrium with a price of 100,000 rubles and quantity of 20,000 seats a year.

On the demand side, as we explained in chapter 2, each person will buy enough to balance his or her marginal benefit with the price of travel, and this is true for every buyer. In a perfectly competitive market, all buyers face the same price; hence, their respective marginal benefits will be equal. This is the first condition for economic efficiency. Note that, in deciding on his or her purchases, every individual is acting selfishly – no one is thinking about economic efficiency.

What about the airlines? On the supply side, as we explained in chapter 4, each airline will expand up to the point where the marginal cost of a larger scale of operations just balances the price. This scale of operations maximizes profit. Again, in a perfectly competitive market, all airlines face the same price. Thus, with each airline selfishly maximizing profits, every airline will be operating at the same marginal cost. This is the second condition for economic efficiency.

We have seen that all buyers balance marginal benefit with price and all airlines balance marginal cost with price. But, in a market equilibrium, all buyers and all airlines face the same price. Therefore, marginal benefit and marginal cost must balance. This is the third condition for economic efficiency. So, a perfectly competitive market satisfies all three requirements for economic efficiency.

This example illustrates the power of Adam Smith's "invisible hand." The market price guides multiple buyers and sellers, all acting independently and selfishly, to achieve economic efficiency.

Maximum Buyer and Seller Surplus

In discussing markets, we have used the concepts of buyer and seller surplus extensively. Let us now show that economic efficiency is equivalent to maximizing the sum of market buyer surplus and market seller surplus. Recall that economic efficiency is defined by three conditions. Let us relate each of them to buyer and seller surplus.

First, if not all users achieve the same marginal benefit, then market buyer surplus could be increased by reallocating some quantity from users with lower marginal benefit to users with higher marginal benefit. Second, if not all suppliers operate at the same marginal cost, market seller surplus could be increased if suppliers with lower marginal cost produced more and suppliers with higher marginal cost produced less. Third, if not every user's marginal benefit is equal to every supplier's marginal cost, the sum of buyer and seller surplus could be increased by reducing production if marginal cost exceeds marginal benefit or, if otherwise, by raising production.

Accordingly, economic efficiency is equivalent to maximizing the sum of market buyer and seller surplus. Moreover, since perfect competition achieves economic efficiency, it also must maximize the sum of market buyer and seller surplus.

To illustrate, consider the market for air travel in figure 6.1. Suppose that the quantity produced is 16,000 seats a year, which is less than the equilibrium quantity of 20,000. Then, by increasing the quantity to the equilibrium quantity, the sum of market buyer and seller surplus will increase by the shaded area *bca*. Likewise, if the quantity of air travel is 24,000 seats a year, which exceeds the equilibrium quantity of 20,000, then a reduction to the equilibrium quantity will increase the market buyer and seller surplus by the area *ade*. These arguments demonstrate that, with perfect competition, the market equilibrium maximizes the sum of market buyer and seller surplus.

Market System

Adam Smith's invisible hand is the market price. A price performs two roles. First, it communicates all the necessary information: the price tells buyers how much to purchase and tells sellers how much to supply. Second, it provides a concrete incentive for each buyer to purchase the quantity that balances marginal benefit with the market price: by purchasing this quantity, the buyer achieves the maximum net benefit.

Similarly, the price provides a concrete incentive for every seller to supply the quantity that balances marginal cost with the market price: By supplying this quantity, the seller maximizes its profit.

> The **market** or **price system** is the economic system in which resources are allocated through the independent decisions of buyers and sellers, guided by freely moving prices.

We give the name of **market system** or **price system** to an economic system in which resources are allocated through the independent decisions of buyers and sellers, guided by freely moving prices. The alternative names, *market system or price system*, recognize the key role of prices in markets. The role of the invisible hand in achieving economic efficiency is the intellectual foundation of the market system.

Fall of Communism

The 1917 Bolshevik Revolution established the world's first communist government in the Soviet Union. During and after World War II, communism spread through Eastern Europe and Asia. Under a communist system, the government owns all property including factories, farms, housing, and mines, and every citizen is a government employee. The government directs and manages economic activity through central planning rather than a market system.

By contrast with a market system, under communism the Central Planning Bureau must collect information about each buyer's marginal benefit and each seller's marginal cost. Then the bureau must calculate the economically efficient purchases and sales. Finally, the bureau must persuade each buyer to purchase the efficient quantity and each seller to supply the efficient quantity.

Let us note just one difficulty for the Central Planning Bureau in collecting the required information and implementing the planned quantities. Suppose that the managers and staff of some factory decide to reduce their workload. The factory could report that it lacks sufficient personnel so that the central planning bureau would allocate more funds and workers. With the additional resources, the managers and staff of that factory will have an easier time. Indeed, one of the key problems with a centrally planned system is that work incentives are very weak. Under communism, workers receive the same wages whether they work hard or slack off.

In 1978, some 60 years after the Bolshevik Revolution, Chinese leader Deng Xiao Ping replaced communist central planning in favor of "socialism with Chinese characteristics." This Chinese brand of socialism bore several hallmarks of a market system, including private property and competitive markets. Then, in just two years, between 1989 and 1990, almost all the communist governments in Eastern Europe gave way to democracy and the market system. Why did China and most of Eastern Europe abandon central planning in favor of market systems?

The invisible hand explains why China and Eastern Europe abandoned central planning. Prior to World War II, East and West Germany were a single country with the same income throughout the nation. When Germany was defeated in 1945, it was divided into a Western part that adopted a market system, and an Eastern part that came under Communist central planning. After 50 years of central planning,

East Germany had fallen far behind West Germany. It reunited with the West to regain an equal standard of living. The example of East and West Germany clearly proved the superiority of a market system in allocating resources. By switching to a market system, China and Eastern Europe hoped to replicate the economic success of West Germany and other market economies.

Progress check

Progress Check 6B   Some agricultural experts forecast that China's continuing economic and population growth will lead to severe shortages of grain. Explain how the invisible hand can help.

The Limits to Growth: 30 years afterward

By contrast with the pessimistic tenor of *The Limits to Growth*, the world did not collapse: none of the book's scary predictions has even come close to being realized. Far from presaging disaster, the sharp increases in mineral prices were a critical step by which resource markets adjusted to increasing consumption and diminishing stocks.

Consider the market for oil. On the demand side, higher prices encouraged users to conserve, switch to other sources of energy, and use alternative materials. For instance, between 1975 and 1997, the average fuel efficiency of American passenger cars rose by 55% from 13.9 to 21.5 miles per gallon.

On the supply side, higher prices stimulated producers to seek out new sources of supply, and encouraged businesses to develop new energy sources and alternative materials. Between 1973 and 1999, the world's proven reserves of oil increased by 79% from 577 to 1,033 billion barrels. Note that reserves increased even as the world continued to consume over 20 billion barrels of oil a year.

Sources: U.S. Department of Transportation, Bureau of Transportation Statistics *National Transportation Statistics 1999* (http://www.bts.gov/ntda/nts/NTS99/ch4index.html); and *BP Statistical Review of World Energy, 1999* (http://www.bp.com/worldenergy/index.htm).

◂◂ 4 Decentralized Management

We have shown that the concept of economic efficiency can guide the best use of scarce resources within individual organizations as well as across whole economies. An entire economy can apply the invisible hand to achieve economic efficiency. Let us now see how an individual organization can also apply the invisible hand.

The invisible hand in the electromagnetic spectrum: licenses for personal communications services

The Federal Communications Commission (FCC) regulates telecommunications and broadcasting in the United States. As the electromagnetic spectrum is limited, one of the FCC's major responsibilities is to allocate licenses to use frequencies for wireless telecommunications and broadcasting. Until 1994, the FCC assigned licenses by administrative fiat. Administrative law judges held hearings to decide which of the many applicants deserved the limited number of licenses. When this method proved too time consuming, the FCC turned to allocating licenses by lottery. Some lotteries attracted over 500,000 applications!

In August 1993, with a view to developing a new source of revenue, Congress mandated the FCC to award licenses by competitive auction. The FCC adopted an auction procedure suggested by Stanford University professors Paul Milgrom and Robert Wilson and University of Texas (Austin) professor Preston McAfee. In July 1994, the auction for narrowband Personal Communications Services (PCS) licenses raised $617 million, while in March 1995, the auction for broadband PCS licenses raised $7.7 billion.

There are two major differences between allocation by administrative fiat and by auction. One, as emphasized by Congress, is revenue. The other is that the auction will be much more likely to assign licenses to the applicants with the highest marginal benefit. Those applicants will be willing to pay the highest bids.

When there is a limited number of items, it is economically efficient to allocate the items to the users with the highest marginal benefit. The auction will be more likely than administrative fiat to allocate licenses in an economically efficient way.

Source: Peter C. Cramton, "Money out of Thin Air: the Nationwide Narrowband PCS Auction," *Journal of Economics and Management Strategy* 4, (1995) pp. 267–343.

Internal Market

Recall that Moonlight Paper needs to organize production and delivery of wood. Suppose that there is a competitive market for the wood used to make paper. One approach is central planning: the company headquarters can collect information about production costs and revenues from all the various forests and mills, and then decide how much each forest should produce and deliver to each mill.

An alternative for Moonlight is to decentralize management of wood production in the following way. Moonlight should direct the managers of every forest to maximize profit and sell wood at the market price, whether to the company's own paper mills or outside buyers. Similarly, Moonlight should direct every mill to maximize profit and allow mills the freedom to buy wood from any supplier, whether it be one of the company's own forests or an outside source.

> A **transfer price** is the price charged for the sale of an item within an organization.

Under the decentralized policy, if one of Moonlight's forests sells wood to one of Moonlight's mills, the forest must charge the market price. As this sale is a transfer within the same organization, the corresponding price is called a **transfer price**. Moonlight should set the transfer price for wood equal to the market price.

With the decentralized policy, each paper mill will buy wood up to the point that its marginal benefit balances the market price. Since all mills face the same market price, their marginal benefits will be equal. Similarly, each forest will produce up to the point that its marginal cost balances the market price. As all forests face the same market price, their marginal costs will be equal. Since the mills and the forests face the same market price, marginal benefit will be equal to marginal cost. Thus, the decentralized policy achieves the three conditions for economic efficiency within the same organization. Essentially, by decentralizing wood production, Moonlight is establishing an internal market that is integrated with the external market.

Implementation

The Moonlight example illustrates two general rules that an organization should follow when decentralizing control over an internal resource. First, if there is a competitive market for the item, the transfer price should be set equal to the market price. If there is no competitive market for the item, then the appropriate transfer price is more complicated. We discuss transfer pricing more generally in chapter 7.

> **Outsourcing** is the purchase of services or supplies from external sources.

The second general rule of decentralized management is that producing units should be allowed to sell the product to outside buyers and consuming units should be allowed to buy the product from external sources. Purchase of services or supplies from external sources is described as **outsourcing**.

To explain why the right of outsourcing is crucial, suppose that Moonlight required all mills to buy wood only from the company's own forests. Then, the forests would have market power, and as we show in chapter 8, they would charge a price above the competitive market level. As a result, the mills would no longer purchase the economically efficient quantity of wood. A similar argument shows why it is necessary to allow producing units to sell the product to outside buyers.

Any organization that uses resources or products for which there are competitive markets can apply decentralization to achieve internal economic efficiency. For example, financial institutions can apply decentralization to manage the internal use of funds, oil companies can apply the technique to manage production and use of crude oil, and auto manufacturers can apply it to manage production and use of components.

Progress Check 6C Bank Luna has two divisions, corporate lending and consumer lending. Both divisions draw funds from a central treasury. Explain how the bank can use decentralization to ensure efficient use of the funds.

Progress check

Half an invisible hand: pricing supplies at the Anderson School

In 1989, UCLA's Anderson Graduate School of Management adopted a pricing system to encourage members of the faculty and staff to economize on services and supplies. The dean's office allocated a budget for services and supplies to each academic department. In turn, the dean's office charged each department for telephone calls, photocopying paper, and other services and supplies. For administrative convenience, the dean's office excluded some basic items from the new pricing system. One of the omitted items was bond paper.

The new system was very effective in cutting the school's consumption of photocopying paper. At the same time, however, there was a significant jump in the use of bond paper and breakdown of photocopying machines. The reason soon became very obvious: because the pricing system excluded bond paper, secretaries throughout the Anderson School had switched to feeding bond paper into their photocopying machines.

‹‹ 5 Capital Markets

For economic efficiency, the marginal benefit must balance the marginal cost in all markets, including those for capital. In a market system, there are markets for shares, bonds, and loans. These markets extend beyond these organized exchanges like the New York and London Stock Exchanges to banks, other financial intermediaries, insurance companies, and individual investors.

Allocation of Capital

A **capital market** comprises buyers and sellers of investment funds in communication with one another for voluntary exchange. Capital markets channel funds from individuals and institutions with surplus funds to those in need of funds. Owing to the central role of capital markets, another name for a market system is the *capitalist* system.

A **capital market** comprises buyers and sellers of investment funds in communication with one another for voluntary exchange.

By contrast with a market system, under central planning, the government owns all property and there are no capital markets. Instead, the Central Planning Bureau allocates funds for investments. Traditional Marxist principles emphasized heavy industries such as coal mining, rail transportation, chemicals, and steel. Accordingly, the Communist governments of Eastern Europe and China directed resources toward heavy industry and away from agriculture and light industry.

For instance, in the 1950s, China's economy was predominantly agricultural and the country had relatively little capital. Nevertheless, the government depressed the prices of raw materials and capital to subsidize the development of heavy industries such as chemicals and steel. Following Deng Xiao Ping's "Four Modernizations," however, the Chinese government relaxed the emphasis on heavy industry and also encouraged private investment. The result was a boom in agriculture, light manufacturing such as toys and clothing, and services such as entertainment and travel.

We are not saying that heavy industries such as chemicals and steel are necessarily bad or that light manufacturing is necessarily good. Rather, we mean that there should be a balance between heavy industry and other sectors and that this balance should depend on the country's economic resources. For instance, Germany, one of the world's leading market economies, has the world's three largest chemical manufacturers and a substantial steel industry. It makes sense that a rich country like Germany should focus on capital-intensive businesses. By contrast, China, which has relatively more human resources, should focus on labor-intensive production. To achieve an economically efficient balance, it is best to leave the balancing process to the invisible hand.

An economy that employs central planners instead of the invisible hand runs the risk of resources being misallocated. The central planners may not be able to get all the information necessary to manage the economy, they may not be able to persuade all individuals to comply with central directives, or they may even deliberately direct resources in an inefficient way.

Progress check   **Progress Check 6D**   At one time, the Soviet Union produced more steel than the United States. The Communist government hailed this as a great achievement and proof of the Soviet Union's economic success. Do you agree?

Bankruptcy

As we have just stressed, in a market system, investment funds are channeled through capital markets. In capital markets, the supply side includes lenders as well as investors in shares and bonds. Lenders and investors devote considerable effort to assessing potential borrowers and investments. Lenders want to know potential borrowers' ability to repay. Investors want to know how much profit they can expect. Since no one can perfectly predict the future, some lenders and investors will make mistakes. A market system provides for this possibility through the institution of bankruptcy.

Bankruptcy is a set of legal provisions that take effect when an entity (person, partnership, or company) cannot meet its obligations to lenders. Bankruptcy is a distinctive feature of a market system.

> **Bankruptcy** is a set of legal provisions that take effect when an entity cannot meet its obligations to lenders.

Let us see how bankruptcy works. Suppose that Sol Trucking is over-staffed relative to its fleet, so its costs are higher than those of competing carriers. Then society would be better off with Sol's human and physical resources reallocated toward the lower-cost carriers. Society could get the same amount of service at lower cost. In a market system, Sol will accumulate losses and, eventually, reach a point where it cannot pay its bills. At that point, Sol's lenders may institute bankruptcy proceedings to close the carrier and recover their loans.

We should emphasize that, when Sol goes bankrupt, nothing will necessarily be destroyed. For instance, Sol's trucks may be sold to other carriers and Sol's personnel

The aftermath of bankruptcy: Barings PLC

Barings PLC, the 233-year-old British investment bank, collapsed on the weekend of February 26, 1995. Management disclosed that Barings' Singapore futures trading business had amassed losses of £827 million. These losses far exceeded Barings' equity capital of £325 million. Britain's central bank, the Bank of England, tried to arrange a rescue. When this attempt failed, Barings was forced into administration, which is a form of bankruptcy in the British legal system.

Some of Barings' businesses, however, were deemed to be very sound. Only 10 days later, on March 6, Internationale Nederlanden Groep NV (ING), a Dutch financial services group, purchased Barings' asset-management, banking, and securities subsidiaries. ING quickly injected £660 million of new capital, which allowed these businesses to resume normal operations.

ING, however, stopped short of buying Barings PLC, the publicly listed holding company; neither did it assume responsibility for the holding company's debt and preferred shares. Barings' ordinary shares became worthless.

ING retained most of Barings' asset-management, banking, and securities personnel. To dissuade key Barings personnel from quitting, ING even provided £95 million to pay bonuses for 1994. The new owners dismissed just two dozen senior executives, whom it held responsible for the collapse. Peter Baring and Andrew Tuckey, respectively chairman and deputy chairman of Barings, were among those who resigned or were fired.

Sources: "Gone Dutch," *Economist*, March 11, 1995, p. 89; "ING Baring Unit is Denied Deals by U.K. Firms," *Asian Wall Street Journal*, March 20, 1995, p. 1; "ING Drops Axe on 21 at Barings," *South China Morning Post*, May 2, 1995, Business, p. 12.

No way out: business in India

Although India encourages private enterprise, the government restricts some rights to which businesses in other countries are accustomed. Under Indian labor laws, a business must get official permission to dismiss workers or shut down. For fear of powerful labor unions, however, the government is rarely willing to grant such permission.

This means that, even when business prospects are poor, investors cannot shut down and instead must accumulate losses until they have exhausted their entire capital. For example, in the center of Bombay, a large number of old textile mills occupy some of the most expensive real estate in the world. An economically efficient solution would be to relocate the mills to areas with cheaper land and cheaper labor, then to redevelop their present sites for commercial or residential use. Without government permission, however, the mills cannot move, and they continue to creak along.

Not only do India's labor laws prevent reallocation of resources, they also deter new investment. In a system where investors lack the option of shutting down, the risk of making an investment is higher and hence the supply of new investment is smaller.

Sources: "How to Keep Investors Out," *Economist*, June 11, 1994, p. 27; "The Most Expensive Slum in the World," *Economist*, May 6, 1995, pp. 29–30.

will find employment elsewhere. Indeed, these movements are necessary steps in the process of reallocating Sol's human and physical resources to more effective management.

Although employees in weak businesses live in fear of bankruptcy, the institution of bankruptcy is good from a social standpoint. Bankruptcy helps to improve the allocation of resources. Indeed, one of the conditions for a market to be perfectly competitive is that there be no barriers to exit. The institution of bankruptcy facilitates exit and hence helps to make a market more competitive.

By contrast, in a centrally planned economy, the government supports all enterprises, whether they make profits or losses: bankruptcy does not exist. Consequently, there is no pressure to reallocate resources from inefficient to efficient uses.

◂◂ 6 Price Ceilings

We have discussed two extreme models of economic management: central planning and the market system. Even within a market system, however, the government may choose to intervene with the market outcome. The intervention may take the form of controls on prices or taxes. Let us now analyze the effects of government controls on prices.

Rent Control

Housing is considered a necessity, and so, it attracts considerable government attention. The supply of housing tends to be fairly inelastic especially in the short run. When rising incomes and population growth cause demand to increase, the result is rapid increases in rents and a shortage of "affordable" housing.

One response to rising rents is rent control. Rent control, so the argument goes, makes housing more affordable and protects poor tenants from rapacious landlords. In reality, does rent control relieve shortages of affordable housing? Who benefits from rent control and who loses?

New York and Los Angeles are just two of the many American cities that regulate residential rents. Supposing that New York's apartment market were perfectly competitive, let us apply demand–supply analysis to learn the effects of New York's rent control. First, we draw the demand for residential rental units and then the supply of rental units in figure 6.2. Suppose that the equilibrium is at point *b*, with a rental of $1,000 per month and 300,000 units rented.

Rent control is a **price ceiling**: it sets an upper limit to the rent that landlords can charge and renters can pay. If the limit exceeds the free-market equilibrium rent, then the rent control is irrelevant. The rent control bites only when the limit falls below the free-market equilibrium rent.

> A **price ceiling** is an upper limit to the price that sellers can charge and buyers can pay.

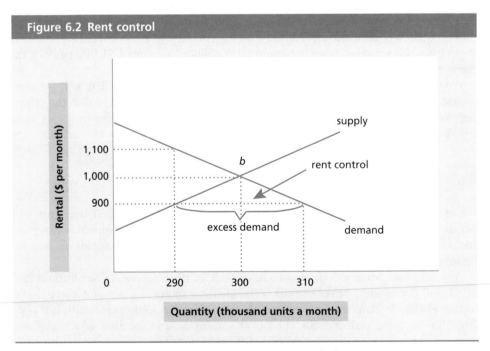

Figure 6.2 Rent control

The rent control of $900 per month results in excess demand of 20,000 units.

Suppose that the typical controlled rent is 10% below the free-market equilibrium. To illustrate this, on figure 6.2, we mark the point $900 on the monthly rent axis and draw a horizontal line outward. This $900 line first crosses the supply curve, showing that landlords will supply 290,000 units at $900 per month. Then the $900 line crosses the demand curve, showing that renters will demand 310,000 units at $900 per month.

At a rent of $900 per month, quantity demanded exceeds quantity supplied by 310,000 − 290,000 = 20,000 units per month. There is an excess demand of 20,000 units per month. So, far from alleviating the shortage of affordable housing, rent control exacerbates the problem by stimulating demand and discouraging supply. The result is that the number of renters seeking housing exceeds available quantity. In general, whenever the government sets a price ceiling below the free-market equilibrium, there will be excess demand.

What determines the degree of shortage? In our example, a 10% reduction in rent from $1,000 to $900 per month caused landlords to reduce the quantity supplied by 3.33% from 300,000 to 290,000 units per month. So, the price elasticity of supply at a rent of $1,000 was 3.33/10 = 0.33.

Suppose, instead, that the price elasticity of supply had been 0.5. Then the 10% reduction in rent would have caused landlords to change quantity supplied by 0.5 × (−10)%; that is, reduce it by 5%. This means that the number of units available at a $900 per month rent would be 0.95 × 300,000 = 285,000 units. Generally, the more elastic is the supply, the greater will be the shortage. Similarly, the more elastic is the demand, the greater the shortage that rent controls will create.

The amount of excess demand (or shortage) also depends on the controlled rent. The higher the controlled rent, the more units landlords will supply and the fewer units renters will demand; hence, the excess demand will be smaller. In particular, if the control is set at or above the free-market equilibrium rate of $1,000 per month, there will be no excess demand.

Whenever there is a shift in demand or supply, buyers and sellers will be concerned about the effects on prices and sales. From chapter 5, we know that the effects depend on the elasticities of demand and supply. We have just shown the same is true when the government sets a price ceiling.

Gains and Losses

When the government sets a price ceiling, an important concern is the costs and benefits to buyers and sellers. For instance, in the case of rent control, who gains and who loses? We can apply the concepts of buyer and seller surplus to address these questions.

First, consider renters. Referring to figure 6.3, at the free-market equilibrium rate of $1,000 per month, buyer surplus is the area *acb* under the demand curve down to the $1,000 level. With rent control, the rent drops to $900 per month but only 290,000 units are available. So, the buyer surplus is now the area *afed* under the demand curve down to the rental of $900 per month and limited by the quantity of 290,000 units per month.

Figure 6.3 Buyer surplus

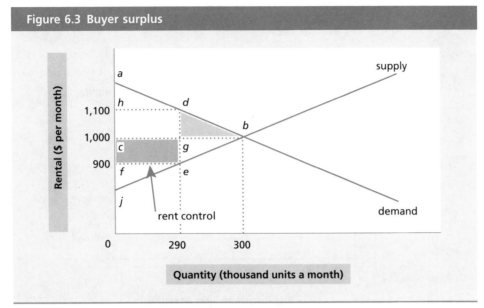

The rent control increases buyer surplus by the area *cfeg* as some tenants get units for $100 a month lower rent. The rent control reduces buyer surplus by the area *dgb* because some renters who are willing to pay $1,000 per month cannot get housing.

Thus, as a result of rent control, buyer surplus increases by the shaded area *cfeg* as some tenants get units for $100 a month less than before. On the other hand, buyer surplus falls by shaded area *dgb* as some renters who are willing to pay $1,000 per month cannot get housing. Our analysis indicates that some renters benefit from rent control, while others lose. The gains may outweigh the losses or they may be smaller than the losses. In general, we cannot say whether buyer surplus will rise or drop on a net basis.

The picture on the supply side is much simpler. Referring to figure 6.4, at the free-market equilibrium, seller surplus is the area *cjb* above the supply curve up to the $1,000 level. With rent control, the rent drops to $900 per month and landlords cut back quantity supplied to 290,000 units. Seller surplus now is the area *fje* above the supply curve up to the $900 level. Hence, seller surplus clearly falls: some landlords withdraw from the market (shaded area *geb*) and landlords who continue in business receive $100 less rent (shaded area *cfeg*). So, seller surplus unequivocally falls.

Deadweight Loss

The buyer surplus increases by the shaded area *cfeg* and falls by the shaded area *dgb*. So, part of the landlords' loss, the shaded area *cfeg*, is the tenants' gain: the

Figure 6.4 Seller surplus

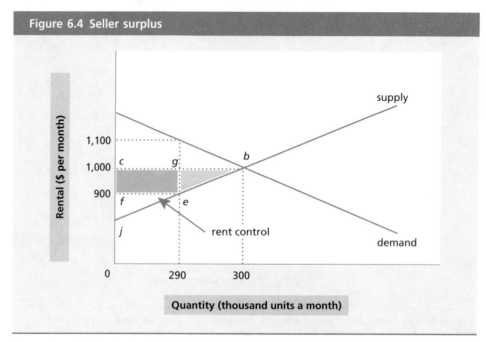

The rent control reduces seller surplus by the shaded area *geb* as some landlords withdraw from the market and by the shaded area *cfeg* as other landlords who continue in business receive $100 less rent.

> A **deadweight loss** is any loss of buyer or seller surplus that is not transferred to another party.

reduction in rent for the units that continue in the market is a pure transfer from landlords to tenants. Part of the landlords' loss, the shaded area *geb*, however, is a complete loss in the sense that it does not show up as a gain to renters.

This difference is called a **deadweight loss**. A *deadweight loss* is any loss of buyer surplus or seller surplus that is not transferred to another party. Buyer surplus falls by the shaded area *dgb*. This loss does not accrue to any other party; hence, it is also a deadweight loss. Accordingly, the total deadweight loss arising from the rent control is the shaded areas *dgb* and *geb*. Figure 6.5 shows the deadweight loss.

Generally, a deadweight loss arises whenever sellers are willing to provide an item at a price that buyers are willing to pay and that provision does not occur. In the case of the rent control, figure 6.5 shows that, between the quantities of 290,000 and 300,000, landlords are willing to rent 10,000 units at a marginal cost lower than the corresponding marginal benefit to renters. As a result of the rent control, however, these units are not provided. Accordingly, there is a deadweight loss.

When the marginal benefit is not equal to the marginal cost, the allocation of resources violates the third condition for economic efficiency. This suggests another way to calculate the deadweight loss: it is the sum of the differences between the buyers' marginal benefits and the sellers' marginal costs for all the units that are not provided.

Figure 6.5 Deadweight loss

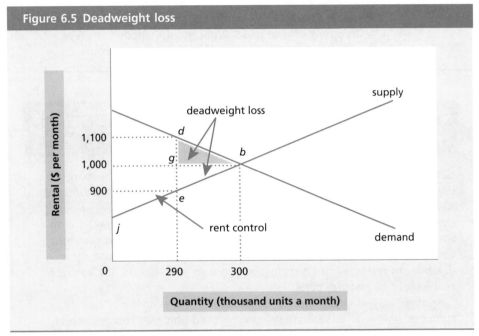

Rent control causes a deadweight loss of the shaded areas *dgb* and *geb*. The more inelastic demand is, the larger the area *dbg* will be. The more elastic supply is, the larger the area *geb* will be.

Price Elasticities

The magnitude of the deadweight losses depends on the price elasticities of demand and supply. In the case of the rent control, referring to figure 6.5, given that the quantity supplied falls to 290,000 units, area *dgb* will be larger the more inelastic is demand. Intuitively, the less sensitive renters are to rent increases, the greater will be the pain that they will suffer from having fewer units to rent.

Similarly, the more elastic the supply, the greater will be the cut in quantity supplied resulting from the 10% rent cut. The bigger the cut in quantity supplied, the larger will be area *geb*. Intuitively, the more sensitive are landlords to a cut in rent, the more units they will take off the market; hence, the fewer the units there will be for renters.

The rent control example highlights a general point: The deadweight loss will be relatively larger when demand is more inelastic or supply is more elastic. Deadweight losses arise whenever sellers are willing to provide an item at a price buyers are willing to pay and that provision does not occur. Deadweight losses are a serious cost of government interference with a competitive market.

Progress Check 6E In figure 6.5, mark the deadweight loss with a rent control of $800 per month. Shade the areas representing the changes in buyer and seller surplus.

Circumventing rent control: obituary pages and key money

Generally, when a market is out of free-market equilibrium, the marginal benefit is not equal to the marginal cost. Then, there is an opportunity to make a profit by resolving the economic inefficiency. In the case of rent control, landlords and renters resort to a number of creative mechanisms. Some New Yorkers regularly scan newspaper obituary pages to spot rent-controlled units that might become available. These activities are deadweight losses, as the costs incurred in such activities do not accrue as a benefit to another party.

Another way of circumventing rent control is "key money." The owner or holder of a lease on a rent-controlled unit may charge a hefty nonrefundable fee to change the locks on the unit. Key money is a pure transfer from tenants to landlords, so it is not a deadweight loss. To the extent that renters can indirectly pay more than the regulated rent, the quantity of units supplied will be increased. Key money is an illicit way of pushing the rent, and hence the quantity of units supplied to the free market equilibrium. To the extent that key money is effective in increasing the number of apartments for rent, it reduces the deadweight loss.

Price ceilings and the profitability of China's state-owned enterprises

Shanghai Petrochemical is listed on the Hong Kong and New York Stock Exchanges. In 1993, the company was among the first of China's state-owned enterprises to be restructured and listed on an international exchange. The following year, securities analysts applauded when the company announced its annual results. The company had achieved a 73% increase in profit to 1.78 billion yuan.

A closer look at the company, however, provided a different picture. In 1994, Shanghai Petrochemical was able to raise prices of synthetic fibers by 30–35%, as the Chinese government relaxed restrictions on the prices of chemicals.

Crude oil accounted for almost half of Shanghai Petrochemical's costs. The Chinese government supplied Shanghai Petrochemical with 4.5 million metric tons of crude at a government-controlled price of 689 yuan. Compared with the free-market price of 1,100 yuan, this was an implicit subsidy of 1.85 billion yuan. When this subsidy was deducted from the company's reported profit of 1.78 billion yuan, the financial picture did not look so rosy after all. In fact, the company's profitability depended critically on continued government support.

Shanghai Petrochemical's use of oil was not economically efficient. It was using oil at a price 35% below the market price that other manufacturers had to pay. Hence, the allocation of oil did not meet the equal marginal benefit condition for economic efficiency.

Source: I. P. L. Png and Changqi Wu, "A Tale of Two Companies," *Far Eastern Economic Review*, October 12, 1995, p. 39.

◂◂ 7 Price Floors

Rent control is an example of a price ceiling. Another way by which governments intervene in markets is to set a floor below the market price. A **price floor** is a lower limit to the price that sellers can charge and buyers can pay. A minimum wage is a price floor in the labor market. In the United States, the federal government stipulates a minimum wage that applies throughout the country. As table 6.1 shows, individual states may set minimum

> A **price floor** is a lower limit to the price that sellers can charge and buyers can pay.

Table 6.1 State minimum wages

State	Minimum Wage ($ per hour)
California	5.75
District of Columbia	6.15
Hawaii	5.25
Massachusetts	6.00
Oregon	6.50
Washington	6.50
Federal	5.15

Source: U.S. Department of Labor.

wages above the federal minimum. Some Asian and many European countries also set minimum wages.

Minimum Wage

How does a minimum wage affect wages, earnings, and employment? We use demand–supply analysis to address these questions. We will see that, under some conditions, a minimum wage can reduce the total earnings of workers.

Suppose that the market for labor is perfectly competitive. In figure 6.6, we mark the wage rate on the vertical axis and quantity of labor on the horizontal axis. Then we draw employers' demand for labor and workers' supply of labor. Suppose that the equilibrium is at point b, with a wage is $4.00 per hour and that, at that wage, employment is 3 billion worker-hours a week.

To have any effect, the minimum wage must exceed the free-market equilibrium. Suppose that the minimum wage is $4.20 per hour, which is 5% above the equilibrium wage. The higher the wage rate, the less labor employers will want to hire. Suppose that the elasticity of labor demand with respect to the wage is −0.6. Then, the rise in the wage to $4.20 per hour will change the quantity of labor demanded

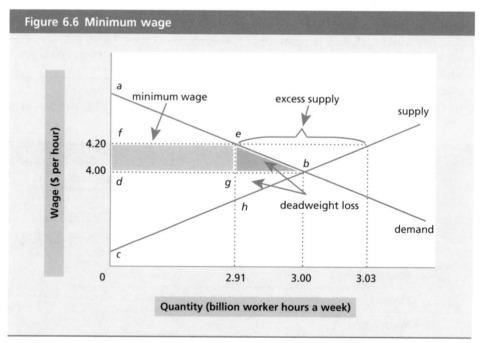

Figure 6.6 Minimum wage

The minimum wage of $4.20 results in excess supply of 120 million worker-hours a week and deadweight loss equal to area *egb* and *ghb*.

by $-0.6 \times 5 = -3\%$; that is, reduce it by 3%. Hence, referring to figure 6.6, at the wage of $4.20 per hour, the quantity of labor demanded would be 2.91 billion worker-hours.

A higher wage, however, increases the quantity supplied as more people enter the labor force and part-timers switch to full-time work. Suppose that the elasticity of labor supply with respect to the wage is 0.2. Then, the 5% wage increase will increase the quantity of labor supplied by $0.2 \times 5 = 1\%$. Hence, referring to figure 6.6, at the wage of $4.20 per hour, the quantity supplied of labor is 3.03 billion worker-hours. The result of the minimum wage is excess supply of $3.03 - 2.91 = 0.12$ billion worker-hours or 120 million worker-hours.

Compared with the free-market equilibrium, the wage is higher but total employment is lower. Let us consider the impact on total earnings. Total earnings equal the wage multiplied by number of hours worked. With a free market, total earnings are $4.00 \times 3.0 = \$12$ billion a week. With the $4.20 minimum wage, total earnings are $4.20 \times 2.91 = \$12.22$ billion, which is $220 million higher than the free-market equilibrium.

Suppose, however, that the demand for labor is more elastic. Specifically, suppose that the wage elasticity is -1.2. Then, the 5% increase in the minimum wage will cause the quantity demanded of labor to fall by $1.2 \times 5 = 6\%$. With a 6% reduction, the quantity demanded of labor will become 2.82 billion worker-hours a week. Then, total earnings with the minimum wage would be $\$4.20 \times 2.82 = \$11.844$ billion a week. As calculated previously, with a free market, total earnings are $12 billion a week. Hence, the minimum wage reduces total earnings by $12 - 11.844 = \$0.156$ billion or $156 million a week.

This example shows that whether a minimum wage raises or reduces total earnings depends on the wage elasticity of demand for labor. The more elastic is the demand for labor, the more likely is it that a minimum wage will reduce total earnings. By contrast, if the demand for labor is inelastic, a minimum wage will increase total earnings.

Gains and Losses

Let us also consider the costs and benefits of the minimum wage in terms of buyer and seller surplus. In the labor market, the buyers are businesses and the sellers are people. Referring to figure 6.6, at the free-market equilibrium, the buyer surplus is area *adb*. With the minimum wage, the buyer surplus becomes the area *afe*. Hence, the minimum wage reduces buyer surplus by the shaded area *fdge* and the shaded area *egb*.

At the free market equilibrium, the seller surplus is area *dcb*. With the minimum wage, the seller surplus becomes the area under the wage of $4.20 and above the supply curve up to the quantity that employers demand, that is, 2.91 billion hours a week. This area is *fche*. Hence, as a result of the minimum wage, the seller surplus falls by the area *ghb*, as some workers lose employment, and increases by the area *fdge*, as those workers who retain employment gain a higher wage.

Accordingly, the minimum wage may increase or reduce seller surplus, depending on whether area *fdge* is greater or smaller than area *ghb*. Essentially, the less elastic the demand for labor, the more likely it is that the minimum wage will increase seller surplus.

Part of the buyers' loss of surplus (shaded area *fdge*) accrues to sellers in the form of a higher wage. The other part (shaded area *egb*), is a deadweight loss. There is also deadweight loss (shaded area *ghb*) on the seller side. The total deadweight loss is the areas *egb* and *ghb*.

Intuitively, the deadweight loss arises because workers willing to provide labor at a wage of $4.00, which buyers are willing to pay, cannot provide that labor. Hence, another way to calculate the deadweight loss is the sum of the differences between the buyers' marginal benefits and the sellers' marginal costs for all the work that is not provided.

The deadweight loss will be relatively larger when demand is more elastic or supply is more inelastic. The more sensitive employers are to an increase in the wage, the more they will cut back employment. The less sensitive workers are to wage changes, the greater will be the pain that they will suffer from having less employment.

Progress check   **Progress Check 6F**   In figure 6.6, mark the deadweight loss with a minimum wage of $4.50 per hour. Compare it with the deadweight loss at the $4.20 minimum.

Heterogeneous Labor

So far, we have treated all labor as homogeneous and, hence, traded in a single market. Realistically, there are many different grades of labor. The equilibrium wage for skilled labor is much higher than the legal minimum, so the minimum wage does not have a significant direct effect on the market for skilled labor.

There may be an indirect effect, however. By raising the cost of low-skilled labor, the minimum wage encourages employers to substitute away from low-skilled labor toward more automated operations. This will increase the demand for skilled labor. Thus, while an increase in the minimum wage will reduce employment of low-skilled labor, it may increase the employment of skilled labor.

In most countries, a relatively larger proportion of skilled workers join unions. Accordingly, unions tend to represent the interests of skilled workers. Our explanation of the effect of a minimum wage on the demand for skilled labor explains why unions often favor increases in the minimum wage, even though their members earn far more than the minimum.

PURPA and the market for wind-generated electricity

The Public Utility Regulatory Policies Act (PURPA) of 1978 required electric power utilities to purchase (wholesale) electricity at a fixed price from producers of renewable energy. PURPA gave birth to the California wind power industry. Under the terms of state-mandated contracts, utilities had to buy electricity at a wholesale purchase price that was fixed on the assumption that the price of oil would exceed $30 per barrel. By 1985, a total of 1,000 megawatts of wind-powered electric generating capacity had been installed, mainly in the Tehachapi and Altamont Passes.

Meanwhile, the price of oil fell to a low of $10.91 per barrel in July 1986, and then oscillated between $10 and $20 over the next ten years. In the mid-1990s, one of California's major utilities, Pacific Gas and Electric, was paying over 7 cents per kilowatt hour for wind-generated electricity when it could generate electricity by conventional means for less than 3 cents per kilowatt hour.

With cheap oil, the market demand from electric power utilities for wind-generated electricity was low. In a free market equilibrium, the price of electricity generated by wind power would not diverge by much from that of electricity generated by other means. However, by fixing the price of wind-generated electricity above the market equilibrium, PURPA stimulated an excess supply.

California electric power utilities incurred about $1 billion a year in additional costs to pay for electricity from renewable energy producers under the state-mandated contracts. These costs were passed on to their business and residential consumers.

Source: Richard T. Stuebi, "The Rise, Fall and Rebirth of Wind Energy in California: Lessons for the Renewable Energy Industry," *NextWave Energy*, March 1999.

◀◀ 8 Taxes

Governments all over the world depend on tax revenues to support public services such as national defense, administration of justice, and public health. Some taxes are levied on consumers, others on businesses, and some are levied on both. For instance, the United States government imposes an airport tax on airlines for every passenger that they carry. By contrast, many Asian governments collect the airport tax from the passenger. What difference would it make if the U.S. government switched to the Asian system?

To address this question, we must first understand the impact of taxes on a market. Let us apply the demand–supply framework to investigate the effect of taxes on market price and quantity. Specifically, suppose that the U.S. government levies a $10 tax on international airline tickets. How would this affect the market for air travel between Chicago and London?

Buyer's vis-à-vis Seller's Price

We assume that the market is perfectly competitive. The demand comes from business and leisure travelers, while American and foreign airlines provide the supply. Since this market is subject to a tax, it is necessary to make one change to the usual demand–supply analysis. We must distinguish the price that buyers pay (buyer's price) from the price that sellers receive (seller's price). The seller's price is the buyer's price minus the amount of the tax.

We draw the demand and supply curves in figure 6.7. Suppose that, initially, there is no tax on airline tickets and the equilibrium is at point *b*, with a price of $800. Since there is no tax, $800 is the buyer's price as well as the seller's price. At the price of $800, airlines sell 920,000 tickets a year.

Now the federal government requires airlines to pay a tax of $10 on each ticket. This raises the marginal cost of delivering economy class air travel between Chicago and London by $10. Note that the same $10 applies, regardless of the number of

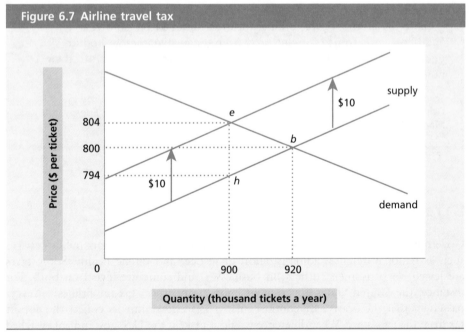

Figure 6.7 Airline travel tax

The tax of $10 per ticket raises the marginal cost of supplying air travel, increases the buyer's price to $804, and reduces the quantity to 900,000 tickets a year.

tickets that the airlines sell. Accordingly, the $10 tax increases the airlines' marginal cost at all quantities of tickets. Graphically, in figure 6.7, we represent the tax by shifting the entire supply curve up by $10.

As a result of the tax, there will be a new equilibrium at point *e*, with a price of $804 and quantity of 900,000 tickets a year. The price is higher and the quantity of travel is smaller. Now that there is a tax, the buyer's price differs from the seller's price. The buyer's price is $804, while the seller's price is the buyer's price less the $10 tax, or $794. In the new equilibrium, the seller's price of $794 is lower than the original seller's price with no tax, which was $800.

Incidence

What determines the extent to which the buyer's price increases, the seller's price falls, and the quantity falls? In general, the effect on prices and quantity depends on the price elasticities of demand and supply. With moderate demand and supply elasticities, the buyer's price will rise by less than the amount of the tax, the seller's price will drop by less than the amount of the tax, and the quantity will fall by some amount.

Referring to figure 6.8, the buyer's price rises to $804, the seller's price falls to $794, and the quantity falls to 900,000 tickets. Recall from chapter 5 that *incidence*

Figure 6.8 Gains and losses from tax

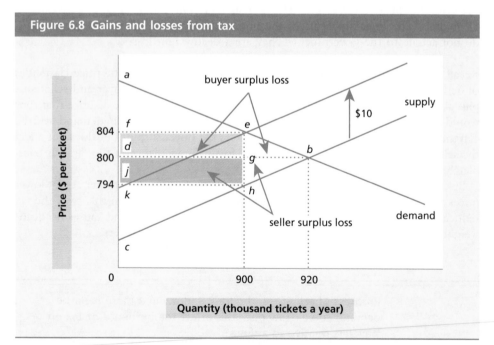

The tax reduces buyer surplus by the shaded area *egb* because travelers make fewer trips and by the shaded area *fdge* because travelers must pay $4 more. The tax also reduces seller surplus by the shaded area *ghb* because airlines sell fewer tickets and by the shaded area *djhg* because they receive $6 less for each ticket.

Tax incidence describes the actual burden of a tax in terms of the price or buyer/seller surplus.

is the change in the price for buyer or seller resulting from shift in demand or supply or some other condition. In the same way, tax experts use **tax incidence** to describe the actual burden of a tax. In our example, the change in the buyer's price is $804 − $800 = $4, hence, the incidence on the demand side is $4. The change in the seller's price is $800 − $794 = $6, so the incidence on the supply side is $6.

Another way of looking at incidence is to consider the effect on buyer and seller surplus. Before the tax, the buyer surplus was area *adb*, and after the tax, the buyer surplus is area *afe*. Accordingly, the tax affects the buyer surplus in two ways. First, it reduces the buyer surplus by the area *egb* because travelers make fewer trips. Second, it reduces the buyer surplus by the shaded area *fdge* because they must pay $4 more for each trip that they do make.

Before the tax, the seller surplus was area *dcb*, and after the tax, the seller surplus is area *fke*. By geometry, area *fke* is exactly equal to area *jch*. So, effectively, the tax affects the seller surplus by the difference between areas *dcb* and *jch*. This means that the tax affects the seller surplus in two ways. First, it reduces the seller surplus by the area *ghb* because airlines sell fewer tickets. Second, it also reduces the seller surplus by the shaded area *djhg* because they receive $6 less for each ticket that they do sell.

Part of the loss of buyer and seller surplus, the shaded areas *fdge* and *djhg*, accrue to the government as tax revenue. These areas represent a sum of $10 × 900,000 = $9 million. The remaining part of the buyer and seller loss, the areas *egb* and *ghb*, do not accrue to the government. They are a deadweight loss.

Recall that the effect of a tax on price and quantity depends on the price elasticities of demand and supply. Accordingly, the effect of a tax on the buyer and seller surplus also depends on these elasticities. If travelers are so insensitive to price that they would rather accept higher prices than cut back on flying, then demand will be extremely inelastic. In this case, the tax reduces the buyer surplus but does not affect the seller surplus and causes no deadweight loss. The incidence of the tax falls completely on the buyers.

By contrast, if airlines are so insensitive to price that they would rather accept lower prices than cut back on sales, then supply is extremely inelastic. In this case, the tax reduces the seller surplus but does not affect the buyer surplus and causes no deadweight loss. The incidence of the tax falls completely on the sellers.

Progress check	**Progress Check 6G** In figure 6.8, draw in a more inelastic demand curve. How does this affect the incidence of tax on travelers relative to airlines?

Ecology taxes on gasoline

European governments levy heavy taxes to discourage gasoline consumption. At the time of writing, taxes accounted for 65–77% of the retail gasoline price in France, Italy, and the United Kingdom. In Germany, the government of Chancellor Gerhard Schroeder imposed a phased "ecology tax" on gasoline, with the tax rising by 6 pfennig per liter in each phase. By contrast, the average tax in the United States is only 24%, with the precise amount varying with differences in state sales taxes and state gasoline duties.

The effectiveness of a gasoline tax in reducing consumption depends on the price elasticity of demand. Over a hundred studies of the demand for gasoline have been published. The median estimate of the short-run price elasticity of demand is −0.23. This suggests that a tax that raises the price of gasoline by 1% would reduce consumption by 0.23%.

Further, the demand for gasoline is significantly less elastic in the United States than Europe. This suggests that a gasoline tax would be relatively less effective in reducing short-run consumption in the United States.

The median estimate of the long-run price elasticity of demand is −0.43. This suggests that a tax that raises the price of gasoline by 1% would reduce consumption by 0.43%. Hence, a gasoline tax will be more effective in reducing consumption in the long run than the short run. There is, however, no significant difference in the long-run elasticity of demand between the United States and Europe.

Source: Molly Esprey, "Gasoline Demand Revisited: an International Meta-analysis of Elasticities," *Energy Economics* 20, no. 3 (June 1998), pp. 273–95.

The ideal tax?

From a social standpoint, the cost of raising revenue through taxes is the resulting deadweight loss. The ideal tax is one that causes no deadweight loss. Generally, the deadweight loss from a tax will be smaller if the demand and the supply are less elastic. Accordingly, governments should focus taxes on items for which either demand or supply is relatively inelastic.

The supply of land is quite inelastic. If there is a fall in the price of land, the quantity supplied will not fall by very much. Over the long term, the supply may be somewhat elastic as landowners reduce investments in drainage and protection against erosion. But, relative to most other items, the supply of land is quite inelastic. Accordingly, a tax on land ownership would be a relatively efficient way to raise revenue.

Collecting Taxes

We are now ready to address the introductory question of the effects of a switch to collecting an airport tax from passengers rather than airlines. This is just one specific case of the general issue of whether a tax should be imposed on the buyers or the sellers.

Obviously, there may be differences in administrative costs and perhaps psychological differences between collecting the tax from passengers rather than airlines. For instance, since there are relatively fewer airlines than passengers, it may be less costly to collect the tax from airlines.

Aside from administrative and psychological differences, however, we claim that the effect of a tax will be the same, whether it is collected from the buyers or the sellers. To explain this point, let us consider again the effect of a $10 tax on the market for economy class air travel between Chicago and London. Figure 6.7 showed the U.S. practice, which is to collect the tax from airlines. The $10 tax raised the buyer's price to $804, reduced the seller's price to $794, and reduced travel to 900,000 tickets. By contrast with the USA, many Asian governments collect air travel taxes from travelers.

Suppose that the U.S. government were to adopt the Asian method of collecting the tax from travelers. Then, flying from Chicago to London would mean paying a

Figure 6.9 Collecting the air travel tax from passengers

The $10 tax reduces travelers' willingness to pay. The new buyer's price, the seller's price, and the quantity of tickets are the same whether the government collects the tax from airlines or travelers.

price to an airline and the $10 tax to the government. The $10 tax reduces travelers' willingness to pay airlines at all quantities of tickets. Graphically, in figure 6.9, we represent the tax by shifting the entire demand curve down by $10. As a result of the tax, the equilibrium shifts from the original point *b* to a new point *t*: both the seller's price and the quantity of tickets drop.

Now compare triangle *ehb* in figure 6.7 with triangle *utb* in figure 6.9. Point *b* is common to both triangles, both lines *eh* and *ut* represent $10, both *be* and *bu* are segments of the original demand curve, and both *hb* and *tb* are segments of the original supply curve. So, the two triangles must be identical. This means the new buyer's price, the seller's price, and the quantity of tickets are the same whether the government collects the tax from the airlines or travelers.

To reiterate, regardless of who pays the tax, the outcome is identical. Our demand–supply analysis simply reflects common sense. If airlines pay the tax, the increase in costs will lead them to charge higher prices to the extent that airlines are not willing to accept lower prices and travelers are willing to absorb higher prices. By contrast, if passengers pay the tax, they would pay less in price to airlines to the extent that airlines are willing to accept lower prices and travelers are not willing to bear higher prices.

We have shown that the incidence on passengers relative to airlines does not depend on which side pays the tax. Incidence depends only on the price elasticities of demand and supply. Generally, the effect of a tax will be the same, whether it is collected from the buyers or the sellers.

◂ 9 Summary

The central idea in this chapter was Adam Smith's invisible hand. Free-market competition will ensure that the allocation of resources is economically efficient. Although the buyers and sellers act selfishly, the net outcome is at least as good as the best efforts of the most enlightened and well-informed central planner. This applies to markets for goods and services as well as capital.

The same principle applies within an organization. Through decentralization, management can achieve efficient use of scarce internal resources. This means charging a transfer price for items produced and consumed within the organization.

Government policies such as price ceilings, price floors, and taxes cause deadweight losses and impede economic efficiency. The extent of these deadweight losses depends on the price elasticities of demand and supply. There will be no deadweight loss if either the demand or the supply is extremely inelastic.

Key Concepts

economically efficient	transfer price	price ceiling
technical efficiency	outsourcing	deadweight loss
invisible hand	capital market	price floor
market or price system	bankruptcy	tax incidence

Further Reading

Steven E. Landsburg provides a detailed analysis of market efficiency in chapter 9, "Knowledge and Information," of *Price* *Theory and Applications*, 4th ed. (South-Western College Publishing, 1998).

Review Questions

1. In 1987, Soviet leader Mikhail Gorbachev complained that children were kicking bread in games of football. Consider this observation in terms of the conditions for economic efficiency.

2. The external auditor of the local school system has found that some schools are paying 20% more for cleaning services than other schools in the same area. Which condition of economic efficiency is being violated?

3. Consider a competitive labor market. Explain how the invisible hand ensures that the allocation of labor is economically efficient.

4. If no resources were scarce, would central planning be less effective than a market system?

5. Using relevant examples, explain the concept of a transfer price.

6. Venus Fruit produces apples that the company uses to make juice as well as for sale to external customers. The apple market is perfectly competitive. How much should Venus charge the juice division for apples?

7. Super Pied is considering where to establish a new rubber shoe factory. Super Pied will produce for two years. If the demand is insufficient, it will shut down and move the equipment elsewhere. Country A has an effective bankruptcy law, while country B does not allow factories to shut down. Which country has higher barriers to exit?

8. Consider a competitive capital market. Explain how the invisible hand ensures that the allocation of capital is economically efficient.

9. Using relevant examples, explain the differences between
   (a) a price floor;
   (b) a price ceiling.

10. Explain why deadweight losses from rent controls will be larger
    (a) if demand is more inelastic;
    (b) if supply is more elastic.

11. Suppose that the government is planning to raise the minimum wage. Will the increase in the minimum wage have a greater effect on employment among lawyers or janitors?

12. Explain why deadweight losses from a minimum wage will be larger
    (a) if demand is more elastic;
    (b) if supply is more inelastic.

13. Explain the difference between the payment and incidence of a gasoline tax.

14. In the United States, the federal income tax applies to all earned income exceeding a specific threshold. Does the income tax affect economic efficiency in the labor market? If so, explain how.

15. The market for telephones is competitive. Demand is very inelastic, while supply from factories in Asia is very elastic. Suppose that the government were to impose a tax on telephones. How much will this affect a manufacturer of telephones?

Discussion Questions

1. Luna Mining operates silver mines in Colorado and Peru. Until recently, corporate headquarters set production targets for each mine based on average production costs. Then, on the recommendation of a management consultant, the company changed its production policy. Under the new policy, each mine must aim to maximize profits given the prevailing price of silver.
   (a) Under Luna Mining's old production policy, which condition(s) for economic efficiency might not be satisfied?
   (b) Does the new production policy improve economic efficiency?
   (c) Explain the role of price under the new policy.

2. Tickets to popular musical and sporting events, like the U2 world tour and the Super Bowl, often sell out. Devoted fans must either spend long hours waiting in line for a limited supply of tickets or pay a premium price to scalpers or touts. Scalpers and touts buy tickets to resell.
   (a) When tickets sell out, which condition(s) for economic efficiency might not be satisfied?
   (b) Do scalpers and touts improve economic efficiency?

3. In January 1984, a court decree required telecommunications monopoly AT&T to focus on long-distance service and divest the Bell operating companies (BOCs) through which it provided local telephone service. At the time, AT&T's principal long-distance competitor was MCI. The newly independent BOCs asked their subscribers to select a long-distance carrier. Millions of subscribers, however, did not bother to express a preference. A major issue for the Federal Communications Commission (FCC) was what to do with these "silent" subscribers.
   (a) *Default Plan.* One theory proposed to the FCC was that the silent subscribers were implicitly choosing the incumbent carrier, AT&T. Which long-distance carrier does this proposal favor?

(b) *Market Share Plan.* Another proposal to the FCC was to consider the choices of the subscribers who did exercise a preference and then to allocate the silent subscribers in the same proportions among the various carriers. Would MCI prefer the default plan or the market share plan?

(c) *Auction Plan.* UCLA professors Ivan Png and Eric Rasmusen suggested that the FCC require long-distance carriers to bid for the rights to serve the silent subscribers. Compare this proposal with the Default Plan and the Market Share Plan in terms of economic efficiency.

4. For many years, the Japanese Government supported large banks, builders, and real estate developers that had incurred massive losses and were technically insolvent. The government did not provide the same help to smaller companies. However, in 1997, the government rescinded its "too large to fail" policy and decided to allow the bankruptcy of large institutions including the Long-Term Credit Bank of Japan and the Sogo department store chain.

(a) In a competitive capital market, what is the function of bankruptcy?

(b) How did the Japanese Government's "too large to fail" policy affect the allocation of financial resources across large as compared with small businesses?

5. Consider a company that manages a network of hospitals across several counties in one state. Household incomes and the cost of living are higher in urban than rural areas. The company, however, has set the same prices for pharmaceuticals and services in all of its hospitals. It has also paid the same salaries for doctors, nurses, and other professional staff throughout the state.

(a) Management has noticed that there are long waiting lists for treatment at its urban hospitals. Can you explain this problem?

(b) The company has had great difficulty in recruiting professional staff for its urban hospitals. Can you explain this problem?

(c) What advice would you give to management?

6. In 1994, one-quarter of all British workers were engaged in part-time employment. The European Union proposed to require that part-time workers receive similar benefits to full-time workers. This would mean better redundancy pay and maternity benefits for many part-time workers. Britain's employment minister Michael Portillo vetoed the proposal ("European Summit: The Black Cloud," *Economist*, December 10, 1994, pp. 45–6).

(a) A disproportionate number of part-time workers are young people and women. How would the proposed directive affect them?

(b) In 1993, the European Union unemployment rate was almost 10% among the general population and almost 20% among workers aged below age 25. How would the proposed directive affect these rates?

(c) Explain why British trade unions supported the European Union proposal.

7. In 1985–86, the Singapore Government noticed that, at prevailing fares, there were long lines for taxis. The government decided to raise taxi fares to the equilibrium level.

(a) Assuming that all rides are identical, illustrate the fare increase on an appropriate demand–supply diagram. Identify the effects on the buyer and seller surpluses.

(b) In estimating the supply curve, the government did not appreciate that about one-third of all holders of taxi licenses were inactive or semiactive. How would the increase in fares affect this group of licensees? What would be the effect of this mistake on the estimate of the impact on the seller surplus as compared with the original estimate given in (a)?

(c) Unfortunately, the increase in fares coincided with the onset of Singapore's severest economic recession in two decades. On your diagram, show how the economic downturn would affect the market for taxi rides.

8. The U.S. Government assists farmers by buying specified quotas of their peanuts at a guaranteed support price. At times, the government incurs a loss as it sells the peanuts at prices below the guaranteed support price. In June 2000, with the almost unanimous support of Alabama and Georgia representatives, Congress passed a $35 million subsidy to make up for the losses incurred by the peanut support program.

(a) How do price supports affect the market for peanuts?

(b) Explain why the government ends up selling the peanuts at prices below the guaranteed support price.

(c) Argentina is one of the world's leading exporters of peanuts. How does the U.S. peanut support program affect Argentinian peanut farmers?

9. Throughout the world, governments target cigarettes and alcohol for especially high taxes. Let us consider the arguments in favor of these so-called sin taxes.

(a) Suppose that the demand for alcohol is relatively inelastic compared with the demand for other products. Compare the deadweight loss resulting from a tax on alcohol compared with a tax on other products.

(b) Suppose that the demand for alcohol is relatively elastic. How would a tax on alcohol affect consumption?

10. In Switzerland, the federal government levies a social security tax, partly on employers and partly on employees. Employers and employees pay equal percentages of the employee's salary in tax.

(a) Using relevant demand–supply analysis, explain the effect of the social security tax on wages, employment, and the buyer and seller surpluses.

(b) Suppose that the government changed its policy and decided to collect the entire tax from employees. How would this new policy benefit employers?

11. The West African country of Nigeria is a major producer and exporter of oil. The Nigerian government subsidizes domestic gasoline sales. In May 2000, the retail price was about 76 U.S. cents per gallon.

(a) A tax can be represented by shifting up the supply curve. How would you represent a subsidy?

(b) Using a relevant demand–supply diagram, explain the effect of a subsidy on retail price and sales.

(c) Do you expect Nigerians to have bigger or smaller cars relative to residents of another country with a similar income but no subsidy on gasoline?

Part *II*

Market Power

Chapter 7

Costs

Upon graduating from the University of Kansas, reclusive billionaire Philip F. Anschutz joined his father's oil wildcatting business. He made his first billion in oil and then diversified into the rail industry. In 1988, Mr Anschutz bought the Southern Pacific Railroad, and sold it eight years later to the Union Pacific Corporation for a $1.4 billion profit. Significantly, he retained the rights to build a nationwide broadband telecommunications network along the rights-of-way of the railroad tracks. Mr Anschutz hired AT&T veteran Joseph P. Nacchio to head the new business, named Qwest Communications.[1]

In 1999, Qwest completed its 18,500 mile trans-continental Macro Capacity network linking 150 cities in the United States. The network consisted of 48 strands of fiber-optic cable, each capable of conveying data at a rate of 10 Gigabits per second (Gbps). The capacity of fiber-optic cable was so large that just four strands were sufficient to carry all of the country's long-distance telecommunications traffic at the time. Qwest put two strands into operation, leaving the remaining 46 strands as "dark fiber", to be activated later.

Internationally, Qwest's network extended 1,400 miles into Mexico, and was linked by trans-Atlantic cable to KPNQwest, a joint venture with the Dutch telecommunications carrier KPN. By 2001, KPNQwest was expected to complete a 9,100 mile broadband network linking 39 European cities. In addition, Qwest owned part of a 13,125 mile trans-Pacific submarine cable linking California with Japan and East Asia.

Traditionally, long-distance telecommunications companies such as AT&T provided voice and data communications over separate networks, using distinct technologies. By contrast, Qwest applied Internet Protocol technology to carry both voice and data over its single Macro Capacity network.

▼

[1] The following analysis is based in part on "One Word for Phil Anschutz: Private," *Los Angeles Times*, Sunday, October 10, 1999; "Qwest," *Research*, October 1999, and "The Bandwidth Barons," *Data Communications*, July 1998, pp. 44–56.

In 1999, Qwest acquired US West, the dominant provider of local telephone and high bandwidth Internet access in the West and Midwest. Qwest forecast that the acquisition would bolster "scope and scale" through reducing operating expenses by $4.4 billion and capital expenditure by $2.2 billion over the period 2000–2005.

That year, Qwest's revenue from communications and construction services was $3.928 billion, operating expenses were $3.604 billion, and hence net earnings were $323 billion. Qwest's interest expense was $151 million, and after-tax profit was $459 million.

Why did Qwest build its trans-continental network with 23 times excess capacity? What advantages did Qwest gain over competitors like AT&T from being able to provide voice and data communications over a single network? If Qwest had financed its operations with more equity and less borrowing, its interest expense would have been lower and its after-tax profit would have been higher. Should Qwest have borrowed less?

For many important business decisions – including pricing, deciding whether to outsource, assessing performance, and planning investments – managers must have accurate information about costs. In chapter 4, we introduced the concepts of fixed, variable, marginal, and average costs. Now, we build on this foundation and present two basic principles to guide managers in understanding business costs.

The first principle is to consider how costs depend on the scale and scope of the business. The scale refers to the production rate, while the scope means the variety of different products. This principle can guide managers on the issues of whether to operate on a small scale or a large scale and whether to offer many products or focus on a single item. The effect of scale can explain why Qwest built 23 times excess capacity. The effect of scope can explain Qwest's advantage from providing voice and data communications over a single network.

The second principle is relevance: managers should consider only relevant costs and ignore all others. To identify what costs are relevant, a manager needs to consider the alternative courses of action. This approach will reveal costs not shown in accounting statements, called *opportunity costs*. Conventional accounting statements ignore the opportunity cost of equity capital, hence a company that issues more debt will report a higher profit than one that borrows less. The concept of *economic value added* aims to correct this distortion.

The principle of relevance also shows that some expenses that are recorded in accounting statements are not relevant. We explain that, for effective managerial decisions, these *sunk costs* should be ignored.

◂◂ 2 Economies of Scale

A fundamental issue for any business is whether to operate on a small scale or large scale. Large-scale production means mass marketing and relatively low pricing; by contrast, small-scale production is associated with niche marketing and relatively high pricing. Here, we shall analyze how costs depend on the scale or rate of production. (We shall treat the *scale* and *rate* of production as synonymous.) It is important, however, to note that the decision on scale also depends on market demand and competition. We will analyze these factors in chapters 8 and 10.

To understand how costs depend on the scale of production, let us recall the distinction between the fixed and variable costs introduced in chapter 4. The *fixed cost* is the cost of inputs that do not change with the production rate. The *variable cost* is the cost of inputs that change with the production rate.

In chapter 4, we introduced fixed and variable costs in a short-run planning horizon. The same distinction applies in the long run as well and explains how costs depend on the scale of production.

Fixed and Variable Costs in the Long Run

To illustrate the distinction between long-run fixed and variable costs, let us consider the production of an old-fashioned newspaper, the *Daily Globe*. The production process begins when the typesetting department receives the text ("copy") of the forthcoming edition from the editorial and the advertising departments. The typesetters compose the copy in type, which are metal pieces with raised shapes. The type is then mounted on electric-powered printing presses. Once the type has been set, the presses can be switched on and fed a continuous flow of newsprint and ink to produce the printed product.

We asked the management of the *Daily Globe* to estimate the daily expenses required for production rates up to 90,000 copies a day. Table 7.1 reports this information in the four categories of labor, printing press, ink and paper, and electric power. For simplicity, we ignore other costs.

Table 7.1 Daily expenses

Daily production (thousands)	Labor	Printing press	Ink and paper	Electric power	Total
0	$5,000	$1,000	$0	$200	$6,200
10	$5,000	$1,500	$1,200	$300	$8,000
20	$5,000	$2,000	$2,400	$400	$9,800
30	$5,000	$2,500	$3,600	$500	$11,600
40	$5,000	$3,000	$4,800	$600	$13,400
50	$5,000	$3,500	$6,000	$700	$15,200
60	$5,000	$4,000	$7,200	$800	$17,000
70	$5,000	$4,500	$8,400	$900	$18,800
80	$5,000	$5,000	$9,600	$1,000	$20,600
90	$5,000	$5,500	$10,800	$1,100	$22,400

Table 7.2 Analysis of fixed or variable costs

Daily production (thousands)	Fixed cost	Variable cost	Total cost	Marginal cost	Average fixed cost	Average variable cost	Average cost
0	$6,200	$0	$6,200				
10	$6,200	$1,800	$8,000	$0.18	$0.62	$0.18	$0.80
20	$6,200	$3,600	$9,800	$0.18	$0.31	$0.18	$0.49
30	$6,200	$5,400	$11,600	$0.18	$0.21	$0.18	$0.39
40	$6,200	$7,200	$13,400	$0.18	$0.16	$0.18	$0.34
50	$6,200	$9,000	$15,200	$0.18	$0.12	$0.18	$0.30
60	$6,200	$10,800	$17,000	$0.18	$0.10	$0.18	$0.28
70	$6,200	$12,600	$18,800	$0.18	$0.09	$0.18	$0.27
80	$6,200	$14,400	$20,600	$0.18	$0.08	$0.18	$0.26
90	$6,200	$16,200	$22,400	$0.18	$0.07	$0.18	$0.25

Consider each category of expense. The cost of labor is $5,000, and does not vary with the size of the print run. The labor required to produce the paper is the same whether the newspaper plans to print 10,000 or 90,000 copies a day. Accordingly, the labor is a fixed cost of newspaper production.

Next, the cost of the printing press ranges from $1,000 with no production up to $5,500 at a production rate of 90,000. The cost of the press includes a fixed cost of $1,000. The remainder is a variable cost.

The cost of ink and paper is nothing with no production; hence, this item is completely variable. For a print run of 10,000 copies, the cost of ink and paper is $1,200, while for a run of 20,000 copies, the cost is $2,400. The cost of ink and paper is proportional to the production rate.

The cost of electricity is also partly fixed and partly variable. There is a $200 cost of power for lighting which does not vary with the production rate. It is a fixed cost. By contrast, the cost of powering the presses is variable. It increases by $100 for every 10,000 copy increase in the production rate.

In table 7.2, we assign the costs of newspaper production – labor, printing press, ink and paper, and electric power – into the two categories of fixed and variable costs. There is a fixed cost of $6,200. A substantial fixed cost is a fact in producing a newspaper. The industry has given the name *first copy cost* to the fixed cost. It is the cost of producing just one copy a day.

By contrast, as the print run increases from 0 to 90,000 copies a day, the variable cost rises from nothing to $16,200. By distinguishing between fixed and variable costs, the management of a business can understand which cost elements will be affected by changes in the scale of production.

Marginal and Average Costs

Applying the analysis of fixed and variable costs, we can see how costs depend on the scale of production. In chapter 4, we also introduced the concepts of marginal and average costs. Recall that the marginal cost is the change in total cost due to the production of an additional unit. The average (or unit) cost is the total cost divided by the production rate or scale.

Let us study the marginal and average costs of production of the *Daily Globe*. Referring to table 7.2, as the print run increases from 0 to 90,000 copies a day, the total cost of production increases from $6,200 to $22,400.

The marginal cost of the first 10,000 copies is $8,000 − $6,200 = $1,800, or $1,800/10,000 = 18 cents per copy. The marginal cost is constant at 18 cents at all scales of production. From chapter 4, we know that the marginal cost equals the rate of change of the variable cost. For the *Daily Globe*, the average variable cost remains constant at 18 cents per copy. Hence, the marginal cost is also constant at 18 cents per copy.

Dividing total cost by the scale of production, we can obtain the average cost. The average cost drops from 80 cents at a scale of 10,000 copies a day to 25 cents at 90,000 copies a day. To understand why the average cost decreases with the scale of production, recall that the average cost is the average fixed cost plus the average variable cost. The average fixed cost is the fixed cost divided by the production scale. With a larger scale of production, the fixed cost will be spread over more units of production and the average fixed cost will be lower.

The average variable cost is constant at 18 cents per copy. Therefore, the average cost declines as the scale of production increases. In figure 7.1, we graph the marginal, average variable, and average costs against the scale of production. The marginal and average variable cost curves are identical and flat. The average cost curve slopes downward.

A business for which the average cost decreases with the scale of production is said to exhibit **economies of scale** or *increasing returns to scale*. With economies of scale, the marginal cost will be lower than the average cost. Since the marginal unit of production costs less than the average, any increase in production will reduce the average. Therefore, the average cost curve slopes downward.

> **Economies of scale** (increasing returns to scale) means that the average cost decreases with the scale of production.

Intuitive Factors

Scale economies arise from two possible sources. One is significant fixed inputs, that is, those that can support any scale of production. At a larger scale, the cost of the fixed inputs will be spread over more units of production, so that the average fixed cost will be lower. If the average variable cost is constant or does not increase very much with the scale of production, then the average cost will fall with the scale. Newspaper production illustrates economies of scale arising from substantial fixed inputs.

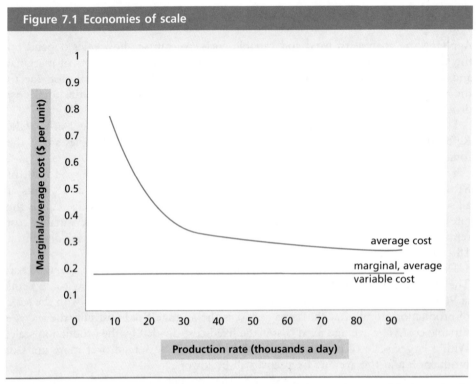

Figure 7.1 Economies of scale

The marginal and average variable costs are identical and do not change with the scale of production. The average cost decreases with the scale of production.

Any business with a strong element of composition, design, or invention has significant fixed inputs. For instance, the cost of developing a new pharmaceutical is fixed. Regardless of the production rate, the development cost will remain the same. Similarly, the cost of preparing the computer code for a software package is fixed. It is the same whether the publisher distributes 1 million copies or only 1. Accordingly, there are strong economies of scale in these businesses. Indeed, for pharmaceuticals and software, the marginal production cost is tiny compared with the average cost.

The other reason for scale economies is if the average variable cost falls with the scale of production. Generally, an increase in scale may increase or reduce the average variable cost. Whether the average variable cost increases or falls depends on the particular technology of the business.

For example, a distributor of gas needs a pipeline to transport its product. The transmission capacity of a pipeline depends on its cross-sectional area, which increases with the square of the radius of the cross section. By contrast, the amount of material required to build the pipeline depends on the circumference of the pipeline, which increases with the radius of the cross section. Accordingly, a 10% increase in the transmission capacity of the pipeline requires less than 10% additional materials. In this case, the average variable cost falls with the scale of operations. This factor tends to generate economies of scale in pipeline operations.

Progress Check 7A Using the data in table 7.2, draw the average fixed cost in figure 7.1.

Progress check

Diseconomies of Scale

A business where the average cost increases with the scale of production is said to exhibit **diseconomies of scale** or *decreasing returns to scale*. A business will have diseconomies of scale if the fixed cost is not significant and the variable cost rises more than proportionately with the scale of production.

> **Diseconomies of scale** (decreasing returns to scale) means that the average cost increases with the scale of production.

To illustrate diseconomies of scale, let us consider Angela's hair-dressing salon. The salon does not involve a significant fixed cost. The main variable cost is labor. Angela estimates that the cost of labor rises more than proportionately with the scale of production.

The average cost is the average fixed cost plus the average variable cost. For the salon, the average cost initially decreases with the scale because of the decreasing average fixed cost. Since the variable cost rises more than proportionately with the scale of production, the average variable cost is increasing. Hence, there is a scale where the decreasing average fixed cost is outweighed by the increasing average variable cost. Then, the average cost reaches a minimum and rises with further increases in the scale. The average cost curve is shaped like the letter U. As we explained in chapters 4 and 5, the average cost curve of a perfectly competitive business is U-shaped.

Strategic Implications

The relation between average cost and the scale of production influences the structure of the industry. If there are economies of scale, a business operating on a relatively large scale will achieve a lower average cost than smaller-scale competitors. Large-scale production means mass marketing and relatively low pricing. An industry where individual suppliers have economies of scale tends to be concentrated, with a few suppliers serving the entire market. In chapter 8, we analyze the extreme case of a monopoly, where there is only one supplier.

By contrast, in a business with diseconomies of scale, the management should aim at a relatively small scale. Small-scale production is associated with niche marketing and relatively high pricing. Industries where individual suppliers have diseconomies of scale tend to be fragmented. The extreme case is the model of perfect competition in chapter 5, where there are many sellers, none of whom can influence the market demand.

Technology and economies of scale: processing credit card transactions

Changes in technology can affect the extent of scale economies. Consider, for instance, the processing of credit card transactions. Credit cards are issued by businesses ranging from banks and credit unions to oil companies and department stores. In the past, every transaction made with a credit card was processed manually.

Automation, however, has changed the processing of credit card transactions into a production-line operation. Automated processing requires significant fixed investments in computer systems. Consequently, the processing of credit card transactions is now a business with economies of scale. It is no longer cost-efficient for each issuer of credit cards to process its own transactions on a small scale.

The efficient scale of processing exceeds the volume of transactions at many individual credit card issuers. As a result, specialized firms have arisen to process the credit card transactions of issuers.

In line with scale economies, the credit card processing industry has become increasingly concentrated. For instance, in six years, Nova Corporation and PMT acquired over 130 other credit card processors, and finally, in June 1998, Nova acquired PMT. Nova Chairman Edward Grzedzinski explained: "This is a scale business, and by adding PMT's volume to our operating platform there is a tremendous advantage economically."

The following year, Nova had become the third largest processor with an 8% market share. The largest processor was giant First Data, with a commanding 44% market share, followed by National Processing with 13%.

Source: "Credit-Card Processor Nova to Buy PMT in Stock Accord Valued at $1.23 Billion," *Wall Street Journal*, June 19, 1998, p. A4; and Nilson Report.

◀◀ 3 Economies of Scope

> **Economies of scope** means that the total cost of production is lower with joint than with separate production.

A fundamental strategic issue for any business is whether to offer many different products or focus on a single item. The answer to this question depends in part on the relation between cost and the scope of production. There are **economies of scope** across two products if the total cost of production is lower when two products are produced together than when they are produced separately. Conversely, there are

Table 7.3 Expenses for two products

Organization	Daily production (thousands)	Labor	Printing press	Ink, paper, electric power	Total cost
Separate production					
Daily Globe	50	$5,000	$3,500	$6,700	$15,200
Afternoon Globe	50	$5,000	$3,500	$6,700	$15,200
Combined production	100	$10,000	$3,500	$13,400	$26,900

diseconomies of scope across two products if the total cost of production is higher when two products are produced together.

> **Diseconomies of scope** means that the total cost of production is higher with joint than with separate production.

Joint Cost

Let us consider how costs depend on the scope of production through the following example. Suppose that the management of the *Daily Globe* is considering whether to launch an afternoon paper, the *Afternoon Globe*. Table 7.3 shows three categories of expenses required to produce the *Daily Globe* and the *Afternoon Globe*, assuming a print run of 50,000 copies a day for each paper.

If the two newspapers are printed in separate facilities, then the total production cost is $15,200 a day for each paper, or $30,400 for the two papers. If, however, both newspapers are printed in the same facility, then the total cost of producing the two newspapers is $26,900. The cost of producing both newspapers in the same facility is 11.5% lower than if they were produced separately.

What explains the difference in cost? The key is that the same printing press can be used in the night to print the morning paper, and in the late morning to print the afternoon paper. To produce the *Daily Globe* by itself, the publisher must spend $3,500 a day on the printing press. Likewise, to produce the *Afternoon Globe* by itself, the publisher must spend $3,500 a day on the printing press. To produce both newspapers from the same facility, however, the publisher spends $3,500 only once.

> The **joint cost** is the cost of inputs that do not change with the scope of production.

The expense of the printing press is a **joint cost** of the morning and afternoon newspapers. The *joint cost* is the cost of inputs that do not change with the scope of production. Economies of scope arise wherever there are significant joint costs.

Strategic Implications

Where two products are linked by economies of scope, it will be relatively cheaper to produce the products together. Then, a supplier of both items can achieve a relatively lower cost than competitors that specialize in one or the other product. Subject to conditions of market demand and competition, the management should offer both products. Multiproduct suppliers dominate industries with economies of scope.

Telecommunication and broadcasting provide an important example of scope economies. Fixed-line telephone service requires a wire network connecting all potential subscribers. Similarly, cable television requires a wire network connecting all potential subscribers. In this case, the cost of building and maintaining the network is a significant joint cost. Consquently, there are very substantial economies of scope across the telephone and television businesses. Combined providers of telephone and television service can deliver the products at relatively lower cost than specialized services. Throughout the world, telephone and cable television companies are expanding into each other's businesses.

Economies of scope in advertising and promotion are essential for the strategy of *brand extension* in marketing. When Kimberly-Clark spends $1 to advertise Kleenex, it is promoting the sales of every product carrying the Kleenex brand. Accordingly, the expenditure on advertising a brand is a joint cost of marketing all the products marked with the brand. This joint cost gives rise to economies of scope in advertising and promotion. Through a brand extension, the owner of an established brand can introduce new products at relatively lower cost than a competitor with no established brand.

Economies of scope also underlie the strategic concept of *core competence*. A *core competence* is generalized expertise in the design, production, and marketing of products based on common or closely related technologies. For instance, a manufacturer with a core competence in small liquid crystal displays can apply this as a basis for manufacturing pocket calculators as well as digital watches. It can produce these items at a relatively lower cost than a specialized competitor. Essentially, a core competence is a joint cost that gives rise to economies of scope.[2]

Diseconomies of Scope

There are diseconomies of scope across two products if the total cost of production is higher when the two items are produced together than when they are produced separately. Diseconomies of scope arise where joint costs are not significant and making one product increases the cost of making the other in the same facility.

To illustrate diseconomies of scope, consider two retail businesses: basic clothing and fast food. Both cater to a similar mix of customers looking for good value. Why then does some entrepreneur not sell clothing together with fast food?

Such a combined business would probably encounter diseconomies of scope. There is no significant joint cost between the two products. Further, people consuming fast food might wander over to the clothing section and spill food and drinks on the merchandise. So, the fast food service increases the cost of selling clothing in

---

[2] This discussion in based on Paul Milgrom and John Roberts, *Economics, Organization, and Management* (Englewood Cliffs, NJ: Prentice Hall, 1992), pp. 107–9.

the same facility. Given these difficulties, it would be less costly to sell the two products in separate facilities.

Where diseconomies of scope prevail, it will be relatively cheaper to produce the various items separately. Hence, specialized producers can achieve relatively lower costs than competitors that combine production. In such circumstances, the management should aim for a narrow scope and focus on one product.

Progress Check 7B Referring to table 7.3, suppose that, with combined production, the expenses on the printing press would be $7,000 a day. Are there economies or diseconomies of scope?

Progress check

Economies of scale and scope in gold mining

Echo Bay Mines Limited owns the Cove open-pit mine in Nevada. The company exploits economies of both scale and scope in operating the mine. Given the fixed cost of keeping the mining pit free from water, it is relatively cheaper to blast rock at a rate exceeding 100,000 tons a day.

The rock is removed from the pit and separated into three categories. The high-grade ore-bearing rock is ground in a mill, after which the metal is extracted by a physical or chemical process. The low-grade ore-bearing rock is collected in a large heap on an impermeable pad and leached with a solvent to dissolve the metal. Finally, the unusable rock is dumped on a waste pile.

The rock contains both gold and silver. Removing the rock from the pit is a joint cost of producing gold and silver. Instead of dumping the silver-bearing rock on the waste pile, the company recovers the silver as well as the gold. In 1999, Cove produced 9.4 million ounces of silver as well as 124,500 ounces of gold.

Source: Echo Bay Mines Ltd., *1994 and 1999 Annual Reports.*

◀◀ 4 Opportunity Cost

We have seen how business costs depend on economies of scale and scope. To actually determine the extent of scale and scope economies, we must know how to measure costs. Analyses of costs usually begin with the accounting statements. These, however, do not always provide the information appropriate for effective business decisions. It is often necessary to look beyond the conventional accounting statements.

Here, we present a key principle to guide managers in measuring costs. That principle is **relevance**: managers should consider only relevant costs and ignore all others. There is no simple definition of which costs are relevant. Which costs are relevant depends on the alternative courses of action for the decision at hand.

Alternative Courses of Action

The following example shows how an analysis of the alternative courses of action will uncover relevant costs that conventional accounting statements leave out. Suppose that, in 1960, Eleanor Williams bought a warehouse in an industrial area that has since been transformed into a tourist zone. Eleanor paid $300,000 for the warehouse, using $200,000 of her own money and a bank loan of $100,000. She has since repaid the loan in full.

Table 7.4 presents the most recent income statement for her warehouse. Eleanor's annual sales revenue is $700,000, her cash outlays are $220,000, hence her profit is $480,000. She is making a return on sales of $480/700 = 69\%$. Eleanor's warehouse business seems to be doing very well.

We contend, however, that this assessment of performance overlooks some significant costs of Eleanor's warehouse business. To evaluate Eleanor's business, we should investigate her alternative courses of action. Since the area has become a tourist zone, an obvious alternative is to redevelop the warehouse into a tourist facility such as a shopping center or entertainment complex.

Suppose that a developer were willing to buy the warehouse for $2 million. If Eleanor sells the warehouse, she could invest the proceeds in government bonds and get a secure income of, say, 8% a year, which works out to $2 million $\times 0.08 = $160,000$. Moreover, Eleanor could then work elsewhere for a salary of, say, $400,000. Thus, if Eleanor were to sell the warehouse, she could earn $560,000 a year. This is more than she earns from continuing in the warehouse business. So, if Eleanor considers the alternative of selling the warehouse, she will soon see that this is better than continuing in business.

This example highlights a major deficiency of the conventional income statement: it does not present the revenues and costs of the alternative courses of action. In table 7.5, we present an expanded income statement that explicitly shows the revenues and costs of Eleanor's two alternatives. It is then very clear that Eleanor should sell the warehouse.

Table 7.4 Conventional income statement	
Revenue	$700,000
Expenses	$220,000
Profit	$480,000

Table 7.5 Income statement showing alternatives, I

	Continue warehouse operations	Shutdown
Revenue	$700,000	$560,000
Expenses	$220,000	$0
Profit	$480,000	$560,000

Table 7.6 Income statement reporting opportunity costs

Revenue	$700,000
Cost	$780,000
Profit	–$80,000

Opportunity Cost Defined

By continuing in the warehouse business, Eleanor foregoes the opportunity to earn $560,000 a year. The **opportunity cost** of the current course of action is the net revenue from the best alternative course of action. In Eleanor's case, the opportunity cost of continuing in the warehouse business is $560,000 a year.

> The **opportunity cost** is the net revenue from the best alternative course of action.

We can apply the concept of opportunity cost to present the revenues and costs of continuing in the warehouse business in another way. This includes opportunity costs among the costs of the business. Table 7.6 presents a single income statement, in which costs include both the cash outlays and the opportunity cost. The cost of $780,000 consists of $220,000 in outlays plus $560,000 in opportunity cost.

Using the opportunity cost approach, we find that Eleanor is incurring a loss of $80,000 a year; hence, she should get out of the warehouse business. This approach leads to the same decision as in table 7.5, where we explicitly show the two alternative courses of action.

Uncovering Relevant Costs

Thus, there are two ways to uncover relevant costs: explicitly consider the alternative courses of action or use the concept of opportunity cost. When applied correctly, both approaches lead to the same business decision.

In Eleanor's case, there was one alternative to the existing course of action. Where there is more than one alternative, the explicit approach still works well. The opportunity cost approach, however, becomes more complicated: we must first identify the best of the alternatives and then charge the net revenues from that alternative as an opportunity cost of the existing course of action.

Conventional methods of cost accounting focus on the cash outlays associated with the course of action that management has adopted. This means that they do not consider the revenues and costs of alternative courses of action; hence, they ignore costs that are relevant but do not involve cash outlays. One reason for these omissions is that alternative courses of action and opportunity costs change with the circumstances and hence are more difficult to measure and verify. Conventional methods of cost accounting focus on easily verifiable costs. Accordingly, they overlook opportunity costs.

Progress check **Progress Check 7C** Suppose that government bonds pay an interest rate of 3% a year. Revise tables 7.5 and 7.6. Should Eleanor continue in the warehouse business?

Opportunity cost: a downtown department store

The main store of the Wing On chain is one of the few department stores in Hong Kong's central district. The store occupies 25,000 square feet on the ground floor and 64,000 square feet on three other floors of the Wing On Centre. The tenants of street-level floors of other nearby buildings include banks, fast-food chains, and jewelers. In 1993, the Wing On department stores reported revenues of HK$2,236 million, costs of HK$2,210 million, and a profit of HK$26 million.

At the time, the market rent for retail space around the Wing On Centre was HK$100–150 per square foot for ground floors and HK$30–50 for other floors. Let us use this data to estimate the opportunity cost of the premises used by Wing On's main store. To be conservative, we use the lower figures of HK$100 and HK$30 a month. Then, on an annual basis, the opportunity cost of the ground-floor space was HK$(25,000 × 100 × 12) = HK$30 million, while the opportunity cost of the other floors was HK$(64,000 × 30 × 12) = HK$23 million. The total opportunity cost was HK$53 million a year.

To evaluate the performance of its department stores, the Wing On Group should take account of the HK$53 million a year income that it could earn by leasing space to other tenants such as banks and fast-food chains.

Source: Wing On Group, *1993 Annual Report*, pp. 25–6.

Free lunch: Picasso versus Rockefeller

The following story is apocryphal. Nelson Rockefeller (a member of the wealthy New York family that controlled the Chase Manhattan Bank) and the famous European artist Pablo Picasso had lunch at the Four Seasons restaurant in New York City. At the end of a fine meal, Picasso reached for the bill, "Let me pay. I'll write a personal check, draw a few squiggles, and sign it. The manager won't ever cash it. She will display it as a work of art. And we'll have a free lunch."

Rockefeller would not agree. "No, allow me to write a personal check. Remember, this is New York City. Here, our Rockefeller name is as good as gold. The manager won't cash my check. She can use it just like money and our lunch will be free."

Who was right? Picasso or Rockefeller? The correct answer to the puzzle is that neither Picasso nor Rockefeller was right. By drawing a few squiggles, Picasso was adding to the world's stock of his works. The increase in the supply would reduce the price that he could get for future works. Picasso would not get a free lunch – he was bartering a picture for a lunch.

Rockefeller was also wrong. Each check that he wrote added to his stock of debts and, ultimately, reduced his creditworthiness. He could not create an unlimited number of checks. So, by creating a check, Rockefeller was exchanging a lunch for a reduction in his creditworthiness. In believing that they could get a free lunch, both Pablo Picasso and Nelson Rockefeller overlooked opportunity cost.

Source: Frank Rabinovitch, personal communication, 1984.

Opportunity Cost of Capital

Conventional accounting methods require the expensing of interest payments but do not require expensing of expected dividends. Consequently, a business that is partly financed by debt will appear to be "less profitable" than an otherwise identical business that is completely financed by equity. Indeed, many loss-making businesses have returned to profit by persuading their creditors to convert their loans to shares.

However, from a managerial perspective, equity capital is not costless; it has an opportunity cost. The shareholders of a business would like management to earn a rate of return on equity that at least matches the return from other investments with the same risk profile. Managers who evaluate business performance in terms of accounting profit will tend to be biased in favor of capital-intensive activities.

Management consultants Stern Stewart developed and trademarked the concept of *economic value added* as a better measure of business performance than accounting

> **Economic value added** is net operating profit after tax subject to adjustments for accounting conventions less a charge for the cost of capital.

earnings. The definition of **economic value added** is net operating profit after tax subject to adjustments for accounting conventions less a charge for the cost of capital. Managers who evaluate business performance in terms of economic value added will make better decisions. In particular, they are less likely to be biased in favor of capital-intensive activities.

The appropriate mix between debt and equity as sources of investment funds is a deep and complicated issue of corporate finance. It is beyond the scope of a managerial economics book. Here, we confine ourselves to the point that a complete measure of business performance should take account of the opportunity cost of equity capital.

Loewen Group: life after death

In June 1999, the Loewen Group operated more than 1,100 funeral homes and 400 cemeteries in Canada, the United Kingdom, and the United States. Historically, the Group had emphasized the operation of funeral homes. It then expanded into cemeteries, partly financed by $2 billion of bonds and $300 million of bank loans.

For the six months ending June 30, 1999, Loewen's revenues were $566 million, operating expenses were $493 million, and operating earnings were $73 million. However, interest expenses of $77 million, and other non-operational expenses dragged the group down to a pre-tax loss of $88 million. Faced with the prospect of further losses, Loewen filed for bankruptcy protection in Canada and the United States.

Chairman John Lacey explained that Loewen would refocus on funeral home operations and away from cemeteries. Saying that bondholders supported the bankruptcy filing, he called on them to convert "hundreds of millions of dollars" of bonds into equity.

Following the conversion of bonds into equity, Loewen's interest expense would be reduced. But the financial engineering alone would not change the revenues and operational expenses of the group. Conversion of debt to equity would "reduce" losses only in a financial sense and only because accounting standards do not require expensing of expected dividends. However, the debt–equity conversion would not change the group's business situation.

Sources: "Loewen Group Seeks Bankruptcy Protection in U.S., Canada," *Dow Jones Business News*, June 1, 1999; "The Loewen Group Reports Second Quarter 2000 Results," The Loewen Group, Inc., Press Release, July 31, 2000.

Figure 7.2 Transfer price

Mercury's semiconductor division has a maximum capacity of 200,000 chips a month. Mercury maximizes its overall profit at a production rate of 160,000 chips a month, where the semiconductor division's marginal cost equals the consumer electronics division's marginal benefit.

◂ 5 Transfer Pricing

Chapter 6 introduced the concept of a transfer price, which is charged for the sale of an item within an organization. Suppose that the Mercury Group consists of two divisions – semiconductors and consumer electronics. The semiconductor division supplies chips to the consumer electronics division for use in manufacturing personal digital assistants. How should these chips be priced?

Figure 7.2 shows the semiconductor division's marginal cost of manufacturing the chip. It also shows the consumer electronics division's marginal benefit from the chip, which reflects the additional profit generated by one more chip. Mercury's overall profit would be maximized at a quantity of 160,000 chips per month, where the consumer electronics division's marginal benefit equals the semiconductor division's marginal cost.

Suppose that Mercury sets the transfer price at $2 per chip, and allows the consumer electronics division to buy as many chips as it wants at that price. Comparing its marginal benefit with the transfer price, the consumer electronics division will buy 160,000 chips per month, which is exactly the quantity that maximizes Mercury's overall profit.

> The **transfer price** of an internally produced input should be set equal to its marginal cost.

Generally, to maximize the profit of the entire organization, the **transfer price** of an internally produced input should be set equal to its marginal cost, which is the change in total cost due to the production of an additional unit. There are two important special cases, which we discuss below.

Perfectly Competitive Market

One special case is where there is a perfectly competitive market for the input. We discussed this case in chapter 6 when considering decentralized management. Rather than measure the marginal cost, it is simpler to set the transfer price equal to the market price. A profit-maximizing business would produce the input at a rate where its marginal cost equals the market price. Hence, the transfer price (set at the market price) will also be the marginal cost.

Full Capacity

The other special case is where the (upstream) division that supplies the input is operating at full capacity. Then, the marginal cost of the input is not well defined. For instance, referring to figure 7.2, if Mercury's semiconductor division is producing at a rate of 200,000 chips a month, the marginal cost curve is vertical and hence the marginal cost of a chip is not defined.

In this case, the transfer price should be set equal to the opportunity cost of the input, which is the marginal benefit that the input provides to the current user. To understand why, suppose that Mercury re-allocates one chip away from the consumer electronics division to some other use. Since the semiconductor division's total production remains the same, there will be no effect on its production costs. However, the re-allocation will result in an opportunity cost – the reduction in profit for the consumer electronics division.

To ensure that the alternative use of the chip raises overall profit, the transfer price should be set equal to the consumer electronics division's marginal benefit from that chip. The alternative user will only buy the chip if the benefit exceeds the transfer price, and hence only if its benefit exceeds the consumer electronics division's benefit. Accordingly, this rule will maximize the profit of the entire organization.

◂◂ 6 Sunk Costs

For effective business decisions, managers should take account of all relevant costs. We have just seen that, because conventional accounting methods do not present alternative courses of action, they may fail to reveal important relevant costs. We shall next consider situations where some of the costs reported in conventional accounting statements are not relevant, and should be ignored.

In chapter 4, we introduced the concept of a sunk cost, which is a cost that has been committed and so cannot be avoided. Since sunk costs cannot be avoided, they are not relevant to business decisions. As with opportunity costs, the easiest way to identify sunk costs is to consider the alternative courses of action.

Alternative Courses of Action

The following example shows how an analysis of the alternative courses of action will identify sunk costs in a conventional accounting statement. Suppose that Sol Athletic is about to launch a line of new athletic shoes. Some months ago, management prepared an advertising campaign and booked space in *Road Runner* magazine and the *Daily Globe* newspaper. The total budget for the new advertisements was $310,000.

Sol forecast that the advertisements would generate sales of 20,000 units. The unit contribution margin, which is price less average variable cost, would be $20. Hence the contribution margin, which is revenue less variable cost, would be $20 × 20,000 = $400,000. Thus, the new product would yield a profit of $400,000 – $310,000 = $90,000.

Recently, however, one of Sol's major competitors also launched a new product. Sol now estimates that its own launch will generate sales of only 15,000 units. The unit contribution margin would still be $20; hence, the contribution margin would only be $20 × 15,000 = $300,000. This seems to be less than the cost of the advertisements. Should Sol cancel the launch?

To address this question, we should carefully lay out the revenues and costs associated with the alternative courses of action. Table 7.7 shows the required information.

Supposing that Sol continues with the launch, the contribution margin would be $300,000. Sol must pay $50,000 to a graphic arts consultant for artwork, $60,000 to *Road Runner* magazine, and $200,000 to the *Daily Globe*. The total advertising cost would be $310,000, hence Sol's profit would be –$10,000.

By contrast, if Sol cancels the launch, the contribution margin would be $0. Even if it cancels the launch, Sol must still pay something to the graphic arts consultant, the magazine, and newspaper. Table 7.7 shows the amounts that Sol must pay in

Table 7.7 Income statement showing alternatives, II		
	Continue product launch	Cancel launch
Contribution margin	$300,000	$0
Graphic arts consultant fee	$50,000	$50,000
Road Runner charge	$60,000	$30,000
Daily Globe charge	$200,000	$20,000
Profit	($10,000)	($100,000)

Table 7.8 Income statement omitting sunk costs	
Contribution margin	$300,000
Graphic arts cost	$0
Road Runner cost	$30,000
Daily Globe cost	$180,000
Profit	$90,000

the event of cancellation. Hence, if Sol decides to cancel the launch, the total advertising cost would be $100,000; thus, its profit would be –$100,000.

By this analysis, Sol should continue with the product launch. Continuation yields a loss of $10,000, which is less than the loss of $100,000 from cancellation.

Avoidable Costs

By canceling the launch, Sol does not save the entire advertising budget of $310,000. Some expenses already have been committed and are now sunk. Sol can correctly decide whether or not to continue the launch by using a single income statement that omits sunk costs and includes only avoidable costs.

Table 7.8 presents this information. The contribution margin is $300,000. Note that table 7.8 presents costs rather than expenses. The total (avoidable) cost of the advertising plan is $210,000. If Sol continues with the launch, it will earn a profit of $90,000. Accordingly, the correct decision is to continue with the launch.

Strategic Implications

Generally, managers should ignore sunk costs and consider only avoidable costs. Sunk costs, once incurred, are not relevant for pricing, investment, or any other business decision. Managers who consider sunk costs may stumble into serious mistakes.

From a prospective viewpoint, managers should be very careful before committing to costs that will become sunk, since such commitments cannot be reversed. In chapter 10, we discuss how businesses can exploit investments in sunk costs as a way to strategically influence the behavior of competitors.

We have shown two ways of dealing with sunk costs: explicitly consider the alternative courses of action or remove all sunk costs from the income statement. When applied correctly, both approaches lead to the same business decision.

In Sol's case, there was one alternative to the existing course of action. Where there is more than one alternative, the explicit approach still works well. The sunk cost approach, however, becomes more complicated. Which costs are sunk depends on the alternative at hand. Accordingly, it is easier to consider the alternative courses of action explicitly.

Conventional methods of cost accounting focus on the cash outlays associated with the course of action that management has adopted. These methods report all costs that involve cash outlays, even sunk costs. To make effective business decisions, managers must look beyond conventional accounting statements to consider only relevant costs. This means ignoring sunk costs.

Commitments and the Planning Horizon

To identify sunk costs, managers should consider two factors: past commitments and the planning horizon. Suppose that Sol Athletic has engaged an advertising agency on a retainer basis with a minimum monthly fee. The contract requires six months' notice of termination. Then, from the current standpoint, the advertising agency's minimum fee is sunk for a six-month planning horizon but not for the seventh and following months.

If Sol's commitment had been different, the sunk cost picture would also be different. Suppose that the contract provided for only three months' notice of termination. Then, from the current standpoint, the advertising agency's minimum fee is sunk for only the next three months. For planning beyond the fourth month, the fee is avoidable.

This example also illustrates how the extent to which a cost is sunk depends on the planning horizon. Generally, the longer the planning horizon, the more time there will be for past commitments to unwind and hence the greater will be management's freedom of action.

In chapter 4, we distinguished between short-run and long-run planning horizons. The short run is a time horizon in which at least one input cannot be adjusted. By contrast, the long run is a time horizon long enough that all inputs can be freely adjusted. Consequently, in a short-run planning horizon, there will be some sunk costs, while in a long-run horizon, there will be no sunk costs.

Progress Check 7D Suppose that Sol has made no commitments to the suppliers of artwork or advertising space. Revise tables 7.7 and 7.8. Should Sol cancel the launch?

Progress check

Apple Computer's 1-megabit DRAMs

Apple Computer manufactures the Macintosh line of personal computers. During the first half of 1988, the company's sales of high-end Macintosh machines equipped with larger memory had been unexpectedly strong. By the summer, management had become concerned about the company's stocks of 1-megabit DRAMs. Moreover, Apple's DRAM suppliers were falling behind in their deliveries. Chairman and Chief Executive Officer, John Sculley, explained: "We also thought that 1-megabit chips supplies would get even tighter towards the end of the year."

Consequently, Apple bought several hundred million dollars' worth of 1-megabit DRAMs, at an average cost of $38 per chip. This was significantly higher than the cost earlier in the year. To recoup the higher cost of memory, management raised prices across the entire Macintosh line. The company based the differential in price between machines with larger memory and those with smaller memory on the DRAM cost of $38.

By January 1989, however, shortages in the DRAM market eased and the price dropped to $23. This exposed a problem with Apple's pricing. Computer resellers such as Computerland undercut Apple's high-end machines by adding memory and hard disks from third-party sources to basic Macintosh computers. Moreover, resellers enjoyed higher margins on third-party components than Apple Computer products.

Apple's sales of high-end Macintoshes collapsed and millions of excess DRAMs accumulated in inventory. Consequently, Apple's gross margin fell from 51.5% in the third quarter of 1988 to 46.2% in the second quarter of 1989. For a company with quarterly sales of $1.25 billion, each 1% of gross margin amounted to $12.5 million.

What went wrong at Apple? In January 1989, the historical cost of each 1-megabit DRAM was $38, but the market value was only $23. By then, the $15 difference was a sunk cost. Apple's management should have faced the fact that anyone could buy DRAMs at $23; hence, the relevant cost of Apple's DRAMs, new or old, was $23.

Apple's management, however, did not follow this principle. It maintained prices for the entire Macintosh line based on a cost of $38 per DRAM. Apple's high-end Macintosh computers were too expensive relative to the basic machines. Consequently, sales of the high-end machines collapsed, and the company's quarterly profit slumped.

Source: "Apple Slips as Result of Hoarding Chips," *Wall Street Journal*, January 30, 1989, p. A6; Apple Computer, *1989 Annual Report*, pp. 19–20.

Sunk vis-à-vis Fixed Costs

In popular as well as professional discussion, the term *fixed cost* is often used in two different senses: a cost that cannot be avoided once incurred (what we call *sunk cost*) and the cost of inputs that do not change with the production rate (what we call *fixed cost*).

For the sake of clarity, we distinguish these two meanings with two different terms. It is important to understand this distinction very clearly because the two types of costs have very different implications for business decisions. Managers should ignore sunk costs that have been incurred, as these cannot be avoided. By contrast, the presence of fixed costs in the long run tends to give rise to economies of scale, and so management should aim to operate on a large scale.

Some fixed costs become sunk once incurred. For instance, suppose that the soles of Sol Athletic's jogging shoes are made of molded rubber. For each size of shoe, Sol Athletic must have at least one pair of molds (left and right). So, the cost of designing the molds is a fixed cost. Moreover, once the molds have been designed, the cost has been committed and cannot be avoided. Hence, the design cost is a sunk cost, once incurred.

Not all sunk costs, however, are fixed in the sense of supporting any scale of operations. Having designed the molds, Sol must manufacture one set of molds to begin production of shoes. The cost of making the molds is sunk, once incurred. If the demand for the shoes is sufficiently high, Sol might have to invest in a second production line. Then it will need a second set of molds, which requires an additional investment. So, the cost of making molds is not a fixed cost. Rather, it depends on the scale of operations.

Likewise, not all fixed costs become sunk when incurred. For instance, Sol must have at least one production operator on each production line. Accordingly, the wage of a production operator is a fixed cost of making a particular model of shoes. If, however, the demand for that model of shoes should fall, Sol can close the line and shift the operator to another model. Thus, the production operator's wage need not be sunk.

Figure 7.3 illustrates a basic approach to analyzing costs. First, we divide costs into sunk and avoidable. This division depends on past commitments and the current planning horizon. Managers should ignore all costs that are sunk for the planning horizon at hand. Next, we can analyze avoidable costs into variable and fixed elements. This division depends on the technology of the business. The presence of substantial long-run fixed costs gives rise to economies of scale. Then, management should aim to operate on a relatively large scale.

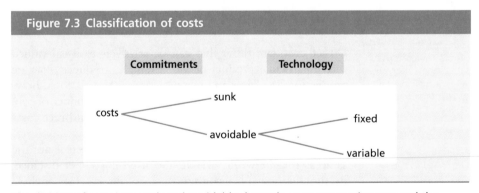

Figure 7.3 Classification of costs

The division of costs into sunk and avoidable depends on past commitments and the current planning horizon. The division of avoidable costs into variable and fixed elements depends on the technology of the business.

Why Qwest built in 2,300% excess capacity

Broadband communications provider Qwest built its Macro Capacity network with 48 strands of 10 Gbps fiber optic cable. The telecommunications provider activated 20 Gbps while leaving the other 460 Gbps as "dark fiber." Building 2,300% excess capacity would be highly unusual in most other industries. A hospital is not likely to build facilities for 4,800 patients when currently serving only 20. Similarly, an automobile manufacturer will not build a factory with capacity for 480,000 cars a year while making only 20,000.

A key difference between broadband telecommunications and other businesses is that two major costs of constructing a broadband network are fixed. The costs of securing the right of way and digging the trench do not vary with the network capacity. Whether Qwest laid 1 strand or 48, these costs would be the same. The variable costs of additional network capacity were the price of the extra strands, the incremental cost of installing them (beyond the cost of installing the first strand), and the network equipment connecting the strands.

Qwest deliberately installed 46 extra strands of "dark fiber" for possibly two reasons. One was that the economies of scale in the construction of a broadband network were so large that it was worthwhile to build the additional capacity in anticipation of future demand. The other reason was that the cost of building the excess capacity was sunk, once incurred. As we explain in chapter 10, large sunk investments may be effective in deterring potential competitors.

Source: "The Bandwidth Barons", *Data Communications*, July 1998, pp. 44–56.

◀◀ 7 Direct and Indirect Costs[3]

A **direct cost** is a cost that can be relatively easily identified with a particular product or job

An **indirect (overhead) cost** is a cost that cannot be easily identified with a particular product or job.

Direct costs are those that can be relatively easily identified with a particular product or job. Examples of direct costs are production-line labor and material inputs. Not all costs, however, can be easily identified with a particular product or job. Those costs that cannot be easily identified are **indirect costs** (also called *overhead* costs).

The distinction between direct and indirect costs is not the same as that between variable and fixed costs. For instance, in the business of repairing tractors, direct costs include

---

[3] This section may be omitted without loss of continuity.

mechanics' labor and major parts but not grease and screws. If the mechanics repair one more tractor, they will use more grease and screws. Accordingly, grease and screws are a variable cost. Generally, direct costs may be variable or fixed, and similarly, indirect costs may be variable or fixed.

Many businesses, whether in manufacturing or services, produce multiple products. In a multiproduct business where indirect costs represent a significant proportion of total costs, an important issue is how to allocate the indirect costs among the various products. For pricing and other business decisions, it is vital to allocate indirect costs in a reasonable way. One method is called *activity-based costing*.

Activity-Based Costing

To explain activity-based costing, let us consider the following example. Suppose that Luna Machining produces two models of cast-iron pulleys for the elevator industry, the Alpha and the Beta. To set prices, management would like to know the cost of each model, including direct costs as well as relevant indirect costs.

Luna Machining produces 20 units of the Alpha and 60 units of the Beta each week. Using specialized equipment, Luna's workers machine cast-iron pieces to produce high-quality pulleys. Both the Alpha and the Beta require 5 hours of direct labor at an average cost of $15 per hour. Both products require material inputs of $10.20 per unit and take the same amount of machine time, at a cost of $6.80 per unit.

For simplicity, we suppose that the only indirect cost is a Shipping Section, whose annual expenses are $50,000, consisting of $48,000 in wages and $2,000 in telephone and fax charges. So, the issue is how to allocate the cost of the Shipping Section between the two products.

The first step in activity-based costing is to identify the expenses and activities of the Shipping Section. By interviewing the shipping supervisor, we learn that the section spends most of its time on two activities: processing shipments and dealing with customer inquiries. The main expenses are wages and telephone and fax charges. Table 7.9 presents the expenses.

Table 7.9 Analyzing expenses and activities

Item	Expenses	Activity: Shipments	Activity: Customer inquiries	Allocation method
Wages	$48,000	$30,000	$18,000	Worker-hours
Telephone and fax	$2,000	$0	$2,000	Identified
Total	$50,000	$30,000	$20,000	

Table 7.10 Allocating expenses to activities

	Activity	
	Shipments	Customer inquiries
Alpha	500	1,000
Beta	800	1,600
Total activity	1,300	2,600
Annual expenses	$30,000	$20,000
Weekly expenses	$600	$400
Allocation: Alpha	$231	$154
Allocation: Beta	$369	$246

We must then learn how the expense categories are divided among the activities. The shipping supervisor estimates that the section spends 62.5% of its time on shipments and 37.5% on customer service. Taking the total of $48,000 in wages, we then allocate $48,000 × 0.625 = $30,000 to shipments and the balance of $18,000 to customer service. The supervisor believes that all the telephone and fax charges are associated with customer inquiries.

We compile this information in columns 3 and 4 of table 7.9. The total cost of shipments is $30,000, while the total cost of servicing customer inquiries is $18,000 + $2,000 = $20,000.

The next step is to learn the relationship between the two products and the activities of the Shipping Section. Continuing the interview, we learn that the Alpha requires 500 shipments a year while the Beta requires 800 shipments a year. Further, the Alpha involves 1,000 customer service inquiries a year, while the Beta involves 1,600 inquiries a year. We compile this information in the top part of table 7.10.

From table 7.9, the total cost of shipments is $30,000. Assuming 50 working weeks a year, this is equivalent to $30,000/50 = $600 a week. We then allocate this $600 weekly cost in proportion to the shipments of the two products. For the Alpha, the allocated shipment cost is $600 × (500/1300) = $231, while for the Beta, the allocated shipment cost is $600 − $231 = $369.

Also from table 7.9, the cost of customer service is $20,000 a year, or $20,000/50 = $400 a week. We then allocate this weekly $400 cost in proportion to the number of inquiries for the two products. For the Alpha, the allocated inquiries cost is $400 × (1,000/2,600) = $154, while for the Beta, the allocated shipment cost is $400 − $154 = $246. With these calculations, we complete the lower part of table 7.10.

Table 7.11 Allocated costs

Model	Weekly output	Direct labor	Direct materials	Machine time	Shipments	Customer inquiries	Total cost	Average cost
Alpha	20	$1,500	$204	$136	$231	$154	$2,225	$111
Beta	60	$4,500	$612	$408	$369	$246	$6,135	$102

Finally, in table 7.11, we combine the information on direct costs with the allocations of indirect costs. The calculations show, as we might intuitively expect, that the Alpha, which is a low-volume product, has a higher average cost than the Beta, the high-volume product.

Intuitively, shipping involves some fixed costs. It does not cost three times as much to support the Beta as the Alpha. So, the higher-volume product has a lower average cost.

To summarize, the procedure in **activity-based costing** is to first identify the activities that are undertaken by the group incurring indirect costs. The next step is to systematically investigate how the various products drive the indirect activities, and, accordingly, to allocate the costs of the activities among the products. The final step is to combine the allocated indirect costs with the direct costs.

In conventional methods of cost accounting, the indirect costs are allocated in proportion to direct costs. Conventional methods ignore the possibility that there are fixed elements in the way that indirect activities support the various products. The result is a tendency to overstate the costs of high-volume products and understate the costs of low-volume products.

Notice that, in compiling table 7.10, we implicitly assumed that the costs of the shipments and dealing with customer inquiries were proportionate. Should management consider whether there are fixed elements in these activities? The answer depends on the balance between the marginal benefit and the marginal cost of accuracy.

> **Activity-based costing** consists of identifying the activities undertaken by the group incurring indirect costs, investigating how the various products drive these indirect activities, allocating the costs of the activities among the products, and combining the allocated indirect costs with the direct costs.

Progress Check 7E Referring to tables 7.10 and 7.11, suppose that the Beta product requires 1,500 shipments and 3,000 customer inquiries a year. Under this assumption, compare the average cost of the two products.

Progress check

Activity-based costing at Harris Semiconductor

In 1989, the Harris Corporation acquired General Electric's semiconductor business. The business, however, did not perform well. A year after the acquisition, Harris wrote off $72.9 million in restructuring expenses. The following year, Harris semiconductor sector reported a loss of $75.5 million, which led to management being replaced.

Phillip Farmer, the new president of the semiconductor sector, discovered that the company had no accurate information on costs. Semiconductor manufacturing involves relatively small direct costs. Harris produced a wide spectrum of products, ranging from basic memories to specialized chips. The company should have paid close attention to the allocation of indirect costs.

Farmer introduced activity-based costing. The new system revealed that margins on logic and memory chips were low, while specialized chips for automobiles and medical equipment were much more profitable. By laying off 2,400 of 11,500 employees, including more than a third of middle management, and by refocusing sales on the higher-margin products, Farmer restored the semiconductor business to profit by the middle of 1992.

Source: "Harris Finally Digests Big Semiconductor Acquisition," *Wall Street Journal*, October 13, 1992, p. B6.

◀◀ 8 Statistical Methods[4]

We have presented three principles to guide managers in analyzing business costs. While these principles are very clear, in practice, managers are often confronted with a mass of disparate information. Under these circumstances, it helps to use statistical methods, specifically, multiple regression, to understand the data. These methods are also useful in making forecasts about costs.

Multiple regression can help in many analyses of costs, including researching the relationship between costs and the scale and scope of production and also understanding how indirect costs depend on various indirect activities.

Multiple Regression

In the following example, we show how to use multiple regression analysis to investigate the extent of fixed costs and economies of scale. Suppose that, from past experience, the management of Mercury Elevator has identified four major factors

▼

[4] This section is more advanced. It may be omitted without loss of continuity.

Table 7.12 Elevator manufacturing costs

Direct cost (thousand $)	Capacity (thousand kg)	Speed (m/s)	Travel (m)	Landings
65	1.60	1.6	21.0	2
63	0.71	1.6	47.5	8
64	0.85	1.6	47.5	8
39	1.00	0.6	15.0	6
59	0.90	1.0	45.2	9
50	0.90	1.0	28.6	6
56	0.90	1.6	60.9	6
35	0.80	1.0	6.9	2
58	0.54	1.0	40.6	15
45	0.54	1.0	40.7	8
68	0.82	1.0	43.8	16

in the direct manufacturing cost of an elevator system: the rated capacity and speed, the distance through which the elevator travels, and the number of landings.

To support its pricing, Mercury would like to understand how its direct cost depends on the four factors. It would also like to know whether there are significant fixed elements in the direct cost. Fixed costs would give rise to economies of scale in production.

We can use multiple regression to address these questions. First, we collect data on the direct cost and the corresponding characteristics for some recent projects (see table 7.12).

In the multiple regression analysis, we specify direct cost as the dependent variable and four independent variables: capacity (in thousand kilograms), speed (in meters per second), travel (in meters), and number of landings. Table 7.13 reports the results of the analysis.

Referring to table 7.13, the F-statistic is 27.79, and the probability that all the coefficients are 0 is 0.00. Accordingly, we can be very confident that the regression equation is statistically valid. The R-squared is 0.95; hence, the equation explains a very high percentage of the variation of the cost.

The intercept is −5.51, which is negative. The probability that the intercept is 0 is 0.41. If there is a fixed direct cost in manufacturing, then the direct cost would be positive even with all the independent variables being equal to 0. Hence, the fixed cost would be reflected in the intercept. We find, however, that the intercept

Table 7.13 Multiple regression analysis estimates

Regression statistics:	
R-square	0.95
Standard error	3.23
Number of observations	11
F-statistic	27.79
Significance	0.00

Independent variable	Coefficient	Standard error	t-statistic	Significance
Intercept	−5.51	6.16	−0.89	0.41
Capacity	21.20	4.77	4.44	0.00
Speed	19.63	4.80	4.09	0.01
Travel	0.04	0.12	0.35	0.74
Landings	2.19	0.36	6.12	0.00

is negative and not statistically significant. This suggests that there are no significant fixed elements in manufacturing.

The coefficients for capacity, speed, and landings are positive. The probability that each of these coefficients is 0 is less than 0.05. Hence, we can be very confident that these variables are significant factors in the direct cost of manufacturing an elevator.

The coefficient for travel is positive, but the probability that this coefficient is 0 is 0.74. This suggests that, contrary to management's belief, the distance of travel is not a significant factor in the direct manufacturing cost.

Forecasting

A multiple regression equation can be used to forecast the dependent variable when the independent variables take different values. For this, we need a statistically significant multiple regression equation that explains a high percentage of the variation of the dependent variable.

Referring to table 7.13, the equation for Mercury Elevator meets these conditions. Management can use the equation to forecast the cost of any future project. For instance, suppose that a client has requested a quotation for a system with the following characteristics: capacity of 1,000 kilograms, speed of 1.0 meter per second, travel of 20 meters, and four landings. Then, the estimated cost (in thousands of dollars) would be

$$-5.51 + (21.20 \times 1) + (19.63 \times 1) + (0.04 \times 20) + (2.19 \times 4) = 44.88, \qquad (7.1)$$

or \$44,880.

Other Applications

We have just seen how multiple regression can be used to research the presence of fixed costs. Managers can also apply multiple regression to investigate the presence of joint costs across two products. To research this question, we need data about average costs when different quantities of the two products are produced together and when they are produced separately.

In the regression equation, the dependent variable should be the average cost and there should be three independent variables: the quantities of the two products and an indicator that takes the value of 1 where the two products are produced together and the value of 0 where the two products are produced separately. If there are joint costs, then the coefficient of the indicator should be negative and statistically significant.

Previously, we discussed how to use activity-based costing in allocating indirect costs. We implicitly assumed that we could proportionately allocate each indirect activity to the various products. If this is not reasonable, then managers can use multiple regression to allocate the costs of each indirect activity. There should be one equation for each indirect activity, in which the dependent variable is the cost of the indirect activity and the independent variables are the quantities of the various products. The regression coefficients will then show how to allocate the cost of the indirect activity to the various products and whether the activity involves a fixed cost.

◂◂ 9 Summary

Conventional accounting statements do not always provide all the information on costs necessary for effective business decisions. Managers should use the principles presented in this chapter to develop accurate information about costs.

Economies of scale arise from either significant fixed costs or variable costs that diminish with the scale of production. An industry where businesses exhibit scale economies will tend to be concentrated. Economies of scope arise from significant joint costs across the production of two or more items. Scope economies drive businesses to supply multiple products.

Opportunity cost is the net revenue from the best alternative course of action. Sunk costs are costs that have been committed and cannot be avoided. For effective business decisions, managers should consider opportunity costs and ignore sunk costs. The transfer price of an item within an organization should be set equal to the marginal cost.

Key Concepts

economies of scale	joint cost	transfer price
diseconomies of scale	relevance	direct cost
economies of scope	opportunity cost	indirect (overhead) cost
diseconomies of scope	economic value added	activity-based costing

Further Reading

For a general introduction to cost accounting, refer to Charles Horngren, George Foster, and Srikant Datar's *Cost Accounting: A Managerial Emphasis*, 10th ed. (Englewood Cliffs, NJ: Prentice Hall, 2000). Chapters 2, 3, 5, 10, 11, and 14 are especially closely related to the concepts presented here. C. K. Prahalad and Gary Hamel launched the concept of core competence in "The Core Competence of the Corporation," *Harvard Business Review*, 68, no. 3 (May–June 1990): pp. 79–91. Alfred Rappaport explains the concept of shareholder value added in *Creating Shareholder Value: A Guide for Managers and Investors* (New York: Free Press, 1998).

Review Questions

1. Define each of the following terms and give an example to illustrate your definition:
   (a) Variable cost.
   (b) Fixed cost.
   (c) Economy of scale.
   (d) Joint cost.
   (e) Economy of scope.

2. Generation of electric power involves significant short-run fixed costs. Owing to the entry of several independent power producers, the demand for Southern Power's electricity has dropped. Management has reduced production. How will this cutback affect Southern Power's average fixed costs?

3. Identify the situation for which economies of scale are more significant (choose a or b).
   (a) Tre Stagioni, which has a permanent staff of two chefs and five waiters.
   (b) Campus Deli, which relies mainly on part-time workers, hired on a monthly basis.

4. The most significant cost in family medicine practice is human resources. To treat twice as many patients, a clinic probably will need twice as many doctors, nurses, and other professional staff. Does this business have economies of scale?

5. Banks and insurers both need distribution networks to sell products and serve their customers. An office that takes deposits and makes loans can just as easily sell insurance policies. In France, many banks sell life insurance. Is the combination of banking and insurance, called *bancassurance*, a result of economies of scale or scope?

6. Hindus must not eat beef, while Moslem people must not consume pork. A restaurant catering to both Hindu and Moslem customers must have separate facilities for preparing Hindu food and Moslem meals. Are there economies or diseconomies of scope across the Hindu and Moslem restaurant businesses?

7. A salesman buys lunch for a potential client. Why is this lunch *not* free for the client?

8. Discuss whether business performance should be measured in terms of economic value added rather than accounting profit.

9. The Director of Executive Education at your school has reported that revenue increased from $5 to $5.5 million, while profit rose from $2 to $2.1 million. How would you consider the use of school facilities and faculty member time in evaluating these results?

10. There is a perfectly competitive market for lumber. How much should Saturn's residential development group pay the building materials division for lumber?

11. "Our costs are very high because of the huge pensions of our retirees." Are the pensions of retired employees relevant for prospective business decisions?

12. For which of the following businesses are sunk labor costs more significant (choose a or b)?
    (a) A Japanese conglomerate that guarantees lifetime employment.
    (b) A U.S. manufacturer that employs workers at will, which means that workers can be dismissed without cause.

13. Consider the costs of offering a freight transport service. In which of the following situations are sunk costs relatively largest?
    (a) The railway company owns the tracks.
    (b) The railway company pays another company to use the track on a long-term contract.
    (c) The truck operator pays tolls to use the highway as and when necessary.

14. Venus Machine Tools has automated production to the point that direct labor and materials accounts for less than 20% of the production cost. Explain why Venus should not allocate indirect costs in proportion to direct labor and materials.

15. Explain the relation, if any, between direct costs, and variable costs.

Discussion Questions

1. Qantas operates a fleet of over 100 Boeing jet aircraft. Commercial passenger jets must be operated by a pilot and co-pilot. Many jets carry cargo in their "bellies," under the passenger seating areas. Consider each of the following costs. Identify which are joint costs of the passenger and belly cargo services, which are fixed costs of passenger services, and which are both.

   (a) *Cockpit personnel.* All jets, large and small, require a pilot and co-pilot. Belly cargo service requires no additional officers in the cockpit.

   (b) *Airport landing fees.* Some airports charge landing fees by weight of the aircraft, while others levy a fixed fee regardless of weight.

   (c) *Fuel.* Larger aircraft and those carrying heavier loads consume relatively more fuel.

2. Elevators generally break down at random times and for different reasons. Elevator maintenance contractors must have trained service personnel to provide routine and emergency service. Shan On Elevator has 200 service personnel to maintain 1,000 elevators.

   (a) Suppose that Shan On has received a contract to maintain an additional 1,000 elevators. Do you expect that Shan On will need to double service personnel? Why or why not?

   (b) Does the example in (a) illustrate economies of scale or scope?

   (c) Escalators and elevators use quite different technology and parts. But many clients operate both escalators and elevators. Are there any economies of scope for a contractor to maintain both escalators and elevators?

3. Applying Internet Protocol technology, Qwest provides nationwide long-distance voice and data communications over a single network. Other carriers provide voice and data communications over separate networks. In 1999, while building networks for local telecommunications access in 25 metropolitan areas, Qwest acquired US West. US West dominated the market for local telephone and high bandwidth Internet access in the West and Midwest. Qwest forecast that the acquisition would bolster "scope and scale" through reducing operating expenses by $4.4 billion and capital expenditure by $2.2 billion over the period 2000–2005.

   (a) Discuss whether the acquisition would expand Qwest's horizontal or vertical boundaries or both.

   (b) To what extent do you expect the acquisition to yield gains from economies of scale?

   (c) To what extent do you expect the acquisition to yield gains from economies of scope?

4. Traditionally, electric power utilities generated electricity in large-scale plants with capacities of hundreds of megawatts. However, the economies of scale in generation had to be balanced against power losses in distribution of electricity, which increase with the distance of transmission. New gas-fired turbine technology allows cost-effective generation of electric power at small scales of 50–100 kilowatts.

(a) Explain the trade-off between economies of scale in power generation and power losses in the distribution of electricity.

(b) How did the development of the new gas-turbine technology affect economies of scale in the generation of electric power?

(c) How will the new gas-turbine technology affect the demand for electricity transmission equipment?

5. Mercury Electronics imports European and Japanese DVD players. In 1999, Mercury bought a shipment of 1,000 Japanese DVD players for $200,000 and another 1,000 DVD players from Europe for $180,000.

(a) In 1999, the yen appreciated by 9%. For purposes of pricing, what is the relevant cost of the DVD players in 2000?

(b) In 1999, the European depreciated by 16%. For purposes of pricing, what is the relevant cost of the European machines?

(c) Use the examples in (a) and (b) to explain the concepts of opportunity cost and sunk cost.

6. Under the Multi-Fiber Agreement, international trade in clothing is governed by export quotas awarded on a country-to-country basis. Until 1987, the Singapore government gave quotas to manufacturers according to their past export record. A recipient was permitted to subcontract the manufacturing of its quota. The Hong Kong government also gives quota allocations to certain selected manufacturers. It allows recipients to sell quotas on a secondary market.

(a) Suppose that Venus Fashion has a Singapore export quota for men's clothing. Consider Venus's internal manufacturing cost relative to that of a subcontractor. Under what circumstances will Venus choose to subcontract manufacturing?

(b) Suppose that Venus has a Hong Kong export quota for men's clothing. Consider Venus's internal manufacturing cost relative to that of other manufacturers. Under what circumstances will Venus choose to sell its quota on the secondary market?

(c) If the Singapore government were to adopt the Hong Kong resale system, what would be the effect on the quantities of clothing produced internally by quota recipients?

7. Over the 1990s, the Loewen Group expanded from funeral homes to cemeteries, partly financed by $2 billion of bonds and $300 million of bank loans. For the six months ending June 30, 1999, Loewen's operating earnings were $73 million. However, interest expenses of $77 million, and other nonoperational expenses dragged the group down to a $88 million pre-tax loss. Faced with the prospect of further losses, Loewen filed for bankruptcy protection in Canada and the United States. Chairman John Lacey called on bondholders to convert hundreds of millions of dollars of bonds into equity.

(a) Discuss whether the Loewen Group expansion from funeral homes to cemeteries affected its horizontal or vertical boundaries or both.

(b) If you had to justify the expansion, would you rely on economies of scale or scope or neither?

(c) Suppose that bondholders converted $500 million worth of bonds to equity. How would this affect Loewen's earnings before income taxes as compared with its economic value added?

8. In April 1996, the Singapore Technologies Group acquired disk-drive manufacturer Micropolis for S$80 million. Micropolis was hit by a severe downturn in the disk drive industry, and despite S$550 million in loans, the company had to be liquidated in late 1997. Liquidators estimated the market value of Micropolis's assets to be S$76 million as compared with their S$274 million book value. Table 7.14 lists the estimates for various categories of assets.

   (a) Which of the following best describes the difference between book value and estimated realizable value: (i) sunk cost, (ii) opportunity cost, (iii) fixed cost? Explain your answer.

   (b) Define "specificity" as the ratio of book value less estimated realizable value to book value, in percentage terms. Calculate the specificity of (i) inventories and work-in-progress, (ii) production equipment, and (iii) factory.

   (c) Explain the relation between sunk costs and specificity.

   (d) Explain why Micropolis's inventories and work-in-progress and production equipment have a higher specificity than the factory.

Table 7.14 Micropolis: Assets, December 1997 S$ million

	Book value	Estimated realizable value
Inventories and work-in-progress	130	13
Production equipment	34	4
Factory	70	45
Other items	40	14
Total	274	76

Source: "STPL's Micropolis Venture May Cost it $575m Loss," *Straits Times*, December 24, 1997, p. 1.

9. In 1979, almost all Middle East oil exports were shipped by tanker through the Persian Gulf. Then war broke out between Iraq and Iran and both countries attacked gulf shipping. By February 1988, a total of 308 tankers had been hit, of which 53 were total losses. To sustain its exports to Europe, Iraq built pipelines to the Red Sea and the eastern Mediterranean. At the end of the Iraq–Iran war, the *Far Eastern Economic Review* posed the issue, "The war's end, if permanent, leaves many uncertainties – its effect on secondhand tanker values for instance, and consequent effects on new buildings in yards around the world" (Michael Westlake, "Less Oil in Troubled Waters," *Far Eastern Economic Review*, (October 20, 1988).

   (a) How would the end of the war affect the cost of conveying a barrel of crude from Iraq to the eastern Mediterranean by pipeline?

   (b) How would the end of the war affect the cost of conveying the same barrel of crude from Iraq to the eastern Mediterranean by tanker?

(c) Which method of transportation involves a larger proportion of sunk costs, once incurred: pipelines or tankers?

(d) Do you expect tankers to recapture a dominant share of the Iraqi export market from the pipelines?

10. This question relies on the direct/indirect costs section. Major law firms organize their lawyers into functional practices, such as corporate law, litigation, real estate, and tax. One of the major indirect expenses of a law firm is the library. Explain how you would allocate the expenses of a library among the functional practices.

11. This question relies on the statistical methods section. Suppose that Mercury Elevator has just discovered a mistake in the data of table 7.12. In the first column, every entry for cost should be $14,000 higher. All other data remain valid.

(a) Estimate the cost equation with the original data (before the revision of the first column).

(b) Estimate the cost equation with the revised data. Does production involve substantial fixed elements?

(c) Using the revised estimates in (b), calculate the cost of a system with the following characteristics: capacity of 1,000 kilograms, speed of 1.0 meter per second, travel of 20 meters, and four landings.

Chapter 8

Monopoly

◂ 1 Introduction

Depression is associated with an imbalance of neurotransmitters, the chemicals that enable nerve cells in the brain to communicate with one another. The selective serotonin re-uptake inhibitor (SSRI) class of drugs helps to control the symptoms of depression by increasing the brain's supply of the neurotransmitter serotonin. Leading SSRIs include Eli Lilly's Prozac, Pfizer's Zoloft, and SmithKline's Paxil.[1]

In December 1987, Prozac became the first SSRI to receive U.S. government approval for treatment of depression. The drug quickly became a blockbuster. By 1999, Lilly's worldwide revenues from Prozac were $2.6 billion a year including $2.1 billion in the United States. Sales were supported by $60.2 million of detailing (visits to) physicians in offices and hospitals, $8.2 million of advertising in medical journals, and just $151,000 of direct-to-consumer advertising. However, Prozac was losing market share to Zoloft and Paxil.

In 1996, generic drug manufacturer Barr Laboratories began legal action to challenge Lilly's patent over Prozac. In the U.S. District Court, Judge Sarah Barker held that Lilly's patent was valid until December 2003. However, the U.S. Court of Appeals for the Federal Circuit overruled the lower court and cleared the way for generic competition from February 2001. Analysts expected Lilly to receive an additional six months' protection by testing Prozac on children and, so, competition would effectively begin only in August 2001.

Lilly priced Prozac at $2.63 for a day's supply. Generally, incremental margins on patented prescription drugs are about 90%, and generics are sold at half the price of branded drugs. Following the U.S. Appeals Court decision, Lilly's stock price fell

▼

[1]   This discussion is based, in part, on "Court Ruling Means Cheaper, Generic Prozac to Hit Market in 2001," *AP Business News*, August 11, 2000; "Prozac® Patent Ruled Invalid by U.S. Court of Appeals," Barr Laboratories Press Release, August 9, 2000; and "Hard to Swallow – America's Soaring Drug Costs," *Wall Street Journal*, November 16, 1998, p. A1.

by $31.86 from $108.55 to $76.69, reducing the company's market capitalization by $36 billion. Barr's stock price rose from $45.75 to $77, raising the company's market capitalization by $1.1 billion.

With the expiry of its patent and the advent of competition from generics, Eli Lilly had to consider whether, and if so, how to revise the price and advertising policy for Prozac. Why did the Appeals Court decision raise Barr's market value by less than the amount by which it reduced Lilly's value?

To address these questions, we must understand the behavior of buyers or sellers that have the power to influence market conditions. A buyer or seller that can influence market conditions is said to have *market power*. A buyer with market power can influence market supply, in particular, the price and quantity supplied. A seller with market power can influence market demand, in particular, the price and quantity demanded.

For simplicity, we will focus on markets in which there is either just one seller or one buyer. If there is only one seller in a market, that seller is called a **monopoly**. If there is only one buyer in a market, that buyer is called a **monopsony**. Monopoly and monopsony are extreme cases: at the opposite extreme lies perfect competition, where there are numerous buyers and sellers, all of whom are small relative to the market. The knowledge of these extremes helps us to understand the intermediate case where there are several buyers or sellers who are large enough to influence market conditions.

> A **monopoly** is the only seller in a market.

> A **monopsony** is the only buyer in a market.

We begin by discussing the sources of market power. Then, we analyze how a profit-maximizing monopoly sets its price and scale of production. This allows us to show how the monopoly should adjust price and production in response to changes in demand and costs. Applying this analysis, we can address the issue of whether and, if so, how Lilly should adjust the price of Prozac when generics enter the market.

Next, we consider how much a monopoly should spend on advertising. Then, we compare prices, production rates, and profits under a monopoly with perfect competition. This explains how competing sellers can benefit by restricting competition among themselves through cartels or horizontal integration. We can apply this analysis to explain why the Appeals Court decision raised Barr's market value by less than it reduced Lilly's.

Finally, we focus on monopsony and analyze how a monopsony that maximizes net benefit will set its price and scale of purchases.

◂◂ 2 Sources of Market Power

Before analyzing how monopolies and monopsonies use market power, we first review the sources of this power. To understand the reasons for a monopoly, we need to ask why other sellers do not enter the market to compete for the business. Generally, the sources of market power are the barriers that deter or prevent entry by other competing sellers. Similarly, the sources of market power for a monopsony are the barriers that deter entry of competing buyers.

Monopoly

UNIQUE RESOURCE   One barrier to entry by competing sellers is access to unique human resources. All team sports regulate the number and roles of players. For instance, football teams are limited to one quarterback and soccer teams to one goalkeeper. A football manager cannot field two quarterbacks nor can a soccer team have two goalkeepers. Under such circumstances, it is not possible to substitute quantity for quality.

Similarly, directors of performing arts such as movies, music, and theater cannot substitute quantity for quality. Imagine *Pulp Fiction* with Uma Thurman, John Travolta, and Bruce Willis replaced by randomly chosen extras from Central Casting. In sport and performing arts, the next-best performer or athlete is a poor substitute for a superstar. Accordingly, the superstar will have substantial market power and earnings that are disproportionate to performance.

By contrast, in many occupations, it is possible to substitute quantity for quality. For instance, a building contractor can replace a superfast bricklayer with two relatively slow bricklayers. Similarly, a restaurant can substitute two slow dishwashers for a single fast one. In occupations such as bricklaying and dishwashing, superior performers have relatively little market power and their earnings will tend to be proportionate to performance.

Another reason why competing sellers cannot enter is that they may be unable to get access to a unique physical or natural resource. Eurostar has exclusive right to use the Eurotunnel linking Britain with the European Continent. Eurostar offers a much faster service than competing rail operators, who must transfer their passengers to ferries for the English Channel crossing. In this case, exclusive access to a physical resource – the Eurotunnel – is the source of market power.

The platinum industry provides an example of natural resources giving rise to market power. Platinum is a relatively inert corrosion-resistant metal with a high electrical resistance that has relatively few substitutes. Anglo-American Corporation, a South African conglomerate, owns over 75% of the world's reserves of platinum. Anglo-American is an example where ownership of a natural resource is the source of market power.

INTELLECTUAL PROPERTY   A second source of market power is control over intellectual property; that is, property over inventions or expressions. To encourage research and development of new products and processes, most governments award patents for new inventions. A patent gives the owner an exclusive right to the invention for a specified period of time. This exclusive right may be a source of market power. Eli Lilly's patent to Zovant, a drug for the treatment of sepsis, provides it with a monopoly over the drug.

Another form of intellectual property is a copyright. A copyright establishes property in published expressions, including computer software and engineering drawings. Microsoft, for example, has the copyright over Office 2000, so it is illegal for another person to copy or manufacture the Office 2000 business software suite. The copyright to Office 2000 gives Microsoft a monopoly over the software. In chapter 11, we discuss the economics of patents and copyrights in greater detail.

ECONOMIES OF SCALE AND SCOPE A third source of market power is economies of scale or scope, as discussed in chapter 7. Electricity distribution illustrates economies of scale. This service requires an extensive network of cables leading from generating stations to the various users, including factories, residences, and offices. To have two competing distributors of electricity would mean duplication of the cable network. So, in electricity distribution, one provider can achieve lower costs than multiple providers. Hence, the industry will tend to be dominated by a single provider.

Cable television and local telephone service illustrate economies of scope. Both services depend on a network of cables from the service provider to the individual subscribers. Owing to economies of scope, a combined provider of television and telephone service can achieve lower average costs than specialized providers. Consequently, these industries will tend to be dominated by a single provider.

REGULATION A fourth source of market power is government regulation. In businesses where economies of scale or scope are strong, the government may decide to award an exclusive franchise to one provider. By deliberately prohibiting competition, the government hopes to avoid duplication and, so, reduce the cost of the service. Examples of businesses in which governments award exclusive franchises include local telephone service, and distribution of electricity and natural gas.

The U.S. Federal Reserve system: a monopoly money machine

In 1913, the U.S. Congress established the Federal Reserve System. The system consists of 12 Federal Reserve Banks, which have the exclusive right to issue currency notes. As of December 1999, $601 billion worth of U.S. currency was in public circulation.

Considering that currency notes are merely high-quality printed paper, it is not surprising that the Federal Reserve's monopoly is extremely profitable. In 1998, the Federal Reserve Banks earned $26.3 billion on revenue of $28.1 billion – a performance that would be the envy of any business.

Although the Federal Reserve System has a monopoly within the United States, it has no such privilege overseas. International business can be transacted in any currency. Despite competition from other currencies, the greenback has held up very well in international transactions. It has been estimated that 70–75% of $100 Federal Reserve notes circulate outside the United States. There was even $600 million in Vietnam at a time when that country did not have diplomatic relations with the United States.

Sources: Board of Governors of the Federal Reserve System, *1999 Annual Report*; U.S. Treasury Department, *The Use and Counterfeiting of United States Currency Abroad*, January 2000; "Hanoi Dictates Currency Clamp," *South China Morning Post*, August 10, 1994, Business, p. 10.

The government itself may also keep a monopoly over specific activities for reasons of national interest. For instance, almost all national governments have monopolies over defense and issuance of currency. In the United States, the Department of Defense monopolizes military services, and the Federal Reserve Board has a monopoly over the issuance of currency notes and coins.

PRODUCT DIFFERENTIATION   Finally, a seller may be able to establish market power by differentiating itself from competitors. Sellers can differentiate their products through advertising, promotion, product design, and location. Coca Cola provides an excellent example of product differentiation. There are many competing colas in the retail market. To differentiate its product, Coca Cola has made intensive investments in its brand that support a price premium over generic colas.

In retailing, an important dimension by which sellers can differentiate themselves is location. Retailers know well that consumer demand varies with location. In city centers, fast-food restaurants try to locate on streets with heavy pedestrian traffic. Gasoline stations prefer to locate at busy intersections.

Monopsony

So far, we have been discussing why a seller may be a monopoly or, more generally, have market power. These same factors explain why a buyer may have market power. There is one additional reason for the presence of a monopsony: the existence of a monopoly. A seller that has a monopoly over some good or service is also

Individual vis-à-vis market demand elasticities

Generally, the products of an entire market have fewer close substitutes than the product of an individual seller. Accordingly, the individual seller's demand will tend to be more elastic than the market demand. At one extreme, if the market is perfectly competitive, the individual seller's demand will be extremely elastic. At the other extreme, if the market is a monopoly, the individual seller's demand will be the same as the market demand; hence, it will have the same price elasticity as the market demand.

Table 8.1 reports the price elasticities of demand for representative individual businesses as compared with their respective markets. In food and apparel, a typical business faces a demand that is almost four times more elastic than the corresponding market demand. By contrast, in paper and petroleum, the individual demand is only slightly more elastic than the market demand. These data suggest that American manufacturers of paper and petroleum have relatively more market power than manufacturers of food and apparel.

Table 8.1 Market and individual demand elasticities

Industry	Price elasticity of demand	
	Market	Individual business
Food	−1.0	−3.8
Textiles	−1.5	−4.7
Apparel	−1.1	−4.1
Paper	−1.5	−1.7
Printing and publishing	−1.8	−3.2
Petroleum	−1.5	−1.7
Rubber	−1.8	−2.3
Leather	−1.2	−2.3

Source: Matthew D. Shapiro, "Measuring Market Power in U.S. Industry," National Bureau of Economic Research, Working Paper no. 2312 (1987).

likely to have market power over the inputs into that item. For instance, a monopoly electricity distributor would have market power over suppliers of electricity meters and high-voltage switch-gear. It would probably also be a monopsony in the market for the services of power engineers.

When AT&T had a near-monopoly over local telecommunications in the United States, it was also the dominant buyer of terminal equipment. Indeed, AT&T established a subsidiary, Western Electric, to manufacture terminal equipment for itself.

Defense provides another example. We have mentioned that national governments monopolize defense. By this monopoly, the government would have market power over suppliers of military equipment and supplies, as well as the services of military personnel.

◂◂ 3 Monopoly Pricing

Having reviewed the sources of market power, let us now consider how a seller can use market power. Suppose that Solar Pharmaceutical has just received a patent for a new drug, Gamma-1, that cures bone-marrow cancer. How should Solar set the price for this drug? The essence of market power is that the seller faces a demand curve that slopes downward. Solar Pharmaceutical, being a monopoly, faces the market demand curve. Unlike a perfectly competitive seller, a monopoly has to consider how its sales will affect the market price.

Given the market demand curve, a monopoly can either set the price and let the market determine how much it will buy, or decide how much to sell and let the market determine the price at which it is willing to buy that quantity. If the monopoly tries to set both the price and sales, the price and the sales may be inconsistent in the sense that, at that price, the market wants to buy more or less than the quantity the monopoly is selling. In terms of a graph, inconsistency means that the monopoly is choosing a combination of price and sales off the demand curve. Accordingly, a monopoly can set either the price or sales but not both.

Suppose that Solar decides to set the price and let the market determine the quantity of sales. A preliminary issue is Solar's objective. We shall assume that Solar aims to maximize profit, which is revenue less cost. This assumption, although not completely realistic, is enough for us to understand a monopoly's pricing strategy and several other practices as well. So, assuming that Solar aims to maximize profit, we must ask how Solar's price affects its revenue and cost.

Revenue

First, let us look at the relationship between price and revenue. Table 8.2 shows the demand for Gamma-1: Specifically, the second column shows, for every price, the quantity of Gamma-1 that Solar expects to sell. We see that the quantity demanded increases by 200,000 units for every $10 reduction in price. Using this information,

Table 8.2 Monopoly revenue, cost, and profit

Price ($)	Sales	Total revenue ($)	Marginal revenue ($)	Total cost ($)	Marginal cost ($)	Profit ($)
200	0.0	0		50		−50
190	0.2	38	190	52	10	−14
180	0.4	72	170	56	20	16
170	0.6	102	150	62	30	40
160	0.8	128	130	70	40	58
150	1.0	150	110	80	50	70
140	1.2	168	90	92	60	76
130	1.4	182	70	106	70	76
120	1.6	192	50	122	80	70
110	1.8	198	30	140	90	58
100	2.0	200	10	160	100	40
90	2.2	198	−10	182	110	16

Note: Sales in millions of units, total revenue, total cost, and profit in millions of dollars.

we can then calculate Solar's *total revenue* for every price, which is price multiplied by sales. From the total revenue, we can then calculate *marginal revenue*, which is the change in total revenue arising from selling an additional unit.

To sell additional units, Solar Pharmaceutical must reduce its price. So, when increasing sales by one unit, Solar will gain revenue from selling the additional (or marginal) unit, but it will lose revenue on the **inframarginal units**. The *inframarginal* units are those other than the marginal unit. Solar would have sold the inframarginal units without reducing the price.

> Inframarginal units are those other than the marginal unit.

For example, referring to table 8.2, to increase sales from 200,000 to 400,000 units, Solar must reduce the price from $190 to $180. Hence, Solar will gain revenue of $180 × 200,000 = $36 million on the additional units, but lose $(190 − 180) × 200,000 = $2 million on the inframarginal 200,000 units that it could have sold at $190. Thus, Solar's revenue for the additional 200,000 units is $36 − $2 = $34 million, which means that marginal revenue is $170 per unit.

In general, the marginal revenue from selling an additional unit will be less than the price of that unit. The reason, as we have explained, is that the marginal revenue is the price of the marginal unit minus the loss of revenue on the inframarginal units.

The difference between the price and the marginal revenue depends on the price elasticity of demand. If demand is very elastic, then the seller need not reduce the price very much to increase sales; hence, the marginal revenue will be close to the price. If, however, demand is very inelastic, then the seller must reduce the price substantially to increase sales; so, the marginal revenue will be much lower than the price.

We should also emphasize that the marginal revenue can be negative, if the loss of revenue on the inframarginal units exceeds the gain on the marginal unit. Table 8.2 shows that, if Solar cut the price from $100 to $90, sales would increase from 2.0 to 2.2 million units. The change in revenue, however, is −$2 million for the additional 200,000 units, which means that marginal revenue is −$10 per unit.

Progress Check 8A If demand is extremely elastic, what will be the difference between the price and the marginal revenue?

Progress check

Costs

We have considered the relation between price and revenue. The other side to profit is cost. Table 8.2 also shows data for Solar Pharmaceutical's production costs. It reports only avoidable costs and omits sunk costs. From the total cost at a zero production scale, we can infer that production requires a fixed cost of $50 million.

Total cost increases with the scale of production. Table 8.2 shows Solar's marginal cost, which is the change in total cost due to the production of an additional unit. The change in total cost arises from change in the variable cost.

Profit-Maximizing Price

With information on both revenue and cost, we can calculate Solar's profit. Profit is total revenue less total (fixed and variable) cost. The last column of table 8.2 reports profit at every quantity of sales. Looking down the column, we see that Solar's maximum profit is $76 million. It achieves this profit with a price of $130 and sales of 1.4 million units.

In addition to calculating the profit from all possible prices or quantities of sales, the **profit-maximizing scale of production** can be identified in another way: determine the scale at which the marginal revenue balances the marginal cost. At the price of $130, Solar's sales are 1.4 million units. The marginal revenue is $70 per unit. The marginal cost is also $70 per unit. So, at the profit-maximizing quantity, the marginal revenue equals the marginal cost.

> The **profit-maximizing scale of production** is where marginal revenue equals marginal cost.

This suggests a general rule: to maximize profit, a monopoly should produce at a scale where its marginal revenue balances its marginal cost. This rule applies to any

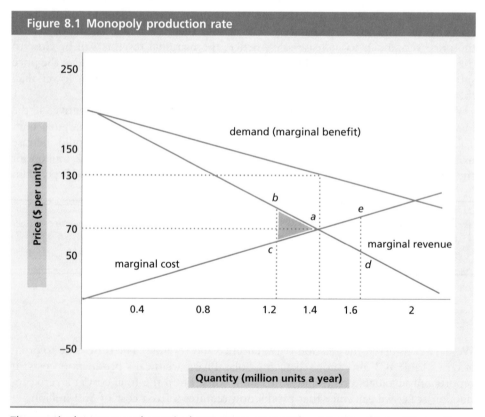

Figure 8.1 Monopoly production rate

The marginal revenue and marginal cost curves cross at the quantity of 1.4 million units. Reading from the demand curve, the profit-maximizing price is $130. The demand curve also shows the marginal benefit. At 1.4 million units, the marginal benefit exceeds the marginal cost.

seller and not only a monopoly. It can be expressed in another way. The **contribution margin** is the total revenue less the variable cost. If the seller sells an additional unit, then its contribution margin will change by the difference between the marginal revenue and the marginal cost. Hence, a seller

> The **contribution margin** is the total revenue less variable cost.

maximizes profit by operating at a scale where the sale of an additional unit will result in no change to the contribution margin.

Let us illustrate the profit-maximizing price and production scale with a diagram. Figure 8.1 shows Solar Pharmaceutical's demand, marginal revenue, and marginal cost curves. The demand curve shows, for every price, the quantity that the market will buy. Equivalently, it shows, for every quantity of purchases (on the horizontal axis), the maximum price (on the vertical axis) that the market will pay for that quantity.

The marginal revenue curve shows, for every quantity (on the horizontal axis), the marginal revenue (on the vertical axis). As we have explained, for every quantity, the marginal revenue is less than the price. Accordingly, at all quantities, the marginal revenue curve lies below the demand curve.

The marginal revenue and marginal cost curves cross at the quantity of 1.4 million units. From the demand curve, we see that the price at that quantity is $130. This is the profit-maximizing price.

Let us understand why a seller maximizes profit at a production scale where marginal revenue balances marginal cost. Suppose that Solar produces at a scale, such as 1.2 million units, where the marginal revenue exceeds the marginal cost. Then, if

Life-and-death monopoly: Glaxo Wellcome and the pricing of AZT

Glaxo Wellcome PLC owns the patent to the antiviral drug AZT. AZT blocks the enzyme that stimulates the HIV virus to proliferate. While the drug does not cure AIDS, it may relieve symptoms and prolong remission.

At one time Glaxo's drug meant the difference between life and death for many people. Even well-informed analysts have been confused into thinking that such a monopoly can make unlimited profit: "Once its products were approved, a big drug firm such as Glaxo could sell them at almost whatever price it wanted" ("Waging Sykological Warfare," *The Economist* (January 28, 1995), pp. 61–2.)

Although AZT was critical for a person with AIDS, Glaxo could not charge an unlimited price for the drug. Glaxo actually could set the price as high as it liked, but it could not force people with AIDS to buy the drug. Glaxo knew that, if it set a higher price, the quantity demanded would be lower. In 1994, the manufacturer set a wholesale price of around £1 per 100 milligram capsules and its total revenues were £207 million.

Source: Letter to shareholders, Glaxo Wellcome PLC (February 15, 1995).

Solar increases production by 200,000 units, its revenue will increase by more than its cost; indeed, it will increase its profit by the area shaded *bca*.

By contrast, suppose that Solar produces at a scale such as 1.6 million units, where the marginal revenue is less than the marginal cost. Then, if Solar cuts production by 200,000 units, its revenue will fall by less than its cost; hence it will increase its profit by the area *ade*. Generally, a seller will maximize profit if it produces at a scale where its marginal revenue balances its marginal cost.

Progress check   **Progress Check 8B** Suppose that, at the current scale of production, Solar's marginal revenue is less than its marginal cost. How should management adjust its price?

Economic Inefficiency

Figure 8.1 reveals an important aspect of a monopoly's profit-maximizing production scale. At the quantity of 1.4 million units, the price is $130. Recall that the demand curve also shows the marginal benefit for every quantity of purchases. Hence, the marginal benefit at 1.4 million units is $130.

By contrast, the marginal cost at 1.4 million units is $70. Hence, the marginal benefit exceeds the marginal cost. This means that some buyers are willing to pay more than the marginal cost for the item but cannot get it. In chapter 6, we explained that such a divergence between the marginal benefit and the marginal cost is economically inefficient.

The managerial implication of this economic inefficiency is that a profit can be made through bridging the gap to provide the item to those buyers. Since they are willing to pay more than the marginal cost, the difference is the potential profit to be made by supplying them. In chapter 9, we discuss various pricing policies through which a seller can increase profit by bridging the inefficiency.

Demand and Cost Changes

How should a monopoly respond to changes in demand? For instance, suppose that demand for Solar's Gamma-1 shifts outward. How should Solar adjust its price? To address this question, figure 8.2 shows the new demand curve. From the new demand curve, we can calculate the new marginal revenue curve.

The new marginal revenue curve lies further to the right. Since the upward-sloping marginal cost curve does not change, the new marginal revenue curve crosses the marginal cost curve at a larger scale. Specifically, the two curves cross at a scale of about 1.5 million units, and the new profit-maximizing price is around $135.

Although the change was only in demand, we must consider both the new marginal revenue and the original marginal cost to obtain the new profit-maximizing sales and price.

Figure 8.2 Demand increase

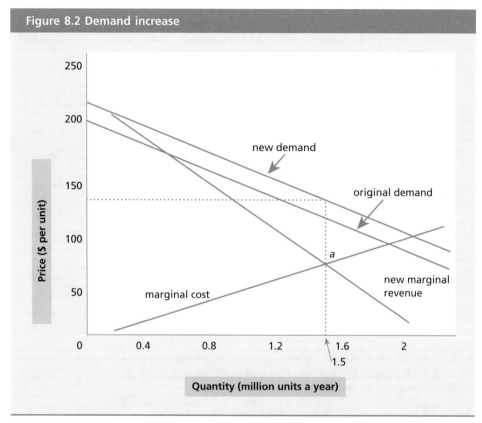

The new marginal revenue curve crosses the marginal cost curve at the quantity of 1.5 million units. The new profit-maximizing price is around $135.

We can use a similar approach to understand how a monopoly should respond to a change in the marginal cost. Suppose, for instance, that, relative to the data reported in table 8.2, the marginal cost drops by half at all scales of production. Should Solar reduce the price of the drug by half as well?

To address this question, consider figure 8.3, which shows Solar's marginal revenue and the new marginal cost. The marginal revenue and the new marginal cost cross at a quantity of about 1.7 million units. The new profit-maximizing price is around $120. Notice that Solar maximizes profits by cutting its price by about $10, which is proportionately less than the fall in the marginal cost. Further, although the change was only in the marginal cost, Solar must consider the marginal revenue as well as the new marginal cost to obtain the new profit-maximizing price and sales.

Generally, when there is a change in either demand or cost, the extent to which a monopoly should adjust its price depends on the shapes of both its marginal revenue and marginal cost curves. It should adjust the price until its marginal revenue equals its marginal cost and low marginal costs.

Figure 8.3 Reduction in marginal cost

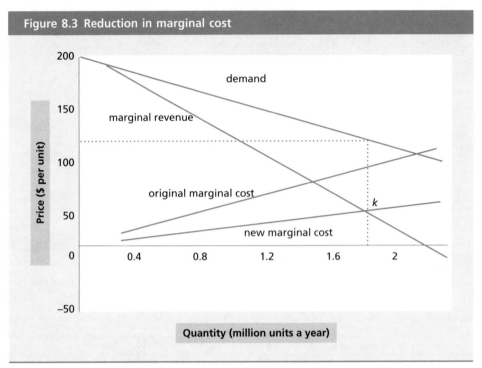

The marginal revenue and the new marginal cost cross at a quantity of about 1.7 million units. The new profit-maximizing price is around $120.

We should stress that a monopoly's profit-maximizing price and sales do not depend in any way on the fixed cost (so long as it is not too large). Suppose that Solar Pharmaceutical must incur an additional fixed cost of $40 million a year to maintain its production line. In table 8.3, we show Solar's revenues and costs with the higher fixed cost. The profit-maximizing price and sales are still $130 and 1.4 million units, respectively.

There is another way to see that the profit-maximizing price and sales do not depend on the fixed cost. Recall that a monopoly maximizes profit by operating at the scale where its marginal revenue equals its marginal cost. Changes in the fixed cost will not affect the marginal cost curve; hence, they will not affect the profit-maximizing price.

If, however, the fixed cost is so large that the total cost exceeds total revenue, then the monopoly will prefer to shut down. In Solar's case, if the fixed cost exceeds $126 million, the company will close. Unless the fixed costs are so large, they do not affect the profit-maximizing price and sales.

The general point that the profit-maximizing price and sales do not depend on the level of fixed cost is crucial for technology-intensive businesses. These businesses are characterized by relatively high fixed costs and low marginal costs.

Table 8.3 Increase in fixed cost

Price ($)	Sales	Total revenue ($)	Marginal revenue ($)	Total cost ($)	Marginal cost ($)	Profit ($)
200	0.0	0		90		−90
190	0.2	38	190	92	10	−54
180	0.4	72	170	96	20	−24
170	0.6	102	150	102	30	0
160	0.8	128	130	110	40	18
150	1.0	150	110	120	50	30
140	1.2	168	90	132	60	36
130	1.4	182	70	146	70	36
120	1.6	192	50	162	80	30
110	1.8	198	30	180	90	18
100	2.0	200	10	200	100	0
90	2.2	198	−10	222	110	−24

Note: Sales, total revenue, total cost, and profit in millions of dollars.

Progress Check 8C In figure 8.1, show how the monopoly should adjust price if marginal cost increases everywhere by $10.

Progress check

Planning Horizon

We have been considering how a monopoly should set prices and sales. Up to this point, we have not mentioned the length of the planning horizon. Let us now empha-size that the procedure for determining the profit-maximizing price and sales is essen-tially the same in the short and long runs. In a short-run planning horizon, the monopoly should aim to balance short-run marginal revenue and marginal cost; in a long-run planning horizon, it should balance long-run marginal revenue and marginal cost.

License auctions and the cost of mobile telecommunications

Telecommunications regulators around the world are concerned about how to allocate new licenses for mobile services. The German, U.K., and U.S. Governments have used multiple-round sealed bid auctions. Other regulators worry about the impact of license auctions on the cost of telecommunications services. Hong Kong Director-General of Telecommunications, Anthony Wong, remarked, "There's good and bad in auctioning off spectrum . . . it may raise costs for telecoms providers."

In fact, regulators need not worry at all. Typically, the auction price is a lump sum that does not vary with the quantity or variety of services that the telecommunications provider will offer. Accordingly, the auction price is a fixed cost with respect to the scale and scope of operations, and would not affect the marginal cost at all. Hence, the auction price would not affect the price of telecommunications services to end-users.

Even if a telecommunications provider were to over-bid and eventually suffer losses and become bankrupt, the license would still exist and could be sold to another provider. At that stage, the price originally paid for the license at auction would be a sunk cost, and would not affect its resale price to the new licensee.

Source: "Telecoms Chief Sees Further Fall in Long-Distance Tariffs," *South China Morning Post*, December 31, 1999, Business 1.

◂◂ 4 Advertising

> **Promotion** is the set of marketing activities that a business undertakes to communicate with its customers and sell its products.

A monopoly, and more generally, any seller with market power can influence the demand for its products. **Promotion** is the set of marketing activities that a business undertakes to communicate with its customers and sell its products. It encompasses advertising, sales promotion, and public relations. Let us now consider how much a business should spend on promotion. For convenience, we focus the analysis on advertising by a monopoly. The same principles apply to the other dimensions of promotion and any seller with market power.

Benefit of Advertising

How much should Solar Pharmaceutical spend on advertising its new drug, Gamma-1? Advertising can influence the market demand. Specifically, given Solar's price, expenditure on advertising can increase the quantity of sales by shifting out the demand curve as well as causing it to be less elastic. The additional sales in turn affect Solar's total revenue and variable cost and hence its contribution margin. The benefit of advertising is the change in the contribution margin.

Accordingly, the net benefit from advertising is the change in the contribution margin less the advertising expenditure. To maximize profits, Solar should advertise up to the point that the increase in the contribution margin from an additional dollar of advertising is exactly $1.

Let us understand why this rule maximizes profit. Consider a point at which the increase in the contribution margin from an additional dollar of advertising is more than $1. Then, if Solar spends an additional dollar on advertising, its contribution margin will increase by more than $1, hence Solar will increase its profit. By contrast, at a point where an additional dollar of advertising increases Solar's contribution margin by less than $1, Solar can increase profit by cutting back on advertising expenditure.

Essentially, the rule advises the seller to invest in advertising up to the point that the marginal benefit just balances the marginal cost. To keep a clear distinction between the benefits and the costs of advertising, we measure the benefits by the effect on the contribution margin.

By contrast, some marketing specialists measure the benefit of advertising by the effect on awareness and recall of the featured product or on product sales. We emphasize that it is more appropriate to consider the effect of advertising on the contribution margin generated by the product. The reason is that, ultimately, the aim of most advertisers is to increase the seller's profit rather than awareness or sales as such. Managers who focus on awareness and recall or even sales may overlook the effect on profit.

Profit-Maximizing Advertising

We have just presented a rule for advertising expenditure: to maximize profits, a monopoly should advertise up to the point that the increase in the contribution margin from an additional dollar of advertising is $1. Using the concepts of an *incremental margin* and the *advertising elasticity of demand*, we can derive a simpler version of the rule for the profit-maximizing level of advertising expenditure.

We define the **incremental margin** as the price less the marginal cost. The incremental margin is the increase in the contribution margin from selling an additional unit, holding the price constant. Recall from chapter 3 that the advertising elasticity of demand is the percentage by which the demand will change if the seller's advertising expenditure rises by 1%, other things equal.

In the math supplement, we show that, when the marginal benefit equals the marginal cost of advertising, the **advertising–sales ratio** (the ratio of the advertising expenditure to the sales)

> The **incremental margin** is the price less the marginal cost (which is the increase in the contribution margin from selling an additional unit, holding the price constant).

> The profit-maximizing **advertising–sales ratio** is the incremental margin multiplied by the advertising elasticity of demand.

is the incremental margin multiplied by the advertising elasticity of demand. This provides a simpler rule for the profit-maximizing level of advertising expenditure.

We can apply this rule to determine the profit-maximizing level of advertising expenditure for Solar's new drug Gamma-1. Recall that, with the demand and costs in table 8.2, the profit-maximizing price is $130 per unit and the marginal cost is $70. This means that the incremental margin is $130 – $70 = $60 per unit. Suppose that, at the price of $130, the advertising elasticity of the demand is 0.05. Then the profit-maximizing ratio of advertising expenditure to sales is $60 × 0.05 = $3 per unit.

At the $130 price, Gamma-1 sales are 1.4 million units. Hence, the profit-maximizing advertising expenditure is $3 × 1.4 million = $4.2 million.

Demand and Cost Changes

The rule for advertising expenditures implies that, if the incremental margin is higher, then the seller should spend relatively more on advertising. The reason is that each dollar of advertising produces relatively more benefit as measured by the incremental margin. Accordingly, when the incremental margin is higher, the seller should increase advertising. This means that, whenever a seller raises its price or its marginal cost falls, it should also increase advertising expenditure. By contrast, if a seller reduces its price or its marginal cost rises, it should reduce advertising expenditure.

Further, the rule for advertising expenditures implies that, if either the advertising elasticity of demand or the sales is higher, then the seller should spend relatively more on advertising. Essentially, a higher advertising elasticity of demand or sales means that the influence of advertising on buyer demand is relatively greater. In these circumstances, it makes sense to advertise more.

Progress check   **Progress Check 8D**   Suppose that the profit-maximizing scale of production for Gamma-1 is 1.4 million units. At that scale, the price is $140 per unit, the marginal cost is $70, and the advertising elasticity of demand is 0.01. How much should Solar spend on advertising?

Promotion

Up to this point, we have focused on a monopoly's advertising policy. The same principles apply to promotion, which is the general set of marketing activities encompassing advertising, sales promotion, and public relations. A monopoly should promote up to the point that an additional dollar of promotion increases its contribution margin by one dollar. The profit-maximizing ratio of promotional expenditure to sales is the incremental margin multiplied by the elasticity of demand with respect to an increase in promotion.

Dollar General's new advertising policy

Discount retailer Dollar General operates over 4,000 stores in 24 states, mainly in the midwest and southeast of the USA. The chain targets low and fixed-income families. Two-thirds of customers have household incomes below $30,000. Shoppers spend an average of $8.06 a trip. Of the 3,200 items that Dollar General sells, it prices 1,500 at $1 or lower, and the most expensive at $35. The average size of a Dollar General store is 6,700 square feet, which is smaller than the typical Wal-Mart or Kmart.

In 1998, Dollar General made a significant change to its advertising policy. It discontinued all advertising other than announcements of new stores. Financial analysts worried that sales would drop. With advertising expenditure dropping from 3.8% to 0.2% of sales revenue, sales indeed did fall. However, sales fell by less than Dollar General expected, and the company's profit rose.

Dollar General Chief Executive, Cal Turner, Jr., explained the new advertising policy: "Our customer lives within three to five miles of the store, knows we're there, knows who we are and appreciates the everyday low price."

Source: "Dollar General Sticks to Plan for Prosperity," *Wall Street Journal*, August 16, 1999, p. B11E.

◂◂ 5 Market Structure

Monopoly, the case of a single seller, is one extreme of a range of market structures. At the other extreme lies perfect competition, where there are numerous sellers, each of whom is too small to affect market conditions. How do price and production depend on the competitive structure of the market? Monopoly and perfect competition are extreme cases. Knowledge of these extremes helps us understand the intermediate case, where there are several sellers who are large enough to influence market conditions.

Effects of Competition

To address the question of how price and production depend on the market structure, consider the following example. We take a long-run perspective. Assume that the production of oranges involves no fixed cost and the marginal cost is constant at 30 cents per unit. We will compare price and production when orange growing is perfectly competitive with the outcome when the same industry is a monopoly.

First, suppose that the orange industry is perfectly competitive. Since production requires only a constant marginal cost of 30 cents, all growers will be willing to

Figure 8.4 Market structure

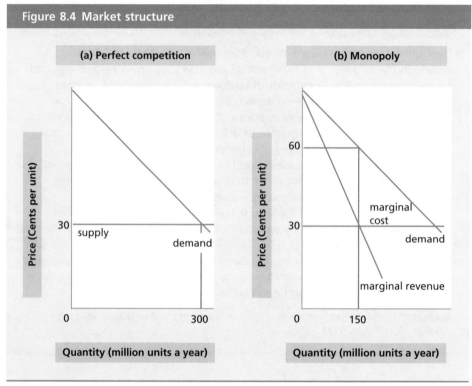

(a) Perfect competition

(b) Monopoly

(a) Under perfect competition, competition drives the market price down toward the long-run average cost of 30 cents. Production is 300 million units.

(b) Under a monopoly, the monopoly restricts production below the competitive level and sets a higher price of 60 cents to obtain larger profit.

supply unlimited quantities at 30 cents per orange. Hence, the market supply will be perfectly elastic at 30 cents per orange. Given the market demand, the supply will balance demand at a price of 30 cents. Figure 8.4(a) illustrates the market equilibrium. The sales and production will be the quantity demanded at a price of 30 cents, say, 300 million units a year. In equilibrium, each grower earns zero profit.

Next, suppose that the orange industry is a monopoly. The monopoly will produce at a scale that balances marginal revenue and the marginal cost of 30 cents. Since the marginal revenue curve lies below the demand curve, marginal revenue equals marginal cost at a quantity of less than 300 million a year. Accordingly, the monopoly will set the price above 30 cents. Suppose that the monopoly price is 60 cents and sales are 150 million units a year. Figure 8.4(b) depicts the monopoly price and sales. The monopoly will enjoy profits of $(0.60 - 0.30) \times 150 = \$45$ million a year.

The orange-growing example illustrates several general points. First, a monopoly restricts production below the competitive level, and by doing so, it can set a relatively higher price, extracting larger profit. By contrast, competition drives the market price down toward the long-run average cost and results in more production. Further, the profit of a monopoly exceeds what would be the combined profit of all the sellers if the same market were perfectly competitive.

Potential Competition

We have just seen that competition will push down the market price toward the long-run average cost. It is worth emphasizing that, under specific conditions, even *potential* competition will be sufficient to keep the market price close to the long-run average cost.

Consider a market in which sellers can enter and exit at no cost. Such a market is called **perfectly contestable**. A monopoly in a perfectly contestable market cannot raise its price substantially above its long-run average cost.

> A perfectly contestable market is a market in which sellers can enter and exit at no cost.

To understand why, suppose that Venus Trucking is the only truck service on the coastal route and that other truckers can easily switch their trucks from other routes to the coast. Now, if Venus raises its price above the long-run average cost, other truckers can profit by entering the coastal route. They will quickly enter to compete for a share of the market. The resulting increase in supply will drive the market price back toward the long-run average cost.

We have shown that a monopoly in a perfectly contestable market cannot raise price substantially above its long-run average cost. The degree to which a market is contestable depends on the extent of barriers to entry and exit. The introduction to this chapter reviewed barriers to entry. To the extent that there are barriers to entry, it will be more difficult for competing sellers to enter and, hence, it will be easier for a monopoly to raise its price above the long-run average cost.

The degree to which a market is contestable also depends on the extent of barriers to exit. Recall that, if Venus Trucking raises its price above long-run average cost, it might attract other truckers to enter the coastal market. These other truckers are lured by the attraction of temporary profits, made possible by Venus's relatively high price. Once Venus lowers its price back toward long-run average cost, these other truckers will leave. But their brief presence in the market will have been profitable.

Now, suppose that these other truckers must incur liquidation costs to exit the coastal market. When deciding whether to enter the market, these other truckers must consider these exit costs. The higher such exit costs are, the less likely these other truckers are to enter when Venus raises its price. This illustrates how barriers to exit affect the degree to which a market is contestable.

Lerner Index

Having understood the potential effect of monopoly on price and production, it is worth considering how to measure monopoly power. One measure is the

The **Lerner Index** is the incremental margin divided by the price, or the incremental margin percentage.

Lerner Index, defined as the incremental margin divided by the price, which is the incremental margin percentage. (This Index was proposed by the economist Abba Lerner.)

In a perfectly competitive market, every seller operates at a scale where its marginal cost equals the market price; hence, its incremental margin is 0. By contrast, a monopoly restricts sales to raise its price above its marginal cost. The more inelastic is market demand, the higher a monopoly can raise its price above its marginal cost. Accordingly, the Lerner Index focuses on the incremental margin, which is the difference between the price and the marginal cost.

The Lerner Index is defined as a ratio (incremental margin divided by price) so that it can be used to compare the degree of monopoly power in markets with different prices. For instance, the price of a floppy disk is much less than a dollar per unit, while the price of a database program may be well over a hundred dollars. It would not make sense to directly compare the incremental margins in floppy disks and database programs. Even if the market for database programs were almost perfectly competitive, the price would be a few dollars above the marginal cost. This difference would be close to the incremental margin in a floppy disk monopoly. Accordingly, to enable comparison of monopoly power in markets with different price levels, the Lerner Index is defined as a ratio.

The Lerner Index also captures the impact of potential competition. If, owing to the presence of potential competitors, a monopoly sets a price close to its marginal cost, then its Lerner Index will also be relatively low. One problem with the index, however, is that it will not detect the power that a monopoly does not exercise. Specifically, if a monopoly faces an inelastic demand but nevertheless sets a price close to its marginal cost, then the Lerner Index will be relatively low, indicating that the market is close to perfectly competitive.

Progress check   **Progress Check 8E**   Referring to table 8.2, calculate the Lerner Index when Solar Pharmaceutical sets a price of $130.

Common Misconception

Finally, let us mention one technical difference between a monopoly and perfect competition. A common mistake is to refer to a monopoly's "supply curve." In fact, there is no such thing. Recall that, to construct a supply curve in a perfectly competitive market, we ask each seller how much it would like to supply under the assumption that it can sell an unlimited amount at the given price. For a perfectly competitive seller, its marginal cost curve is also its individual supply curve.

By definition, a monopoly is large relative to its market, so it faces a downward sloping demand curve. This means that it cannot sell an unlimited amount without affecting the market price. Accordingly, for a monopoly or, indeed, any seller with market power, we cannot construct a "supply curve."

Prozac: value of a monopoly

Eli Lilly's Prozac and other selective serotonin re-uptake inhibitors control the symptoms of depression by increasing the brain's supply of the neurotransmitter serotonin. In 1999, Lilly's worldwide revenues from Prozac were $2.6 billion a year including U.S. revenues of $2.1 billion. In August 2000, the U.S. Court of Appeals overturned the District Court's finding that Lilly's patent over Prozac was valid until December 2003.

Under the extreme assumptions that Lilly would lose its entire sales of Prozac to generics and that all of its manufacturing costs must be written off, Lilly would lose its incremental margin on every unit sold. Supposing this to be 90%, Lilly's loss would be $0.9 \times \$2.6$ billion $= \$2.34$ billion a year.

The U.S. Appeals Court decision effectively shortened Lilly's patent by 26 months (the period between August 2001 and December 2003). Disregarding that a dollar in the future is worth less than a dollar in the present, the Appeals Court decision reduced Lilly's future earnings by $\$2.34 \times 26/12 = \$5.07$ billion. However, the decision reduced Lilly's market capitalization by $36 billion. Apparently, Wall Street had over-reacted.

By contrast, the Appeals Court decision raised the market capitalization of generic drug manufacturer Barr Laboratories by only $1.1 billion. Why did Barr's market value rise by less than the drop in Lilly's value? One reason is that with the expiry of Lilly's patent, any generic drug manufacturer, and not only Barr, could produce Prozac. The other reason is that the new competitors would reduce drug prices, which would hurt drug manufacturers, while benefiting those who pay for medicine.

Sources: "Court Ruling Means Cheaper, Generic Prozac to hit Market in 2001," *AP Business News*, August 11, 2000; "Prozac® Patent Ruled Invalid by U.S. Court of Appeals," Barr Laboratories Press Release, August 9, 2000; and "Hard to Swallow – America's Soaring Drug Costs," *Wall Street Journal*, November 16, 1998, p. A1.

◂◂ 6 Restraining Competition

We have just seen that a monopoly is more profitable than a competitive industry. Accordingly, rather than compete, sellers can increase profits by restraining competition among themselves. If sellers restrain competition to a sufficient degree, they can achieve the profit of a monopoly. Competing sellers can restrain competition in two ways: through agreement or by integration. We now discuss these ways of restraining competition.

Cartels

A **cartel** is an agreement to restrain competition.

A **cartel** is an agreement to restrain competition. A seller cartel is an agreement among sellers to restrain competition in supply, while a buyer cartel is an agreement among buyers to restrain competition in demand. Typically, a seller cartel sets a maximum sales quota for each participant. By limiting each participant's sales, the cartel restricts the quantity supplied and raises sellers' profit above the competitive level. The more effectively the cartel suppresses competition, the closer will the cartel's profit be to the monopoly level.

A seller cartel restrains sales to raise the market price above the competitive level. The higher is the price, however, the more attractive it will be for an individual seller to sell more than its quota. To the extent that any one seller exceeds its quota, the quantity supplied will increase and the market price will fall. So, to be effective, a cartel must have some way to compel each participant to abide by its quota.

Further, if a cartel succeeds in raising the price above the competitive level, it will attract new sellers to enter the market. Hence, another issue for a cartel is how to keep out new entrants. Therefore, the key to an effective cartel, or more generally, effective restriction of competition, is enforcement against existing sellers exceeding their quotas and against the entry of new competitors.

Enforcement

The laws of most developed countries seek to encourage competition and typically do not allow cartels except for specific exemptions. Cartels that are not legal must rely on private enforcement. Generally, the effectiveness of private enforcement depends on several factors. One factor is the number of sellers in the market. Enforcement is easier when there are fewer sellers to be monitored. So, a cartel will be more effective in an industry with relatively few sellers than in a fragmented industry.

Another factor in the effectiveness of a cartel is the relation of industry capacity to market demand. If all sellers are operating near capacity, then it will be difficult for them to expand; hence, there will be little incentive to exceed the specified quotas. By contrast, a seller with substantial excess capacity will have more incentive to exceed its quota.

A third factor is the extent of sunk costs. In the short run, competitive sellers are willing to operate so long as the price covers avoidable cost. Sellers with significant sunk costs will be relatively more willing to cut the price and exceed their quotas.

A fourth factor that influences the effectiveness of a cartel is the extent of barriers to entry and exit. Suppose that all the sellers in a perfectly contestable market form a cartel. Despite their monopoly, they cannot raise the price above the long-run average cost, because that would draw new suppliers into the market, which would drive the market price back down.

Finally, the nature of the product also influences the effectiveness of a cartel. If the product is homogeneous, then each individual seller faces a relatively elastic demand, so it can easily sell more than its quota. On the other hand, if the product is homogeneous, it is easier for the cartel to monitor the various sellers. Frequently, sellers circumvent cartels by attributing increases in sales to items not covered by the cartel agreement. If the product is homogeneous, such subterfuge is no longer possible; hence, it will be easier to enforce the cartel.

Labor Unions

Labor unions are probably the most widespread cartels. Unions organize workers to negotiate with employers over wages and conditions of work. Negotiations in which workers are represented by a union are called *collective bargaining*. Unions are explicit seller cartels: their primary purpose is to gain higher wages and better conditions than workers could obtain through individual negotiation. Developed countries have encouraged workers to form unions, and most have laws that specifically allow workers the right to form labor unions.

Recall from our earlier analysis that a monopoly restrains production to raise the price and gain larger profit. In the case of a labor union, it must restrain the amount of employment so as to raise wages above the competitive level. Accordingly, to the extent that a union succeeds in raising wages, it must restrict employment. This means that it must exclude some workers from work.

Nonunion workers present a major threat to labor unions. To prevent such competition, a union would ideally like to establish a "closed shop." A factory or other place of employment is a closed shop if the employer commits not to hire nonunion workers. A union with a closed shop has a monopoly over the labor supply. At its

Government enforcement

Some cartels have the advantage of government enforcement. For instance, the U.S. government has instituted Agricultural Marketing Orders in a number of agricultural products. Under these orders, the government regulates how much each farmer or grower may produce and, so, determines total production and the market price. In effect, these Agricultural Marketing Orders are legalized seller cartels enforced by the government.

Another market in which a seller cartel enjoys government support is international air service. International airlines need the permission of at least two governments: those at the points of departure and arrival. Many governments tightly control airline capacity, frequency, and fares through bilateral aviation agreements. Owing to these controls, an airline that cuts fares might not get government permission to expand its flights to meet the increase in quantity demanded. Hence, government regulation inhibits airlines from cutting fares. In addition, regulation also limits the entry of new airlines.

Business triumphs over ideology: De Beers' central selling organization

Until the early 1990s, the government of South Africa practiced an official policy of racial discrimination called *apartheid*. Blacks could not live in areas reserved for whites, a colored (mixed-race) child could not attend a school reserved for blacks, and it was even illegal for persons of different races to engage in sexual intercourse. As a result of the apartheid policy, South Africa was ostracized by the governments of many countries, including the Soviet Union.

At one time, South Africa was the world's leading producer of raw gem-quality diamonds. The De Beers group, which monopolized the South African diamond industry, established the Central Selling Organisation (CSO) to manage the international diamond market. The CSO bought diamonds when it perceived prices to be too low and sold as prices rose.

The Soviet Union's large resources of raw diamonds, however, threatened De Beers' cosy monopoly. Sensing the problem, De Beers sought a deal with Moscow. Although the Soviet government resolutely opposed South Africa's apartheid policy, it recognized the benefits of maintaining control over international diamond sales. In 1959, the Soviet government agreed to channel its diamonds through the CSO.

Over time, other countries came to dominate world production of raw diamonds. By 1992, the world's top three producers were Botswana, Russia, and Angola. While publicly hostile to South Africa, the governments of Angola and Botswana also agreed to cooperate with the CSO, so preserving the CSO's power over the diamond market.

Source: "Russian Diamonds: Disputes are Forever," *Economist*, September 17, 1994, pp. 71–2; "De Beers Supremo Dies at 83 Years," *South China Morning Post*, October 21, 1995, Business, p. 5.

most extreme, a closed shop means that the employer must dismiss all nonunion workers and cannot hire nonunion workers in the future.

Another challenge to a labor union is the extent to which the employer can automate the production process or shift production overseas. Automation is the substitution of equipment for labor; moving to an overseas location is the substitution of foreign labor for domestic labor.

Progress check

Progress Check 8F Recall the five factors that determine the effectiveness of a cartel. How do these apply to a labor union?

The Brisbane concrete cartel

Concrete, a mixture of cement, gravel, sand, and water, is an essential input into building construction. By its very nature, concrete solidifies quickly; hence, once mixed, it cannot be transported over long distances. Suppliers must mix concrete at plants close to their customers' construction sites. The land for mixing plants is a major fixed cost. Physically, concrete is a fairly homogeneous product.

In 1989, five major suppliers – Pioneer, Boral, CSR, Goodmix/Hymix, and Rocla – accounted for about 95% of the concrete market in Brisbane, Australia. Following a price war, the big five agreed to limit competition so that each could maintain its respective historical market share. In particular, they agreed not to poach customers from one another.

The big five held regular meetings to discuss upcoming concrete sales. The meetings allocated each sale to a particular supplier and fixed the price for the sale, with the other suppliers agreeing to quote a higher price or not to quote at all. From time to time, the meetings also arranged to raise the price of concrete.

To discourage cheating, each of the big five reported information on its sales volume, prices, and raw materials costs to a firm of accountants. The accountants collated this information as the Brisbane Concrete Survey. The big five used the survey to verify their respective market shares and to check whether anyone had undercut the agreed prices.

Generally, if a cartel succeeds in raising the price above the competitive level, it will attract new entrants. In 1991, Excel Concrete entered the Brisbane market. The big five responded by targeting Excel's customers with extremely low prices. Further, Excel's concrete plants were subject to opposition in local government councils. Two years later, however, Excel was acquired by the Holderbank group of Switzerland. Once the big five saw that Excel had stronger backing, they changed tack and invited Excel to join the cartel.

After an investigation by the Australian Competition and Consumer Commission, all the big five – Pioneer, Boral, CSR, Goodmix/Hymix, and Rocla – were prosecuted and fined for colluding on prices.

Source: Letter from the Australian Competition and Consumer Commission, December 14, 1995.

The power of Indian banking unions

Indian employers must apply for government permission to dismiss workers. Owing to the fear of increasing unemployment, the government seldom approves the applications. Backed by such laws, labor unions have considerable power over employers. Unions in the banking industry have used this power to block automation. In 1993, the unions forced Indian banks to agree that those with more than 500 branches would computerize at a rate not exceeding 0.5% a year, while those with fewer than 500 branches could computerize at 1% a year.

Source: "How to Keep Investors Out," *Economist*, June 11, 1994, p. 27.

Horizontal Integration

Cartels that are illegal must rely on private enforcement to prevent sellers from exceeding their quotas. However, competing sellers can restrain competition in a way that does not raise the difficulties of enforcement. The alternative is for the competing sellers to integrate.

Acquiring market power in disk drives: Seagate Technology and Conner Peripherals

Computers store data in disk drives. Until September 1995, the world's four largest manufacturers in the $17 billion disk drive industry were Seagate Technology, Quantum, Conner Peripherals, and Western Digital. Then, Seagate announced that it would acquire Conner in an exchange of shares worth over $1 billion.

Among the reasons that industry analysts cited for the acquisition was the effect on competition. The combination of Seagate and Conner commanded more than a third of the worldwide market. According to David Bunzel, of the Santa Clara Consulting Group, "It probably puts [Seagate] into a leadership role that ultimately could benefit the industry."

Seagate's announcement of the acquisition resulted in the shares of Quantum and Western Digital rising by 6.8 and 5%, respectively. These reactions were consistent with the belief that Seagate's acquisition would reduce industry competition and hence result in higher prices for all manufacturers.

Sources: "Disk Drive Maker Seagate Talking Buyout with Conner," *Business Journal* [San Jose], September 25, 1995, Section 1, p. 9; "Seagate to Acquire Conner in $1.04 Billion Stock Swap," *New York Times*, September 21, 1995, Business, pp. 1 and 6.

Consider, for instance, a combination of two sellers, each of which has 50% of a market. The combined business will have a monopoly. While it may be illegal for two independent competitors to fix prices between themselves, it is certainly legal for the two parts of the same company to agree on prices. Hence, a combination that creates a monopoly will certainly be able to set price and sales at monopoly levels, subject, of course, to the entry of potential competitors.

> **Horizontal integration** is the combination of two entities, in the same or similar businesses, under a common ownership.

The combination of two entities, in the same or similar businesses, under a common ownership is called **horizontal integration**. This should be distinguished from **vertical integration**, which describes the combination of the assets for two successive stages of production under a common ownership.

> **Vertical integration** is the combination of the assets for two successive stages of production, under a common ownership.

The horizontal integration of any two businesses with market power will lead to a reduction in the quantity supplied, and hence raise the market price and increase profits. The increase in the market price will benefit competing sellers as they will enjoy higher profits.

◂◂ 7 Monopsony

A monopoly and, more generally, any seller with market power will restrain sales to raise the price and so increase profit. Let us now consider how the behavior of a buyer with market power will differ from that of a perfectly competitive buyer. We focus on a market where there is only one buyer, that is, a *monopsony*. Since there are close parallels between monopoly and monopsony, we will briefly highlight the similarities, while focusing on the important differences.

Benefit and Expenditure

Suppose that a key input into the production of Gamma-1 is a tropical leaf that grows in South America. Solar is the only buyer of this leaf; hence, it is a monopsony. By contrast, many growers produce the leaf. Each grower is too small to affect market conditions, so the supply of the leaf is perfectly competitive.

Since the leaf is a key input into Solar's manufacturing process, it provides a benefit that can be measured as the revenue generated less the costs of other associated inputs. The leaf, however, must be bought from the South American growers. Solar's expenditure is the market price of the leaf multiplied by the quantity purchased. Accordingly, Solar's net benefit from the leaf is its benefit less expenditure. We suppose that Solar's objective is to maximize its net benefit.

Let us determine the quantity of purchases at which Solar will maximize its net benefit. Referring to figure 8.5, Solar's benefit depends on the quantity of its purchases: we suppose that the marginal benefit of a small quantity is very high and that the marginal benefit falls with the scale of purchases.

Figure 8.5 Monopsony purchasing

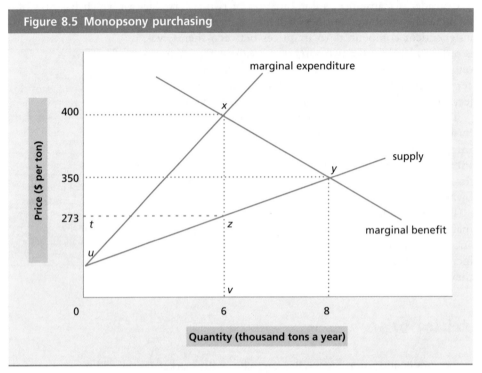

The marginal benefit and marginal expenditure curves cross at a quantity of 6,000 tons. Reading from the supply curve, the price at that quantity is $273. The supply curve also shows the marginal cost. At 6,000 tons, the marginal benefit exceeds the marginal cost.

Also referring to figure 8.5, the supply curve shows, for every quantity, the price at which competitive sellers will provide the leaf. Equivalently, the supply curve represents the monopsony's average expenditure for every possible quantity of purchases. Since the price must be higher to induce a greater quantity of supply, the average expenditure curve slopes upward.

> The **marginal expenditure** is the change in expenditure resulting from an increase in purchases by one unit.

The **marginal expenditure** is the change in expenditure resulting from an increase in purchases by one unit. For the average expenditure curve to slope upward, the marginal expenditure curve must lie above the average expenditure curve and slope upward more steeply.

> The net benefit maximizing scale of purchases is where marginal benefit equals marginal expenditure.

Maximizing Net Benefit

We can now state the following rule: a monopsony or any buyer with market power will maximize its net benefit by purchasing the quantity at which its marginal benefit equals its marginal expenditure. To explain this rule, consider a scale of purchases where Solar's marginal benefit exceeds marginal expenditure. Then, if Solar steps up purchases, its benefit will increase by more than its expenditure; hence it will obtain a larger net benefit. By contrast, if marginal benefit is less than marginal expenditure, Solar should reduce purchases: its benefit will drop by less than its expenditure. Solar will exactly maximize net benefit when it purchases the quantity where its marginal benefit balances its marginal expenditure.

Referring to figure 8.5, the quantity that maximizes net benefit is 6,000 tons. At that quantity, the price is $273 per ton. Notice that the price of $273 per ton is less than the buyer's marginal benefit. By contrast, if the demand side was competitive and the marginal benefit curve represented the market demand, the equilibrium price would be $350 per ton and the quantity would be 8,000 tons. This illustrates a general point: a monopsony restricts purchases to get a lower price and increase its net benefit above the competitive level.

Progress Check 8G In figure 8.5, shade in an area that represents Solar's total expenditure on the tropical leaf.

Progress check

Restraining Competition

A monopsony can use its market power to get a lower price than many small competing buyers. This provides an incentive for competing buyers to restrain purchases collectively and, so, depress the market price below the competitive level. A buyer cartel restrains each participant's purchases to a maximum quota to reduce the market price.

Buyer cartel meets seller cartel: baseball

Generally, U.S. law prohibits buyers as well as sellers from cooperating to fix prices. There has been an exemption for major league baseball, however, since a decision of the U.S. Supreme Court in 1922. By virtue of this exemption, major league baseball restricts entry of new clubs, determines how clubs share revenue from ticket sales and broadcast rights, and regulates player salaries and transfers.

Until the spring of 1976, the owners of baseball teams had considerable monopsony power over baseball players. Then, the owners signed a collective bargaining agreement that allowed free agency for players with over six years' experience. Partly in consequence, the average salaries of baseball players rose from $46,000 in 1975 to over $1 million in 1992.

Alarmed by this rapid increase, the owners sought a cap on players' salaries. In August 1994, the players union rejected the salary cap and declared a strike, which led to the cancellation of the World Series for the first time since 1904.

President Clinton appointed W. J. Usery to mediate between the owners and the players. Negotiations, however, broke down in December. The owners then unilaterally imposed a salary cap, requiring the league's 21 teams to cut salaries by a total of $56 million a year.

Sources: Gerald W. Scully, *The Market Structure of Sports* (Chicago: University of Chicago Press, 1995), pp. 19–40, 49–55; "Owners Cap Pay as Tax Plan Fails," *Eastern Express*, December 24–6, 1994, p. 41.

Cheating on the cartel: The German engineering industry

Under Germany's system of national collective bargaining, an employer federation in each industry negotiates wages and other conditions with the corresponding labor union. By law, the national agreement between the employers federation and the labor union binds the entire industry. The result is wages and conditions that are uniform across the industry.

In the engineering industry, the employers federation Gesamtmetall spans international giants like Daimler and Robert Bosch as well as small businesses such as Bauer and Haeselbarth. IG Metall, representing 3 million engineering workers, is Germany's largest union. In March 1995, negotiators for Gesamtmetall and IG Metall concluded a new collective agreement, raising wages by 3.5%, and cutting working hours from 36 to 35 a week.

Consistent with our analysis of monopsony, major employers have negotiated more favorable separate deals with their own workers. After Robert Bosch threatened to establish a competing factory in Scotland, its workers accepted more flexible working hours. Likewise, Daimler agreed to build a new line of compact cars in Germany only after workers conceded on wages.

The ability of large employers to reach separate deals reduces their incentive to press hard in the collective negotiations. By contrast, smaller companies have no such power. On learning of the new collective agreement, Bauer and Haeselbarth quit the employers federation. Managing director, Erhard Lenz, remarked, "There's no unity among employers anymore."

Source: "German Companies Sour on Centralized Bargaining," *Asian Wall Street Journal*, October 18, 1995, pp. 1 and 12.

The lower the market price is, however, the more attractive it will be for individual buyers to purchase more than their quotas and for new buyers to enter the market. To the extent that individual buyers exceed their quotas, the quantity demanded will increase and the market price will rise. Similarly, if new buyers enter the market, they will increase the demand and raise the market price. Accordingly, the effectiveness of a buyer cartel depends on enforcement against existing buyers exceeding their quotas and against entry of new buyers. The factors that determine the effectiveness of a seller cartel also apply to a buyer cartel.

Instead of forming a cartel, competing buyers can restrain competition through horizontal integration. For instance, a combination of two buyers that each have 50% of the demanded purchases will create a monopsony. The market price under a monopsony will be lower than the price with competition among buyers.

◀◀ 8 Summary

Market power arises from unique resources, intellectual property, scale and scope economies, regulation, or product differentiation.

A seller with market power restrains sales to raise the market price above the competitive level and extract higher profits. It maximizes profit by producing the quantity at which marginal revenue equals marginal cost. The extent to which a monopoly should adjust the price and sales in response to changes in demand or costs depends on the shapes of both the marginal revenue and the marginal cost curves.

The profit-maximizing advertising–sales ratio is the incremental margin multiplied by the advertising elasticity of demand.

A buyer with market power restrains purchases to depress the price below the competitive level and raise its net benefit. Competing sellers and, likewise, competing buyers can restrain competition by forming a cartel or through horizontal integration.

Key Concepts

monopoly	Lerner Index
monopsony	incremental margin percentage
inframarginal units	advertising–sales ratio
contribution margin	cartel
promotion	horizontal integration
incremental margin	vertical integration
perfectly contestable market	marginal expenditure

Further Reading

References on promotion include the classic by Philip Kotler, *Marketing Management*, 10th ed. (Englewood Cliffs, NJ: Prentice Hall, 2000), chapter 19, and Paul R. Messinger's *Marketing Paradigm* (Cincinnati: South- Western Publishing, 1995), chapter 8. Gerald W. Scully provides a detailed analysis of monopolistic and monopsonistic practices in American sports in *The Market Structure of Sports* (Chicago: University of Chicago

Press, 1995). Dennis W. Carlton and Jeffrey M. Perloff provide a more detailed analysis of cartels in *Modern Industrial Organization*, 3d ed. (Reading, MA: Addison-Wesley Longman, 1999), chapter 5.

Review Questions

1. Give one example for each of the following sources of market power:
   (a) a unique human or physical resource;
   (b) an intellectual property;
   (c) economies of scale or scope;
   (d) regulation;
   (e) product differentiation.

2. Explain why marginal revenue is less than or equal to price. How does the difference between price and marginal revenue depend on the price elasticity of demand?

3. Luna Software has priced its new spreadsheet program such that its marginal revenue is more than its marginal cost. Advise the company how to raise its profit.

4. A monopoly restrains its sales to maximize its profit. True or false. Explain.

5. Once the patent on a product expires, others can freely manufacture the same product. Suppose that Solar Pharmaceutical's patent on the antiviral drug Beta-4 is about to expire. How will expiration of the patent affect
   (a) Solar's market power over the drug?
   (b) Solar's price elasticity of demand?

6. Explain why a seller must take into account both the marginal revenue and the marginal cost when considering how to adjust price following a change in costs.

7. The profit-maximizing price for Luna Software's spreadsheet program is $100. At that price, the advertising elasticity of the demand is 0.01 and sales are 500,000 units a year. The marginal cost of production is $40 per unit. How much should Luna spend on advertising?

8. The advertising to sales ratio for some drug exceeds the incremental margin multiplied by the advertising elasticity of demand. How can profit be increased?

9. For which of the following items will the advertising elasticity of demand be relatively higher? (i) item with no substitute; (ii) item with several equally popular competitors.

10. How would the Lerner Index for an industry be affected by a reduction in the degree of potential competition?

11. Suppose that a cable television provider merges with the local telephone company. How would this affect the degree of potential competition in the markets for cable television and local telephone service?

12. Is a cartel easier or more difficult to enforce in a market with a more homogeneous product?

13. Labor unions can use their market power to win higher wages and better working conditions for their members. By doing so, are they also causing unemployment?

14. A monopsony restrains its purchases to maximize its net benefit. True or false? Explain.

15. The National Collegiate Athletic Association (NCAA) restricts the amount that colleges and universities may pay their student athletes. If the U.S. government were to forbid the NCAA from such restrictive practices, what would happen to
    (a) each athlete's earnings?
    (b) the number of athletes?

Discussion Questions

1. Pfizer owns the patent to Viagra, which at the time of writing, was the only approved drug for erectile dysfunction. Bayer manufactures aspirin, which is not covered by patent and is one of several drugs that relieve the symptoms of the common cold.
   (a) Who has relatively more market power: Pfizer over Viagra or Bayer over aspirin?
   (b) How is the difference between price and marginal revenue related to the price elasticity of demand?
   (c) Compare the difference between price and marginal revenue for the two drugs, Viagra and Bayer's aspirin.

2. Table 8.2 describes the demand and costs for Solar Pharmaceutical's Gamma-1 drug. Suppose that the costs have been changed to a fixed cost of $75 million and a constant marginal cost of $50 per unit. The demand remains the same.
   (a) Prepare a new table of revenues and costs according to the new data.
   (b) What is the profit-maximizing price and production scale?
   (c) At that production scale, what are the marginal revenue and the marginal cost?

3. Hong Kong Director-General of Telecommunications Anthony Wong expressed concern about the effect of license auctions on the price of telecommunications: "There's good and bad in auctioning off spectrum . . . it may raise costs for telecoms providers" ("Telecoms Chief Sees Further Fall in Long-Distance Tariffs", *South China Morning Post*, December 31, 1999, Business 1).
   (a) Typically, licenses are transferable, but the one-time license fee, once paid, is not refundable. From an operational standpoint, how does the cost of a license depend on the price, if any, that the owner paid for it?
   (b) How does the one-time license fee affect the marginal cost of providing telecommunications service? How does it affect the profit-maximizing scale of operations?
   (c) Suppose that the one-time license fee is changed to an annual charge based on the telecommunications provider's revenue. How would the new policy affect the service provider's profit-maximizing scale of operations?

4. This question applies the techniques introduced in the math supplement. Suppose that Neptune Music has the copyright to the latest CD of the Heavy Iron band. The market demand curve for the CD is

$$Q = 800 - 100p, \tag{8.1}$$

where Q represents quantity demanded in thousands and p represents the price in dollars. Production requires a fixed cost of $100,000 and a constant marginal cost of $2 per unit.

(a) What price will maximize profits?
(b) At that price, what will be the sales?
(c) What is the maximum profit?
(d) Calculate the Lerner Index at the profit-maximizing scale of production.
(e) Suppose that the fixed cost rises to $200,000. How would this affect the profit-maximizing price?

5. Eli Lilly holds the patent to the antidepressant Prozac. In 1996, generic drug manufacturer Barr Laboratories challenged Lilly's patent. In January 1999, U.S. District Judge Sarah Barker held in favor of Lilly. That year, Lilly reduced its expenditure on direct-to-consumer advertising of Prozac from $37.5 million to just $151,000, while raising the expenditure on detailing to physicians from $49.9 to $60.2 million and advertising in medical journals from $7.9 to $8.1 million. Subsequently, the U.S. Court of Appeals overturned the patent, and generic competition was expected to begin in August 2001.

(a) Was Lilly's decision to redirect promotion spending away from consumers to doctors consistent with Judge Barker's decision?
(b) Following the introduction of generic drugs, how should Lilly adjust the price of Prozac?
(c) Following the introduction of generic drugs, how should Lilly adjust the promotion of Prozac?

6. Discount retailer Dollar General targets low and fixed-income families in the midwest and southeast. The majority of the chain's 3,200 items are priced at $1 or lower. Shoppers spend an average of $8.06 a trip. The average store size is 6,700 square feet. In 1998, Dollar General discontinued most advertising. While financial analysts worried that sales would drop, the company's profit rose. Chief Executive, Cal Turner, Jr., explained: "Our customer lives within three to five miles of the store, knows we're there, knows who we are and appreciates the everyday low price" ("Dollar General Sticks to Plan for Prosperity," *Wall Street Journal*, August 16, 1999, p. B11E).

(a) How could the cut in advertising raise profit while reducing sales?
(b) Explain Mr. Turner's comment in terms of the advertising elasticity of demand.
(c) Relate Dollar General's incremental margin and advertising elasticity of demand to the new advertising policy.

7. The California Public Utilities Commission (PUC) regulates rates charged by the state's $2-billion-a-year trucking industry. In June 1989, a PUC official proposed to allow truckers to reduce rates by up to 10% without PUC approval. Spokespersons for the trucking industry adamantly opposed the proposal, saying that it would allow rates to fall below cost ("Truckers Oppose Rate Change," *Los Angeles Times* (June 8, 1989), Part IV, p. 2).

(a) Suppose that the trucking industry is a cartel. If individual truckers had the freedom to cut rates, what would happen to the market price?

(b) The PUC must approve all changes in rates. How does this requirement help the trucking industry?

(c) From the perspective of the trucking industry, why is it important that the PUC has the power of law?

8. Gesamtmetall is the federation of employers and IG Metall is the labor union in Germany's engineering industry. Under the German system of national collective bargaining, Gesamtmetall and IG Metall negotiate pay and working conditions for the entire industry.

(a) With respect to labor, does Gesamtmetall serve as a buyer cartel or seller cartel? What about IG Metall?

(b) Consider large employers such as Daimler and Robert Bosch. Why might they prefer to negotiate separate deals with their own workers rather than comply with the national collective agreement?

(c) If all large employers negotiate separate deals, how will this affect the wages and conditions that small companies must offer?

9. For many years, the National Basketball Association (NBA) had a monopoly over basketball and, consequently, monopsonized the market for players. This monopsony over players began to erode in 1967 with the formation of the American Basketball Association (ABA). Finally, in 1983, basketball team owners agreed to allow free agency, which removed the restrictions against players moving between teams. An analysis of earnings showed that a player who scored 10% more points would have earned 2.05% more salary between 1968 and 1975, but 3.21% more salary between 1984 and 1988 (Gerald W. Scully, *The Market Structure of Sports* (Chicago: University of Chicago Press, 1995), pp. 50–3.).

(a) Explain the connection between having a monopoly over basketball and a monopsony over basketball players.

(b) Compare the wage rate when the demand side of the market is a monopsony with the perfectly competitive wage.

(c) Explain the difference in player earnings between 1968–75 as compared with 1984–88.

(d) When the ABA and NBA proposed to merge, the basketball players opposed the proposal. Explain why.

10. DaimlerChrysler, Ford, and General Motors dominate American automobile production. Some automobile parts, such as batteries and tires, wear out with use and must be replaced at relatively frequent intervals. Accordingly, suppliers of these parts sell their products both as original equipment to auto manufacturers and as replacement parts to car owners. By contrast, air bags and ignition systems wear out relatively slowly. The bulk of such equipment is bought by auto manufacturers.

(a) Referring to relevant sources of data, calculate the combined share of Daimler-Chrysler, Ford, and General Motors in the American automobile market.

(b) Assess the power of automobile manufacturers over sellers of (i) batteries and tires as compared with (ii) air bags and ignition systems.

(c) For products in which auto manufacturers have monopsony power, do you expect prices to be higher in the original equipment market or the replacement market?

Chapter 8

Math Supplement

Price and Marginal Revenue

We first show that the marginal revenue is always less than the price, and also show how the difference depends on the price elasticity of demand. Let p represent the price of the product, and Q the scale of production. Since total revenue varies with the production scale, let us represent total revenue as a function, $R(Q)$, of Q.

By definition, total revenue is the product of price and sales, while sales is the same as the production scale,

$$R(Q) = pQ. \qquad (8.2)$$

We differentiate total revenue to obtain marginal revenue,

$$\frac{dR(Q)}{dQ} = p + Q\frac{dP}{dQ}. \qquad (8.3)$$

Since the demand curve slopes downward, $dp/dQ < 0$, so

$$\frac{dR(Q)}{dQ} < p. \qquad (8.4)$$

This result holds at all values of Q, hence it proves that the marginal revenue is less than the price at all production scales.

Rearranging equation (8.3), the difference between the price and the marginal revenue,

$$p - \frac{dR(Q)}{dQ} = -Q\frac{dp}{dQ}. \qquad (8.5)$$

By definition, the (own) price elasticity of demand,

$$e_p = \frac{p}{Q}\frac{dQ}{dp}, \qquad (8.6)$$

hence

$$p - \frac{dR(Q)}{dQ} = -\frac{p}{e_p} \qquad (8.7)$$

This shows that the difference between the price and the marginal revenue is inversely related to the absolute value of the price elasticity of demand.

Profit-Maximizing Production

Next, let us prove that a monopoly maximizes profit by producing at the scale where the marginal revenue equals the marginal cost. Since total cost and profit vary with the production scale, we represent them as functions $C(Q)$ and $P(Q)$, respectively. By definition, profit is total revenue less total cost,

$$P(Q) = R(Q) - C(Q). \qquad (8.8)$$

To find the production scale that maximizes profit, we differentiate profit with respect to the production scale, and set the derivative equal to zero. This gives us

$$\frac{dR(Q)}{dQ} = \frac{dC(Q)}{dQ}, \quad (8.9)$$

which implies that, to maximize profit, the seller must operate at a scale such that the marginal revenue just balances the marginal cost.

Let us apply this analysis to a monopoly that faces the market demand curve represented by the equation,

$$Q = 100 - 2p. \quad (8.10)$$

This demand curve is a straight line. Suppose that production requires a fixed cost of 300 and a constant marginal cost of 10 per unit.

Rearranging equation (8.10), the price,

$$p = \frac{100 - Q}{2}, \quad (8.11)$$

hence the total revenue,

$$R(Q) = pQ = \frac{1}{2}(100Q - Q^2). \quad (8.12)$$

Differentiating, the marginal revenue,

$$\frac{dR(Q)}{dQ} = \frac{1}{2}(100 - 2Q). \quad (8.13)$$

We can obtain the profit-maximizing production scale by equating the marginal revenue to the marginal cost.

$$\frac{1}{2}(100 - 2Q) = 10 \quad (8.14)$$

Solving, the profit-maximizing production scale is $Q = 40$. By substituting $Q = 40$ into (8.11), we obtain the profit-maximizing price, $p = 30$. Hence, total revenue

$$R(Q) = pQ = 30 \times 40 = 1200. \quad (8.15)$$

It was given that production requires a fixed cost of 300 and a constant marginal cost of 10 per unit. Accordingly, the total cost of producing $Q = 40$ units is

$$C(Q) = 300 + (10 \times 40) = 700. \quad (8.16)$$

Therefore, the monopoly's maximum profit is $1200 - 700 = 500$.

Advertising

Let us prove that, to maximize profit, a seller should advertise up to the point that an additional dollar of advertising increases the contribution margin by one dollar. In this case, we must recognize that sales depend on advertising expenditure as well as the price. Let A represent the expenditure on advertising and $Q(p, A)$ the sales as a function of price and advertising.

Profit is now total revenue less production cost and less expenditure on advertising,

$$P(Q(p, A)) = pQ(p, A) - C(Q(p, A)) - A. \quad (8.17)$$

To find the profit-maximizing expenditure on advertising, we take a partial derivative of P with respect to A, and set the derivative equal to zero:

$$p\frac{dQ}{dA} - \frac{dC(Q)}{dQ}\frac{dQ}{dA} - 1 = 0. \quad (8.18)$$

We can rearrange this equation as

$$\left(p - \frac{dC(Q)}{dQ}\right)\frac{dQ}{dA} = 1. \quad (8.19)$$

We call the term,

$$\left(p - \frac{dC(Q)}{dQ}\right) \quad (8.20)$$

the *incremental margin*. It is the increase in the contribution margin from selling an additional unit, holding price constant. The other term on the left-hand side of (8.19) is dQ/dA. This is the *marginal sales response*, or the increase in sales that results from an additional dollar of advertising. (The marginal sales response is the derivative of what marketing specialists call the sales-response function.)

Accordingly, (8.19) states that, at the profit-maximizing advertising level, an additional dollar of advertising increases the contribution margin by one dollar.

We can express (8.19) in another form that applies the advertising elasticity of demand. By definition, the advertising elasticity,

$$e_a = \frac{A}{Q}\frac{dQ}{dA} \qquad (8.21)$$

Rearranging, the marginal sales response is

$$\frac{dQ}{dA} = \frac{e_a Q}{A}. \qquad (8.22)$$

Substituting this in equation (8.19) and rearranging, we have

$$\frac{A}{Q} = \left(p - \frac{dC(Q)}{dQ} \right) e_a, \qquad (8.23)$$

which states that the profit-maximizing advertising–sales ratio is the incremental margin multiplied by the advertising elasticity and multiplied by the sales.

Monopsony

Finally, we prove that, for a buyer with market power, if the average expenditure is increasing with purchases, then the marginal expenditure curve must lie above the average expenditure curve and slope upward more steeply. Let E represent expenditure and Q represent purchases. Then the average expenditure is E/Q.

Suppose that the average expenditure is increasing with purchases,

$$\frac{d}{dQ}\left(\frac{E}{Q}\right) > 0. \qquad (8.24)$$

This implies that

$$\frac{1}{Q}\frac{dE}{dQ} - \frac{E}{Q^2} > 0, \qquad (8.25)$$

which simplifies to

$$\frac{dE}{dQ} > \frac{E}{Q}, \qquad (8.26)$$

that is, the marginal expenditure curve lies above the average expenditure curve. By differentiating again, we find that the marginal expenditure curve slopes upward more steeply than the average expenditure curve.

◂◂ 1 Introduction

With $8.5 billion annual revenues from over 56 million passengers, Northwest Airlines is one of the five largest airlines in the United States. In February 2000, economy class passengers on Northwest flight 1017 from Minneapolis to New York City's La Guardia Airport who compared tickets might have been surprised that fares differed by almost a thousand dollars. The unrestricted round-trip fare was $1,267, while the 14-day advance purchase non-refundable fare including a Saturday night overstay and $75 penalty for changes was only $311.[1]

Pricing is crucial for Northwest and other airlines. Travelers vary widely in the amount that they are willing to pay for the identical service. Moreover, when a plane is about to take off, the marginal cost (of filling an empty seat with another passenger) is almost zero. Airlines have invested millions of dollars in reservations and yield management systems with the aim of adjusting fares and allocating seats to increase profit. Between 1995–99, Northwest's passenger load factor, which measures capacity utilization, increased steadily from 71.5% to 74.6%.

Despite the airline's sophisticated systems, many business travelers buy fares that airlines intend for leisure travel. Northwest Vice President for Pricing and Yield Management, Tom Bach, explained, "[B]usiness travelers were contorting their schedules to stay overnight Saturday and qualify for fares with leisure travel restrictions." In February 2000, the airline launched a major pricing innovation to contain such behavior. Northwest introduced a new fare requiring 10-day advance purchase and a minimum stay of one night with a $75 penalty for changes. The new fare cost $765 for a round-trip between Minneapolis and New York.

Besides advance purchase and overnight stay restrictions, Northwest's fares vary on many other dimensions. It offers a 10% discount off adult fares to senior citizens,

---

[1] This discussion is based, in part, on "Northwest Airlines Offers New Type of Business Fare," *New York Times*, February 12, 2000, Business 14; and Northwest Airlines, *1999 Annual Report*.

special convention fares, and fares that are available only outside the United States in conjunction with an international ticket.

Since the marginal cost of a seat is almost zero, why doesn't Northwest fill all its seats and earn more profit? Why does it offer senior citizen discounts? What is the purpose of Northwest's advance purchase and overnight stay restrictions? Why did the airline introduce the new 10-day advance purchase fare?

In this chapter, we systematically tie threads from previous chapters on demand, elasticity, costs, and monopoly to analyze how a seller with market power should set prices to maximize profit. We first apply the price elasticity of demand and marginal cost. Our rule will explain why Northwest doesn't fill all its seats. Essentially, the reason is that, to fill the empty seats, it must cut fares to a point that it would reduce overall profit.

Sellers very commonly set the same price for every unit sold. We show how to raise profit by setting prices that realize different margins from various market segments. This depends on the extent of the seller's information about the individual buyer's demand. We consider situations where the seller has complete information as well as those where the seller has limited information.

Using our framework for segment pricing, we explain why Northwest offers special discounts to senior citizens, the purpose of advance purchase and overnight stay restrictions, and why Northwest introduced the new 10-day advance purchase fare. Any seller with market power can use the methods presented in this chapter to increase profit above the level available from charging the same price for every unit.

◀◀ 2 Uniform Pricing

Whenever managers are asked why do they not set a higher price, the most frequent response is, "Because I would lose sales." This does not, however, answer the question. Unless the demand is completely inelastic, a higher price will always result in lower sales. The real issue is how the increase in price will affect the profit of the business. As we will show, the answer depends on the price elasticity of demand and the marginal cost.

> **Uniform pricing** is a policy where a seller charges the same price for every unit of the product.

In this section, we shall consider only policies where the seller charges the same price for every unit of the product. These are policies of **uniform pricing**. Later in this chapter, we will discuss how a seller can extract higher profit by setting prices so as to realize different margins on various units of the product.

Price Elasticity

Suppose that Mercury Bikes plans to export racing bikes from the United States to Japan. It incurs no fixed cost in supplying the Japanese market. The only cost is a constant marginal cost of ¥30,000 per unit including production and freight. What price should Mercury set in the Japanese market? One proposal, based on the U.S. price and the freight, converted to Japanese yen, is a price of ¥38,000.

Recall from chapter 3 that the own-price elasticity of demand is the percentage by which the quantity demanded will change if the price of the item rises by 1%, other things equal. (In this chapter, we will discuss only one elasticity: the own-price elasticity of demand. For brevity, we shall refer to it simply as the *price elasticity*.) When the demand is elastic, a 1% price increase causes the quantity demanded to drop by more than 1%. By contrast, when the demand is inelastic, a 1% price increase causes the quantity demanded to fall by less than 1%.

Suppose that Mercury estimates that, if it were to set the Japanese price 10% higher, at ¥41,800, then sales (which is the quantity demanded) would be 9% lower. This indicates that the demand is inelastic. Since sales fall less than proportionately with the increase in price, Mercury's total revenue will increase, specifically, by 0.1%. Moreover, lower sales mean lower costs. Hence, in this example, a price increase will raise Mercury's profit. Generally, as we showed in chapter 3, if the demand is inelastic, an increase in price will lead to a higher profit. Accordingly, a seller that faces an inelastic demand should raise the price.

Profit-Maximizing Price

We have seen that, when the demand is inelastic, a seller should raise the price. But what if the demand is elastic? More generally, what price maximizes the seller's profit? In chapter 8, we showed that, at the profit-maximizing sales, the marginal revenue equals the marginal cost. Figure 9.1 shows the profit-maximizing price and sales for Mercury's Japanese business. Managers, however, usually do not readily have information about marginal revenue. They usually have better information about the price elasticity of demand. So, it would be more convenient to have a pricing rule based on elasticity.

> The profit-maximizing price is where the incremental margin percentage equals the reciprocal of the absolute value of the price elasticity of demand.

Fortunately, such a rule is available. This rule applies the concept of the incremental margin percentage. Recall from chapter 8 that the incremental margin percentage is the price less the marginal cost divided by price. It is also known as the Lerner Index.

In the math supplement, we show that, when the marginal revenue equals the marginal cost, then the incremental margin percentage equals the reciprocal of the absolute value of the price elasticity of demand. Equivalently, a seller maximizes profit by setting a price where

$$\text{incremental margin percentage} = -\frac{1}{\text{price elasticity of demand}}. \qquad (9.1)$$

The price elasticity of demand is negative; hence, the minus sign on the right-hand side of the pricing rule ensures that the entire right-hand side is positive.

Let us apply the rule to determine Mercury's price for the Japanese market. Suppose that the price elasticity of demand is –2.2. The pricing rule shows that, for Mercury to maximize its profit, the incremental margin percentage must be 1/2.2, or about

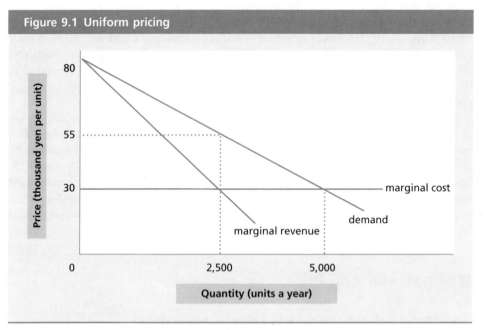

Figure 9.1 Uniform pricing

At the profit-maximizing quantity of sales, the marginal revenue equals the marginal cost. Equivalently, the incremental margin percentage equals the reciprocal of the absolute value of the price elasticity of demand.

45%. Then, representing the price by p, and recalling that the marginal cost is ¥30,000, the rule implies that

$$\frac{p - 30,000}{p} = 0.45. \tag{9.2}$$

By solving this equation, we find that $p = 55,000$. Hence, the price that maximizes Mercury's profit is ¥55,000. (As figure 9.1 shows, we get the same price if we look for the quantity where the marginal revenue equals the marginal cost.)

At the price of ¥55,000, the quantity demanded is 2,500 units a year. Hence, Mercury's total revenue is $55,000 \times 2,500 =$ ¥137.5 million a year. Mercury's total cost is $30,000 \times 2,500 =$ ¥75 million; hence, its profit is $137.5 - 75 =$ ¥62.5 million.

The pricing rule highlights the importance of understanding the price elasticity of demand. In chapter 3, we discussed the intuitive factors that underlie the price elasticity. These factors include the availability of direct and indirect substitutes, buyers' prior commitments, and the cost relative to the benefit of searching for more favorable prices.

The price elasticity may vary along a demand curve. Further, the marginal cost may change with the scale of production. Accordingly, determining the profit-maximizing price typically involves a series of trials with different prices until finding a price such that the incremental margin percentage equals the reciprocal of the absolute value of the price elasticity.

Changes in Demand and Cost

The pricing rule shows how a seller should adjust its price when there are changes in the price elasticity of demand or marginal cost. Consider changes in the price elasticity. If the demand is more elastic, then the price elasticity will be a larger negative number. So, according to the rule, the seller should aim for a lower incremental margin percentage. For instance, suppose that, in Mercury's case, the price elasticity is –2.5 rather than –2.2. Then, the profit-maximizing incremental margin percentage will be $1/2.5 = 40\%$. Letting the price be p, we have $(p - 30{,}000)/p = 0.40$, which implies that the profit-maximizing price is ¥50,000.

By contrast, if the demand were less elastic, say, with an elasticity of –1.5, then the profit-maximizing incremental margin percentage would be $1/1.5 = 67\%$. Again, representing the price by p, we would then have $(p - 30{,}000)/p = 0.67$, which implies that the profit-maximizing price would be ¥90,000.

Next, let us consider changes in the seller's marginal cost. In our original example, the price elasticity was –2.2, while the marginal cost was ¥30,000. Suppose that the marginal cost is ¥6,000 lower at ¥24,000. How should Mercury adjust its price for the Japanese market? Using the pricing rule, the profit-maximizing price must satisfy $(p - 24{,}000)/p = 1/2.2$, which implies that $p = 44{,}000$. Notice that, although the marginal cost is ¥6,000 lower, the profit-maximizing price is ¥11,000 lower.

Similarly, we can show that, if the marginal cost is higher, Mercury should not raise its price by the same amount. The reason is that Mercury must consider the effect of the price change on the quantity demanded.

These examples demonstrate that the way a seller should adjust its price to changes in either the price elasticity or the marginal cost depends on both the price elasticity and the marginal cost. In particular, this means that a seller should not necessarily adjust the price by the same amount as a change in marginal cost.

> **Progress Check 9A** In the case of Mercury Bikes, suppose that the price elasticity of demand is –1.75, while the marginal cost is ¥27,000 per unit. Calculate the price that maximizes the profit.
>
> *Progress check*

Common Misconceptions

The pricing rule applies the concept of incremental margin percentage. In cost accounting, the *contribution margin percentage* is defined as the revenue less variable cost divided by revenue. In the math supplement, we show that the contribution margin percentage equals the price less the average variable cost divided by the price. Accounting systems often assume that costs are proportional; in which case, the marginal cost is the same as the average variable cost. Then, the contribution margin percentage equals what we call the *incremental margin percentage*.

Generally, however, variable costs may be increasing or decreasing with the scale of production, and so, the marginal cost will not be the same as the average variable cost. In this case, it is important to keep a clear distinction between the contribution margin percentage and the incremental margin percentage. Only the latter is relevant for pricing.

A common mistake is the belief that the profit-maximizing price depends only on the elasticity. According to this approach, if the demand is more elastic, the price should be lower, while if the demand is less elastic, the price should be higher. This approach considers only the demand and ignores costs. To maximize profits, however, management should take into account both the demand and costs.

To illustrate the difference between the mistaken thinking and the correct approach, consider the mini-bars provided by many hotels. The mini-bar has considerable market power, especially in the early hours of the morning, when it would be inconvenient if not hazardous to venture out of the hotel for a beverage. Suppose that Heineken beer and Coca Cola have the same price elasticity of demand. Should the hotel set the same price for both items? Absolutely not. According to our pricing rule, the hotel should set the same incremental margin percentage on the two items. Since the marginal cost to the hotel of Heineken beer is higher than that of Coca Cola, the hotel should set a higher price for it.

Consumer goods retailing provides another example. Branded disposable diapers, such as Pampers and Huggies, are available at many supermarkets and drug stores. If one supermarket sets a higher price for Pampers, its customers may buy their Pampers elsewhere. So, the demand for branded diapers at any particular store may be quite elastic. By contrast, the demand for private-label diapers at the same store may be somewhat less elastic because private-label products are available only from the corresponding chain. For instance, only SavOn Drugs stores sell SavOn Drugs diapers. Then, according to our pricing rule, stores should set a higher incremental margin

Price elasticity: who is the customer?

Body shops repair exterior damage to automobiles. Whenever a damaged car arrives at a body shop, one of the first questions that the car owner must answer is, "Do you have insurance for the damage?" Why does the body shop care whether the owner has insurance coverage?

Automobile body repair is a case where there are two persons on the demand side: the car owner who makes the buying decision and the insurer who pays the bill. As a result of this split, the owner of a damaged car will be relatively less sensitive to the price of repairs. Indeed, the owner may ask the body shop to repair some other outstanding damage at the insurer's expense. Realistically, however, the car owner will be concerned about the price of repairs to the extent that his or her future insurance premium or renewal of the policy depends on past claims.

Generally, demand is less sensitive to price whenever there is a split between the party that makes the buying decision and the party that pays the bill. Body shops understand and exploit this split.

percentage for private-label diapers. This does not, however, necessarily mean a higher *price* for private-label diapers.

Another common mistake in pricing is to set the price by marking up average cost. Cost-plus pricing poses several problems. First, in businesses with economies of scale, the average cost depends on the production scale. So, to apply cost-plus pricing, the seller must make an assumption about the scale. But the production scale depends on the price, hence cost-plus pricing leads in a circle.

A further difficulty with cost-plus pricing is that it gives no guidance as to the appropriate markup on average cost. Should a seller apply the same or different markups to different products? Suppose that a seller wants to set the markup to maximize profits. Then, the seller must go back to considering the price elasticity of demand and the marginal cost. Hence, cost-plus pricing is not so simple after all.

Cost-plus pricing: Wang Laboratories

In 1976, Wang Laboratories launched a word-processing machine that took the office market by storm and sales soared. Several years later, however, Apple and then IBM began marketing personal computers. The new personal computers offered a number of business applications, including word processing. Wang did consider whether to introduce a personal computer as well. Management, however, rejected the idea for fear that the new product would cut too much into its word processor sales.

Wang used a cost-plus method to set prices for its word processors. To calculate the appropriate markup, management divided overhead costs by the projected sales volume. By the mid-1980s, personal computers were quickly eroding the demand for Wang's word processor. When Wang's sales did not meet the original projections, management had to recalculate the markup. With the same overhead costs divided by fewer sales, the result was a higher markup and higher prices. The increase in prices made Wang's machines even less attractive vis-à-vis the new personal computers and caused sales to drop even further. Eventually, Wang was forced into bankruptcy.

Source: Thomas T. Nagle and Reed K. Holden, *The Strategy and Tactics of Pricing*, 2d ed. (Englewood Cliffs, NJ: Prentice Hall, 1995), p. 3.

◂◂ 3 Complete Price Discrimination

In the previous section, we introduced a rule for uniform pricing: the seller should set the price so that the incremental margin percentage equals the reciprocal of the absolute value of the price elasticity of demand. In figure 9.2, we illustrate the profit-maximizing uniform price for Mercury Bikes in the Japanese market. On closer

Figure 9.2 Complete price discrimination

With complete price discrimination, the seller prices each unit at the buyer's benefit and sells a quantity such that the marginal benefit equals the marginal cost. The increase in profit over uniform pricing is the shaded area *adb* plus the shaded area *bec*.

examination, however, we can show that uniform pricing does not yield the maximum possible profit. This suggests that we should look for pricing policies that are more profitable than uniform pricing.

Shortcomings of Uniform Pricing

Recall that the demand curve for a product also reflects the marginal benefits of the various buyers. At the price of ¥55,000 per unit, the benefit of a bicycle for the marginal buyer is just equal to the price. For all the other (inframarginal) buyers, who account for 2,499 units, the benefit exceeds the price. Each of these inframarginal buyers is enjoying some buyer surplus. The market buyer surplus is the shaded area *abd*.

With uniform pricing, the inframarginal buyers do not pay as much as they would be willing to pay. This suggests that, by devising a way of taking some of the buyer surplus, Mercury could increase its profit.

Another shortcoming of uniform pricing is that it results in an economically inefficient quantity of sales. The marginal buyer derives a benefit of ¥55,000, while the marginal cost is only ¥30,000. This gap between the marginal benefit and the marginal cost shows that the quantity of sales is not economically efficient. By devising some way to provide the product to everyone whose marginal benefit exceeds the marginal cost, Mercury could also earn more profit.

Progress Check 9B Referring to figure 9.2, shade in the market buyer surplus if Mercury sets a price of ¥30,000 per unit.

Progress check

Price Discrimination

Ideally, Mercury would like to sell each bike at the respective buyer's benefit. Referring to figure 9.2, this would be like selling down the market demand curve. Then, Mercury would earn a higher incremental margin from buyers with higher benefit and a smaller margin from buyers with lower benefit. Any pricing policy under which a seller sets prices to earn different incremental margins on various units of the same or a similar product is called **price discrimination**.

> **Price discrimination** is a policy where a seller sets different incremental margins on various units of the same or a similar product.

We give the name **complete price discrimination** to a pricing policy where the seller prices each unit at the buyer's benefit and sells a quantity such that the marginal benefit equals the marginal cost. This policy is called *complete price discrimination* because it charges every buyer the maximum that he or she is willing to pay for each unit. Hence, the policy leaves each buyer with no surplus.

> **Complete price discrimination** is the policy where a seller prices each unit at the buyer's benefit and sells a quantity such that the marginal benefit equals the marginal cost.

To illustrate complete price discrimination, let us consider Mercury Bikes' pricing. Referring to figure 9.2, the demand curve is a straight line with a slope of $50,000/5,000 = 10$. This means that the first buyer is willing to pay $80,000 - 10 = ¥79,990$ for a bike; the second buyer, $80,000 - 20 = ¥79,980$; and so on. Hence, under complete price discrimination, Mercury should charge ¥79,990 to the first buyer, ¥79,980 to the second buyer, and so on.

Mercury should not stop selling at the 2,500th unit. The reason is that the buyer of the 2,501st unit derives a benefit of $55,000 - 10 = ¥54,990$, which exceeds Mercury's marginal cost of ¥30,000. This means that Mercury could increase its profit by selling a unit to that buyer.

Indeed, Mercury should sell up to the quantity where the marginal benefit just equals the marginal cost. Referring to figure 9.2, this balance occurs at a quantity of 5,000 units a year. The buyer of the 5,000th unit is willing to pay exactly ¥30,000 for a bike, which is Mercury's marginal cost. If Mercury tried to sell beyond 5,000 units, it would make a loss on additional units. Under complete price discrimination, the buyer of the 5,000th unit is the marginal buyer.

With complete price discrimination, Mercury's total revenue will be the area $0fca$ under the demand curve from the quantity of 0 up to 5,000 units a year. This area is $(80,000 + 30,000)/2 \times 5,000 = ¥275$ million a year. As for costs, Mercury's total cost would be area $0fcg$, which is $30,000 \times 5,000 = ¥150$ million a year. (Recall that Mercury incurs no fixed cost.) Hence, with complete price discrimination, Mercury's profit would be $275 - 150 = ¥125$ million a year.

By contrast, in the preceding section, we showed that Mercury's maximum profit with uniform pricing is ¥62.5 million. So, Mercury's profit with complete price discrimination is higher than the profit with uniform pricing.

Comparison with Uniform Pricing

Under a policy of complete price discrimination, the seller should sell each unit for the benefit that it provides its buyer and sell the quantity where the buyer's marginal benefit just equals the marginal cost. The policy resolves the two shortcomings of uniform pricing. First, by pricing each unit at the buyer's benefit, the policy extracts all the buyer surplus. Second, the policy provides the economically efficient quantity; hence, it exploits all the opportunity for additional profit through changes in sales.

Specifically, in the case of Mercury Bikes, the policy of complete price discrimination enables Mercury to extract higher prices for the 2,499 units that would be inframarginal under uniform pricing. This increase in profit is represented by the shaded area *adb* in figure 9.2. Second, with complete price discrimination, Mercury would sell 2,500 more units than with uniform pricing. These additional units raise the profit by the shaded area *bec* in figure 9.2. The total increase in profit is the sum of the shaded areas *adb* and *bec*.

Generally, a policy of complete price discrimination yields more profit than uniform pricing. Complete price discrimination extracts a higher price for units that would be sold under uniform pricing, while extending sales by selling additional units that would not be sold with uniform pricing.

Progress check **Progress Check 9C** We can use figure 9.2 to compare the profits from uniform pricing and complete price discrimination. The difference is areas *adb* and *bec*. Calculate the numerical values of these areas.

Why does the doctor really need to know your occupation?

Price discrimination is common in medical services. Doctors treat patients on an individual basis. A doctor's first step in treatment is always to record the patient's history. This routinely includes questions about the patient's occupation, employer, home address, and scope of insurance coverage. This information is very useful in gauging a patient's ability and willingness to pay as well as the patient's health.

To the extent that a patient is paying her or his own bill, the doctor can easily use this information to charge different prices to various patients for the same treatment. The result is close to complete price discrimination. Indeed, until the 1960s, the American Medical Association required doctors to charge lower prices to poorer patients.

Information

Under complete price discrimination, the seller charges each buyer a different price for each unit of the product. This means that a buyer who is interested in buying more than one unit of the product should be charged a different price for each unit. For instance, suppose that the Miki family is interested in two bikes. One bike is quite essential, as Mrs. Miki will use it every day when shopping for groceries. The second bike is for Grandma who uses the bike far less often. With complete price discrimination, Mercury should charge more for the first bike and less for the second.

Accordingly, to implement complete price discrimination, the seller must know each potential buyer's individual demand curve. It is not enough to know the market demand curve or the price elasticity of the individual demand curves. Rather, the seller must know the entire individual demand curve of each potential buyer. This is a tremendous requirement. In practice, most sellers will not have this amount of information, so, complete price discrimination is usually not feasible.

Since complete price discrimination requires more information than uniform pricing, we should understand when it is relatively more important to implement price discrimination. One factor is the degree to which the individual demands of potential buyers are different. The other factor is the steepness of the individual demand (marginal benefit) curves.

For instance, suppose that there are 8,000 bike buyers, all of whom are identical in that they are willing to pay ¥40,000 for a bicycle and want only one unit. Then the market demand curve will be flat, as shown in figure 9.3. In this case, with uniform pricing, Mercury should set a price of ¥40,000. Under complete price

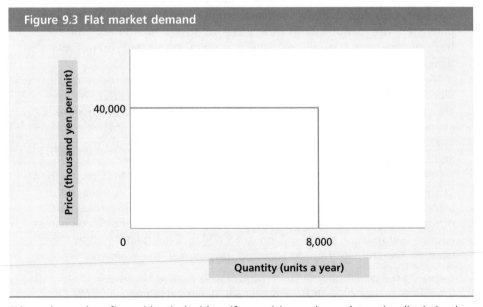

Figure 9.3 Flat market demand

Price, sales, and profit are identical with uniform pricing and complete price discrimination.

U.S. Treasury bill auctions

The U.S. government issues Treasury bills as a way to borrow funds for periods up to one year. The Treasury sells bills in a sealed-bid auction. Each participant sends in a sealed bid. After the close of bids, the Treasury opens the bids and allocates the bills for sale to the highest bidder, then to the next highest bidder, and so on until it has allocated all the bills for sale.

The Treasury has varied the rules of its auctions. At times, the Treasury has stipulated that the auction be *discriminatory* in the sense that each successful bidder must pay the amount that they bid. In a discriminatory auction, different bidders pay different prices for their Treasury bills. By using a discriminatory sealed-bid auction, the Treasury implements price discrimination.

Even though the Treasury's auction is discriminatory, it cannot implement complete price discrimination. The reason is that participating bidders generally shade their bids downward to get some buyer surplus.

Selling down the demand curve: USi

With Internet service becoming pervasive and more reliable, software producers are mimicking automobile manufacturers and movie studios. Not every potential customer derives enough benefit to justify an outright purchase. Auto manufacturers offer leases to drivers who do not wish to buy. Similarly, movie studios sell videos to rental stores that cater to low-benefit viewers.

The same principle applies to software. Systems for enterprise resource planning (ERP) and financial management can be very expensive. Prices are out of reach for many businesses. Yet the marginal cost of software is almost zero. Enter the application service provider to offer software "on tap" through the Internet. The application service provider charges by usage and so reaches down the demand curve to low-benefit users.

Founded in January 1998, USinternetworking (USi) commands over a third of the market for Internet ERP services. With headquarters in Annapolis, Maryland, USi provides services through four data centers in various parts of the world. The application service provider focuses on midsize companies with annual revenue of $50 million to $1 billion. Even giants such as Hershey, General Electric, and Samsung have signed up for service.

Source: "The Application Service Providers Have Landed," *Software Development*, July 2000, (http://www.sdmagazine.com/features/2000/07/f1.shtml).

discrimination, it should set the same ¥40,000 price. The price and sales are identical with uniform pricing and complete price discrimination, hence Mercury's profits will be identical as well.

By contrast, if the buyers differed in their individual demand curves or individuals were willing to buy more at a lower price, then the policy of complete price discrimination would yield more profit than uniform pricing.

◂◂ 4 Direct Segment Discrimination

To implement complete price discrimination, a seller must know the entire individual demand curve of each potential buyer. The seller, however, may not have so much information. Accordingly, we now explore other forms of price discrimination that require less information.

From the viewpoint of the seller's profit, a policy of complete price discrimination is better than uniform pricing, essentially because it sets prices on an individual basis. A seller that lacks sufficient information to price on an individual basis may still be able to discriminate among **segments** of buyers. In the language of marketing, a segment is a significant group of buyers within a larger market.

> A **segment** is a significant group of buyers within a larger market.

Segment Margins

Suppose that Mercury Bikes produces men's and women's versions of its bike at the same marginal cost of ¥30,000 and that men and women buy only men's and women's bikes respectively. Then, Mercury can divide the Japanese market into two segments according to gender. It, however, does not have the information to segment the market beyond the gender of the buyer.

We give the name **direct segment discrimination** to the policy of setting different incremental margins to each identifiable segment. In Mercury's case, there are two identifiable segments: men and women. Lacking the information necessary for further discrimination, Mercury must set a uniform price within each segment. Accordingly, we can determine the profit-maximizing prices for each segment by applying the rule for uniform pricing. The prices are such that the incremental margin percentage for each segment equals the reciprocal of the absolute value of the segment's price elasticity of demand.

> **Direct segment discrimination** is the policy where a seller charges a different incremental margin to each identifiable segment.

Let the men's and women's demands be as shown in figure 9.4. Consider first the demand for men's bikes. Suppose that the profit-maximizing price is m. Through a process of trial and error, we find that, at the price m, the price elasticity of demand is −2.2. Accordingly, Mercury should set the price m so that the incremental margin percentage is $1/2.2 = 45\%$. This means $(m - 30{,}000)/m = 0.45$, hence the price of a man's bike, $m = ¥55{,}000$. At this price, the quantity demanded is 2,500 units.

Figure 9.4 Direct segment discrimination

(a) Men's demand

(b) Women's demand

The demand for men's bikes is relatively less elastic, so the seller should set a relatively higher incremental margin percentage on men's bikes.

Next, we consider the demand for women's bikes. The women derive lower marginal benefits; hence, the women's demand curve is lower than that for men. Suppose that the profit-maximizing price is w. Through another process of trial and error, we find that, at the price w, the price elasticity of demand is -4. Hence, Mercury should set the price w so that the incremental margin percentage is $1/4 = 25\%$. Then, $(w - 30{,}000)/w = 0.25$, which implies that the price for a women's bike is $w = ¥40{,}000$. At this price, the quantity demanded is 1,000 units.

In this example, the men's demand is less elastic. Therefore, Mercury should set a relatively higher incremental margin percentage on the men's bikes. Mercury's profit from the men's segment is $(55{,}000 - 30{,}000) \times 2{,}500 = ¥62.5$ million. Further, its profit from the women's segment is $(40{,}000 - 30{,}000) \times 1{,}000 = ¥10$ million. So, its total profit with direct segment discrimination is ¥72.5 million. By contrast, its profit with complete price discrimination is ¥125 million, while its profit with uniform pricing is ¥62.5 million.

Implementation

To implement direct segment discrimination, the seller must have some way of segregating buyers into distinct segments with different demand curves. This means finding some identifiable and fixed buyer characteristic that segments the market. The characteristic must be fixed; otherwise, a buyer might switch segments to take advantage of a lower price. The seller can then base the price discrimination on this characteristic.

The second condition necessary for direct segment discrimination is that the seller must be able to prevent buyers from reselling the product among themselves. If the segment to whom the seller sets a relatively low price could resell to other buyers, then the seller will not be able to sell anything at the high price.

Typically, it is more difficult to resell services, especially individual services, than goods. For instance, it is more difficult to resell medical treatment than pharmaceuticals, and it is more difficult to resell tax planning advice than tax preparation software. Accordingly, price discrimination is relatively more widespread in services than goods and is especially common in individual services.

The demand for movies and theme parks varies with such buyer characteristics as income, occupational status, and age. Movie theaters and theme parks cannot observe a customer's income, but they can check a customer's age and whether a customer is a student.

Age is a characteristic that fits the conditions for direct segment discrimination. It is easy to identify and impossible to change. A middle-aged adult cannot buy a senior citizen's ticket. Accordingly, movie theaters and theme parks set prices so as to extract lower margins from senior citizens and children. Assuming that the marginal cost of serving all patrons is the same, then the result is lower prices for senior citizens and children and higher prices for middle-aged adults.

Resale is the major hurdle to price discrimination between college students and other adults. Providers recognize this problem. Most movie theaters mark their tickets as "Not Transferable." To the extent that theaters can prevent buyers from reselling tickets, they can discriminate between college students and other adults.

Generally, with a policy of direct segment discrimination, prices should be set to derive a relatively lower incremental margin percentage from the segment with the more elastic demand and a relatively higher incremental margin percentage from the segment with the less elastic demand.

In the example of Mercury Bikes, the marginal cost was a constant. By constrast, a seller that faces the constraint of a fixed capacity may have a constant marginal cost for wide ranges of output. Near to the capacity limit, however, the marginal cost is increasing. Consider, for instance, a local telephone company. Its network has a fixed capacity, and it would like to directly discriminate between the residential and business segments. How should it set prices to the two segments when the marginal cost is increasing?

The telephone company should follow the same general rule: it should set prices so that the incremental margin percentage for each segment equals the reciprocal of the absolute value of the segment's price elasticity of demand. With an increasing marginal cost, however, any change in the price for one segment that affects sales will affect the marginal cost and, hence, the incremental margin percentage for the other segment. Accordingly, when the marginal cost is increasing, the seller must conduct the trial and error search for the prices to both segments at the same time.

Segment Discrimination in E-commerce

The *New Yorker* once published a cartoon entitled, "On the Internet, nobody knows you're a dog" (July 5, 1993, p. 61). Clearly, direct segmentation by age, gender, and other personal characteristics is more difficult in business-to-consumer (B2C) e-commerce than conventional retailing.

The degree of difficulty depends on whether the item is delivered through conventional means or the Internet. Many airlines sell tickets through the World Wide Web, either directly through their own websites or indirectly through intermediaries. While passengers may buy tickets over the Internet, they must eventually check in at an airport. Hence, airlines can still set prices to extract different margins from different segments.

Other goods, including newspapers, books, and music, are now delivered through the Internet. Every device connected to the Internet must have an identity so that other devices can communicate with it. For instance, suppose that Max logs on to the Internet and clicks on Amazon.com. Then, Amazon's computers must know where to send its webpage. The Internet standard for identification is the "IP address", a set of numbers that uniquely identifies a device connected to the Internet. For instance, the IP address of one Pacific Internet server is 192.169.41.36.

IP addresses are scarce, and so, Internet access providers typically do not assign dial-up users a fixed IP address, but rather assign addresses to users dynamically from a pool, as and when they log on. Users accessing the Internet through organizational networks are identified by the IP address of the organization's computer.

Under these circumstances, segment discrimination is relatively difficult. A middle-aged adult could pose as a child or senior citizen, and someone in Los Angeles could pose as living in New York. To this extent, sellers of goods delivered through the Internet are more likely to fall back upon uniform pricing.

Profit Ranking

The Mercury example illustrates the differences in profit from the various pricing policies. The seller's profit is highest with complete price discrimination, next with direct segment discrimination, and lowest with uniform pricing.

It is obvious that direct segment discrimination would be less profitable than complete price discrimination. Direct segment discrimination uses uniform prices within each segment; hence, it suffers from the same shortcomings as uniform pricing: within each segment, it does not completely extract the buyer surplus and it provides economically inefficient quantities. (The exception arises when all the buyers within a segment are identical. In this case, the profit from direct segment discrimination is equal to that with complete price discrimination.)

Direct segment discrimination, however, is more profitable than uniform pricing. Through direct segmentation, the seller can reduce the margin to the segment with the more elastic demand and hence expand the quantity of sales closer to the point where the marginal benefit equals the marginal cost. Direct segmentation may also enable the seller to raise the margin to the segment with the less elastic demand and so extract more of its buyer surplus.

> **Progress Check 9D** Referring to figure 9.4, suppose that the marginal cost is ¥35,000 per unit. Use the figure to illustrate the new prices for men's and women's bikes.
>
> *Progress check*

Heinz ketchup: "Not for retail sale"

The market for ketchup consists of a retail consumer segment and an institutional segment. Institutional customers include restaurants, catering services, and airlines. The demand curves of retail and institutional customers are quite different. Institutions order larger amounts and often have professional purchasing staff who aim to secure better deals. Typically, the institutional demand is more price elastic than the retail demand.

Ketchup manufacturers supply institutional customers directly and retail consumers through distribution channels such as supermarkets and grocery stores. To the extent that manufacturers can prevent institutional customers from reselling ketchup to retail consumers, they can implement direct segment discrimination. This means setting prices for a lower incremental margin from institutional customers. It is no coincidence that every bottle of Heinz ketchup served in a restaurant is marked "Not for Retail Sale."

Discriminating between residential and business users: local telephone service

The business demand for telephone service is less price elastic than the residential demand. The provider of local telephone services can raise its profit by extracting more buyer surplus from business customers. Assuming that the costs of serving the two segments are identical, a policy of direct segment discrimination would mean setting a higher price for business customers.

Verizon is the dominant provider of telephone services in New York City. In 2000, it charged $16 a month for a residential line and $23 a month for a business line.

How can the telephone company prevent a business from posing as a residential subscriber to take advantage of the lower price? For fixed-line service, the telephone company can check the customer's location physically. The inspection will deter many businesses from posing as residential subscribers.

Another factor is listings in the telephone directory. A business depends on its directory listing to reach potential customers. A business that poses as a residential subscriber will not be listed in the business telephone directory. It will lose potential customers searching in the telephone directory or yellow pages.

Microsoft Office 2000 Pro

Microsoft sells various versions of its hugely popular Office 2000 suite of business software. The Standard edition includes Excel, PowerPoint, Outlook, and Word, while the Professional edition includes the four basic elements plus Access and Publisher.

Microsoft's pricing of Office 2000 varies internationally. Direct segmentation by country is feasible to the extent that Microsoft can prevent resale across national borders. Table 9.1 reports the regular prices of Office 2000 Pro in three countries. Supposing that there are no differences in marginal cost, Microsoft's incremental margin is highest in the U.K. and lowest in Singapore.

Microsoft also segments between students and others through academic discounts. Relative to users in general, students are probably more price sensitive. They have low incomes, and possibly, more opportunities to share and copy software. Microsoft has another motivation to provide academic discounts – to lock in users for future purchases at full price. Table 9.1 shows that academic prices for Office 2000 Pro are 65–70% lower than the corresponding regular prices.

Table 9.1 Microsoft Office 2000 Pro

	Singapore	United Kingdom	U.S.A.
Regular price	S$929 = $540.68	£419.89 = $629.41	$599
Academic price	S$289 = $168.20	£154.99 = $232.33	$193

Sources: Challenger Superstore, Singapore; Insight UK (http://www.insight.com/); World of Web Academicware (http://www.wowa.org/); author's calculations.

◂◂ 5 Location

| A free on board (FOB) price does not include delivery. |

To the extent that a product is costly to transport and the seller can identify a buyer's location, the seller can discriminate on the basis of the buyer's location. Generally, there are two ways of pricing to buyers in different locations. One way is to set a common price to all buyers that does not include delivery. Such a price is called ex-works or **free on board** (**FOB**). In this case, each buyer pays the FOB price plus the cost of delivery to its respective location. With FOB pricing, the differences among the prices at various locations are exactly the differences in the costs of delivery to those locations.

The alternative way of pricing to buyers at different locations is to set prices that include delivery. This practice is called **delivered pricing**, and the price is called **cost and freight** (**CF**). With delivered (CF) pricing, the differences among the prices at various locations need not correspond to the differences in the cost of delivery to the respective locations.

> **Delivered pricing** is the policy where a seller's price includes delivery.

> A **cost including freight (CF)** price includes delivery.

FOB or CF

Let us compare FOB and CF pricing in the context of pricing to an export market. First, we illustrate FOB pricing. Suppose that Mercury Bikes sets a price of $350 in its domestic market. For its price in Japan, it plans to add the freight of $30 and convert the total to yen. Hence, with an exchange rate of ¥100 to the dollar, Mercury's Japanese price is $380 \times 100 = ¥38,000$.

FOB pricing, however, ignores the differences between the price elasticities of demand in the various markets. The alternative is CF pricing, which can yield higher profit. In Mercury's case, assuming that it can prevent buyers in one country from reselling bicycles to the other country, it can implement direct segment discrimination across the two countries. This means setting prices so that its incremental margin percentage in each country balances the reciprocal of the absolute value of the price elasticity of demand.

If the Japanese demand is more elastic than American demand, then Mercury should set prices so that its incremental margin percentage is lower in Japan than the United States. A lower margin, however, does not necessarily mean a lower price, because Mercury's marginal cost of supplying the Japanese market includes transportation. Hence, the marginal cost in Japan will be higher than the marginal cost in the United States.

By contrast, if the Japanese demand is less elastic than American demand, then Mercury should set prices so that its incremental margin percentage is higher in Japan than the United States. Taking into account the higher marginal cost of supplying the Japanese market, this definitely means that Mercury's price in Japan should exceed that in the United States.

Thus, to the extent that Mercury can prevent buyers in one country from reselling bicycles to the other country, it can aim for different incremental margin percentages in each market. Then, it will be setting CF prices in the two markets; that is, prices including delivery, rather than FOB prices.

With CF pricing, the difference in the prices between the two markets will simply be the result of the different incremental margin percentages and the different marginal costs of supplying the two markets. In particular, the price difference need not necessarily be the cost of shipping the product from the domestic to the foreign market. Depending on the price elasticities and the marginal costs, the difference may be larger or smaller than the freight cost.

For instance, earlier, we showed that, when the price elasticity of demand in the Japanese market is −2.2 and the marginal cost of supplying the Japanese market is ¥30,000, the profit-maximizing price is ¥55,000. At the exchange rate of ¥100 to

$1, this price is $550. By contrast, Mercury's price in the United States was $350. The difference between the Japanese and American prices is $200, which far exceeds the $30 freight cost.

<table>
<tr><td>*Progress check*</td><td>**Progress Check 9E** Suppose that, for the Japanese market, the price elasticity of demand is –2.5 and the marginal cost including freight is ¥30,000. Calculate Mercury's CF Japanese price. If Mercury's U.S. price is $350, what is the difference between the Japanese and American prices?</td></tr>
</table>

Restricting Resale

If a seller is to succeed in discriminating on the basis of a buyer's location, the various buyers must not be able to adjust location to take advantage of price differences. For most goods, the seller can control only the location at which it sells the product and cannot directly monitor the buyer's location.

For instance, if Mercury sets a higher margin in Japan than the United States, some Japanese consumers may buy bikes in the United States and ship them back to Japan. Worse still, some Japanese bicycle retailers may establish a "gray market," in which they purchase large quantities of Mercury bikes in the United States for resale in Japan.

Asian Wall Street Journal: print and Internet editions

The *Asian Wall Street Journal* is printed daily in Hong Kong, Singapore, and Tokyo for same-morning delivery. The newspaper charges widely varying prices in the three cities. In August 2000, the prices for a twelve-month subscription were HK$2,298 ($294.60) in Hong Kong, ¥94,500 ($871.29) in Tokyo, and S$298 ($173.64) in Singapore.

A business newspaper is particularly suited to discrimination by location. Few business people are interested in trading off a lower price for old news. Hence, the *Asian Wall Street Journal* can maintain a price in Tokyo that is five times higher than that in Singapore.

By contrast, it is relatively difficult to pinpoint the location of an Internet subscriber. Accordingly, the *Wall Street Journal Interactive Edition* charges the same price of $59 for a twelve-month subscription to every subscriber. Generally, retailers of items that are both sold *and* delivered over the Internet have not been able to discriminate by location.

A seller of durable products can limit such reselling by restricting warranty service to the location of purchase. Mercury might refuse to provide warranty service in Japan for bikes purchased in the United States. This is a way by which a seller can ensure that consumers buy in their respective locations and not elsewhere.

◂◂ 6 Indirect Segment Discrimination

For a policy of direct segment discrimination, the seller must be able to identify some fixed buyer characteristic that divides the market into segments with different demand curves. A seller may know that specific segments have different demand curves but cannot find a fixed characteristic with which to discriminate directly. Under these circumstances, the seller may be able to apply another policy, which uses an indirect means to discriminate on price.

Suppose that Pluto Airways operates a passenger service between Toronto and Miami. Pluto has four potential customers. Maria and Tom are private bankers based in Toronto who are visiting wealthy clients in Miami. Robin and Leslie are traveling on vacation. Table 9.2 shows the benefit that each of these travelers will derive from (unrestricted) air travel. Clearly, there are two segments, business persons and vacationers, with the business travelers willing to pay more. If traveling to Miami is too expensive, Robin and Leslie could take their vacation elsewhere, so, they are not willing to pay as much.

We use the information from table 9.2 to construct the market demand curve for air travel in figure 9.5. The market demand is discrete; hence the demand curve, as shown in figure 9.5, is a series of steps. By contrast, Mercury Bikes' demand in figure 9.2 is a smooth curve.

Suppose that Pluto's marginal cost is constant at \$200 per seat and the airline has no other costs. Then, each potential traveler gets a benefit that exceeds the marginal cost. If Pluto could implement complete price discrimination, it would set four different fares and sell tickets to each of the four travelers.

Table 9.2 Benefits from air travel			
		Benefit	
Traveler	Segment	Unrestricted travel ($)	Restricted travel ($)
Maria	Business	1,000	200
Tom	Business	900	180
Robin	Vacation	500	400
Leslie	Vacation	280	224

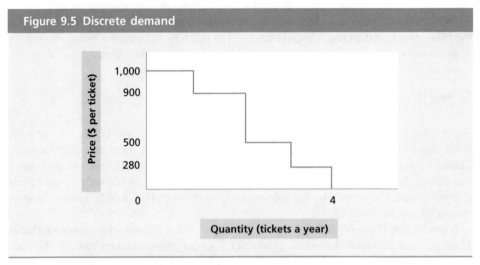

Figure 9.5 Discrete demand

A discrete demand curve consists of a series of steps.

It is not likely, however, that Pluto will be able to charge a different price to each traveler. Assuming that Pluto can directly identify business and vacation travelers, the next best alternative is direct segment discrimination. When the segment demands are discrete, the procedure for determining the prices with direct segment discrimination is to calculate the profits from each of the possible prices as in table 9.3. The profit-maximizing prices are a business fare of $900 and a vacation fare of $500. The airline's profit would be $1,700.

We should, however, consider whether Pluto can distinguish business from vacation travelers. The airline's check-in staff might ask every traveler to declare what he

Table 9.3 Air travel, direct segment discrimination

Fare ($)	Sales	Total revenue ($)	Marginal revenue ($)	Marginal cost ($)	Total cost ($)	Profit ($)
Business segment						
1,000	1	1,000	1,000	200	200	800
900	2	1,800	800	200	400	**1,400**
					Maximum segment profit	
Vacation segment						
500	1	500	500	200	200	**300**
280	2	560	60	200	400	160
					Maximum segment profit	

or she is planning to do in Miami. Then, every passenger would claim to be going on vacation. Alternatively, Pluto's staff might check whether passengers are wearing casual clothes or business attire. Then, even business travelers would dress casually to check in. Pluto might have to x-ray passengers' luggage to check for business suits and documents. Clearly, it is very difficult to discriminate directly between business and vacation travelers.

Structured Choice

Let us now consider another form of price discrimination that may be feasible when Pluto cannot directly identify business and vacation travelers. This pricing policy uses an indirect means to discriminate between the two segments. Consider the travelers' plans in more detail. Vacationers such as Robin and Leslie can book well in advance and usually want to stay through the weekend. By contrast, business travelers are less able to book early and often prefer to return home for the weekend. So, business travelers and vacationers are differentially sensitive to these features.

Pluto could offer two fares: an unrestricted fare and a fare subject to the restrictions of advance booking and weekend stay. To evaluate this policy, we must know the benefits that the various travelers get from restricted travel. Table 9.2 provides this information. All four get more benefit from unrestricted than restricted travel. The bankers, Maria and Tom, however, get relatively more benefit from unrestricted travel and relatively less benefit from restricted travel.

Note that unrestricted and restricted fares are substitutes offered by the same seller. Since Pluto cannot directly identify business and vacation travelers, each customer can choose between the two fares. This means that the demand for unrestricted travel depends on the price that Pluto sets for restricted travel. Likewise, the demand for restricted travel depends on the price of unrestricted travel.

Suppose, for instance, that Pluto sets a restricted-travel fare of $401. Table 9.2 shows that this price exceeds the benefit of every traveler from restricted travel. This means that no one will buy the restricted fare. Hence, the demand for unrestricted travel will be the same as if no restricted fare were available. Using the data from table 9.2, we can construct the demand for unrestricted travel when the restricted fare is $401. Figure 9.6(a) illustrates the demand curve.

Next, suppose that Pluto sets a restricted fare of $300. If Robin buys restricted travel, she will get a buyer surplus of $400 − $300 = $100. So, Robin will buy unrestricted travel only if it provides her at least $100 of buyer surplus. By table 9.2, Robin would get a benefit of $500 from unrestricted travel; hence, she will buy unrestricted travel only if the price, u, is sufficiently low that $500 − u \geq 100$, or $u \leq \$400$. Since the restricted fare of $300 exceeds the benefit of each of the other three travelers, they definitely will not buy restricted travel.

Using this information about Robin and the data from table 9.2, we now can construct the demand for unrestricted travel when the restricted fare is $300. If the price of unrestricted travel is between $901 and $1,000, only Maria will buy. If the price is between $401 and $900, both Maria and Tom will buy. If the price is between

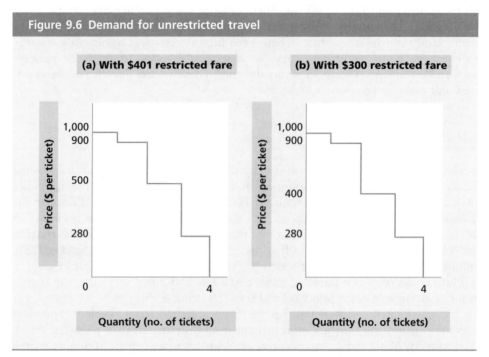

Figure 9.6 Demand for unrestricted travel

(a) With $401 restricted fare

(b) With $300 restricted fare

If the price of restricted travel is lower, then the demand curve for unrestricted travel will be lower.

$281 and $400, then Maria, Tom, and Robin will buy. Finally, if the price is less than or equal to $280, all four travelers will buy. Figure 9.6(b) illustrates the demand curve.

Comparing figures 9.6(a) and (b), we see that the demand for unrestricted travel depends on the price of restricted travel. Generally, if the price of restricted travel is lower, then the demand curve for unrestricted travel will be lower. Accordingly, to calculate the profits from the alternative prices for restricted and unrestricted travel, we must take account of the substitution between the two products. To find the profit-maximizing prices, we must calculate the profits from every combination of unrestricted and restricted fares.

In table 9.4, we calculate the profit from an unrestricted fare of $900 and a restricted fare of $399. With these fares, Maria would get some buyer surplus from unrestricted travel, while the restricted fare is more than her benefit. Accordingly, Maria would buy an unrestricted fare. Similarly, Tom would buy an unrestricted fare. By contrast, Robin would get some buyer surplus from restricted travel, while the unrestricted fare is more than her benefit. So, Robin would buy a restricted fare. For Leslie, both of the fares are more than the respective benefits, so she will not buy either fare. Thus, Pluto sells two unrestricted fares and one restricted fare.

With the $900 unrestricted fare and $399 restricted fare, Pluto's total revenue would be $900 × 2 + $399 = $2,199. The total cost would be $200 × 3 = $600;

Table 9.4 Air travel, indirect segment discrimination

Product	Fare ($)	Sales	Total revenue ($)	Total cost ($)	Profit ($)
Unrestricted	900	2	1,800	400	1,400
Restricted	399	1	399	200	199

hence its profit would be $2,199 – $600 = $1,599. By checking all the other combinations of unrestricted and restricted fares, we can show that this is the maximum profit.

Pluto Airways faces two segments, business travelers and vacation travelers, with different demand curves. The airline, however, has no way to directly identify the segments. Instead, it structures a choice between unrestricted and restricted travel to exploit the differential sensitivity of business and vacation travelers to restrictions on travel. Given this choice, the business travelers voluntarily choose the unrestricted fare, while one of the vacationers voluntarily chooses the restricted fare. The choice enables Pluto to discriminate indirectly between the segments.

> **Indirect segment discrimination** is the policy where a seller structures a choice for buyers so as to earn different incremental margins from each segment.

We give the name **indirect segment discrimination** to the policy of structuring a choice for buyers so as to earn different incremental margins from each segment.

Implementation

Two conditions are necessary for indirect segment discrimination. First, the seller must have control over some variable to which buyers in the various segments are differentially sensitive. The seller then can use this variable to structure a set of choices that will discriminate among the segments. In Pluto's case, the discriminating variable is the restriction on travel.

The other condition necessary for indirect segment discrimination is that buyers must not be able to circumvent the discriminating variable. Suppose, for instance, that Pluto allowed travelers holding restricted tickets to return without staying over the weekend. Then some business travelers might switch from unrestricted to restricted fares. Such switching will undermine the segment discrimination. Accordingly, Pluto must strictly enforce the conditions of restricted fares.

As we explain later, sellers discriminate indirectly because they cannot directly identify the customer segments. Since indirect segment discrimination means giving every buyer a choice of products, the seller obviously cannot prevent buyers from reselling the product. What is necessary for indirect segment discrimination is that buyers must not be able to circumvent the discriminating variable.

The policy of indirect segment discrimination uses product attributes to discriminate indirectly among the various buyer segments. Essentially, the product attributes are a proxy for the buyer attributes. To determine the profit-maximizing prices, the seller must consider that buyers might substitute among the various choices. Hence, the seller must analyze how changes in the price of one product affect the demand for other choices. Accordingly, the seller must not price any product in isolation. Rather, it must set the prices of all products at the same time.

Ideally, the seller should design each of the alternative product choices to maximize the difference between the buyer's benefit and the seller's cost. The difference between the benefit and the cost is the maximum available profit. It will not always be possible to attain this ideal, however. For instance, in Pluto's case, vacationer Robin chooses restricted travel. The restricted fare gives Robin less benefit than unrestricted travel, but the marginal cost of both fares is the same. If Pluto could implement complete price discrimination, it would make more profit by selling unrestricted travel to Robin. This, however, is not possible with indirect segment discrimination. In a later section of the chapter, we discuss the issue of choosing the discriminating variable in more detail.

Profit Ranking

Indirect segment discrimination uses product attributes to discriminate indirectly among the various buyer segments. By contrast, with direct segment discrimination, the seller can discriminate directly on the buyer's attributes. The seller can identify each buyer segment and prevent one segment from buying the product targeted at another segment. Hence, the seller can set prices without worrying about buyers switching among the products.

Direct discrimination on buyer attributes is more profitable than indirect discrimination through product attributes. One reason is that the products under indirect discrimination may provide less benefit than those with direct discrimination. For instance, with indirect discrimination, Pluto must sell restricted travel to the vacationers, which provides less benefit than the unrestricted travel. By contrast, with direct discrimination, Pluto can sell unrestricted travel to all the passengers and so earn a higher profit.

Another reason why indirect discrimination is less profitable is that it may involve relatively higher costs. For instance, consumer products manufacturers use cents-off coupons to indirectly discriminate among consumers with different price elasticity. Coupons impose costs on both the issuers and users.

Finally, indirect discrimination relies on the various segments voluntarily identifying themselves through the structured choice. This may not always work perfectly: consumers in one segment may buy the item aimed at the other segment. Such leakage will also reduce the profitability of indirect discrimination.

Table 9.5 ranks the various pricing policies in decreasing order of profitability. The most profitable is complete price discrimination, with direct segment discrimination second, indirect segment discrimination third, and uniform pricing as least profitable.

Table 9.5 Ranking of pricing policies		
Profitability	Policy	Information Requirement
Highest	Complete price discrimination	Highest
	Direct segment discrimination	
	Indirect segment discrimination	
Lowest	Uniform pricing	Lowest

Progress Check 9F   Referring to table 9.3, suppose that the value of Maria and Tom's benefits from restricted travel change to $600 and $500, respectively. With these changes, can Pluto implement indirect segment discrimination?

Progress check

Cents-off coupons: consumer time and price elasticity of demand

In 1999, American businesses distributed 256 billion coupons with a face value of over $180 billion. Of these, consumers redeemed only 2%. An intriguing marketing issue is why sellers do not directly cut product prices. Considering the low redemption rate of coupons, direct price cuts would seem to be a more cost-effective way of promoting product sales.

From the consumer's viewpoint, a major difference between direct price cuts and coupons is the time and effort needed to redeem a coupon. The more valuable a consumer's time, the higher the cost of redeeming a coupon will be.

Consumers differ in their price elasticity of demand. Ideally, a seller would like to set prices so as to achieve lower margins from consumers whose demand is more elastic and higher margins from those with less elastic demand. To the extent that consumers whose time is more valuable are also those whose demand is less elastic, sellers can use coupons to implement indirect segment discrimination. Buyers whose time is more valuable will tend not to redeem coupons. Only those whose time is relatively cheap will use coupons.

By issuing coupons, a seller can target a discount at the consumer segment that is relatively more price elastic. In contrast, a direct price cut will benefit all buyers, regardless of their price elasticity. Hence, a direct price cut will be less profitable than the policy of issuing coupons.

Source: NCH (http://www.nuworld.com/).

Northwest Airlines' new 10-day advance purchase fare

In the U.S. airline industry as a whole, business travel accounts for 40% of passengers but over 50% of revenue. Many business travelers fly at the expense of others. For this and other reasons, they are willing to pay more than leisure travelers. Airlines use reservations and yield management systems to target higher unrestricted fares at business travelers and lower restricted fares at leisure travelers.

Despite the airlines' sophisticated systems, many business travelers buy restricted fares. Northwest Vice President for Pricing and Yield Management Tom Bach explained, "[B]usiness travelers were contorting their schedules to stay overnight Saturday and qualify for fares with leisure travel restrictions". In February 2000, the airline launched a major pricing innovation to contain such behavior. Northwest introduced a new fare requiring 10-day advance purchase and a minimum stay of one night with a $75 penalty for changes.

At $765 for a Minneapolis–New York round trip, the new fare was positioned about midway between the $1,267 unrestricted round-trip fare, and the 14-day advance purchase non-refundable fare of $311. The 14-day advance purchase fare required a Saturday night overstay and $75 penalty for changes. Over most routes, however, the 14-day advance purchase fare and the new 10-day advance purchase fare were respectively about 50% and 60% of the unrestricted fare.

Northwest believed that the new fare would attract 20% of business travelers, of whom half would switch from full fares and the other half would move up from more deeply discounted fares. On balance, Mr. Bach estimated that the new fare would raise annual revenues by about $50 million.

Sources: "Northwest Airlines Offers New Type of Business Fare," *New York Times*, February 12, 2000, Business 14; and *S&P Industry Surveys: Airlines*, vol. 167, no. 18, section 1 (May 6, 1999).

◂◂ 7 Bundling

Bundling is the combination of two or more products into one package with a single price.

Indirect segment discrimination usually involves a structured choice that persuades the various buyer segments to identify themselves through their choices. One method of indirect segment discrimination, however, deliberately restricts buyer choices. This is **bundling**, which is the combination of two or more products into one package with a single price.

Table 9.6 Benefits from cable television				
Segment	Population	Educational channel ($)	Music channel ($)	Bundle ($)
Conservatives	4,000	20	2	22
Middle-of-the-road segment	6,000	11	11	22

Pure Bundling

Cable television providers make extensive use of bundling in their pricing. To illustrate this pricing policy, suppose that Venus Cable has an educational channel and a music video channel. There are two segments among the viewer population: conservatives and a middle-of-the-road segment. Table 9.6 shows the segment sizes and their monthly benefits from the two channels. Venus Cable incurs a fixed cost of $100,000 a month, while the marginal cost of providing each channel is nothing.

Suppose that Venus Cable can implement direct segment discrimination. This means setting prices so as to obtain a different margin for each channel from each segment. Since the marginal cost is nothing, Venus should provide both channels to both segments. It should set the prices equal to the segment's benefits. For instance, the prices of the educational and music channels to the conservative segment should be $20 and $2 per month, respectively. The contribution margin will be ($20 × 4,000) + ($2 × 4,000) = $88,000. For the middle-of-the-road segment, both channels should be priced at $11, yielding a contribution margin of ($11 × 6,000) + ($11 × 6,000) = $132,000. Venus's profit would be $88,000 + $132,000 − $100,000 = $120,000.

What if Venus lacks sufficient information to implement direct segment discrimination? Another way to set prices yields an equally large profit. Let Venus offer the two channels as a bundle. Table 9.6 also shows the benefits provided by the bundle. Both segments value the bundle at the same amount of $22 a month. If Venus offers the bundle at a uniform price of $22, then everyone will buy the bundle. The profit will be $22 × (4,000 + 6,000) − $100,000 = $120,000.

In this example, the seller offered only a bundle of the two channels. A pricing policy that offers only a bundle and does not allow the alternative of buying the individual products is called *pure bundling*. Next, we will consider policies that do offer the alternative of the individual products.

With bundled pricing, Venus earns the same profits as from direct segment discrimination. Generally, the bundling strategy will be more profitable than uniform pricing, but less profitable than direct segment discrimination.

Mixed Bundling

In the preceding example, the seller offered only a bundle. Typically, however, the seller can make more profit by allowing buyers a choice between the bundle and the individual products. To illustrate, suppose that Venus incurs a marginal cost of $5 per channel for each customer. The fixed cost remains $100,000 and table 9.6 still represents the buyers' benefits.

Suppose that Venus Cable can implement direct segment discrimination. Consider the prices Venus should set to the conservative segment. Venus should not provide these viewers with the music channel as their benefit of $2 is less than the $5 marginal cost. They should be sold only the educational channel at a price of $20. Venus will earn a contribution margin of $(20 − 5) × 4,000 = $60,000. As for the middle-of-the-road segment, the benefit to these viewers for each channel exceeds the marginal cost. Hence, they should be provided both channels at a price of $11 each, yielding a contribution margin of $(11 − 5) × 6,000 + $(11 − 5) × 6,000 = $72,000. Venus's profit would be $60,000 + $72,000 − $100,000 = $32,000.

Now suppose that Venus Cable lacks sufficient information to implement direct segment discrimination. Pure bundling at a $22 price would be economically inefficient because it would provide both channels to the conservatives. This means that the conservatives would get the music channel, for which their benefit is less than the marginal cost. If it could avoid this inefficiency, Venus could earn a higher profit.

The economic inefficiency can be resolved through mixed bundling, which offers buyers a structured choice between the bundle and the individual products. Let Venus offer the bundle at a price of $22, and the educational channel separately at just under $20. What will the conservatives buy? If they buy the bundle, they will get no buyer surplus. If, however, they buy only the educational channel, they will get a little buyer surplus. Hence, they will choose the educational channel, and Venus will earn a contribution margin of just under $(20 − 5) × 4,000 = $60,000.

As for the middle-of-the-road viewers, they will get no buyer surplus from the bundle. Since the price of the educational channel exceeds the benefit, they will not buy the educational channel. Hence, they will choose the bundle, and Venus will earn a contribution margin of $(22 − 5 − 5) × 6,000 = $72,000. Venus's total profit would be just under $60,000 + $72,000 − $100,000 = $32,000. This is only a little less than the profit with direct segment discrimination.

Mixed bundling is a form of indirect segment discrimination. In this example, the conservatives and the middle-of-the-road segments are differentially sensitive to the product structure. The conservatives benefit relatively more from the educational channel, while the middle-of-the-road segment benefits relatively more from the music channel. Through mixed bundling, Venus attracts only the middle-of-the-road segment to choose the bundle, and persuades the conservatives to choose the educational channel.

Application

Bundling is relatively more useful under three conditions: where there is substantial disparity among the segments in their benefits from the separate products, where the benefits of the segments are negatively correlated in the sense that a product that is extremely beneficial to one segment provides relatively little benefit to another, and where the marginal cost of providing the product is low.

With the first and second conditions, the benefit from the bundle will be relatively less disparate across the segments than the benefits from the separate products. The third condition means that relatively little economic inefficiency will accrue from providing the bundle to all buyers.

In the Venus Cable example, each channel provides widely disparate benefits to each of the two segments. The bundle, however, provides exactly the same benefit of $22 to both segments. Accordingly, it is easy to set a price for the bundle.

When provision of the product involves a substantial marginal cost, a seller should consider mixed bundling. This is essentially a form of indirect segment discrimination. By structuring a choice among the bundle and the separate products, the seller can persuade the various segments to identify themselves through their product choice. In this way, the seller can avoid the economic inefficiency of providing a product for which the marginal cost is less than the buyer's benefit.

As already mentioned, bundling is ubiquitous in cable television. Another example of bundling is packaged holidays. A package consisting of airline travel and rooms in a beach resort will be relatively more attractive to vacationers than business travelers.

Avis Switzerland: bundling unlimited mileage

The market for car rentals, like that for airline services, consists of business and vacation segments. To the extent that employers or clients pay for business rentals, the demand of business drivers is relatively less elastic. A challenge for car rental agencies is how to discriminate between business and vacation drivers. Since rental agencies cannot discriminate directly, they need some variable with which to discriminate indirectly.

Suppose that vacationers tend to drive long distances, while business renters drive relatively shorter distances. Accordingly, these segments are differentially sensitive to mileage charges. Then, a rental agency can use mileage charges to discriminate between business and vacation drivers. Specifically, it should structure two choices. One choice combines a relatively high daily charge with a low mileage charge to draw vacationers. In the extreme, this could offer unlimited mileage. The other choice should have a lower daily charge with a higher mileage charge to attract business drivers.

Essentially, the unlimited mileage rate is a bundle of two products: the car and unlimited usage. The time and mileage rate sets separate prices for the two products.

In 1995, Avis Switzerland offered an Opel Vectra for weekday rental at an unlimited mileage rate of Fr 296 (Swiss francs) per day or a time and mileage rate of Fr 127 per day plus Fr 1.37 per kilometer. The break-even mileage between the two rates was 123 kilometers. Provided that most business renters drove less than 123 kilometers a day, the Avis pricing policy would succeed in indirect segment discrimination.

Given a choice of airline travel and a package holiday at a somewhat higher price, business travelers are relatively more likely to choose the separate airline travel, while vacationers will prefer the package.

Progress check

Progress Check 9G Referring to table 9.6, suppose that the conservatives derive a benefit of $19 from the educational channel, and $1 from the music channel. The marginal cost of providing each channel is $5. What prices should Venus set with mixed bundling?

◂◂ 8 Selecting the Discriminating Variable[2]

We have discussed how a seller can discriminate even when it cannot directly identify the various buyer segments. Indirect segment discrimination proceeds by offering buyers a choice of several alternatives, structured so that each segment makes a different choice. One issue that we have not yet considered is how to select the discriminating variable. For instance, should an airline require 7, 14, or 21 days' advance purchase for a restricted fare?

We now address this issue, and for simplicity, we do so in a context where the seller can choose among many different levels of the discriminating variable.

Suppose that Jupiter Suds has identified two segments in the market for its laundry detergent. There are 100,000 singles and 100,000 families. Figure 9.7(a) shows a single's demand for detergent, while figure 9.7(b) shows a family's demand for detergent. Families need more detergent than singles, hence have a higher demand curve. Jupiter's marginal cost of laundry detergent is constant at 10 cents per ounce and there are no other costs.

Consider the singles market. If Jupiter could directly identify single buyers, it would manufacture a bottle of the size at which a single person's marginal benefit equals the marginal cost. By figure 9.7(a), this size is 5 ounces. A single person's benefit from a 5-ounce bottle is the area $a0db$, under the demand curve up to 5 ounces. This area is $1/2 \times (10 + 90) \times 5 = \$2.50$. Hence, if Jupiter charges $2.50 for a 5-ounce bottle, every single will buy one bottle and get zero buyer surplus.

The cost of the 5-ounce bottle is $5 \times 10 = \$0.50$, hence the incremental margin from each bottle is $\$2.50 - 0.50 = \$2.00$. Since there are 100,000 singles and no other costs, the profit is $\$2.00 \times 100,000 = \$200,000$.

Similarly for families, if Jupiter could directly identify the families, it would manufacture a size that balances a family's marginal benefit with the marginal cost. By figure 9.7(b), this size is 10 ounces, and a family would pay up to area $e0gf$, or $1/2 \times (10 + 110) \times 10 = \$6.00$ for a 10-ounce bottle.

---

[2] This section is more advanced. It may be omitted without loss of continuity.

Figure 9.7 Demand for laundry detergent

(a) Single's demand

(b) Family's demand

With direct segment discrimination, Jupiter would sell a 5-ounce bottle to singles and a 10-ounce bottle to families. The singles would pay area *a0db* = $2.50 per bottle, and families would pay area *e0gf* = $6.00 per bottle.

The cost of the 10-ounce bottle is $10 \times 10 = \$1.00$; hence, the incremental margin from each bottle is $6.00 - \$1.00 = \$5.00$. Since there are 100,000 families and no other costs, the profit is $5.00 \times 100,000 = \$500,000$. Therefore, with direct segment discrimination, Jupiter's total profit would be $200,000 + \$500,000 = \$700,000$.

Cannibalization

Consider, however, a family's choice if Jupiter allowed it to choose between the 5- and 10-ounce bottles at prices of $2.50 and $6.00, respectively. A family would get zero buyer surplus from a large bottle at $6.00.

What if it were to buy the small bottle? Figure 9.8 shows both the family's and a single's demand curves. If it bought a 5-ounce bottle at $2.50, the family would get buyer surplus equal to the area *e0dh*, under the family's demand curve up to 5 ounces, minus $2.50. The area *e0dh* is $1/2 \times (110 + 60) \times 5 = \$4.25$, hence the family's buyer surplus would be $4.25 - \$2.50 = \$1.75$. This exceeds the buyer surplus from a large bottle; hence, every family would buy the 5-ounce bottle.

Graphically, referring to figure 9.8, the area *a0db* is $2.50. Since the area *e0dh* represents the family's benefit from the 5-ounce bottle, we can represent the family's

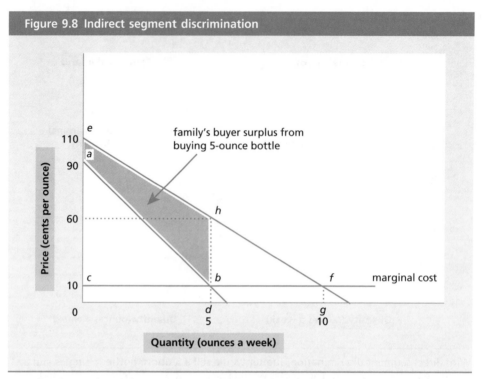

Figure 9.8 Indirect segment discrimination

For a family to voluntarily choose the 10-ounce bottle, the maximum that it can be charged is slightly less than area *e0gf*, under a family's demand curve up to 10 ounces, less the shaded area *eabh*, the buyer surplus that a family would get from the 5-ounce bottle.

> **Cannibalization** occurs when the sales of one product reduce the demand for another product with a higher incremental margin.

buyer surplus from the 5-ounce bottle by the shaded area *eabh*. The shaded area *eabh* is $1.75.

In marketing language, if Jupiter offers the 5- and 10-ounce bottles at prices of $2.50 and $6.00, respectively, the small bottle would **cannibalize** the demand for the large bottle. Cannibalization occurs when sales of one product reduce the demand for another product with a higher incremental margin.

The fundamental reason for cannibalization is that Jupiter has no way to distinguish families from singles directly; hence, it cannot prevent families from buying the bottle aimed for the singles segment. Accordingly, Jupiter must fall back on indirect segment discrimination. This means designing and pricing the two bottles so that families voluntarily choose the large bottle.

Suppose that Jupiter offers the 5-ounce bottle at $2.50. Then, as we have calculated already, every family will derive buyer surplus of $1.75 from the 5-ounce bottle. So, Jupiter must ensure that a family will get buyer surplus of slightly more than $1.75 from the 10-ounce bottle. Let *p* represent the price of the 10-ounce bottle. Referring to figure 9.8, if a family buys the 10-ounce bottle, its benefit will be area $e0gf$, which is $6.00; hence, its buyer surplus will be $6.00 − p.

For a family to get buyer surplus of slightly more than $1.75 from the 10-ounce bottle, the price that Jupiter charges must satisfy $6.00 − p > 1.75$. Thus, the maximum price is p = $4.24. Graphically, referring to figure 9.8, the maximum that Jupiter can charge for the 10-ounce bottle is slightly less than area $e0gf$, under a family's demand curve up to 10 ounces, less the shaded area $eabh$, the buyer surplus that a family would get from the 5-ounce bottle.

Accordingly, if Jupiter offered a 5-ounce bottle at $2.50 and a 10-ounce bottle at $4.24, singles would buy the 5-ounce bottle, while families would buy the 10-ounce bottle. With these prices, Jupiter could discriminate between singles and families.

Let us calculate Jupiter's profit. The cost of the 5-ounce bottle is 5 × 10 = $0.50; hence, the incremental margin from each bottle is $2.50 − $0.50 = $2.00. The cost of the 10-ounce bottle is 10 × 10 = $1.00, hence the incremental margin from each bottle is $4.24 − $1.00 = $3.24. Since there are 100,000 singles and 100,000 families and no other costs, Jupiter's profit is ($2.00 × 100,000) + ($3.24 × 100,000) = $524,000.

Progress Check 9H With indirect segment discrimination, if Jupiter reduces the price of the 5-ounce bottle to $2.00, how much can it charge families for the 10-ounce bottle?

Progress check

Degrading Quality

So far, we have assumed that Jupiter offers a 5-ounce bottle at $2.50. Notice from figure 9.9 that, at every quantity, a single person's marginal benefit from detergent is lower than a family's marginal benefit.

Suppose that Jupiter were to reduce the small bottle by 0.1 ounce to 4.9 ounces. Then, it must reduce the price of the small bottle by the marginal benefit to a single person of the 4.9th ounce. According to figure 9.9, this marginal benefit is area $bkjd$, or $(11.6 + 10)/2 × 0.1 = 1.08$ cents. Recall that the marginal cost of detergent is 10 cents per ounce. So, by cutting the size of the small bottle, Jupiter will reduce its cost by 10 × 0.1 = 1 cent per bottle. Thus, the incremental margin from the 4.9-ounce bottle will be $(1.08 − 1) = 0.08$ cent less than from the original 5-ounce bottle.

With the small bottle reduced to 4.9 ounces, a family's buyer surplus from the small bottle will fall by area $hmkb$, or $(49.4 + 50)/2 × 0.1 = 4.97$ cents. Hence, Jupiter can raise the price of the 10-ounce bottle and still attract families to buy the 10-ounce bottle. Specifically, Jupiter can raise the price by 4.97 cents, which increases its margin by 4.97 cents.

The net effect of these changes is to raise Jupiter's profit by a total of $(4.97 × 100,000) − (0.08 × 100,000) = $4,890$. Accordingly, Jupiter can increase its profit

Figure 9.9 Mitigating cannibalization

A 0.1-ounce reduction of the smaller bottle mitigates the extent to which it cannibalizes the demand for the 10-ounce bottle. Hence, the seller can extract the shaded area *mkbh* in additional contribution margin from buyers of the 10-ounce bottle.

Cellular telephone service: how many choices to offer

Indirect segment discrimination is widespread in cellular telephone service. Table 9.7 reports AT&T's Digital One rates. The company offered a choice of four plans, differing in the monthly basic charge, the quantity of free airtime, and the rates for additional airtime.

To decide how many alternatives to offer buyers, a seller should consider the number of segments in the market. Generally, the number of alternatives should not exceed the number of segments. Owing to the problem of cannibalization, however, it may not be profitable to discriminate among all segments. In this case, a seller may choose to provide buyers with fewer alternatives and so allow some market segments to choose the same product.

Table 9.7 AT&T Digital One Calling Plans		
Monthly fee	Inclusive airtime (minutes)	Additional airtime (per minute)
$59.99	300	35¢
$89.99	600	25¢
$119.99	1,000	25¢
$149.99	1,400	25¢

Source: http://www.attws.com/personal/.

by downgrading the smaller bottle. Essentially, this downgrading mitigates the extent to which the smaller bottle cannibalizes the demand for the larger bottle and, so, allows Jupiter to extract more profit from families.

Generally, Jupiter should downgrade the small bottle to a size such that the marginal reduction in profit from singles equals the marginal gain in profit from families. This balance depends on the single relative to the family demand and the number of singles relative to families. In the extreme case, if the demand from singles is very low and there are very few singles, Jupiter may decide to sell only a large bottle and cater only to families.

Cannibalization: is an Audi worth 40% more?

The Volkswagen Group (Audi, Skoda, SEAT, and VW), accounts for over 9% of the world automobile market. Like other major car manufacturers, Volkswagen economizes on development and manufacturing costs by using a set of common chassis and engines across its various brands. For instance, the high-end Audi A6 and the lower-end VW Passat share the same 1.8 and 2.8-liter engine and body. The Audi is differentiated through superior paneling, instrumentation, and other electronic equipment.

The Audi is priced at a 40% premium to the VW. Owing to their basic similarities, however, the VW has cannibalized the demand for the Audi. Some German buyers of large numbers of cars for fleets reportedly switched their purchases to the VW. Tynan's, a VW dealer in Aurora, Colorado, even mounted a Web-page entitled "Volkswagen's Passat vs Audi A6" to compare the relative value of the two cars.

Source: "Let's Make a Deal," *Time*, January 25, 1999, pp. 35–6.

◂◂ 9 Summary

The simplest way to set price is through uniform pricing. At the profit-maximizing uniform price, the incremental margin percentage equals the reciprocal of the absolute value of the price elasticity of demand. The most profitable pricing policy is complete price discrimination, where each unit is priced at the benefit that the unit provides to its buyer. To implement this policy, however, the seller must know each potential buyer's individual demand curve and be able to set different prices for every unit of the product.

The next most profitable pricing policy is direct segment discrimination. For this policy, the seller must be able to directly identify the various segments. The third most profitable policy is indirect segment discrimination. This involves structuring a set of choices around some variable to which the various segments are differentially sensitive. Uniform pricing is the least profitable way to set a price.

A commonly used basis for direct segment discrimination is location. This exploits a difference between free on board and cost including freight prices. A commonly used method of indirect segment discrimination is bundling. Sellers may apply either pure or mixed bundling.

Key Concepts

uniform pricing
price discrimination
complete price discrimination
segment
direct segment discrimination
free on board (FOB)

delivered pricing
cost including freight (CF)
indirect segment discrimination
bundling
cannibalization

Further Reading

Thomas T. Nagle and Reed K. Holden provide a comprehensive economic analysis of pricing in *The Strategy and Tactics of Pricing*, 2d ed. (Englewood Cliffs, NJ: Prentice Hall, 1995).

Review Questions

1. Many supermarkets sell both branded and private-label merchandise. Suppose that some supermarket estimates that the demand for its private-label cola is less elastic than the demand for Coca Cola. Does this mean that it should set a higher price for private-label cola?

2. Sol Electric manufactures long-life light bulbs. The marginal production cost is

50 cents per unit. Sol estimates that the price elasticity of demand is −1.25. Assuming that Sol will set a uniform price, what is the profit-maximizing price?

3. Saturn Tire has found a way to reduce the marginal cost of a tire from $50 to $40. Should Sol reduce the selling price of a tire by $10?

4. Give an example of direct segment discrimination. Discuss whether the product meets the conditions for such discrimination.

5. Some department stores offer a free delivery service. For stores that do, is the FOB price of goods less than, equal to, or greater than the CF price?

6. Sol Electric is planning to export light bulbs to Germany and South Africa. The marginal production cost is 50 cents per unit. The cost of shipping is 5 cents to Germany and 10 cents to South Africa. The price elasticity of demand is −1.2 in Germany and −1.5 in South Africa. What prices should Sol set in the two export markets?

7. On which of the following products would it be easier to discriminate by the buyer's location? Newspapers or scientific journals? Explain your answer.

8. Microsoft priced Office 2000 Pro with a higher incremental margin in the USA than in Singapore. Relate this difference to the greater availability of pirated software and opportunities for copying in Singapore.

9. Give an example of indirect segment discrimination. Discuss whether the example meets the conditions for such discrimination.

10. The *Wall Street Journal Interactive Edition* charges a lower subscription fee to those who already subscribe to the print edition. Explain this practice.

11. AT&T Cellular offers a menu of pricing plans. Plans with higher monthly charges include a larger number of "free minutes." What is the purpose of this menu?

12. Hertz imposes a charge for gasoline if a renter returns a car without refueling. Typically, Hertz's price for gasoline is much higher than that at nearby gas stations. Explain how this indirectly segments between drivers who are paying for a rental themselves and those who are renting at the expense of others.

13. Use pure bundling to explain the following comment on cable television business strategy: "[I]f every segment . . . was wild about one thing and hated the rest, they have done their job. If all their programmes are mildly, but not very interesting to everybody, they haven't" ("Getting better all the time," *Economist*, November 21, 1998).

14. Some restaurants offer a choice between à la carte and all-you-can-eat self-service buffets. Explain how this choice will indirectly discriminate between consumers with small and big appetites.

15. Venus Airways offers business class and economy class. Which of the following factors should the airline consider in deciding how much to invest in upgrading its economy class service?
    (a) The effect on sales of business class fares.
    (b) The effect on sales of economy class fares.

Discussion Questions

1. Most international airlines offer special excursion fares, which are subject to restrictions such as a minimum three nights' stay at the destination. Regular economy class fares carry no such restrictions. A study of North Atlantic airline services found that the price elasticity of demand was −1.30 for regular economy class and −1.83 for excursion fares (J. Cigliano, "Price and Income Elasticities for Airline Travel: The North Atlantic Market," *Business Economics*, September 1980).
   (a) Explain why the demand for regular economy class is less elastic than the demand for excursion fares.
   (b) Assume that one airline has a monopoly over the North Atlantic routes and that travelers cannot substitute between regular economy and excursion fares. How can it use the data on price elasticities to set the two fares?
   (c) In reality, travelers can substitute between regular economy and excursion fares. Explain how the demand for one product depends on the price of the other.

2. Major industrial corporations often borrow money through loans that are syndicated among multiple banks. The managers of the syndicated loan may specify the interest rate as the London Interbank Offer Rate (LIBOR) plus a "spread" to account for the riskiness of the borrower. Most banks prefer to source funds from savings and time deposits as the rates on these deposits are usually lower than the London Interbank market.
   (a) Does LIBOR reflect a typical bank's average or marginal cost of funds?
   (b) For purposes of pricing, which is relevant – average or marginal cost?
   (c) In addition to the riskiness of the borrower, should banks consider the borrower's price elasticity of demand when setting spreads on syndicated loans?

3. Doctors routinely ask patients about their occupation, employer, home address, and scope of insurance coverage. How do the following factors affect the scope for price discrimination in medical services?
   (a) Characteristics such as occupation and home address are quite fixed.
   (b) It is physically impossible to transfer medical treatment from one person to another.
   (c) Doctors treat patients on an individual basis.

4. Referring to figure 9.1, suppose that Mercury Bikes' marginal revenue and demand curves cross the marginal cost curve at quantities of 3,000 and 6,000 units a year, respectively. All other data remain the same.
   (a) Calculate the profit under policies of (i) uniform pricing, and (ii) complete price discrimination.
   (b) Suppose that Mercury is implementing complete price discrimination. Explain why it should sell up to the quantity where the buyer's marginal benefit equals Mercury's marginal cost.
   (c) Explain why Mercury's profit is higher with complete price discrimination than with uniform pricing.

5. Microsoft offers special discounts to students. Other publishers have developed special "student" editions of their software with fewer features than the regular packages.
   (a) Why do publishers offer discounts to students?
   (b) What is the purpose of developing less powerful "student" editions?
   (c) Should software publishers also offer discounts to senior citizens or develop "senior citizen" editions?

6. Some Japanese consumer electronics manufacturers set higher prices in Tokyo than in Hong Kong. This, however, has created a "gray market" through which Japanese retailers buy cheap products in Hong Kong and ship them back to the Japanese market.
   (a) By considering price elasticities of demand and production and shipping costs, explain why some Japanese manufacturers set higher prices in Tokyo than in Hong Kong.
   (b) Why does the gray market present a problem?
   (c) Compare the gray market problem for big-screen TVs relative to cosmetics.

7. Airlines measure passenger service capacity by "available seat-miles," which is the number of seats multiplied by the miles flown; sales volume by "revenue passenger-miles," which is the number of fare-paying passengers multiplied by the miles flown; and average price collected by the "revenue per passenger-mile," which is passenger revenues divided by the revenue passenger-miles. Table 9.8 reports financial data for Northwest Airlines between 1994 and 1999.

Table 9.8 Northwest Airlines

	1999	1998	1997	1996	1995	1994
Available seat-miles (millions)	99.4	91.3	97.0	93.9	87.4	85.0
Revenue passenger-miles (millions)	74.1	66.7	72.0	68.6	62.5	57.9
Revenue per passenger-mile (cents)	11.72	13.22	12.25	12.53	12.42	13.36

Source: Northwest Airlines, *1999 Annual Report*.

   (a) Considering the demand for passenger service, do you expect Northwest's revenue passenger-miles and revenue per passenger-mile to be positively or negatively related?
   (b) Comment on the following criticism: "No self-respecting yield management system should allow a plane to take off with empty seats. Every seat should be sold, even if only for a few dollars".
   (c) Northwest gives seniors a 10% discount. Suppose that, without the discount, no seniors would have traveled on Northwest. Discuss how the senior discount would affect Northwest's revenue per passenger-mile. If Northwest maximizes revenue per passenger-mile, would it also be maximizing profit?

(d) Some seniors, however, would have bought the adult fare even without the discount. Discuss how the senior discount would in fact affect Northwest's profit.

8. Each year, consumer products manufacturers spend millions of dollars distributing cents-off coupons to consumers. Why do manufacturers not directly cut the wholesale prices of the products? A direct price cut would be much cheaper to administer than coupons.

(a) Some say that retailers would absorb a direct wholesale price cut instead of passing it on to consumers. They argue that, by contrast, retailers cannot absorb the value of coupons. Suppose that the retail sector is perfectly competitive. Compare the demand–supply equilibrium in the retail market with (i) a wholesale price cut of 50 cents and (ii) widespread distribution of 50-cent coupons. For this part, you may assume that all consumers use coupons.

(b) Would there be any difference between the wholesale price cut and using coupons if the retailer were a monopoly? (Continue to assume that all consumers use coupons.)

(c) Explain how coupons may be used to discriminate among consumers on price.

9. The Chinese Embassy in Singapore charges different fees for visas according to the number of times that the visitor wishes to enter China and the requested processing time (see table 9.9). Assume that the costs of preparing single and double entry visas are the same, and that the costs of processing over 1, 3, and 5 days are the same. Explain the Embassy's pricing policies in terms of indirect segment discrimination between tourists and business travelers.

Table 9.9 Visa Fees, Chinese Embassy, Singapore

	Processing time		
	1 day	3 days	5 days
Single entry	75	60	25
Double entry	85	70	35

Source: Chinese Embassy, Singapore, July 2000.

(a) Explain the Embassy's pricing policies in terms of indirect segment discrimination between tourists and business travelers.

(b) The Embassy charges a premium of $10 for double entry visas relative to single entry visas. Consider intuitively what premium it should charge for double entry visas.

(c) Should the Chinese Government set the same schedule of visa fees at all of its overseas embassies?

10. Refer to the example of Jupiter Suds. Suppose that Jupiter's marginal cost is 5 cents per ounce, while the demands of singles and families remain unchanged.

(a) Calculate the profit-maximizing bottle sizes and prices with direct segment discrimination.

(b) Suppose that Jupiter offers the bottle sizes and prices in (a). How much buyer surplus would a family get from buying the small bottle?

(c) Suppose that Jupiter offers the bottle sizes in (a) and sets the price of the small bottle as in (a). What is the maximum that Jupiter could charge a family for the large bottle?

11. This question applies the technique for the profit-maximizing uniform price presented in the math supplement. Consider a business that faces a demand curve represented by $Q = 12 - p$. Production requires a fixed cost of 5 and a constant marginal cost of 2 per unit.

(a) Using the rule that equates the incremental margin percentage with the reciprocal of the absolute value of the price elasticity of demand, calculate the profit-maximizing price and quantity.

(b) Suppose that the marginal cost is 3 rather than 2 per unit. How would this affect the profit-maximizing price and quantity?

Chapter 9

Math Supplement

Uniform Pricing: Profit-Maximizing Price

Let us prove the rule for a profit-maximizing price in terms of the price elasticity of demand: the incremental margin percentage equals the reciprocal of the absolute value of the price elasticity. Let Q represent sales, and $R(Q)$ and $C(Q)$ represent total revenue and total cost, respectively. Then, a seller's profit is total revenue less total cost:

$$P = R(Q) - C(Q). \qquad (9.3)$$

From chapter 9, we know that, at the profit-maximizing amount of sales, the marginal revenue equals the marginal cost:

$$\frac{dR(Q)}{dQ} = \frac{dC(Q)}{dQ} \qquad (9.4)$$

Now the marginal revenue is

$$\frac{dR(Q)}{dQ} = \frac{d}{dQ}(p \times Q)$$

$$= p + Q\frac{dp}{dQ}. \qquad (9.5)$$

Substituting in (9.4), we have

$$p + Q\frac{dp}{dQ} = \frac{dC(Q)}{dQ}. \qquad (9.6)$$

By the definition of the price elasticity of demand,

$$e_p = \frac{p}{Q}\frac{dQ}{dp}; \qquad (9.7)$$

hence,

$$Q\frac{dp}{dQ} = \frac{p}{e_p}.$$

Substituting in (9.6), we have

$$\frac{p - dC(Q)/Q}{p} = -\frac{1}{e_p} \qquad (9.8)$$

This states that, at the profit-maximizing price, the incremental margin percentage equals the reciprocal of the absolute value of the price elasticity.

Let us apply this analysis to a business that faces the straight-line demand curve represented by the equation

$$Q = 100 - 2p. \qquad (9.9)$$

Differentiating with respect to p,

$$\frac{dQ}{dp} = -2. \qquad (9.10)$$

Suppose that production requires a fixed cost of 300 and a constant marginal cost of 10 per unit, hence $dC(Q)/dQ = 10$. Rearranging equation (9.9), the price,

$$p = \frac{100 - Q}{2} = 50 - \frac{Q}{2}. \qquad (9.11)$$

Substituting the marginal cost of 10 and the price,

$$\frac{p - dC(Q)/dQ}{p} = \frac{40 - Q/2}{(100 - Q)/2}. \qquad (9.12)$$

Substituting from (9.10) and (9.11) in (9.7), the price elasticity,

$$e_p = \frac{50 - Q/2}{Q}(-2) = -\frac{100 - Q}{Q}. \qquad (9.13)$$

Substituting from (9.12) and (9.13) in (9.8),

$$\frac{40 - Q/2}{(100 - Q)/2} = \frac{Q}{100 - Q}, \qquad (9.14)$$

which implies that $Q = 40$. Hence by (9.11), $p = 30$. The profit-maximizing price is 30 and the corresponding quantity is 40 units.

Contribution Margin Percentage

Next, we prove that the contribution margin percentage is equal to the price less the average variable cost divided by the price. In cost accounting, the contribution margin percentage is defined as total revenue less variable cost divided by total revenue, or

$$CM\% = \frac{R(Q) - V(Q)}{R(Q)}. \qquad (9.15)$$

Dividing both the numerator and the denominator by sales (or the quantity demanded), we have

$$CM\% = \frac{R(Q)/Q - V(Q)/Q}{R(Q)/Q}. \qquad (9.16)$$

Consider the first term in the numerator and the same term in the denominator:

$$\frac{R(Q)}{Q} = \frac{p \times Q}{Q} = p \qquad (9.17)$$

Hence, the contribution margin percentage simplifies to

$$CM\% = \frac{p - V(Q)/Q}{p}, \qquad (9.18)$$

which is the price less the average variable cost divided by the price.

◄◄ 1 Introduction

Soft drinks are America's single most popular beverage, accounting for one in four beverages consumed, up from one in five over a decade ago. The average American consumes almost 55 gallons a year, equivalent to 2.4 eight-ounce servings a day. Coca Cola, with a 45% market share, followed by Pepsi with 30%, and Cadbury Schweppes with 14%, dominate the U.S. soft drink industry. With the top three manufacturers accounting for almost 90% of the market, the industry is highly concentrated.[1]

Despite the high industry concentration, Coke and Pepsi competed intensely on price, and their profits slipped. Then, in November 1999, Coke made a fundamental change in strategy, announcing a 7% increase in the price of concentrate to bottlers, which translated into a 5% retail price increase. Within a week, Pepsi followed suit, raising the price of concentrate by 6.9%, which led to a 5% retail price increase.

Why did the two arch-rivals succeed in raising prices after the long, sustained price war? Standard and Poors analyst Richard Joy pointed to a significant change in Pepsi's organizational architecture: "The creation of the Pepsi Bottling Group . . . had the effect of reducing price competition at the retail level. . . . Now that it is no longer shielded by the corporate umbrella of PepsiCo, Pepsi Bottling Group needs to produce profits, and thus appears unlikely to discount its brands."

Historically, Coke was vertically separated: the Coca Cola Company, headquartered in Atlanta, owned the brand and sold concentrate to Coca Cola Enterprises and other franchised bottlers. By contrast, PepsiCo had been vertically integrated. Then, in March 1999, PepsiCo spun off the Pepsi Bottling Group (PBG). Following the spin-off, PepsiCo managed the brand and sold concentrate. PBG and other

---

[1] This discussion is based, in part, on *Standard & Poor's Industry Surveys: Foods & Nonalcoholic Beverages*, 166, no. 22, section 1 (June 3, 1999), p. 3; "Coca Cola Shifts Strategy In Effort to Boost Profit," *Wall Street Journal Interactive Edition*, November 16, 1999.

franchised bottlers used the concentrate to manufacture soft drinks for sale in supermarkets and other distribution channels.

A **strategy** is a plan for action in a situation where the parties actively consider the interactions with one another in making decisions. Consider Coke's decision whether to raise its price. The soft drink industry is so concentrated that it surely must consider the reactions of Pepsi and Cadbury Schweppes. Coke was making a *strategic* decision.

> A **strategy** is a plan for action in a situation where the parties actively consider the interactions with one another in making decisions.

Contrast Coke's pricing decision with a sugar beet farm's choice of how much to plant for the next season. The farm is too small to affect the price of sugar, hence it need not consider its impact on other farms. The farm's decision is not strategic.

In this chapter, we consider how to organize thinking about strategic decisions, choose among alternative strategies, and make better strategic decisions. This chapter is based on a set of ideas and principles to guide strategic thinking called **game theory**.

> **Game theory** is a set of ideas and principles that guides strategic thinking.

Game theory explains why Coke and Pepsi were able to raise their prices only after Pepsi vertically separated into independent brand and bottling businesses. Pepsi's vertical separation mitigated the intensity of price competition, and paved the way for the two arch-rivals to raise prices.

The ideas and principles of game theory provide an effective guide to strategic decision-making in many businesses. Corporate financiers apply game theory in takeover contests. Telecommunications and media providers apply it in bidding for licenses. And, of course, game theory is useful to any business with market power in analyzing competitive strategy.

Before going further, we should note that a decision-maker always has the option of acting nonstrategically. Obviously, there will be situations where the cost of strategic thinking outweighs the benefit. In this chapter, however, we shall focus on situations where it is worthwhile to act strategically.

Progress Check 10A Explain why the decisions of a presidential election candidate are strategic.

Progress check

◂◂ 2 Nash Equilibrium

We introduce a framework for strategic decisions that must be taken simultaneously in the context of the following example. Radio Jupiter and Merkur Radio, each with 50% of the audience, dominate the market for the adult contemporary (AC) format. After many successful years, Jupiter is considering a shift to the "Hot AC" format, which would mean a larger proportion of new pop/rock releases. Meanwhile, Merkur is debating a shift towards the easier listening "Lite AC" format.

The dilemma for Jupiter is that its best decision depends on whether Merkur shifts format. If Merkur does not change, then Jupiter can raise its audience share to 60% by shifting to Hot AC. However, if Merkur does change, then Jupiter can raise its share to 70% by sticking with the current format. How should Jupiter decide without knowing Merkur's choice?

Strategic Form

The battle for the adult contemporary audience is clearly a strategic situation. Jupiter's dilemma is that its best decision depends on what it believes Merkur would do. Jupiter might place itself in Merkur's shoes to figure out which format Merkur would choose. But Merkur might be doing the same. Jupiter is faced with a problem of *infinite regress*: its best decision depends on how it expects Merkur to act, which in turn depends on how Merkur expects Jupiter to act, and so on.

Let us try to clarify Jupiter's position in the following way. Recall that a strategy is a plan for action in a situation where the parties actively consider interactions with one another in making decisions. Jupiter must decide on a strategy. Jupiter has a choice of two alternative strategies, switch to Hot AC or do not change, and likewise, Merkur has a choice of two strategies, switch to Lite AC or do not change.

Accordingly, there are four possible outcomes: Jupiter shifts to Hot AC and Merkur shifts to Lite AC, Jupiter shifts to Hot AC while Merkur does not change format, Jupiter does not change while Merkur shifts to Lite AC, and both stations do not change. For each of these outcomes, we know the audience shares of the two stations.

Next, we gather this information in table 10.1 as follows. We mark Jupiter's alternative strategies along the rows, and Merkur's strategies along the columns. The columns and rows delineate four cells, each representing one of the four possible outcomes. In each cell, we record the consequences for Jupiter and Merkur, respectively. For instance, in the cell where Jupiter shifts to Hot AC and Merkur shifts to Lite AC, we mark "J: 60" to represent Jupiter's audience share, and then "M: 40" to represent Merkur's share.

Table 10.1 Battle of the radio stations

	Merkur	
	Lite AC	No change
Jupiter Hot AC	J: 60, M: 40	J: 60, M: 40
No change	J: 70, M: 30	J: 50, M: 50

Table 10.1 is called a **game in strategic form**. It is a very useful way to organize thinking about strategic decisions that parties must take simultaneously. Let us use the game in strategic form to consider how Jupiter should move. First, look at the situation from Merkur's position. If Jupiter shifts to Hot AC, then Merkur will get a 40% share whether it changes to Lite AC or not. If Jupiter does not change format, then Merkur is better off with no change. So, regardless of Jupiter's move, Merkur should not change. For Merkur, the strategy of switching to Lite AC is **dominated** by the strategy of no change of format.

A strategy is *dominated* if it generates worse consequences than some other strategy, regardless of the other parties' choices. It makes no sense to adopt a dominated strategy.

For Merkur, switching to Lite AC is a dominated strategy. Accordingly, Jupiter can figure out that Merkur will not change its format. Given that Merkur will not change, Jupiter must choose between switching to Hot AC and getting a 60% audience share, and not changing, which would mean a 50% share. Clearly, Jupiter should switch to Hot AC.

> A **game in strategic form** is a tabular representation of a strategic situation, showing one party's strategies along the rows, the other party's strategies along the columns, and the consequences for the parties in the corresponding cells.

> A **dominated strategy** is a strategy that generates worse consequences than some other strategy, regardless of the choices of the other parties.

Progress Check 10B Check whether any of Jupiter's strategies in table 10.1 is dominated.

Progress check

Definition

The pair of strategies – Jupiter switches to Hot AC and Merkur does not change – is the obvious way for the two stations to act. Moreover, this pair of strategies is a stable situation in the following sense. Even if Merkur knows that Jupiter will switch to Hot AC, Merkur will be indifferent between switching to Lite AC and not changing format, so it will not change. Likewise, even if Jupiter knew that Merkur would not change, Jupiter would still switch to Hot AC.

In a strategic situation, a **Nash equilibrium** is a set of strategies such that, given that the other parties choose their Nash equilibrium strategies, each party prefers its own Nash equilibrium strategy. In the battle of the radio stations, the pair of strategies in which Jupiter switches to Hot AC and Merkur does not change is a Nash equilibrium.

> A **Nash equilibrium** is a set of strategies such that, given that the other players choose their Nash equilibrium strategies, each party prefers its own Nash equilibrium strategy.

What justifies a Nash equilibrium as a reasonable way for the relevant parties to act? One reason is that a Nash equilibrium provides a logically consistent solution to the problem of infinite regress that strategic decisions present. Jupiter could have placed itself in Merkur's shoes to guess Merkur's strategy, but Merkur could do likewise. The result is a problem of infinite regress: to identify Merkur's best strategy, we must know Jupiter's strategy, but to identify Jupiter's strategy, we must know Merkur's strategy. The Nash equilibrium provides a logically consistent solution to this problem of infinite regress.

Another reason to act according to Nash equilibrium strategies is that, in many typical strategic situations that we analyze later, the Nash equilibrium strategies seem like the most reasonable and obvious way to behave. By extension, this provides ground for believing that, in other, less familiar settings, the relevant parties should also act according to Nash equilibrium strategies. Accordingly, the Nash equilibrium strategies provide a focal point for strategic decision making.

Solving the Equilibrium

The formal way to find a Nash equilibrium is, first, to rule out dominated strategies and, next, to check all the remaining strategies, one at a time.

A simple, informal method of finding a Nash equilibrium is to draw arrows between the cells as follows. Supposing that Merkur switches to Lite AC, then for Jupiter, draw an arrow from 60 in the top left-hand cell pointing toward 70 in the bottom left-hand cell. Next, supposing that Merkur does not change, then for Jupiter, draw an arrow from 50 in the bottom right-hand cell pointing toward 60 in the top right-hand cell.

Now, supposing that Jupiter switches to Hot AC, then for Merkur, draw a double-pointed arrow linking 40 in the top left-hand cell with 40 in the top right-hand cell. Finally, supposing that Jupiter does not change, then for Merkur, draw an arrow from 30 in the bottom left-hand cell pointing toward 50 in the bottom right-hand cell.

Using this "arrow" technique, we can easily see if a strategy is dominated. A strategy is dominated if the row or column corresponding to the strategy has all the arrows pointing out. From table 10.1, Merkur's strategy of switching to Lite AC is dominated. The arrow technique also easily identifies an equilibrium. If there is a cell with all arrows leading in, then the strategies marking that cell are a Nash equilibrium.

A Cartel's Dilemma

A particularly useful application of game theory is to analyze the behavior of participants in a cartel. Recall from chapter 8 that competing sellers can raise their profit by organizing a cartel. A cartel agreement restricts the sales of each individual seller to a specific quota. The total quota is set below the quantity that a competitive market would supply; hence, the cartel can increase its profit above the competitive level.

Suppose, for instance, that Hilda, Inc., and Sharon Corporation dominate the market for truck rentals. The managements of the two companies have discussed a cartel agreement limiting each company to a specific quota of truck rentals a year. The quotas have been set to maintain the price at the monopoly level.

Game theory at war: Battle of the Bismarck Sea

In late February 1943, Japanese commander Rear-Admiral Kimura had assembled a convoy of sixteen transport ships and destroyers at the port of Rabaul. Admiral Kimura's mission was to bring the convoy to Lae, on the mainland of New Guinea. American Lieutenant-General Kenney, commander of Allied Air Forces in the area, was ordered to intercept and destroy the Japanese convoy.

Admiral Kimura had to choose between sailing along a northern route through the Bismarck Sea and a southern route. Meteorologists forecast that there would be rain on the northern route, which would reduce visibility. Weather on the southern route, however, would be fine.

General Kenney had to decide the direction in which to concentrate his reconnaissance aircraft. Once his aircraft spotted the Japanese convoy, Kenney would dispatch his bombers. The dilemma for Kenney was that his best decision depended on what he believed Kimura would do.

Table 10.2 represents the Battle of the Bismarck Sea in strategic form. In each cell, the first entry represents the number of days of bombing that Kenney could inflict on the Japanese, while the second entry represents the number of days of bombing that Kimura would suffer.

Using the arrow technique, we can solve the Nash equilibrium, which is for Kenney to fly north and Kimura to sail north. Indeed, on February 28, Admiral Kimura set out on the northern route. General Kenney's reconnaissance planes discovered the Japanese convoy on March 2. In two days of massive aerial raids, Kenney's bombers destroyed the Japanese convoy.

Sources: O. G. Haywood, "Military Decision and Game Theory," *Journal of the Operations Research Society of America* 2, no. 4 (November 1954): pp. 365–85; Eric Rasmusen, *Games and Information*, 2d ed. (Cambridge, MA: Basil Blackwell, 1994), chapter 1; and J. Rohwer and G. Hummelchen, *Chronology of the War at Sea, 1939–45*, vol. 2, trans. Derek Masters (London: Ian Allan, 1974), p. 306.

Table 10.2 Battle of the Bismarck Sea

		Kimura	
		North	**South**
Kenney	North	Ken: 2, Kim: –2	Ken: 2, Kim: –2
	South	Ken: 1, Kim: –1	Ken: 3, Kim: –3

Table 10.3 Cartel's dilemma			
		Sharon	
		Follow quota	Produce more
Hilda	Follow quota	H: 15, S: 10	H: 10, S: 13
	Produce more	H: 19, S: 5	H: 12, S: 8

This discussion of cartels, however, has ignored the incentives of the individual sellers. Each seller makes an independent decision on its sales. Accordingly, it is important to ask, will the individual sellers comply with their quotas?

To address this question, suppose that Hilda and Sharon each have two alternatives: either follow the quota or produce more. Table 10.3 is a game in strategic form that describes the cartel comprising Hilda and Sharon. In each cell, the first entry is Hilda's annual profit in millions of dollars and the second entry is Sharon's profit.

Consider Hilda's decision. Assume that Sharon follows its quota. Then, if Hilda follows its quota, its profit will be $15 million, while if it produces more than its quota, its profit will be $19 million. Hence, if Sharon follows its quota, Hilda should produce more than its quota. Similarly, if Sharon produces more than its quota, Hilda should also produce more than its quota. From Hilda's standpoint, following its quota is a dominated strategy. No matter what Sharon does, the best strategy for Hilda is to exceed its quota.

Similarly for Sharon, following its quota is a dominated strategy. Hence, for both companies, the Nash equilibrium strategy is to produce more than the quota.

We call this situation a *cartel's dilemma* because both companies know that, if they can cooperate, then they can increase their profit. The snag, however, is that when each individual company acts independently, it will decide to exceed its quota. The final outcome is that the two companies produce at a competitive rather than monopoly level.

Progress check **Progress Check 10C** Referring to table 10.3, use the arrow technique to identify the Nash equilibrium strategies.

Nonequilibrium Strategies

We have explained how to analyze a strategic situation using the concept of a Nash equilibrium. Given that the other players choose their Nash equilibrium strategies, each party's best choice is its own Nash equilibrium strategy. But, what if some party does not follow its Nash equilibrium strategy? Then the other parties may find it better to deviate from their respective Nash equilibrium strategies.

For example, refer to table 10.1, which describes the strategic situation between Merkur and Jupiter. Jupiter's Nash equilibrium strategy is switching to Hot AC, while Merkur's Nash equilibrium strategy is not to change. Suppose, however, that Merkur decides, for some reason, to switch to Lite AC and that Jupiter has this information. Then, Jupiter can win a bigger audience share by not changing format.

Accordingly, in the battle between the radio stations, if one party does not follow its Nash equilibrium strategy, then it may be better for the other party to choose a strategy that is not a Nash equilibrium strategy.

In other situations, however, it may be better for a party to stick to its Nash equilibrium strategy even if the other does not follow its Nash equilibrium strategy. These are cases where the other strategies are dominated.

Consider, for instance, the cartel's dilemma in table 10.3. Suppose that Sharon decides to follow its quota. Hilda should still produce more than its quota. The alternative strategy – following the quota – is dominated.

OPEC: dilemma of an oil cartel

The Organisation of Petroleum Exporting Countries (OPEC) includes major oil producers Saudi Arabia, Iran, Kuwait, and Venezuela. Like any other cartel, OPEC suffers from the problem that individual members prefer to exceed their quotas. From a short-term perspective, no matter what others do, each member's best strategy is to cheat.

In November 1994, OPEC members met to decide production quotas for the following year. Iran's oil minister Gholamreza Aqazadeh remarked, "it will be very good for the market . . . I hope everybody will agree to the quota without violations". Twelve months later, it was estimated that Venezuela had exceeded its 2.359 million barrel per day (bpd) quota by 300,000 bpd.

Besides cheaters within the cartel, OPEC had also to contend with high output from non-member countries. In June 1998, OPEC agreed that its members would reduce production by 2.6 million bpd, and non-members Mexico, Norway, Oman, and Russia by 500,000 bpd. Saudi oil minister Ali Ibrahim Naimi was cautiously optimistic: "I don't think that anybody expects 100% compliance. . . . Is three million [bpd] going to be pulled out of the market? Probably not. But is 2.5 million? That is still good."

Sources: "Producers Maintain Oil Output Ceilings," *South China Morning Post*, November 23, 1994, Business Post, p. 14; "OPEC Fears Quota Cheats May Hurt Price," *South China Morning Post*, November 23, 1995, Business Post, p. 9; "Saudi Minister Expects Nations to Cheat on New Oil-output pact," *Asian Wall Street Journal*, June 26–27, 1998, p. 27.

Prisoners' dilemma

The cartel's dilemma is just one concrete application of a general strategic situation called the *prisoners' dilemma*. Greg and Susan stole a handbag and have been apprehended by the police. The police do not have sufficient evidence to convict them of theft. The only witnesses to the theft are the two suspects.

The police chief has put Greg and Susan into separate interview rooms. In each room, the police interrogator is offering a deal: "If the other suspect doesn't confess, but you do, we'll give you a reward of $1,000." Each suspect knows that if neither confesses, they will be let off. If one confesses while the other does not, then the confessing suspect will receive the $1,000 reward, while the other will be fined $2,000. If both confess, each will be fined $1,000.

Each suspect must choose between confessing and not confessing. Table 10.4 represents the game in strategic form.

For Greg, the strategy of not confessing is dominated by the strategy of confessing. The same is true for Susan. The Nash equilibrium is for both suspects to confess – even though both would be better off if they did not confess.

Source: A. W. Tucker, "A Two-Person Dilemma," mimeo, Stanford University, May 1950.

Table 10.4 Prisoners' dilemma

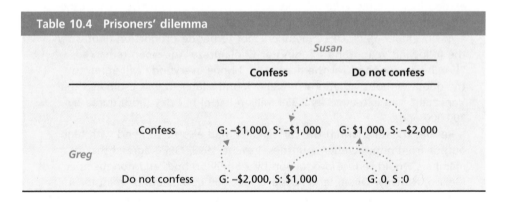

		Susan	
		Confess	**Do not confess**
Greg	Confess	G: –$1,000, S: –$1,000	G: $1,000, S: –$2,000
	Do not confess	G: –$2,000, S: $1,000	G: 0, S :0

◂◂ 3 Randomized Strategies[2]

When the various parties act strategically, it seems reasonable for them to choose Nash equilibrium strategies. In some situations, however, there is no Nash equilibrium

[2] This section is more advanced. It may be omitted without loss of continuity.

Table 10.5 Modified battle of the radio stations

| | | Merkur | |
		Lite AC	No change
Jupiter	Hot AC	J: 60, M: 40	J: 40, M: 60
	No change	J: 40, M: 60	J: 60, M: 40

of the type that we have been considering. To illustrate, let us modify the situation between Radio Jupiter and Merkur Radio. Suppose that table 10.5 represents the game in strategic form.

For Merkur, switching to Lite AC no longer is dominated by no change. Specifically, if Jupiter switches to Hot AC, then Merkur would get a higher audience share from no change than by switching to Lite AC (60% as compared with 40%), hence Merkur will prefer not to change. However, if Jupiter does not change, then Merkur will prefer switching to Lite AC (getting 60% audience share as compared with 40% from no change).

By applying the arrow technique to table 10.5, we can see that there is no Nash equilibrium in "pure strategies": no cell has all the arrows leading inward. A *pure strategy* is one that does not involve randomization. In table 10.5, Jupiter has two pure strategies, switch to Hot AC and no change, and Merkur also has two pure strategies, switch to Lite AC and no change.

Although there is no Nash equilibrium in pure strategies, there is another way for Jupiter and Merkur to act. Essentially, Jupiter does not want Merkur to know or predict which format it will choose. One way by which Jupiter can keep Merkur in the dark is to randomize the choice between switching to Hot AC and no change. If Jupiter randomizes its choice, the station itself will not know whether it will switch or not change. Then, of course, Merkur will not know either.

Similarly, Merkur does not want Jupiter to know or predict its choice of format. If Merkur randomizes its decision, Jupiter cannot guess or learn Merkur's format.

Under a **randomized strategy**, the party specifies a probability for each of the alternative pure strategies and chooses a pure strategy randomly according to the probabilities. The various probabilities must add up to 1.

> A **randomized strategy** is a strategy for choosing among the alternative pure strategies in accordance with specified probabilities.

Nash Equilibrium in Randomized Strategies

Suppose that Jupiter adopts the following randomized strategy: switch to Hot AC with probability 1/2 and no change with probability 1/2. To implement this strategy,

Jupiter's president marks a coin with "Hot AC" on one side and "no change" on the other side, then gives the coin to the station manager. Jupiter then orders the station manager to toss the coin and fix the format according to which side of the coin faces up.

Given that Jupiter has chosen this randomized strategy, how should Merkur act? Referring to table 10.5, let us calculate the expected consequence for Merkur from switching to Lite AC. Its audience share would be 40% if Jupiter switches to Hot AC, or 60% if Jupiter does not change format. Hence, Merkur's expected return from switching to Lite AC is $(40 \times 1/2) + (60 \times 1/2) = 50\%$. Similarly, we can calculate that, if Merkur does not change format, its expected audience share would be $(60 \times 1/2) + (40 \times 1/2) = 50\%$, which is identical to the expected consequence of switching to Lite AC.

What should Merkur do? Since it gets the same expected consequence from its two pure strategies, it is indifferent between the two. Accordingly, it would be willing to randomize between them. Specifically, suppose that Merkur switches to Lite AC with probability $1/2$.

Then, we must consider how Jupiter will act. If Jupiter switches to Hot AC, its expected audience share would be $(60 \times 1/2) + (40 \times 1/2) = 50\%$. If Jupiter does not change format, its expected audience share would be $(40 \times 1/2) + (60 \times 1/2) = 50\%$, which is identical to its expected audience share from switching to Hot AC. Therefore, given Merkur's strategy, Jupiter is indifferent between switching to Hot AC and no change.

A Nash equilibrium in randomized strategies is like a Nash equilibrium in pure strategies: given that the other players choose their Nash equilibrium strategies, each party's best choice is its own Nash equilibrium strategy. The following randomized strategies constitute a Nash equilibrium in the modified battle of the radio stations: Jupiter switches to Hot AC with probability $1/2$ and Merkur switches to Lite AC with probability $1/2$.

Suppose that Jupiter has adopted the Nash equilibrium strategy of switching to Hot AC with probability $1/2$. Suppose further that Merkur has learned Jupiter's strategy through a spy. How can Merkur exploit this information? The answer is that it cannot – as we have calculated earlier, whether Merkur switches to Lite AC or doesn't change, its expected audience share will be 50%. Generally, whenever a party adopts a Nash equilibrium strategy, the other parties cannot benefit from learning the strategy.

By contrast, suppose that Jupiter decides to switch to Hot AC with certainty, which is not a Nash equilibrium strategy. Then, if Merkur learns this strategy, Merkur will not change format with certainty, thus reducing Jupiter's audience share to 40%. For Jupiter, this is worse than its expected audience share of 50% from the Nash equilibrium with randomized strategies.

We should emphasize that the advantage of randomization comes from being *unpredictable*. To implement the randomized strategy, Jupiter must leave the direction of its visit to the coin toss. Jupiter must not make any conscious decision on the choice of format. If it chooses its format in a conscious way, Merkur may be able to guess or learn Jupiter's decision and act accordingly.

Figure 10.1 Randomization

Merkur's audience share

Merkur's audience share if it doesn't change format

60

60

40

40

Merkur's audience share if it switches to Lite AC

0

1/2

1

Probability with which Jupiter switches to Hot AC

If Jupiter switches to Hot AC with probability 1/2, then Merkur will receive the same consequences whether it switches to Lite AC or does not change format.

Progress Check 10D Referring to table 10.5, suppose that Jupiter switches to Hot AC with probability 2/5. Calculate the expected consequences for Merkur if it (1) switches to Lite AC, and (2) does not change.

Progress check

Solving the Equilibrium

Having understood the usefulness of randomization, we must learn how to determine the Nash equilibrium probabilities. We can do so by using figure 10.1, where the horizontal axis shows the probability with which Jupiter switches to Hot AC, and the vertical axis shows Merkur's audience share.

We draw two lines in figure 10.1. The downward-sloping line shows Merkur's audience share from switching to Lite AC as a function of the probability that Jupiter switches to Hot AC. The higher the probability that Jupiter switches to Hot AC, the lower will be Merkur's audience share from switching. The upward-sloping line shows Merkur's audience share from not changing format as a function of the probability that Jupiter switches to Hot AC.

At the crossing point of the downward- and upward-sloping lines, Merkur's audience share will be the same whether if switches to Lite AC or not. That point marks Jupiter's Nash equilibrium probability of 1/2. We can draw a similar diagram for Merkur to find its equilibrium probability, which is also 1/2.[3]

---

[3] This technique is based on Avinash Dixit and Barry Nalebuff, *Thinking Strategically: The Competitive Edge in Business, Politics, and Everyday Life* (New York: W. W. Norton, 1991), chapter 7.

Another way to find the Nash equilibrium probabilities is to use algebra. In equilibrium, both Merkur and Jupiter must randomize. Suppose that Jupiter switches to Hot AC with probability q. For Merkur to be willing to randomize, it must be indifferent between its alternative pure strategies: switching to Lite AC and not changing format. This means that Merkur must receive the same expected return from the two pure strategies.

To calculate Merkur's expected consequences from switching to Lite AC, we refer to table 10.5. If Merkur switches to Lite AC, its share would be 40 if Jupiter switches to Hot AC, which occurs with probability q, while its share would be 60 if Jupiter doesn't change format, which occurs with probability $1 - q$. Hence, Merkur's expected audience share is $40q + 60(1 - q) = 60 - 20q$. Similarly, we can calculate Merkur's expected share from not changing format to be $60q + 40(1 - q) = 40 + 20q$. Equating these expected shares, we have $60 - 20q = 40 + 20q$, and hence $q = 1/2$.

Likewise, we can determine Merkur's Nash equilibrium strategy. Suppose that Merkur switches to Lite AC with probability p. For Jupiter to be indifferent between its alternative pure strategies, it must receive the same expected share from switching to Hot AC and not changing format. This means that $60p + 40(1 - p) = 40p + 60(1 - p)$, or $p = 1/2$.

Price promotions: randomization in retailing

For retailers such as supermarkets, a major competitive challenge is how to attract price-sensitive customers without sacrificing profit from the less price-sensitive segment. The typical retailer has two alternative pure strategies: maintain a high price or offer a discount price.

Consider the high-price strategy. This may extract the buyer surplus of the less price-sensitive customers but fails to attract the price-sensitive customers. Further, it exposes the retailer to a competitor setting a discount price. By contrast, if the retailer chooses the alternative discount-price strategy, it will attract price-sensitive customers but must forgo the full buyer surplus of the less price-sensitive customers.

There is an intermediate alternative: randomize between the high price and the discount price. When a retailer adopts a randomized pricing strategy, its pricing will not be predictable. It then will be more difficult for competitors to take away potential customers. In retailing, a strategy of randomization is an effective way of mitigating the intensity of competition.

Note that the retailer should discount its price at random and not in a predictable way. Suppose, for instance, that Safeway Supermarket announces that it will cut the price of Huggies diapers by 10% in the first week of every month. Competing stores can then respond with even lower prices in the first week of each month, thus, undermining Safeway's discount. This example shows that price discounts must be random and not predictable.

◂◂ 4 Competition or Coordination

In the battle of the radio stations (table 10.1), if we add the consequences for Jupiter and Merkur in each cell, we get a sum of 100 in every cell. The situation is a *zero-sum game*.

A **zero-sum game** is a strategic situation where one party can become better off only if another is made worse off. A zero-sum game is the extreme of competition: there is no way for *all* parties to become better off.

> A **zero-sum game** is a strategic situation where one party can become better off only if another is made worse off.

Note that a strategic situation can be a zero-sum game even if the consequences for the various parties do not add up to 0 in every cell of the game in strategic form. If the consequences for the various parties add up to the same number in every cell of the game in strategic form, then one party can become better off only if another is made worse off. Accordingly, such a strategic situation is also a zero-sum game.

Coordination

Many strategic situations are not zero-sum games. Consider the following example. Suppose that there are two different technologies for a database program: Orange and Green. From the user's viewpoint, the two technologies are equally effective. However, it would be beneficial if all users adopt the same software, as this would facilitate the sharing and exchange of data.

This example of database software illustrates a *network effect*. A **network effect** arises whenever a benefit or cost depends on the total number of other users.

> A **network effect** arises when a benefit or cost depends on the total number of other users.

Table 10.6 presents a game in strategic form that describes the situation facing two potential users, Venus, Inc., and Sol Corporation. Each must choose between the Orange and Green database programs. In table 10.6, each cell shows the consequences for Venus and Sol, respectively. Recall that the two users will benefit if they both adopt the same software. Hence, we represent the benefit to Venus and Sol by 1.5 each when they both choose the Orange program. If they choose different programs, then each will get a benefit of 1. The two programs are equally effective; hence, if both companies choose the Green program, their benefits are also 1.5 each.

Table 10.6 Adopting database software

		Sol Corp.	
		Orange	Green
Venus, Inc.	Orange	V: 1.5, S: 1.5	V: 1, S: 1
	Green	V: 1, S: 1	V: 1.5, S: 1.5

A **positive-sum game** is a strategic situation where one party can become better off without another being made worse off.

Let us check whether the strategic situation facing Venus, Inc., and Sol Corporation is a zero-sum game. If both choose the Orange program, their total benefit is $1.5 + 1.5 = 3$ units. If they choose different programs, their total benefit is $1 + 1 = 2$ units. If they both choose the Green program, their total benefit is $1.5 + 1.5 = 3$ units. Accordingly, Venus and Sol do not face a zero-sum game. Rather, their situation is a **positive-sum game**. In a *positive-sum game*, one party can become better off without another being made worse off.

As table 10.6 suggests, the situation of Venus and Sol is essentially one of coordination rather than competition. If the two users can coordinate on the same software, both will benefit. If, however, they fail to coordinate, both will suffer. Strategic situations involving coordination are positive-sum games.

Let us apply the arrow technique to analyze the Nash equilibria in table 10.6. There are two Nash equilibria in pure strategies. In one, both users choose the Orange program; in the other equilibrium, both users choose the Green program.[4]

Progress check

Progress Check 10E Check whether the cartel's dilemma (table 10.3) is a zero-sum game.

Focal Point

Previously, we discussed why it is reasonable to adopt a Nash equilibrium strategy. In situations of coordination, there is an additional reason to adopt a Nash equilibrium strategy. Suppose that the various parties are able to talk to one another before making their choices and they agree on how to act. Then, a Nash equilibrium is a good basis for discussion because, by definition, Nash equilibrium strategies are self-enforcing in the sense that, if one party expects the others to follow their Nash equilibrium strategies, then its best choice is its own Nash equilibrium strategy.

For instance, in the choice of database software, there are two Nash equilibria in pure strategies. This presents the companies with the question of which strategy to adopt. Since the essential issue is coordination between the two companies, it is reasonable that they meet to agree on one choice.

If Venus and Sol discuss their choices, they might easily agree on one program, say, the Orange software. Then, when they make their purchases, if each expects the other to buy the Orange software, its own best choice is also the Orange software. In this way, a Nash equilibrium provides a focal point for discussion and action by the two parties.

▼

[4] In addition to the two Nash equilibria in pure strategies, there is also a Nash equilibrium where both parties randomize with probability $1/2$.

Rockwell vs US Robotics in 56k modems

For dial-up access to the Internet, a user needs a modem to convert digital data from the computer into analog signals for transmission over telephone circuits. At the other end, the Internet access provider needs a matching modem to convert the analog signals back to digital data. In the mid-1990s, the dominant standard for modems was the V.34, providing a speed of 28.8 or 36.6 kilobits per second (kbps).

In Autumn 1996, four manufacturers – Rockwell, U.S. Robotics, Lucent, and Motorola – launched next-generation 56 kbps modems. These were based on Brent Townshend's insight that most Internet access providers had digital connections to the telephone company and hence the conversion from digital to analog and back to digital between them could be eliminated.

Lucent and Motorola soon joined forces with Rockwell around the K56Flex standard. U.S. Robotics separately pushed its own X2 standard for 56 kbps modems. However, the two technologies were incompatible. Demand failed to take off as end-users as well as Internet access providers waited to see which standard would dominate. Neither technology secured a critical mass of adopters.

The Rockwell and U.S. Robotics camps battled for months, rejecting the International Telecommunications Union's (ITU) efforts at standardization. The deadlock was broken only when 3Com (a supporter of Rockwell's K56Flex) acquired U.S. Robotics. In December 1997, an ITU working group of engineers from 32 companies resolved the discrepancies between the two competing technologies and agreed on the new 56 kbps V.90 standard.

Following the ITU's release of V.90 in February 1998, demand took off. By July, America Online had fully deployed the new modems. After further revisions, the V.90 standard was ratified in mid-September 1998.

Source: http://www.V90.com/.

Co-opetition

Some situations involve elements of both competition and coordination. Consider a city with two TV stations, Channel Zeta and Channel Delta. Market research shows that the demand for a news program peaks at 8:00 p.m., so both stations want to schedule their evening news at 8:00 p.m. If, however, both stations broadcast their news at the same time, they will both be worse off than if one broadcasts at 8:00 p.m. and the other at 7:30 p.m.

We construct the strategic form of this situation in table 10.7. Each station has two pure strategies: broadcast at 7:30 p.m. or at 8:00 p.m. In each cell, we present the profits to Channels Zeta and Delta, respectively. If both stations broadcast their news at 7:30 p.m., then they will get a profit of $1 million a month each. If one broadcasts at 7:30 p.m. while the other takes the 8:00 p.m. slot, then the station

Table 10.7 Battle for the evening news			
		Channel Delta	
		7:30 p.m.	8:00 p.m.
Channel Zeta	7:30 p.m.	Z: 1, D: 1	Z: 3, D: 4
	8:00 p.m.	Z: 4, D: 3	Z: 2.5, D: 2.5

with the 7:30 p.m. slot will earn $3 million, while the station with the 8:00 p.m. slot will earn $4 million. Finally, if both stations broadcast their news at 8:00 p.m., then they will get a profit of $2.5 million each.

By adding the profits of the two TV stations in each cell of table 10.7, we see that the situation is a positive-sum game. The total profit of the two TV stations is not a constant. It is largest when they take different time slots. The next highest total profit arises when both stations broadcast at 8:00 p.m. The total profit is lowest when both stations broadcast at 7:30 p.m. The two TV stations need to coordinate and avoid scheduling their evening news at the same time.

While the battle for the evening news involves coordination, it also has an element of competition. Both stations will be better off if they schedule their news at different times. But one station will benefit relatively more – the station that gets the 8:00 p.m. slot. Accordingly, there are elements of competition as well as coordination.

Applying the arrows technique, we can find the Nash equilibria. As in the situation of choosing the database software, there are two Nash equilibria in pure strategies: Channel Zeta gets the 8:00 p.m. slot and Channel Delta takes 7:30 p.m., or Delta gets the 8:00 p.m. slot and Zeta takes 7:30 p.m.[5]

Co-opetition is a strategic situation that involves elements of both competition and coordination.

Strategic situations that involve elements of both competition and coordination have been described as **co-opetition**.[6] The battle for the evening news illustrates co-opetition: the two TV stations would certainly cooperate to avoid the outcome where both schedule their news at the same time. They would, however, compete for the 8:00 p.m. slot.

Even the cartel's dilemma (table 10.3) is a situation of co-opetition. Both producers would like to cooperate and avoid production at the competitive level. The problem, however, is that following the quota is a dominated strategy, and the result is that both produce more than the quota.

In a later section, we show that cooperation may arise when the strategic situation of co-opetition is repeated. By conditioning their actions on either external events or the previous actions of the other party, the parties involved may be able to avoid the undesirable outcomes of one-shot situations.

▼

[5] There is also an equilibrium in randomized strategies, where each station chooses 7:30 p.m. with probability 1/7 and 8:00 p.m. with probability 6/7.
[6] Adam M. Brandenburger and Barry J. Nalebuff, *Co-opetition* (New York: Doubleday, 1996).

Progress Check 10F Explain why the battle for the evening news is not a zero-sum game.

Progress check

◄◄ **5 Sequencing**

So far, we have focused on situations where the various parties move simultaneously. However, in many business situations, the parties move one at a time. We shall see that the best strategy may be quite different if the parties move in sequence. To organize thinking about a strategic situation in which the various parties act in sequence, we use the **game in extensive form**. An *extensive form* explicitly shows the sequence of moves and the corresponding outcomes. It consists of nodes and branches: a node represents a point at which a party must choose a move, while the branches leading from a node represent the possible choices at the node.

> A **game in extensive form** is a graphical representation of a strategic situation, showing the sequence of moves and the corresponding outcomes.

Let us apply this concept to the battle for the evening news where Channel Zeta can schedule its news before Delta. Figure 10.2 is a game in extensive form that represents the situation of the two TV stations. The first node, *A*, is on the extreme left. At that node, Channel Zeta must choose between 7:30 p.m. (the upper branch) and 8:00 p.m. (the lower branch). Channel Delta has the next move. Delta's node

Figure 10.2 Battle for the evening news: extensive form

At node *B*, Delta will choose 8:00 p.m. At node *C*, Delta will choose 7:30 p.m. By backward induction, at node *A*, Zeta will choose 8:00 p.m.

depends on Zeta's choice. If Zeta has chosen 7:30 p.m., then Delta will be at node *B* and must decide between the two branches of 7:30 p.m. and 8:00 p.m. If Zeta has chosen 8:00 p.m., then Delta will be at node *C* and must decide between the two branches of 7:30 p.m. and 8:00 p.m.

The consequences for Channel Delta of 7:30 p.m. or 8:00 p.m. depend on Zeta's choice. At the end of each branch, we mark the profits to Zeta and Delta, respectively. If Zeta chooses 7:30 p.m. and Delta also chooses 7:30 p.m., they both receive $1 million profit. If Zeta chooses 7:30 p.m. while Delta chooses 8:00 p.m., then Zeta makes $3 million and Delta earns $4 million. If Zeta chooses 8:00 p.m. while Delta chooses 7:30 p.m., then Zeta makes $4 million and Delta earns $3 million. Finally, if both stations choose the peak time of 8:00 p.m., they both earn $2.5 million.

Backward Induction

> Backward induction is a procedure for solving games in extensive form, looking forward to the final nodes and reasoning backward toward the initial node.

How should the two stations act? We solve the extensive form by **backward induction**, which means looking forward to the final nodes and reasoning backward toward the initial node. We can use this procedure to identify the best strategies for the two stations. There are two final nodes: *B* and *C*. At node *B*, Channel Delta can choose 7:30 p.m., which yields $1 million, or it could choose 8:00 p.m., which yields $4 million. Clearly, at node *B*, Delta would choose 8:00 p.m. Accordingly, we cancel the 7:30 p.m. branch. Now, consider node *C*. Here, Delta must choose between 7:30 p.m., which yields $3 million, or 8:00 p.m., which yields $2.5 million. It will choose 7:30 p.m., so we cancel the 8:00 p.m. branch.

Having determined how Channel Delta will act at each of its two possible nodes, *B* and *C*, we work back to consider the initial node, *A*. At node *A*, if Zeta chooses 7:30 p.m., it can foresee that Delta will choose 8:00 p.m., so Zeta will earn $3 million. On the other hand, if Zeta chooses 8:00 p.m., it can foresee that Delta will choose 7:30 p.m., so Zeta will earn $4 million. Therefore, Zeta should choose 8:00 p.m. Accordingly, in the battle for the evening news, when Zeta can move first, it will choose the 8:00 p.m. slot, while Delta will take the 7:30 p.m. time.

Equilibrium Strategy

> An **equilibrium strategy** in a game in extensive form is a sequence of the best actions, where each action is decided at the corresponding node.

In a game in extensive form, a party's **equilibrium strategy** consists of a sequence of its best actions, where each action is decided at the corresponding node. In the battle for the evening news, when Channel Zeta can move first, Zeta's equilibrium strategy is to choose the 8:00 p.m. slot, while Channel Delta's equilibrium strategy is take the 7:30 p.m. time.

We have assumed that Channel Zeta could move before Channel Delta. If Delta can move first, then the game in extensive form will be like figure 10.2, except that Delta would schedule its broadcast time at node A, and Zeta would schedule its broadcast time at node B or C. Then, Delta's equilibrium strategy would be to take the 8:00 p.m. slot, and Zeta's equilibrium strategy would be to settle for 7:30 p.m.

To decide on a strategy in a situation where the parties move in sequence, the basic principle is to look forward and anticipate the other parties' responses. So, when Channel Delta can set its schedule before its competitor, Delta must look forward and anticipate how Zeta will respond to each of Delta's choices. In this way, Delta anticipates that, if it chooses 7:30 p.m., then Zeta would choose 8:00 p.m., while if it chooses 8:00 p.m., then Zeta would choose 7:30 p.m. By this procedure of backward induction, Delta and Zeta can determine their equilibrium strategies.

The concept of equilibrium strategy in a game in extensive form is different from that of the Nash equilibrium strategy in a game in strategic form. In a strategic form, the parties act simultaneously, and a party's Nash equilibrium strategy is the best strategy given that the other parties adopt their respective Nash equilibrium strategies. By contrast, in an extensive form, the parties move in sequence, and a party's equilibrium strategy is the sequence of the best actions for that party, where each action is decided at the corresponding node.

In the battle for the evening news, we have shown that, when the two stations move simultaneously, there are two Nash equilibria in pure strategies. But when the stations move in sequence, there is only one equilibrium. In the battle for the evening news, the equilibrium in the extensive form is also a Nash equilibrium in the corresponding strategic form. In other cases, however, the equilibrium in the extensive form may not be a Nash equilibrium in the corresponding strategic form. Accordingly, when analyzing a strategic situation, it is important to consider carefully the structure of the moves: do the parties move simultaneously or sequentially?

Progress Check 10G Suppose that Channel Delta can set its schedule before Zeta. Using a suitable game in extensive form, illustrate this sequence of moves and analyze the two stations' equilibrium strategies.

Progress check

◂◂ 6 Strategic Moves

Lithography is a process by which an artist creates a stone or metal plate, then treats the plate with ink, and prints pictures. Most lithographers specify the number of copies that they will print from each plate and mark each print with a serial number. For instance, the mark "5/30" means the 5th of 30 copies. Some lithographers destroy their plates after printing the specified number of copies. Why do lithographers engage in such practices?

To address these questions, we consider lithography from the customer's standpoint. The value of a lithograph, like any other work of art or indeed any product

Figure 10.3 Lithographer's incentive

At node *C*, the lithographer will generate more prints. By backward induction, at node *B*, consumers will choose not to buy.

in general, depends on the supply. In the case of a lithograph, the supply is the number of copies that the artist has printed or will print.

Lithography is a business with significant economies of scale. Once the cost of preparing the plate has been incurred, the lithographer can generate more prints for the minor cost of ink and paper. So, after producing an initial 10 prints, the lithographer may consider selling another 10 at a lower price. Provided that the marginal revenue covers the marginal cost, the lithographer will earn additional profits. Indeed, having sold the second batch of 10, the lithographer may produce a third batch. Generally, the lithographer always has an incentive to continue producing more prints so long as the marginal revenue covers the marginal cost.

We can represent the lithographer's actions by a game in extensive form, figure 10.3. To analyze the situation, we must look forward to the final nodes and reason backward toward the initial node. At node *C*, the lithographer considers whether the marginal revenue of additional sales will cover the marginal cost. If so, she will then generate more prints. Working back to node *B*, consumers will decide not to buy: they would rather wait for the lithographer to cut the price at node *C*.

The lithographer needs some way to convince potential buyers that she will not keep producing more prints. One way is to specify the total number of prints and number each copy; for instance, "5/30" means the 5th of 30 copies. Numbering the prints, however, does not affect the lithographer's incentive to produce more copies in the future, so potential buyers may still be wary.

> A **strategic move** is an action to influence the beliefs or actions of other parties in a favorable way.

A definitive way to resolve this problem is for the lithographer to destroy the plates after printing the initial set of copies. Then, buyers can be confident that there will be no further prints, and they will be more willing to purchase.

Pepsi's strategic move: spinning off the bottling group

Until 1999, Coca Cola's organizational architecture differed sharply from that of Pepsi. Coke was vertically separated: the Coca Cola Company, headquartered in Atlanta, owned the brand and sold concentrate to about 100 franchised bottlers, the largest of which was Coca Cola Enterprises. By contrast, PepsiCo was vertically integrated from brand marketing through production of concentrate to bottling.

Then, in March 1999, PepsiCo spun off the Pepsi Bottling Group (PBG) in one of the largest initial public offerings on the New York Stock Exchange. Following the spin-off, PBG became an independent profit-driven business and responsible to its own shareholders. PepsiCo managed the brand and sold concentrate to PBG and other franchised bottlers. The bottlers used the concentrate to manufacture soft drink for sale in supermarkets and other distribution channels.

PBG accounted for 55% of Pepsi's sales in Canada and the United States and had considerable market power in its territories. Chapter 8 on Monopoly showed that, if a seller with market power experiences a reduction in marginal cost, it would reduce its price by an amount proportionately less than the marginal cost reduction.[7] Accordingly, if PepsiCo reduced the price of concentrate, PBG would reduce its retail price, but by a proportionately smaller amount.

In this light, Pepsi's vertical separation was a critical strategic move to mitigate the intensity of retail price competition. After the spin-off, Pepsi could not directly control retail prices. Further, PBG had an incentive to dampen price cuts. Indeed, Standard & Poor's analyst, Richard Joy, remarked: "Now that it is no longer shielded by the corporate umbrella of PepsiCo, Pepsi Bottling Group needs to produce profits, and thus appears unlikely to discount its brands."

Mr Joy's prediction was soon borne out. In November 1999, Coke announced a 7% increase in the price of concentrate, which translated into a 5% retail price increase. Within a week, Pepsi followed suit, raising the price of concentrate by 6.9%, which led to a 5% rise in retail prices.

Sources: Standard & Poor's Industry Surveys: Foods & Nonalcoholic Beverages 166, no. 22, section 1 (June 3, 1999), p. 3; "Coca Cola Shifts Strategy in Effort to Boost Profit," Wall Street Journal Interactive Edition, November 16, 1999.

[7] Strictly, this is true for straight-line market demand curves.

The lithographer's destruction of her plates is an example of a **strategic move**. A *strategic move* is an action to influence the beliefs or actions of other parties in a favorable way. Typically, a strategic move requires the party making the move to deliberately restrict its own freedom of action. For instance, by destroying her plates, the lithographer prevents herself from producing more prints in the future. This self-imposed restriction is a way to assure collectors that the supply will be limited.

Notice that the lithographer's strategic move involves a real cost. Once the plates have been destroyed, it will not be possible to produce more prints even if all the initial buyers want to have more.

Credibility

The battle for the evening news is another setting where strategic moves are possible. By table 10.7, if both stations move simultaneously, then there are two possible Nash equilibria in pure strategies: One station (either Channel Delta or Channel Zeta) gets the 8:00 p.m. slot and the competitor settles for 7:30 p.m. By contrast, if one station can set its schedule before the other, then it can secure the lucrative 8:00 p.m. slot.

Suppose that Delta announces that it wants the 8:00 p.m. slot. Is this sufficient to persuade Zeta to settle for 7:30 p.m.? Probably not. Delta's announcement may prompt Zeta to make its own announcement that it is scheduling its news at 8:00 p.m. A strategic move must be credible to influence the beliefs or actions of other parties. A mere announcement is not very credible.

For a strategic move to be credible, it must involve sufficient commitment to persuade other parties to change their beliefs or actions. Suppose that Delta contracts with several major advertisers to broadcast their advertisements during the 8:00 p.m. news. Further, the contracts provide that Delta must pay several million dollars in compensation if the station changes the time of the evening news. Then, these advertising contracts are a commitment and may be enough to persuade Channel Zeta to take the 7:30 p.m. slot.

Let us consider another possible setting for strategic moves. Suppose that Agua Luna and Moonlight Water dominate the market for bottled water. Their products are differentiated: Agua Luna is natural spring water, while Moonlight produces distilled water. Each manufacturer must decide whether to produce 1 or 2 million bottles a year. Table 10.8 presents the game in strategic form. If both manufacturers produce

		Moonlight Water			
		Produce 1 million bottles		Produce 2 million bottles	
Agua Luna	Produce 1 million bottles	AL: $750,000	MW: $750,000	AL: $700,000	MW: $1,100,000
	Produce 2 million bottles	AL: $1,100,000	MW: $700,000	AL: $600,000	MW: $600,000

Table 10.8 Competing on production capacity

1 million bottles a year, they will get a profit of $750,000 a year each. If one manufacturer produces 2 million bottles while the other produces 1 million, then the larger producer will earn $1.1 million, while the smaller producer will earn $700,000. Finally, if both manufacturers produce 2 million bottles a year, then each will get a profit of $600,000.

Assuming that the two manufacturers decide on production simultaneously, there are two Nash equilibria in pure strategies: Agua Luna produces 2 million bottles a year and Moonlight Water produces 1 million or Moonlight produces 2 million and Luna produces 1 million.

Now suppose that Agua Luna can set its production before Moonlight Water. By analyzing the game in extensive form, we can show that, in equilibrium, Agua Luna will produce 2 million bottles a year, while Moonlight Water will produce 1 million. By contrast, if Moonlight can move first, it will produce 2 million bottles a year, while Agua Luna will produce 1 million.

Moonlight would like to produce 2 million bottles a year and persuade Agua Luna to produce only 1 million. As in the battle for the evening news, a mere announcement would not be credible. A credible commitment would be for Moonlight to sign contracts with major buyers, such as catering services and supermarkets, committing it to supply 2 million bottles a year.

Sunk investments are another strategic move that might persuade Agua Luna to produce 1 million bottles a year. Manufacturing bottled water requires the construction of a production facility and acquiring materials, labor, and utilities. Suppose that the production facility is a large proportion of the total cost and that Moonlight builds a 2-million bottle a year facility. Will this convince the competing manufacturer, Agua Luna, to produce 1 million bottles a year?

The answer depends on the extent to which Moonlight's facility is a *sunk* cost of the bottled water business. Recall from chapter 7 that *sunk* costs are costs that have been committed and cannot be avoided. If the entire facility cost is sunk, Agua Luna will understand that Moonlight is committed to producing 2 million bottles a year. Then, Agua Luna is likely to acquiesce.

By contrast, if Moonlight also intends to expand its beer business and could easily convert the facility from water to beer, then the facility cost will not be so much sunk to the bottled water business. In this case, construction of the facility is not such a strong commitment to producing 2 million bottles of water a year.

Progress Check 10H Suppose that Agua Luna can set its production before Moonlight Water. By analyzing the game in extensive form, identify the equilibrium strategies.

Progress check

First Mover Advantage

In the battle for the evening news, the station that is first to commit its schedule will make the larger profit. Similarly, in the bottled water example, the manufacturer

A **first mover advantage** gives the party that moves first an advantage over parties that move later.

that is first to commit its production will make the larger profit. In these settings, the first mover has the advantage. There is **first mover advantage** in any strategic situation where the party that moves first has an advantage over parties that move later. To identify whether a strategic situation involves first mover advantage, it is necessary to analyze the game in extensive form.

The first mover advantage is a concept that corporate strategists emphasize a great deal. Note, however, that the first mover advantage is not a universal rule in business or other strategic situations. In some circumstances, the follower has an advantage. For instance, in retail pricing, if one store sets its price first, then its competitors will have the opportunity to undercut it with lower prices. Similarly, in military confrontations, the party that moves first may reveal its strategy and the other side can take advantage of that information.

In the introduction of a new product category, later movers have some advantage over earlier movers. A business introducing a new product category must make considerable investments in advertising and promoting the new category as distinct from its own particular product. These expenditures on advertising and promotion of the new category will benefit all businesses introducing new products in the same category. Hence, later movers can piggyback on the advertising and promotion expenditures of the pioneer.

Marketing Jack Nicholson: first and second mover advantage

In situations where the first mover has an advantage, the various parties will compete to move first. By contrast, where later movers have an advantage, the various parties will jockey and maneuver for the opportunity to move later. Two movies starring Jack Nicholson provide a vivid example.

The six-week Christmas season is a prime time for the movie exhibition industry. In 1992, two major studios, Columbia and Fox, both planned to release movies starring Jack Nicholson. Columbia had scheduled to release *A Few Good Men* on December 18. When Fox announced that it planned to open *Hoffa* on December 11, Columbia then advanced the release of *A Few Good Men* by one week from December 18 to December 11.

Finally, Fox postponed the opening of *Hoffa* by two weeks to December 25. The studio's executive vice-president, Tom Sherak, explained, "If *A Few Good Men* is as strong as we think it'll be, we'll get a lot of publicity for our own very good Jack Nicholson film."

Source: "Yule Laugh, Yule Cry," *Business Week*, November 2, 1992.

◀◀ 7 Conditional Strategic Moves

Destroying plates is a costly way for a lithographer to convince art collectors that she will not make more prints in the future. In some situations, it is possible to influence the actions or beliefs of others at lower cost through **conditional strategic moves**. There are two types of conditional strategic moves: threats and promises. A **threat** is a strategic move that imposes costs under specified conditions to change the beliefs or actions of other parties. By contrast, a **promise** is a strategic move that conveys benefits under specified conditions to change the beliefs or actions of other parties.

To the extent that a threatened or promised action need not actually be carried out, the conditional strategic move has no cost. A more accurate name for an action like destroying the plates is an *unconditional strategic move* because the party taking the action does not condition it on any eventuality. An unconditional strategic move usually involves a cost under all circumstances.

> A **conditional strategic move** is an action under specified conditions to influence the beliefs or actions of other parties in a favorable way.

> A **threat** imposes costs under specified conditions to change the beliefs or actions of other parties.

> A **promise** conveys benefits under specified conditions to change the beliefs or actions of other parties.

Threats

To understand threats, let us consider how companies can fend off hostile takeovers. An effective way of deterring a hostile takeover is the so-called scorched earth defense, which means destroying the company. The scorched earth defense is a very costly strategic move. Clever bankers and lawyers have devised more sophisticated defenses that are much less costly. One example is the shareholder rights plan, which has also been called the *poison pill*. As we will explain, this plan is a conditional strategic move: it comes into action only in the event of a hostile takeover.

Suppose that Sharon Corporation has 1 million shares, with a value of $2 each, hence, a total value of $2 million. The company has adopted a shareholder rights plan that created one right for every share of the company. Under the plan, if any party acquires 100,000 or more of Sharon's shares, then Sharon's management can activate the rights. Each right could be exercised to buy additional shares of the company at half their value. Any rights owned by the party whose acquisition activated the rights, however, would be canceled.

Hilda, Inc., is potentially interested in taking over Sharon Corporation. Let us construct a game in extensive form to analyze the strategic interaction between Hilda and Sharon. Referring to figure 10.4, at node *A*, Hilda must decide whether to acquire 100,000 Sharon shares with the attached rights. At node *B*, Sharon's management must choose whether to activate the rights.

Suppose that, at node *B*, Sharon's management activates the rights. This cancels Hilda's 100,000 rights. The holders of the remaining 900,000 rights will now buy

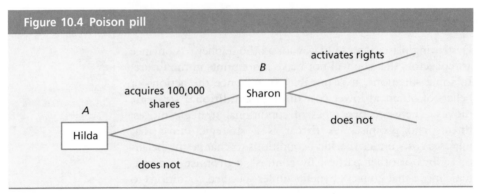

Figure 10.4 Poison pill

At node *B*, Sharon will activate the rights. By backward induction, at node *A*, Hilda will choose not to acquire the 100,000 shares.

an additional 900,000 shares at half their value. The activation increases the number of shares by 900,000 to 1.9 million and also draws more money into Sharon as the holders of the 900,000 rights pay for their additional shares. The number of shares, however, increases proportionately more than the value of the company; hence, the value of each share will fall. Specifically, it may be shown that the activation reduces the value of each share to $1.38.[8]

The activation has two implications for Hilda. First, it raises the cost to Hilda of acquiring 100% of Sharon. If Sharon's management does not activate the rights, there are 900,000 remaining shares and Hilda must pay $2 × 900,000 = $1.8 million to buy them. By contrast, if Sharon's management does activate the rights, there will be 1,800,000 remaining shares, and Hilda must pay $1.38 × 1,800,000 = $2.484 million for them.

Second, the activation of the rights causes a reduction in the value of Hilda's 100,000 shares from $2 × 100,000 = $200,000 to $1.38 × 100,000 = $138,000. So, Hilda will suffer a 31% loss on its investment. It is no wonder that such shareholder rights plans have been given the nickname of a *poison pill*.

In the case of Sharon Corporation, a potential bidder will look ahead from node *A* and see how Sharon's management could raise the costs of a takeover bid. Accordingly, the establishment of a shareholder rights plan significantly reduces the likelihood of a hostile takeover. If the plan succeeds in discouraging hostile takeovers, the rights need never be activated.

▼
[8] Suppose that Sharon's management activates the rights and cancels Hilda's 100,000 rights. Let the value of each share become $v. The holders of the remaining 900,000 rights will now buy an additional 900,000 shares at $0.5v each. Their payments for these shares will increase the value of the company by $0.5v × 900,000 = $450,000v to $2 million + $450,000v.

Since the activation increases the number of shares by 900,000 to 1.9 million, the value of each share is now $v = $(2,000,000 + 450,000v)/1,900,000. Solving, we have 2,000,000 = 1,450,000v, which implies that v = 1.38.

Threats in corporate finance: the two-tier takeover

In December 1994, Williams Companies, a natural gas producer and pipeline operator, announced a two-tier bid for Transco Energy Co. Williams's first tier offered to buy up to 60% of Transco's common shares for $17.50 in cash. The first-tier cash offer expired within one month and was conditional on Williams securing at least 51% of Transco's shares.

The second tier of the takeover bid would come into effect if Williams received 51% or more of Transco's shares through the cash offer. In the second tier, Williams would exercise its majority control to convert all remaining Transco shares into 5/8ths of a Williams common share. After Williams announced its takeover bid, the price of its shares dropped to $24 on the New York Stock Exchange. At this price, the value of the second tier was $5/8 \times 24 = \$15$ for each Transco share.

The two-tier structure implies a threat: A Transco shareholder who does not sell his or her shares in the first tier would be squeezed out for a lower price in the second tier.

Suppose that Sally owns one share of Transco. How should she respond to Williams's first-tier offer? Figure 10.5 presents the game in extensive form between Williams and Sally. For brevity, the figure shows only the outcomes for Sally at the ends of the final branches.

Suppose that, at node B, Sally accepts the $17.50 first-tier offer. At node C, we draw a circle to indicate that the ensuing consequences depend on the decisions of the other shareholders. (Neither Williams nor Sally makes a move at node C.) If Williams gets 51% or more of the shares and gains control over Transco, then it would proceed to the second-tier squeeze out. Since Sally accepted the first-tier offer, she would have $17.50. If, however, Williams fails to secure 51% of the shares in the first tier, it would return all the shares and Sally would be back to holding one share of Transco.

Suppose, instead, that, at node B, Sally rejects the $17.50 first-tier offer. At node D, we again draw a circle to indicate that the ensuing consequences depend on the decisions of the other shareholders. If Williams wins control over Transco, then it would proceed to the second-tier squeeze out. Since Sally rejected the first-tier offer, she would be squeezed out in the second tier and end up with $15. If, however, Williams fails to win control in the first tier, it would return all the shares and Sally would continue to hold one share of Transco.

Looking forward from node B, not to accept the first-tier offer is a dominated strategy for Sally. However the other shareholders act, Sally will be no worse off by accepting the first-tier offer. Accordingly, Sally should accept the first-tier offer. Indeed, all the shareholders of Transco should accept the first-tier offer. Through a two-tier offer, Williams can be assured of winning control of Transco.

Source: "Williams to Buy Transco Energy for $3 Billion," *Asian Wall Street Journal*, December 13, 1994, p. 2.

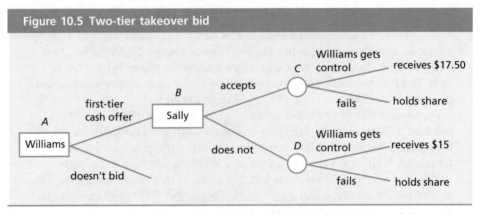

Figure 10.5 Two-tier takeover bid

The outcomes at nodes *C* and *D* are uncertain, depending on the decisions of the various shareholders. By backward induction, at node *B*, for Sally, the outcomes if she does not accept are dominated by the outcomes if she accepts, so she will accept. At node *A*, Williams will make the first-tier cash offer.

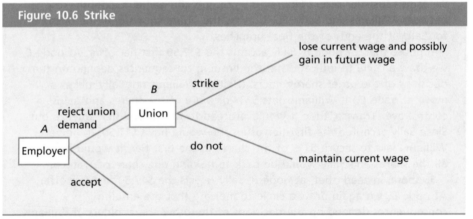

Figure 10.6 Strike

If the workers' union strikes, it will lose current wages and possibly gain higher wages in the future. If it does not strike, then it will maintain the current wage.

Threats are frequently used in negotiations. In negotiations with employers, unions may threaten a strike: "If you don't agree to raise wages by at least 7%, we will strike." Employers fear the disruption to operations resulting from a strike. The threat of a strike may persuade an employer to concede on wages. The occurrence of strikes, however, varies with the industry.

In professional American football, for instance, strikes are rare. To understand why, we analyze whether a union's threat of a strike is credible. Credibility is an issue because a strike also imposes costs on the workers themselves. During a strike, the workers must forgo part or all of their wages. In figure 10.6, at the node B, where the union decides whether to proceed with a strike, the union must compare the consequences of a strike with those from no strike.

If the union proceeds with the strike, the workers will lose some current wages, and they may be able to convince their employer to increase their future wages. If the union decides to cancel the strike, then the workers will continue to receive their current wage. For the threat of a strike to be credible, the workers must expect to gain more from a strike than by continuing to work normally.

Compared with many other workers, the career of a professional American football player is relatively short. Like other workers, if football players strike, they are trading off current loss of income against higher wages in the future. As football players have short careers, they are not so attracted by higher wages in the future. Accordingly, football players are relatively less likely to strike than those in other sports.

Promises

Besides threats, the other type of conditional strategic move is promises. For an outstanding example of a promise, we turn to banking. Most governments are concerned about the stability of their banking systems. Banks take deposits in checking and savings accounts and lend the funds to short- and long-term borrowers. This means that, generally, banks do not have enough cash at hand to repay all their depositors on short notice.

Consider a typical depositor. Every day, she must choose between maintaining her savings account with a bank and withdrawing the deposit to get cash. Cash, of course, is the safest possible investment. It, however, yields no interest. Other things equal, the depositor would rather keep the money in the savings account. If, however, she hears a rumor that the bank is in trouble, she will rush to withdraw her deposit. As all depositors rush to withdraw, the bank may run short of funds. So, rumors can bring down even financially sound banks.

To ensure the stability of the banking system, many governments provide deposit insurance. This means that, if a participating bank cannot repay the money deposited, then the government will pay all its depositors. Deposit insurance is a conditional strategic move: the government pays only in the event that the bank cannot repay.

Official promise: The Federal Deposit Insurance Corporation

In the United States, the Federal Deposit Insurance Corporation (FDIC) guarantees deposits of up to $100,000 at participating banks. The FDIC aim is to forestall bank runs on the scale that exacerbated the Great Depression in the early 1930s. As result of FDIC insurance, holders of insured bank deposits need not worry about the financial condition of the bank. FDIC insurance can effectively prevent bank runs. If the FDIC covers only sound banks, then the banks that it insures will not fail and the FDIC need never pay out any money.

Now, consider the effect of deposit insurance. The depositor need not worry about rumors. Even if the rumors are true, she will still get her money back, in this case, from the government. Accordingly, depositors will not withdraw their deposits when they hear rumors that their banks are in difficulties. Thus, deposit insurance can effectively prevent bank runs. If the government insures only sound banks, then government need never pay out any compensation. That is the beauty of a conditional strategic move.

◂ 8 Repetition

So far, we have considered strategic interactions that take place only once. Many strategic interactions, however, are repeated. Generally, the range of possible strategies is much wider in repeated interactions than in one-shot scenarios. In situations that involve coordination, the wider range of strategies may enable the various parties to achieve better outcomes than in interactions that occur only once.

With repeated interaction, a party may condition its action on either external events or the previous actions of the other party. Such conditional strategies may yield a better outcome than the equilibrium of the one-shot scenario.

Conditioning on External Events

Let us consider strategies that condition actions on external events in the context of the battle for the evening news. With simultaneous moves on a one-shot basis, each station will jockey and manuever for the first-mover advantage. Suppose, however, that the stations look at their situation as a repeated interaction. Then other strategies become possible. In particular, a station could adopt a strategy under which its schedule is conditioned on some independent variable.

For instance, Channel Delta could condition its news schedule on the month: broadcast at 8:00 p.m. in odd months and at 7:30 p.m. in even months. Likewise, one of Channel Zeta's strategies is to broadcast at 7:30 p.m. in odd months and at 8:00 p.m. in even months. These two strategies are an equilibrium in the repeated battle for the evening news.

Essentially, the stations alternate between the two time slots. By alternating, the stations can ensure that they achieve the efficient outcome where one station broadcasts at 8:00 p.m. and the other broadcasts at 7:30 p.m. Each will have an equal share of the premium 8:00 p.m. slot. The alternating strategy will be better than fighting over the 8:00 p.m. slot on a one-shot basis, which might result in both stations broadcasting their news at the same time.

Conditioning on Other Party's Actions

Strategies in repeated strategic situations can also be conditioned on the previous actions of the other party. Let us see how such strategies can improve the outcome in the context of the cartel's dilemma.

Every member of a cartel knows that, if all sellers cooperate in restricting production, they will collectively be able to increase their profits. In one-shot cartels, however, individual members have an overwhelming incentive to exceed their quotas. Table 10.3 shows the game in strategic form: following the quota is a dominated strategy.

Let us now consider a repeated cartel, that is, a cartel that continues over an extended period of time. In a repeated cartel, a seller can adopt a strategy under which it conditions its production on the actions of another party at a earlier time. One such strategy is tit for tat: I will begin with following my quota and will continue until you exceed your quota, in which case, I shall produce more than my quota in the following month, and thereafter, I will follow your move.

A tit-for-tat strategy combines a promise with a threat. The promise is to abide by quota if the other seller follows its quota. When all sellers abide by their quotas, they can achieve profits above the competitive level. The threat is to produce more than one's quota if the other seller exceeds its quota. Whenever a seller exceeds its quota, it will depress the market price and, hence, reduce the profits of other sellers.

Is tit-for-tat an equilibrium strategy for all parties in the repeated cartel? Referring to table 10.3, suppose that both Hilda and Sharon adopt a tit-for-tat strategy. Each begins by following its quota, with Hilda earning $15 million and Sharon earning $10 million. However, at some time, Sharon cheats and produces more than quota, while Hilda follows the quota. Sharon will earn $13 million instead of $10 million, gaining $3 million.

In the following month, Hilda would retaliate and produce more than quota. What should Sharon do? She could continue cheating, and then Hilda would continue to retaliate. In this case, Sharon would earn $8 million indefinitely. Alternatively, Sharon could go back to following the quota, and so restore cooperation thereafter. In this case, Sharon would earn $5 million for one month and $10 million every month afterward.

Tit-for-tat is an equilibrium strategy for Sharon if the one-time $3 million gain is outweighed by the future losses due to Hilda's retaliation. This depends on two factors. One is how Sharon values $1 in a future month relative to $1 in the present, or the financial concept of discounting. The less Sharon values money in the future, the more likely it is that Sharon will cheat. The other factor is the likelihood that the cartel will be terminated in the future due to the obsolescence of the product or entry of new competitors. The shorter the expected life of the cartel, the more likely it is that Sharon will cheat.

Accordingly, under certain conditions, tit-for-tat is an equilibrium strategy in a repeated cartel. In the tit-for-tat equilibrium, every individual seller will restrict production. Thus, when competing sellers interact over an extended period of time, it is possible to maintain a cartel and achieve profit above the competitive level.

A cartel can further improve the likelihood that individual sellers will restrict production if it extends agreement to several different markets. In a cartel that covers several markets, a seller can condition its production on the preceding actions of another party in all the markets.

For instance, in a cartel that encompasses the markets for equipment leasing and truck rentals, a seller could adopt the following tit-for-tat strategy: I will begin with abiding by my quota and will continue until you exceed your quota in any market, in which case, I shall produce more than my quota in both markets; and thereafter, I will follow your move in both markets.

The tit-for-tat strategy is an equilibrium strategy. In a cartel that extends to several markets, the tit-for-tat strategy promises a greater benefit: increased profit in all the markets if sellers restrict production. Moreover, the tit-for-tat strategy threatens a greater punishment: reduced profit in all the markets if sellers exceed their quotas.

Tit-for-tat wins again

Political scientist Robert Axelrod invited a number of scholars to submit computer programs specifying strategies for a prisoners' dilemma repeated 200 times. Dr. Axelrod pitted each program against the others in a round-robin tournament, and recorded its total score over 200 repetitions against all the other programs.

Programs that were "nice" in the sense of not being first to cheat performed better than those that were not nice. The winning strategy was tit-for-tat. Dr. Axelrod announced these results and held a second tournament. Despite the opportunity to devise better strategies, no scholar could beat tit-for-tat, and the simple strategy also won the second tournament.

Based on the results of his tournaments, Dr. Axelrod put forward four simple rules for success in repeated strategic interactions:

1. do not strike first;
2. reciprocate both good and bad;
3. act simply and clearly;
4. do not be envious.

Source: Robert Axelrod, *Evolution of Cooperation* (New York: Basic Books, 1984).

◂◂ 9 Summary

In strategic situations, when the parties move simultaneously, there are several useful principles to follow: avoid using dominated strategies, focus on Nash equilibrium strategies, and consider randomizing. When the parties move sequentially, a strategy should be worked out by looking forward to the final nodes and reasoning back to the initial node.

Restricting competition in building materials

Boral, CSR, and Pioneer International are leading manufacturers of building materials with operations throughout Australia. In 1989, the three corporations, together with Goodmix/Hymix and Rocla, supplied 95% of the market for ready-mix concrete in Brisbane. The five companies formed a cartel and agreed not to poach customers from one another. They held regular meetings to allocate sales and fix prices. The Brisbane concrete cartel continued until mid-1994.

Boral, CSR, and Pioneer were also involved in cartelizing other markets for building materials elsewhere in Australia. The three corporations fixed the prices of ready-mix concrete in Melbourne in 1978–79, as well as roof tiles in Adelaide. The geographical and product spread of the cartel would have helped to increase the incentive of individual members to abide by their quotas in each market.

Sources: "CSR, Pioneer, Boral Are Fined for Price-Fixing," *Asian Wall Street Journal,* December 5, 1995, p. 5; letter from James Lambie, Australian Competition and Consumer Commission (December 14, 1995).

Through conditional or unconditional strategic moves, it may be possible to influence the beliefs or actions of other parties. In some settings, the first mover has the advantage; in others, the first mover is at a disadvantage. Finally, it is important to consider whether the situation will be played just once or repeated. The range of possible strategies is wider in a repeated situation.

In a zero-sum game, one party can become better off only if another is made worse off. In a positive-sum game, one party can become better off without another being made worse off.

Key Concepts

strategy	co-opetition
game theory	game in extensive form
game in strategic form	backward induction
dominated strategy	equilibrium strategy in a game in extensive form
Nash equilibrium	strategic move
randomized strategy	first mover advantage
zero-sum game	conditional strategic move
network effect	threat
positive-sum game	promise

Further Reading

Two entertaining and very readable books on strategic thinking are Avinash Dixit and Barry Nalebuff's best seller, *Thinking Strategically: The Competitive Edge in Business, Politics, and Everyday Life* (New York: W.W. Norton, 1991), and Thomas C. Schelling's classic, *The Strategy of Conflict* (Cambridge, MA: Harvard University Press, 1980). Avinash Dixit and Susan Skeath's *Games of Strategy* (New York: W. W. Norton, 1999), provides a more formal yet approachable review of game theory.

Review Questions

1. Speedy Snaps is a small public company in the perfectly competitive fastener industry. Which of the following choices by Speedy are strategic?
   (a) Switching deposits from Citibank to Chase Manhattan Bank.
   (b) Hiring another worker for the night shift.
   (c) Adopting a poison pill.

2. Explain the following concepts:
   (a) Dominated strategy.
   (b) Nash equilibrium.

3. Which of the following are reasons to adopt a Nash equilibrium strategy?
   (a) I can minimize my expected loss.
   (b) I can guarantee a minimum level of payoff.
   (c) Even if the other party knows my strategy, it cannot take advantage of that information.

4. This question relies on the randomized strategies section. Referring to table 10.6, calculate the Nash equilibrium in randomized strategies.

5. This question relies on the randomized strategies section. Some right-handed boxers also train themselves to box with their left hands. Which of the following strategies will be more effective?
   (a) Throw a left-hand punch after every three right-handers.
   (b) Box mainly with the right hand and throw a left-hand punch at random.

6. While shopping at Bloomingdales in Manhattan, you suddenly realize that you have been separated from your boyfriend. Both your boyfriend and you must simultaneously decide where to look for the other person. Explain why there are many possible Nash equilibria: one corresponding to every place in the store. Explain why the customer service counter is a focal point.

7. Suppose that, in some game in strategic form, the payoffs to the two players in every cell add up to −10. Is this a zero-sum game?

8. Recall the choices of Venus and Sol between the Orange and Green database software (please refer to table 10.6). Suppose that Venus can move first. Using an extensive form, analyze the equilibrium.

9. Explain the following:
   (a) A strategic move.
   (b) A promise.
   (c) A threat.

10. Compare the following actions by a lithographer. Which is more credible to buyers?
    (a) She announces that she will print only 30 copies.
    (b) She destroys the plates after printing 30 copies.

11. What's wrong with analyzing a game in extensive form by reasoning forward from the initial node?

12. Some say that a manufacturer can gain a first-mover advantage by investing in production capacity. Why is it important that the capacity cannot be easily switched to another use?

13. Generally, why are conditional strategic moves better than unconditional strategic moves?

14. Loan sharks are not allowed to use the legal system to collect debts. Does this explain why they employ violence?

15. How do strategies in repeated strategic situations differ from those that occur only once?

Discussion Questions

1. The National Collegiate Athletic Association (NCAA) restricts the amount that colleges and universities may pay their student athletes. Suppose that there are just two colleges in the NCAA: Ivy and State. Each must choose between paying athletes according to NCAA rules or paying more.
   (a) Construct a game in strategic form to analyze the choices of Ivy and State.
   (b) Identify the equilibrium or equilibria.
   (c) The NCAA rules have government backing. How will this affect the equilibrium or equilibria?

2. The demand for most new films is highest in the first few days after opening, then tapers off. Two key factors affecting potential demand are the season (Summer and Christmas are the best times) and the timing of other releases. Suppose that both Studio Luna and Moonlight Movies are producing major action movies.
   (a) The two studios simultaneously must choose between release on December 11 or 18. If both films open on December 11, each will sell 200,000 tickets. If one opens on December 11 and the other on December 18, then the early release will sell 350,000 tickets, while the later release will sell 150,000. If both open on December 18, each will sell 100,000 tickets.

Construct a game in strategic form to illustrate the situation and identify the equilibrium or equilibria.

(b) Now suppose that the publicity surrounding one movie will increase the demand for the other film. Specifically, each studio will sell 70,000 more tickets if both open on the same day. Adjust the data in (a) according to this new information. How does this affect the equilibrium or equilibria?

3. Dial-up Internet users need modems to convert digital data into analog signals and Internet access providers (IAPs) need matching modems to convert the analog signals back to digital data. In the mid-1990s, the dominant standard for modems was the V.34, providing a speed of 28.8 or 36.6 kilobits per second (kbps). In Autumn 1996, two incompatible technologies for 56 kbps modems – Rockwell's K56Flex and U.S. Robotics's X2 – were launched.

(a) Construct the following game in strategic form. End-users choose among the three alternatives of buying K56Flex, buying X2, or remaining with the old technology, while IAPs have the same choice. If both end-users and IAPs choose K56Flex, each group receives a net benefit of 100, and similarly, if both groups choose X2. If end-users or IAPs buy K56Flex or X2, while the other does not buy the matching technology, the buyer receives a net benefit of –50. Anyone that remains with the old technology receives 0. Identify the equilibrium/equilibria in pure strategies.

(b) In February 1998, Rockwell and U.S. Robotics agreed on a common V.90 standard. How did this affect the game and its equilibrium/equilibria?

4. Suppose that Eastern Airways and Aero Sol charge $400 for a round-trip economy class fare and that, presently, each airline has an equal market share. Each airline believes that, if it cuts its price by 10% while the other airline maintains its price, the elasticity of demand will be –4.0. Half of the additional customers will be new flyers, while the other half will switch from the higher-priced airline. If both airlines cut their prices by 10%, then each will have a demand elasticity of –2.0. In this case, all of the additional customers will be new flyers. Let the unit cost of each seat be constant at $200 for both airlines.

(a) Use a game in strategic form to analyze this situation. For each airline, the possible strategies are to maintain its price or to cut its price 10%. What will be the equilibrium?

(b) Suppose now that the two airlines form a revenue pool. Under this arrangement, they will contribute all their revenues to a common pool and each will get a half share of the pooled revenues. Each, however, must pay its own costs. Use a game in strategic form to analyze this revised situation. For each airline, the possible strategies are the same as in (a). What will be the equilibrium?

5. The Spanish conquistador Hernando Cortés led an expedition from the island of Cuba to conquer Mexico on the American mainland. The Spanish were outnumbered by the Mexican armies, and after landing in Mexico, some of Cortés's followers tried to escape back to Cuba. Cortés, however, believed that, if every knight and soldier in his expedition fought with complete determination, they would succeed in conquering Mexico. He also knew that, without total commitment, they would lose.

In a historic move, Cortés ordered his carpenters to dismantle all their ships, and to use the timber and metal in the landward expedition. Using a game in extensive form, explain Cortés's decision (Bernal Diaz del Castillo, *The Discovery and Conquest of Mexico, 1517–1521*, trans. A.P. Maudslay (New York: Harper & Brothers, 1928), pp. 168–9).

6. Linux is an open-source operating system for workstations. The open-source movement marshals the efforts of thousands of volunteer software developers who receive no direct pay for their contributions. For Linux to unseat Microsoft's Windows operating system, it must persuade end users to adopt the new operating system and induce independent software publishers to develop applications software based on Linux.
   (a) Identify the interactions between end-users' decisions whether to adopt Linux and independent software publishers' decisions whether to develop Linux applications.
   (b) Using a suitable strategic form, identify the possible equilibria of the decisions of end-users and independent software publishers.

7. The Organisation of Petroleum Exporting Countries (OPEC) includes Saudi Arabia, Iran, Kuwait, and Venezuela, but not Mexico, Russia, and several major oil exporters. Throughout the 1990s, OPEC sought to raise the price of oil by limiting production without much success. Finally, in 1999, after years of steady decline, the price of oil turned upward to the levels of a decade before.
   (a) Referring to the cartel's dilemma, explain OPEC's difficulty in raising price.
   (b) Compare the incentive of an OPEC member such as Venezuela to cut price with that of a non-member such as Mexico.
   (c) Saudi Arabia's marginal cost of oil production is among the lowest in the world. Traditionally, it played the role of "OPEC policeman," increasing output whenever it detected others cheating on the cartel. Explain why the Saudis were well placed to discipline the cartel.
   (d) During 1998, as the price of oil hit new lows, oil companies throughout the world reduced exploration and production expenditure by $25 billion. How did this cut back affect the effectiveness of OPEC?

8. German telecommunications provider Deutsche Telekom is rated Aa2 by Moody's on a scale ranging from the highest grade of Aaa through Aa, A, Baa, Ba, B, to the lowest grade of Caa. In its June 2000 bond issue worth $14.5 billion, Deutsche Telekom promised to increase the interest payment by 0.5% if its credit rating should fall below A.
   (a) For simplicity, assume that the normal interest on the bonds is $870 million a year. Suppose that, some years later, Telekom will choose between two investments. For the risky investment, it must issue new bonds with annual interest of $130 million. The risky investment will generate a cash flow of $1.5 billion with 50% probability, and $1 billion otherwise. The safe investment will not require additional borrowing and will yield $1.07 billion for sure. Using a game in extensive form, illustrate this choice, while ignoring the promise. At each final node, show the net cash flow (net of interest on all loans).

(b) Now suppose that the additional borrowings for the risky investment would reduce Telekom's credit rating below A and trigger its promise to raise the interest payment by $0.5\% \times \$14.5 = \$72.5$ million. Suppose that banks will not lend if there is any possibility of negative net cash flow. How does Telekom's promise affect the game in extensive form?

9. In December 1994, the Williams Companies made a two-tier bid for the common shares of Transco Energy. In the first tier, Williams offered $17.50 per share in cash; in the second tier, Williams offered stock worth $15. Before the bid was announced, Transco shares were trading at $12.625. Williams conditioned its first-tier cash offer on receiving 51% or more of Transco's shares. Only if Williams gained control through the first-tier cash offer would it be able to effect the second-tier squeeze-out.

   (a) Using a suitable extensive form, analyze how a Transco shareholder should respond to the cash offer.

   (b) Suppose, instead, that Williams's first-tier cash offer had been unconditional. How should a Transco shareholder respond under the following conditions:

      (i) She believes that Williams will get control through the first-tier cash offer.

      (ii) She believes that Williams will not get control through the first-tier cash offer.

10. Lithograph collectors fear that the lithographer will use the same plates to produce more prints in the future.

    (a) Explain why some lithographers destroy their plates after making a specified number of prints.

    (b) Suppose a lithographer promises to buy back his prints at any time at the original sale price. Explain how this buyback offer affects the lithographer's incentive to produce additional prints.

    (c) Compare the strategic moves in (a) and (b) as ways of assuring art collectors that the lithographer will not use the same plates to produce more prints.

11. Explain whether it will be relatively easy or difficult to maintain a cartel in the following industries:

    (a) Semiconductors, where the pace of technological progress is so fast that the effective selling life of each new model is 50% shorter than that of the preceding generation.

    (b) Rice, where the crop is grown throughout the world and there is a high turnover among producers.

    (c) Refined oil, where the industry is relatively stable with the same producers dominating the market for many years.

Part III

Imperfect Markets

Chapter 11

Externalities

◀◀ ## 1 Introduction

America Online Inc. (AOL) was founded in 1985 to provide online access to a proprietary network. Subscribers dialed up to use exclusive information, entertainment, and email services. By 1993, when AOL had grown to 500,000 subscribers, Microsoft CEO, Bill Gates, famously threatened to "buy or bury" AOL.[1]

With the invention of the Web browser, the Internet graduated from an academic tool to a mass communications technology. AOL acquired Global Network Navigator to provide Internet service. In late 1995, the Microsoft Network (MSN) was launched and enrolled more than 500,000 members within three months. Microsoft announced a partnership with the television network NBC to create an interactive on-line news service for MSN. About that time, AOL's membership reached 3 million.

In the following year, AOL agreed to adopt Microsoft's Internet Explorer in exchange for Microsoft including an AOL icon in all Windows-95 systems. In early 1998, AOL acquired ailing online access provider CompuServe and positioned it as a low-end $9.95 a month service.

In 1999, six years after Bill Gates's threat, AOL was still independent and far from dead. Microsoft Vice President, Brad Chase, threatened a price war in Internet access: "AOL might think about it [access] as a profit center. That's not how we think about it." MSN regularly charged $21.95 a month for Internet access. It then bundled discounts through computer retailers that effectively lowered the price to $10.95 a month.

AOL Chief Operating Officer, Brad Pittman, professed not to be worried. AOL had recently raised the price of its premium AOL service to $21.95 a month from $19.95 without affecting subscriber growth. Two of AOL's most popular services were AOL Instant Messenger and ICQ. These free instant messaging services alerted a subscriber whenever designated "buddies" connected to the Internet.

---

[1] This analysis is based in part on "America Online: Pricks and Kicks," *Economist*, August 14, 1999, pp. 52–3, and Microsoft Museum Timeline (http://www.microsoft.com/MSCorp/Museum/timelines/microsoft/timeline.asp/).

AOL licensed ICQ and Instant Messenger to Mindspring, Earthlink, and other Internet service providers but not MSN. In July 1999, MSN launched an instant messaging service to interconnect with AOL Instant Messenger. AOL quickly blocked access to MSN users. A cat-and-mouse game ensued with Microsoft engineers probing the AOL system and AOL blocking their entry. Finally, in November 1999, Microsoft conceded defeat by issuing a new version of MSN Messenger that did not interconnect with AOL.

At the time of Mr. Chase's warning, AOL had 17.6 million subscribers, while CompuServe and MSN had 2 million each. By March 2000, AOL's membership had grown to 22 million, while that of CompuServe exceeded 2.5 million. By August 1999, the AOL Instant Messenger service had 45 million users. By March 2000, ICQ had 53.1 million registered users, more than two-thirds of whom lived outside the United States.

Why did Bill Gates encounter so much difficulty in carrying out his threat to "buy or bury" AOL? Why did Microsoft engineers try so hard to interconnect their instant messaging service with AOL Instant Messenger? What was the cost to AOL of licensing ICQ and Instant Messenger to Mindspring, Earthlink, and other Internet service providers? These questions may be answered through the concepts of externality and public good.

> An **externality** arises when one party directly conveys a benefit or cost to others.

An **externality** arises when one party directly conveys a benefit or cost to others (not through a market). Instant messaging services provide communications. The benefit of communications depends on the number in the network. When another person joins AOL Instant Messenger, he or she generates an externality to all other subscribers by adding to the number with whom the others can communicate.

The externalities among the subscribers to ICQ and AOL Instant Messenger tie them strongly to the AOL Internet service. AOL's hold on its members is further strengthened by externalities among users of chat-rooms, forums, and other services within AOL's walled garden of content and services. These externalities explain why Microsoft was unable to bury AOL.

MSN Messenger's network of users was smaller than that of AOL. By interconnecting with AOL Instant Messenger, Microsoft could immediately and sharply increase the number with whom MSN users could communicate. This would substantially raise the benefit of MSN service to its users, and raise the demand for MSN.

> An item is a **public good** if one person's increase in consumption does not reduce the quantity available to others.

An item is a **public good** if one person's increase in consumption does not reduce the quantity available to others. Technology is a public good. Once AOL had written the software underlying its Instant Messenger, the cost to AOL of providing the technology to Mindspring, Earthlink, and other Internet access providers was zero.

This chapter introduces the concept of an externality, characterizes its economically efficient degree, and discusses how that might be achieved through either merger or joint action by the entities involved. We then discuss the particular concepts of network externalities and network effects, which underlie the rapid growth of the Internet. Finally, we introduce the concept of a public good and discuss its provision.

◂◂ 2 Benchmark

To introduce the concept of an externality, we consider the following example. Luna, a major department store, is opening a 50,000-square-foot store on Main Street. To obtain the site, Luna outbid several other major chains and raised the general level of rents along Main Street. The increase in rents affects other stores in the area, but this increase is not an externality because it passes through the real estate market.

Luna's new store affects other retailers in another way. Specialty retailers sell smaller ranges of products, for instance, casual wear, flowers, or shoes. Luna's new store will draw more shoppers to Main Street and, hence, generate more business for nearby specialty retailers. There is no market through which specialty retailers pay Luna for the additional business, however. Accordingly, the additional business is an externality from Luna to the specialty retailers.

Alternatively, Luna's new store may take customers away from other department stores on Main Street. The cut in business does not pass through any market; hence, it is an externality from Luna to other department stores.

Externalities can be positive or negative. A **positive externality** arises when one party directly conveys a benefit to others. The additional business that Luna generates for specialty retailers is a positive externality. By contrast, a **negative externality** arises when one party directly imposes a cost on others. The business that Luna's new store takes away from other department stores along Main Street is a negative externality.

> A **positive externality** arises when one party directly conveys a benefit to others.

As the Luna example suggests, there are significant positive externalities in real estate. In Britain, leading banks, insurers, and other financial institutions congregate in the one square mile City of London to benefit from positive externalities among themselves. The same is true in many other countries: financial institutions and associated professionals such as lawyers and accountants tend to cluster in the same area.

> A **negative externality** arises when one party directly imposes a cost on others.

Construction of transportation facilities provides another example of externalities in real estate. Whenever the government builds a mass transportation system, it generates externalities for the owners of nearby property. For instance, construction of a subway will raise the value of retail businesses such as grocery stores and restaurants located close to the subway stations. By improving access, a subway may also raise the value of commercial and residential property.

Positive Externalities

By definition, an externality conveys a benefit or cost directly rather than through a market. So, in deciding on the levels of externalities, the source considers only the benefits and costs to itself, while ignoring the benefits and costs to others.

In the case of Luna's investment in its new Main Street store, Luna will consider its own benefit and cost and ignore the benefits and costs to other stores. Let us assume that Luna aims to maximize the profit from its investment. Our analysis will be easier if we segregate the cost of sales from the cost of the investment in the following way. Luna's profit is the difference between its benefit (revenues less the cost of sales) and the cost of the investment. To maximize profit, Luna should invest up

Externalities in talent: Silicon Valley

There is an exceptional concentration of computer, electronics, and related businesses in the peninsula between the San Francisco Bay and the Pacific Ocean. The area, aptly nicknamed *Silicon Valley*, is home to high-technology leaders such as Apple Computer, Hewlett-Packard, Sun Microsystems, and Varian Associates.

Two institutions, Stanford University and the Xerox Palo Alto Research Center (PARC), played key roles in fostering the development of Silicon Valley. Basic and applied research at the two institutions has provided the foundation for many successful high-tech products.

A local area network links separate personal computers over short distances. Robert Metcalfe and David Boggs invented the Ethernet local area network at the Xerox PARC. In 1979, Metcalfe left the Xerox PARC to found 3Com (the three "coms" being computer, communication, and compatibility), which commercialized the Ethernet technology. 3Com has since grown to become the world's second largest manufacturer of data networking systems.

Stanford University staff and students personally established several of the most successful Silicon Valley businesses. Routers are devices that link computer networks that use different protocols. Sandy Lerner and Len Bosack started Cisco Systems while working at Stanford University. In 1986, they left the university to run Cisco full time. The company has grown to become the world's largest manufacturer of routers and other data-networking systems.

In April 1994, two graduate students in Stanford's electrical engineering department, David Filo and Jeff Yang, started an index to the Internet. Their hobby quickly grew into Yahoo!, one of the most popular guides to the Internet's multimedia World Wide Web. More recently, two Stanford computer science graduate students launched Google, which is fast becoming the premier search engine for the Web.

Sources: Douglas K. Smith and Robert C. Alexander, *Fumbling the Future* (New York: William Morrow, 1988), pp. 95–103; letter from Robert Metcalfe (July 16, 1996); letter from Cisco Systems (May 23, 1996); World Wide Web pages www.cisco.com and www.3com.com (May 22, 1996), www.yahoo.com (June 25, 1996).

to the point that the marginal benefit from an additional dollar in investment equals the marginal cost.

At this level of investment, however, Luna may be ignoring opportunities for additional profit from positive externalities. To understand this point, let us change our earlier setting. Suppose now that the Luna department store belongs to Group Luna and the group also owns a florist shop and a shoe store already on Main Street. Then, when deciding on the level of its investment, the group will consider the benefits and the costs to all of its stores.

The total benefit from Luna's investment is the sum of the benefits to every store in the group, including the new store. The group's marginal benefit from investment in the new store is the increase in benefit to the group resulting from an additional dollar of investment in the new store. The additional dollar of investment will generate benefits for all the stores. Accordingly, the group's marginal benefit is the sum of the individual marginal benefits to each of the stores.

In figure 11.1, we illustrate the marginal benefits from investment in the new store for the new store and the two other stores. Note that each store may receive a different marginal benefit. The stronger the positive externality, the higher the recipient's marginal benefit curve will be.

Graphically, the group's marginal benefit is the *vertical sum* of the individual marginal benefits. A vertical sum means that, at every quantity of investment, we add the corresponding heights on each of the individual marginal benefit curves. For instance, referring to figure 11.1, if Luna invests $100,000, the florist's marginal benefit is $360,000, the shoe store's marginal benefit is $80,000, and Luna's own marginal benefit is $900,000. Hence, the sum of the marginal benefits is $1,340,000, which marks the corresponding point on the group marginal benefit curve.

In figure 11.1, we also draw the marginal cost of investment in the new store. If Luna considers only the benefit and the cost for the new store, it would maximize profit where the store's marginal benefit equals the marginal cost, which is at an investment of $900,000. This, however, ignores the positive externalities. If Luna considers the benefits and the costs for the entire group, then it would maximize profit at the level of investment where the group marginal benefit equals the marginal cost. Referring to figure 11.1, the profit-maximizing investment would be $929,000.

As this example shows, when the source of a positive externality considers only the benefit and the cost for itself, it overlooks an opportunity for additional profit. Referring to figure 11.1, by increasing its investment from $900,000 to $929,000, the group can gain the shaded area in additional profit.

Progress Check 11A Referring to the preceding discussion and to chapter 2, explain the difference between the following: (1) the horizontal sum of individual demand curves is the market demand curve, and (2) the vertical sum of individual marginal benefit curves is the group marginal benefit curve.

Progress check

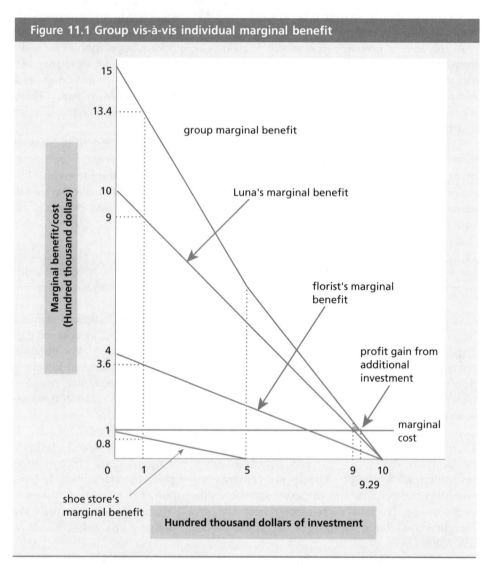

Figure 11.1 Group vis-à-vis individual marginal benefit

The group's marginal benefit is the vertical sum of the individual marginal benefits. At every quantity of investment, we add the corresponding heights on each of the individual marginal benefit curves. The group maximizes profit at an investment of $929,000, where the group marginal benefit equals the marginal cost. If Luna considers only the benefit and the cost for itself, it would invest only $900,000. By increasing its investment to $929,000, the group could gain the shaded area in additional profit.

Negative Externalities

Having considered positive externalities, we next consider how to take account of negative externalities. Recall that Luna's new store will take away business from other Main Street department stores. Changing our earlier setting, let us now suppose that the Group Luna owns two department stores, the Luna as well as the existing Sol store on Main Street, but does not own any specialty retailers. When deciding on its investment in the new Luna store, the group should consider the benefits and the costs to both department stores.

The total cost of investment in the new Luna store is the sum of the costs to both stores in the group. Accordingly, the group's marginal cost of investment in the new store is the increase in cost to the group resulting from an additional dollar of investment in the new store. This group marginal cost is the sum of the individual marginal costs for each store. For the new store, the marginal cost of an additional dollar of investment is just $1. For the existing store, the marginal cost is the reduction in profit arising from an additional dollar of investment in the new store.

In figure 11.2, we illustrate the marginal costs from investment in the new store for the new store itself and the existing store. Graphically, the group's marginal cost

Figure 11.2 Group vis-à-vis individual marginal cost

The group's marginal cost is the vertical sum of the individual marginal costs. The group maximizes profit at an investment of $750,000, where the group marginal benefit equals the marginal cost. If Luna considers only the benefit and the cost for itself, it would invest $900,000. By reducing its investment to $750,000, the group could gain the shaded area *abc* in additional profit.

is the vertical sum of the individual marginal costs. A vertical sum means that, at every quantity of investment, we add the corresponding heights on each of the individual marginal cost curves. For instance, at an investment of $500,000, the marginal cost for the Luna store is $100,000, while the marginal cost for the Sol store is $100,000; hence, the group marginal cost is $200,000.

In figure 11.2, we also draw the marginal benefit from investment in the new store. If Luna considers only the benefit and the cost for the new store, it would maximize profit where the marginal benefit equals Luna's marginal cost, which is at an investment of $900,000. If, however, Luna considers the benefits and the costs for the entire group, then it would maximize profit at the level of investment where the group marginal benefit equals the marginal cost. Referring to figure 11.2, the profit-maximizing investment is $750,000.

As this example shows, when the source of a negative externality considers only the benefit and the cost for itself, its profit will be less than the maximum possible. By figure 11.2, if the group would reduce its investment from $900,000 to $750,000, it could increase its profit by the shaded area *abc*.

Progress check   **Progress Check 11B** Referring to figure 11.2, suppose that the negative externality to the Sol store is stronger. How will this affect (1) Sol's marginal cost curve and (2) the level of investment that maximizes the group profit?

Externalities in General

We have separately discussed positive and negative externalities. Generally, if a group has a member that generates positive as well as negative externalities, then the group maximizes profit at the following benchmark: where the sum of the marginal benefits equals the sum of the marginal costs.

> An **externality is resolved** when the sum of the marginal benefits equals the sum of the marginal costs.

We say that an **externality is resolved** when the sum of the marginal benefits equals the sum of the marginal costs. Recall from chapter 6 that this benchmark also defines the economically efficient level of the activity generating the externalities. Hence, we can also say that the externality is resolved at the economically efficient level.

In developing the benchmark, we took the viewpoint of a group that included the source as well as recipients of the externalities. We next show that the same benchmark applies when the source is separate from the recipients.

Consider a positive externality and suppose that the sum of its marginal benefits exceeds the marginal cost. Then, if the source increases the externality, the marginal benefits will be greater than the marginal cost; hence, there will be a net benefit. This is a profit opportunity for an intermediary, which could collect fees from the recipients to pay the source to increase the externality. The set of transactions is feasible since the intermediary could set the fee to each recipient at less than its marginal benefit and the payment to the source to cover its marginal cost.

There will be an opportunity for such a profit whenever the sum of marginal benefits exceeds the marginal cost. Accordingly, the intermediary will pay the source to increase the externality up to the point where the sum of the marginal benefits equals the marginal cost, which defines the economically efficient level of the activity generating the positive externality. At that point, the externality is resolved.

A similar argument applies to negative externalities: an intermediary maximizes profit when it arranges for the source to resolve the externality, that is, choose the economically efficient level of the activity generating the externality. At that point, the intermediary maximizes profit. Accordingly, the benchmark of economic efficiency applies whether the source of the externality is separate or integrated with the recipients.

So far, we have considered externalities that affect the revenues and costs of the recipients, which can be measured directly in terms of dollars and cents. The benefits and costs of some externalities, however, are not in monetary form. For instance, suppose that there is a large church on Main Street. The church expects Sunday attendance to fall as people are attracted to Luna's new department store. The negative externality that Luna imposes on the church is not only monetary. Similarly, the new Luna store may generate positive externalities that are not monetary.

To take account of externalities in nonmonetary form, we require only that the recipients be able to measure the benefits and costs in terms of money. We suppose that, rather than maximizing profit, these recipients aim to maximize their net benefit, which is the benefit less the cost. Where all externalities are in monetary form, the net benefit simplifies to the profit.

◄◄ 3 Resolving Externalities

We have identified the benchmark for an externality as the economically efficient level. In chapter 6, we showed that, in a perfectly competitive market, the invisible hand ensures economic efficiency. By definition, however, externalities do not pass through markets. Hence, externalities will be resolved only through deliberate action. We now turn to consider practical ways to resolve externalities.

Merger

In the case of Luna's new store, we saw that, when a single entity owns all the stores along Main Street, it considers all the benefits and costs of its investments; hence, it will invest up to the economically efficient level. This suggests how to resolve an externality: the source and the recipient of the externality should merge into a single entity.

A merger can be effected in one of three ways. Either the recipient of the externality acquires the source, the source of the externality acquires the recipient, or a third party acquires both the source and the recipient. In the case of Luna's new store, either the existing Main Street retailers should acquire Luna, Luna should buy all the retailers presently on Main Street, or Luna and the existing retailers should all sell out to a third party.

From the viewpoint of resolving externalities, it does not matter who buys whom. Once the source and the recipient of the externality are combined, the single entity will take account of all the benefits and the costs of its investments and will invest up to the economically efficient level.

Let us justify this claim for Luna's positive externalities. First, suppose that the existing florist and shoe store on Main Street acquire the Luna department store to form the Main Street group. Then, the total benefit of the group consists of the benefit from the three stores. To maximize profit, the group should invest up to the point that the group marginal benefit equals the marginal cost. The group marginal benefit is the sum of the marginal benefits from the three stores. Hence, referring to figure 11.1, the profit-maximizing investment level is $929,000.

Next, suppose Luna buys the two specialty retailers to form Group Luna. Again, the total benefit of the group consists of the benefit from the three stores. To maximize the group profit, it should invest up to the point that the sum of the marginal benefits from the three stores equals the marginal cost. Again, referring to figure 11.1, the profit-maximizing investment level is $929,000.

Mickey Mouse externalities

The Walt Disney Company owns and manages Disneyland in Anaheim, California. This theme park is surrounded by hundreds of businesses, including motels, restaurants, souvenir stores, and transportation services. Disneyland visitors are the major source of income for these neighboring businesses.

In the late 1980s, the Walt Disney Company decided to embark on a large program of investments to upgrade Disneyland. Before commencing construction, the company bought much of the property around the theme park. The company paid $200 million for the Disneyland Hotel.

By purchasing the surrounding property, the Walt Disney Company ensured that it would capture relatively more of the benefits from new attractions. Consequently, the company had a greater incentive to make the economically efficient level of investment in new attractions at the theme park.

The Walt Disney Company continued to buy real estate around Disneyland. In December 1995, it acquired the Pan Pacific Hotel, which was renamed the Disneyland Pacific Hotel.

Source: Gary Wilson, Chief Financial Officer, Disney Company, speech at the Anderson School, UCLA, March 15, 1989; "Walt Disney Co.," *Asian Wall Street Journal*, December 13, 1995, p. 22.

Academic externalities: a free campus

In May 1995, the regents of the University of California met to choose the location for its proposed San Joaquin campus, to be the 10th branch of the university. The regents considered two alternatives: a 2000-acre site at Lake Yosemite offered free of charge by the Virginia Smith Trust and another site near the city of Fresno that would be purchased. Swayed in part by the free land, the regents voted for Lake Yosemite.

The Virginia Smith Trust owned 7,000 acres of land by Lake Yosemite. When the trust made the offer to the university, its land was used to graze cattle. The trust projected that, with establishment of the new campus, it could earn $350 million from development of the remaining 5,000 acres of real estate.

The positive externalities generated by the new campus were sufficient to justify the "gift" of 2,000 acres to the University of California.

Source: "Lake Yosemite Selected for Proposed Campus," UC Focus [Office of the President, University of California] 9, no. 5 (June–July 1995), pp. 1 and 7.

Finally, suppose that Luna and the two specialty retailers all sell out to a third party, Moonlight Holdings. In this case, Moonlight Holdings owns the three stores. As in the two previous cases, the owner of the three stores will maximize profit by investing $929,000, the point where the sum of the marginal benefits from the three stores equals the marginal cost.

We have shown that, for a positive externality, the level of investment will be economically efficient if the source and the recipient of the externality are combined. It does not matter how the combination takes place. The same is true for a negative externality and, generally, for an activity that generates both positive and negative externalities. Regardless of how the source and the recipient of the externality are combined, the combined entity will choose an economically efficient level of investment.

Joint Action

We have seen how the affected parties can resolve externalities through merger. Merger, however, is not always feasible. For instance, recall the negative externality that Luna's new department store would impose on the church. A merger would mean combining the church and the Luna store under a common ownership. Such a combination may not be feasible.

Accordingly, it is important to explore the alternative approach to resolving an externality: joint action. To resolve an externality through joint action, the source and the recipient of the externality must negotiate and agree on how to resolve the externality. Joint action is a feasible way to resolve the negative externality from Luna's new store to the church. For instance, the church may offer Luna the use of its parking area if Luna agrees not to open on Sunday mornings. Such a deal is a way of jointly resolving the negative externality.

Joint action is also a way by which the positive externalities from Luna to the specialty retailers can be resolved. Since Luna's investment increases the revenues of the florist and the shoe store, the two specialty retailers would like Luna to increase its investment.

Suppose that the florist pays Luna a contribution equal to its marginal benefit from Luna's investment and that the shoe store does likewise. Then Luna's total benefit will be the benefit from its own store plus the contributions from the two specialty retailers. Luna's profit will be its total benefit less the cost of the investment. Therefore, it will maximize profit by choosing the level of investment where the sum of the marginal benefits equals the marginal cost. Referring to figure 11.1, that level of investment is $929,000. Accordingly, joint action can give Luna sufficient incentive to look beyond its own benefits and costs and resolve its positive externalities.

With joint action, the source and the recipient of the externality remain separate entities. Joint action to resolve an externality requires two steps. First, the affected

Cooperative advertising: resolving "Intel Inside"

Compaq is one of the world's leading manufacturers of IBM-compatible personal computers. Intel is the dominant manufacturer of IBM-compatible microprocessors. Compaq spends millions of dollars each year on advertising. Many of these advertisements feature "Intel Inside," the mark that a computer is powered by an Intel microprocessor. By publicizing Intel, these advertisements boost the demand for the products of other manufacturers using Intel microprocessors.

From Intel's standpoint, the economically efficient amount of "Intel Inside" advertising by Compaq balances the marginal benefit to all manufacturers with the marginal cost to Compaq. In planning its advertising, however, Compaq might ignore the positive externalities to other manufacturers.

Intel resolves these externalities through cooperative advertising: the microprocessor manufacturer shares the cost of advertising by personal computer makers that features "Intel Inside." This subsidy encourages manufacturers of personal computers to invest the appropriate amount of resources in advertising Intel microprocessors.

Source: "Compaq and Intel Renew Old Alliance," *South China Morning Post,* January 23, 1996, Technology, p. 6.

parties must agree on how to resolve the externality. This step involves collecting information about the benefits and costs to the various parties, and then planning the level of the activity that generates the externality. The second step is to enforce compliance with the agreed plan. Enforcement includes monitoring the source of the externality and applying incentives to ensure that the source complies with the planned level of the externality-generating activity.

Free Rider Problem

Externalities can be resolved through merger or joint action. There are, however, some hurdles, however, in the way. To illustrate, suppose that Luna and the two specialty retailers aim to resolve the externalities through joint action. Then the three parties must agree on the marginal benefit that Luna's investment will generate for the florist. This will determine the florist's contribution to Luna's investment.

To reduce its contribution, the florist may claim that its marginal benefit from Luna's investment is low. Since the florist will probably have better information than the other two parties about its own marginal benefit, it may be difficult for the other two parties to know whether the florist is bluffing. The result may be that the parties cannot agree and the positive externality would not be resolved.

Similarly, differences in information about the shoe store's marginal benefit from Luna's investment might also prevent resolution of the externality to the shoe store. As these examples show, differences in information may prevent the affected parties from reaching an agreement on how to resolve an externality.

Differences in information can be compounded in the following way. It is difficult for Luna to exclude the florist from receiving the positive externality. Hence, the florist can still benefit from Luna's investments even if it contributes less than its marginal benefit. When the florist considers its contribution from a purely selfish viewpoint, it will maximize its own profit by underreporting its marginal benefit.

In this example, the florist is taking a free ride on Luna's investment. Generally, a **free rider** understates its benefit from an externality and contributes less than its marginal benefit to resolution of the externality. In the extreme, the free rider claims that it derives no benefit and avoids all contribution. The incentive to take a free ride arises whenever it is costly to exclude particular individuals from receiving an externality.

> A **free rider** contributes less than its marginal benefit to the resolution of an externality.

The incentive to take a free ride is stronger when the externality affects many recipients and these recipients differ widely in their marginal benefits. When an externality affects many recipients, the contribution of any particular recipient is relatively small. Hence, the other recipients may resolve the externality even if some recipients take a free ride. When the recipients of the externality differ widely in their marginal benefits, there is relatively more scope for an individual recipient to claim a low marginal benefit.

Fisheries I: joint action

There are significant negative externalities among producers in the fisheries industry. The more that one fisher catches, the less there will be available for others. Fishers, however, may engage in practices that are privately beneficial but are not economically efficient. Such practices include indiscriminate fishing methods that catch young as well as mature fish. As a result of overfishing, many marine resources are being exhausted.

   The fisheries industry also provides an example where some of the affected producers have resolved the negative externalities through joint action. The American state of Maine is famous for its lobsters. Lobster catchers in some areas organized to restrict catching with very dramatic results. In the restricted areas, the number of lobsters per trap was 60% higher than in unrestricted areas and the average weight of caught lobsters was 67% higher.

Source: James A. Wilson, "A Test of the Tragedy of the Commons," in *Managing the Commons*, ed. Garrett Hardin and John Baden (San Francisco: W. H. Freeman, 1977), pp. 96–111.

Fisheries II: the limits to joint action

International waters are marine areas beyond the jurisdiction of a single country. Marine resources in international waters attract fishers from all over the world. Consequently, joint action to resolve negative externalities among fishers can be problematic. Even if the parties involved can agree on how much to catch, it may be difficult to enforce compliance.

   Turbot, also known as Greenland halibut, found in the Grand Banks off Newfoundland, attract trawlers from Canada, Portugal, Spain, and other countries. The Northwest Atlantic Fisheries Organization (NAFO) regulates turbot fishing in the Grand Banks. In September 1994, the organization set a quota of 16,200 metric tons for Canada and 3,400 tons for the European Union. Despite the quotas, there have been serious disagreements among the NAFO member countries. Canada, for instance, has accused Spanish trawlers of flouting the quotas. In March 1995, the dispute escalated when Canadian Navy ships fired warning shots to force the Spanish trawler *Estai* into the Canadian port of St John's.

   The Antarctic provides another example. The International Whaling Commission has banned the commercial hunting of whales in the Antarctic since December 1994. Nevertheless, Japan has exploited a loophole to catch several hundred whales for "scientific purposes." Caught in the name of science, these whales provide meat to Japanese restaurants for sale at $160 a pound.

Sources: "Spanish Vessel Seized," *South China Morning Post*, March 11, 1995, p. 14; "Hunters Defy Ban on Killing Minke Whales," *South China Morning Post*, February 16, 1995, p. 14.

◂◂ 4 Network Externalities

The Internet is a global network of computers based on the communications protocol TCP/IP. The World Wide Web is a set of standards that defines access to multimedia resources over the Internet. With the development of the Web and invention of the Web browser, the Internet graduated from an academic tool to a mass communications technology. Web browsing and electronic mail fueled the exploding demand for Internet access. In 1981, the Internet consisted of just over 200 hosts. The number grew to over 300,000 in 1990, and over 72 million by 2000. (For the most recent count, please refer to the Internet Software Consortium at http://www.isc.org/.)

The essential reason for the accelerating growth of the Internet is *network externalities*. A **network externality** arises when a benefit or cost directly conveyed to others depends on the total number of other users.

> A **network externality** arises when a benefit or cost directly conveyed to others depends on the total number of other users.

To understand the meaning of a network externality, suppose that Joy is the only user connected to the Internet. To whom could she send electronic mail? When Joy is the only subscriber, Internet electronic mail service is worthless.

Suppose, by contrast, that there are 20 million other users on the Internet. Then, Joy could use electronic mail to communicate with 20 million other persons. The benefit of Internet electronic mail to Joy depends on the total number of other users, regardless of how close or distant they may be. The adjective *network* emphasizes that the externality is generated by the entire network of users.

In chapter 2, we discussed the factors – including price, buyer income, and prices of related products – that affect the marginal benefit and demand for an item. The marginal benefit and demand for an item that exhibits network externalities depends on one additional factor, which is the total number of other users. When another person joins the Internet, the marginal benefit and demand curves of all existing users will shift up. Network externalities explain why the demand for Internet access grew at an accelerating rate.

As with externalities in general, the benchmark for an item that exhibits network externalities is economic efficiency: the sum of marginal benefits equals the sum of marginal costs. The presence of network externalities or network effects (which we explain next) implies that the character of demand and competition will differ from that in conventional supply–demand markets in several important ways. Before analyzing these implications, we distinguish network externalities from network effects.

Network Effects

As we explained in chapter 10, a *network effect* arises whenever a benefit or cost depends on the total number of other users. A network externality is transmitted directly, while a network effect acts through a market.

To illustrate a network effect, consider telephone service. The benefit that one subscriber derives from telephone service definitely depends on the total number of other subscribers. Hence, connections to telephone service generate network effects. Are these effects also network externalities? Note that there is a market for telephone service: the service provider can increase its profits by resolving the effect from one subscriber's connection to the benefit of other subscribers. Thus, connections to telephone service generate network externalities only to the extent that they are not resolved by the service provider.

The market for Internet access exhibits both network externalities and network effects. As we have already explained, the marginal benefit of Internet electronic mail depends on the number of other users in the network. The market for Internet access, however, is quite fragmented. A single access provider may not completely resolve the network externality – because part of the additional profit from resolution will accrue to other access providers. Accordingly, there may remain unresolved network externalities in the market for Internet access.

Why is it important to understand the distinction between network externalities and network effects? If a network externality is completely resolved, and so is classified as a network effect, there is no further opportunity for profit from resolving the externality. If the network externality is not completely resolved, then there exist opportunities for profit from resolving the difference between the sum of marginal benefits and the sum of marginal costs.

Progress check

Progress Check 11C   Which of the following are network externalities?

(a)   An increase in the number of people speaking French benefits existing French speakers.

(b)   An increase in the number of merchants accepting a new credit card benefits existing cardholders.

Critical Mass

> The **critical mass** is the number of users at which the quantity demanded becomes positive.

The first important way in which markets with network externalities/effects differ from conventional markets is that the demand is zero unless the number of users exceeds critical mass. The **critical mass** is the number of users at which the quantity demanded becomes positive. For instance, in the case of the Internet, there is some number of users below which the quantity demanded will be 0. Supposing that the number is 100, then the critical mass for Internet is 100 users. This means that there will be a positive demand for the Internet only when the price or other factors are sufficient to attract 100 users.

The demand for some items depends on the presence of complementary hardware. For instance, the demand for Internet access depends on the number of personal computers, personal digital assistants, and other devices that provide Internet access. Similarly, the demand for telephone service depends on the number of telephones.

In these cases, the **installed base** is the quantity of the complementary hardware in service.

Suppose that each user needs one separate unit of the complementary hardware. Then an alternative way to measure the number of users is the size of the installed base. Further,

> The **installed base** is the quantity of the complementary hardware in service.

an alternative specification of the critical mass is in terms of the installed base of the complementary hardware. In our earlier hypothetical example of Internet access, the critical mass was 100 users. Then, equivalently, the critical mass is an installed base of 100 units of personal computers, personal digital assistants, and other access devices.

Expectations

The second important feature of markets with network externalities/effects is the role of user expectations. Chapter 10 introduced the concept of Nash equilibrium for games in strategic form. We showed that, in positive-sum games, there might be more than one equilibrium.

Referring again to our hypothetical example of Internet access, there are two possible equilibria. In the good equilibrium, every potential Internet user expects the others to subscribe to Internet access, and accordingly subscribes. Then demand exceeds critical mass and the service succeeds as expected. By contrast, in the bad equilibrium, potential users are pessimistic. Each person expects fewer than 100 others to subscribe, and so, does not subscribe. Then, indeed, demand fails to reach critical mass and the service flops as expected.

The role of expectations is a major difference between markets with network externalities/effects and conventional markets. How can the expectations of potential users be influenced? One way is through commitments that effectively guarantee or provide a strong assurance of critical mass. This explains why sellers of items generating network externalities/effects often give away large quantities in order to establish a sufficient installed base.

Another way of influencing expectations is hype. For instance, a grand launch attended by many dignitaries may generate the self-fulfilling prophecy that demand for the item will attain critical mass. Music publishers invest heavily to get their CDs to the top of the charts in order to persuade consumers to buy.

Tipping

The third important feature of markets with network externalities/effects concerns the character of competition. The demand in markets with network externalities/effects is extremely sensitive to small differences among competitors. Suppose there are several competing products, all of which have attained a critical mass of demand. Then, a small increase in the user base of one product can *tip* the market demand toward that product. **Tipping** is the tendency

> **Tipping** is the tendency for the market demand to shift toward a product that has gained a small initial lead.

for the market demand to shift toward a product that has gained a small initial lead.

To illustrate the phenomenon of tipping, suppose that there are two global computer networks, the Internet and the Total-Net, each with 100 users. The two networks are incompatible; hence, Internet subscribers cannot communicate with Total-Net subscribers and vice versa.

Now, suppose that 10 users decide to switch from the Internet to the Total-Net. Then, the Internet will have 90 subscribers, while the Total-Net will have 110 subscribers. Consider Max, a typical Internet subscriber: with 10 users switching, he can now communicate with only 89 other people. Hence, the number of Internet users has dropped below the critical mass. So, Max switches from the Internet to the Total-Net. Every other Internet user also switches. Ultimately, the initial switch by 10 users tips everyone toward the Total-Net.

In a market for competing products that generate network externalities, the likelihood of tipping means that one product will eventually dominate the market. Any slight movement in demand toward one product will tip all the users to that product. Consequently, it is unlikely that several competing products will coexist for an extended period of time.

By contrast, in a conventional market, several competitors of similar size may continue profitably for a long time. Even if one seller gains an advantage in pricing or product quality, the entire market demand will not tip in its favor.

Price Elasticity

Chapter 3 introduced the concept of (own) price elasticity of demand, which is the percentage by which the quantity demanded changes if the price of the item rises by 1%, holding all other factors unchanged. The presence of network externalities/effects affects the price elasticity in different ways depending on whether the market demand has reached critical mass and the relation among competing sellers.

When the market demand is below critical mass, the demand will be zero, and hence extremely price inelastic. Neither price increases nor reductions will affect the demand at all.

The demand will be sensitive to price only when it exceeds critical mass. In this case, if the price rises by 1%, the number of users and quantity demanded will be lower. These reductions will feed back through the network externality/effect to reduce the quantity demanded still further. The network externality/effect tends to amplify the effect of a price increase on the quantity demanded. Similarly, the network externality/effect would amplify the effect of a price reduction. Accordingly, the network externality/effect causes the market demand to be relatively more elastic.

If there are several competing products, all of which have attained a critical mass of demand, then the market demand could tip in favor of one that gains a small advantage. This means that the individual demand for each product will be extremely price elastic.

Microsoft: Got Netscape but not AOL

Personal computer software giant Microsoft was relatively late to appreciate the business potential of the Internet. During this window of opportunity, Netscape unseated Mosaic as the dominant Web browser and Sun positioned Java as the programming language of choice for the Web.

Importantly, the Netscape browser and Java applications were designed to operate on any computer, regardless of the underlying operating system. With the Netscape–Java combination, key software could be moved away from the desktop to powerful machines called servers providing software through the Internet.

Bill Gates recognized the threat to Microsoft's market power over personal computer software: "A new competitor 'born' on the Internet is Netscape. Their browser is dominant, with 70% usage share, allowing them . . . to commoditize the underlying operating system." Microsoft quickly bundled version 2.0 of its Internet Explorer browser free with the Windows 95 operating system.

Microsoft easily defeated Netscape. The reason is that most World Wide Web content was written in simple hypertext markup language (HTML) that could be read equally well with many browsers including Netscape Navigator and Internet Explorer. As such, there was no strong network externality/effect binding users to a choice of Web browser. Netscape users could easily switch to Internet Explorer. By the end of 1997, Netscape's market share of usage had fallen below 40%.

By contrast, Microsoft has so far failed to either "buy or bury" AOL. The network externality/effect among the subscribers to ICQ and AOL Instant Messenger ties them strongly to AOL Internet service. AOL's hold on its members has been further strengthened by network externalities/effects among users of chat-rooms, forums, and other services within its walled garden of content and services.

Owing to these network externalities/effects, the demand for AOL's premium service was extremely inelastic. This explains, in part, why AOL was not perturbed by Microsoft's threat of a price war. The other reason was that AOL had protected its low end by positioning CompuServe to price-sensitive subscribers.

Sources: "America Online: Pricks and Kicks," *Economist*, August 14, 1999, pp. 52–3; Positive Support Review, Inc., Press Release, January 8, 1998; *U.S. v. Microsoft: Proposed Findings of Fact*, Section VII.

◂◂ 5 Public Goods

Every Fourth of July, millions of Americans gather to watch Independence Day fireworks. These displays attract more people than top football and baseball games. Clearly, there is a huge pent-up demand for fireworks. Why don't some entrepreneurs provide this form of entertainment on a commercial basis?

> Consumption is **nonrival** if one person's increase in consumption does not reduce the quantity available to others.

To address this question, we apply the concept of a public good. As explained in the Introduction, an item is a public good if one person's increase in consumption does not reduce the quantity available to others. Equivalently, a public good provides nonrival consumption. Consumption is **nonrival** if one person's increase in consumption does not reduce the quantity available to others.

Open-air fireworks are an example of a public good. For instance, if Joy comes to watch a show of open-air fireworks, she does not reduce the quantity available for other people. Hence, open-air fireworks provide nonrival consumption and are a public good.

Another way of understanding nonrival consumption is through the concept of scale economies. Given that open-air fireworks are being provided to one viewer, the marginal cost of providing the same display to additional viewers is nothing. There is an extreme economy of scale in providing a public good: provision involves only a fixed cost and the marginal cost of serving additional consumers or users is 0.

As suggested by the question of why there is little or no commercial provision of open-air fireworks, the provision of public goods is a complicated issue. To lay the foundation for an answer, we first discuss the differences between public and private goods, and then consider the economically efficient provision of a public good.

> An item is a **private good** if one person's increase in consumption by some quantity reduces the total available to others by the same quantity.

Rivalness

Public goods lie at one end of a spectrum of rivalness, with *private goods* at the other extreme (figure 11.3). An item is a **private good** if one person's increase in consumption by some quantity reduces the total available to others by the same quantity. Equivalently, a private good provides **rival** consumption, which means that one person's increase in consumption by some quantity reduces the total available to others by the same quantity.

> Consumption is **rival** if one person's increase in consumption by some quantity reduces the total available to others by the same quantity.

Food and clothing, for instance, are private goods. If Lucas eats a four-ounce frozen yogurt, then there will be four ounces less for other consumers. If Max is wearing a new polo shirt, no one else can wear it at the same time. The professional services of accountants and lawyers are also private goods: if an accountant is attending to one client, then there will be less of his or her time available for other clients.

Figure 11.3 Rivalness

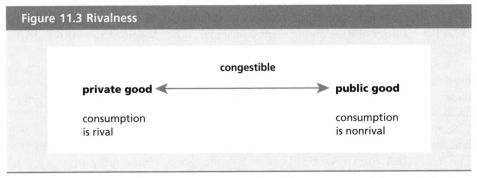

A private good provides rival consumption. At the other extreme, a public good provides nonrival consumption.

Some items are neither public nor private. An example are items that provide **congestible** consumption. This means that one person's increase in consumption by some quantity reduces the total available to others but by less than that quantity. Congestible items are public goods when consumption is low but are private goods when consumption is high.

> Consumption is **congestible** if one person's increase in consumption by some quantity reduces the total available to others but by less than that quantity.

For instance, entertainment by a juggler is congestible: several people can comfortably watch a juggler, but after some number, additional viewers will get in the way and reduce the quantity of entertainment available to other viewers. The Internet is also congestible. At off-peak times, an increase in usage by one person will not reduce the service to others. At peak times, however, the more users connect to the Internet, the slower will be the service for others.

Progress Check 11D On the spectrum of figure 11.3, mark the following items: (1) services of a mainframe computer, (2) computer monitor, (3) technique for coronary bypass operation, (4) cardiac (heart) surgeon's services, and (5) bottled oxygen.

Progress check

Content vis-à-vis Delivery

To understand the degree of rivalness, it is important to distinguish between content and delivery. For instance, television programming can be broadcast in a number of ways: over the air from land-based transmission towers, directly to receivers from orbiting satellites, or by cable.

Regardless of the method of delivery, the content of broadcast television is non-rival. If Maria switches on her television to watch the evening news, she does not affect the quantity of the evening news available to other people. This is true whether the signal comes over the air or by cable.

The method of delivery, however, may be a public or private good. Delivery by over-the-air transmission is a public good. The same signal can serve any number of television sets within the transmission range. Delivery by cable, however, is a private good. One cable serves only one television set.

Scientific knowledge provides another illustration of the distinction between content and delivery. Consider, for instance, this textbook on managerial economics. The intellectual content of this book is a public good. If one more person understands the principles of managerial economics, she or he does not reduce the quantity available to other people.

On the other hand, the principles of managerial economics are delivered through the medium of a textbook. The textbook is a private good: if one person is using a copy of this book, that copy is unavailable to others.

As we shall discuss later in this chapter, the distinction between content and delivery is important for commercial provision of public goods. The basis of commercial provision of many public goods is to deliver them in the format of private goods.

Economic Efficiency

Previously, we showed that, when an externality is at an economically efficient level, there are no further opportunities to profit from adjusting the activity generating the externality. Let us now show the same for a public good. Suppose that there are three viewers of open-air fireworks – Alan, Mary, and Peter – with marginal benefits as shown in figure 11.4. The figure also shows the marginal cost of open-air fireworks, which we suppose to be a constant $5.60 per minute.

Consider the provision of one minute of fireworks. Since fireworks are a public good, there will be one minute for each of the three viewers. Accordingly, each would be willing to pay her or his marginal benefit for that minute. By figure 11.4, the sum of the marginal benefits to the three viewers is $0.80 + $3.60 + $4.50 = $8.90. The cost of one minute is $5.60, hence there is an opportunity to make a profit by providing one minute of fireworks. This same argument applies for additional quantities up to four minutes.

At four minutes of fireworks, the sum of the individual marginal benefits equals the marginal cost. Can someone make money by increasing provision to five minutes? By figure 11.4, the fifth minute provides an additional benefit to Alan and Mary only. The sum of their marginal benefits is $2.00 + $2.50 = $4.50. Since the cost of each minute is $5.60, providing the fifth minute would result in a loss.

We have shown that opportunities for profit are exhausted at the point where the vertical sum of the individual marginal benefits equals the marginal cost. By the definition in chapter 6, this is the economically efficient quantity of the public good.

Figure 11.4 Economically efficient provision of public good

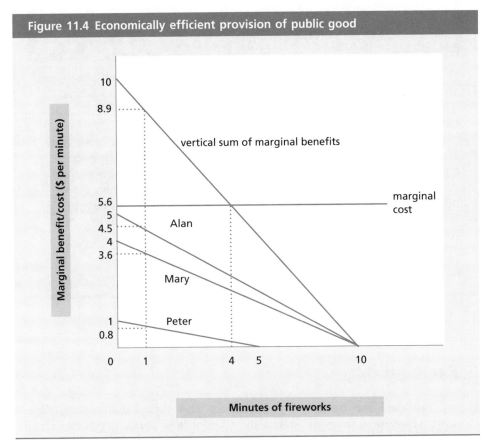

At the economically efficient quantity of a public good, the sum of the individual marginal benefits equals the marginal cost. Every individual marginal benefit curve lies below the marginal cost of $5.60; hence, no individual person would be willing to buy even one minute of fireworks. If each individual tries to get a free ride, it might not be possible to provide even one minute of fireworks on a commercial basis.

Accordingly, at the economically efficient quantity, there are no further opportunities to profit from adjusting the provision of the public good.

In figure 11.4, notice that each of the individual marginal benefit curves lies below the marginal cost of $5.60. Hence, no individual person would be willing to buy even one minute of fireworks. The sum of the individual marginal benefit curves, however, lies above the marginal cost curve at quantities of between zero and four minutes. Since a public good provides nonrival consumption, the three persons' willingness to pay is given by the vertical sum of the individual marginal benefit curves. While no single person would buy even one minute of fireworks, they collectively would be willing to pay for four minutes.

Managing congestion: waiting times and the price of gasoline

The pumps at a gasoline station are a congestible facility. At off-peak times, an increase in usage by one driver will not reduce the service to others. At peak times, however, the more drivers are filling up, the slower will be the service for others.

Gasoline stations resolve the congestion through pricing. For many years, at the corner of Le Conte and Gayley Avenues in Westwood, Los Angeles, a Chevron station charged lower prices than the Shell station across the street. A station that sets higher prices will draw fewer customers; hence, it implicitly offers faster service. One estimate shows that, on average, drivers are willing to pay a 1% higher price for a 6% reduction in congestion.

Source: I. P. L. Png and David Reitman, "Service Time Competition," *RAND Journal of Economics* 25, no. 4 (Winter 1994), pp. 619–34.

◂ 6 Excludability

Having discussed the nature of public goods and their economically efficient quantity, we are now ready to address the issue of how public goods can actually be provided. Many private goods are provided on a commercial basis. There is a fundamental condition for commercial provision of any product that is easy to overlook. That condition is that, to sell a product, the seller must be able to exclude those who do not pay. The condition is crucial in the commercial provision of public goods.

> Consumption is **excludable** if the provider can exclude particular consumers.

Consumption is **excludable** if the provider can exclude particular consumers. Excludability is a fundamental requirement for commercial provision of any item.

When consumption of an item is not excludable, commercial provision will be difficult. To illustrate the problem, let us suppose that Luna Entertainment wants to provide one minute of open-air fireworks to Alan, Mary, and Peter. Referring to figure 11.4, Luna knows that, at that quantity, the individual marginal benefits of Alan, Mary, and Peter are $4.50, $3.60, and $0.80 respectively. If Luna charges each person a price equal to her or his marginal benefit, then Luna will collect $4.50 + $3.60 + $0.80 = $8.90 from Alan, Mary, and Peter. Luna's cost of providing one minute of fireworks is $5.60; hence, it will realize a profit of $3.30.

Peter, however, might reason that if he refuses to pay, while Alan and Mary do pay, then Luna would collect $4.50 + $3.60 = $8.10, which would be enough to cover the cost of $5.60. Then, Luna would provide the one minute of fireworks and, since viewing open-air fireworks is not excludable, Peter would enjoy a free show. Alan and Mary, however, might also think in similar ways. If everyone tries to get a free show, Luna will incur a loss from the fireworks. Hence, in the extreme, the incentive to get a free show prevents the provision of even one minute of fireworks on a commercial basis.

The basic problem is that, whenever consumption of some item is nonexcludable, individual consumers will have an incentive to take a free ride. Free riding will cut into the seller's revenues and, so, reduce the seller's profit and hamper commercial provision of the item.

Many public goods provide consumption that is not excludable. Accordingly, to understand the scope for commercial provision of public goods, we must consider the degree of excludability. This depends on two factors: law and technology.

Law

In the previous section, we explained that scientific knowledge is a public good. An example of scientific knowledge is the formula for an antiviral drug. If Luna Pharmaceuticals uses the formula to manufacture the drug, it will not affect the availability of the formula for other users. Hence, the formula is a public good. Similarly, the formulas for other drugs and chemical processes are public goods.

Through the concept of a **patent**, however, the law has made the use of many scientific formulas excludable. A *patent* is a legal, exclusive right to a product or process. It is illegal to manufacture a product or use a process covered by a patent without the permission of the patent owner. Such illegal activity is called *infringement*. The owner of a patent can sue infringers for a court order to stop the infringement as well as an award of damages.

> A **patent** is a legal, exclusive right to a product or process.

With legal authority, the owner of a patented antiviral drug can exclude those who do not pay from getting the drug. Accordingly, commercial production is feasible.

Patents provide the basis for the commercial provision of scientific knowledge in the chemicals, electrical and electronic equipment, and pharmaceutical industries. The development of a new pharmaceutical, for instance, can take a decade and cost several hundred million dollars. Private enterprises are willing to invest large amounts in research and development only because of the profits that are possible with patent protection. Past scientific discoveries that have been covered by patents include aspirin, the light bulb, and the transistor. More recently, patented products include AZT and the Pentium microprocessor.

Like scientific knowledge, artistic, literary, and musical compositions are also public goods. The content of the *Oxford English Dictionary* may be used any number of times without affecting its availability to other users. Similarly, the content of Mozart's piano concertos, Madonna's songs, the movie *Pulp Fiction*, and computer software is also nonrival.

> A **copyright** is a legal, exclusive right to an artistic, literary, or musical expression.

The law, however, has made the use of artistic, literary, and musical expression excludable through the concept of **copyright**. A *copyright* is a legal, exclusive right to an artistic, literary, or musical expression. It is illegal to reproduce a copyrighted expression without the permission of the copyright owner. The owner of a copyright can sue infringers for a court order to stop the infringement as well as an award of damages.

Copyright gives the owner the authority to exclude those who do not pay from using the material. Commercial provision of literary and musical compositions and computer software is possible only with copyright law. For instance, if there were no copyright protection for personal computer software, all users could freely copy the products and the business of software development would not be commercially viable.

Patent and copyright are two forms of rights over intellectual property, which is the legal concept for ownership of ideas. The law deliberately creates these exclusive rights to encourage investment in creating new scientific knowledge, literary and musical compositions, and computer software.

Patents and copyrights are limited to specific periods of time. Once the patent on a product or process has expired, the owner loses the exclusive right and anyone can freely imitate the item. Similarly, after the expiration of the copyright on a literary or musical work, anyone is free to copy or use the work. For instance, the copyright on Mozart's piano concertos expired long ago, hence advertising agencies and movie studios can freely use Mozart's works.

The law can establish excludability through intellectual property. The effectiveness of exclusion, however, depends on enforcement. Consider, for instance, the process

Patents: seventeen years was not long enough for the real thing

Coca Cola, one of the world's most famous products, has not been patented, and deliberately so. The reason is that the applicant for a patent must submit a detailed description of the product or process for which it seeks protection. This information becomes part of the public record, so that others can avoid infringing the patent. Potential competitors, however, can refer to the public records for details of the product or process. Once the patent expires, they are free to imitate the product or process.

If Coca Cola had filed for a patent, it would have enjoyed only 17 years of protection. (Beginning in 1995, U.S. patents were extended to 20 years.) Then, on the expiration of the patent, anyone – even Coca Cola's arch-rival, Pepsi – could manufacture the "real thing." The Coca Cola Company decided not to obtain a patent and chose instead to keep its formula a trade secret. Over 100 years later, the company continues to have a monopoly over the real thing.

for distilling water: heat the water to its boiling point, recover the steam, and then cool the steam and collect the condensate. Even if the law allowed a patent on this process, the right would be nearly impossible to enforce. Imagine trying to exclude particular high-school students, engineers, or household cooks from using the process to distill water.

By contrast, a patent on the formula for an antiviral drug is quite enforceable. The only potential commercial users of the formula are pharmaceutical manufacturers. To make money from the drug, a manufacturer must produce it on a large scale and sell it on the open market. This means that use of the formula will be relatively easy to detect. Accordingly, the owner of the patent can effectively exclude particular persons from usage.

Computer software provides another example of the distinction between establishing and enforcing intellectual property. Millions of people have personal computers and use spreadsheet and word-processing programs. Any one can quite easily copy personal computer software. By contrast, the number of mainframe computers is relatively small, which in turn limits the demand for mainframe software. Accordingly, it is much easier to enforce intellectual property over software for mainframe computers than personal computers.

Technology

In addition to the law, the other factor affecting excludability is technology. Recall Luna Entertainment's difficulty in marketing an open-air fireworks show: it could not exclude particular persons, so some if not all of the viewers might refuse to pay. Suppose, however, that Luna could produce fireworks that could be seen only through a special set of viewing glasses. Then, it could charge a price for the special glasses. In this example, a change of technology transforms the consumption of the product from being nonexcludable to excludable.

We have mentioned that the content of television programming is a public good. Whether, however, consumption of broadcast television is excludable depends on the technology of delivery. Consumption of free-to-the-air television is not excludable. The station cannot prevent particular individuals from watching a broadcast.

With scrambling technology, however, the consumption of over-the-air television can be made excludable. If a station scrambles its signal, only viewers who pay for decoding equipment can watch the programs. In this case, scrambling technology has transformed the medium of delivery from being nonexcludable to excludable.

Consumption of television programming that is broadcast by cable is very easily excludable. A cable television station simply disconnects viewers who do not pay.

Software provides another example. The intellectual content of a new computer program is a public good. Suppose that the publisher distributes the program through the Internet. Whether the delivery is excludable depends on the technology implemented by the publisher. If access is open, then anyone can go to the publisher's site and download the program. On the other hand, the publisher could restrict access to users with an authorized password. Then the delivery would be excludable.

Commercial provision without exclusion? free-to-the-air TV

We have claimed that commercial provision of a public good is difficult when consumption is nonexcludable. Consumption of free-to-the-air television is nonexcludable. In America, however, four major networks provide free-to-the-air television on a commercial basis. Far from limping along, the business has flourished. What is the television networks' secret?

Commercial television networks such as Fox and NBC get no revenues directly from their viewers. Their primary source of revenues is advertising. In 1996, NBC sold 30-second spots during the prime-time Summer Olympics for up to $400,000. While viewers of Fox and NBC do not directly pay for television, they do pay indirectly. They pay by increasing their purchases of the products advertised on television. If television advertising had no effect on consumer demand, would Anheuser-Busch, General Motors, and Visa spend millions of dollars each year on advertising? Obviously not.

Commercial Provision

Generally, the commercial provision of a public good depends on the extent to which the seller can exclude those who do not pay from consumption. In figure 11.5, we present a spectrum of excludability, with items whose consumption is excludable at one extreme and those whose consumption is nonexcludable at the other extreme.

Considering scientific knowledge, the formula for an antiviral drug is at the excludable end, while the process for distilling water is at the nonexcludable end. With regard to broadcast television, cable television is excludable, while free-to-the-air television is nonexcludable.

We have discussed how excludability depends on law and technology. Neither of these factors, however, is fixed. Like technology, the law can change with time, and

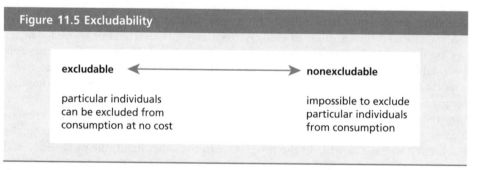

Figure 11.5 Excludability

excludable ⟷ nonexcludable

particular individuals can be excluded from consumption at no cost

impossible to exclude particular individuals from consumption

Consumption ranges from being excludable at one extreme to being nonexcludable at the other extreme.

so a public good may change from being excludable to nonexcludable or vice versa. Moreover, the scope of intellectual property differs among legal jurisdictions. For instance, discoveries that can be patented in one country may not get protection elsewhere. Accordingly, it is important to pay attention to differences in law and technology over time and place.

> **Progress Check 11E** Using the spectrum of figure 11.5, mark the following items: (1) mainframe computer services; (2) Ohm's Law, which relates electric voltage, current, and resistance; (3) a technique for a coronary bypass operation; and (4) a cardiac (heart) surgeon's services.
>
> *Progress check*

◂◂ 7 Summary

An externality arises when one party directly conveys a benefit or cost to others. A network externality arises when a benefit or cost directly conveyed to others depends on the total number of other users. An item is a public good if one person's increase in consumption does not reduce the quantity available to others. Equivalently, a public good provides nonrival consumption.

The benchmark for externalities and public goods is economic efficiency. At that point, all parties maximize their net benefits. Externalities can be resolved through merger or joint action, but resolution may be hampered by differences in information and free riding. Similarly, the commercial provision of a public good depends on being able to exclude free riders. Excludability depends on law and technology.

Markets with network externalities differ from conventional markets in several ways. Demand is insignificant until a critical mass of users is established. Expectations of potential users help to determine the attainment of critical mass.

Key Concepts

externality	network externality	rival
public good	critical mass	congestible
positive externality	installed base	excludable
negative externality	tipping	patent
externality is resolved	nonrival	copyright
free rider	private good	

Further Reading

A symposium in the *Journal of Economic Perspectives* (8, no. 2 [Spring 1994]: pp. 93–150) reviews network effects and externalities. Carl Shapiro and Hal R. Varian analyze business strategy in the new economy more generally in *Information Rules: A Strategic Guide to the Network Economy* (Boston, MA: Harvard Business School Press, 1999).

Review Questions

1. Give one example each of
    (a)   a negative externality;
    (b)   a positive externality.

2. When the sum of the marginal costs from a negative externality is greater than the marginal benefit to the source, an intermediary could collect fees from the recipients to pay the source to cut back on the externality. Please explain.

3. Which of the following actions will help to resolve the externalities generated by a new subway line?
    (a)   The subway system buys the property around the new stations.
    (b)   The owners of property near the new stations buy shares in the subway system.
    (c)   The subway system buys a competing bus company.

4. Luna City lies two miles off Interstate Highway 105. Several of the city's leading property owners have proposed to build an exit from the interstate to attract traffic into the city. Moonlight Properties, which owns several motels, has refused to contribute any money for the new exit.
    (a)   How will the new exit affect Moonlight's business?
    (b)   Use this example to explain the "free rider incentive."

5. Explain the externalities among fishers. In which of the following cases will it be more difficult to resolve the externalities (choose a or b)?
    (a)   trout in a small lake within an Indian tribal reservation;
    (b)   tuna in the Pacific Ocean.

6. Give an example of a network externality. Explain the concepts of a critical mass and tipping.

7. Explain why there are few, if any, network externalities/effects in consumers' choice of Web browsers.

8. Does the presence of network effects cause demand to be more or less price elastic?

9. Where are technical standards relatively more important? In markets with network effects or those without? Explain your answer.

10. Give an example of a public good. Explain how the use of the good is nonrival.

11. Which of the following are public goods? (i) CBS, a free-to-the-air network TV channel, and (ii) video-on-demand from a broadband service provider.

12. For a public good, why is the group marginal benefit the sum of the individual marginal benefits?

13. Which of the following services is excludable?
    (a)   cable television;
    (b)   free-to-the-air television;

(c)   wireless telephone service;

(d)   a page on the World Wide Web.

14. Explain the differences between patent and copyright.

15. Give examples of public goods that have been made excludable through
    (a)   copyright law.
    (b)   patent law.

Discussion Questions

1. A study of leasing practices among U.S. shopping malls reported that, on aver-
    age, department stores paid rent of $2.24 per square foot. After controlling
    for differences in sales per square foot among stores of different types, the study
    calculated that the average rent for a specialty store was $11.88 per square foot.
    (*Source*:   B. Peter Pashigian and Eric D. Gould, "Internalizing Externalities: the
    Pricing of Space in Shopping Malls," *Journal of Law and Economics*, vol. 41,
    no. 1 (April 1998), pp. 115–42.)
    (a)   Compare the development of a new department store along an open street
          with one in a shopping mall. In which case are the externalities more likely
          to be resolved?
    (b)   Explain why shopping malls charge department stores much lower rent than
          specialty retailers.

2. From an economic and technical standpoint, there is an optimal rate at which
    to extract oil from an oil field. In the mid-1990s, Mobil was producing 60,000
    barrels of oil per day (bpd), and Shell was producing 75,000 bpd from adjacent
    fields in California.
    (a)   What are the externalities between the production of the two oil companies?
    (b)   If the two companies negotiate an agreement, should they aim to increase
          or reduce production?
    (c)   Assess the likelihood that the externality would be resolved.

3. Most local telephone service providers publish Yellow Page telephone direc-
    tories. They distribute these directories free of charge to all telephone subscri-
    bers. As the Yellow Pages are an effective way of attracting customers, businesses
    are willing to pay for listings. The Yellow Pages provide local telephone com-
    panies with a lucrative source of revenue.
    (a)   How does one telephone subscriber's acquisition of telephone service
          affect other subscribers?
    (b)   How should a telephone company adjust the price of Yellow Page listings
          according to the circulation of the directory?
    (c)   Compare two telephone companies. Southern Telephone publishes Yellow
          Pages, while Northern Telephone does not. Which operator has a higher
          marginal revenue from telephone service?

(d) Assuming that Southern Telephone and Northern Telephone face the same marginal cost of providing telephone service, which will operate on a larger scale?

4. With populations growing, an increasing number of people are choosing to live in multifamily dwellings such as condominiums. Condominiums have rules that specify the rights and the obligations of the owners and residents.
   (a) By considering the demand and supply of land, explain why condominiums are becoming relatively more popular.
   (b) Give examples of negative externalities that condominium residents can generate for one another.
   (c) Should the law require the residents of a condominium to comply with the condominium rules?
   (d) Some residents in a condominium are annoyed by the barking of other residents' dogs. How could they jointly resolve this externality?

5. Radisson is an international chain of more than 400 hotels in over 50 countries. Many of the hotels are owned and operated by franchisees with contracts to use the Radisson business format. A franchisee might free ride by compromising on its own service, while depending on the overall Radisson brand to attract customers. To ensure a consistent standard throughout the chain, each Radisson District Director inspects at least one hotel a week.
   (a) Explain the negative externality among franchisees.
   (b) Why would a franchisee want Radisson to inspect other franchisees?
   (c) Will the free rider problem be more or less severe in a chain of hotels that are all in a single city as compared with an international chain?

6. With the growth of international trade and travel, more and more people are learning English. Major European companies have adopted English as a common language. English is also the standard language for communication among aircraft pilots and air-traffic controllers. France, however, has passed a law to restrict the use of English.
   (a) Compare the benefit of speaking a common language among (i) truckers, and (ii) pilots.
   (b) Does the growth of English generate a positive or negative externality for (i) people who are already fluent in English and (ii) people who do not speak English?
   (c) What are the prospects for French as an international language?

7. Kevin Kelly, Executive Editor of *Wired* Magazine, has written that network effects are pervasive: "the more plentiful things become, the more valuable they become . . . cotton shirts, bottles of vitamins, chain saws . . . will also obey the laws of plentitude" ("New rules for the new economy," *Wired*, September 1997).
   (a) If more people were to consume some brand of vitamins, how would your marginal benefit from that brand be affected?
   (b) Must the number of chain saw users exceed a critical mass before the demand becomes positive?
   (c) Are there network effects in the demand for vitamins, cotton shirts, and chain saws?

8. Plain text email can be sent and received from a multiplicity of email systems, including those based on the PC like Eudora and others provided through the World Wide Web like Hotmail and Yahoo mail. By contrast, the recipient of email attachments such as Microsoft Word and Lotus Notes files needs the corresponding applications software. This difficulty can be resolved by converting attachments into Adobe Acrobat's pdf (portable document format). Pdf files can be read with the Acrobat Reader, which Adobe distributes free through the Web.
   (a) Which demand exhibits stronger network effects? That for text email or that for Microsoft Word and Lotus Notes email attachments?
   (b) How does Adobe Acrobat's pdf affect the network effects in the demand for Microsoft Word and Lotus Notes software?
   (c) Adobe sells the Acrobat program to create pdf files while distributing the Acrobat Reader free through the Web. How does the installed base of Acrobat Readers affect the demand for the Acrobat document creation program?

9. Cheryl, who lives in London, and Zak, who lives in Brooklyn, agreed to meet in Manhattan one weekend. As Cheryl was leaving her apartment, she collected her camera bag. Her boyfriend remarked that they need not bring a camera since Zak surely would. Suppose that the cost of carrying a camera is 1/2 and that the benefit to each party, if there is at least one camera, is 1. Additional cameras do not increase anyone's benefit.
   (a) Using a suitable game in strategic form, analyze the situation between the two friends.
   (b) Identify the equilibrium or equilibria of the situation.
   (c) What should Cheryl do?
   (d) How would your answer to (c) change if, just before leaving London, Cheryl could leave a message for Zak to tell him whether she would bring a camera?

10. The United States and most other developed countries provide copyright protection for personal computer software such as Microsoft Word and Lotus Notes.
   (a) Compare the demand for software that can be copied and used by many persons in a local area network with the demand for software that cannot be copied and can be used only on a single machine.
   (b) By comparing the prices under the two scenarios in (a), explain why some publishers do not copy-protect or limit the multiple usage of their software.
   (c) The effectiveness of copyright protection varies among countries. From the standpoint of maximizing profits, should a software publisher charge a higher or lower price in a country where copyright protection is relatively weak?

11. This question applies the techniques presented in the math supplement. Let b represent marginal benefit and q the amount of Luna's investment in the new Main Street store. Suppose that the investment generates marginal benefits, $b = 15 - q$ for Luna, $b = 4 - 0.4q$ for the florist, and $b = 5 - 0.5q$ for the shoe store. Luna's marginal cost is 1.
   (a) Calculate the group marginal benefit from Luna's investment.
   (b) On a suitable diagram, draw the group marginal benefit and Luna's marginal cost.
   (c) Calculate the economically efficient quantity of investment.

Chapter 11

Math Supplement

Let us first show how to obtain the group marginal benefit curve from individual marginal benefit curves. Let b represent marginal benefit and q the amount of Luna's investment in the new Main Street store. Suppose that the investment generates marginal benefits, $b = 10 - q$ for Luna, $b = 4 - 0.4q$ for the florist, and $b = 1 - 0.2q$ for the shoe store.

We draw these marginal benefit curves in figure 11.1. Notice that Luna's marginal benefit is positive for q in the interval [0, 10], the florist's marginal benefit is positive for q in the interval [0, 10], while the shoe store's marginal benefit is positive for q in the interval [0, 5].

Over the interval [0, 5], the vertical sum of the individual marginal benefits is

$$b = (10 - q) + (4 - 0.4q) + (1 - 0.2q)$$
$$= 15 - 1.6q. \qquad (11.1)$$

Over the interval [5, 10], the vertical sum of the individual marginal benefits is

$$b = (10 - q) + (4 - 0.4q)$$
$$= 14 - 1.4q. \qquad (11.2)$$

Accordingly, the group marginal benefit is

$$b = 15 - 1.6q \qquad (11.3)$$

for q in the interval [0, 5], and

$$b = 14 - 1.4q \qquad (11.4)$$

for q in the interval [5, 10]. We draw this in figure 11.1.

Next, given the marginal cost of 1, let us calculate the economically efficient quantity. By figure 11.1, the group marginal benefit will cross the marginal cost with investment in the interval [5, 10]. In that interval, the group marginal benefit is

$$b = 14 - 1.4q. \qquad (11.5)$$

Equating this to the marginal cost of 1, we have

$$q = 13/1.4 = 9.29. \qquad (11.6)$$

Accordingly, the efficient amount of investment is $929,000.

Similarly, we can derive the group marginal cost as the vertical sum of the individual marginal cost curves and calculate the economically efficient investment. We do not elaborate, as the procedure is similar to that for marginal benefits.

Chapter *12*

Asymmetric Information

◄◄ 1 Introduction

With assets exceeding S\$5 billion and annual premium income of S\$1.2 billion, NTUC Income is one of Singapore's largest life and general insurers. By contract with the Singapore Government, NTUC Income underwrites the public officers group insurance scheme. This group scheme provides *optional* term life insurance for all civil servants. NTUC Income also offers term life insurance to the general public.

In May 2000, for a 43 year-old civil servant, the annual premium for a S\$200,000 term life policy through the public officers group insurance scheme was S\$240. The premium was identical for female and male participants. By contrast, for the same coverage through an individual policy, NTUC Income quoted premiums of S\$991 for a female and S\$1,849 for a male.

The public officers group insurance scheme sets a ceiling of S\$300,000 coverage for participants aged below 45, and S\$200,000 for those older than 45. NTUC Income has contractually agreed to accept any applicant for the scheme without medical examination.

NTUC Income's practices for individual policies are quite different. It offers individual term life policies for coverage of S\$1 million and above. However, it requires every applicant to undergo a medical examination.

Sellers of most goods and services do not limit the quantity that a customer may buy. Also, sellers of many goods and services offer quantity discounts – the more that a customer buys, the lower is the unit price. Business practices in life insurance are quite different: the public officers group insurance scheme limits the amount of insurance cover. Civil servants who seek higher coverage must buy an individual policy, which is much more expensive than the group scheme.

The basic reason for the puzzling discrepancies between group and individual insurance is **asymmetric information** between the insurer and the party seeking life insurance. In a situation

> In a situation of **asymmetric information**, one party has better information than another.

of asymmetric information, one party has better information than another. A person's likelihood of death depends on his or her health. She or he has better information about her own health than NTUC Income. Accordingly, there is asymmetric information between NTUC Income and the applicant for life insurance.

Many other markets are characterized by asymmetric information. In credit markets, borrowers have better information about their ability to repay than lenders. In labor markets, workers have better information about their productivity than potential employers.

Recall from chapter 5 that a condition for perfect competition is that buyers and sellers have equal information. Hence, a market where information is asymmetric cannot be perfectly competitive. The better-informed party will take advantage of its superior information, and the allocation of resources will not be economically efficient.

This chapter focuses on business practices that resolve asymmetric information. We use asymmetric information to explain the systematic difference in premium between group and individual insurance policies. Essentially, individual insurance policies tend to attract applicants with relatively worse health or who are relatively more pessimistic about their life expectancy. One reason is that insurers provide larger coverage through individual than group policies.

Insurers like NTUC Income require applicants for individual policies to undergo a medical examination. This is one way to resolve the asymmetric information between the insurer and applicant for insurance. Generally, the medical examination illustrates the use of appraisal to resolve asymmetric information.

Appraisal does not always resolve asymmetric information completely. Accordingly, we also discuss three indirect methods of resolving asymmetric information – screening, signaling, and contingent contracts. These play a major role in credit, labor, and other markets characterized by asymmetric information.

◀◀ 2 Imperfect Information

> **Imperfect information** is the absence of certain knowledge.

Before analyzing situations of asymmetric information, we should understand the concept of **imperfect information**. To have *imperfect information* about something means not having certain knowledge about that thing. Most people have imperfect information about future events such as next Monday's Standard & Poor's 500 Index, the severity of the coming winter, and the next year's growth in employment. It is also possible to have imperfect information about things in the present or past. For instance, do you know precisely the height above sea level of Mount Kilimanjaro or the distance between Berlin and Kansas City?

Imperfect vis-à-vis Asymmetric Information

A single person can have imperfect information. By contrast, asymmetric information involves two or more parties, one of whom has better information than the other or others. Asymmetric information will always be associated with imperfect information, because the party with poorer information definitely will have imperfect information. For instance, if the seller of an antique knows whether the item is genuine or fake but a potential buyer does not, then the buyer has imperfect information. The item could be a genuine antique or a fake, but the buyer does not know which for sure.

Although the concepts of asymmetric and imperfect information are related, it is important to remember the difference between the two. The reason is that a market can be perfectly competitive even when buyers and sellers have imperfect information, so long as they all have the same (imperfect) information. In a perfectly competitive market, the forces of demand and supply will channel resources into economically efficient uses; hence, no further profitable transactions are possible.

For instance, the current demand for heating oil depends on expectations about temperatures in the coming winter. Buyers and sellers have equal access to meteorological forecasts. Based on these forecasts, each buyer determines its demand for heating oil. In a market equilibrium, the quantity demanded equals the quantity supplied and the marginal benefit equals the marginal cost. Hence, any further sales would be unprofitable.

By contrast, a market where information is asymmetric cannot be perfectly competitive. This means that, if buyers and sellers can resolve the information asymmetries, they can increase their benefits by more than their costs.

Risk Defined

When information is imperfect, there is risk. To understand the meaning of *risk*, let us consider the following example. Hilda knows, with probability 1.5%, that someone will steal her $20,000 car within the next 12 months. If that were to happen, Hilda would lose $20,000. If Hilda's car is not stolen, however, Hilda would lose nothing. The probability that her car will not be stolen is $100 - 1.5 = 98.5\%$.

Hilda has imperfect information about her future losses, because she does not know for sure whether her car will be stolen. Hilda bears a **risk**: either she will lose $20,000 with probability of 1.5% or she will lose nothing with probability of 98.5%. **Risk** is uncertainty about benefits or costs and arises whenever there is imperfect information about something that affects benefits or costs.

> **Risk** is uncertainty about benefits or costs.

If Hilda knew for sure that her car would not be stolen within the next 12 months, then she would not bear any risk. Similarly, if she knew for sure that her car would be stolen, she would also not bear any risk. It is because her information is imperfect that she faces risk.

To explain the distinction between risk and imperfect information, consider Max, who is unrelated to Hilda. Max also has imperfect information about whether Hilda's car will be stolen. But the fate of Hilda's car does not affect Max's benefits or costs. Hence, Max does not bear any risk with regard to Hilda's car.

Risk Aversion

A **risk averse** person prefers a certain amount to risky amounts with the same expected value.

How a person responds to situations involving risk depends on the extent to which he or she is **risk averse**. A person is *risk averse* if she or he prefers a certain amount to risky amounts with the same expected value. A person is **risk neutral** if she or he is indifferent between a certain amount and risky amounts with the same expected value.

A **risk neutral** person is indifferent between a certain amount and risky amounts with the same expected value.

Given Hilda's possible losses and the probabilities, her expected loss is ($20,000 × 0.015) + ($0 × 0.985) = $300. If Hilda is risk averse, she will prefer to lose $300 for certain than to lose $20,000 with probability of 1.5%, or lose nothing with probability of 98.5%. If Hilda is risk neutral, she will be indifferent between losing $300 for certain and the risk of losing $20,000 with probability of 1.5%, or losing nothing with probability of 98.5%.

Insurance is the business of taking certain payments in exchange for eliminating risk.

Risk-averse persons will pay to avoid risk. **Insurance** is the business of taking certain payments in exchange for eliminating risk. Suppose that an insurer offers Hilda an insurance policy that pays her $20,000 if her car is stolen but pays nothing if her car is not stolen. If Hilda has the policy and her car is stolen, she loses the car but receives $20,000, so on balance, she gains and loses nothing. If her car is not stolen, the insurer will not pay her anything, so she gains and loses nothing. Thus, the insurance policy eliminates the risk that Hilda must otherwise bear. Recall that, without insurance, Hilda's expected loss is $300. Hence, if she is risk averse, she would pay at least $300 for the insurance policy.

How much risk-averse persons are willing to pay for insurance depends on their degree of risk aversion in that situation. A more risk-averse person will be willing to pay a larger amount to avoid risk. By contrast, a risk-neutral person will not pay anything to avoid risk. For instance, suppose that Lucas faces the same situation as Hilda. If Lucas is risk neutral, he would pay no more than $300 for the insurance policy.

It is important to understand the meaning of risk and risk aversion because, whenever information is asymmetric, the less-informed party has imperfect information. To the extent that this means uncertainty about benefits or costs, the less-informed party faces risk.

Progress check

Progress Check 12A Suppose that Hilda buys the insurance policy that pays her $20,000 if her car is stolen but pays nothing if her car is not stolen. Who of the following has imperfect information and who faces risk: (1) Hilda; (2) the insurer?

◂◂ 3 Adverse Selection

The cost of producing a fake antique can often be very low compared to the value of the genuine article. If fakes are sufficiently convincing, they present a serious problem for the legitimate market. Under such circumstances, potential buyers will be concerned whether they are getting a fake or the genuine article. By contrast, sellers will be much better informed about the true provenance of what they are selling. In these circumstances, information is asymmetric.

Let us use the antiques example to understand the implications of asymmetric information. Specifically, we will consider the nature of market equilibrium and the effect of price changes on the quantity demanded and supplied.

Market Equilibrium

Initially, suppose that sellers offer only genuine antiques. The stock of antiques is fixed (or almost fixed, since a small number are always being discovered). The supply for sale at any one time, however, is more elastic: it depends on existing owners' willingness to sell. In figure 12.1, we show the supply and the demand for genuine antiques.

Figure 12.1 Market with adverse selection

The supply and demand for genuine antiques is in equilibrium at point *b*, with a price of $500 per unit and a quantity of 3,000 units. The combined supply of genuine antiques and fakes begins with 1,000 fakes at no cost, then jumps up and runs parallel to the supply of genuine antiques. The actual demand, which reflects the probability of getting a fake, is the demand curve for genuine antiques shifted down by the proportion 1/Q. The actual demand and the combined supply cross at point *a*, where the price is $300 per unit and quantity is 2,000 units a month.

In equilibrium at point *b*, the price would be $500 per unit and 3,000 units of antiques would be sold each month.

Now suppose that forgers produce a quantity of 1,000 fakes at no marginal cost. In principle, there could be two markets: one for fakes and another for genuine antiques. Suppose, however, that potential buyers cannot distinguish genuine antiques from fakes. Then, there will be only one market. In that single market, fakes trade alongside genuine antiques, so the supply of genuine antiques and fakes is combined.

Graphically, in figure 12.1, since forgers produce 1,000 fakes at no marginal cost, the combined supply of genuine antiques and fakes begins with 1,000 fakes at no cost, and then, at that quantity, the supply curve jumps up and runs parallel to the supply of genuine antiques.[1]

What about the demand side of the market? Each individual buyer has a marginal benefit curve for genuine antiques. Buyers, however, know that they might get fakes. Suppose that all buyers derive no marginal benefit from a fake. So, taking into account the probability of getting a fake, the actual marginal benefit is lower than the marginal benefit from a genuine antique.

Suppose that all buyers are risk neutral and that they purchase a total of Q thousand pieces, of which 1,000 are fake. Then each buyer has a probability $1/Q$ of getting a fake and a probability $(Q-1)/Q$ of getting a genuine antique. Since all buyers are risk neutral, each buyer's actual marginal benefit is only $(Q-1)/Q$ of the marginal benefit for genuine antiques. So, a buyer's actual marginal benefit curve, which reflects the probability of getting a fake, is his or her marginal benefit curve for genuine antiques, shifted down by the proportion $1/Q$ at every quantity.

Accordingly, the actual demand for antiques, which reflects the probability of getting a fake, is the demand curve for genuine antiques shifted down by the proportion $1/Q$. Equivalently, at every possible quantity, the buyers' actual willingness to pay is only a fraction $(Q-1)/Q$ of their willingness to pay for the same of quantity of antiques that are definitely genuine.

Having laid out the demand and the supply, we can study the equilibrium. The actual demand and the combined supply cross at point *a*, where the price is $300 per unit and the quantity is $Q = 2,000$ units a month. Hence, the probability that a buyer gets a fake is $1,000/2,000 = 50\%$ and the probability of getting a genuine antique is 50%.

What if the quantity of fakes were different? If, for instance, there are 500 fakes, then the actual demand will be higher and the combined supply of genuine antiques and fakes will be further to the left. Then, the equilibrium will have a higher price. The equilibrium quantity, however, may be higher or lower: the demand is higher, but supply is further to the left.

By contrast, if the quantity of fakes is larger, then the actual demand will be lower and the combined supply will be further to the right. Hence, the market price will be lower. Again, sales may be higher or lower, depending on the balance between demand and supply.

▼

[1] This model is adapted from B. Peter Pashigian, *Price Theory and Applications* (New York: McGraw-Hill, 1995), pp. 520–6.

Let us consider the effect of a price reduction on the antiques market. The marginal cost curves of legitimate sellers slope upward. So, when the market price is lower, each of them supplies a smaller quantity. By contrast, a drop in the market price does not affect the quantity of fakes supplied. Hence, the drop in the market price increases the proportion of fakes, leaving buyers with an **adverse selection**.

> In an **adverse selection**, the party with relatively poor information draws a selection with relatively less attractive characteristics.

The problem of an *adverse selection* arises in situations of asymmetric information: the party with relatively poor information will draw a selection with relatively less attractive characteristics. In the antiques case, the buyers have less information and draw a mixture of fakes and genuine antiques, which is an adverse selection of items.

Progress Check 12B   Using figure 12.1, illustrate the market equilibrium with 500 fakes. Will the market price be higher or lower than when there are 1,000 fakes?

Progress check

Economic Inefficiency

How does the introduction of fakes affect buyer and seller surplus? Buyer surplus falls as some buyers receive fakes. On the other hand, buyer surplus rises to the extent that the market price falls. Buyer surplus may also increase if sales are higher. Accordingly, the effect on buyers is ambiguous. As for sellers, we must distinguish those who sell fakes from those who sell genuine antiques. Legitimate sellers definitely are worse off: they get a lower price and they sell fewer units (as genuine antiques get crowded out by lower-cost fakes). Sellers of fakes are the only group that are definitely better off from the entry of fakes into the antiques market.

Is the market equilibrium with fakes economically efficient? Each buyer purchases up to the point that its actual marginal benefit (adjusted for the probability of getting a fake) balances the market price. Similarly, each legitimate seller supplies up to the point that its marginal cost balances the market price. Since fakes provide no marginal benefit, in equilibrium, buyers who get fakes will have a marginal benefit less than the legitimate sellers' marginal cost. On the other hand, buyers who get genuine antiques will have a marginal benefit higher than the legitimate sellers' marginal cost. Accordingly, the equilibrium is not economically efficient.

Specifically, referring to figure 12.1, if sellers offered only genuine antiques, then in equilibrium, the price would be $500 per unit and 3,000 units would be sold. At this quantity, the marginal benefit and the marginal cost are both $500. When the supply includes 1,000 fakes, however, the price falls to $300 per unit and the equilibrium quantity drops to 2,000 units. The equilibrium quantity of genuine antiques is 2,000 − 1,000 = 1,000 units. The supply curve for genuine antiques shows that the marginal cost of the 1,000th unit is $300. The demand curve for genuine antiques shows that the marginal benefit of the 1,000th unit is $700. Hence, in equilibrium, the marginal benefit exceeds the marginal cost, so the quantity traded is not economically efficient.

If, somehow, another genuine antique could be sold, then there would be a buyer willing to pay almost $700 for that item and there would be a seller willing to provide it for a little above $300. Accordingly, there is potential gain of just under $400.

We can relate this analysis to chapter 11 on externalities. Sellers of fakes impose a negative externality on sellers of genuine antiques and buyers. From our study of externalities, we know that, unless it is resolved, there will be too much of a negative externality relative to the economically efficient level. This means that a profit can be made by resolving the externality, which in this case, means resolving the information asymmetry.

Market Failure

Before considering how to resolve an asymmetry of information, let us look at an extreme possibility in the antiques example. Suppose that there are F fakes. Referring to figure 12.2, the combined supply of genuine antiques and fakes has a kink at point c. Now suppose that the number of fakes is so large that the actual demand crosses the combined supply at some point d below the kink. In this case, there

Figure 12.2 Market failure

Supposing that the actual demand crosses the combined supply at point d, then the entire supply will be fakes. The actual demand curve must coincide with the horizontal axis, so the actual demand cannot cross the combined supply at point d. Generally, there cannot be an equilibrium with the actual demand curve crossing the combined supply above but close to the kink.

will be no supply of genuine antiques and the entire supply will be fakes. Then, a buyer's probability of getting a genuine antique is 0. This means that the actual marginal benefit and the actual demand curve must coincide with the horizontal axis. Thus, the initial supposition that the actual demand crosses the combined supply at some point d is not valid.

This discussion shows that there cannot be an equilibrium with the actual demand curve crossing the combined supply below the kink. Indeed, the same logic also shows that there cannot be an equilibrium with the actual demand curve crossing the combined supply above but close to the kink. If there cannot be an equilibrium, then buyers and sellers cannot trade. This means that the intrusion of fakes has caused the entire market to fail!

Let us view the market failure from another perspective. We will show that a change in price has very different effects in a perfectly competitive market as compared with a market subject to adverse selection. Suppose that, in a perfectly competitive market, the quantity supplied exceeds the quantity demanded. Then, a price reduction will reduce the quantity supplied and raise the quantity demanded. A sufficient reduction of the market price will restore equilibrium.

By contrast, suppose that the antiques and fakes market is out of equilibrium, with the quantity supplied greater than the quantity demanded. Consider a reduction in the price. This will cause some genuine sellers to withdraw, hence increasing the proportion of fakes. Thus, buyers will face a worse adverse selection and their willingness to pay and the demand curve will drop. Reducing the price cuts the demand as well as the quantity of supply, so it will not necessarily restore the equilibrium. In the extreme, if the price is sufficiently low, the actual demand curve will drop down to zero and there will be no sales at all. In this case, the fakes have destroyed the market completely.

Generally, the market equilibrium will belong to one of two classes. In one class, the number of fakes is sufficiently small that the actual demand will balance the upward sloping portion of the combined supply well above the kink at point c. Then, in an equilibrium, the supply consists of both fakes and genuine antiques. In the other class, so many fakes have flooded the market that the actual demand curve will drop down to zero and the market will fail.

Lending and Insurance

In the antiques market, sellers have better information about their own characteristics than buyers. In other markets, buyers have better information about their own characteristics than sellers. Consider the market for residential mortgages. One question is at the forefront of any lender's mind: if the value of the property falls below the amount of the outstanding principal, will the borrower default? To *default* means to stop paying the interest and principal.

When the property value is less than the outstanding principal, the borrower's equity in the property is negative. If he or she then defaults on the loan, the borrower is effectively selling the property to the lender for the outstanding principal. Some borrowers will not hesitate to default, while others will continue to make payments, even when they have negative equity.

To the extent that borrowers have better information about their personal willingness to default, there is asymmetric information between borrowers and lenders. Generally, a lender will have some chance of lending to a (bad) borrower who would readily default and some chance of lending to a (good) borrower who would be reluctant to default. If the lender raises the interest rate, it will draw an adverse selection of borrowers: the higher the interest rate, the fewer good borrowers will want loans and the higher will be the proportion of bad borrowers. This explains why a bank will not necessarily agree to lend more if a borrower offers a higher interest rate.

Insurance is another market where buyers have better information about their own characteristics than do sellers. Life insurance is insurance against the possibility of death. (It would be more accurate, but much less appealing, to call it *death insurance*.) The likelihood that a person will die within the next 12 months depends on her or his state of health and style of life. For instance, the probability of death is higher among people with heart trouble, those who engage in rock climbing and scuba diving, and those who have unprotected sex with many different partners.

Resolving adverse selection in insurance: public officers group insurance scheme

A person's likelihood of death depends on his or her health, as well as lifestyle, for instance, how frequently he or she exercises and whether he or she engages in risky sports. People differ in health and lifestyle. NTUC Income, like other life insurers, fears that its policies will attract an adverse selection of applicants.

The design of the public officers group insurance scheme aims to mitigate the problem of adverse selection. The ceiling on coverage limits NTUC Income's risk in the event of a policyholder's death. Further, a person who is relatively pessimistic about his or her life expectancy will seek larger coverage. Hence, the ceiling on the group scheme also serves to discourage people with poor health and unfavorable lifestyles.

To the extent that a group policy mitigates adverse selection, the expected claims will be lower. The mitigation of adverse selection and lower marketing and administrative costs explain the vast disparity in the premiums between the public officers group insurance scheme and NTUC Income's individual term life insurance policies.

The ceiling on coverage, however, tends to defeat the objective of insurance, which is to help a person to avoid risk. The ceiling limits the extent of insurance, and hence forces the person to bear risk above the ceiling. In designing the ceiling to the group scheme, NTUC Income must balance the avoidance of adverse selection against the loss of potential business from people who seek higher coverage.

It is difficult for an insurer to obtain all the relevant information about an applicant's state of health and style of life, however. Hence, there is asymmetric information between insurers and applicants for insurance.

The price that an insurer charges for an insurance policy is called a *premium*. Life insurers face an adverse selection problem: if an insurer charges a high premium, it is likely to draw applicants who know that they are in relatively poor health or who maintain risky lifestyles. Life insurers need some way to resolve the asymmetry of information.

Progress Check 12C Suppose that a life insurer presently has a high percentage of high-risk policyholders. If the insurer reduces its premiums, what will be the effect on the percentage of high-risk policyholders?

Progress check

⯇⯇ 4 Appraisal

Our discussion of fakes in the antiques market illustrates that, when information is asymmetric, the market outcome will not be economically efficient. Generally, if the information asymmetry can be resolved, then benefits will increase by more than costs and, hence, there is room to make a profit.

The most obvious way to overcome asymmetric information is to obtain the information directly. In the antiques market, a collector could engage an expert to appraise a potential purchase. Referring to figure 12.1, in the equilibrium at point *a*, the marginal benefit of a genuine antique is $700, while the market price is $300. For that marginal buyer, there is a potential gain of almost $400 by identifying a genuine antique. Provided that an appraisal costs less than the potential gain, then the buyer will purchase the appraisal.

This argument applies to all buyers for whom the marginal benefit of a genuine antique exceeds the market price by more than the cost of appraisal. To the extent that buyers obtain appraisals, there will be a separate market for genuine antiques. In that market, buyers and sellers will have equal information and, so, perfect competition will lead to economic efficiency. The buyers, however, must pay the cost of appraisals. (Recall from chapter 5 the distinction between paying and bearing a cost. Who bears the cost of appraisals depends on the elasticities of demand and supply.)

There are some buyers whose marginal benefit from a genuine antique is relatively low, however, so that the difference between their marginal benefit and the market price does not cover the cost of appraisal. These buyers will choose not to get appraisals; hence, they cannot distinguish genuine antiques from fakes. The information asymmetry means that they will suffer from an adverse selection.

For an information asymmetry to be resolved directly, the asymmetry must satisfy two conditions. First, the characteristic about which information is asymmetric must be objectively verifiable. If an expert cannot objectively distinguish genuine antiques from fakes, then appraisals will not resolve the information asymmetry between buyers and sellers. The verification must be objective: if different appraisers give different opinions, then buyers' and sellers' information will still be asymmetric.

The second condition is that the potential gain from resolving the asymmetric information must cover the cost of appraisal. The maximum potential gain is the difference between the marginal benefit and the marginal cost. Buyers, however, focus on the difference between the marginal benefit and the market price, which is a smaller difference. Sellers focus on the difference between the market price and their marginal cost. Generally, if the potential gain is too small, then the information asymmetry will not be resolved.

Progress check **Progress Check 12D** Will appraisals be more common in the market for cheap or more expensive antiques?

Procuring the Appraisal

In the antiques example, we supposed that the buyers procured expert appraisals to resolve the information asymmetry. Recall that the intrusion of fakes hurts sellers of genuine antiques. Hence, sellers of genuine antiques may pay for expert appraisals to distinguish themselves from sellers of fakes.

Indeed, it is more economical for sellers to procure the appraisals. The seller of an item can obtain one appraisal and present the results to many potential buyers. The appraisal is a public good: any number of potential buyers can use the same information. Hence, it is less costly for the seller to get an appraisal than for every potential buyer to procure an appraisal of the same item.

Under what circumstances should a seller rather than potential buyers obtain the appraisal? One factor is the number of potential buyers. If there is only one potential buyer, then the expenditure will be the same whether the seller or the buyer procures the appraisal. By contrast, if there are many potential buyers, then there will be a relatively greater saving if the seller procures the appraisal.

Another factor is the extent to which the various potential buyers seek the same information about the item. If different potential buyers have different considerations, then it may be difficult for the seller's appraisal to provide all the required information. In this case, each potential buyer might prefer to obtain an individual appraisal.

Appraising Borrowers

In the market for loans, borrowers have better information about their ability and willingness to repay than potential lenders. To guard against adverse selection, lenders can also appraise applicants for loans. One input into the appraisal is a credit check. This shows the applicant's outstanding debts and record in repaying loans and other forms of credit. A credit check provides information about a borrower's ability and willingness to repay. Many lenders will also check a loan applicant's employment record, which is another indicator of ability to repay.

Credit checks and employment reports can help borrowers with some history to resolve their asymmetry of information with lenders. What about borrowers such as new immigrants and graduating students who have little prior credit history or employment record? They may have no way to directly resolve the information asymmetry.

◂◂ 5 Screening

We have discussed how asymmetric information can be directly resolved through appraisal. Since appraisal is costly and not always feasible, however, it is important to consider indirect alternatives. Generally, asymmetric information can be resolved in three indirect ways. We discuss one in this section, and the others in later sections.

In a situation where one party has better information about its own characteristics, the less-informed party may be able to elicit another party's characteristics indirectly through **screening**. *Screening* is an initiative of a less-informed party to indirectly elicit the other party's characteristics. It exploits

> **Screening** is an initiative of a less-informed party to indirectly elicit the other party's characteristics.

Moody's: appraising debt

Private and public corporations, municipalities, sovereign governments, and international organizations raise funds through issuance of debt obligations such as commercial paper and bonds. These securities may be sold to numerous investors, dispersed all over the world. A major concern for investors is the possibility that the issuer will default. Issuers, however, have better information about their own financial condition and likelihood of default.

Issuers can address this asymmetry by obtaining an independent rating of their debt. Moody's Investors Service was founded in 1909 to rate railway bonds. At the request of an issuer, Moody's will rate a debt obligation on a scale ranging from the highest grade of Aaa through Aa, A, Baa, Ba, B, to the lowest grade of Caa. The issuer can then provide the rating to potential investors.

Empirical studies show that issuers with lower Moody's ratings have been systematically more likely to default. Over the period 1920–99, the average 10-year default rate was 4.85% among investment-grade (Baa and higher) issuers, and 25.31% among speculative-grade (Ba and lower) issuers.

Sources: "Rating the Rating Agencies," *Economist*, July 15, 1995, pp. 61–2; Moody's web page (http://www.moodys.com/) March 10, 1999.

How's your health?

Applicants for life insurance have better information about their health and lifestyles than potential insurers. Life insurers are aware of this information asymmetry and the associated problem of adverse selection. The Prudential Insurance Company, American's largest insurer, requires some applicants for life insurance to undergo a medical examination. The company will not provide insurance to applicants who refuse the examination.

Typically, life insurers require more stringent and comprehensive physicals for applicants who are older and seek larger policies. Both factors help guard against adverse selection. From the insurer's perspective, a medical examination helps to weed out applicants who are in relatively poor health.

The insurer's benefit from this weeding is greater for older applicants because there is greater variation in health among older than younger people. Further, the insurer's benefit from the physical is greater for larger policies.

The cost of the medical examination, however, does not vary with the applicant's age and policy amount. Accordingly, life insurers typically require more stringent and comprehensive physicals for applicants who are older and seek larger policies.

| In **self-selection**, parties with different characteristics choose different alternatives. |

the sensitivity of the better-informed party to some variable that the less-informed can control. The less-informed party must design choices around that variable to induce **self-selection**, meaning that parties with different characteristics choose different alternatives.

The ancient Jewish king Solomon provided the classic example of screening. Two women came before him, one holding a dead boy and the other a living boy. Each woman claimed the living boy to be her son. Solomon had to decide:

> [T]he king said, "Bring me a sword . . . Divide the living child in two, and give half to the one, and half to the other." Then the woman whose son was alive said to the king, because her heart yearned for her son, "Oh, my lord, give her the living child, and by no means slay it." But the other said, "It shall be neither mine nor yours; divide it." Then the king answered and said, "Give the living child to the first woman, and by no means slay it; she is the mother." (1 Kings 3.16–27 RSV)

In this famous case, Solomon was the less-informed party: he did not know which woman was truly the mother of the living boy. He did know, however, that the true mother would not allow her son to be killed, while the false mother might be indifferent. The two women were differentially sensitive to Solomon's proposal to divide the boy. The king exploited this differential to good effect. The true mother and the false mother quickly identified themselves.

"Points": screening home mortgage borrowers

In the United States, financial institutions making residential mortgage loans face borrowers with different horizons. Some borrowers plan to repay within a short time, while others intend to keep their loans for a longer period. The longer the period, the more profit the lender will earn from the loan.

Lenders, however, cannot directly distinguish borrowers with different horizons. They do so indirectly through an up-front charge called *points*. The charge is set as a percentage of the principal. So, for instance, the charge on a $100,000 loan that bears 1.5 points is $1,500.

Lenders typically offer borrowers a choice among loans with different interest rates and points. Loans with lower interest rates bear higher points. For instance, in March 1999, Countrywide Home Loans advertised 30-year fixed interest loans of less than $203,150 as follows: a rate of 6.75% with 1.0 point, and a rate of 7.00% with 0.25 point.

By offering these alternatives, Countrywide can screen among borrowers according to how long they plan to hold their loans. A borrower who plans to repay his or her loan within a short time horizon will prefer a loan with low points. Such a borrower would rather pay a higher interest rate for a relatively short period of time. By contrast, a borrower who plans to hold the loan for a long time will prefer a loan with a lower interest rate and higher points. The savings on interest will make up for the higher up-front charge in points.

The choice between high points or a high interest rate effects self-selection among the borrowers. Loans with high points and low interest rates draw longer-term borrowers, while those with lower points and higher interest rates attract borrowers with shorter horizons.

If, however, both women had been indifferent to cutting the boy, then Solomon's proposal would have failed to induce self-selection between the two women. Screening is possible only if the less-informed party can control some variable to which the better-informed parties are *differentially* sensitive. By contrast with direct appraisal, screening elicits the characteristics of the better-informed party indirectly. Screening is an indirect way of resolving an information asymmetry.

Indirect Segment Discrimination

One of the key business applications of screening is to pricing policy. In chapter 9, "Pricing Policy," we gave the name *indirect segment discrimination* to pricing policies that apply screening to induce self-selection among buyers with different characteristics.

Generally, to effect indirect segment discrimination, the seller must identify some variable to which the segments are differentially sensitive and then structure a set of alternatives that will induce self-selection.

Airlines offer a choice between unrestricted and restricted fares to screen between business and leisure travelers. Business travelers cannot book far in advance and do not wish to stay away for the weekend. Airlines charge a higher price for fares that do not require advance booking or weekend overstay and a lower price for restricted fares. The unrestricted fares attract business travelers, while the restricted fares draw leisure travelers.

Similarly, consumer products manufacturers also engage in indirect segment discrimination. They use cents-off coupons to screen between customers with higher and lower price elasticity of demand. The customers with more elastic demand are more likely to use the coupons and hence get a lower price. The customers with inelastic demand are less likely to use the coupons and hence pay a higher price.

Cable television providers also engage in indirect segment discrimination. They apply bundling to screen between customers with different preferences. Bundled channels attract viewers with relatively middle-of-the-road preferences, while separate channels draw viewers with more extreme tastes.

Differentiating Variable

In some instances, the less-informed party may have the choice of several differentiating variables. Ideally, the less-informed party should structure the choice that drives the biggest possible wedge between the better-informed parties with the different characteristics.

The less-informed party must consider the effectiveness of each differentiating variable in driving a wedge between the various segments. This means comparing the differential sensitivity of the segments to each variable. The less-informed party should place relatively more emphasis on the more effective variable.

For instance, airlines could use clothing as a differentiating variable, offering a lower fare to travelers wearing casual clothing and a higher fare to travelers in business attire. Business travelers could easily circumvent this differentiating variable; hence, it is not effective. By contrast, airlines have found advance booking and weekend stayover to be effective differentiating variables.

The most effective screening may involve a combination of the differentiating variables. For instance, airlines use a combination of restrictions, advance booking and weekend stayover, and a separation between first class and coach to screen leisure from business travelers.

Multiple Unobservable Characteristics

In some cases, the information asymmetry between two parties concerns not just one but several characteristics. Then, if the less-informed party screens on a single differentiating variable, the resulting choices may not resolve the asymmetry.

Consider the following example. Comprehensive automobile insurance covers loss or damage to a car arising from all causes, including fire and theft. The likelihood of loss or damage depends on the driver's behavior. It is lower for a careful driver who parks in secure, well-lighted places and uses a steering lock and car alarm. By contrast, the likelihood of loss or damage is higher for less careful drivers.

The demand for comprehensive insurance arises from risk-averse drivers: they would rather pay a fixed premium than face the risk of loss or damage. The insurer, however, cannot directly observe either the driver's carefulness or degree of risk aversion.

Many automobile insurers offer comprehensive insurance with a choice of several deductibles, where the insurer compensates loss or damage only in excess of the specified deductible. Insurers charge relatively higher premiums for policies with lower deductibles.

The choice of deductible can screen drivers by their carefulness. Careful drivers will select cheaper policies that carry higher deductibles. Less careful drivers will prefer expensive policies with low deductibles. The choice of deductibles, however, also screens drivers by their degree of risk aversion. Less risk-averse drivers will prefer cheaper policies with high deductibles, while more risk-averse drivers will prefer policies with lower deductibles.

The choice of deductibles screens two characteristics: carefulness and risk aversion. A single variable, the deductible, cannot resolve the asymmetry of information over two characteristics. For instance, the insurer will not know whether those choosing the high-deductible policies are more careful drivers or less risk averse.

Screening not permitted: the right to remain silent

Criminal trials provide a clear example of asymmetric information. The defendant knows much more about his or her past conduct than does the prosecuting lawyer, the judge, or the jury. In American and English criminal courts, every person who takes the witness stand may be examined by the lawyers for the prosecution as well as the defense. If a defendant were to testify, then she or he might be subject to cross-examination by the prosecution. So, a defendant with something to hide would rather not take the witness stand.

This suggests a very obvious screening mechanism: every defendant should be permitted to choose whether to take the witness stand, but the court can draw a negative inference about one who elects not to testify. This policy should induce self-selection among defendants according to whether they are concealing evidence of their own guilt.

American and English criminal law, however, allows every defendant the right to remain silent but prohibit the court from inferring anything from the defendant's decision. This right nullifies what would otherwise be a very effective screening procedure.

Generally, to resolve information asymmetries through screening, the less-informed party needs as many differentiating variables as there are characteristics that it cannot observe.

Progress check

Progress Check 12E Collateral is property that a borrower provides to a lender as a security for a loan. If the borrower defaults on the loan, the lender can seize the collateral. Explain how a lender can use requirements for collateral to screen among borrowers with different willingness to repay.

◂◂ 6 Auctions[2]

We have discussed how businesses can apply screening to discriminate among buyers who are willing to pay different prices. Let us now discuss auctions, a pricing technique that screens by exploiting strategic interaction among potential buyers.

Consider the following example. Venus Paper wants to sell a tract of forest. There are many potential buyers and Venus wants to get the highest possible price. In this case, it does not seem feasible to apply indirect segment discrimination: what set of choices would induce self-selection? One feasible approach is to negotiate with all the possible buyers on an individual basis. Individual negotiation, however, would take a lot of time. An alternative is for Venus to conduct an auction.

An auction applies competitive pressure to the participating bidders. Each bidder must act strategically since its best bid depends on the competing bids: If the other bids are low, then a bidder can win with a relatively low bid, while, if the other bids are high, then a bidder must bid relatively high to win. Each bidder faces a fundamental trade-off. By bidding more aggressively, it will improve its chances of winning the auction. On the other hand, if it bids more aggressively, it will get a smaller profit from winning the auction.

The differentiating variable in an auction is the probability of winning. A bidder with a higher value for the item will gain relatively more from winning the auction and hence will pay relatively more for a higher probability of winning. Thus, the auction induces self-selection among the participants according to their respective values for the item.

Auction Methods

The **reserve price** is the price below which the seller will not sell the item.

There are various methods of conducting an auction. The bidding could be open or sealed. The seller may or may not specify a **reserve price**, below which it refuses to sell the

---

[2] This section is more advanced. It may be omitted without loss of continuity.

item. In an auction for multiple items, each winning bidder could be required to pay the price that she or he bid or the price bid by the marginal winning bidder.

How the method of auction affects bidding depends on various factors, including the extent to which bidders share the same value for the item on sale, the bidders' uncertainty about the true value, and bidders' risk aversion. Rather than investigate all of these factors in detail, we discuss some implications that apply generally.

Auction houses such as Christie's and Sotheby's use open auctions to sell jewelry, real estate, and works of art. The auctioneer calls out prices in an ascending sequence, and the bidders indicate whether or not they wish to continue participating. By contrast, other auctions allow only sealed bids. One factor in the choice between open and sealed-bid auctions is the potential for collusion among the bidders. As we discussed in chapter 8, competing buyers can increase their net benefit by colluding to depress the price. This principle applies to auctions as well: competing bidders can benefit by agreeing on a low price.

The bidders in an open auction can see each other's behavior. This means that colluding bidders can observe whether they are each abiding by their collusive agreement. If one bidder cheats by bidding above the agreed price, another bidder can raise the price and prevent the cheater from winning the auction. By contrast, in a sealed-bid auction, a bidder can easily cheat on the collusive agreement with a bid exceeding the agreed price. The other bidders will learn about the cheating only when the seller announces the result of the auction. At that time, it would be too late to rein in the cheater.

Another difference between open and sealed-bid auctions concerns the character of information revealed during bidding in an open auction. We consider this difference later in this section.

We have discussed how open auctions are more vulnerable to collusion among bidders than sealed-bid auctions. The seller in open auction, however, can counteract collusion by applying a reserve price. A bidder must exceed the reserve price to get the item. The major reason for a seller to set a reserve price is to defeat collusion among the bidders. A reserve price forces bidders to bid higher or face the prospect of not getting the item.

The downside of a reserve price is that all the bids may fall below the reserve price. In this case, the sale will fail and the seller gets no revenue. Accordingly, in setting a reserve price, the seller must balance the increased revenue from a sale against the probability of no sale. A factor in this trade-off is the number of bidders: when there are many bidders, it is more likely that at least one bidder will exceed the reserve price.

> In a **discriminatory auction**, each winning bidder pays the price that she or he bid.

In a **discriminatory auction**, each winning bidder pays the price that she or he bid. By contrast, in a **nondiscriminatory auction**, each winning bidder pays the price bid by the marginal winning bidder. Since a winning bidder at a nondiscriminatory auction pays the price of the marginal

> In a **nondiscriminatory auction**, each winning bidder pays the price bid by the marginal winning bidder.

winning bidder, a bidder at a nondiscriminatory auction should bid relatively higher than at a discriminatory auction.

This, however, does not necessarily imply that the seller will get higher revenue from a nondiscriminatory auction. Although bidders make relatively higher bids, the seller collects only the price bid by the marginal bidder for each item sold. Whether a seller gets a higher revenue from a discriminatory or nondiscriminatory auction depends on the balance between the two factors.

Winner's Curse

In addition to not knowing their competitors' strategies, the bidders participating in an auction may also be uncertain about the value of the item for sale. For instance, in the example of Venus Paper, the various bidders may be unsure about the quantity of wood pulp that the trees will yield. Let us see how this uncertainty can affect the outcome of bidding.

Suppose that Joy is one of four bidders at the auction and that her estimate of the yield is 4,000 tons of pulp a year, while the other bidders have lower estimates. Then, Joy will probably make the highest bid and win the auction. On the basis of the information of all four bidders, however, Joy probably has overestimated the true yield. It is even possible that Joy's estimate is so high that her bid exceeds the true yield, so that she will incur a loss on the deal.

> The **winner's curse** is that the winning bidder overestimates the true value of the item for sale.

Joy's example illustrates the **winner's curse**. The *winner's curse* arises in an auction where the various bidders are uncertain about some common element in the value of the item for sale. A bidder whose estimate of that common element is about right will probably not win the auction. On the other hand, a bidder whose estimate is too high has a higher probability of winning. Hence, on average, the winning bidder is one who has overestimated the true value of the item.

A bidder should take account of the possibility of the winner's curse by bidding more conservatively, that is, aiming for a larger margin between his or her estimate of the value of the item and his or her bid. By bidding conservatively, he or she can reduce the likelihood of overbidding for the item.

The winner's curse is more severe when the number of bidders is larger, when the true value of the item is more uncertain, and in a sealed-bid compared with an open auction. If there are 20 bidders, then the winner will probably be one whose estimate is higher than 19 other estimates. By contrast, if there are four bidders, then the winner's estimate is probably higher than three other estimates. An estimate that is higher than 19 others is more likely to exceed the true value than an estimate that is higher than three others.

If the true value of the item is more uncertain, then the probability that the highest estimate exceeds the true value will be higher. Consider, for instance, an ounce of gold. There is no uncertainty about the true value of an ounce of gold. Every bidder would know the value to be the prevailing market price, and hence all their estimates and bids would be the same. The winner's curse arises only when there is uncertainty about the true value of the item for sale. The greater the uncertainty about the true value, then the greater will be the extent of the winner's curse.

In an open auction, bidders with relatively low values for the item will drop out progressively as the price ascends. Since the record of bidding is open, the remaining bidders can see the prices at which the various bidders drop out. The price at which a bidder drops out reveals information about her or his estimate of the true value of the item. The remaining bidders can use this additional information to refine their estimate of the true value. Hence, open bidding mitigates the winner's curse.

We have discussed three factors that affect the extent of the winner's curse. Whenever the winner's curse is relatively more severe, a bidder should adjust by bidding more conservatively.

Progress Check 12F   Venus Paper has procured an independent appraisal of the tract that it is selling by auction.

Progress check

(a) Should it provide this information to the bidders?
(b) How will this affect the extent of the winner's curse?

Winner's curse: the Los Angeles Metro

Governments frequently use auctions to procure goods and services. The principles of an auction to buy are exactly the same as for an auction to sell. In an auction where the bidders are competing to supply an item and they are uncertain about some common cost element, the winner's curse is the prospect of bidding *less* than the true cost. The following example illustrates the winner's curse in a procurement auction.

In late 1987, the Southern California Rapid Transit District (RTD) called tenders to build an underground Los Angeles Metro station at the intersection of Seventh and Flower Streets. There were eight bids for this project, ranging from $37.8 to $58.1 million, with an average bid of $46.6 million.

The RTD awarded the contract to the Granite-Marmolejo joint venture, which bid $42.5 million. Four years later, on completing the project, Granite-Marmolejo filed a claim for an additional $27 million, which amounted to 64% of its original price. The contractor claimed that it had incurred the extra costs to deal with unforeseen difficulties that the RTD had not disclosed during the tender. These difficulties included unmarked utility lines, unstable soil, and underground obstacles.

Source: "Metro Rail 64% over Budget, Builder Says," *Los Angeles Times*, February 4, 1992, p. B1.

◄◄ 7 Signaling

In a situation where information is asymmetric, the marginal benefit does not equal the marginal cost; hence, a profit can be made by resolving the asymmetry. We have considered an indirect solution – screening, an initiative of the less-informed party to elicit the characteristics of the better-informed party.

> **Signaling** is an action by the better-informed party to communicate its characteristics in a credible way to the less-informed party.

Another indirect way of resolving an information asymmetry is through the initiative of the better-informed party. **Signaling** is an action by the better-informed party to communicate its characteristics in a credible way to the less-informed party.

To illustrate the concept of signaling, let us consider again a market where buyers of antiques cannot distinguish between genuine items and fakes. In this market, the unknown characteristic is the true nature of an item. With the intrusion of fakes, the market outcome is not economically efficient. Since sellers of genuine antiques clearly suffer from the fakes, they may take the initiative to resolve the asymmetry of information.

Suppose that an antiques dealer guarantees to buy back anything that it sells at the original sale price at any time. To assure potential customers that the offer is legitimate, the dealer posts a sufficiently large bond with a reputable bank. Can this buyback offer effectively signal that the dealer is indeed selling a genuine antique? Equivalently, is the buyback offer a credible signal?

The answer depends on whether the seller of a fake will also make such a buyback offer. Assuming that buyers of fakes eventually discover the truth, a dealer who sells fakes and makes the buyback offer would eventually have to buy back all the fakes that it has sold. Accordingly, sellers of fakes would prefer not to make buyback offers. The buyback offer makes sense only for sellers of genuine antiques. Thus, it credibly distinguishes sellers of genuine antiques from sellers of fakes.

By contrast with direct appraisal, signaling communicates the characteristics of the better-informed party indirectly. Signaling is an indirect way of resolving an information asymmetry. For instance, the antiques dealer does not directly declare its item to be genuine. Rather, the dealer makes a commitment that indirectly and credibly communicates that it is selling a genuine item. Because sellers of fakes would not make the same commitment, the buyback offer is a credible signal.

Credibility

To be credible, a signal must induce self-selection among the better-informed parties. Specifically, the cost of the signal must be sufficiently lower for parties with superior characteristics than for parties with inferior characteristics. Then, only those with superior characteristics will offer the signal. For instance, in the case of the antique dealers, if buyers of fakes eventually discover the truth, then the cost of the buyback offer is lower for sellers of genuine antiques than for sellers of fakes. This cost difference drives the self-selection among the various sellers.

Suppose that Mercury Antiques posts a sign "All genuine" outside its store. Will this be a credible signal? The answer depends on whether it is relatively more costly for the seller of a fake to post the sign. The cost of posting an "All genuine" sign is the same for sellers of genuine antiques and fakes. Hence, such a sign alone will not induce self-selection among sellers and cannot be a credible signal.

Advertising and Reputation

We have just claimed that an "All genuine" sign cannot be a credible signal that a seller is offering genuine antiques. Let us next consider a somewhat different proposal. Suppose that Mercury Antiques spends several thousand dollars to advertise that it deals only in genuine articles. If, however, Mercury pushes out fakes, then buyers will discover the subterfuge and the word will spread. If the word spreads quickly enough, Mercury will not recover the investment in its advertising. In this case, the advertising expenditure is an investment that pays off only if Mercury does indeed deliver genuine antiques.

A sunk investment that pays off only if the seller does indeed deliver good quality can be a credible signal. This signaling depends on three conditions. First, the investment must be sunk. If the advertising expenditure is reversible, then a seller of low quality can also make the same investment, pass out inferior products, and get its money back. A reversible investment would not be a credible signal.

Second, buyers must be able to detect poor quality fairly quickly. If a seller can fool buyers for a long time, then even one offering poor quality can afford the sunk investment. Many car owners purchase rust treatment: It is almost impossible for any individual driver to tell whether the treatment is effective. Automobile rust treatment is a product for which a sunk investment may not be a credible signal.

The third condition is that word of poor quality must spread and cut into the seller's future business. A one-time seller can afford to pass off poor quality because it will never face the punishment of losing repeat business. Fast-food restaurants along highways serve many customers on a one-time basis. If a restaurant provides poor quality, its customers may notice but they might never pass the same way again, so the restaurant does not lose.

Any investment that meets these three conditions can be a credible signal of good product quality. An "All genuine" sign may not be meaningful for a seller with a short time horizon. By contrast, a seller who has been in business for many years can build up a reputation. This is a sunk investment that would not make sense for a seller offering inferior quality.

Progress Check 12G Explain the difference between screening and signaling. *Progress check*

Branding: signaling service station quality

Service stations market a variety of products ranging from hot dogs to gasoline and repair service. The seller's reputation is a potentially credible signal of good product quality. But, it would be credible only to customers who are likely to come back. What about one-time customers?

The asymmetry of information can be resolved through branding. A brand attaches its reputation to many service stations, all over the country. Hence, if one station provides poor service, it affects the reputation of the entire brand, and customers will cut back their patronage of all the stations with the same brand. The owner of the brand will invest effort in monitoring the various stations to maintain quality, and so avert a brandwide drop in business.

Service stations along highways have a higher proportion of one-time relative to repeat customers. Hence, they have greater need for branding as a way to assure customers of product quality. An empirical study of service stations in eastern Massachusetts showed that stations along highways were 19% more likely to be affiliated with a major brand than stations off highways.

Source: I. P. L. Png and David Reitman, "Why are Some Products Branded and Others Not?" *Journal of Law and Economics* 38, no. 1 (April 1995), pp. 207–24.

Signaling privacy: BBBOnline

The Internet holds forth the promise of a borderless market. Californian connoisseurs buy South African wines and consumers all over the world buy Australian Merino sweaters through the Internet. With minimal investment, almost anyone, anywhere can engage in e-commerce. Many thousands of e-tailers seek to emulate the successes of Amazon, eBay, and Yahoo!

A major obstacle to business-to-consumer (B2C) e-commerce, however, is Internet consumers' concern about privacy. Online vendors amass considerable information about visitors and customers through registration forms, cookies, and other sources. The various pieces of information can be assembled to form comprehensive profiles of consumers who buy through the Internet.

How can a new e-commerce vendor credibly commit to its privacy policy and communicate it to potential consumers? One answer is BBBOnline. Better Business Bureaus are private nonprofit organizations supported largely by dues paid by business and professional members. They have had a long history of providing information on business and charities, and helping to resolve consumer disputes.

In 1999, riding on the reputation of the Bureaus, the Council of Better Business Bureaus established BBBOnline. To qualify for the BBBOnline Privacy Seal, a business must pass a comprehensive review of its privacy policy and procedures, and participate in BBBOnline's dispute resolution program. BBBOnline engaged Underwriters Laboratories to verify Web vendor compliance with the Privacy Seal guidelines.

Source: Web pages (http://www.bbbonline.org/), August 1, 2000.

◂◂ 8 Contingent Payments

We have discussed two ways of indirectly resolving an information asymmetry: screening and signaling. Let us now consider a third indirect approach, which is to use a **contingent payment**. A *contingent payment* is a payment made if a specific event occurs. Bets are contingent payments: you get a dollar from me if the coin turns up heads, while I will get a dollar from you if it turns up tails. In this bet, the specific event is the side of the coin that faces up after the toss.

> A contingent payment is a payment made if a specific event occurs.

All insurance policies make use of contingent payments. A life insurance policy makes a payment in the contingency of death, a health insurance policy makes payments in the contingency of illness, and a driver's liability policy makes a payment in the contingency of an automobile accident.

Let us consider how contingent payments can be used to signal information. Recall Venus Paper's auction of a tract of forest. Suppose that Venus knows that these trees will yield an exceptional quantity of wood pulp, say, 6,000 tons a year. It, however, has no independent appraisal or other information that would directly convince potential buyers.

What if Venus were to specify that it would sell the tract for a share of the pulp production rather than a straight cash payment? By asking for a share, Venus is taking a payment that is contingent on the yield from the tract. If the tract produces a high yield, then Venus will get a higher payment, while if it produces a low yield, then Venus's payment will be low.

Selling the tract for a share of the production is a way by which Venus can signal its information to potential buyers. Other things equal, sellers of average or relatively low-yielding trees would prefer to sell for straight cash. Hence, those selling relatively better trees can distinguish themselves by selling for a share of the production. Accordingly, the share induces self-selection among sellers offering products of different quality.

Contingent payments can be used to screen as well as signal. In the example of Venus's trees, the seller can retain a share of the production as a way of signaling its information. On the other hand, a potential buyer could take the initiative of offering the seller a choice between payment in a share of the production or straight cash. A seller who chooses straight cash is implicitly admitting that the production will be relatively low. A seller of relatively high-yielding trees is more likely to choose the payment with a share of production.

The market for legal services provides another example of how contingent payments can resolve asymmetries of information. Suppose that Heather was hurt in an automobile accident. She has consulted a lawyer about suing the other driver. The lawyer has advised Heather that she can get at least $100,000 in damages.

Realistically, an experienced lawyer will be better informed than Heather about the amount that she can expect to recover in a law suit. In the United States, lawyers

Buyback in international investment

Many developing countries want to boost their exports of manufactured products. With this aim, they actively promote the acquisition of production technology and equipment from foreign suppliers. The developing countries use these to produce manufactured items for export to the world market.

Compared with large multinational companies, however, developing countries suffer from an information asymmetry. They have relatively poor information about current technology and world market conditions. They worry that foreign suppliers are palming off old write-offs rather than providing the most cost-effective technology and equipment. They also worry that the foreign suppliers may exaggerate the market potential for the manufactured product.

One way to resolve the information asymmetry is to require the foreign supplier of production technology and equipment to buy back a specified quantity of future production of the manufactured item. The foreign suppliers' sales will depend on the quality of production technology and facilities that it had supplied to the developing country. The sales will also depend on the world market conditions.

Through the arrangement, the payment to the foreign supplier becomes contingent on the quality of production technology and equipment supplied and the supplier's estimate of world market conditions. The foreign supplier will then have a strong incentive to supply the most cost-effective technology and equipment and provide a realistic projection of the market potential for the manufactured product.

Source: Jean Francois Hennart, "The Transaction-Cost Rationale for Countertrade," *Journal of Law, Economics, and Organization* 5, no. 1 (Spring 1989), pp. 127–53.

may be paid a contingency fee, under which the lawyer receives a percentage of the amount recovered from the other side. A lawyer on a contingency fee who loses the case will receive nothing.

The contingency fee can help to resolve the asymmetry of information between client and lawyer about the expected recovery from a law suit. A lawyer on a contingency fee will not have an incentive to exaggerate the expected recovery.

◂◂ 9 Summary

In situations of asymmetric information, the allocation of resources will not be economically efficient. The asymmetry can be resolved directly through appraisal or indirectly through screening, signaling, or contingent payments. The indirect methods depend on inducing self-selection among parties with different characteristics.

Screening is an initiative of the party with less information, while signaling is an initiative of the party with better information.

A key business application of screening is indirect segment discrimination in pricing. A related application is auctions, which exploit strategic interaction among competing bidders to force bidders with higher values to pay higher prices.

When the distribution of information is asymmetric, one or more parties will have imperfect information and hence bear risk. The distribution of risk may conflict with the self-selection needed to resolve the asymmetric information.

Key Concepts

asymmetric information	insurance	discriminatory auction
imperfect information	adverse selection	nondiscriminatory auction
risk	screening	winner's curse
risk averse	self-selection	signaling
risk neutral	reserve price	contingent payment

Further Reading

For more on the economics of asymmetric information generally, see Michael L. Katz and Harvey Rosen, *Microeconomics* (Homewood, IL: Irwin McGraw-Hill, 1998), chapter 17, and Eric Rasmusen, *Games and Information* (Cambridge, MA: Basil Blackwell, 1994). Paul Milgrom and John Roberts apply the economics of asymmetric information to corporate finance in chapter 15 of *Economics, Organization, and Management* (Englewood Cliffs, NJ: Prentice-Hall, 1992).

Review Questions

1. Explain the difference between imperfect information and risk.

2. In the following situations, explain the asymmetry of information, if any.
   (a) Investors cannot perfectly predict the next day's Standard & Poor's 500 Index.
   (b) Acquirer is planning a takeover bid for Target at $50 a share, which is 25% above the current market price of $40. Directors of Acquirer are secretly buying shares of Target for their personal accounts.

3. True or false?
   (a) Where there is asymmetric information, there will be imperfect information.
   (b) Whenever people face risk, they will seek insurance.

4. Bohemian Clothing, a manufacturer of women's fashions, pays its production workers through a piece rate. The Human Resources manager has proposed to

offer workers the alternative of a fixed salary. Will this alternative draw an adverse selection of workers?

5. Toshi is about to buy a secondhand Nissan. The seller is offering a below-market price. The seller has assured Toshi that the car is in perfect mechanical condition. Explain why Toshi should get an expert to evaluate the car.

6. Give an example of screening. Explain
    (a) the asymmetry of information;
    (b) how screening works through self-selection.

7. An automobile insurance policy with a $2,000 deductible only covers loss in excess of $2,000. Typically, automobile insurers offer policies with a choice between higher deductibles and higher premiums. Explain how this choice can screen among drivers with different probability of accident.

8. During peak hours, the demand for road space exceeds the available capacity. Drivers differ in their value of time. From the standpoint of economic efficiency, the road space should be allocated to the drivers who value time most highly. Explain how a toll on road usage can screen among drivers with different value of time.

9. This question relies on the auctions section. Explain the impact of the following on collusion among bidders at an auction:
    (a) using open bidding vis-à-vis sealed bids;
    (b) setting a reserve price.

10. This question relies on the auctions section. In which of the following auctions for the rights to extract oil will the winner's curse be more serious?
    (a) The seller provides all available geological information to the bidders.
    (b) The seller has made a geological study but is keeping it secret.

11. Give an example of signaling. Explain
    (a) the asymmetry of information;
    (b) how signaling works.

12. Intuit, the publisher of Quicken, a financial management program, once offered full refunds to any dissatisfied purchaser. Is the refund policy a credible signal of product quality?

13. If a borrower defaults on a secured loan, the creditor can seize and sell the item against which the loan is secured. Explain why the interest rate on secured loans is lower than that on unsecured loans.

14. Early in the twentieth century, Chinese leader Sun Yat Sen proposed a reform of property taxation. Every landowner would be asked to report the value of his land. The tax authority would then be allowed to choose between accepting tax based on the reported value and buying the land at the reported value. Explain how this mechanism would persuade landowners to report their land value truthfully.

15. Acquirer is interested in making a takeover bid for Target. Acquirer, being unsure about Target's true value, decides to offer an exchange of shares rather pay cash for Target. Explain how the exchange of shares resolves asymmetric information between Acquirer and Target.

Discussion Questions

1. Pedro farms wheat. Each season, he sells his crop of 100,000 bushels to a general trading company.
   (a) Explain how the future price of wheat will affect Pedro's sales. For simplicity, suppose that the future price of wheat will be either $4 or $5 per bushel with equal probability.
   (b) Assuming that Pedro has imperfect information about the future price of wheat, what risk does he bear?
   (c) Pedro is averse to risk. The trading company has offered to buy Pedro's crop in advance at a fixed price of $4.45 per bushel. Explain how this will eliminate Pedro's risk.

2. Many countries have a consumers' association that assesses the quality and prices of consumer goods and services. Consumers pay for most of these assessments. Some countries also have institutions that test products according to specified standards. Testing institutions include the British Standards Institute, the TUV in Germany, and the Underwriters' Laboratory in the United States. Typically, manufacturers pay for their products to be tested.
   (a) Identify the consumers association and testing institution in your country.
   (b) Which are relatively more subjective: (i) product assessments by a consumer association or (ii) tests by a testing institution?
   (c) Based on your answer to (b), can you explain why consumers pay for most product assessments by consumer associations, while manufacturers pay for most tests by testing institutions?

3. Under California law, the owner of car must show proof of valid insurance to renew automobile registration. Drivers with poor records have difficulty securing insurance. Fortunately for them, Save-On Insurance Services of Los Angeles advertises "Lowest Rates, Low Monthly Payments, No One Refused."
   (a) What type of drivers will Save-On attract?
   (b) Compare the premiums for automobile insurance provided to all applicants ("No One Refused") with that for a select group such as government employees.
   (c) Is Save-On offering a good or bad deal?

4. Medical insurance covers the cost of the treatment and prescriptions necessary for the insured party to recover from an illness or accident. Some medical insurance policies also cover medical expenses associated with pregnancy.
   (a) Explain the asymmetry of information between the insurer and insured party.
   (b) Why do some insurers require a minimum deductible no matter how much an applicant is willing to pay?
   (c) Unlike falling sick or meeting with accidents, in many cases, women voluntarily enter into pregnancy. If a medical insurer covers pregnancy, will it encounter an adverse selection?
   (d) Suppose that an insurer decides to cover pregnancy. Should it offer pregnancy coverage as an option or as part of the basic coverage?

5. Consider a final examination where students must choose between Exam E (Easy) and Exam D (Difficult) without seeing either in advance. Exam E is straightforward and the average student may expect to answer it correctly. Exam D is trickier: Only those who have understood the relevant topics very well will be able to answer it correctly. Average students can expect lower marks on Exam D than Exam E. However, to earn a final course grade of A– or higher, a student must answer Exam D successfully.
   (a) Explain what information the instructor is hoping to learn from the student's choice between E and D.
   (b) How might strong differences in students' degree of risk aversion affect the result of this choice?
   (c) Will the screening work if students are allowed to look at E and D *before* making their choice?

6. This question relies on the auctions section. Suppose that the government is selling the rights to mine silver from a tract of federal land by sealed-bid auction. Luna Mining's geologists estimated that the tract would yield 2.2 million ounces of silver. Luna, however, has learned that a competitor's estimate of the recoverable silver is 2.5 million ounces.
   (a) Explain the winner's curse in the context of this example.
   (b) How should Luna adjust its estimate of the recoverable silver in light of the competitor's estimate?
   (c) If the government switches to an open auction, should Luna bid more or less aggressively?

7. American automobile manufacturers are very keen to persuade consumers that their cars are of high quality. Explain which of the following actions by a manufacturer will credibly signal the superior quality of its car.
   (a) Requiring all employees to buy the car.
   (b) Offering a longer product warranty.
   (c) TV commercials showing a typical American family endorsing the car.

8. A major obstacle to business-to-consumer (B2C) e-commerce is Internet consumers' concern about privacy. BBBOnline's Privacy Seal, TRUSTe, and other services have arisen to certify Web vendors' compliance with privacy guidelines. BBBOnline was established by the Council of Better Business Bureaus, while TRUSTe was founded by CommerceNet, the Electronic Frontier Foundation, and the Boston Consulting Group.
   (a) Would a certification service started by some college students be as effective as BBBOnline's Privacy Seal and TRUSTe?
   (b) TRUSTe systematically "seeds" participating Web sites with user information to monitor whether the data are collected and used in conformance with stated privacy policies. Why does TRUSTe do this?
   (c) Some major e-commerce vendors, including Amazon and Yahoo!, do not carry any third-party privacy seal. Explain why they have less need for external certification.

9. Automobile repair is a service that most consumers purchase relatively infrequently. It is also difficult for a consumer to assess the quality of a repair: did the car break down because of a poor repair or because it was in bad shape anyway?

(a) Explain the asymmetry of information between buyers and sellers of automobile repair service.

(b) How can sellers resolve this asymmetry through reputation and branding?

(c) Explain how buyers can resolve this asymmetry by getting an independent opinion.

(d) Will the unresolved divergence between the buyer's marginal benefit and the seller's marginal cost be larger or smaller for major as compared with minor repairs?

10. Established after World War II, the Long-Term Credit Bank of Japan (LTCB) helped to finance Japan's industrial miracle. LTCB, however, strayed from its original mission into real estate lending. When the Japanese real estate market collapsed, many of LTCB's loans turned sour. In June 1998, with its share price at ¥50, down more than 90% in nine months, LTCB arranged a merger with Sumitomo Trust and Banking. Announcing the deal, LTCB President, Matsunobu Ohnogi, declared, "We are not insolvent." Sumitomo President, Atsushi Takahashi, however, was not convinced, "If [LTCB] is insolvent, then we will get public money."

(a) Explain the asymmetry of information between the managements of LTCB and Sumitomo.

(b) Sumitomo did not proceed with the rescue, and the Japanese Government had to take over LTCB. In late 1999, American investor group Ripplewood Holdings bought LTCB. The government promised to buy back LTCB's outstanding loans at book value if their value fell by more than 20%. Explain how this guarantee could resolve asymmetric information between the Japanese Government and Ripplewood.

(c) Compare the Japanese Government's buy-back promise with an alternative scheme under which Ripplewood paid for LTCB in shares rather than cash.

11. This question applies the technique for deriving a market equilibrium with adverse selection presented in the math supplement. Suppose that the demand for genuine antiques is $D = 4 - p$ and the supply is $S = p - 2$, where D and S are in thousands of units a month and p represents price in hundreds of dollars. In addition, some sellers produce 500 fakes at no marginal cost.

(a) In a market of purely genuine antiques, what will be (i) the buyers' marginal benefit from a quantity Q, (ii) the sellers' marginal cost of providing a quantity Q, and (iii) the market equilibrium price and quantity.

(b) In a market including both genuine antiques and fakes, what will be (i) the buyers' marginal benefit from a quantity Q, (ii) the sellers' marginal cost of providing a quantity Q, and (iii) the market equilibrium price and quantity.

Chapter 12

Math Supplement

In an early section of the chapter, we presented a market equilibrium with adverse selection. Let us now derive the equilibrium precisely using algebra. Suppose that the demand for genuine antiques is

$$D = 8 - p \qquad (12.1)$$

and the supply is

$$S = p - 2, \qquad (12.2)$$

where D and S are in thousands of units a month and p represents price in hundreds of dollars.

Since the demand for genuine antiques is $D = 8 - p$, the buyers' marginal benefit from a quantity Q of genuine antiques is $(8 - Q)$. Since the supply of genuine antiques is $S = p - 2$, the sellers' marginal cost of providing a quantity Q of genuine antiques is $(2 + Q)$.

In a market of purely genuine antiques, the market equilibrium will be at the price where $D = S$; that is,

$$8 - p = p - 2, \qquad (12.3)$$

or $p = 5$. At this price, $D = S = 3$.

Now, suppose that some sellers produce 1,000 fakes at no marginal cost. The market equilibrium includes both genuine antiques and fakes. Suppose that the equilibrium quantity is Q (in thousands of units a month). Then, a buyer's probability of getting a genuine antique is

$$(Q - 1)/Q. \qquad (12.4)$$

We have shown the buyers' marginal benefit from a quantity Q of genuine antiques is $(8 - Q)$. Hence, with the fakes, the buyers' actual marginal benefit is

$$(Q - 1)/Q \times (8 - Q). \qquad (12.5)$$

On the other side, the market supply consists of 1,000 fakes plus the genuine supply. Referring to figure 12.1, for any quantity Q, the marginal cost of the genuine and fake antiques is $2 + (Q - 1)$.

At the market equilibrium, the buyers' actual marginal benefit equals the sellers' marginal cost, which in turn is the market price:

$$(Q - 1)/Q \times (8 - Q) = 2 + (Q - 1), \qquad (12.6)$$

or

$$2Q^2 - 8Q + 8 = 0, \qquad (12.7)$$

which implies that $Q = 2$. By (12.5), the buyers' actual marginal benefit, and the market price, is $1/2 \times 6 = 3$.

Thus, the market equilibrium with both genuine antiques and fakes is at a price of $300 per unit and quantity of 2,000 units a month.

Previously, we also showed that the antiques market will fail if the quantity of fakes is too large. We can illustrate this with the mathematical model. Suppose that, in the preceding scenario, there are 2,000 rather than 1,000 fakes. Then, the buyers' actual marginal benefit will be

$$(Q - 2)/Q \times (8 - Q). \qquad (12.8)$$

The sellers' marginal cost will become $2 + (Q - 2) = Q$.

In equilibrium, the buyers' actual marginal benefit equals the sellers' marginal cost:

$$(Q - 2)/Q \times (8 - Q) = Q, \qquad (12.9)$$

or

$$2Q^2 - 10Q + 16 = 0. \qquad (12.10)$$

This equation has no real roots, which implies that there is no equilibrium. In intuitive terms, the market has failed.

Chapter 13

Incentives and Organization

◂ 1 Introduction

Until 1970, Boeing and other American manufacturers dominated the world market for large commercial aircraft.[1] Then, the governments of France and Germany established Airbus. Today, Airbus and Boeing are the world's two leading commercial aircraft manufacturers. They, however, had very different organizational architectures. Boeing was an integrated manufacturing company that is publicly traded on the New York Stock Exchange. By contrast, Airbus was a sales, marketing, and customer-support organization, established under French law as a tax-free "groupement d'interêt economique."

At the time of writing, Airbus was owned by Aerospatiale–Matra (37.9%), British Aerospace (20%), Construcciones Aeronauticas (CASA) (4.2%) and Daimler Aerospace (DASA) (37.9%). The four partners performed dual roles as shareholders of Airbus and industrial contractors, carrying out most of the design and all aircraft manufacturing.

Most major decisions required unanimous approval of the shareholders. Owing to its shareholders' dual role, Airbus was obliged to distribute production work among the partners according to political as well as economic considerations.

For instance, when final assembly of the new A-318 was assigned to DASA's Hamburg plant, Aerospatiale demanded a share of DASA's work on the older A-319 model. Consequently, A-319 production was split between DASA in Hamburg and Aerospatiale in Toulouse. Another symptom of Airbus's peculiar organization is that it operates a dedicated fleet of huge transport aircraft to shuttle aircraft fuselage sections among the various production facilities.

---

[1] This discussion is based on "European Aerospace: Airbusiness as Usual," *Economist*, June 19, 1999, p. 73; "BAe Expects Value of its 20% Holding in Airbus to Double," *Asian Wall Street Journal*, October 27, 1999, p. 23; "Airbus Rolls the Dice, Prepares to Make Bold Moves", seattletimes.com, August 8, 1999; and Airbus web pages (http://www.airbus.com/about_overview.html).

The governments of Britain, France, Germany, and Spain recognized the difficulties with Airbus's organizational structure. They pressed for Airbus to be converted into a limited company that integrated design and production with sales, marketing, and customer support. Airbus Chief Executive, Noel Forgeard, was hopeful about the benefits of injecting a private-sector culture. They included estimated annual savings of 350 million Euros through elimination of duplicative management, streamlining of production, and reduction of inventories. For instance, the various Airbus partners could save a substantial sum by consolidating their purchases of aluminum alloy.

Some, however, resisted the organizational change. Former Aerospatiale Chairman, Yves Michot, dismissed corporatization as merely a "legal" issue and preferred Airbus to continue as an "industrial project." The corporatization of Airbus was also hampered by disagreement among the partners on the values of their respective assets that would be pooled into the new company.

The architecture of an organization comprises the distribution of ownership, incentive schemes, and monitoring systems.[2] The Airbus example demonstrates the tremendous importance of **organizational architecture**: management estimated that corporatization could reduce costs by 350 million Euros, which was significant for an entity with 17.8 billion Euros annual revenues.

> **Organizational architecture** comprises the distribution of ownership, incentive schemes, and monitoring systems.

This chapter presents a framework for analyzing organizational architecture. An efficient organizational architecture resolves four internal issues – holdup, moral hazard, monopoly power, and economies of scale. A holdup is an action to exploit the dependence of another party. For instance, when Aerospatiale demanded a share of A-318 production, it exploited Airbus's dependence on it for supply of cockpits and forward fuselage sections.

Moral hazard arises when one party's actions affect but are not observed by another party, and the two parties have different interests. Airbus's production partners sold their services at fixed transfer prices. Each production partner had more incentive to economize on its own work, where it would enjoy the whole gain, than on the product of Airbus as a whole, from which it derived only a part of the gain.

As the management of Airbus well knows, changes in organizational architecture can help to resolve moral hazard and the potential for holdup. These changes can also influence costs through their impact on internal monopoly power and the realization of economies of scale and scope. The framework of analysis presented in this chapter can also be applied to address the important managerial issue of vertical integration and how to manage the related question of whether to "make or buy."

---

[2] Brickley, Smith, and Zimmerman (1997) coined the term "organizational architecture". This chapter draws heavily from chapters 9 and 10 of their book and chapters 5–7, 9, and 16 of Paul Milgrom and John Roberts's *Economics, Organization, and Management* (Englewood Cliffs, NJ: Prentice Hall, 1992).

◂ 2 Moral Hazard

Suppose that Luna Supermarket acquires a fleet of trucks and hires personnel to estab-lish a delivery department. Mary is a delivery person in the afternoon shift. By the very nature of her job, a delivery person operates independently. Hence, it is difficult for Luna to monitor Mary's work. She alone decides how fast to drive and where to park; she alone determines how quickly to move goods from her truck into a customer's home.

Another feature of Mary's job is that she and her employer may disagree over how hard she should work. Luna wants her to exert the maximum effort and deliver the goods as quickly as possible. For instance, this may mean carrying goods up a stair-case rather than waiting for an elevator. Mary, however, prefers to take the day at a more leisurely pace.

> **Moral hazard** exists when one party's actions affect but are not observed by another party with whom it has a conflict of interest.

In this example, Mary is subject to **moral hazard**. A party is subject to moral hazard if its actions affect but are not observed by another party with whom it has a conflict of inter-est. Mary's actions certainly affect Luna Supermarket. Luna, however, does not monitor her throughout the day. There is a conflict of interest between Mary and her employer over her level of effort since she prefers less effort while her employer prefers her to exert more.

Sales representatives provide another example of moral hazard. They must work independently. It is difficult enough for an employer to monitor a salesperson's hours, for instance, whether he or she began sales calls at 8:00 a.m. or 9:00 a.m. It is even more difficult to monitor how much effort a salesperson puts into his or her work. Further, there is a conflict of interest between the salesperson and the employer: the salesperson bears the entire cost of effort, but the profit from additional sales accrues to the employer.

Moral hazard also arises in large publicly listed corporations. A large publicly-listed company may have many diverse shareholders ranging from pension funds with million-dollar holdings to individuals with several hundred shares. Few shareholders consider it worthwhile to monitor the managers of the company. Further, there may also be a conflict of interest between shareholders and management. While share-holders are primarily concerned about the value of their shares, senior managers may have other objectives such as building a large corporate empire or hobnobbing with fashionable artists.

Asymmetric Information about Actions

If Mary's employer could freely monitor her at all times, then it could direct her to use staircases rather than wait for elevators, take shortcuts rather than the easier but slower route, and the like. Then Mary would not be subject to moral hazard. As this discussion shows, moral hazard arises because information is asymmetric. The employer depends on the worker's effort but cannot observe it.

In chapter 12, we discussed asymmetric information in situations such as buying and selling antiques where the buyer is uncertain about the true provenance of an item, an application for life insurance where the applicant has better information about his or her health, and an application for a loan where the borrower has better information about his or her ability and willingness to repay. In all of these cases, the asymmetry of information concerned some individual characteristic of the better-informed party.

By contrast, in the example of Luna Supermarket, the delivery person has better information about her future actions. In this case, the asymmetry of information concerns some future action of the better-informed party. This information asymmetry is a necessary condition for there to be moral hazard.

Economic Inefficiency

Let us analyze the Luna Supermarket example to understand the effect of moral hazard on the relevant parties. The degree of effort that a delivery person exerts at work affects the employer's revenues and costs and, hence, profit. Let us separate the wages and other incentives that the employer pays to the worker from the employer's other costs. We call the employer's revenue less the other costs, the employer's benefit. Then the employer's profit is its benefit less the wages and other incentives paid to the worker.

For the worker, her net benefit is these wages and incentives less the cost of her effort. Considering the worker and the employer as a group, the group's net benefit from the worker's effort is the employer's benefit less the worker's cost of effort.

If a delivery person increases her effort, the resulting change in the employer's profit is its marginal benefit from the worker's effort. The additional cost required to increase effort is the worker's marginal cost of effort. In figure 13.1, we draw the employer's marginal benefit from the delivery person's effort and the worker's marginal cost of effort.

From the perspective of maximizing the group's net benefit, the worker should put in the amount of effort that balances the employer's marginal benefit with the worker's marginal cost. By the definition in chapter 6, this also characterizes the economically efficient level of effort. Referring to figure 13.1, the employer's marginal benefit equals the worker's marginal cost at an effort of 120 units. There, the employer's marginal benefit is 60 cents per unit of effort, which equals the worker's marginal cost of 60 cents per unit of effort.

Recall, however, that the worker acts independently. Hence, the worker does not consider the employer's marginal benefit but rather her personal marginal benefit from effort. Her personal marginal benefit depends on the structure of her wages and other incentives. In figure 13.1, we also draw the worker's personal marginal benefit from effort. The worker chooses the level of effort that balances her personal marginal benefit with her marginal cost. This is the level of effort that will actually be realized.

Referring to figure 13.1, the worker's marginal benefit equals her marginal cost at an effort of 100 units. At that level, the worker's marginal benefit and marginal cost are

Figure 13.1 Economically efficient effort

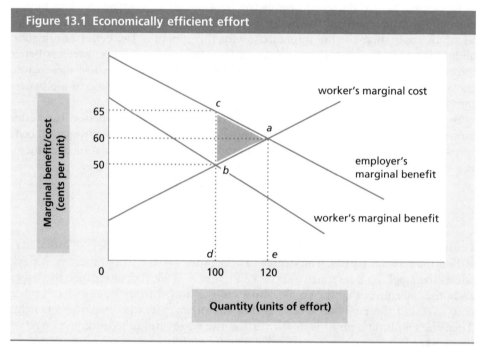

The economically efficient level of effort, 120 units, balances the employer's marginal benefit with the worker's marginal cost. Mary, the worker, chooses 100 units of effort, which balances her personal marginal benefit with her marginal cost. The lower is the worker's marginal benefit relative to the employer's marginal benefit, the lower will be the effort that the worker chooses relative to the economically efficient level.

both equal to 50 cents. At 100 units of effort by the worker, however, the employer's marginal benefit is 65 cents. This exceeds the worker's marginal cost of 50 cents.

Generally, a party that is subject to moral hazard will choose to act according to its own marginal benefit and marginal cost. As a result, its behavior will diverge from the economically efficient choice.

Suppose that the worker could be induced to increase her effort to 120 units. Then the additional benefit to the employer would be the area *cdea* under the employer's marginal benefit curve, between 100 and 120 units of effort. The additional cost to the worker would be the area *bdea* under the worker's marginal cost curve, between 100 and 120 units of effort. Hence, the additional benefit to the employer would exceed the additional cost to the worker by the shaded area *acb*. This represents the amount of profit that can be earned by resolving the worker's moral hazard. The challenge then is how to resolve the moral hazard.

Degree of Moral Hazard

Suppose that there were no conflict of interest between Mary and Luna Supermarket. This means that the worker's marginal benefit from effort would coincide exactly with the employer's marginal benefit from effort. Then, the worker would choose the economically efficient level of effort. Under these conditions, there will be no moral hazard.

Referring to figure 13.1, the lower the worker's marginal benefit relative to the employer's marginal benefit, the lower will be the effort that the worker chooses relative to the economically efficient level.

This example suggests that we can measure the degree of moral hazard by the difference between the economically efficient action and the action chosen by the party subject to moral hazard. The larger this difference, the greater will be the degree of moral hazard and the gain in net benefit that can be realized by resolving the moral hazard.

Progress Check 13A Suppose that the worker's marginal cost of effort in figure 13.1 were higher. Draw the new marginal cost curve. How does this affect (1) the economically efficient level of effort and (2) the effort that the worker actually chooses?

Progress check

Moral hazard at the top

American Express, listed on the New York Stock Exchange, is a global provider of travel and financial services. In December 1992, following pressure from major shareholders, the company announced that its long-time chairman and chief executive James Robinson would step down. Within a day of the announcement, the price of the company's common shares jumped 6%, increasing the market value of American Express by $667 million.

Under Robinson, American Express had expanded into credit cards by launching the Optima card and into investment banking through the acquisition of Shearson Lehman Brothers. Robinson's successor, Harvey Golub, chose a strategy that Wall Street much preferred. He spun off the investment bank and refocused the company on its travel-related and charge card businesses.

Sources: Corporate Governance and Pension Plans, Wharton impact conference, University of Pennsylvania (May 5, 1995); World Wide Web page, www.kiplinger.com/magazine/jul96/dow10k2.html (October 30, 1996).

Moral hazard in medicine: what did the doctor order?

Patients rely on doctors for advice and, often, get treatment from the doctor providing the advice. Consequently, the doctor is subject to moral hazard. The more treatment a doctor recommends, the more he or she will earn.

Obstetricians are doctors who specialize in treating pregnant women and delivering babies. Babies can be delivered either naturally through the vagina or by cesarean section. Obstetricians earn higher fees from cesarean sections. In 1989, the average charge for a cesarean section was $2,053, or 28% more than that for a vaginal delivery. Obstetricians also prefer cesarean sections because these can be scheduled in advance and may take less time than vaginal deliveries.

The demand for obstetric services depends crucially on the rate at which women become pregnant. Between 1970 and 1982, the U.S. fertility rate fell by 13.5% from 1.84 to 1.59 per hundred population. This decline in fertility would have substantially cut obstetricians' incomes. By a happy coincidence, however, the proportion of deliveries by cesarean section increased by 240% over the same period.

The increase in cesarean sections was not such a coincidence. Obstetricians exploited their informational advantage and substituted cesarean sections for vaginal deliveries. In this way, they could maintain their incomes even as fertility declined.

Source: Jonathan Gruber and Maria Owings, "Physician Financial Incentives and Cesarean Section Delivery," *RAND Journal of Economics* 27, no. 1 (1996), pp. 99–123.

◄◄ 3 Incentives

We have identified the potential gains from resolving moral hazard. Generally, there are two complementary approaches to resolve moral hazard. One is to invest in monitoring, surveillance, and other methods of collecting information about the behavior of the party subject to moral hazard. The other approach is to align the incentives of the party subject to moral hazard with those of the less-informed party.

Monitoring systems and incentive schemes are two elements of organizational architecture. They are complementary because all incentives must be based on behavior that can be observed, so the better is the available information, the wider will be the choice of incentive schemes. Ideally, the relevant parties would like to completely resolve the moral hazard, so that the better-informed party will make the economically efficient choice. Let us now discuss how to resolve the moral hazard of a worker relative to her employer.

Monitoring

The simplest monitoring system focuses on objective measures of performance. Most employers require workers to punch a card to record the time at which they arrive and depart work. The time clock is a basic and almost universal monitoring system. In the case of a delivery person, another simple monitoring system is a vehicle log, in which the worker records every point of collection and delivery. The employer can compare the log with the mileage on the truck's meter.

Hours on the job, however, is distinct from effort. A worker can arrive at 8:00 a.m. and leave at 5:00 p.m., but do nothing during that time. Accordingly, employers need monitoring systems that provide more than basic objective information.

One method that employers frequently use to collect information is to hire supervisors. It is not cost effective for supervisors to monitor workers all the time, however. Hence, supervisors should make only random checks. In chapter 10, we

Monitoring truck drivers: onboard computers

Truck drivers must operate independently and may travel far from base. Some trucks are equipped with onboard computers. There are two types of onboard computers – trip recorders and electronic vehicle-management systems (EVMSs). A trip recorder provides an electronic record of speed, idle time, and other data. An EVMS includes the functions of a trip recorder and, in addition, provides real-time information about the vehicle location and a communications system to allow the dispatcher to direct the driver.

The management of a trucking business can use trip recorders and EVMSs to monitor its drivers. A study of the U.S. trucking industry found significant differences in the adoption of onboard computers between owner- and employee-operated trucks, and between trucks driven over short as compared with long distances.

Only 7% of owner-operated trucks were equipped with onboard computers, as compared with 19% of employee-operated trucks. An owner-operator would not need to monitor himself, hence derives less benefit from an onboard computer.

Only 6% of trucks that operated at fewer than 50 miles from base were equipped with an onboard computer. By contrast, 19% of trucks operated at distances of 100–200 miles had onboard computers. Truckers who operate at greater distance will be more difficult to monitor through personal supervision. Hence, management derives a greater benefit from installing an onboard computer to monitor such drivers.

Source: Thomas N. Hubbard, "The Demand for Monitoring Technologies: the Case of Trucking," Working Paper, University of Chicago, 1999.

discussed the advantages of randomization. The same principle applies to supervision: the supervisor should check workers at random, rather than according to some regular pattern.

Employers can also enlist customers to monitor worker performance. Customers have a natural advantage in monitoring workers, such as delivery persons and sales representatives, who spend more time with customers rather than at the employer's location. Employers can encourage customers to report worker performance and then follow up by investigating reports of especially poor or good performance.

Performance Pay

The counterpart to monitoring systems is incentive schemes. Incentive schemes resolve the moral hazard by tying payments to some measure of performance. The schemes depend on a link between the unobservable action and some observable measure of performance. Generally, the scope of incentive schemes depends on what indicators of the unobservable action are available.

An employer can use the information provided by monitoring systems to structure incentives for its workers. For instance, in the case of Luna Supermarket, the employer cannot observe Mary's effort. But it can monitor the number of deliveries. Then it could base incentives on the number of deliveries.

> **Performance pay** is an incentive scheme that bases pay on some measure of performance.

One common incentive scheme is **performance pay**, which bases a worker's pay on some measure of performance. Let us consider performance pay in the example of the Luna Supermarket. Suppose first that Luna pays Mary a fixed daily wage of $50 and that Luna does not monitor Mary at all, not even using a time clock or vehicle log. Then, Mary cannot affect her earnings in any way, whether she starts early or late and whether she works quickly or slowly. Her personal marginal benefit from effort will be zero. In figure 13.2, the worker's personal marginal benefit with a fixed daily wage is the horizontal axis. This is lower than the worker's marginal cost at all levels of effort. Hence, with a fixed daily wage, the worker chooses no effort.

Now, suppose that Luna pays Mary $2 for each delivery that she makes. This is an example of payment based on performance. The more deliveries that Mary makes, the more she will earn. With this incentive scheme, her personal marginal benefit from effort will be positive. The height and slope of the personal marginal benefit curve depend on how the worker's effort affects the number of deliveries.

In figure 13.2, we also show the worker's personal marginal benefit with a commission of $2 per delivery. This crosses her marginal cost at an effort of 80 units. With a commission of $2 per delivery, the worker chooses effort of 80 units. Accordingly, the commission helps to resolve the worker's moral hazard.

An incentive scheme is relatively "stronger" if it provides a higher personal marginal benefit for effort. Suppose that the employer strengthens the incentive scheme by raising the commission to $3 per delivery. Then the worker's personal marginal benefit

Figure 13.2 Performance pay

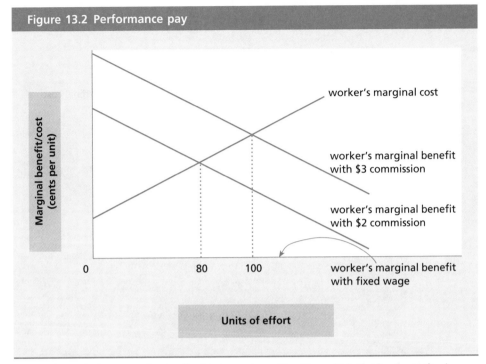

With a fixed daily wage, the worker's personal marginal benefit is the horizontal axis. A commission of $3 leads the worker to choose more effort than a $2 commission.

curve would be higher, and it would cross the marginal cost curve at a higher level of effort, say, at 100 units of effort. This shows that, the stronger is the incentive scheme, the higher will be the worker's effort.

> **Progress Check 13B** Using figure 13.2, draw a personal marginal benefit curve such that the worker would choose the economically efficient level of effort.
>
> *Progress check*

Performance Quota

If Luna paid a large enough commission, Mary's personal marginal benefit would be sufficiently high that she would choose the economically efficient 120 units of effort. This, however, may mean paying a large sum of money in commissions.

Let us explore another way to induce a worker to choose the economically efficient level of effort. Suppose that Luna establishes the following incentive scheme for Mary:

Figure 13.3 Performance quota

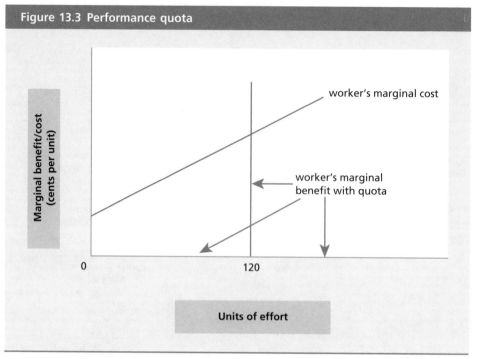

With a quota of 20 deliveries a day, the worker's personal marginal benefit curve has three parts, and the worker chooses 120 units of effort.

> A **performance quota** is a minimum standard of performance, below which penalties apply.

Luna will pay a fixed daily wage provided that Mary performs a specified quota of deliveries each day; otherwise, she will be dismissed. A **performance quota** is a minimum standard of performance, below which a worker is subject to penalties. The penalties could include deferral of promotion, reduction in pay, or even dismissal.

To apply a performance quota, Luna Supermarket must identify the number of deliveries that would result if Mary chose the economically efficient 120 units of effort. Suppose that 120 units of effort would generate 20 deliveries a day. Then the employer should set the performance quota at 20 deliveries a day. In figure 13.3, we show the worker's personal marginal benefit curve with a quota of 20 deliveries a day.

The worker's personal marginal benefit curve has three parts. Recall that the employer pays the worker a fixed daily wage provided that he or she meets the quota; otherwise that worker will be dismissed. At 119 units of effort and below, the worker will be dismissed. Additional effort does not affect her earnings; hence, her personal marginal benefit is zero.

The incentive scheme pays the worker no extra for additional effort above 120 units. Accordingly, at 121 units of effort and above, the worker's personal marginal benefit also is zero. The personal marginal benefit, however, is very high at exactly 120 units of effort. An increase in effort from 119 to 120 units is just enough to satisfy the quota and hence allows worker to get the daily wage and retain her job.

Thus, the worker's personal marginal benefit curve follows the horizontal axis from 0 to 119 units of effort, spikes up at 120 units, and then follows the horizontal axis again at 121 units of effort and above. Therefore, the personal marginal benefit curve crosses the marginal cost at 120 units of effort. Accordingly, the worker chooses 120 units of effort.

A performance quota is a cost-effective way of inducing the worker to choose the economically efficient level of effort. It is cost-effective because it does not reward effort below or above the economically efficient level. It focuses the incentive at the economically efficient level of effort.

Progress Check 13C Suppose that 100 units of effort would generate 18 deliveries a day. Using figure 13.3, illustrate the worker's marginal benefit if the employer specifies a quota of 18 deliveries a day.

Progress check

Smog check: "Don't pass, don't pay"

To reduce lead emissions, the state of California requires all new automobiles to be equipped with catalytic converters and to use unleaded gasoline. Where leaded gasoline is cheaper than unleaded, many drivers are tempted to fuel their cars with leaded gasoline. To deter such switching, the state government requires each car to undergo a smog check every two years.

The California Bureau of Automotive Repair licenses service stations to conduct the smog checks. It also conducts random roadside inspections of cars. The bureau's records show that 5% of all cars failed the biennial smog check. By contrast, 25% of cars checked in the roadside inspections had defective emissions control equipment.

Who was responsible for this disparity? The obvious suspects were the mechanics and service stations that performed the smog checks. They have an incentive to pass their customers. Some stations even go so far as to advertise "Smog Check: Don't Pass, Don't Pay."

Source: "Smog Checks to Get in Gear with Air Act," *Los Angeles Times*, February 28, 1991, pp. A3 and A31.

Stanford University Hospital: paying doctors more to do less

Patients rely on doctors for advice and treatment. For various reasons, doctors may have an incentive to prescribe excessive tests, treatment, and drugs. To the extent that a patient's medical costs are covered by insurance or a managed health care plan, he or she will not be sensitive to the cost of excessive care. After all, a third party pays the bills.

Large third-party payers including the federal government, managed health care plans, and medical insurers have reacted to the doctors' moral hazard. The federal Medicare program for elderly patients instituted a fixed price for each case, regardless of actual treatment costs. Likewise, many providers of managed health care are pressing doctors and hospitals to accept a fixed fee per patient.

Stanford University Hospital has been caught between major customers who want to cut costs and doctors who prescribe premium care. For instance, HealthNet, a major provider of medical benefits, warned Stanford that it might withdraw its business unless the hospital could reduce its costs.

Stanford responded to these pressures by merging the medical faculty with the hospital to form Stanford Health Services. The new organization ties the doctor's pay more closely to the hospital's profit. University administrators believe that this tie will give doctors a stronger incentive to consider the cost of tests, treatment, and drugs to the hospital and so find ways to reduce the cost of medical care.

For instance, through careful re-examination of its procedures, the Department of Cardiothoracic Surgery was able to cut the price of heart transplants by over 20%. Other doctors are researching standard patterns of treatment to cut the cost of treating common illnesses such as asthma.

Source: George Anders, "Prescription for Change: Stanford Hospital Confronts the Cost-Conscious '90s," *Stanford Magazine* 23, no. 1 (March 1995), pp. 36–41.

◄◄ 4 Risk

Incentive schemes resolve moral hazard by tying payments to some observable indicator of the unobservable action. But, what if the indicator is affected by factors other than the unobservable action? Then, the payments will depend on these other factors. A party who is subject to moral hazard and has imperfect information about these factors will face risk.[3]

---

[3] The reader may wish to refer to the section on imperfect information in chapter 12.

For instance, in the example of Luna Supermarket, the supermarket may base Mary's incentives on the number of deliveries a day. The number of deliveries, however, may also depend on other factors such as customers' orders, traffic congestion, and the weather. An incentive scheme based on the number of deliveries will impose a risk on Mary. Specifically, it is possible that, even when she puts in a great deal of effort, her deliveries will be hindered by traffic congestion or bad weather.

Risk arises whenever incentives are based on an indicator that depends on extraneous factors and the party subject to the moral hazard has imperfect information about those factors. The incentive scheme that maximizes net benefit, that is, the economically efficient scheme, must balance the incentive for effort with the cost of risk.

Costs of Risk

The cost imposed by risk depends on three factors. The first is the structure of the incentive scheme. Generally, as we showed in the preceding section, a stronger incentive scheme would induce the worker to increase her effort. A stronger incentive scheme, however, would impose a heavier burden of risk on the party subject to moral hazard.

For example, in figure 13.2, if the commission per delivery were raised from $2 to $3, the worker would increase the effort from 80 to 100 units. With the larger commission, however, a bigger part of worker's income will depend on the number of deliveries. This means that the worker will bear more risk.

The second factor that affects the risk-bearing cost is the degree of risk aversion in the party subject to moral hazard. If the party is risk neutral, then the risk imposes no cost. Risk imposes a cost only if the party is risk averse. The more risk averse that the party is, then the larger will be the cost imposed by risk.

The third factor is the influence of the uncertain factors on the indicator that forms the basis for the incentive scheme. The strength of this influence depends on the way in which the indicator depends on these factors and the extent to which these factors can vary. For instance, if the indicator were sensitive to these factors and the factors were subject to wide swings, then the risk would be relatively large. By contrast, if the indicator were insensitive to these factors or the factors would not vary much, then the risk would be relatively smaller.

Generally, the incentive scheme should be stronger if the party subject to moral hazard is relatively less risk averse and the extraneous factors are weaker. Conversely, the incentives should be weaker if the risk aversion is higher and extraneous factors have a stronger influence.

Progress Check 13D Alan and Mary are delivery persons for Luna Supermarket. Alan is more risk averse than Mary. Whose incentive scheme should be stronger? *Progress check*

Comprehensive auto insurance: balancing moral hazard and risk

Comprehensive automobile insurance covers loss or damage to a car arising from all causes, including fire and theft. The likelihood of theft depends on the driver's behavior: taking care to park in secure, well-lighted places; using a steering lock; and activating the car alarm. Short of hiring a full-time private detective, it is difficult for an insurer to monitor the driver's behavior completely.

A driver who has comprehensive automobile insurance, however, may take fewer precautions. For instance, the driver may sometimes neglect to engage the steering lock or, in a pinch, park in dark alley. While the driver personally bears all the costs of precautions, a large part of the benefit in terms of reduced likelihood of theft accrues to the insurer.

Many insurers offer comprehensive automobile insurance only with a minimum deductible. Such policies provide compensation only to the extent that the loss exceeds the deductible. A driver will benefit from precautions against loss to the extent of her or his deductible. Accordingly, the deductible helps to resolve the driver's moral hazard.

The deductible, however, imposes risk on the driver. Drivers buy insurance because they are averse to risk. Ironically, the insurer must limit the extent of insurance to resolve the problem of moral hazard.

Relative Performance Incentives

In some situations, the moral hazard can be resolved in a very natural way without imposing risk. Suppose that Mary is just one of many delivery persons working for Luna Supermarket. Then Luna could adopt the following incentive scheme, which is based on *relative* performance. Using records of the deliveries made by the various workers, Luna can calculate the average number of deliveries. It can then pay Mary a fixed daily wage plus a $2 commission for each delivery that she performs in excess of the average for all delivery personnel.

Luna's incentive scheme will not penalize Mary for an extraneous factor like bad weather. Suppose that the weather is bad. This will hamper all delivery persons and cut the average number of deliveries. If Mary exerts relatively more effort, she will still achieve more deliveries than the average and hence will earn the $2 commission.

By gauging performance on a relative basis, the incentive scheme cancels out the effect of extraneous factors to the extent that they affect all workers equally. This reduces the risk due to extraneous factors.

Even with a relative incentive scheme, however, a worker must continue to bear the risk due to idiosyncratic factors that do not affect the average worker to the same extent. For instance, if Mary's territory is relatively more prone to traffic congestion, she will suffer relatively more risk from this factor.

Generally, an incentive scheme based on relative performance will eliminate the risk due to extraneous factors that affect all parties equally. Relative incentive schemes are most useful where common extraneous factors are important.

Evaluating managerial performance

A common way of evaluating the performance of company management is through the stock price. AT&T is a leading international telecommunications provider. AT&T common shares rose by 44% between 1993–98. Should investors cheer?

Not if they consider their alternatives. Figure 13.4 shows the cumulative total shareholder returns from investments in AT&T shares as compared with the Standard & Poor's Telephone Index, which is an index of shares of major telecommunications providers. An investment in the Telephone Index would have been much more profitable.

This example suggests that a more reasonable way of evaluating managers is to measure their performance against that of other companies in the same industry. Relative performance evaluation cancels out background factors over which managers have no control. This yields a more accurate measure of management's performance.

Source: AT&T, proxy statement pursuant to Section 14A of the Securities Exchange Act of 1934 (March 25, 1999).

Figure 13.4 AT&T relative performance

Source: AT&T proxy statement (March 25, 1999).

Between 1993–98, the cumulative total shareholder return from investments in AT&T shares was 140%, as compared with 199% from the Standard & Poor's Telephone Index.

◀◀ 5 Multiple Responsibilities

Until this point, we have focused on situations where the moral hazard concerns a single action or responsibility. In many cases, however, the party subject to the moral hazard has multiple responsibilities. For instance, a supermarket may want delivery persons to carry out their work quickly as well as in a polite and friendly way that will encourage repeat customers. In a department store, a salesclerk may be required to make new sales, process returns, as well as look out for shoplifters.

Consider situations where the moral hazard concerns multiple responsibilities. This means that the party subject to moral hazard takes multiple actions that affect but are not observed by another party with whom it has a conflict of interest.

Ideally, an incentive scheme should aim to balance the multiple responsibilities. This means that there should be some investment in monitoring each of the unobservable actions and incentives based on the corresponding indicators.

Balancing multiple responsibilities becomes harder when it is more difficult to measure performance for some responsibilities than others. An incentive scheme may focus

---

Balancing multiple responsibilities: Hong Kong's traffic wardens

In Hong Kong, traffic wardens have two responsibilities: static traffic control duty and enforcement against illegal parking and unpaid use of parking meters. For the individual traffic warden, strict enforcement of parking regulations means intensive patrolling and possibly receiving verbal or other abuse from drivers. By avoiding enforcement, a traffic warden can pass the day quietly and peacefully.

When the government Audit Department monitored a random sample of traffic wardens, it discovered that those who were monitored issued 69 to 215% more parking citations than the average traffic warden. The Audit Department proposed to resolve the moral hazard problem by assigning each traffic warden a quota of citations.

The proposed quota would surely induce traffic wardens to put more effort into enforcement of parking regulations. The Audit Department, however, overlooked an important side effect of its proposal. Traffic wardens are also responsible for static traffic control duty. The quotas on parking citations would induce traffic wardens to reduce their attention to traffic control. Overall, the quotas would improve parking regulation enforcement but lead to worse traffic control.

Source: Hong Kong, Director of Audit, Report no. 23, *The Royal Hong Kong Police Force*, chapter 7, "The Performance of the Traffic Warden Corps" (Hong Kong: Audit Department, 1994).

on a particular responsibility because that dimension is relatively easier to monitor. As we emphasized previously, the scope of an incentive scheme depends on the available indicators of the unobservable action.

Suppose, however, that the incentive scheme focuses on just one responsibility. Then, it will induce better performance on that dimension but have the side effect of aggravating the moral hazard with regard to the other responsibilities.

For instance, Luna Supermarket wants Mary to carry out deliveries quickly and in a polite and friendly way. Performance in politeness and friendliness, however, is much more difficult to measure than the number of deliveries. If Luna adopts a strong incentive scheme for the number of deliveries, Mary will speed up her work, but this will undercut the goal of polite and friendly service.

Incentive schemes focus on actions for which there are reliable measures of performance. If, however, there are important responsibilities for which it is difficult to measure performance, then it will be better to adopt relatively weak performance incentives. A deliberate use of weak incentives is a way to achieve a balance among multiple responsibilities.

> **Progress Check 13E** Suppose that a department store has switched its salesclerks from a straight salary to a salary plus a commission on sales. How will this affect the salesclerks' incentive to process returns?
>
> *Progress check*

◂◂ 6 Holdup

The architecture of an organization includes incentive schemes and monitoring systems. It can help to resolve holdup as well as moral hazard.

To understand the meaning of a *holdup*, suppose that Luna Supermarket engages Speedy Deliveries to deliver grocery orders. According to their contract, Speedy makes two rounds of deliveries a day, one beginning at 12:00 noon and another at 4:00 p.m. One day, however, Luna received so many delivery orders that it asked Speedy to make a third round. Sensing that Luna was in a desperate situation, Speedy refused to make the additional delivery unless Luna paid twice the usual price.

In this example, Speedy took advantage of Luna's special need to *hold up* the supermarket. A **holdup** is an action to exploit another party's dependence. A holdup is distinct from moral hazard in that it does not require asymmetric information. For example, when Luna requested the extra delivery, Speedy openly refused. Luna could clearly observe Speedy's action: hence, there was no asymmetry of information. A holdup is similar to moral hazard in that it arises only when there is a conflict of interest between the parties.

> A **holdup** is an action to exploit another party's dependence.

Speedy's holdup has implications beyond the exceptional price that Luna paid on that one occasion. The prospect of a holdup in the future will lead Luna to take precautions and avoid depending too much on Speedy. For instance, Luna might warn customers that delivery cannot be assured on the same day, it might limit the number of orders for delivery each day, or it might establish its own delivery service.

Limiting the number of orders for delivery each day will reduce Luna's benefit from Speedy's service. Establishing its own delivery service will add to Luna's costs. Luna's precautions either reduce its benefit from Speedy's service or increase its own costs.

Generally, whenever there is the prospect that someone will engage in a holdup, other parties will take precautions to avoid dependence. These precautions either reduce the benefit from the relationship or increase costs. Thus, the potential for a holdup reduces the group's net benefit.

Specific Investments

One particular type of precaution against a holdup is not so obvious and, hence, should be highlighted. Suppose that, to optimize delivery time and fuel, Speedy has installed a computerized route planning system on every truck. To use this system, every package must be marked with a suitable barcode strip. Then, the driver scans the packages so that the onboard computer can prepare the optimal delivery route.

Luna must prepare a delivery order for each package. The easiest way of preparing the route planning barcodes is to generate them with the delivery orders. This, however, requires Luna to integrate Speedy's bar codes with its delivery system. Integration will make Luna relatively more dependent on Speedy and, hence, more vulnerable to a holdup. Accordingly, Luna will be reluctant to invest in such integration.

In this example, integrating the barcodes is an investment by Luna that is specific to its relationship with Speedy. The **specificity** of an investment in an asset is the percentage that will be lost if the asset is switched to another use.

> **Specificity** is the percentage of the investment that will be lost if the asset is switched to another use.

For instance, suppose that Luna must spend $5,000 to integrate Speedy's barcodes with its delivery system. Of the $5,000 investment, $2,000 is for a barcode printer, while the remaining $3,000 pays for tailor-made software specified by Speedy. If Luna switches to another delivery contractor, it will lose the $3,000 specialized investment. Hence, the integrated barcode system is 3,000/5,000 = 60% specific to the relationship with Speedy.

By contrast, suppose that Luna buys several mobile phones to contact delivery persons when they are on the road. The same phones, however, can be used by any delivery contractor. Hence, these are nonspecific assets. The prospect that Speedy might act opportunistically will have relatively little impact on Luna's investments in such non-specific assets.

Specific assets can be physical; for instance, plant and equipment. Specific assets also encompass human capital. Many businesses provide new recruits with introductory training. Through on-the-job training programs, employees are making investments in specific human capital. The prospect of a holdup will deter investments in all forms of specific assets.

Progress Check 13F Which of the following requires you to invest relatively more in specific human capital: a university degree program or on-the-job training?

Progress check

Avoiding specificity in electric power investments: floating power plants

Smith Cogeneration International of Oklahoma City manufactures electric power plants. In 1993, the company was invited to supply a power plant in the Dominican Republic. However, it learned that over 20 other potential suppliers had refused to bid. Owing to the political and economic risks of investment, the other suppliers could not secure the several hundred million dollars of financing necessary for construction.

Taking inspiration from sailboat racing, company president Donald Smith contracted to supply a *floating* plant. The company built a gas turbine plant on a barge at a Beaumont, Texas, yard and then towed it across the Caribbean Sea to the Dominican Republic.

The barge had two advantages over a conventional land-based plant. First, in the event of default by the host government, Smith could actually float the plant away. The extent of its specific investment was much lower than with a land-based plant. The second advantage was faster delivery. Smith did not have to send personnel to the Dominican Republic and thus saved six months in construction time.

Source: "Power Plants Atop Barges Will Make Waves in Asia," *Asian Wall Street Journal*, May 23, 1996, pp. 1 and 6.

Incomplete Contracts

Suppose that the contract between Luna and Speedy had specified conditions under which Luna could request an additional delivery and the corresponding price. Then, Speedy would not have been able to hold up Luna. Generally, the scope for a holdup depends on the extent to which a contract is incomplete. A **complete contract** specifies what each party must

> A **complete contract** specifies what each party must do and the corresponding payments under every possible contingency.

do and the corresponding payments under every possible contingency. By contrast, a contract is incomplete if it does not specify duties or payment in some contingency.

It would be extremely costly for Luna and Speedy to prepare and agree on a complete contract. A huge number of contingencies would have to be covered: the need for a fourth delivery, the possibility that Speedy's truck may break down, and the possibility of an earthquake are just a few. Rather than consider every such detail, the two parties will probably agree on an incomplete contract.

As this example suggests, in practice, all contracts are incomplete, and deliberately so. The issue then is how incomplete the contract should be. Generally, the answer depends on two factors: the potential benefits and costs at stake and the extent of the possible contingencies.

Let us consider the first factor: the potential benefits and costs at stake. The larger are the stakes, the more the parties should invest in preparing the contract. Compare, for instance, Luna's purchases of sundry hardware and dairy products. Sundry hardware such as nails and screws is a minor item in Luna's sales. By contrast, dairy products account for a large part of Luna's sales and are much more important. Accordingly, Luna might not need a contract with its supplier of sundry hardware, but it will need a detailed contract with its supplier of dairy products.

The second factor in the incompleteness of the contract is the extent of the possible contingencies. Consider again Luna's purchases of sundry hardware and dairy products. Hardware is a durable item with relatively slow sales. By contrast, dairy products are perishable and sold in high volume, hence Luna needs frequent supply. The supply of dairy products, however, is relatively more vulnerable to disruptions by bad weather, transportation problems, and labor disputes. Accordingly, Luna will seek relatively more assurance about the supply of dairy products. This means a relatively more detailed contract.

Gains from Resolution

In general, contracts are deliberately incomplete. This incompleteness gives rise to the possibility of a holdup. In turn, this leads the affected parties to take precautions such as avoiding investments in specific assets. These precautions reduce the net benefit of the various parties from the relationship. If, however, the potential for holdup can be resolved, then the additional benefit will exceed the additional cost. Accordingly, a profit can be made by resolving the potential for holdup.

An obvious way to resolve the potential for holdup is for the relevant parties to specify contracts in greater detail. We have already discussed the factors to consider when deciding on the degree of contractual incompleteness.

Another way to resolve holdup is through changing the ownership of the relevant assets. In the next section, we discuss the meaning of ownership.

◂◂ 7 Ownership

Ownership means the rights to **residual control**, which are those rights that have not been contracted away. To explain the meaning of *residual control*, suppose that Moonlight Properties borrowed $5 million from a bank to develop a supermarket, which it has rented to Luna on a five-year lease.

> **Ownership** means the rights to residual control.

> The rights to **residual control** are those rights that have not been contracted away.

The bank has a mortgage against the building. This means that, if Moonlight fails to make the loan payments on time, the bank will have the legal right to take possession of the building. This is a right that Moonlight contracted away to get the loan.

Moonlight has also entered into a five-year lease with Luna Supermarket. Through the lease, Luna has the right to use the property for five years. This is another right that Moonlight has contracted away.

As owner, Moonlight has residual control. This means that it has all rights except those contracted away. For instance, it may have the right to enter into a second mortgage on the building, and it has the right to use the building after the expiration of Luna's lease.

A transfer of ownership means shifting the rights of residual control to another party. Suppose that Luna buys ownership of the supermarket building from Moonlight. Then, Moonlight no longer will have the right to enter into a mortgage on the building. Such rights now belong to the new owner, Luna.

Residual Income

One dimension of residual control particularly is worth emphasizing. The owner of an asset also has the right to receive the **residual income** from the asset, which is the income remaining after payment of all other claims.

> **Residual income** is the income remaining after payment of all other claims.

To illustrate, suppose that Moonlight collects $100,000 a month in rent from Luna. Moonlight's expenses include $50,000 in interest and principal to the bank as well as $20,000 in taxes and other expenses. As owner of the building, Moonlight receives the residual income of $100,000 − $50,000 − $20,000 = $30,000.

As the recipient of the residual income, the owner gets the full benefit of changes in income and costs. For instance, if Moonlight can raise the rent by $5,000 to $105,000, then its profit will increase by $5,000 to $35,000. Similarly, if Moonlight can reduce expenses by $2,000, then its profit will increase by $2,000 to $32,000. On the other hand, if Moonlight's expenses increase by $5,000, then its profit would fall by $5,000 to $25,000.

Table 13.1 Vertical integration				
Acquirer		Target		Source
Company	Business	Company	Business	
Walt Disney Co.	Production of films and television programming	CapCities/ABC	Television broadcasting	a
Broken Hill Proprietary Co.	Copper mining	Magma Copper	Copper smelting	b
Loral Space & Communications	Manufacturing of satellites	Space Systems/ Loral	Satellite communications services	c
Dominion Resources	Electric power utility	Consolidated Natural Gas	Natural gas production	d

Sources:
[a] "Disney's Kingdom," *Business Week*, August 15, 1995, p. 33.
[b] "Broken Hill Proprietary Sets Perpetual Growth Plan," *Wall Street Journal*, January 10, 1996, p. B4.
[c] "Loral Space Posts Net, Seeks Control of Unit," *Asian Wall Street Journal*, October 30, 1996, p. 11.
[d] "Energy, the New Convergence," *Economist*, May 29, 1999, pp. 67–8.

Vertical Integration

> **Vertical integration** is the combination of the assets for two successive stages of production under a common ownership.

Chapter 8 introduced the concept of vertical integration. To recall, **vertical integration** is the combination of the assets for two successive stages of production under a common ownership. Table 13.1 lists some recent examples of vertical integration.

Vertical integration is downstream or upstream, depending on whether it involves the acquisition of assets for a stage of production nearer to or further from the final consumer. Suppose, for instance, that a food manufacturer acquires a supermarket. Since the supermarket operates a stage of production nearer to the final consumer, this is an example of downstream vertical integration. By contrast, if the food manufacturer were to acquire a grower of fresh fruit, it would be vertically integrating upstream.

The decision to vertically integrate upstream is often characterized as the choice of whether to "make or buy." The food manufacturer can either *buy* fruit from growers or establish its own fruit-growing operation to *make* the input for its production.

Vertical integration or disintegration changes the ownership of assets, and hence alters the distribution of the rights to residual control and residual income. As we explain in the next section, these in turn affect the degree of moral hazard and the potential for holdup.

Progress Check 13G Referring to table 13.1, identify the examples as upstream or downstream vertical integration.

Progress check

◂◂ 8 Organizational Architecture

In chapter 1, we discussed the vertical and horizontal boundaries of an organization. An oil company that both produces crude and sells gasoline is more vertically integrated than one that only produces crude. A media organization that publishes newspapers and provides cable television and Internet service has wider horizontal boundaries than one that specializes in cable television service.

Vertical and horizontal boundaries are just two implications of the architecture of the organization, which comprises the distribution of ownership, incentive schemes, and monitoring systems. The design of organizational architecture depends on a balance among four issues – holdup, moral hazard, internal monopoly, and scale and scope economies – and the mechanisms by which these issues may be resolved.

Holdup

First, let us consider how the potential for holdup can be resolved by changing the ownership of the relevant assets. Recall that, when Luna requested an additional delivery on short notice, Speedy extracted double the usual price for the service. What if Luna had an in-house delivery service? To make the additional delivery, it might have to order a driver to work overtime. The driver could respond by striking to demand a special overtime payment. By doing so, however, the driver runs the risk that Luna may replace her with another worker.

If the driver strikes, the cost imposed on Luna is the cost of hiring a replacement driver on short notice. This will be lower than the cost of hiring a replacement truck and driver which would be necessary if Speedy should withhold its services.

As this example suggests, even an employee can engage in holdup. However, an employee is less likely than an external contractor to engage in holdup and would impose lower costs if it did so. The reason is that the external contractor owns the assets necessary to provide the service. Residual control of an asset includes the right to withhold its services. Hence, an external contractor has the power to withhold the services of its assets.

By contrast, an employee has no such power since the assets on which she works belong to the employer. With its smaller power, the employee is less likely to behave opportunistically and engage in a holdup and would impose lower cost if it did so. Accordingly, the potential for holdup can be mitigated through vertical integration into the relevant stage of production.

Moral Hazard

We have discussed how a change in the ownership of an asset can affect the likelihood and cost of a holdup. A change in ownership will also affect the degree of moral hazard.

Earlier, we considered the moral hazard of an employee relative to an employer. Generally, the employer's marginal benefit diverges from the worker's personal marginal benefit. Since the worker chooses effort according to her personal marginal benefit, she chooses less than the economically efficient level of effort.

By contrast, suppose that the employee owns the business. In this case, the worker receives the residual income of the business. Hence, if the worker exerts an additional unit of effort, she will receive the entire marginal benefit. By contrast, if the worker did not completely own the business, she would receive only a part of the marginal benefit.

Corporatizing Airbus

Airbus's organizational architecture required it to divide manufacturing work among its shareholders. For instance, Aerospatiale manufactured cockpits and forward fuselage sections, DASA was responsible for major fuselage sections and the tail, while British Aerospace manufactured the wings. These sections were then transported to either Hamburg (DASA) or Toulouse (Aerospatiale) for final assembly. To support this division of work, Airbus operated a dedicated fleet of huge transport aircraft.

Airbus purchased sections and services from its production partners at fixed transfer prices. Each production partner had more incentive to economize on its own work, where it would enjoy the whole gain, than on the product of Airbus as a whole, from which it derived only a part of the gain.

In 1999, Airbus decided that the newest A-318 model would be assembled in DASA's Hamburg plant. Aerospatiale threatened to withdraw from the program unless it received an equal share of work. The organization succumbed and agreed to re-assign a share of A-319 final assembly from DASA to Aerospatiale. The result of the holdup was that Airbus split assembly of the A-319 between two locations, and hence diluted economies of scale in manufacturing.

Despite all these anomalies, Airbus claimed to have one of the most efficient production systems in the world, with about 95% of its manufacturing work performed by its shareholders.

Source: "Airbus Rolls the Dice, Prepares to Make Bold Moves," *Seattletimes.com, Business*, August 8, 1999.

Likewise, a worker who reduces effort by one unit will suffer the entire reduction in the marginal benefit. Thus, when balancing her marginal benefit with the marginal cost, the worker will choose the economically efficient level of effort. Giving ownership to the worker will resolve the moral hazard.

Generally, since the owner of an asset receives its residual income, it will aim to maximize the net benefit, which means using the asset in an economically efficient way. This explains why many businesses pay senior managers through shares and stock options. To the extent that these managers have a share of ownership, their interests will be more closely aligned with those of the business, which reduces the degree of the moral hazard.

How does this analysis apply to Luna's in-house delivery service? It implies that Mary's moral hazard will be relatively low if she owned the service. The delivery person's moral hazard would be higher if the service were owned by the supermarket. So, if Luna vertically integrates into the delivery business, it will increase the delivery person's degree of moral hazard.

Vertical integration changes ownership: it transforms a supplier of a service from an owner into an employee. An employee is subject to relatively greater moral hazard than an owner. Accordingly, vertical integration increases the degree of moral hazard.

Internal Monopoly

Another consideration in organizational architecture is the extent to which an internal provider exploits monopoly power. If Luna establishes its own delivery service, it will prefer using its own delivery service to engaging an external contractor. This is a reasonable policy to the extent that some of the costs of the in-house delivery service are sunk.

The preference in favor of an internal provider, however, means creating an internal monopoly. In chapter 8, we showed that a seller with market power will restrict production and raise price. An internal provider may also use its market power to raise its price. Then, the organization as a whole will find that the cost of internal provision may rise above the price charged by external contractors. This higher cost must be borne by the organization.

One way of resolving the problem of an internal monopoly is to outsource whenever the internal provider's cost exceeds that of external sources. *Outsourcing* is the purchase of services or supplies from external sources. It subjects internal providers to the discipline of market competition and, so, limits the extent to which the cost of internal provision diverges from the competitive level.

Economies of Scale and Scope

Finally, a decision on organizational architecture should also take account of scale and scope economies. Recall from chapter 7 that, if there are economies of scale, then the average cost of provision will be lower with a larger scale. Typically, an internal provider will operate at a smaller scale than an external contractor. It then is necessary to consider how the average cost varies with the operating scale.

For instance, in Luna's case, the supermarket's deliveries may occupy a truck and driver for only four hours a day. If Luna were to set up its own delivery service, its utilization of the assets and human resources would be relatively low. By contrast, an external delivery contractor may get 10 or 12 hours a day of work from its equipment and personnel. The external contractor would have better capacity utilization and hence a lower average cost. To this extent, it would be less costly to purchase the service from the external contractor.

We can also illustrate the significance of scale economies by comparing a supermarket's need for delivery service with that for armored truck service to convey cash and checks. While some supermarkets have their own delivery service, almost none have their own armored trucks. A major reason for this difference is economies of scale. It hardly would be efficient for a supermarket to buy an armored truck that makes one daily trip to the bank.

From chapter 7, if there are economies of scope across two products, then the total cost of production will be lower when the two products are produced together than when they are produced separately. Economies of scope are a key reason for the growth of supermarkets at the expense of traditional stores. A supermarket can supply a wide range of items at a relatively lower cost than more specialized stores such as bakeries, groceries, and newsstands.

Economies of scope are the major factor in favor of wide horizontal organizational boundaries. However, scope economies must be balanced against moral hazard within a large organization. The management of a supermarket chain must find some balance. The family that owns and operates the corner grocery may have stronger incentives for effort than the employees of a national supermarket chain. At some point, the scope economies are outweighed by the degree of moral hazard within the various operational units of the organization.

Balance

The decision on organizational architecture depends on a balance among all the factors that we have discussed: the scope for holdup, the degree of moral hazard, internal monopoly power, and the extent of economies of scale and scope. Further, it also depends on other ways to resolve these issues. Specifically, holdup can be resolved through investment in more detailed contracts, moral hazard can be resolved through performance incentives, and internal monopoly power can be resolved through outsourcing. Generally, the economically efficient solution will involve a mix of all policies.

Let us illustrate the application of this framework with two examples. One concerns the vertical boundaries of the organization, while the other concerns its horizontal boundaries. The two examples show that the same framework can be applied to address both vertical and horizontal dimensions of organizational architecture.

Figure 13.5 Vertical integration

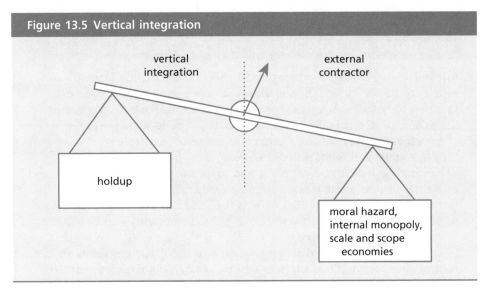

The scope for a holdup weighs in favor of vertical integration, while the degree of moral hazard, internal monopoly power, and the extent of economies of scale and scope weigh against it.

A function that many organizations consider whether to "make or buy" is information technology services. As figure 13.5 shows, this decision resolves to a balance among four factors. The factor in favor of "make" is the extent to which the potential for holdup cannot be cost-effectively reduced through more detailed contracts. There are three factors in favor of "buy." The first is the extent to which moral hazard among the internal information technology group cannot be cost-effectively resolved through incentive schemes and monitoring systems. The second is the extent to which the internal group's monopoly power cannot be cost-effectively redressed through out-sourcing. The third is the extent to which the internal group will lack economies of scale.

Decisions whether to "make or buy" concern the vertical boundaries of the organization. An organization must also consider its horizontal boundaries. For instance, should a bus operator also be in the trucking business? As the businesses are not vertically related, holdup and internal monopoly power are not major issues. The key factor in favor of owning both businesses is economies of scope, while the factor against is the extent to which moral hazard in the trucking group cannot be cost-effectively resolved through incentive schemes and monitoring systems.

Progress Check 13H Jupiter Bank has 1 million credit card accounts, while Mercury Bank has only 1,000 accounts. Explain why Jupiter chooses to own and operate its own credit card processing, while Mercury contracts out for that service.

Progress check

B2C e-commerce:
to build warehouses or not to build

Established in 1995, Amazon.com quickly became the world's leading online retailer of books, music CDs, and videos, and one of the preeminent B2C (business-to-consumer) portals. Founder Jeff Bezos began with the sale of books and located his new business in Seattle, close to a major wholesaler of books. In this way, Amazon could economize on inventory.

By late 1998, with annual sales exceeding $600 million and a product line extending into toys, electronics, and tools, Amazon changed its strategy to embrace bricks and mortar. Amazon already had two relatively old warehouses, in Seattle and Delaware. It then decided to invest $300 million to build five state-of-the-art warehouses across the country – in Georgia, Kansas, Kentucky, and Nevada.

Amazon justified the vertical integration into distribution in terms of control over holdup. Chief Logistics Officer, Jimmy Wright, explained: "[O]ur distribution center associates are the last people to touch an order before it reaches our customers – that's why we do our own shipping." Vice President Andrew N. Westlund feared that independent distributors would pass on Amazon's innovations in customer service to competing retailers: "We would be the teacher and then they would offer those services to our competitors."

By comparison with Amazon, online video retailer BigStar Entertainment is a minnow. Commenting on Amazon's integration into distribution, BigStar Chief Executive, David Friedensohn, remarked, "I don't want 1,000 hourly workers sitting in a warehouse wrapping presents. There are plenty of people bidding for that business." One factor in the difference in the degree of vertical integration between Amazon and BigStar is the difference in their scale and scope.

Sources: "Amazon's Risky Christmas," *New York Times*, November 28, 1999, Money and Business, p. 1; "Amazon.com to Open Two Kentucky Distribution Centers to Meet Rapid Growth," *PRNewswire*, May 25, 1999.

Tracking stock:
a new horizontal architecture

Telecommunications giant AT&T provides local, long-distance, and international fixed-line and wireless telecommunications, and broadband and cable services to consumer and business customers. Relative to the remainder of the company, the AT&T Wireless Group is essentially a horizontal extension.

In 2000, AT&T created the AT&T Wireless Group tracking stock to reflect earnings of the wireless businesses. AT&T sought to preserve a common ownership and hence economies of scope between itself and the wireless businesses. Accordingly, it did not divest the wireless businesses. Instead, AT&T established the tracking stock, which was listed on the New York Stock Exchange.

One of AT&T's primary reasons for creating the tracking stock was to strengthen incentives for the management and staff of the Wireless Group. Historically, incentive stock options for Wireless Group employees were based on the shares of AT&T as a whole, which meant that their compensation depended on the performance of other divisions. Along with the creation of the AT&T Wireless Group tracking stock, AT&T established a stock option plan based on the tracking stock. The stock options accounted for about 65 million shares of the AT&T Wireless Group tracking stock.

The tracking stock was a clever balance between retaining the economies of scope among wireless telecommunications, fixed-line telecommunications, cable and broadband service that flowed from common ownership, while sharpening the incentives for the employees of the Wireless Group.

Source: AT&T Proxy Statement, January 26, 2000, and AT&T Wireless Group Tracking Stock, Prospectus, April 26, 2000.

◂◂ 9 Summary

The architecture of an organization comprises the distribution of ownership, incentive schemes, and monitoring systems. Ownership means the rights to residual control. Incentive schemes and monitoring systems are related as incentives must be based on behavior that can be observed. An efficient incentive scheme balances the incentive for effort with the cost of risk.

An efficient organizational architecture resolves four internal issues – holdup, moral hazard, monopoly power, and economies of scale. Holdup and moral hazard arise between parties with a conflict of interest. Additionally, moral hazard depends on one party not being able to observe the actions of the other. Holdup can also be resolved through more detailed contracts, moral hazard through incentive schemes and monitoring systems, and internal monopoly power through outsourcing.

Key Concepts

organizational architecture	relative performance	ownership
moral hazard	holdup	residual control
performance pay	specificity	residual income
performance quota	complete contract	vertical integration

Further Reading

The key reference is Paul Milgrom and John Roberts's *Economics, Organization, and Management* (Englewood Cliffs, NJ: Prentice Hall, 1992). Professors Milgrom and Roberts apply state-of-the-art scholarship to the issues of incentives and organization. See especially their chapters 5–7, 9, and 16. James A. Brickley, Clifford W. Smith, Jr., and Jerold L. Zimmerman, *Managerial Economics and Organizational Architecture* (Boston, MA: Irwin McGraw Hill, 1997), chapters 9 and 10, provide a complementary perspective.

? Review Questions

1. In the context of your business or organization, explain the meaning of organizational architecture.

2. Explain the moral hazard in the following situation. Leah has just bought comprehensive insurance on her car. This covers loss and damage for any reason including theft. Her insurer is concerned that she may take fewer precautions against theft.

3. By considering benefits and costs to the various parties, explain why a profit can be made by resolving moral hazard.

4. Compare the following ways of paying a lawyer in terms of the incentive for effort.
   (a) Hourly rate, in which the lawyer receives a fixed dollar amount for each hour of work on the case.
   (b) Contingency fee, in which the lawyer receives a portion of the amount that the client recovers. If the client loses the legal action, the lawyer gets nothing.

5. A department store employs both sales staff and delivery drivers. Explain how incentives based on relative performance can be structured to achieve the following objectives:
   (a) motivating salespersons to promote merchandise;
   (b) motivating drivers to maintain their vehicles carefully and avoid breakdowns.

6. A secretary's job includes typing letters, answering telephone calls, and handling visitors as well as other responsibilities. Comment on a proposal to pay a secretary according to the number of letters that he types.

7. For each of the following investment funds, suggest an appropriate benchmark against which the fund performance might be measured:
   (a) a fund specializing in small stocks;
   (b) a U.S. Government bond fund;
   (c) a Japanese stock fund.

8. Maria is a pilot. Which of the following investments is the relatively more specific?
   (a) An executive MBA program for middle managers.
   (b) Training on an Airbus A-340 simulator.

9. Why do businesses enter into contracts that are deliberately incomplete?

10. In the context of an incorporated business, explain the meaning of (i) residual control, and (ii) residual income.

11. Give an example of a holdup. Explain how this will induce the affected parties to avoid specific investments.

12. True or false? An aircraft manufacturer has experienced holdup by its supplier of avionics. The aircraft manufacturer could resolve all incentive problems by producing the avionics internally.

13. How can outsourcing resolve the monopoly power of an internal supplier?

14. Explain the difference between vertical and horizontal integration.

15. A property management business is considering whether to set up its own cleaning service to replace an outside contractor. What are the arguments for and against this proposal?

Discussion Questions

1. Alan is a sales representative for a cellular telephone manufacturer. He must operate independently, calling on clients. Some of his clients are difficult and troublesome, while others are pleasant and easygoing. Spending one hour with a difficult client requires much more effort than four hours with an easy client.
   (a) Is Alan subject to moral hazard?
   (b) From the company's perspective, how much effort should Alan put into promoting sales?
   (c) Comment on a proposal to pay sales representatives by the number of hours that they spend with clients.

2. In 1996, the Aetna Life and Casualty Company acquired U.S. Healthcare for $8.8 billion. At the time, Aetna was a leading provider of medical insurance. Medical insurance allows the insured party a relatively free choice of doctors and treatment centers. By contrast, U.S. Healthcare specialized in managed health care, under which covered patients could get treatment only from specific doctors and at specified facilities ("Aetna to Buy U.S. Healthcare in Big Move to Managed Care," *New York Times*, April 2, 1996, p. A1).
   (a) A medical insurer pays the bills, while a doctor decides on tests, treatment, and prescriptions. Explain the moral hazard between doctors and medical insurers.
   (b) A managed health care plan may restrict coverage to treatment by the plan's own employees and facilities. Compare the extent of a doctor's moral hazard under managed health care relative to medical insurance.
   (c) Using your answer to (b), explain why managed health care is less costly than medical insurance.

3. The market for rental apartments includes both unfurnished and furnished units. Landlords of furnished units must make allowance for depreciation of the appliances and furniture.
   (a) Explain how the depreciation of appliances and furniture depends on the behavior of the tenants.
   (b) Which of the following items is relatively more sensitive to misuse by tenants: a sofa or a TV set?
   (c) Explain why furnished apartments usually include sofas but not TV sets.

4. AT&T is a major provider of local and long-distance telecommunications, and wireless, cable, and Internet service. AT&T's incentive scheme for senior management includes stock options, which are the right to buy shares at a fixed exercise price. In 1995, Chairman and Chief Executive Officer Robert E. Allen received options to buy 108,000 shares at an exercise price of $49.9375.
   (a) Explain how the stock options were intended to motivate Mr. Allen.
   (b) Suggest an incentive scheme based on relative performance and compare it with AT&T's stock option scheme.
   (c) Mr. Allen also received a salary and bonus from AT&T. How would the stock options affect the risk that he bore?

5. Hong Kong traffic wardens prefer a quiet peaceful day to vigorous enforcement against illegal parking and unpaid parking meters. The government Audit Department proposed to resolve the moral hazard by assigning each traffic warden a quota of parking citations.
   (a) The extent of illegal parking varies by the time of day and day of the week. What risk will the quota impose on traffic wardens?
   (b) Please suggest how an incentive scheme based on relative performance can resolve the problem in (a).
   (c) Consider the game in strategic form as depicted in table 13.2. Show that there is no equilibrium in pure strategies.

Table 13.2 Traffic warden vs. driver

		Driver	
		Parks illegally	Does not
Traffic warden	Enforces	TW: 2, D: −1	TW: −1, D: 0
	Does not	TW: 0, D: 1	TW: 0, D: 0

6. The Sol Department Store pays large commissions to its sales staff. Salespersons, however, have other duties in addition to promoting merchandise. These include answering customers' telephone enquiries and processing returns.
   (a) Recently, a Sol customer complained that a salesperson did not attend to her when she asked to return several items. Explain how the salesperson's behavior is related to the company's policy of paying large commissions on sales.
   (b) Should Sol pay a commission to salespersons for processing returns as well?

(c) Comment on the alternative solution of centralizing returns in the customer service section, where the staff do not receive commissions.

7. Mineral-rich Papua New Guinea (PNG) is separated from the Australian state of Queensland by the Coral Sea. Chevron Services is developing extensive natural gas fields in PNG. To bring the gas to market, it contracted for a 2,100 kilometer pipeline costing A$1.5 billion from PNG to Gladstone in Queensland. The Australian Gas Light Company and Petronas, Malaysia's national oil company, will build and operate the gas pipeline. Australian Gas Light already owns a 1,580 kilometer network for distribution of natural gas in Queensland. Other potential buyers of the PNG gas in Gladstone included aluminum smelter Comalco Ltd and electric power generator NRG Asia Pacific ("Australian Gas, Petronas Sign Pipeline Deal," *Asian Wall Street Journal*, August 7–8, 1998, p. 19; "Boost for PNG, WA Gas Lines," *Australian Financial Review*, August 20, 1998, p. 20).
   (a) In the context of the new pipeline, explain the meaning of "sunk costs."
   (b) By considering possible moral hazard, explain why it is desirable that the builder of the pipeline also be engaged to operate it.
   (c) Identify the specific investments involved in the agreements among the three parties – gas producer, pipeline, and gas customers.
   (d) What are the potential holdup problems among the three parties?
   (e) If Chevron decided to build and operate the pipeline itself, what problems would be resolved, and what new problems would arise?

8. Airbus was owned by Aerospatiale-Matra (37.9%), British Aerospace (20%), Construcciones Aeronauticas (CASA) (4.2%) and DaimlerChrysler Aerospace (DASA) (37.9%). Most major decisions by Airbus required unanimous shareholder approval. In 1999, Airbus decided that the newest A-318 model would be assembled in DASA's Hamburg plant. Aerospatiale threatened to withdraw from the program unless it received an equal share of work. The organization succumbed and agreed to re-assign a share of A-319 final assembly from DASA to Aerospatiale.
   (a) The potential for holdup by a supplier may lead a customer to contract with a back-up supplier. (This practice is called "second-sourcing".) Explain why second-sourcing may be inefficient in terms of scale economies.
   (b) Explain how the potential for holdup by a customer may lead a supplier to avoid specific investments.
   (c) Upon corporatization, the management of Airbus would need unanimous shareholder approval only for three-year business plans, corporate changes exceeding $500 million, and a few other major business decisions. Referring to the episode with Aerospatiale over the A-318 and A-319, explain how corporatization might increase Airbus's earnings.

9. In 1995, the Walt Disney Company acquired Capital Cities/ABC Inc. for $19 billion. Through the acquisition, the Disney Company, which produces films and television shows, gained ownership of a major customer, the ABC television network. *Business Week* remarked that the deal would give Disney "a guaranteed platform for its first-run syndication programs – shows that might otherwise die on the vine" ("Disney's Kingdom," *Business Week*, August 15, 1995, p. 33).

(a) Use this example to explain the meaning of downstream vis-à-vis upstream vertical integration.

(b) Considering the ABC television network as a division of the Walt Disney Company, explain the meaning of outsourcing.

(c) From the perspective of maximizing the company's overall profit, does it make sense for Disney to force ABC to broadcast programs that "might otherwise die on the vine"?

10. One disadvantage of vertical integration is that the in-house provider may be too small to achieve the efficient scale. To what extent does this factor explain the following differences?

(a) Building contractors usually employ their own bricklayers and carpenters but hire subcontractors for electrical work and elevators.

(b) Large commercial buildings have their own teams of cleaners but hire external contractors for maintenance of heating, ventilation, and air-conditioning equipment.

11. General Motors and Toyota are two of the world's largest automobile manu-facturers. The two companies differ significantly in the degree of vertical integ-ration. While General Motors produces many components itself, Toyota tends to buy components from external suppliers.

(a) A consultant has measured labor productivity among automobile manu-facturers by the number of cars produced per employee. On this measure, labor productivity is much lower at General Motors than Toyota. Comment on this measure.

(b) External subcontractors may be able to achieve a more efficient scale than an internal provider. Does this factor apply to Toyota?

(c) One reason for producing components in-house is to avoid a holdup by external suppliers. Suppose that, owing to long-term relationships, Toyota's suppliers are relatively less opportunistic. How does this affect Toyota's degree of vertical integration?

(d) Strategy professor, Jeffrey H. Dyer, observed that suppliers to Japanese automobile manufacturers made more specific investments than their American counterparts ("Dedicated Assets," *Harvard Business Review*, November–December 1994, pp. 174–8). Dyer attributed the relative inefficiency of American automobile manufacturers to the low level of specific investments by their suppliers. Comment on this explanation.

Regulation

◄◄ 1 Introduction

Until the late 1990s, the Consolidated Edison Company of New York had a legal monopoly over the market for electricity in New York City and Westchester County. Like many other U.S. electric power utilities, Con Edison was vertically integrated from generation of electric power through transmission and distribution to retail sale.[1]

Under the terms of its franchise, Con Edison was subject to regulation by the New York State Public Service Commission. The Commission restrained Con Edison's exercise of monopoly power by limiting the company to a maximum rate of return on its investments.

Despite regulation, the price of electricity in New York State rose steadily through the 1980s and into the early 1990s. By 1995, the average price reached 12 cents a kilowatt, which exceeded the national average by over 50%. Moreover, the disparity between New York State and the national average was on an increasing trend.

The State then decided on two changes. First, it re-directed the focus of price regulation from an allowed rate of return to a price cap. The State linked Con Edison's prices to those of a peer group of other Northeast electric utilities.

Second, and more fundamentally, the State decided to re-structure the entire electric power industry. Con Edison and other electric power utilities were required to divest their power generation businesses, and to focus on transmission and distribution. The State encouraged the entry of new Energy Service Companies and required Con Edison and other utilities to transport their electric power supply.

Why did New York State award Con Edison a monopoly over electricity in New York City and Westchester County? Why did the State shift from rate of return regulation to a price cap? Why did the State re-structure the entire industry, forcing Con Edison to sell all of its electric power plants?

▼
[1] New York State Public Service Commission, *Annual Reports, 1993–94, 1995–96, 1998–99.*

This chapter addresses these and other issues that arise where the invisible hand fails. Buyers and sellers, acting independently and selfishly, do not equalize marginal benefit and marginal cost; hence, the allocation of resources is not economically efficient.

If the resource allocation is economically inefficient and private action fails to resolve the inefficiency, then there may be a role for government action. The government can act through regulation. If government regulation can resolve the divergence between the marginal benefit and the marginal cost, then it will increase net benefit for society.

To understand the role of government regulation, we consider the various sources of economic inefficiency: market power, asymmetric information, externalities, and public goods. In each case, we then analyze the conditions under which the government should intervene and the appropriate form of regulation.

In our analysis of economic inefficiency due to market power, we explain why a government may award legal monopolies for businesses with significant economies of scale relative to demand. One example is electricity distribution. This explains Con Edison's monopoly over electricity in New York City and Westchester County, and the monopoly structure of the U.S. electricity industry until the late 1990s.

We compare regulation by rate of return with direct regulation of price. The difference explains why New York State shifted from rate of return regulation to a price cap. We also discuss how to regulate an industry in which some parts have strong economies of scale or scope, while other parts do not. This explains why New York and many other states have re-structured their electricity industries to separate power generation from transmission and distribution.

The invisible hand may also fail because of information asymmetries. We consider how these may be resolved through regulation of disclosure, conduct, and business structure. We also consider how industry can apply self-regulation as an alternative to government intervention.

The third group of reasons for failure of the invisible hand is externalities and public goods. We consider how the government can resolve externalities through standards and user fees, and resolve the provision of public goods through an appropriate legal framework.

◀ 2 Natural Monopoly

Recall from chapter 8 that a monopoly will restrict sales to a quantity where the price exceeds the marginal cost. If buyers have no market power, they each purchase a quantity where the price equals the marginal benefit. Hence, at the monopoly price, some buyers will be willing to pay more than the seller's marginal cost but cannot get the product. This outcome is not economically efficient.

If monopolies cause economic inefficiency, why have governments all over the world awarded exclusive franchises to electricity distributors? To address this question, we must consider the technology of the business and, specifically, the presence of substantial economies of scale or scope.

Electricity is distributed through a network of cables running from a central source to every user. Consider a town in which there are two separate electricity distributors. Then, two sets of cables would run into every home, office, and factory. In the

electricity distribution business, having more than one provider could mean wasteful duplication.

A market is a **natural monopoly** if the average cost of
production is minimized with a single supplier. Examples of
natural monopolies include distribution of electricity, gas,
and water, and collection of sewage. In all of these markets,
the economies of scale may be large relative to the market

> A **natural monopoly**
> is a market where
> the average cost
> of production is
> minimized with
> a single supplier.

demand. Consequently, the average cost of production is lowest when there is only
one supplier. Similarly, in a market with economies of scope that are large relative
to the market demand, the average cost of production will be minimized with a
single supplier.

If a market is a natural monopoly, the government should prohibit competition and
award an exclusive franchise to a single supplier. This will establish the conditions
for production at the lowest average cost.

The monopoly, however, might exploit its exclusive right to raise its price at the
expense of its customers. The increase in the price will force the marginal benefit
above the marginal cost. Accordingly, to ensure economic efficiency, the government must establish controls on the monopoly.

A monopoly can be controlled in two ways: the government itself can own and
operate the business, or a monopoly franchise could be awarded to a commercial
enterprise that would be subjected to government regulation. Historically, government ownership of natural monopolies was relatively more common in Europe and
developing countries, while private ownership subject to government regulation was
more common in the United States. Since the 1980s, however, there has been a
worldwide trend to adopt the American model and privatize government enterprises.

Government Ownership

The major reason for privatization is that government-owned enterprises tend to
be relatively inefficient. One problem is that they are more prone to be coopted by
employees, so that the enterprise serves its employees rather than its customers. Some
symptoms of employee control are high wages and over-staffing, both of which inflate
the cost of production.

Another problem for government-owned enterprises is their dependence on the
government for investment funds. The national government budget must finance
everything from social welfare to military equipment. A government-owned enterprise must compete with other priorities for an allocation from the budget. Unlike
a commercial enterprise, a government-owned enterprise cannot borrow or raise
capital independently. The reason is that lenders cannot prevent the government
from spending the funds on military equipment or other purposes. By contrast,
a privately-owned enterprise can commit to invest borrowed funds or capital in its
own business.

Owing to these problems, government-owned natural monopolies may fall far short
of resolving economic inefficiency in their respective markets. We have mentioned

> **Privatization** is the transfer of ownership from the government to the private sector.

that there has been a worldwide trend toward privatization. **Privatization** means transfering ownership from the government to the private sector. It does not necessarily mean allowing competition. Indeed many privatized enterprises continue to have exclusive franchises in their respective businesses.

Government vis-à-vis private ownership: Telmex

For many years, the Mexican government owned most of the national telecommunications carrier, Telefonos de Mexico (Telmex). Owing to the government's fiscal difficulties, Telmex lacked funds to keep up with customer demand. The carrier provided only 6.5 lines per 100 residents, well below the world average of 9 lines per 100 residents. Moreover, the service was notoriously poor: the waiting list for telephone lines was 1 million long, the system did not complete a high percentage of calls, and fewer than 30% of lines were digital.

In December 1990, the government sold control of Telmex to a consortium of Mexican investors, Southwestern Bell, and France Telecom. The next year, Telmex was listed on the New York Stock Exchange. The company retained its monopoly over local, long-distance, and international services. The government allowed competition in cellular services, however.

Following privatization, Telmex embarked on a $11 billion program of investment. By 1995, its provision exceeded 9 lines per 100 residents, the waiting list had been eliminated, the call-completion rate was much higher, and almost 90% of lines were digital. Between 1989 and 1995, earnings per share rose six times from 39 cents to $2.40.

Sources: "Slim Competition," *Economist*, April 27, 1996, p. 81; *Value Line Survey*, Telefonos de Mexico, April 12, 1996, p. 797; "Market: The Mexican Model," *Ericsson Connexion*, no. 1 (March 1994).

Price Regulation

If the government awards an exclusive franchise for a natural monopoly to a commercial enterprise, then the government must regulate the monopoly. How should the government carry out the regulation?

Recall from chapter 6 that the provision of any good or service will be economically efficient at the level where the marginal benefit equals the marginal cost. Suppose that the government awards an exclusive franchise for gas distribution to Pluto Gas. Pluto's costs include a fixed cost and a constant marginal cost of 15 cents per cubic foot. Figure 14.1 shows the distribution cost and the demand for gas.

Figure 14.1 Marginal cost pricing

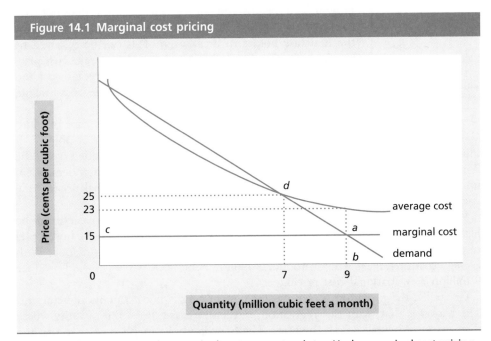

The demand curve crosses the marginal cost curve at point a. Under marginal cost pricing, the provider sets a price of 15 cents per cubic foot and the market quantity demanded is 9 million cubic feet a month. The demand curve crosses the average cost curve at point d. Under average cost pricing, the provider sets a price of 25 cents and the market quantity demanded is 7 million.

Suppose that the government requires the franchise holder to set its price equal to its marginal cost and to meet the quantity demanded. Then, referring to figure 14.1, at every possible quantity, the price will be the marginal cost. In effect, the government's policy forces the franchise holder to behave like a perfectly competitive supplier. This policy is called **marginal cost pricing**.

> **Marginal cost pricing** is the policy in which the price is set equal to the marginal cost and the provider must supply the quantity demanded.

The demand curve crosses the marginal cost curve at point a. If Pluto sets a price of 15 cents a cubic foot, the market quantity demanded will be 9 million cubic feet. Under the regulation, Pluto must meet the quantity demanded; hence, it must produce 9 million cubic feet. Recall that each customer buys the quantity that balances the marginal benefit with the price. Thus, the marginal benefit equals the marginal cost, which is the condition for economic efficiency.

Pluto's revenue is represented by area 0*bac*, which is $0.15 × 9 million = $1.35 million a month. The average cost at the 9 million production rate is 23 cents per cubic foot, which means that the total cost of production is $0.23 × 9 million = $2.07 million. Accordingly, the government must provide a subsidy of $2.07 − $1.35 million = $720,000 a month to ensure that the franchise is financially viable. In this case, the subsidy is necessary to achieve economic efficiency.

How should the government regulate Pluto if it does not wish
to provide a subsidy? In this case, the regulation must allow
the franchise holder to break even. This can be achieved by
requiring the franchise holder to implement **average cost pricing**, which means setting the price equal to average cost and
meeting the quantity demanded. With average cost pricing,
the franchise holder will exactly cover its costs.

Let us illustrate average cost pricing in the case of Pluto
Gas. In figure 14.1, the demand curve crosses the average cost curve at point *d*. If
Pluto set a price of 25 cents a cubic foot, the market quantity demanded would be
7 million cubic feet. Under the regulation, Pluto must meet the quantity demanded:
it must produce 7 million cubic feet. Its total revenue would exactly balance its total
cost; hence, it would break even.

Where there are economies of scale in production, the average cost curve will be
higher than the marginal cost curve. Then, average cost pricing leads to a lower level
of provision than marginal cost pricing. Pluto Gas illustrates such a situation. With
average cost pricing, it would produce 7 million cubic feet, while it would produce
9 million with marginal cost pricing.

Generally, the provision under average cost pricing is not economically efficient.
The reason is that, with this regulation, buyers purchase up to the quantity where
their marginal benefit equals the price. The franchise holder's price is set so that the
price equals the average cost. Hence, the quantity of provision is such that the marginal
benefit equals the average cost and not the marginal cost.

In Pluto's case, with average cost pricing, the franchise holder produces a quantity of 7 million cubic feet. At this quantity, the marginal benefit is 25 cents per
cubic foot, while the marginal cost is 15 cents. Hence, the provision is not economically efficient.

A major difficulty arises in the implementation of price regulation based on the
franchise holder's costs: such regulation gives the franchise holder an incentive to
persuade the regulator that its costs are higher than they actually are. Then the
regulator will allow the franchise holder to set a higher price, closer to the
monopoly level, which means a higher profit.

Note that the incentive is for the franchise holder to exaggerate its *reported* costs.
Since the regulated price is fixed, the franchise holder will not try to inflate its
actual costs. An increase in the franchise holder's actual costs would cut into its own
profit.

Progress check **Progress Check 14A** Referring to figure 14.1, suppose that
the franchise holder is subject to average cost pricing.
It reports to the regulator that its average cost curve is
10% higher than the true curve. Draw the new regulated
price and show the franchise holder's profit.

Rate of Return Regulation

To implement price regulation, the regulator needs information about the franchise holder's costs. We have seen that this gives the franchise holder an incentive to exaggerate its reported costs. The alternative to price regulation is rate of return regulation. This avoids the issue of costs by focusing on the franchise holder's profit. The regulator allows the franchise holder to set prices freely, provided that it does not exceed the maximum allowed profit.

Under rate of return regulation, the regulator specifies the franchise holder's maximum allowed profit in terms of a maximum rate of return on the value of the **rate base**, which is the assets to which the regulation applies. Whenever the franchise holder's rate of return exceeds the specified maximum, it will be required to reduce its prices.

> The **rate base** is the assets to which the rate of return regulation applies.

Suppose, for instance, that Pluto Gas is subject to rate of return regulation with a maximum 12% rate of return, and the rate base consists of all plant and equipment used for producing and distributing gas. The value of this plant and equipment is $100 million. Then, Pluto's maximum allowed profit will be $0.12 \times \$100$ million = $12 million a year.

Rate of return regulation presents three major difficulties for the regulator. The first is determining the maximum permissible rate of return. Since the rate base is typically a very large number, a small difference in the allowed rate of return will translate into a large sum of money. There is considerable room for dispute over the appropriate rate of return because the franchise holder is a monopoly, which means that there will be few comparable investments.

The second problem is that there will be disputes over what assets are needed to provide the regulated service and, hence, should be counted in the rate base. The franchise holder will seek the widest possible definition to increase its profit.

The third problem with rate of return regulation is that it creates an incentive for the franchise holder to invest beyond the economically efficient level. Specifically, if the franchise holder enlarges its rate base, the allowed rate of return will be applied to a larger base; hence, the franchise holder can earn a larger profit.

For example, the demand for electric power varies over time: The peak demand from commercial and industrial customers occurs during working hours, while the peak demand from residential customers occurs in the early morning and late evening. Suppose that there are two neighboring electric power utilities, one catering to mainly commercial and industrial demand and the other serving mainly residential users. It would be efficient for the two utilities to share generating capacity to meet differences in their peak demands. However, if they are subject to rate of return regulation, each may prefer to build more generating plants to increase its rate base.

Hong Kong's power failure

In Hong Kong, the supply of electric power is monopolized by two vertically integrated companies. Hong Kong Electric supplies Hong Kong Island, while China Light and Power supplies Kowloon and the New Territories. The Hong Kong Government subjects each company to a "Scheme of Control" that limits its profit to a 15% maximum rate of return on its rate base.

Since the adoption of the Scheme of Control, the Hong Kong economy has been transformed. Many manufacturers shifted their factories to Mainland China, to benefit from lower costs of labor, real estate, and other resources. Consequently, the industrial demand for electricity steadily declined. This decline had a relatively larger impact on China Light as most factories were located in Kowloon and the New Territories.

Meanwhile, Hong Kong's population and household incomes continued to grow. This increased the residential demand for electricity and benefited both China Light and Hong Kong Electric.

For China Light, the fall in industrial demand outweighed the growth of residential demand, and by 2000, it had over 50% excess generating capacity. Yet, the company sought government approval to invest HK$30 billion to upgrade its Castle Peak power plant and network. Its motivation was clear – to increase its rate base and hence its allowed profit.

Another symptom of the Scheme of Control is that the networks of China Light and Hong Kong Electric are not inter-connected. Although their networks are less than a mile apart, the two companies have not arranged to transmit electric power to each other. Inter-connection would have increased economic efficiency but reduced both companies' rate bases.

Testifying on the electric power industry before Hong Kong's Legislative Council, senior regulator, Maria Kwan, remarked, "I feel like I am a little bit of a failure."

Source: "The SAR's Greatest Power Failure," *South China Morning Post*, June 10, 2000, p. 16.

◄◄ 3 Potentially Competitive Market

By contrast with a natural monopoly, a potentially competitive market is one where economies of scale or scope are small relative to market demand. A market can switch from a natural monopoly to potentially competitive or vice versa with changes in demand or technology. The mathematical supplement provides a formal analysis of such a change.

If perfect competition prevails over a potentially competitive market, the invisible hand will ensure economic efficiency. Some potentially competitive markets, however, have government protection through exclusive franchises or restrictions against foreign imports. From the standpoint of economic efficiency, these markets should be opened to competition.

In most jurisdictions, the policy regarding competition depends on whether the industry is subject to government regulation. (A jurisdiction could be a state, country, or collection of countries.) Unregulated industries are subject to general competition law, while regulated industries are further subject to laws specific to the industry.

Cable television: still a natural monopoly?

For over three decades, AT&T Cable Services and its predecessors held San Francisco's only franchise for cable television services. In mid-2000, AT&T Cable, whose franchise was valid until 2005, had over 190,000 subscribers. Then, the city of San Francisco licensed a competitor. It granted RCN Telecom Services a 15-year franchise to provide cable television, broadband Internet, and telephone service.

In many cities across the United States, competition in cable television was permitted. For years, however, the cost of laying new cables deterred the entry of new providers. In effect, the cable television market was a natural monopoly.

Then, the Federal Communications Commission de-regulated the local telephone service industry to allow competition, and consumer demand for high-speed Internet service took off. With these two developments, cable providers could expect revenues from two additional sources – telephone and Internet service.

Existing cable companies like AT&T had to re-build their legacy networks to provide telephone and Internet service. New providers such as RCN Telecom Services considered the combination of revenues from cable television, broadband Internet, and telephone service sufficiently attractive to build new networks.

Source: "First for S.F. – Cable TV, Phone, Internet Rivalry," *San Francisco Chronicle*, July 21, 2000, p. A15.

Competition Laws

Table 14.1 lists the key laws regarding competition in several jurisdictions. In addition to these laws, individual countries within the European Union and individual American states may have their own competition laws. Table 14.1 also lists the agencies responsible for enforcing competition laws in the various jurisdictions.

Generally, the competition laws prohibit competitors from colluding on price and prohibit mergers or acquisitions that would create monopolies or monopsonies. In

Table 14.1 Competition laws		
Jurisdiction	Law	Enforcement Agency
Australia	Trade Practices Act, 1974 Competition Law Reform Act, 1995	Australian Competition and Consumer Commission
Canada	Competition Act, 1976	Bureau of Competition Policy
European Union	Treaty of Rome, 1957, Article 87	European Commission
Japan	Anti-monopoly Act, 1947	Fair Trade Commission
United Kingdom	Fair Trading Act, 1973 Resale Prices Act, 1976 Restrictive Trade Practices Act, 1976	Office of Fair Trading Monopolies and Mergers Commission
United States of America	Sherman Act, 1890 Clayton Act, 1914 Robinson-Patman Act, 1938 Federal Trade Commission Act, 1915	U.S. Department of Justice Federal Trade Commission

addition, the laws may prohibit or restrict specific anticompetitive business practices such as control over resale prices and exclusive agreements. What exactly is prohibited varies from one jurisdiction to another.

The role of the competition agency is to enforce the competition laws. Enforcement involves two dimensions. One is prosecution against those who violate the laws. The competition agency will prosecute competing sellers or competing buyers that engage in price collusion. The agency is also responsible for prosecuting anyone involved in anticompetitive practices.

The other major dimension of enforcement is to review proposals for mergers and acquisitions. Each jurisdiction has its own set of criteria regarding mergers and acquisitions. The competition agency must ensure that all proposals meet the criteria. The agency may approve a merger or acquisition subject to specific conditions. For instance, the agency may require divestment of particular businesses to mitigate the anticompetitive impact of a merger or acquisition.

In addition to government enforcement, the competition laws may provide for persons affected by anticompetitive behavior to sue in civil court. Under American laws, for instance, plaintiffs in civil actions can recover three times the damages they suffered. Further, civil plaintiffs can petition the courts for an order to stop anticompetitive conduct.

Structural Regulation

The fact that one market is a natural monopoly does not necessarily mean that related upstream or downstream markets are also natural monopolies. In natural gas, for

Platinum and the European Commission

Platinum is an inert metal that is resistant to corrosion and has a high
electrical resistance. It is mainly used as a chemical catalyst for electrical
contacts and in laboratory apparatus. The market for platinum is global.
The world supply of platinum is highly concentrated, with just three South
African companies – Anglo-American Platinum, Gencor, and Lonrho –
accounting for 72% of total production.

When Gencor and Lonrho proposed to merge their platinum businesses, the
European Commission blocked the merger. The Commission found that Lonrho
had played a major role in lowering the price of platinum and that the merger
would have reduced competition in a highly concentrated industry.

The reduction in competition would have harmed European users of
platinum. The members of the European Union account for a large portion
of world platinum usage. That is why a merger of two South African
companies motivated the European Commission to act.

Source: "Lonrho–Gencor Platinum Merger is Rebuffed by EU Commission,"
Asian Wall Street Journal, April 25, 1996, p. 2.

A multinational marriage: Kleenex and Viva

A merger that creates substantial market power within a jurisdiction may
require government approval. A merger that spans several jurisdictions
may require the approval of all the relevant competition agencies. Each
agency will apply its own criteria and specify its own set of conditions for
approval.

Kimberly-Clark is a leading manufacturer of synthetic and natural fiber
products whose most famous product is Kleenex tissues. In July 1995,
Kimberly-Clark announced that it would acquire the Scott Paper Company.
At the time, Scott was the world's largest manufacturer of beauty and
bathroom tissues with operations in 22 countries. Scott's brands included
Andrex, Cottonelle, Scott, and Viva.

To secure approval of the acquisition by the U.S. Department of Justice,
Kimberly-Clark agreed to divest its Scott Baby Fresh Wipes and Scotties
facial tissues businesses, as well as three tissue mills in the United States.
For approval of the European Commission, Kimberly-Clark had to sell the
Kleenex Velvet bathroom tissue businesses in the United Kingdom and
Ireland and one English bathroom tissue mill. In addition, Kimberly-Clark
also sought clearance from the Canadian Bureau of Competition Policy and
the Federal Competition Commission in Mexico.

Source: Kimberly-Clark Corporation, Form 10-K, fiscal year ending December 31, 1995.

instance, production may be potentially competitive even while distribution is a natural monopoly. Likewise, distribution of water may be a natural monopoly, while production is potentially competitive.

Under such circumstances, the government must consider how to preserve the benefits of monopoly in one market while fostering competition in the other. A special challenge to the regulator arises when the monopoly franchise holder also participates in the potentially competitive market.

To illustrate the issues, suppose that the government awarded a monopoly franchise for water distribution to Agua Fresca, while allowing competition in production of water. Since Fresca has a monopoly over distribution, it has a monopsony over the purchase of water. Hence, the government must regulate Fresca's monopoly over water distribution as well as its monopsony over water purchases.

Now, suppose that Fresca has vertically integrated upstream into the production of water. Then, Fresca may have an incentive to extend its monopoly upstream by discriminating against external water producers. An external source of water might offer a lower price with slightly different technical specifications. It may not be easy for the regulator to distinguish legitimate engineering reasons against the outside source of water from spurious arguments. Hence, external sources may be at a disadvantage.

This particular problem arises when the monopoly and the potentially competitive market occupy successive stages of production. One solution is structural regulation to separate the natural monopoly from the potentially competitive market. Applied to the example of Agua Fresca, the regulator may require Fresca to separate its water

Re-structuring the electric power industry

The State of New York began to re-structure the electricity industry in 1995. Con Edison projected that the re-structuring would yield $1.6 billion in savings, including $1.2 billion in rate reductions, over the following five years. By 1998, the average price of electricity in New York State had fallen to 11.5 cents per kilowatt, and was predicted to drop below 11.0 cents by 2002.

A major reason for the re-structuring was a change in power generation technology that resulted in generation becoming a potentially competitive industry. Traditionally, New York utilities had generated electricity in large-scale fossil fuel (coal, fuel oil, or natural gas) or hydro-electric plants.

New generation technology based on natural gas, however, allowed cost-efficient generation on a much smaller scale. It allowed industrial users to generate their own power at a lower cost than the prices charged by the electric power utility. Consequently, power generation ceased to be a natural monopoly.

Table 14.2 reports the worldwide pattern of electricity de-regulation. The common thread has been the vertical separation of power generation from transmission and distribution. While power generation is deemed to be potentially competitive, many regulators continue to view transmission and distribution as being natural monopolies.

Year	Jurisdiction	Actions
Table 14.2 Electric power: worldwide de-regulation		
1990	England	Central Electricity Generating Board divided into two generating companies (National Power and PowerGen), a transmission company, and twelve regional electricity distributors. Competition allowed in power generation. Each regional distributor granted exclusive franchise for its territory.
1993–4	Victoria, Australia	State Electricity Commission of Victoria divided into five generating companies, two transmission companies (PowerNet Victoria and Victorian Power Exchange), and five distribution companies. Each regional distributor granted exclusive franchise for its territory.
1998	Ontario, Canada	Ontario Hydro divided into three parts: nonprofit Independent Electricity Market Operator, and two commercial organizations, Ontario Power Generation and Ontario Hydro Services Company. Competition allowed in power generation, while Ontario Hydro granted monopoly in transmission and distribution.

Sources: "How Britain Changed from Public to Private Power – Overnight," *Power Engineering*, vol. 95, no. 2 (June 1991), pp. 42–3; U.S. Department of Energy, "Electricity Reform Abroad and U.S. Investment" (http://www.eia.doe.gov/emeu/pgem/electric/ch3.html); Ministry of Energy, Science, and Technology, Ontario (http://www.est.gov.on.ca/english/am/am_faq.html).

distribution and production businesses. An extreme form of structural regulation would be to require that Fresca divest itself of the production business.

> **Progress Check 14B** Suppose that the production of natural gas is potentially competitive and its distribution is a natural monopoly. Explain how structural regulation can ensure economic efficiency in the two markets.
>
> *Progress check*

◀◀ 4 Asymmetric Information

The second situation in which the invisible hand may fail is where there is asymmetric information about some characteristic or future action. Then, from chapters 12 and 13, we know that, if the information asymmetry is not resolved, the marginal benefit will diverge from the marginal cost and the allocation of resources will not be economically efficient.

Consider, for instance, the market for medical services. Patients rely on doctors for advice as well as treatment. Owing to the asymmetry of information between doctor and patient, the doctors are subject to moral hazard. Specifically, doctors can overprescribe treatment and so increase their incomes.

Figure 14.2 Moral hazard in medical services

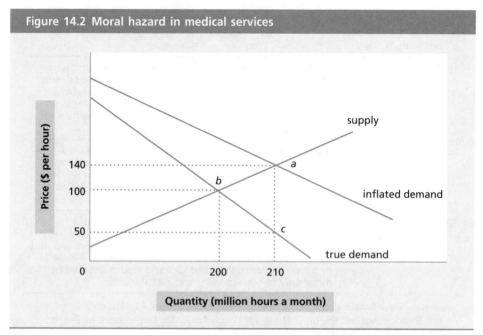

The inflated demand is higher than the true demand. The market equilibrium lies at point *a*, where the inflated demand crosses the supply. The price is $140 per hour and the quantity is 210 million hours a month. If the moral hazard can be resolved, the inflated demand will shift down to the true demand and the equilibrium will be at point *b*, where the true marginal benefit equals the marginal cost.

Figure 14.2 illustrates the market equilibrium. The true demand reflects the patients' marginal benefit if they and their doctors had equal information. The inflated demand is the demand that is actually realized and reflects the asymmetry of information. The inflated demand is higher than the true demand to the extent that doctors induce patients to get excessive treatment.

The inflated demand crosses the supply of medical services at point *a*. In the market equilibrium, the price is $140 per hour and the quantity of treatment is 210 million hours a month. At that quantity, the true marginal benefit of medical services is $50, which is the height of the true demand curve. The marginal cost of medical services is $140, the height of the supply curve at the equilibrium quantity. In equilibrium, the marginal cost exceeds the true marginal benefit by $90. This economic inefficiency is the result of the asymmetry of information between doctors and patients.

Supposing that doctors and patients could not privately resolve the information asymmetry, how can regulation help? In markets with asymmetric information, the regulator can resolve the asymmetry in three ways. First, the regulator can require the better-informed party to disclose its information. Second, it can regulate the conduct of the party with better information. Third, it can impose regulations on the business structure of the better-informed party.

Disclosure

The most obvious way to resolve asymmetric information is to require the better-informed party to disclose its information truthfully. In an unregulated market, parties may supply false information. For instance, dealers in fake antiques may falsely claim to be selling the genuine item, a service station may pass off regular low-octane gasoline as high-octane premium, or an obstetrician may exaggerate a pregnant woman's need for a cesarean section.

A regulatory requirement for disclosure will be meaningful only if the information can be objectively verified. Of the three examples mentioned – fake antiques, substituted gasoline, and an unnecessary cesarean section – disclosure works best for the substituted gasoline. The regulator can require service stations to mark each pump with the octane content of the gasoline and randomly inspect the pumps to ensure that the gasoline matches the specified octane level.

Whether disclosure can resolve the asymmetry of information between sellers and buyers of antiques depends on whether fakes can be distinguished objectively from genuine antiques. Disclosure will not be so helpful if the distinction between fakes and genuine antiques depends on individual judgment. Similarly, the need for a cesarean section is a matter of professional judgment; hence, disclosure may not resolve the information asymmetry.

Regulation of Conduct

Instead of directly resolving an information asymmetry, an alternative is to regulate the conduct of the better-informed party and limit the extent to which he or she can exploit the informational advantage. If parties with better information cannot exploit their advantage, then they are more likely to assist in resolving the asymmetry.

For example, in the market for medical services, a regulation may prohibit doctors from advertising. This may help to prevent further inflation of demand. Another possible regulation is a requirement that doctors recommending major procedures must advise their patients to get a second opinion. The second opinion provides a check against excessive treatment. Doctors could also be required to give patients a minimum time during which to decide on a major procedure. To the extent that these checks are effective, the inflated demand in figure 14.2 will shift down toward the true demand and the equilibrium will be closer to point *b*, where the true marginal benefit equals the marginal cost.

Another example of asymmetric information arises in the market for real estate. Typically, a seller will have better information about her or his property than potential buyers. A seller may use this advantage to pressure a potential buyer. For instance, the seller may say, "Ten other people came this morning, and three of them are making offers. You'd better move fast or you'll lose this house." A regulator can restrict such high-pressure sales tactics by stipulating a minimum waiting period during which a buyer can cancel a purchase at no cost.

Another way by which to ensure proper conduct in real estate transactions is to require that all agreements be in writing and witnessed. This will restrict the scope for a seller to provide misleading information and rush potential buyers into a purchase.

Structural Regulation

In addition to regulating conduct, a way to limit the extent to which a better-informed party can exploit an informational advantage is structural regulation. By enforcing separation of different businesses, a regulator may reduce the opportunities for exploiting superior information.

The market for medical services provides one example of structural regulation. Doctors providing medical advice will have much less incentive to overprescribe if the treatment is provided by others. Hence, a structural regulation requiring doctors to specialize in either providing advice or providing treatment would mitigate the moral hazard problem. While reducing the demand for medical services, this mandatory specialization would increase the cost of the services actually provided. Accordingly, the benefit of the specialization would have to be weighed against the cost.

Mandatory specialization is not as outlandish as might be thought. In some parts of the world, doctors are allowed to sell medicines and medical supplies in their clinics. Under these circumstances, the doctors will have an incentive to overprescribe these items. In other countries, doctors are prohibited from selling medicines and medical supplies. This regulation effectively separates medical services from retailing of medicines and medical supplies and dissuades doctors from excessive prescriptions.

Another example of structural regulation arises in the market for real estate transactions. Suppose that one agent represents both the seller and the buyer of some real estate. Then, the agent will suffer a conflict of interest between the seller and the buyer. The agent, for instance, may learn how much the buyer is willing to pay and convey that information to the seller. Such conflicts of interest can be prevented by a regulation requiring that the seller and the buyer must have separate representation.

Self-Regulation

> **Self-regulation** is the regulation of practitioners by a professional organization.

To forestall direct government regulation, some professions subject themselves to **self-regulation**. This means that a professional organization licenses all practitioners. The organization sets conditions for licensing and rules of conduct. The licensing conditions may include specific preparatory education and training, and examinations.

The professional organization may also regulate conduct such as advertising, pricing, and business structure. For instance, some professional organizations prohibit their members from incorporating with limited liability. Other organizations publish set prices and restrict advertising. Some professional organizations require that members undergo continuing education.

Typically, as a quid pro quo for self-regulation, the government gives the professional organization an exclusive right to license practitioners. Accordingly, one important issue is whether professional organizations use self-regulation as a cover to limit competition. Some rules may have anticompetitive effects. For instance, restrictive admission standards may pose a barrier to entry of new professionals. Further, guidelines on pricing and limits on advertising may also restrict competition among professionals.

Regulating the American securities markets

Following the great stock market crash of 1929, the United States established the Securities Exchange Commission (SEC). The SEC makes wide use of disclosure in regulating the securities markets. For instance, it requires the underwriters of a new share issue to publish a prospectus explaining the business purpose of the issue and possible risks. The SEC also requires publicly listed companies to provide quarterly and annual reports to their shareholders.

The SEC also regulates the conduct of participants in securities markets. For instance, the securities laws prohibit insider trading and market manipulation. The laws also specify rules of conduct for broker-dealers with regard to segregation of customer funds, financial responsibility, and minimum net capital.

Finally, the securities markets are also subject to structural regulation. Under the Glass–Steagall Act, commercial banks may not underwrite, sell, or distribute securities, while securities brokers and dealers may not take deposits. The act imposed a statutory wall between the banking and securities industries.

Source: William A. Lovett, *Banking and Financial Institutions Law in a Nutshell* (St. Paul, MN: West Publishing, 1992).

Self-regulation of lawyers: the state Bar of California

The state Bar Association of California is the self-regulatory authority for lawyers in California. The bar's admission requirements include a specified number of years of law school and a membership examination. The bar regulates advertising by lawyers. This may be a way to prevent lawyers from inflating the demand for their services. However, it has not prevented ambulance chasers from promoting their services on late-night television.

The bar also prohibits lawyers from forming partnerships with accountants. This restriction is a structural regulation to ensure that clients receive independent opinions on legal and financial issues.

The California Bar Association will not automatically grant admission to lawyers from other states. Each state bar sets its own standards of admission. The differences in these standards hinder lawyers from crossing between states, hence, constitute a barrier to competition.

◂ 5 Externalities

Externalities arise when the markets for some costs or benefits fail to exist. Absent a market, the invisible hand cannot work. In chapter 11, we considered how externalities can be resolved through private action. Some externalities, for instance, aircraft noise and automobile emissions, involve hundreds if not thousands of parties. In these cases, the difficulty of organizing all the sources and the affected parties means that private action will probably fail to resolve the externality. Government regulation may be the only solution.

To analyze how to regulate such widespread externalities, let us consider the emissions that create smog. Smog results from a complicated chemical reaction between nitrogen oxides and volatile organic compounds (VOCs). Chapter 6 showed that, for an economically efficient allocation of resources, every good or service must be provided up to the level that the marginal benefit balances the marginal cost. Although emissions are bad, the same principle applies: the economically efficient quantity of emissions balances the marginal benefit of emissions with the marginal cost, taking into account both private benefits and costs and external benefits and costs.

The major benefit of emissions is that the sources can avoid the cost of technologies that generate fewer emissions. Fixed sources of VOCs include petroleum refineries, chemical plants, and furniture manufacturers, while mobile sources include cars, boats, and lawn mowers. Furniture makers, for instance, could switch to less volatile paints and varnishes, and automobiles could use cleaner fuels such as methanol.

The cost of smog is chest pain and the increased risk of asthma attacks among people and damage to crops. Smog is ambient: it affects victims over a wide area and each victim suffers to an equal degree. For example, if a bus service adds a new vehicle, the additional emissions affect all neighboring residents to the same extent. If one victim increases his or her exposure to the emissions, this does not mean that another would be affected less. Accordingly, the marginal cost to society is the *sum* of the marginal costs to the various victims.

As depicted in figure 14.3, the economically efficient rate of emissions is 8,000 tons a year, where the marginal benefit equals the marginal cost to society. Having identified the economically efficient rate of emissions, the remaining issue is how to achieve it. Generally, there are two approaches. One aims to mimic Adam Smith's invisible hand: allow all sources to emit as much as they like provided that they pay a user fee. The other approach is to control emissions directly through standards.

User Fee

Referring to figure 14.3, at the economically efficient rate of emissions, the marginal cost to society is $35 per ton. Suppose that the regulator sets a user fee for emissions of $35 per ton and allows every source (user) to buy as much emissions as it would like at that price.

Figure 14.3 Economic efficiency in emissions

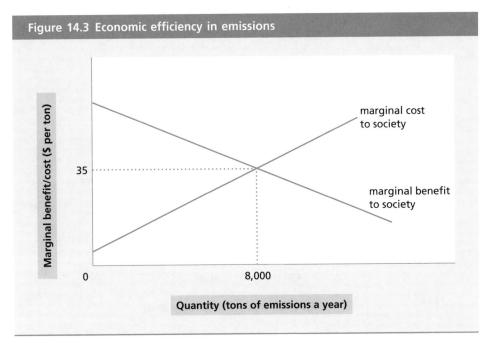

The economically efficient rate of emissions is 8,000 tons a year, where the marginal benefit and the marginal cost to society are both equal to $35 per ton.

Consider an oil refinery that emits pollutants. To maximize profits, the refinery should buy emissions up to the rate where the marginal benefit of emissions balances the $35 fee. Suppose that, as shown in figure 14.4, the refinery's marginal benefit balances the $35 fee at an emissions rate of 500 tons a year.

To see why 500 tons maximizes profit, consider emissions of less than 500 tons a year, say, 400 tons. Then, as figure 14.4 shows, the marginal benefit will be $45, which exceeds the $35 fee; so, by increasing emissions, the refinery can increase profits. Consider, instead, emissions of more than 500 tons a year, say, 600 tons. Then, the marginal benefit will be $25, which is less than the $35 fee; so the refinery should cut back on emissions. Accordingly, the refinery maximizes profit at the emissions rate where its marginal benefit equals the fee.

Other sources of emissions such as furniture manufacturers will make the same calculation: each will emit up to the point that its marginal benefit equals $35. Since the regulator charges the same $35 fee to all sources, the marginal benefits of all sources will be equal.

Since the regulator set the fee at the social marginal cost of emissions, it balances the marginal benefit with the marginal cost of emissions to society. Accordingly, the user fee achieves the economically efficient rate of emissions.

Figure 14.4 User fee

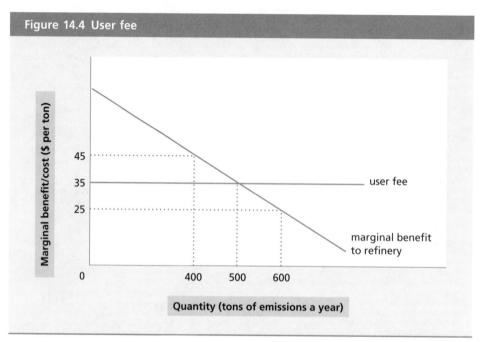

Quantity (tons of emissions a year)

The refinery's marginal benefit equals the $35 fee at an emissions rate of 500 tons a year. If the refinery emitted 400 tons, the marginal benefit would be $45, which exceeds the $35 fee, so by increasing emissions, the refinery could increase profits. If the refinery emitted 600 tons, then the marginal benefit would be $25, which is less than the $35 fee, so the refinery should cut back on emissions.

Fees in action: gasoline taxes

Most governments levy excise taxes on gasoline sales. In addition to raising revenue, a gasoline tax serves as an implicit fee for automobile emissions. In 1994, a Royal Commission on Environmental Pollution recommended that the British government increase fuel taxes by 100% to reduce emissions from cars.

Taxes on fuel can also be used to reflect differences in the external cost of different types of fuel. For instance, the Singapore government levies a lower excise tax on unleaded gasoline than on leaded gasoline. The difference in tax rates is effectively the fee for lead emissions.

Source: Royal Commission on Environmental Pollution, *Transport and the Environment* (London: HMSO, 1994).

Standard

The alternative to charging a fee for emissions is to regulate directly through standards. From figure 14.3, the economically efficient emissions rate is 8,000 tons a year, which is the appropriate standard. There are many sources of emissions, however. How should the regulator allocate the 8,000 tons a year among the various sources?

The answer depends on the cost of monitoring. Suppose that the emissions of all sources can be monitored at relatively low cost. The regulator could issue licenses for 8,000 tons of emissions a year and sell them through public auction. Potential sources of emissions will provide the demand for the licenses. The demand of each source for licenses will be the same as its marginal benefit from emissions. The market demand will be the horizontal sum of the individual demand curves. So, the market demand curve will be identical to the social marginal benefit curve in figure 14.3.

The supply of licenses would be perfectly inelastic at 8,000. In equilibrium, the market demand will balance the supply at a quantity of 8,000 licenses a year. Now, by figure 14.3, the marginal benefit of the 8,000th ton of emissions is $35. Thus, the equilibrium price of a license will be $35. Each source will buy licenses up to the point that its marginal benefit balances the price of $35. As a result, each source's emissions will be economically efficient and the total emissions will be at the economically efficient rate of 8,000 tons a year.

Trading in emissions licenses: curbing acid rain

Emissions of sulfur dioxide cause acid rain. Beginning in 1977, the Clean Air Act required all new power plants to install flue-gas desulfurization equipment ("scrubbers"). The problem was how to reduce sulfur dioxide emissions from existing power plants. It did not seem economical to require scrubbers in older plants.

Congress decided to allow existing plants to reduce emissions by any means including installing scrubbers, switching to low-sulfur coal, and paying other sources to reduce their emissions by more than their own requirement. The latter option created a market in emissions rights.

In 1995, the first year of emissions trading, the Clean Air Act required large electric power plants to reduce sulfur dioxide emissions from 10 to 8.7 million tons. In fact, the value of the emissions rights encouraged power plants to reduce emissions to 5.3 million tons. The trading scheme is estimated to have reduced emissions $2–3 billion more cheaply than if all existing plants had been required to retrofit with scrubbers.

Sources: Paul R. Portrey, "Economics and the Clean Air Act," *Journal of Economic Perspectives*, Fall 1990, pp. 133–81; "Clean Air Sale," *Washington Post*, August 8, 1999.

By selling emissions licenses, the regulator is effectively charging a user fee that is determined by a competitive market. The license scheme, however, may be difficult to implement for small mobile sources such as power-boats and lawn mowers. It will be relatively expensive to monitor emissions from these sources. In such cases, it may be better for the regulator to specify directly the type and size of engine and fuel.

Progress check **Progress Check 14C** Referring to figure 14.3, compare the social welfare with user fees of $25 per ton and $45 per ton.

Regional and Temporal Differences

The efficient degree of an externality balances the marginal benefit with the marginal cost. Many externalities that need regulatory action are regional problems. For instance,

Clean Air Act: federal vis-à-vis state standards

The Clean Air Act, passed by the U.S. Congress in 1970, imposes uniform federal standards for air quality throughout the United States. The Act has substantially enhanced the American quality of air. By 1995, emissions of lead had been cut by over 95%, and smog-forming organic compounds had been reduced by almost 25%.

The federal Environmental Protection Agency (EPA) has specified controls on petroleum refineries, chemical plants, and even dry cleaners. Further, in several especially polluted areas, the EPA has required gasoline stations to sell only reformulated gasoline, which causes less pollution but also provides lower mileage.

The annual cost of complying with the Clean Air Act, however, exceeded $30 billion in 1990 and was estimated to reach $60 billion by 2005. The costs of compliance led some states to seek novel solutions. For instance, in Wisconsin, small engines generate 11% of emissions. The state offered to buy old outboard motors in exchange for credits toward new motors.

In southern California, the oil company Unocal was required to cut emissions from its marine terminal. The conventional approach would have been to install a vapor-recovery system. Instead, Unocal bought and destroyed 350 old cars, so reducing emissions by the required amount at much lower cost.

Sources: National Air Quality and Emissions Trends Report, EPA-450/4-90-002, U.S. Environmental Protection Agency (March 1990); "Clean Air (1)," *Economist*, March 4, 1995, p. 36.

smog above Los Angeles does not affect Chicago. Further, the marginal benefit and the marginal cost of an externality may vary from one place to another.

If the benefits and costs of an externality are confined to a region, then it is economically efficient to allow each region to determine its own degree of the externality. Uniform national standards may result in economic inefficiency.

National or international standards, however, are necessary for externalities that cross boundaries. For instance, sulfur dioxide emitted by coal-fired electric power plants in the American Midwest causes acid rain in the Northeast and Canada. Chlorofluorocarbons from all over the world damage the ozone layer in the atmosphere. Federal regulation is necessary to resolve externalities among states, and international regulation for externalities among countries.

If the marginal benefit and the marginal cost of an externality vary over time, then the efficient degree of the externality will also vary with time. This is most obvious with noise. Society may be relatively more willing to tolerate noise during working hours than at night or on weekends. The same principle also applies over longer periods of time. As victims become more sensitive to air pollution or new technologies to reduce emissions become available, the economically efficient rate of emissions will fall.

Accidents

As discussed earlier, private action may fail to resolve externalities that involve large numbers of parties. A specific class of such externalities is accidents. When Joy drives out of her house onto the main road, she joins an anonymous stream of other cars, buses, and trucks. She has no way of knowing the other drivers, let alone negotiating and agreeing with them on how to deal with an accident.

Yet each driver influences the likelihood and severity of accident by the care that he or she takes in driving. The economically efficient degree of care balances the marginal benefit to society (in terms of the reduced expected damage from accidents) with the marginal cost of care to the driver. We illustrate this balance in figure 14.5.

Private action, however, may fail to resolve the externality imposed by one driver on another. It is difficult for every driver to negotiate with every other driver about their respective degrees of care in driving and even more difficult to enforce compliance. Accordingly, government intervention is necessary to balance the marginal benefit and the marginal cost.

> The **law of torts** is the law governing interactions between parties that have no contractual relationship.

Typically, the government does not intervene directly. Rather, the government establishes a legal framework to deal with accidents. The legal framework consists of laws and the court system. The **law of torts** governs interactions between parties that have no contractual relationship. The court system provides the mechanism by which the victim of an accident can enforce her or his legal rights.

> **Liability** is the set of conditions under which one party must pay damages to another party.

The law of torts specifies the **liability** of the parties to an accident. Liability is the set of conditions under which one party

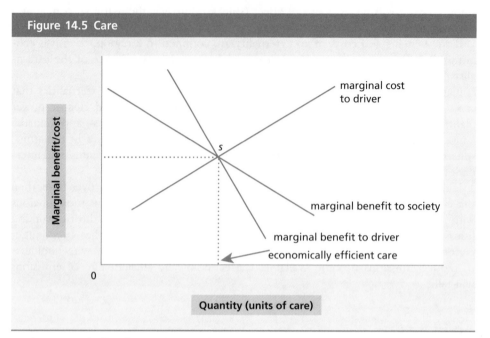

Figure 14.5 Care

At the economically efficient degree of care, the marginal benefit to society equals the marginal cost of care to the driver. If the marginal benefit of care to the driver balanced the marginal cost at the economically efficient level, then the driver would choose the economically efficient degree of care.

must pay damages to another party. The law regarding liability varies from one jurisdiction to another. For instance, in some jurisdictions, the injurer is liable only if he or she was negligent, and in other jurisdictions, the injurer is not liable if the victim contributed to the occurrence of the accident.

The law of torts also specifies the amount that the injurer must pay in damages to the victim. Generally, the damages include compensation for the victim's loss, including medical expenses and lost earnings. Again, the precise rules on damages vary among jurisdictions.

In effect, by specifying liability and damages, the law of torts establishes a price for causing an accident or, equivalently, a price for failing to take care. Unlike prices in competitive markets, the price for an accident is paid only after the event. This legal framework is less costly than requiring every potential injurer to negotiate and agree with every potential victim in advance.

Within this framework, each potential injurer will balance the private marginal benefit of care (in terms of the reduced expected liability for damages) against the marginal cost. If the law specifies liability and damages appropriately, then the potential injurer will choose the economically efficient level of care. Referring to figure 14.5, this will happen if the marginal benefit of care to the driver balances the marginal cost at the economically efficient level.

> **Progress Check 14D** Suppose that, relative to the situation in figure 14.5; the courts double the damages that injurers must pay accident victims. How will this affect a driver's choice of care?
>
> *Progress check*

◂◂ 6 Public Goods

A public good provides nonrival consumption or use. Private enterprises provide many public goods, including free-to-the-air television, literary and musical works, and software on a commercial basis. Usually, a public good can be provided commercially only if the consumption or use of the item is excludable. If a provider could not exclude free riders, then it would be very difficult to sell the item. As we discussed in chapter 11, excludability depends on law and technology.

Here, we discuss the legal framework for excludability and show that regulators must balance two factors: that excludability is necessary for private provision and that private provision may result in less than the economically efficient level of provision. We then discuss the alternative to private provision, which is provision by charity or the government.

Legal Framework

In chapter 11, we considered two forms of intellectual property – copyright and patent – that make the use of scientific knowledge excludable. A copyright is a legal, exclusive right to an artistic, literary, or musical expression. The concept extends protection to software. Similarly, a patent is a legal, exclusive right to a product or process.

Suppose that the owner of a copyright or patent aims to maximize profit and applies uniform pricing. Each individual user will purchase the quantity of the copyrighted or patented item where the marginal benefit equals the price. Hence, the marginal benefit equals the price. But the profitmaximizing uniform price exceeds the marginal cost. This means that each user's marginal benefit will exceed the marginal cost and the use will be less than the economically efficient level.

For economic efficiency, a public good should be provided up to the quantity that the marginal benefit equals the marginal cost. A public good provides nonrival use; hence, the marginal cost of additional provision is nothing. Thus, the public good should be provided up to the quantity that the marginal benefit is zero for each user. A profit-maximizing owner applying uniform pricing will not achieve this level of provision.

We have just shown that copyright and patent protection may result in use at less than the economically efficient level. On the other hand, without such protection, there would be little incentive for commercial creation of scientific knowledge. Accordingly, society faces a trade-off between the incentive to create scientific knowledge and inefficient use.

This trade-off explains why copyrights and patents have limited lives. Under U.S. law, copyrights last for the life of the creator plus 70 years, while patents are valid for 20 years. On the expiration of a copyright, anyone can freely copy or use the material. Similarly, once a patent has expired, anyone can freely imitate or use the product or process.

The expiration of a copyright or patent allows free use of the formerly protected scientific knowledge. Usage will extend to the point where the marginal benefit equals zero, which is the economically efficient level. During the life of a copyright or patent, however, the owner has an exclusive right and society bears the cost of less than efficient usage.

Progress check   **Progress Check 14E**   If society wants to increase the usage of existing scientific knowledge, should it reduce or extend the validity of copyrights and patents?

Legalizing My.MP3.com

At the time of writing, one of the World Wide Web's most popular services was distribution of music in MP3 digital format. Riding on the wave, My.MP3.com offered a service to store digital copies of music CDs. Any user who proved ownership of a CD could store its content on My.MP3.com and use it through the Internet. My.MP3.com soon assembled a large database of digital music copied from 45,000 CDs.

The world's five leading music publishers – BMG Entertainment, Warner Music, EMI Recorded Music, Universal Music, and Sony Music Entertainment – sued My.MP3.com for copyright infringement. In April 2000, U.S. federal District Judge Jed S. Rakoff ruled in favor of the publishers. Several months later, My.MP3.com settled with BMG and Warner Music for tens of millions of dollars and entered into licensing agreements for future use.

Warner Music executive vice-president, Paul Vidich, hailed the settlement: "This is an important moment for recording artists and copyright owners. The settlement agreement clearly affirms the rights of copyright owners to be compensated for use of their works on the Internet."

Source: "MP3.com Reaches Settlement with 2 Labels over Online Music," *Wall Street Journal Interactive Edition*, June 9, 2000.

Public Provision

For some public goods, it would be difficult or impossible to exclude people who do not pay. For instance, if the air circulating above Houston becomes cleaner, it would be difficult to exclude specific persons from enjoying the cleaner air. The same is true of national defense: during an enemy bomb raid, anti-aircraft batteries cannot protect some people without protecting everyone else in the neighborhood.

For other public goods, exclusion may be possible but only against some users. Consider the process for distilling water. Suppose that the law allowed a patent on this process. The owner of the patent could probably enforce it on large-scale users such as commercial suppliers of distilled water. It would be nearly impossible to exclude high-school students or household cooks from using the process, however.

Typically, if use of a public good is nonexcludable or difficult to exclude, it can be provided only by charities or the government. Some of the public goods provided by charities are medical and scientific research, public health, and free-to-the-air radio and television. The public goods that are provided by government include civil laws, environmental protection, and national defense. Table 14.3 lists some providers of scientific research.

In addition to the issue of excludability, there is another reason for charitable or government provision of a public good. To the extent that these providers do not charge a price for the use of the good, it will be used up to the quantity where the marginal benefit equals zero. Hence, the use will be economically efficient.

It is important to distinguish public goods from goods provided by the government, however. Not all items provided by the government sector are public goods. Compare, for instance, public health programs such as the eradication of communicable diseases with medical treatment. The eradication of communicable diseases such as tuberculosis is a public good. Once tuberculosis is wiped out, everyone benefits to an equal degree. By contrast, medical treatment is a private good: a doctor that spends more time treating one patient will have less time for other patients.

Table 14.3 Funding for scientific research

Jurisdiction	Organization	Research Area
Australia	CSIRO	Science and technology
Canada	National Research Council	Science and technology
Japan	Science and Technology Agency	Science and technology
United Kingdom	Medical Research Council Science Research Council Wellcome Foundation	Medicine Science Medicine
United States of America	National Institutes of Health National Science Foundation	Medicine Science and technology

Governments provide many private goods such as food, education, housing, and medical services. By providing these private goods, the government may be aiming to equalize the distribution of wealth and provide equal opportunity for future generations.

Congestible Facilities

The use of facilities such as tunnels is excludable. Such facilities often have a capacity that is relatively large compared with demand, causing them to be natural monopolies. Hence, for economically efficient usage, they must be prevented from exercising monopoly power. In principle, these facilities could be provided by a commercial operator subject to regulation. Some, however, are provided by the government.

The demand for such facilities usually varies with time. Outside of peak hours, the facility provides nonrival use. By contrast, during peak hours, each additional user adds to congestion, the costs of which include delays, additional fuel, and an increase in accidents; hence, usage is a private good.

Consider a tunnel that can smoothly convey up to 30 vehicles a minute. When 30 vehicles a minute already are entering the tunnel, however, additional drivers will cause congestion. From the standpoint of economic efficiency, traffic through the tunnel should be managed so that the marginal benefit of each user balances the marginal cost. When there are fewer than 30 vehicles a minute, the marginal cost of a crossing is nothing. So, the tunnel should not exclude any driver.

When, however, 30 vehicles per minute are in the tunnel, the marginal cost becomes positive. For economic efficiency, the tunnel should set a toll equal to the marginal cost. This will ensure that the only drivers who enter the tunnel are those whose benefit exceeds the marginal cost.

What if the tunnel does not charge a toll? Consider the decision of a marginal driver (the 31st) whether to enter the tunnel or wait until there is less traffic. If the driver enters immediately, she will save some time. In making the decision, that driver compares her private benefit from crossing at that time with her private cost and ignores the additional costs on other drivers. Owing to this negative externality, the number of drivers entering the tunnel tends to exceed the economically efficient number. The solution is for the tunnel to charge a toll equal to the marginal cost of a crossing.

Generally, for economic efficiency, congestible facilities should levy a price, set equal to the marginal cost of use, where the cost includes the externalities imposed on other users. As the marginal cost varies with the time of day, so should the price. This pricing would ensure economically efficient usage of facilities such as bridges, tunnels, roads, and subways.

Progress check **Progress Check 14F** Suppose that a local telephone service provider sets the same price for local calls at all times of the day. Would this lead to economically efficient usage?

Congestion in space

Satellites provide a convenient platform for transmission of electromagnetic signals over long distances, especially in relatively undeveloped regions. In recent years, the rapid growth of international broadcasting and telecommunication has boosted the demand for satellite transmission.

To operate effectively, a communications satellite must remain within the line of sight of all its corresponding earth stations. For this, the satellite should be positioned at a height of 35,784 kilometers, so that it will remain stationary relative to its position over the earth. This position is called a *geosynchronous orbit*.

Since transmissions from one satellite can interfere with those of another, it is important that there be adequate spacing between satellites. Consequently, there is a limit to the number of geosynchronous positions.

The International Telecommunications Union regulates the positioning of communications satellites. It stipulates a 3–4° angular spacing between satellites, depending on the frequencies at which the satellites are transmitting.

In July 1994, a Chinese consortium launched and positioned its Apstar 1 at 131° East, with only a 1° spacing from the Japanese Sakura satellite at 132° East and the Russian Rimsat at 130° East. Predictably, the Apstar 1 interfered with the Sakura's communications.

The Japanese Government protested vigorously. Eventually, the Chinese consortium moved the Apstar 1 to 138° East.

Sources: William Stallings and Richard Van Slyke, *Business Data Communications*, 2d ed. (New York: Macmillan, 1994), pp. 110–18; "Chinese Satellite Launch Condemned by Japan," *New Straits Times*, July 23, 1994, p. 19.

◂◂ 7 Summary

The marginal benefit of an item may diverge from the marginal cost for three basic reasons: market power, asymmetric information, and externalities and public goods. This divergence results in economic inefficiency. Government regulation may help where private action fails to resolve the economic inefficiency.

Generally, the government can regulate conduct, information, and structure. Specifically, the conduct of a franchised monopoly may be regulated directly through price or indirectly through the rate of return. Competition law regulates the conduct and structure of businesses in general. In situations of asymmetric information, mandatory disclosure is one form of regulation.

Externalities may be regulated through fees or standards. The efficient degree of an externality depends on location and time. The government can help to resolve inefficiency in accidents and public goods by providing an appropriate legal framework.

The laws regarding copyrights and patents must balance the incentive for new research against inefficient use of existing knowledge.

Key Concepts

natural monopoly

privatization

marginal cost pricing

average cost pricing

rate base

self-regulation

law of torts

liability

Further Reading

West Publishing publishes simple and useful guides to many areas of United States law and regulation. Relevant titles include Ernest Gellhorn and William Kovacic's *Antitrust Law and Economics in a Nutshell*, 4th ed. (1994); Roger W. Findley and Daniel A. Farber's *Environmental Law in a Nutshell*, 3d ed. (1992); and Arthur R. Miller and Michael H. Davis's *Intellectual Property – Patents, Trademarks and Copyright in a Nutshell*, 2d ed. (1990).

Review Questions

1. Using relevant examples, explain the following concepts:
    (a) a natural monopoly;
    (b) a rate base;
    (c) self-regulation.

2. Name one franchised monopoly from which you buy services. Is the monopoly subject to regulation on any of the following?
    (a) price;
    (b) rate of return;
    (c) structure.

3. Explain the differences between price and rate of return regulation.

4. Why do competition laws generally restrict mergers and acquisitions that create monopolies or monopsonies?

5. Explain the differences between
    (a) privatization;
    (b) allowing competition.

6. Name one self-regulated monopoly. Does it regulate disclosure, conduct, or structure?

7. At one time, U.S. law prohibited movie producers from owning theaters. Use this example to explain
   (a) vertical integration;
   (b) structural regulation.

8. True or false? Mandatory disclosure is always the best way to resolve asymmetric information.

9. Explain how regulation of conduct and business structure can resolve asymmetric information.

10. Explain how the following policies can be used to control noise pollution by construction equipment:
    (a) user fee;
    (b) standard.

11. True or false? The economically efficient degree of an externality can only be achieved through a standard.

12. How do copyrights and patents contribute to excludability of consumption or usage of a public good?

13. Which of the following situations involves externalities?
    (a) The workers in a factory may injure themselves on the production equipment.
    (b) Two ships may collide while passing through a narrow channel at night.

14. A charitable foundation sponsored the development of a drug that cures bone-marrow cancer. The foundation has patented the drug and is selling it on a commercial basis. Will the use of the drug be economically efficient?

15. Explain the differences among a private good, congestible facility, and a public good.

Discussion Questions

1. In July 2000, the San Diego Water Authority charged its 23 member agencies a uniform price of $439 per acre-foot of water. (An acre-foot is the volume of water that would cover one acre to a depth of one foot, or about 326,000 gallons.) Suppose that the Water Authority practices marginal-cost pricing and its marginal cost of water is increasing and begins at $0.
   (a) Illustrate the current price and quantity on an appropriate diagram.
   (b) The Water Authority negotiated with the Imperial Irrigation District to buy 200,000 acre-feet of Colorado River water at $245 per acre-foot. Show how this purchase would affect the Authority's marginal cost of water.
   (c) Assume that the Water Authority continues to practice marginal cost pricing. On your diagram, show the increase in buyer and seller surplus that

San Diego as a whole will achieve from the acquisition of the water rights to 200,000 acre-feet.

2. With over 10 million subscribers, AT&T Cable is one of the nation's largest cable television providers. The cable industry also includes many small operators that serve a few thousand subscribers each.
   (a) For over 20 years, there was only one cable television provider in Louisville, Kentucky. Explain how the cost of laying a network causes cable television to tend towards a natural monopoly.
   (b) Considering an area with a single cable service provider, discuss whether the provider would have greater market power over its consumers if it were AT&T Cable or a small independent operator.
   (c) With de-regulation of the local telephone industry and growing demand for the Internet, cable companies found new opportunities in providing local telephone and Internet access service. Existing cable providers, however, had to re-build their legacy networks to provide the new services. Has the cable business ceased to be a natural monopoly?

3. Which of the following practices are illegal under the competition laws of your jurisdiction?
   (a) The suppliers of 95% of the ready-mix concrete market organize a cartel to limit sales and raise prices above the competitive level.
   (b) An electronics store offers different prices to different customers.
   (c) A pharmaceutical manufacturer's contracts with its retailers provide that the retailers must set prices above a specified minimum, failing which the manufacturer will stop further shipments.

4. In the United States, all stockbrokers must insure customer accounts up to a minimum level with the Securities Investor Protection Corporation (SIPC). This insurance covers customers against default by the broker.
   (a) What is the minimum required level of SIPC insurance?
   (b) Can you explain this requirement in terms of asymmetric information between brokers and investors?
   (c) Many brokers purchase private insurance to cover losses that exceed the minimum SIPC cover. Please explain this practice as a way by which brokers can signal their financial reliability.

5. Consider the following practices of the Hong Kong medical profession. Do they serve to resolve economic inefficiency or limit competition?
   (a) Doctors are not allowed to advertise.
   (b) Doctors can sell medicines from their clinics. Until recently, they could dispense drugs in unmarked containers without indicating the medicine. At the time of writing, they were not required to mark the expiration date of the medicine.
   (c) Doctors admitted in Ireland can practice freely in Hong Kong, but doctors who are qualified in California must undergo special training and a rigorous examination.

6. Leaded gasoline is a major source of lead emissions. Compare these two alternative ways of reducing lead emissions:
   (a) Requiring all new automobiles to be equipped with catalytic converters so that they can operate on unleaded gasoline. The catalytic converter will be damaged if it is used with leaded gasoline. The requirement does not apply to older cars.
   (b) Setting a lower excise tax on unleaded gasoline than on leaded gasoline so that unleaded is cheaper at the pump.

7. Marine traffic through the Luna Straits is very heavy, and especially at night, there is a significant risk of collision between passing vessels.
   (a) Using a suitable diagram, analyze the marginal benefit and marginal cost of care to society in navigation through the Luna Straits.
   (b) Suppose that the law of torts provides that any ship that fails to take due care must bear liability for accidents. Using the diagram in (a), explain how a typical ship's master will choose care.
   (c) Suppose that the courts reduce the damages that ships must pay to victims of accidents. How will this change affect masters in their degree of care in the straits?

8. The U.S. Federal Aviation Administration (FAA) classifies all civil transport aircraft according to noise. The categories range from Stage 1, which is the noisiest, to Stage 3, which is the quietest category.
   (a) If one airport prohibits landings by Stage 1 and 2 aircraft, will it impose externalities on other airports?
   (b) Who should regulate aircraft noise, the federal government or local airport authorities?
   (c) Suppose that an airport has specified standards for aircraft noise. Some airlines operate older, noisier aircraft than others. Should the airport create permits for aircraft noise and allow airlines to trade these permits?

9. Prentice Hall owns the copyright to Professor Philip Kotler's best-selling textbook *Marketing Management*. Prentice Hall earns revenues from sales to students and libraries.
   (a) Explain the sense in which the content of Professor Kotler's book is a public good.
   (b) Students who photocopy a library copy of the book are breaching Prentice Hall's copyright. Compare the following proposals in terms of rewarding authors and administrative cost: (i) The government imposes a levy on all copies made on library photcopying machines. It distributes the revenues from the levy to authors. (ii) The government bans photocopying machines from libraries.

10. Internet users connect either by dial-up service, or continuously through digital subscriber line, cable modem, or corporate network. Among those who dial up, some pay a usage charge for each minute, while others subscribe to unmetered service for a flat monthly fee. The various uses of the Internet range in data intensity. Simple email is the least demanding, while video and audio streaming require transfer of huge quantities of data. Usage of the Internet varies with the time of day.

(a) Explain why unmetered service results in economically inefficient usage of the Internet.

(b) Some Internet access providers charge per minute usage fees that are fixed throughout the day. Should they charge fees that vary with the time of the day?

(c) While users do not mind if email is delayed, they do care about the speed of Web pages. Do the existing pricing mechanisms cater for this difference?

11. This question applies the mathematical technique for analyzing a natural monopoly presented in the math supplement. The demand for electric power in Sol Province is $p = 20 - 20q$, where p and q represent the price in thousands of dollars and the quantity in megawatt-hours, respectively. Suppose that an electricity plant generates power at a constant marginal cost of $1,000 per megawatt-hour up to a capacity of 10 megawatt-hours. Sol Province requires the plant to implement marginal cost pricing.

(a) Illustrate the price and quantity with marginal cost pricing.

(b) Suppose that demand grows to $p = 20 - 0.1q$. At a price of $1,000 per megawatt-hour, what is the minimum number of plants needed to produce the quantity demanded?

Chapter 14

Math Supplement

Let us apply a numerical example to see how a natural monopoly can evolve into a potentially competitive market. Suppose that the demand for electric power is

$$p = 10 - q, \qquad (14.1)$$

where p and q represent price in thousand dollars and quantity in megawatt-hours, respectively. All generating plants have a capacity of 10 megawatt-hours. Generation involves a fixed cost of $50,000 and a constant marginal cost of $1,000 per megawatt-hour.

Figure 14.6 depicts the demand and costs. The demand curve intersects the marginal cost at the quantity where

Figure 14.6 Demand and market structure

original demand curve

new demand curve

capacity of single plant

Price/marginal cost (thousand $ per megawatt-hour)

Quantity (megawatt-hours)

With the original demand curve, generation is a natural monopoly. With the new demand curve, the economies of scale are now small relative to the market demand; hence, the market is close to being potentially competitive.

$$1 = 10 - q \qquad (14.2)$$

or $q = 9$.

Hence, at the intersection, the quantity demanded is 9 megawatt-hours. A single plant can produce this quantity at a total cost of $50,000 + $1,000 × 9 = $59,000, or an average cost of $59,000/9 = $6,556 per megawatt-hour. If, however, two plants were generating, then each would incur the fixed cost of $50,000, hence the total cost would be $109,000, implying an average cost of $109,000/9 = $12,111 per megawatt-hour. In this case, generation is a natural monopoly.

Now, suppose that the demand grows to $p = 10 - 0.05q$. This new demand curve will cross the marginal cost at a quantity of $1 = 10 - 0.05q$, or $q = 9/0.05 = 180$. If every plant operates at full capacity, 18 plants would be needed to meet this quantity demanded. The economies of scale are now small relative to the market demand. The market is no longer a natural monopoly but is close to being potentially competitive.

◄ Guide to Data Sources

Managerial economics is driven by data: the theory must be systematically verified with empirical data, and the concepts can be applied to actual numbers. This guide provides links to sources that the author has found to be particularly useful. It does not aim to be comprehensive or exhaustive. To access the most recent version of this guide, visit http://www.comp.nus.edu.sg/~ipng/mecon.htm and click on "Guide to data sources."

Global Economics and Finance

General business newspapers including the *Financial Times* and the *Wall Street Journal* provide daily stock, bond, commodities, and derivatives prices, exchange rates, interest rates, and other financial information. Proprietary online databases such as the *Dow Jones Interactive* and *Lexis–Nexis* provide general business and economic information in full text.

The following sources provide current and historical data.

- **General**. The World Bank (http://www.worldbank.org/data/) provides a wide range of data, including primary commodity prices, exchange rates, interest rates, and statistics on income, education, nutrition, and other variables relevant to economic and human development. The Organization of Economic Co-operation and Development (http://www.oecd.org/std/index.htm) focuses on statistics for the developed economies.

- **Exchange rates**. Professor Werner Antweiler of the University of British Columbia provides the PACIFIC Exchange Rate Service (http://pacific.commerce.ubc.ca/xr/), a comprehensive source for exchange rates on daily and monthly basis.

- **Market share and growth**. Euromonitor (http://www.euromonitor.com/) publishes market share and growth information for a wide range of consumer and industrial products in many countries. The data are available on CD-ROM and online.

- **Trade.** World Trade Organization (http://www.wto.org/english/res_e/statis_e/statis_e.htm).

United States

Two good starting points for general demographic, economic, financial, and social data of the United States are *Fedstats: One Stop Shopping for Federal Statistics* (http://www.fedstats.gov/), and the *Statistical Abstract of the United States* (http://www.census.gov/statab/www/). Specialized sources worth highlighting are:

- **Macroeconomics and finance**. The *Economic Report of the President* (http://w3.access.gpo.gov/eop/) is published annually by the President's Council of Economic Advisors. It reviews the economy and analyzes current government policy.

- **Money, banking, and finance**. Federal Reserve Board (http://www.federalreserve.gov/rnd.htm).

- **Labor markets and cost of living**. U.S. Bureau of Labor Statistics (http://stats.bls.gov/datahome.htm).

- **Media**. Gale Database of Publications and Broadcast Media.

- **Transportation**. U.S. Bureau of Transportation Statistics (http://www.bts.gov/btsprod/nts/).

Industries and Companies

The following are useful sources for data on particular markets:

- **Agriculture**. United Nations Food and Agriculture Organization (http://apps.fao.org/).

- **Automobiles**. *Automotive News International* (http://www.autonewsinternational.com/).

- **Energy**. *Oil and Gas Journal* (http://ogj.pennnet.com/cd_anchor_home/); *BP Statistical Review of World Energy, 1999* (http://www.bp.com/worldenergy/index.htm); and U.S. Energy Information Administration (http://www.eia.doe.gov/).

- **Semiconductors**. American IC Exchange (http://www.aice.com/).

- **Telecommunications**. International Telecommunication Union (http://www.itu.int/ti/).

- **Transportation: Air**. International Air Transport Association
  (http://www.iata.org/air/).

- **Transportation: Maritime**. *Platou Report*
  (http://www.platou.com/platoureport.htm);
  and Organisation for Economic Co-operation and Development, *Maritime Statistics* (http://www.oecd.org/dsti/sti/transpor/sea/index.htm).

Every company listed on a U.S. stock exchange must file annual and quarterly reports with the Securities and Exchange Commission. These reports are available through the Commission's EDGAR Database (http://www.sec.gov/edgarhp.htm). Corporate data are also available through Yahoo! (http://www.yahoo.com/) and other financial portals.

◄ Answers to Progress Checks and Selected Review Questions

◄ Chapter 1 Introduction to Managerial Economics

1A. The managerial economics of the "new economy" emphasizes network effects in demand and scalability.

1B. Vertical boundaries delineate activities closer to or further from the end user. Horizontal boundaries are defined by the scale and scope of operations.

4. No, models must be less than completely realistic to be useful.

5. (a) Average price per minute = $(360 + 210 \times 4)/5$ = ¥240 per minute.
   (b) Price of marginal minute = ¥210.

6. (a) Flow.
   (b) Stock.
   (c) Stock.

7. (a) The electricity market includes buyers and sellers.
   (b) The electricity industry consists of sellers only.

8. (a) False.
   (b) False.

12. (a) Intel.

13. (b).

14. (a) and (b).

◄ Chapter 2 Demand

2A. The theater must cut its price by $5 from $7.50 to $2.50.

2B. (1) It slopes downward because of diminishing marginal benefit.

(2) Assuming that black-and-white TVs are an inferior product, the drop in the consumer's income will cause the demand curve to shift to the right.

2C. Video rentals are a substitute for movies. A fall in the price of video rentals will cause the demand curve for movies to shift to the left.

2D. An increase in the price of a complement would cause the market demand to shift to the left.

2E. If the price of movies is $5, Joy's buyer surplus would be the area *dcba*.

2F. It can increase its profit by reducing labor to 1,000 worker-hours.

3. Introduction of the new diaphragm will
   (a) reduce the demand for male condoms;
   (b) reduce the demand for birth control pills.

7. (a) The demand for Marriott rooms will increase.
   (b) Assuming that Motel 6 rooms are an inferior product, the demand for Motel 6 rooms will decrease.

8. Mont Blanc fountain pens are a luxury item and more sensitive to income distribution.

9. (a), (b), and (c).

10. The carrier should set the price so that the consumer has no buyer surplus.

◀◀ Chapter 3 Elasticity

3A. The residential demand for water is relatively less elastic than the industrial demand.

3B. The demand curve is a straight line. At a price of $11,000, the quantity demanded would be 14,000 while at a price of $12,000, the quantity demanded would be 12,000. Accordingly, the proportionate change in the quantity demanded is $-2,000/13,000$ and the proportionate change in the price is $1,000/11,500$. Hence, by the arc approach, the own-price elasticity of demand is -1.77.

3C. The demand for liquor is relatively more income elastic than the demand for cigarettes.

3D. For a durable, the short-run demand could be more or less elastic than the long-run demand.

3E. The advertising elasticity of demand is $0.03 \times 446.67/88.93 = 0.15$.

5. Rise.

7. (a) True.
   (b) True.

8. (b) Complements.

10. The increase in quantity demanded would be $1.3 \times 5 = 6.5\%$.

11. Advertising by one particular brand will draw customers from customers of other brands as well as increase the demand for beer in general. Advertising of beer in general can only increase the market demand.

12. More elastic in the long run.

15. A cross section records all the data at one time, while a time series records changes over time.

◄◄ Chapter 4 Supply

4A. The total cost curve would be higher but the variable cost curve would not change.

4B. The marginal and average variable cost curves would not change, but the average cost curve would be lower.

4C. To maximize profit, Luna must produce at the rate where marginal cost equals 75 cents. Please refer to figure 4C.

4D. If the market price of eggs is $1.31, Luna should produce 8,000 dozen eggs a week and its revenue would be $1.31 × 8,000 = $10,840, hence its profit would be $10,480 − $7,232 = $3,248.

4E. See figure 4E.

4F. See figure 4F.

4G. Proportionate change in quantity = (6,500 − 5,800)/6,150 = 11%. Proportionate change in price = (90 − 80)/85 = 12%. Hence, the price elasticity = 11/12 = 0.9.

Figure 4C Answer to Progress Check 4C

Figure 4E Answer to Progress Check 4E

Figure 4F Answer to Progress Check 4F

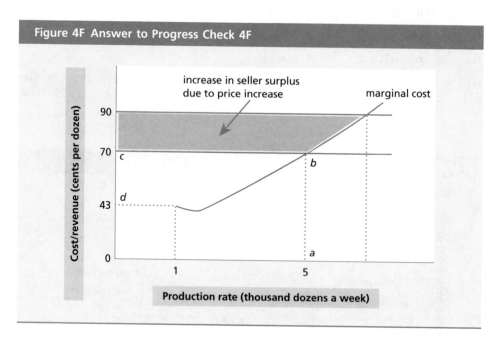

1. The short run is a time horizon within which a seller cannot adjust at least one input. By contrast, the long run is a time horizon long enough that the seller can adjust all inputs. Assuming that all fixed costs are also sunk, while all variable costs are not sunk, then there are fixed costs only in the short run, while all costs are variable in the long run.

2. This statement confuses average with marginal cost. The average cost is $2. The marginal cost may be greater than, equal to, or less than $2, depending on the production technology.

5. Since the price of Mercury's output is less than the marginal cost, Mercury can raise profit by reducing production.

6. The analysis underestimates the increase in profit: it considers only the increase in profit on the existing production, and ignores the increase in profit resulting from an increase in production.

7. (a) Increases both average and marginal cost curves.
   (b) No effect.
   (c) Reduces both average and marginal cost curves.

11. (a) Movement along the market supply curve.
    (b) Shift of the entire market supply curve.
    (c) Shift of the entire market supply curve.

12. The buyer should design its order to leave the seller with zero seller surplus.

13. (a) False.
    (b) True.

15. The supply will be relatively more elastic in the long run.

◂ Chapter 5 Competitive Markets

5A. A seller with market power could affect the selling price; hence, it could not answer the question, "How much would you sell, assuming that you could sell as much as you would like at the going price?" Thus, it is not possible to construct a market supply curve.

5B. See figure 5B.

5C. (1) False.
    (2) True.

5D. See figure 5D.

5E. See figure 5E.

5F. The price will be 1.33% lower at $19.73, and the quantity will be 2.66% higher at 10.27 million.

5G. See figure 5G.

5H. See figure 5H.

1. In entertainment, the market that better fits the model of perfect competition is (b), while for energy, it is (b), and for investments it is (a).

2. True.

Figure 5B Answer to Progress Check 5B

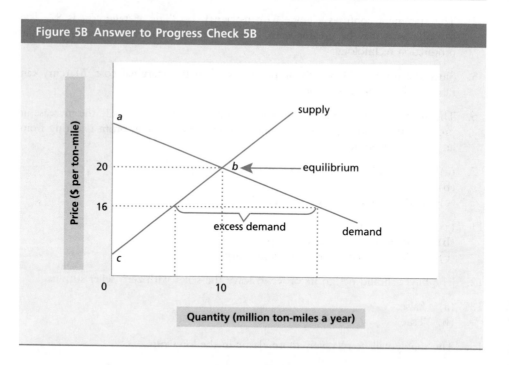

Figure 5D Answer to Progress Check 5D

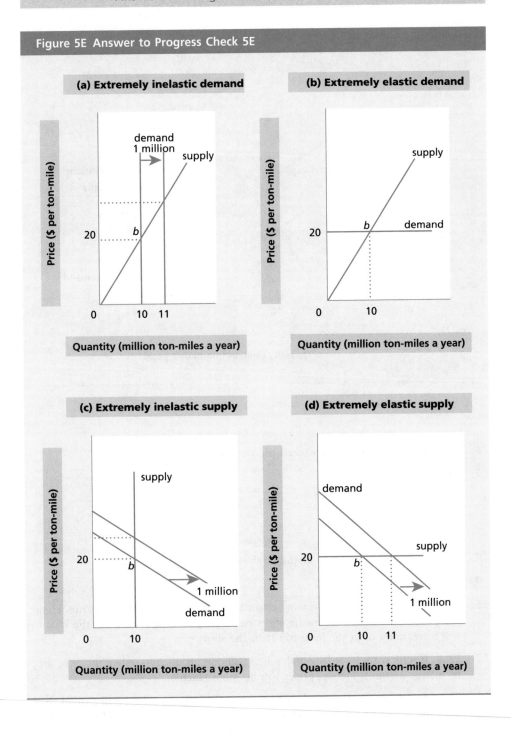

Figure 5E Answer to Progress Check 5E

Figure 5G Answer to Progress Check 5G

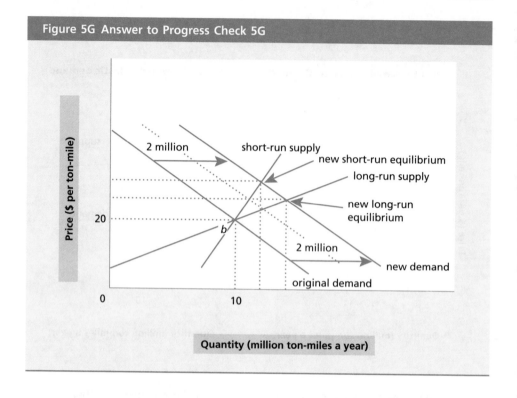

6. The quantity supplied will exceed the quantity demanded.

7. (a) Reduce the supply.
   (b) Increase the supply.
   (c) Reduce the demand.
   (d) Increase the demand.
   (e) No effect.

8. If the demand is extremely elastic or the supply is extremely elastic.

9. (c).

11. The supply of new housing is more elastic in the long run than the short run. Hence, the price will rise further in the short run than the long run, while the quantity will increase more in the long run than the short run.

12. False. If sunk costs are substantial, sellers will quit production only if the price drops by a large amount. Hence, prices will be more volatile.

15. The retailers receive the wholesale price cut. In a competitive retail market, however, the wholesale price cut will increase the supply. The new equilibrium will have a lower retail price. Consumers benefit from a lower retail price, so part of the wholesale price cut will be incident on consumers.

Figure 5H Answer to Progress Check 5H

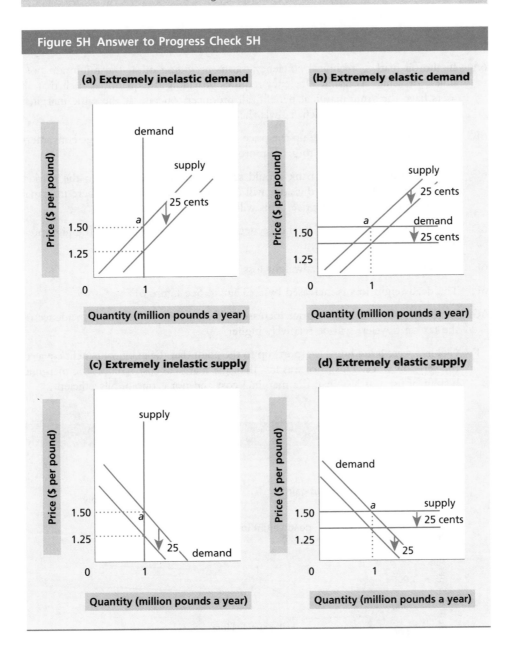

◀◀ Chapter 6   Economic Efficiency

6A. In the oil market, technical efficiency means providing oil at the minimum possible cost, while economic efficiency requires providing the quantities such that all users have the same marginal benefit, all producers operate at the same marginal cost, and the marginal benefit equals the marginal cost.

6B. The invisible hand will drive up the price of grain, which will encourage consumers to conserve and producers to grow more.

6C. With decentralization, the bank should set the transfer price equal to the market price of funds. Then, both divisions will use funds up to the point where marginal benefit equals the transfer price. This will ensure economic efficiency.

6D. No. If the marginal cost of steel exceeded the marginal benefit, then the high production rate was not efficient.

6E. See figure 6E. The new deadweight loss is area *mnb*.

6F. The deadweight loss is increased by area *mnhe*. See figure 6F.

6G. See figure 6G. The buyer's price increases relatively more. Hence, the incidence of the tax on travelers will be relatively higher.

 1. Children were using bread (in sport) up to the point that the marginal benefit equaled the very low price. This price was less than the marginal cost. Hence, the marginal benefit of use was less than the marginal cost and not economically efficient.

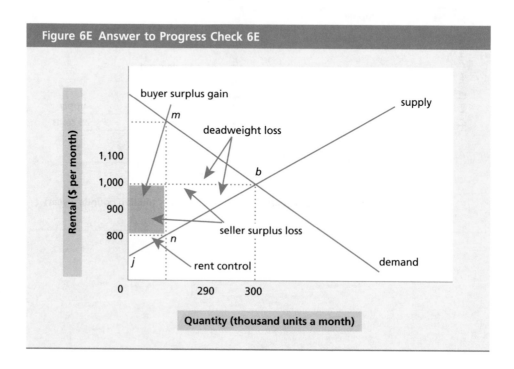

Figure 6E Answer to Progress Check 6E

Figure 6F Answer to Progress Check 6F

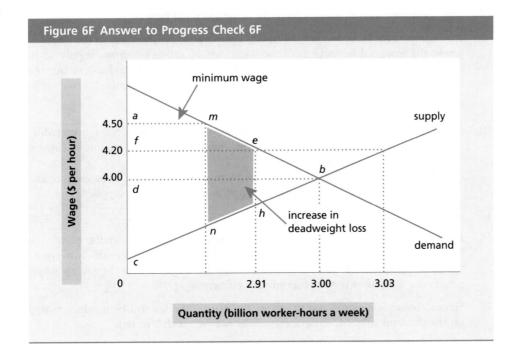

Figure 6G Answer to Progress Check 6G

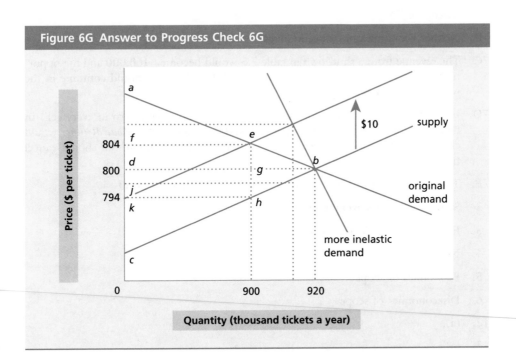

2. The condition that all users receive the same marginal benefit.

3. In a competitive labor market, all buyers (employers) purchase up to the quantity where the marginal benefit equals the wage, and all sellers (workers) supply up to the quantity where the marginal cost equals the wage. Buyers and sellers face the same wage; hence, the allocation of labor is economically efficient.

7. Country B has higher barriers to exit.

10. (a) If demand is more inelastic, renters are less sensitive to price. So, a given reduction in the quantity will cause a larger reduction in the buyer surplus among those who cannot get apartments.
    (b) If supply is more elastic, landlords are more sensitive to price. So, a given reduction in rent will induce a larger reduction in the quantity supplied.

11. The effect will be greater among janitors.

14. Employers buy labor up to the quantity where the marginal benefit equals the buyer's wage. Workers supply up to the quantity where the marginal cost equals the seller's wage. With an income tax, the buyer's wage exceeds the seller's wage; hence, the allocation is not economically efficient.

15. Since demand is inelastic and supply is very elastic, the tax will be incident mostly on the demand side. Manufacturers would not be much affected.

◀◀ Chapter 7   Costs

7A. See figure 7A.

7B. Neither economies nor diseconomies of scope.

7C. The revenue from a shutdown in table 7.5 would become $460,000 and the opportunity cost in table 7.6 would become $680,000. Eleanor should continue in the warehouse business.

7D. In table 7.7, the columns for "Cancel Launch" would have zero in every cell. In table 7.8, the graphics consultant cost would be $50,000, the *Road Runner* would charge $60,000, and the *Daily Globe* would charge $200,000. Sol should cancel the launch.

7E. The average cost of both models would be identical at $104.50.

2. Southern Power's average fixed cost will rise.

3. Economies of scale are more significant in (a).

4. No.

5. Economies of scope.

6. Diseconomies of scope.

12. (a).

13. (a).

Figure 7A Answer to Progress Check 7A

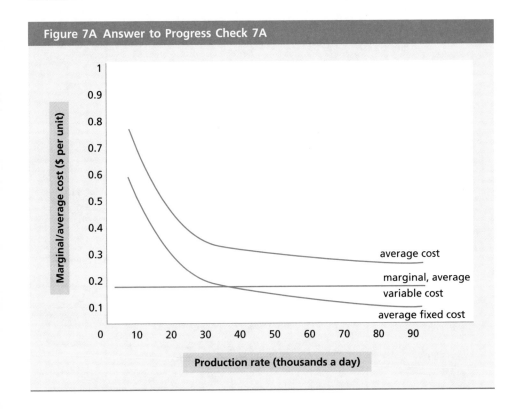

14. Direct labor and materials may not be the drivers of the indirect costs. Allocating indirect costs according to direct labor and materials may result in misleading cost calculations.

◄◄ Chapter 8 Monopoly

8A. No difference: the price would be identical to the marginal revenue.

8B. It should raise price, so reducing sales up to the quantity where its marginal cost equals its marginal revenue.

8C. See figure 8C.

8D. The advertising expenditure should be $(140 − 70) × 0.01 × 1.4 = $0.98 million.

8E. Lerner Index = (130 − 70)/130 = 0.46.

8F. A union will be relatively more effective in a market with relatively few workers, if all workers are working full time, if workers have few commitments to employers, and if there are significant barriers to entry and exit. The fifth factor is ambiguous.

Figure 8C Answer to Progress Check 8C

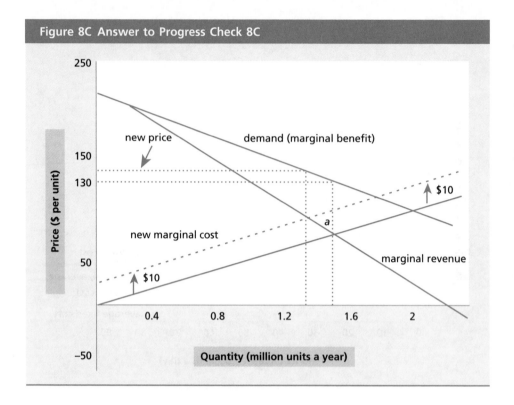

8G. Solar's total expenditure is represented by either the area *u0vx* under the marginal expenditure curve from a quantity of 0 to 6,000 tons or the rectangle *t0vz*.

2. To sell additional units, a seller must reduce its price. So, when increasing sales by one unit, the seller will gain the price of the marginal unit but lose revenue on the inframarginal units. Hence, the marginal revenue is less than or equal to the price. If the demand is very elastic, then the marginal revenue will be close to the price. If, however, the demand is very inelastic, then the marginal revenue will be much lower than the price.

3. Reduce the price, and so increase sales.

4. True.

5. Expiration of the patent will
   (a) reduce Solar's market power;
   (b) raise the price elasticity of demand.

6. The profit-maximizing quantity is such that the marginal revenue equals the marginal cost. Hence, after a change in costs, the seller should look for the quantity where the marginal revenue equals the new marginal cost. So, it must consider both the marginal revenue and the marginal cost.

7. Advertising expenditure = $(100 - 40) \times 0.01 \times 500,000 = \$0.3$ million.

13. Yes.

14. True.

15. If the U.S. government were to forbid the NCAA from restrictive practices,
    (a) athletes' earnings would rise;
    (b) the number of athletes would increase.

◀◀ Chapter 9 Pricing Policy

9A. The profit-maximizing price is ¥63,000.

9B. The market buyer surplus is the area *agc*.

9C. Area *adb* = ¥31.25 million. Area *bec* = ¥31.25 million.

9D. See figure 9D.

9E. CF with the Japanese price = ¥50,000 = $500. The difference with the American price = $150.

9F. No, the two segments will not be differentially sensitive.

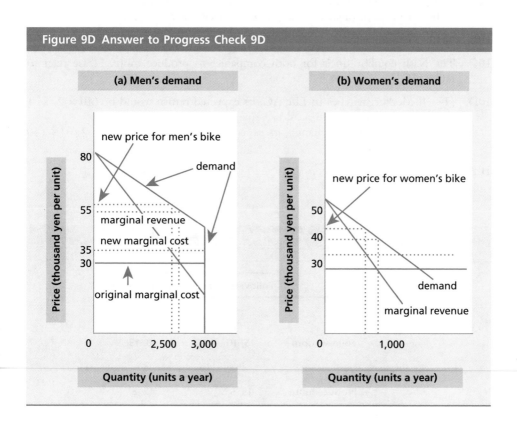

Figure 9D Answer to Progress Check 9D

(a) Men's demand

(b) Women's demand

new price for men's bike

demand

marginal revenue

new marginal cost

original marginal cost

new price for women's bike

demand

marginal revenue

Price (thousand yen per unit)

Price (thousand yen per unit)

Quantity (units a year)

Quantity (units a year)

9G. Price the bundle at $22 and the educational channel at $19.

9H. The maximum price of the large bottle = $3.74.

1. Not necessarily. The price also depends on the marginal cost.

2. The profit-maximizing price = $2.50.

3. No.

5. Equal.

6. The price in Germany = $3.30; the price in South Africa = $1.80.

7. It would be easier to discriminate against newspapers because they have time value and are priced low relative to transportation cost.

14. Consumers with small appetites prefer a la carte to buffets; big eaters prefer the buffets. The result is indirect segment discrimination.

15. (a) and (b).

◀◀ Chapter 10   Strategic Thinking

10A. A presidential election candidate must consider how other candidates will react to her or his decisions. Accordingly, these decisions are strategic.

10B. Neither is dominated.

10C. The Nash equilibrium is for both companies to produce more. Please refer to table 10C.

10D. (1) If Merkur switches to Lite AC, its expected return would be $(40 \times 2/5) + (60 \times 3/5) = 52$.
   (2) If Merkur doesn't change, its expected return would be $(60 \times 2/5) + (40 \times 3/5) = 48$.

10E. It is not a zero-sum game.

Table 10C Answer to Progress Check 10C

		Sharon	
		Follow quota	Produce more
Hilda	Follow quota	15, 10	10, 13
	Produce more	19, 5	12, 8

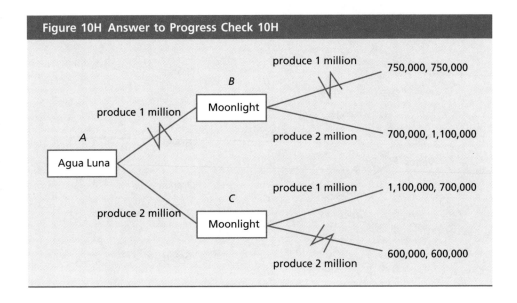

Figure 10H Answer to Progress Check 10H

10F. If the two stations take different time slots, their combined profit will be higher than if they take the same time slot. Accordingly, the situation is not a zero-sum game.

10G. Delta would choose 8:00 p.m. and Zeta would choose 7:30 p.m.

10H. Agua Luna would produce 2 million bottles, and Moonlight would produce 1 million bottles. See figure 10H.

1. (c).

2. (a) A dominated strategy generates worse consequences than some other strategy, regardless of the other parties' choices. It makes no sense to adopt a dominated strategy.
   (b) Given that the other parties choose their Nash equilibrium strategies, each party prefers its own Nash equilibrium strategy. It is a logically consistent solution to the problem of infinite regress. It also provides a focal point for strategic decision making.

3. (c).

4. Venus chooses Orange with probability 0.5 and chooses Green with probability 0.5; and Sol does the same.

5. (b).

8. Venus will choose either Orange or Green – either way, it will receive 1.5. Please refer to figure RQ7.

Figure RQ7 Answer to Review Question 7

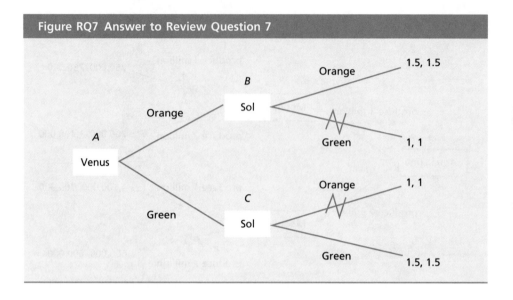

9. (a)   A strategic move is an action to influence the beliefs or actions of other
        parties in a favorable way. Typically, the move involves a deliberate restric-
        tion of the party's freedom of action.
   (b)   A promise conveys benefits under specified conditions to change the beliefs
        or actions of other parties. It is effective only if it is credible.
   (c)   A threat imposes costs under specified conditions to change the beliefs or
        actions of other parties. It is effective only if it is credible.

10. Strategy (b) is more credible.

◀◀ Chapter 11   Externalities

11A. (1)   The horizontal sum of individual demand curves is the market demand curve:
          At every price, we add the *quantities* demanded by the individuals to get
          the market quantity. The curves are added in a horizontal direction.
     (2)   The vertical sum of individual marginal benefit curves is the group marginal
          benefit curve: At every quantity, we add the *marginal benefits* of the
          individuals to get the group marginal benefit. The curves are added in a
          vertical direction.

11B. (1)   Sol's marginal cost curve will be higher, and (2) the level of investment that
          maximizes the group profit will be lower. Please refer to figure 11B.

11C. (a)   is a network externality;
     (b)   is a network effect.

11D. See figure 11D.

Figure 11B Answer to Progress Check 11B

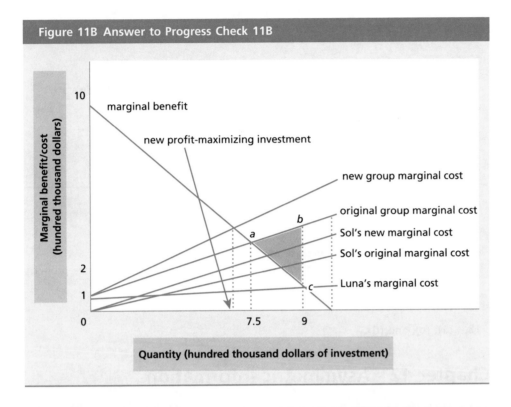

Figure 11D Answer to Progress Check 11D

11E. There are only a few users of techniques for coronary bypass, hence, usage is relatively easy to monitor. See figure 11E.

2. The amount that the recipients of the negative externality are willing to pay for a marginal reduction is less than or equal to the marginal cost. The amount that the source is willing to accept for a marginal reduction is greater than or equal to the marginal benefit. Since the sum of the marginal costs exceeds the marginal benefits, the intermediary could make money.

3. (a) and (b).

Figure 11E Answer to Progress Check 11E

excludable ←————————————————→ nonexcludable

mainframe services   coronary bypass   Ohm's Law
cardiac surgeon's   technique
service

   4. (a) The new exit will increase Moonlight's business.
      (b) Moonlight is taking a free ride on the investments by the other property owners.

   5. (b).

  13. (a), (c), and (d).

◄◄ Chapter 12   Asymmetric Information

12A. Hilda has imperfect information but does not face risk. The insurer has imperfect information and faces risk.

12B. The market price will be higher, as shown in figure 12B.

12C. The percentage of high-risk policyholders will fall.

12D. Appraisals will be more common in the market for more expensive antiques.

12E. Borrowers who are more willing to repay will be relatively more likely to post collateral.

12F. (a) It should provide the information to the bidders.
     (b) This information will reduce the extent of the winner's curse.

12G. Screening is an initiative of the less-informed party, while signaling is an initiative of the better-informed party.

   2. (a) No asymmetry.
      (b) The directors of Acquirer have better information than the general investor.

   3. (a) True.
      (b) False. Risk neutral persons will not want insurance.

   4. Yes, this will draw relatively less hardworking persons.

   5. The seller has an interest not to reveal negative information about the car.

Figure 12B Answer to Progress Check 12B

9. (a) Open bidding allows the participants to observe the bids of others. This supports collusion.
   (b) Setting a reserve price will put a limit to collusion.

10. (b).

12. Yes.

◀◀ Chapter 13   Incentives and Organization

13A. The new marginal cost curve lies above the original. Please refer to figure 13A.
   (1) The economically efficient effort will be lower.
   (2) The effort that the worker actually chooses will be lower.

13B. Draw any personal marginal benefit curve that crosses the marginal cost curve at 120 units of effort.

13C. See figure 13C.

13D. Mary's incentive scheme should be stronger.

13E. The salesclerk's incentive to process returns will be reduced.

13F. On-the-job training.

13G. Walt Disney integrated downstream; Dominion integrated upstream. Broken Hill integrated downstream; Loral integrated downstream.

Figure 13A Answer to Progress Check 13A

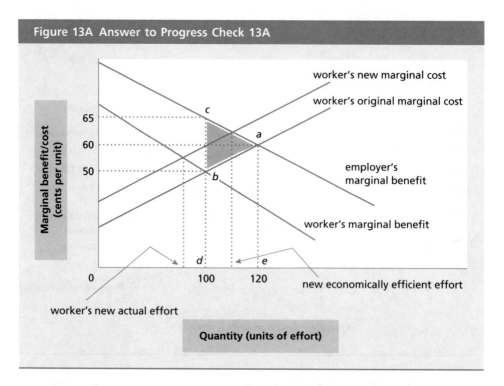

Figure 13C Answer to Progress Check 13C

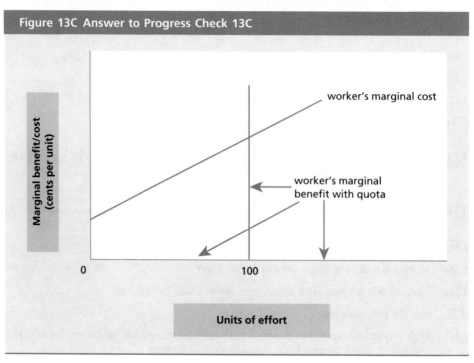

13H. There are scale economies in processing credit card transactions. Mercury is too small to operate the service efficiently.

2. Regarding asymmetry, it is costly for the insurer to monitor Leah's precautions. There is a conflict of interest because, with insurance, Leah bears the cost of precautions but receives only part of the benefit.

3. With moral hazard, the marginal benefit of effort exceeds the marginal cost. By resolving the moral hazard, the potential profit is the marginal benefit less the marginal cost.

4. Method (b) provides more incentive to the lawyer.

5. (a) Pay or quotas based on sales relative to the average.
   (b) Rewards or quotas based on the number of accidents or breakdowns relative to average.

6. The scheme will reduce the secretary's incentive for effort in the other tasks.

7. (a) Index of small stocks.
   (b) Index of U.S. government bonds.
   (c) Index of Japanese stocks.

8. (b).

14. Vertical integration involves combining assets for the two successive stages of production under common ownership. Horizontal integration involves combining assets for the same stage of production under common ownership.

15. For: reduces potential for hold up. Against: increases moral hazard, creates internal monopoly, does not benefit from scale economies.

◀◀ Chapter 14   Regulation

14A. See figure 14A.

14B. One operator should be given a monopoly franchise for distribution of gas. It should be either not allowed to produce natural gas or required to separate its distribution and production businesses.

14C. See figure 14C. With a $25 per ton user fee, sources of emissions will emit 13,000 tons a year. Social benefit would be area $0agn$, under the marginal benefit curve up to 13,000 tons a year. Social cost would be area $0dfn$, under the marginal cost curve up to 13,000 tons a year. There would be a net social gain of area aed less area efg.

   With a $45 per ton user fee, there would be a net social gain of area $abcd$. Neither the $25 nor the $45 fee is optimal. Which is preferable depends on the balance between area bec and area efg.

14D. See figure 14D. The new care would exceed the economically efficient level.

Figure 14A Answer to Progress Check 14A

Figure 14C Answer to Progress Check 14C

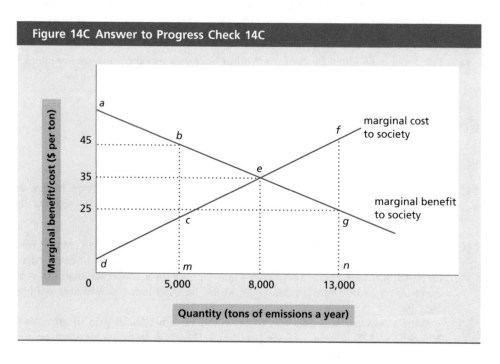

Figure 14D Answer to Progress Check 14D

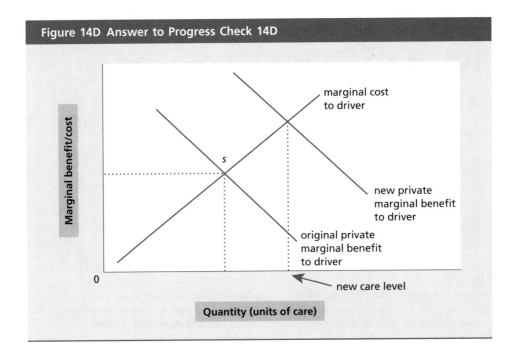

14E. Reduce.

14F. Assuming that demand varies over the day, the marginal cost of usage will also vary. Economically efficient usage requires the price to vary with the marginal cost.

4. Monopolies restrict provision to raise the price, while monopsonies restrict purchases to reduce the price. In both cases, the outcome is not economically efficient.

5. Privatization means transferring ownership from the public to the private sector. Allowing competition means removing an exclusive right.

7. (a) A movie producer that owns a theater is vertically integrated into the downstream stage of production.
    (b) The law that prohibited movie producers from owning theaters is a structural regulation to separate the movie production and exhibition businesses.

8. False.

10. (a) The regulator could charge a fee for noise generated by the construction equipment.

    (b) The regulator could set a standard and make it illegal for construction equipment to generate noise exceeding the standard.

13. (a) Not an externality because all the parties belong to the market for production workers.
    (b) This is an externality.

14. No.

◀◀ Index of Companies and Organizations

◀◀ Subject Index